CONTROLLING IMMIGRATION

CONTROLLING IMMIGRATION

A GLOBAL PERSPECTIVE
THIRD EDITION

EDITED BY

JAMES F. HOLLIFIELD,

PHILIP L. MARTIN,

AND PIA M. ORRENIUS

STANFORD UNIVERSITY PRESS
Stanford, California

Stanford University Press
Stanford, California

Library of Congress Cataloging-in-Publication Data

Controlling immigration : a global perspective / edited by James F. Hollifield, Philip L. Martin, and Pia Orrenius. — Third edition.
     pages cm
  Includes bibliographical references and index.
  ISBN 978-0-8047-8626-3 (cloth : alk. paper)—ISBN 978-0-8047-8627-0 (pbk. : alk. paper)
  1. Emigration and immigration—Government policy—Cross-cultural studies.   2. Immigrants—Government policy—Cross-cultural studies.   3. Human rights—Cross-cultural studies.   I. Hollifield, James Frank, editor of compilation.   II. Martin, Philip L., editor of compilation.   III. Orrenius, Pia M., editor of compilation.
  JV6271.C66 2014
  325′.1—dc23
                                                                                    2013043603

ISBN 978-0-8047-8735-2 (electronic)

Typeset by Newgen in 10/14 Minion

CONTENTS

PREFACE

The idea for this book began in 1990 at the Center for US-Mexican Studies at the University of California at San Diego (UCSD) with a National Science Foundation (NSF) research project comparing national efforts to manage migration under the direction of Wayne A. Cornelius, Philip L. Martin, and James F. Hollifield. National studies of migration data and control systems that grew out of the NSF project were published as the first edition of this book in 1994 by Stanford University Press. A second edition appeared in 2004.

The third edition continues the effort to use systematic, cross-national research to examine the gap between the goals and outcomes of immigration policies in the major immigrant-receiving countries. A generation of scholars and students has wrestled with this question, which continues to drive research agendas in the multidisciplinary field of migration studies. We hope that the third edition will shed new light on the dilemmas of immigration control and help to advance the comparative study of immigration policy.

This book is divided into three parts: (1) nations of immigrants, in which immigration is part of the founding national ideal; (2) countries of immigration, in which immigration has come to play an important role in social and economic development but is not part of the process of nation building; and (3) latecomers to immigration — countries that once sent migrants abroad but in the past few decades made the transition from sending to receiving societies. Each country study is followed by one or more commentaries by scholars and policymakers who offer a critique and, in some cases, an alternative interpretation of policy developments. While keeping the focus on the major receiving countries of North America, Europe, Australia, and East Asia, we have added new chapters on Scandinavia and Switzerland, as well as a special section on the European Union and the global governance of migration.

Our work has benefited from the input of migration scholars and students from around the globe. The workshop for the second edition was hosted by the Center for Comparative Immigration Studies at UCSD, and the third conference, the basis for this edition, was organized by the John Goodwin Tower Center for Political Studies at Southern Methodist University (SMU) in conjunction with the Federal Reserve Bank of Dallas.

We are grateful to all who participated in this conference and to the staff of the Tower Center and the Dallas Fed for their invaluable administrative support. The project was underwritten by the Marian Tower International Conference Fund of the Tower Center at SMU, and supported by the Dallas Fed and the Canadian government. We would like specifically to thank Paula Caldwell St-Onge, Consul General of Canada for the South Central United States, for her support and that of her government. The editors and contributing authors are solely responsible for the information and views presented in this book, which do not necessarily represent those of the Federal Reserve Bank of Dallas or the underwriters.

Special thanks go to Ryan Swick, assistant to the director of the Tower Center, and Jieun Pyun, Communications Director of the Tower Center, for their tireless work on the project, and to Geoffrey Burn, executive editor of Stanford University Press, and his colleagues. Without their extraordinary patience, skill, and support, the third edition of *Controlling Immigration* might never have seen the light of day. To them we are deeply grateful.

James F. Hollifield
Philip L. Martin
Pia M. Orrenius
Dallas, Texas
March 2013

CONTRIBUTORS

RUT BERMEJO CASADO is a lecturer on politics at Rey Juan Carlos University in Madrid. Her publications on border controls and immigration policies include, most recently, "Política migratoria y fronteras: La gestión de la inmigración mediante agencias" in *Fronteras en movimiento: Migraciones en el contexto del euromediterráneo* (2012); "El proceso de institucionalización de la cooperación en la gestión operativa de las fronteras externas de la UE" in *Revista CIDOB d'Affairs Internationals* (2010); and "Migration and Security in the EU: Back to Fortress Europe?" in the *Journal of Contemporary European Research* (2009). Her current research deals with immigration politics and policy design in Spain and the European Union.

ALEXANDER BETTS is university lecturer in refugee and forced migration studies in the Department of International Development at the University of Oxford. He is author or editor of numerous books, including *Forced Migration and Global Politics* (Wiley-Blackwell, 2009), *Protection by Persuasion: International Cooperation in the Refugee Regime* (Cornell University Press, 2009), *Refugees in International Relations* (with Gil Loescher, Oxford University Press, 2010), *Global Migration Governance* (Oxford University Press, 2011), *UNHCR: The Politics and Practice of Refugee Protection* (with Gil Loescher and James Milner, Routledge, 2012), and *Survival Migration: Failed Governance and the Crisis of Displacement* (Cornell University Press, 2013). He has worked for UNHCR and as a consultant to UNDP, UNICEF, IOM, the Council of Europe, and the Commonwealth Secretariat. He is now director of the Humanitarian Innovation Project at Oxford.

IRENE BLOEMRAAD is the Thomas Garden Barnes chair of Canadian studies and associate professor of sociology at the University of California, Berkeley, as well as a scholar with the Canadian Institute for Advanced Research. Her research examines immigrant incorporation into political and civic life, as well as the consequences of immigration on politics and understandings of membership. Her work reaches a broad, interdisciplinary audience, spanning articles in the *American Journal of Sociology*, the *Canadian Journal of Political Science, Perspectives on Politics*, the *Journal of Interdisciplinary History*, and the *Nonprofit and Voluntary Sector Quarterly*. Her books include *Rallying for*

Immigrant Rights: The Fight for Inclusion in 21st Century America (2011); *Civic Hopes and Political Realities: Immigrants, Community Organizations, and Political Engagement* (2008); and *Becoming a Citizen: Incorporating Immigrants and Refugees in the United States and Canada* (2006).

GRETE BROCHMANN is professor of sociology and head of the Department of Sociology and Human Geography at the University of Oslo. She has published several books and articles on international migration, sending- and receiving-country perspectives, EU policies, and welfare state dilemmas, as well as historical studies on immigration. She served as a visiting scholar in Brussels, Berkeley, and Boston. In 2002, she held the Willy Brandt visiting professorship in Malmö, Sweden, and was recently head of a governmental commission on international migration and the Norwegian welfare model.

STEPHEN CASTLES is research professor of sociology at the University of Sydney and a research associate of the International Migration Institute (IMI), University of Oxford. Until August 2009, he was professor of migration and refugee studies at Oxford and director of IMI. He is a sociologist and political economist, and works on international migration dynamics; global governance, migration, and development; and regional migration trends in Africa, Asia, and Europe. His current research project on social transformation and international migration in the twenty-first century is concerned with the way global forces interact with local factors to shape human mobility. It involves fieldwork in Australia, Turkey, South Korea, and Mexico. His recent books include *The Age of Migration: International Population Movements in the Modern World* (with Mark Miller, 2009); *Migration, Citizenship and the European Welfare State: A European Dilemma* (with Carl-Ulrik Schierup and Peo Hansen, 2006); and as co-editor (with Raúl Delgado Wise), *Migration and Development: Perspectives from the South* (2008).

ERIN AERAN CHUNG is the Charles D. Miller associate professor of East Asian politics and director of the Program in East Asian Studies in the Department of Political Science at Johns Hopkins University, where she specializes in East Asian political economy, international migration, and comparative racial politics. She has been a Japan Foundation fellow at Saitama University, an advanced research fellow at Harvard University's Weatherhead Center for International Affairs, and a program scholar at the Mansfield Foundation US-Japan Network for the Future. Her first book, *Immigration and Citizenship in Japan*, was published by Cambridge University Press in 2010 and translated into Japanese in 2012. She is completing her second book, *Immigrant Incorporation in East Asian Democracies*, for which she was awarded an Abe Fellowship by the Social Science Research Council in 2009.

GIANNI D'AMATO is professor at the University of Neuchâtel and director of the Swiss Forum of Migration and Population Studies (SFM). He is also director of the National Center of Competence in Research on Migration and Mobility and member of the Expert Council of German Foundations on Migration and Integration. His research interests are focused on citizenship, human mobility, populism, and the history of migration. His recent publications include a co-edited volume titled *Critical Mobilities* (Routledge, 2013), and "Monitoring Immigrant Integration in Switzerland" (with Christian Suter) in *Monitoring Integration in Europe* (Netherlands Institute for Social Research/SCP, 2012).

GARY FREEMAN is professor of government at the University of Texas, Austin. His work deals with the politics of immigration in Western Europe, North America, and Australia, and his most recent publications address the linkage between immigration, diversity, and the welfare state.

ANDREW GEDDES is professor of politics at the University of Sheffield (UK). He has published extensively on European and EU migration policy and politics, including *Immigration and European Integration: Beyond Fortress Europe?* (2008) and *Migration and Mobility in the EU* (with Christina Boswell, 2011).

RANDALL HANSEN is a political scientist and historian at the University of Toronto, where he has held the Canada research chair in political science since 2005. He taught at the University of London (Queen Mary), Oxford (where he was a tutorial fellow at Merton College), and Newcastle (where he held an established chair) before taking up his current position. His fields of research are twentieth-century history and public policy. He has authored two books, *Citizenship and Immigration in Postwar Britain* (2000) and *Fire and Fury: The Allied Bombing of Germany 1942–1945* (2008), has co-edited three books, and has published numerous articles and book chapters on immigration, citizenship, and the history of eugenics and forced sterilization.

MIRYAM HAZÁN is the Washington director of Mexicans and Americans Thinking Together (MATT), a Texas-based organization focused on establishing bridges of dialogue between Mexico and the United States, and is a fellow with the Tower Center for Political Studies at Southern Methodist University. She is the author of numerous blogs, journal articles, and book chapters on immigration issues as well as the author of the upcoming book *Mexican Immigrant Politics in America* (Cambridge University Press). An expert on US, Mexican, Central American, and Spanish immigration policies, she has held research and scholarly positions at Demos, Ideas in Action, the Migration Policy Institute, the University of Pennsylvania, Rutgers University, and the Tomas Rivera Policy Institute at the University of Texas, Austin. She has media experience across the Americas, including six years at *El Financiero* in Mexico City.

JAMES F. HOLLIFIELD is the Ora Nixon Arnold professor of international political economy, and the director of the Tower Center at SMU. He has worked for a variety of governmental and intergovernmental organizations and has published widely on international political and economic issues, including *Immigrants, Markets, and States* (Harvard University Press, 1992), *L'immigration et l'Etat Nation* (L'Harmattan, 1997), *Migration Theory* (third edition, Routledge, 2014), and *International Political Economy: History, Theory and Policy* (Cambridge University Press, forthcoming), along with numerous other books and scientific articles. His current research looks at how states manage migration for strategic gains.

GALLYA LAHAV is associate professor of political science at the State University of New York at Stony Brook, where she received the Chancellor's Award for Excellence in Teaching. She holds graduate degrees in political science from the London School of Economics and the Graduate Center, CUNY. In addition to her many peer-reviewed articles and book chapters on migration and European integration, she is the author of

Immigration and Politics in the New Europe (2004) and co-editor of *The Migration Reader* (2006) and *The ISA Compendium on Ethnicity, Nationalism and Migration* (2010). She has also served as a consultant and an expert witness to the UN Population Division, the US Special Operations Forces, the Israel Population and Immigration Authority (PIBA), and the European Parliament on international migration.

WILLEM MAAS holds the Jean Monnet Chair and is associate professor at Glendon College, York University, in Toronto. He is the author of *Creating European Citizens* (2007) and the *Historical Dictionary of the European Union* (forthcoming 2014), the editor of *Multilevel Citizenship* (2013) and *Democratic Citizenship and the Free Movement of People* (2013), and the co-editor of *Sixty Years of European Governance* (forthcoming 2014). Currently, he is writing about the future of citizenship, politics in the Netherlands, and federalism. He co-founded the Migration and Citizenship section of the American Political Science Association, and teaches a range of courses in comparative and European politics, citizenship, and migration.

PHILIP L. MARTIN is professor of agricultural and resource economics at the University of California, Davis. He edits *Migration News* and *Rural Migration News*, has served on several federal commissions, and testifies frequently before Congress. He also works for UN agencies on labor and migration issues in Latin America, Turkey and Eastern Europe, Africa, and throughout Asia and has studied the evolving global wine industry.

MIDORI OKABE is associate professor of international relations in the Faculty of Law at Sophia University in Tokyo. She is a former visiting scholar at the Centre of International Studies, University of Cambridge (2006–2007); academic program associate at the United Nations University in Tokyo (2004–2006); and special advisor to the Japanese Ministry of Foreign Affairs (2000–2002). Her main research interest is EU asylum and immigration policy as well as international relations (especially international institutions). Her recent work includes *The "Outside-In": An Overview of Japanese Immigration Policy from the Perspective of International Relations* (2011); *Labor Migration Control over Five Continents* (2010); "The European Union Policy on Migration Management and Its Potential Relevance to Japanese Politics" (presented at the EU-Japan Conference, Brussels, November 2010); *Managed Rights, Managed Migration: The Case of the European Union and Implications for Japanese Immigration, Commentary on the Policy Innovations* (2010); and "Management from the Inside-Out: Relevance of EU Migration Control to the Non-EU World" (presented at the Seventeenth Conference of the Council for European Studies, Montreal, April 2010).

PIA ORRENIUS is vice president and senior economist at the Federal Reserve Bank of Dallas and an adjunct professor at the Hankamer School of Business, Baylor University. At the Dallas Fed, she is a regional economist working on economic growth and demographic change, while her academic research focuses on the labor market impacts of immigration, unauthorized immigration, and US immigration policy. She is co-author with Madeline Zavodny of the book *Beside the Golden Door: U.S. Immigration Reform in a New Era of Globalization* (2010).

DERYA OZKUL is lecturer and PhD researcher at the University of Sydney. During her doctoral research, she held guest researcher fellowships at the Social Science Research

Centre Berlin (WZB) and the University of Bielefeld. She holds degrees from the London School of Economics and the University of Bogazici. Previously, she contributed to research conducted by the Office of the High Commissioner for Human Rights (OHCHR), the Committee on Migrant Workers, and the International Labour Organization's MIGRANT Department in Geneva. Her work has included research on migrant workers' rights and violations of international human rights treaties in El Salvador, Colombia, Azerbaijan, and Syria. As a researcher, she also worked at the Migration Research Centre at Koc University (MiReKoc) in Turkey. She is a recipient of the Summer School Best Written Essay from the Consortium for Applied Research on International Migration (CARIM) at the European University Institute and the CCH Award for Best Written Paper from University of Sydney Law School. Her publications include "Irregular Migration: Causes, Patterns and Strategies" (with others) in *Global Perspectives on Migration and Development* (2012).

TED PERLMUTTER is adjunct professor at Columbia University as well as technology consultant and information systems architect. He is responsible for website coordination and database development, and has been involved in the Religious Peacemaking Database project. His research interests focus on how Internet technology can promote knowledge networks among political and social activists. His research includes work with Suzette Brooks Masters on a Ford Foundation project, "Networking the Networks: Improving Information Flow in the Immigration Field." He has published numerous articles and book chapters on immigration, refugees, political parties, and civil society, and he has taught in the New York University Political Science Department as a lecturer and an assistant professor (1987–1992). He was also the recipient of a German Marshall Fund Grant for the Study of Germany as well as a Fulbright Commission Fellowship for Study in Italy on xenophobic politics in Europe from 1993 to 1995. And he was a visiting fellow at the Italian Academy for Advanced Italian Studies on America at Columbia University (1997–1998).

JEFFREY G. REITZ is professor in the Department of Sociology and director of Ethnic, Immigration and Pluralism Studies in the Munk School of Global Affairs at the University of Toronto. His primary areas of research are immigration and multicultural issues, emphasizing the case of Canada in comparative perspective. His most recent book is *Multiculturalism and Social Cohesion: Potentials and Challenges of Diversity* (2009). Recent articles include "Race, Religion, and the Social Integration of Canada's New Immigrant Minorities" (2009); "Comparisons of the Success of Racial Minority Immigrant Offspring in the United States, Canada and Australia" (2011); "The Distinctiveness of Canadian Immigration Experience" (2012); and "Immigrant Skill Utilization: Trends and Policy Issues" (2013). Presently he is a Marie Curie international fellow at l'École des Hautes Études en Sciences Sociales (EHESS) in Paris.

MARC R. ROSENBLUM is deputy director of MPI's US Immigration Policy Program, where he works on US immigration policy, immigration enforcement, and US regional migration relations. In 2005–2006, he served as a fellow of the Council of Foreign Relations and International Affairs at the Migration Policy Institute, and served on the staff of the US Senate Judiciary Committee, Immigration Subcommittee. In 2008–2009, he was a member of the Immigration Policy Committee of President-Elect Barack Obama's transition team, and from 2011 to 2014, he was a specialist in immigration policy at the Congressional Research Service. He is the author of over fifty articles, book chapters, and policy briefs on US immigration policy, and he is the co-editor (with Daniel Tichenor) of *The Oxford Handbook of the Politics of International Migration Policy* (2012).

GIUSEPPE SCIORTINO teaches sociology at the Università di Trento in Italy. His research interests are migration and social theory. Among his recent works are *Great Minds: Encounter with Social Theory* (with Gianfranco Poggi, 2011) and *Foggy Social Structures: Irregular Migration, Informal Economy and Welfare Regimes* (edited with Michael Bommes, 2011).

F. LESLIE SEIDLE is research director for the Diversity, Immigration and Integration program at the Institute for Research on Public Policy (IRPP) and a public policy consultant. He previously held senior positions in the government of Canada, including director general of Strategic Policy and Research, Intergovernmental Affairs in the Privy Council Office (1996–2002). He was research director (governance) at IRPP (1992–1996) and senior research coordinator for the Royal Commission on Electoral Reform and Party Financing (1990–1991). He is the author of *Rethinking the Delivery of Public Services to Citizens* (IRPP, 1995) and numerous articles on immigration issues, electoral and constitutional reform, public management and political finance. He has edited/co-edited thirteen books, including *Immigrant Integration in Federal Countries* (McGill-Queen's University Press, 2012) and *Belonging? Diversity, Recognition and Shared Citizenship in Canada* (IRPP, 2007). He holds a DPhil from the University of Oxford.

PATRICK SIMON is director of research at the Institut National d'Etudes Démographiques (National Demographic Institute), where he heads the research unit on international migration and minorities. He is also a fellow at the Center of European Studies (CEE) at Sciences Po, and has chaired the scientific panel on integration of immigrants at the International Union for the Scientific Study of Population (IUSSP) and was a member of the scientific board of the Fundamental Rights Agency of the European Commission in Vienna. He studies antidiscrimination policies, ethnic classification, and the integration of ethnic minorities in European countries. With Victor Piché, he edited *The Challenge of Enumeration*, a special issue of *Ethnic and Racial Studies: Accounting for Ethnic and Racial Diversity* (2012).

DIETRICH THRÄNHARDT is professor emeritus at Universität Münster, Institute of Political Science, and has been a guest professor at the International Christian University (ICU) in Tokyo and a fellow at both the Netherlands Institute for Advanced Study (NIAS) and the Transatlantic Academy. Currently, he edits the journal *Studies in Migration and Minorities*. He has published on comparative migration in Europe, the United States, and Japan and on German politics. He is the author or of 40 books and 170 articles in German and in English, and has been translated into French, Japanese, Dutch, Italian, and Catalan. His most recent book, co-edited with Michael Bommes, is *National Paradigms of Migration Research* (2010). His present research interests include the relationship of migration and development, the contradictory processes of opening the world with globalization, and the buildup of security walls and fences. He has consulted for the

Organisation for Economic Co-operation and Development (OECD); for state and local governments and foundations in Germany; and for science organizations in Austria, Belgium, Luxembourg, the Netherlands, and Switzerland; as well as for several American universities.

DANIEL J. TICHENOR is the Philip H. Knight professor of social science and a senior faculty fellow at the Wayne Morse Center for Law and Politics. His extensive publications concern immigration politics and policy, the American presidency, civil liberties, interest groups, social movements, political parties, and US political development. He has been a faculty scholar at the Center for the Study of Democratic Politics at Princeton University, a research fellow in governmental studies at the Brookings Institution, the Abba P. Schwartz fellow in immigration and refugee policy at the John F. Kennedy Presidential Library, a research scholar at the Eagleton Institute of Politics, a visiting scholar at Leipzig University, and a faculty associate at both the Center for Migration and Development at Princeton University and the Center for Comparative Immigration Studies at the University of California, San Diego. *Dividing Lines: The Politics of Immigration Control in America* (2002) won the American Political Science Association's Gladys M. Kammerer Award for the best book on American national policy.

ELLIE VASTA is associate professor of "social inclusion" at Macquarie University in Sydney. From 2003 to 2009, she was a senior research fellow at the Centre on Migration, Policy and Society (COMPAS) at the University of Oxford. Her recent work in Britain and Europe has focused on immigrant work strategies and networks in London, with specific emphasis on immigrant participation, identity, community, and irregular migration; on racism; and on ideological shifts in the European models of immigrant inclusion, focusing on policies and public discourse. Her current research projects are on belonging and "affinities" in multicultural neighborhoods. Recent publications include "From Ethnic Minorities to Ethnic Majority Policy: Multiculturalism and the Shift to Assimilationism in the Netherlands," *Ethnic and Racial Studies* (2007); "The Controllability of Difference: Social Cohesion and the New Politics of Solidarity," *Ethnicities* (2010); "Immigrants and the Paper Market: Borrowing, Renting and Buying Identities," *Ethnic and Racial Studies* (2011); "Do We Need Social Cohesion in the 21st Century? Multiple Languages of Belonging in the Metropolis," *Journal of Intercultural Studies* (2010); and a monograph, *The Internal Dynamics of Migration Processes and Their Consequences for Australian Government Migration Policies* (with Stephen Castles and Derya Ozkul, 2012).

ESKIL WADENSJÖ is professor of labor economics at the Swedish Institute for Social Research, Stockholm University, and director of Stockholm University's Linnaeus Center of Integration Studies. He holds a PhD in economics from Lund University (his thesis was on the economics of international migration), and his main research fields are immigration and integration, social and occupational insurance, labor market policy, self-employment, temporary employment agencies, and the youth labor market. He has published many articles and books related to these fields and has been a member of and written reports for Swedish governmental and parliamentary commissions and for Danish commissions and international organizations such as the Organisation for Economic Co-operation and Development (OECD) and the International Labour Organization (ILO).

CATHERINE WIHTOL DE WENDEN is director of research at CNRS (CERI) and for thirty years has been a researcher on international migration from a political science and public law perspective. She studied at Sciences Po in Paris and at the University of Paris I (Panthéon-Sorbonne) and received her PhD in political science in 1986. She has published 20 books, alone or as a co-author, and approximately 150 articles. She teaches at Sciences Po and at the University La Sapienza in an EU Socrates program. She is past president of the Research Committee on Migration, ISA–International Sociological Association (2002–2008), and consults for the United Nations High Commissioner for Refugees (UNHCR), the Council of Europe, and the European Commission. Her publications include the following: *Les immigrés et la politique* (1988); *Le défi migratoire* (with Bertrand Badie, 1995); *L'immigration en Europe, La documentation française* (1999); *Faut-il ouvrir les frontières* (1999); *La citoyenneté européenne* (1997); *La beurgeoisie* (with Rémy Leveau, 2001); *Police et discriminations* (with Sophie Body-Gendrot, 2003); *Atlas mondial des migrations* (first edition, 2005; second edition, 2009; third edition, 2012); *Les couleurs du drapeau* (with Christophe Bertossi, 2007); *Sortir des banlieues* (with Sophie Body-Gendrot, 2007); *La globalisation humaine* (2009); *La question migratoire au XXIème siècle* (first edition, 2010; second edition, 2013); and *Les nouvelles migrations* (2013).

TOM K. WONG is assistant professor of political science at the University of California, San Diego (USCD). His research focuses on the politics of immigration, citizenship, and migrant illegality and, because these issues have far-reaching implications, the links between immigration, race and ethnicity, and the politics of identity. He is the creator of UCSD's Center for Comparative Immigration Studies and posts the CIR 2013 blog, which analyzes support for and opposition to comprehensive immigration reform among all current members of Congress. His work on immigration reform has been covered by the *Los Angeles Times*, NPR, and ABC News / Univision, among other media outlets. Among his other projects, he is completing work on a book that analyzes the determinants of immigration control policy across twenty-five Western immigrant-receiving democracies. The forthcoming book is *Rights, Deportation, and Detention in the Age of Immigration Control* (Stanford University Press).

MADELINE ZAVODNY is professor of economics at Agnes Scott College in Decatur, Georgia. She is also a research fellow of the Institute for the Study of Labor in Bonn. She received a BA in economics from Claremont McKenna College and a PhD in economics from the Massachusetts Institute of Technology. Her research areas are labor and health economics and economic demography, and much of her research focuses on economic issues related to immigration. Her publications include, with Pia Orrenius, *Beside the Golden Door: U.S. Immigration Reform in a New Era of Globalization* (2010).

ACRONYMS

AAFI	Australians against Further Immigration
ABS	Australian Bureau of Statistics
ACF	Australian Conservative Foundation
AESP	Australians for an Ecologically Sustainable Population
ALP	Australian Labor Party
AZC	Asielzoekerscentrum (asylum reception center)
BCA	Business Council of Australia
BIMPR	Bureau of Immigration, Multicultural and Population Research
CDA	Christen Democratisch Appel (Christian Democratic Party)
CDU	Christlich Demokratische Union (Christian Democratic Union)
CFTC	Confédération Française des Travailleurs Chrétiens (French Confederation of Christian Workers)
CGIL	Confederazione Generale Italiana del Lavoro (Italian Labor Confederation)
CGP	Commissarait Générale du Travail (General Labor Confederation)
CIC	Citizenship and Immigration Canada
CISL	Confederazione Italiana Sindicati Lavoratori (Confederation of Italian Labor Unions)
CNPF	Conseil National du Patronat Français (National Businessmen's Council)
CSU	Christlich Soziale Union (Christian Social Union)
DACA	Departures and Arrivals Control Act
DIEA	Department for Immigration and Ethnic Affairs
DILGEA	Department of Immigration, Local Government and Ethnic Affairs
DIMA	Department of Immigration and Multicultural Affairs
DIMIA	Department of Immigration Multicultural and Indigenous Affairs
EBSVERA	Enhanced Border Security and Visa Entry Reform Act
EC	European Community
ECC	Ethnic Communities Council
EEA	European Economic Area
EEC	European Economic Community

EMU	Economic and Monetary Union
ES	Employment Service
ESB	English-speaking background
EU	European Union
FAIR	Federation for American Immigration Reform
FDP	Free Democratic Party
FECCA	Federation of Ethnic Communities Councils of Australia
FLN	[Algerian National] Front de Libération Nationale
FN	Front National / National Front
GATS	General Agreement on Trade in Services
GDP	Gross Domestic Product
HRDC	Human Resources Development Canada
IIRIRA	Illegal Immigration Reform and Immigrant Responsibility Act
ILO	International Labour Organization
IMDB	Longitudinal Immigrant Database
INS	US Immigration and Naturalization Service
IPS	International Passenger Survey
IRCA	Immigration Reform and Control Act
JCMK	Joint Committee for Immigrant Workers of Korea
KFSB	Korean Federation of Small Businesses
KITCO	Korean International Training Cooperation Corps
LDP	Liberal Democratic Party
LFS	Labor Force Survey
LPF	Lijst Pim Fortuyn (Pim Fortuyn List)
MRAP	Mouvement contre le Racisme et pour l'Amitié entre les Peuples (Movement against Racism and for Friendship among Peoples)
MRCI	Ministère des Relations avec les Citoyens et de l'Immigration (Ministry of Citizenship and Immigration)
MVV	Matching Voorloping Verblijf (authorization for provisional residency)
NAFTA	North American Free Trade Agreement
NCNP	National Congress for New Politics
NDP	New Democratic Party
NESB	non-English-speaking background
NGO	nongovernmental organization
NKP	New Korea Party
NRC	National Research Council
NTOM	Nieuwe Toelatings en Opvang Model (New Admissions and Reception Policy)
OECD	Organisation for Economic Co-operation and Development
OFPRA	Office Français pour la Protection des Réfugiés et Apatrides (Office for the Protection of Refugees and Stateless Persons)
OMA	Office of Multicultural Affairs
ONI	Office National d'Immigration (National Immigration Office)
PAF	Police de l'Air et des Frontières (border police)

PP	Partido Popular (Popular Party)
PRWORA	Personal Responsibility and Work Opportunity Reconciliation Act
PSOE	Partido Socialista Obrero Español (Spanish Socialist Party)
ROA	Rijksregeling Opvang Asielzoekers (Regulation on the Reception of Asylum Seekers)
RPR	Rassemblement Pour la République (Rally for the Republic)
SAC	special assistance category
SAW	Special Agricultural Worker Program
SGI	Société Générale d'Immigration (Immigration Society, special humanitarian program)
SMBA	Small and Medium Business Administration
SPD	Sozialdemokratische Partei Deutschlands (German Social Democratic Party)
TPV	temporary protection visa
TROO	Tijdelijke Regeling Opvang Ontheemden (temporary measure for displaced persons)
UDF	Union pour la Démocratie Française (Union for French Democracy)
UI	unemployment insurance
UIL	Unione Italiana del Lavoro (Italian Labor Union)
UMP	Union pour la Majorité Présidentielle (Union for a Presidential Majority)
UNHCR	United Nations High Commissioner for Refugees
VVtV	Voorwaardelijke Vergunning tot Verblijf (conditional residence permit)
WABW	Wet Arbeid Buitenlandse Werknemers (Foreign Workers Employment Act)
WAV	Wet Arbeid Vreemdelingen (Foreign Workers Employment Law)

CONTROLLING IMMIGRATION

I

INTRODUCTION

1 THE DILEMMAS OF IMMIGRATION CONTROL

James F. Hollifield, Philip L. Martin, and Pia M. Orrenius

All countries in the world today face the reality of controlling or managing migration. The dilemmas of control are especially acute in the advanced industrial democracies, where economic pressures push for openness to migration while political, legal, and security concerns argue for greater control. How do the major immigrant-receiving countries cope with this dilemma?

This book is a systematic, comparative study of immigration policy in fifteen industrialized democracies and the European Union (EU): the United States, Canada, Australia, Britain, France, Germany, the Netherlands, three Scandinavian countries (Sweden, Denmark, and Norway), Switzerland, Italy, Spain, Japan, and Korea. It has two central, interrelated theses. The first, which we call the "convergence hypothesis," is that there is growing similarity among industrialized, labor-importing countries in terms of (1) the policy instruments chosen for controlling immigration, especially unauthorized immigration and refugee flows; (2) the results or efficacy of immigration control measures; (3) integration policies—that is, the measures adopted by labor-importing countries that affect the rate and extent of social, economic, and political integration among immigrants who become long-term residents; and (4) general-public reaction to current immigrant flows and assessment of government efforts to control or manage them.

Our second hypothesis is that the gap between the goals and results of national immigration policy (laws, regulations, executive actions, and court rulings, to name a few) is growing wider in the major industrial democracies, thus provoking greater public hostility toward immigrants in general (regardless of legal status) and putting pressure on political parties and government officials to adopt more restrictive policies. We refer to this as the "gap hypothesis" (see Hollifield 1986).

Beyond testing these two general hypotheses against the comparative evidence gathered in the fifteen countries and regions represented here, we seek to explain the efficacy of immigration control measures in today's labor-importing countries in an era of globalization and unprecedented international labor mobility (Sassen 1988). In each of the in-depth country and regional profiles, the authors explain why certain immigration control measures were chosen (or not chosen) by that country or region and why these measures either succeeded or failed to achieve their stated objectives. Each chapter is followed by one or two commentaries that offer a critique of its principal findings, supplementing them and, in some cases, offering an alternative interpretation.

Our findings generally support the hypothesis of increased "convergence" among industrialized, labor-importing countries, along the lines described above, as well as the "gap hypothesis" emphasizing the divergence of immigration policy outputs and outcomes. Despite significant increases in immigration control efforts in most of the countries under study and the tightening of entry restrictions and monitoring of unauthorized immigrants already working in those countries, officials acknowledge that the challenge of managing migration is more difficult than ever and that they are less confident that governments can regulate immigration flows. In some countries and sectors, there is a structural element to employer demand for foreign workers, such as in agriculture, construction, health care, domestic help, and hospitality. That is, employers continue to hire foreign workers regardless of legal status and irrespective of the business cycle. If governments continue to find it hard to prevent the entry and employment of foreign labor from lower-wage countries, the gap between immigration policy goals and outcomes is likely to persist.

The country studies here highlight the administrative, political, legal, and economic difficulties of immigration enforcement in relatively open and pluralistic societies. Bureaucratic power in all of these countries is routinely open to contestation by a variety of social and economic groups, and reducing the "demand-pull" factors that attract migrants—shortages of manpower and human capital and demographic decline—is extremely difficult. Competing interests in pluralistic societies lead to policymaking gridlock that, in the face of ever-stronger economic incentives, permits immigration to continue in one form or another. Such policy paralysis sends mixed signals to prospective migrants in the labor-exporting countries, encouraging them to overcome additional obstacles placed in their path at borders (external controls) or in the workplace (internal controls). Moreover, amnesties for settled migrants create a potential moral hazard that makes prospective migrants more likely to risk crossing borders and working illegally.

On the other hand, industrialized countries cannot, at least in the short term, realistically hope to reduce the "supply-push" pressures in the principal labor-exporting countries—rapid population growth combined with low rates of economic growth and high unemployment, especially among the young—to which they are increasingly linked by globalization (Joppke 1998; Hollifield 2004). And severing the family- and employer-based networks that link high-emigration and labor-importing nations is becoming harder rather than easier. If demand-pull and supply-push forces, together with networks that link sending and receiving societies, are the necessary conditions for migration to occur, the granting of some kind of legal status (rights) to foreigners is the sufficient condition. These rights most often derive from domestic sources of law, especially constitutions, but migrants are increasingly protected by international law and human rights conventions. This is especially true in Europe (Joppke 2001; see also Chapter 14). Despite the rise of rights-based politics (Hollifield 1992, Hollifield and Wilson 2011) and regimes that check the action of states trying to control migration, in recent decades policies have increasingly targeted migrant rights (civil, social, and political) as a way of controlling immigration.

Legal and constitutional constraints notwithstanding, "fixing" immigration control systems that are buckling under the pressure of new waves of refugees and economic migrants has become a political imperative in most of the countries we have studied. The principal exceptions are Japan and South Korea, where the numbers of new immigrants are still relatively small, and Canada, where general-public hostility to immigration remains relatively low. The severe recession that began in 2008 has led to a stabilization of flows, especially in the United States, and the politics of immigration has shifted somewhat from control to integration of a large illegal population (Hollifield 2010). Integration dilemmas also are acute in Western Europe and the United States, Canada, and Australia—*nations of immigrants*—where sources of immigration have become much more diverse (Favell 1998; Bloemraad 2006; Schain 2012).

However, even in the de facto *countries of immigration*—France, Germany, the Netherlands, Switzerland, Britain, and the Scandinavian countries—where immigration is not part of the founding ideal as it is in the nations of immigrants, general publics and the politicians and political parties that respond to them are increasingly uneasy about the long-term implications of current immigration flows for maintenance of national culture, language, and identity. Debates over the integration of Muslim immigrants in largely Christian societies have been especially vociferous and divisive in Europe (Kepel 2012). Even if foreign workers and their dependents living in industrialized democracies are not illegal aliens (there are millions of settled, legally admitted foreign "guest workers" in European countries), they are often unwanted as a permanent component of the population for non-economic reasons—specifically, low tolerance for cultural, racial, and ethnic diversity; fear of crime and terrorism; and overcrowding in major urban areas (Fetzer 2000; Sides and Citrin 2007; Brader, Valentino, and Suhay 2008).

Public hostility generates strong incentives for officials in labor-importing industrial democracies to redouble their efforts toward immigration control, by fine-tuning existing control measures like employer sanctions (internal control), investing more heavily in border enforcement (external control), and pursuing new experiments to restore at least the appearance of control (so-called trainee programs in Japan and South Korea). For this reason, the politics of immigration in many receiving countries has a strong symbolic dimension (Rudolph 2006); in addition to the wide gap between policy outputs and outcomes, we observe a similarly puzzling gap between public opinion, which wants immigration reduced, and liberal admissions policies(Freeman 1995; Sides and Citrin 2007). The more advanced agenda of anti-immigration and anti-immigrant forces in these countries today is (1) to curtail the access of illegal immigrants to tax-supported public services, including education and nonemergency healthcare, and roll back social rights in general; (2) to block any policies and programs that would accelerate the socioeconomic and cultural integration of settled immigrants and their offspring, opposing legalization programs and denying voting or political rights; and (3) to take steps to discourage permanent settlement, such as tightening citizenship requirements for legal permanent residents, denying citizenship to the native-born children of illegal immigrants, and generally limiting civil rights. It remains to be seen how much of this anti-immigration agenda can be translated into law and public policy in the labor-importing countries and, if so, whether such measures can serve as an effective deterrent to future unwanted migration.

IMMIGRATION CONTROL AND IMMIGRANT INTEGRATION

Immigration has become a central issue of politics and public policy in the advanced industrial democracies (Messina 2007). In Europe, immigration is already a driving factor in electoral politics (Lubbers, Gijsberts, and Scheepers 2002; Lahav 2004; Givens 2005), and it is becoming an increasingly potent electoral issue in the United States (at least in the five states with large immigrant populations; see Chapter 2). After decades of importing foreign labor as "guests," many European nations are confronted with the challenge of assimilating large numbers of culturally different, permanent resident aliens and their offspring. In Japan and South Korea, the influx of foreign workers, eagerly sought by small and medium-sized labor-hungry employers, into racially and culturally homogeneous societies with large and growing demographic deficits looms as a volatile issue for national policy (see Chapter 13). In the United States, the fourth wave of largely Hispanic and Asian immigrants has provoked nativist reactions, especially at the state and local levels (Ramakrishnan 2005; Hollifield 2010), even though immigration does not have the political salience there that it does in other industrial democracies (Norris 2005).

In addition to its impact on domestic politics, the increasing international mobility of workers and their dependents has had a dramatic effect on international relations. The major labor-importing states have scrambled to find ways to consult with each other and coordinate policies for controlling migration, especially refugee flows (Betts 2011). This new dynamic is particularly evident in Europe, where the relaxation of internal borders (associated with the Dublin and Schengen processes and the drive for greater political and economic integration) is pushing states to seek common visa and asylum policies (Thielemann 2003; see also Chapter 14).

The end of the Cold War contributed to this sea change in international relations by increasing the movement of populations from east to west, without slowing or stopping south-to-north migration flows. As a policy issue, international migration has moved from the realm of "low politics" (i.e., problems of domestic governance, especially labor market and demographic policies) to the realm of "high politics" (i.e., problems affecting relations between states, including questions of war and peace). Haiti and the former Yugoslavia provide early examples of this phenomenon, and political instability—associated with war in South Asia (Afghanistan and Pakistan) and upheavals in North and Sub-Saharan Africa, not to mention the so-called "Arab Spring" in the Middle East—has increased the propensity for migration from south to north. With the rise of terrorism in the first decade of the twenty-first century, many governments have recast migration as a problem of national security, and international organizations such as the United Nations High Commission for Refugees have come under intense pressure to help states manage increasing flows (Greenhill 2010; Rudolph 2006; see also the commentary by Betts in Chapter 14).

Should we conclude that the increasing movement of people across national borders is primarily a function of changes in the international system? Clearly, there is a connection between structural changes in the international political economy and the increasing mobility of people (Sassen 1988; Hollifield 2000, 2004). However, we argue that endogenous factors are the key determinants. As much as the principal immigrant-receiving countries may wish to ignore or avoid dealing with the structural factors that drive the supply of and demand for foreign labor, they must eventually recognize that the "crisis of immigration control" that they are experiencing derives largely from changes occurring in the international political economy. For example, competition for the highly skilled (human capital) is increasingly fierce in a global labor market (Chiswick 2011), and the imbalance in global population growth, between the North and the South, is growing.

On the economic and demographic side of the equation, neoclassical "push-pull" arguments provide us with a simple and straightforward explanation for increases in immigration. Demand-pull in the US and European economies during the 1950s and 1960s was so great as to stimulate large-scale migrations from the poorer economies of the "periphery" (Mexico, Turkey, North Africa, etc.). These labor migrations were initiated and legitimized by the receiving states, in Western Europe through the so-called guest worker programs and in the United States through the Bracero Program of contract labor importation (1942–1964). But what started as an optimal movement of labor from south to north became, in the 1970s and 1980s, a sociopolitical liability as economic growth in Western Europe and North America slowed in the aftermath of the first big postwar recessions, which began with the first oil shock in 1973–1974 (Hollifield 1992).

Stopping immigration, however, even during a period of sharp economic contraction, proved exceedingly difficult, in part because of powerful underlying push-pull factors. Demand-pull migration had initiated processes that continued to have unanticipated consequences, from the micro level—employers wanting to retain their "guest workers" indefinitely—to the macro level—the expanding role of immigration in host-country population and labor force growth as well as the dependence of sending-country economies on multibillion-dollar migrant remittances (Hollifield, Orrenius, and Osang 2006). Moreover, supply-push migration reached new heights as the populations of peripheral countries like Turkey, Mexico, and Algeria grew at a very rapid pace even as their economies slowed as a result of the global recession. Migration networks developed during the years of expansionary immigration policies, helping to spread information about job opportunities, modes of entry, and residence in the receiving countries. These transnational social networks, perhaps more than any other factor, helped to sustain migration—especially family reunification in Europe and illegal labor migration from Mexico to the United States—during periods of high uncertainty regarding employment prospects in the labor-importing countries. Thus, despite a series of economic recessions, culminating in the "great recession" of 2008, immigration has continued at historically high levels, forcing governments to scramble to redesign immigration control and refugee admission policies to cope with the rising tides.

Push-pull forces and the imbalances between the economies of the North and South (as well as the West and East in Europe) provide necessary but not sufficient conditions for immigration, especially on the scale experienced in recent decades. To explain what Myron

Weiner (1995) labeled the "global migration crisis," we must look beyond macro- and microeconomics, and even social networks, to trends in the political development of the major receiving countries.

The difficulties of immigration control today are closely linked to the rise of rights-based politics (Hollifield 1992, 1999, 2008). This new brand of politics is especially evident in debates over immigration, naturalization, and asylum policies in all of the major democracies, which must grapple with the fundamental issues of how many migrants to accept, from which countries, and what rights (status) to provide to them. Civil rights–based policies help immigrants not only to get in but also to remain and settle. At the same time, human rights and refugee conventions have underscored the rights of asylum seekers, migrant workers, and their families. In sum, it is to both political and economic changes within states and internationally that we must look for explanations of immigration policy.

THE "LIBERAL PARADOX"

The extension of rights to minorities and foreigners in the decades following World War II is one of the most salient aspects of political development in the advanced industrial democracies. The creation of new legal spaces for marginal groups (including foreigners) in societies as different as Germany, the United States, and Japan is linked to a much broader change in international and democratic politics, which originated with the adoption of the Universal Declaration of Human Rights in 1948 and in the American civil rights struggles of the 1950s and 1960s. A new type of rights-based politics has taken shape at many levels of the democratic polity and in the international system itself: in legislative acts, partisan and interest group (especially ethnic) politics, and, most important of all, in judicial rulings (Schuck 1998). Judicial activism has gained many supporters and detractors, and has helped to spawn a plethora of advocacy groups ranging from social movements and political parties on the extreme right to new civil and human rights organizations on the left.

Even though the history of rights-based politics in the United States is quite different from that in Europe, its impact on immigration policy has been much the same: expanded rights for marginal and ethnic groups, including foreigners. These historical developments have provoked a rethinking of classical liberal theory in the works of scholars who place civil and human rights at the center of a new social contract (see, for example, Rawls 1971; Walzer 1983; Hirsch 1992; Soysal 1994; Bauböck 1994; Jacobson 1996; Benhabib 2004). Redefining the relationship between the state and individuals and groups, through a process of political struggle, has had a great impact on the capacity of democratic states to control immigration, and it has given rise to a new multiculturalism that in many ways has redefined the social contract (Kymlicka 1995). While legislative acts as well as judicial rulings in recent decades have whittled away at some of the rights and protections accorded to immigrants, the legal and political legacy of the postwar era continues to constrain the executive authorities of democratic states in their attempts to achieve territorial closure and to exclude certain individuals and groups from membership in society (Schuck 1998; Benhabib 2004).

It is the confluence of markets (the push-pull factors described above) and rights that explains much of the contemporary difficulty with immigration control, highlighting what

Hollifield (1992) has called "the liberal paradox." How can a society be open for economic reasons and at the same time maintain a degree of political and legal closure to protect the social contract? This political-economic dynamic has weakened the historically close linkage between business cycles and "admissionist" or "restrictionist" immigration policies (Hollifield and Wilson 2011). Efforts by some states to regain control of their borders all point to a gradual recognition that immigration control may require a rollback of civil and human rights for noncitizens (Canada and to some extent Australia would seem to be notable exceptions; see Chapters 3 and 4). Examples include the 1996 US Illegal Immigration Reform and Immigrant Responsibility Act, which tightened restrictions on legal as well as illegal immigrants, the German decision to amend Article 16 of the Basic Law to restrict the blanket right to asylum, the Pasqua and Debré laws in France in the 1990s, and, in the aftermath of the terrorist attacks of the 2000s, new and often sweeping powers granted to police and intelligence services to carry out surveillance and identity checks and to detain individuals without charge for extended periods.

Ruhs and Martin (2008) have argued that there is a tradeoff between numbers and rights—states can have more foreign workers with fewer rights, or they can have fewer foreign workers with more rights, but they cannot have both high numbers (open labor markets) and rights.

The postwar development of rights-based politics has not prevented nationalist and nativist backlashes against immigration. The French Front National is perhaps the most widely known anti-immigrant political movement, but many others have emerged in almost every industrialized country that has experienced large-scale immigration in recent decades (Kitschelt 1995; Money 1999; Norris 2005; Mudde 2007; Hopkins 2010). These backlashes are nationalist, particularist, and exclusionary. Their principal target is immigrants, but they also level criticism at liberal parties and politicians who support the expansion or preservation of civil and political rights for ethnic minorities.

The growth of extreme right anti-immigrant parties places center-right politicians under tremendous electoral pressures (Thränhardt 1996; Perlmutter 1996; Arzheimer and Carter 2006). How can a "liberal" society tolerate the presence of individuals in it who are members but not citizens? Should not all individuals who are members (i.e., permanent residents) of a liberal society be accorded the full panoply of rights (social and political as well as civil) enjoyed by those who are citizens? This is the paradox or dilemma that "liberals" face, and it is particularly acute in countries that have large, multigenerational resident-alien populations that remain just outside the social contract.

In sum, immigration in most of the countries studied in this book can no longer be debated strictly in economic or demographic terms; citizenship, membership in national and local communities, and basic human rights must also be addressed (Brubaker 1989; Carens 2000).

NATIONS OF IMMIGRANTS

In settler nations like the United States, Canada, and Australia, immigration is part of the founding ideal (or myth). But like all immigrant-receiving countries, these countries must address key issues such as how many foreigners to admit, from where, and with what status. We define as "nations of immigrants" those founded, populated, and built by immigrants in modern times; as a result, immigration is a fundamental part of the founding myth, historical consciousness, and national identity of these countries, which normally anticipate and welcome large numbers of immigrants. This does not mean, however, that they have always been so open; nor does it mean that immigration is not currently a source of social tension and political conflict (see, for example, Schlesinger 1992; Smith 1997; Huntington 2004). Indeed, during the last twenty years the United States and Australia have been nearly as prone as the "reluctant" labor importers (to be discussed) to adopt restrictive measures that roll back immigrant rights and indulge anti-immigrant public opinion.

Of all the countries included in this study, the United States has by far the largest gap between the stated goal of controlling immigration and the actual results of policy: historically high immigration levels and a large and growing illegal immigrant population. Recent US efforts to reduce the influx of unauthorized migrants entering via Mexico—through concentrated border enforcement operations, deportation, and other control measures—have not reduced the stock of such immigrants; instead, they have produced a more stable, settled population (Massey, Durand, and Malone 2002). By the beginning of the twenty-first century, 10 percent of low-wage workers in the United States were unauthorized immigrants; in agriculture, they were between 50 and 60 percent (Martin 2009; see also Chapter 2).

The US insistence on maintaining such ineffective immigration control policies prompts Martin to ask, in Chapter 2, whether those policies are genuine efforts to reduce unauthorized immigration or primarily an attempt to manage public opinion using the illusion that illegal immigration is under control. Although enforcement of immigration laws in the workplace is potentially a much more effective means of immigration control, employer sanctions have been ineffective because of the widespread availability of fraudulent documents among immigrant workers and insufficient numbers of inspectors.

The political debate over immigration in the United States is fueled by the large numbers of unauthorized immigrants who find their way into the country; by the perceived impacts of immigration in general on the life chances of native-born workers; and by the alleged failure of recent immigrants (especially Mexicans) to assimilate into society. The general public continues to assume that immigrants depress wages, compete unfairly (and effectively) for jobs that would otherwise be taken by native workers, and drain public services. Martin notes that most empirical research does not support such assumptions (see also Orrenius and Zavodny 2010).

Martin describes the debate between integrationists (assimilationists) and pluralists (multiculturalists) over the extent and pace of immigrant assimilation into US society. Previous attempts to incorporate immigrants through cultural assimilation have been replaced by a greater multicultural tolerance that enables immigrants to attain socioeconomic mobility while retaining cultural differences. Although the United States does not have an official immigrant integration policy, it has provided immigrants with differential access to rights, benefits, and social services depending on legal status (King 2000; Tichenor 2002). Martin argues, however, that there is a rights-numbers trade-off in the United States, just as there is in other industrialized democracies, which means that countries can have high numbers of immigrants with few rights or low numbers with more rights (see also Ruhs and Martin 2008).

Martin observes that US immigration policy has long followed a "zigzag" pattern, with expansionary periods followed by restrictionist periods. After the terrorist attacks of September 11, 2001, the United States clearly entered a new restrictionist phase, as immigration control was conflated with protection of national security. Tightened border controls, much closer monitoring of foreign students, and ethnic/religious profiling to identify and detain potential terrorists became accepted practice in the post-9/11 era. Nevertheless, as Martin notes, there has been no concerted effort to substantially reduce the number of immigrants admitted, thus demonstrating both the resilience of the ideology that the United States is a nation of immigrants and the power of market forces driving immigration.

Among the countries represented in this book, Canada seems to be the most comfortable with its immigration policy. As Jeffrey Reitz in Chapter 3 makes clear, Canada has a consensual and relatively open approach that is geared more toward nation building and national economic development than is US policy. As a result, Canada has maintained an expansionary, skills-based immigration system that sees three times the number of immigrants admitted per capita than the United States. Despite such high immigration levels, the Canadian public remains quite tolerant of immigrants. Reitz attributes the differences between the United States and Canada to different economic structures, cultural factors, and institutional arrangements. Canada has a fixed-target policy of admitting each year a number of immigrants equal to 1 percent of its population (about 300,000 immigrants per annum), regardless of short-run economic conditions. However, unlike the US system, which is based primarily on family ties, Canada has a carefully managed points system that selects immigrants according to their education, skills, and linguistic ability, in an effort to meet the country's long-term labor needs. In recent years, the selection process has placed more emphasis on attracting the young and skilled. Noneconomic immigrants admitted through family reunification or as refugees are proportionately fewer, although Canada has a relatively liberal policy toward asylum seekers.

Given such clear policy objectives, it is relatively simple to measure gaps between policies and actual outcomes in the Canadian case. In terms of the number of immigrants actually admitted, Canada has consistently and significantly fallen short of its 1-percent-of-population target, which, as Reitz notes, is quite interesting since most countries receive more immigrants than desired. It is more difficult to assess whether Canadian policy has been effective in providing the country with enough highly skilled and economically successful immigrants. In the past, immigrant educational levels were higher than native Canadian levels, but the gap has narrowed and virtually disappears when immigrants are compared to young native-born urban workers. Immigrant earnings are higher than in the United States but not relative to qualifications.

The Canadian case is also distinguished by a relatively high level of public support as compared to the United States and Australia, with majorities of Canadians consistently favoring maintaining or increasing current immigration levels. The political discourse on immigration has also remained positive, with all major political parties officially supporting it. Reitz suggests a number of explanations for this: the positive association of immigration with nation building and population maintenance, a small population of illegal immigrants, and simple cultural tolerance. Another reason for public acceptance of high immigration levels may be Canada's policy of selecting immigrants according to skills and other qualifications to meet labor market needs, which gives the public the impression that immigrants are making a positive contribution to the economy.

Canada gives immigrants immediate access to various social services, settlement programs, and a relatively easy naturalization process. The country's official immigrant integration ideology seems to have followed a course somewhat similar to that of the United States: an earlier assimilationist paradigm has been replaced by a multiculturalist approach. Unlike the United States, however, Canada has an explicit and official multiculturalism policy (see also Kymlicka 1995). The greater feeling of social acceptance that this policy generates among immigrants may be one reason that rates of naturalization are higher than in the United States.

Canada is something of a deviant case among the countries considered in this book because of its reaffirmation of expansionary immigration policies. The September 11 terrorist attacks on the United States did not provoke a restrictive turn in Canadian immigration policy, despite increased cooperation with the United States on border security. But Reitz suggests that the widening gaps between policy and outcomes—that is, Canada's inability to attract a sufficient number of immigrants and the recent downward trends in immigrant job-seeking success and earnings—may erode the currently positive economic perception of immigration. Moreover, there is growing concern about the spatial distribution of immigrants; more than 80 percent of new arrivals head for only three cities: Toronto, Montreal, and Vancouver. Finally, it will become increasingly difficult for Canada to keep the proportion of family-based immigrant admissions low, given that the skills-based immigrants already living in the country eventually will want to bring in family members. Such trends may force the government to adopt policies that converge more with those of the United States.

The immigration histories of Australia and Canada have a number of important similarities. Both countries originated as British colonies and in the past pursued racist (white-only) immigration designed to keep their countries white and European. However, they eventually abandoned such discriminatory policies in favor of a skills-selection (points) system and a multicultural policy toward immigrant integration. Both still regard immigration as a means of economic development and nation building. The critical difference is that Australia is currently much more ambivalent than Canada about high levels of immigrants—especially refugees and asylum seekers.

According to Stephen Castles, Ellie Vasta, and Derya Ozkul in Chapter 4, the Australian government has fashioned a carefully managed immigration program modeled on the Canadian system, one that admits skilled immigrants based on a qualification points test and generates a low proportion of family-based and humanitarian immigrants (refugees and asylum seekers). Australia also has a large temporary foreign worker program for immigrants who are highly skilled. Castles, Vasta, and Ozkul find that the gap between immigration policies and outcomes is rather small in Australia. The points system has been relatively effective in attracting the desired skilled, economically successful immigrants. Indeed, the average skill level of recent immigrants is higher than that of native-born workers, and both first- and second-generation immigrants have experienced substantial occupational mobility. The illegal immigrant population is small, partly a consequence of Australia's geographical isolation from poorer, less developed countries. In terms of immigrant integration, Australia seems to have followed the American and Canadian trajectory: an assimilationist policy has given way to a multiculturalist stance that recognizes the nation's cultural diversity and improves immigrant rights and access to social services and institutions. As in the United States, there is not a large difference in the rights conferred to citizens and permanent residents, and the requirements for naturalization are minimal.

The Australian government seems to have done an effective job of convincing the public that their country primarily admits skilled immigrants who contribute to the economy. However, Castles, Vasta, and Ozkul document growing public ambivalence toward immigration, driven by rising unemployment and economic uncertainty, and the emergence of the anti-immigrant One Nation party. Globalization and increased regional integration (both of which have increased the number of countries sending immigrants to Australia) together with the recent arrival of boat people (undocumented immigrants and asylum seekers) have contributed to a sense that the country's tightly controlled immigration system is under threat. In response to this anti-immigrant backlash, government policies have taken a restrictive turn, marked by a draconian tightening of refugee and asylum policy and stronger border controls. Australia's multiculturalism program has also been downgraded and partly dismantled. However, a pro-immigrant movement is emerging, led by a conglomeration of unions and other NGOs. Although Australia has a bureaucracy-dominated immigration policymaking regime, it actively consults with various interest and advocacy groups and is responsive to public pressure.

COUNTRIES OF IMMIGRATION

Immigration has long been a fact of life in Europe, but it is not part of the founding ideal of any European country. Germans, for example, emigrated across the globe as early as the seventeenth century, but in the last decades of the twentieth century, Germany became a country of immigration, facing the same issues as traditional settler nations. We consider "countries of immigration" those that have a history of immigration but officially deny that they are countries of immigration or that have acknowledged this fact only recently. Immigration has not been a fundamental part of their national identity or their nation-building process, and the attitudes of political elites and general publics toward it generally have been more negative than in the classic nations of immigrants. These countries recruit most migrants temporarily (that is, as guest workers) rather than as permanent additions to the labor force, and in effect they are "reluctant lands of immigration." France, as we will see, is a partial exception because of its revolutionary history and early demographic transition.

James Hollifield argues in Chapter 5 that France has been a relatively liberal immigration country because of the strength of its political ideology of republicanism—initially a form of left-wing, rights-based politics—buttressed by the labor requirements of French capitalism and the policy preferences of government economic planners in the post–World War II era. Liberal immigration and naturalization policies also derived from the early establishment, in the nineteenth century, of a pattern whereby immigrant labor was recruited privately by French industry, often with government sanction but with very little state control. The organization of foreign labor importation by the private sector largely bypassed official institutions created to manage immigration flows. The historical pattern has been for such flows to accelerate to the point where the state is compelled, for political reasons, to try to regain control. However, the general ineffectiveness of France's immigration control policies has created a substantial gap between stated policy objectives and actual outcomes.

Consistent with its republican tradition, France has been willing to accept immigrants and incorporate them into the French nation under a generous naturalization policy and with no significant exclusions from the country's welfare state. However, since World War II there have been repeated efforts to curtail immigrant rights, including limiting family reunification, encouraging repatriation, restricting labor permits and employment opportunities, toughening the asylum adjudication process, and expanding the powers of police to detain and deport unauthorized immigrants. Some of these measures were part of a "grand bargain" struck by left-wing governments, in which tightened control over new immigration flows was accompanied by efforts to accelerate the social integration of immigrants already settled in France, through legalization and the granting of citizenship rights. In recent years, more conservative-minded governments have attempted to make France's citizenship and naturalization laws more exclusionary and to limit the civil and social rights of immigrants, partly in an effort to placate the anti-immigrant National Front and win back its supporters.

France's increasingly negative policy stance on immigration led to strong pro-immigrant reactions from civil society. This is despite public anxiety about the rapidly increasing number of Muslim immigrants (the largest concentration in Western Europe) and the threat of terrorism fed by Islamic fundamentalism. The governments of Jacques Chirac and Nicolas Sarkozy secured the enactment of a national ban on the wearing of Muslim head scarves and other religious symbols in public schools. Although the legislation was justified as necessary to protect France's strict doctrine of separation of church and state (*laïcité*), it was also a clear response to public concerns about immigration and the fact that roughly one in five French voters supported the National Front in the last three presidential elections. Part of the public backlash against Muslim immigrants is a concern that they cannot be assimilated in accordance with the republican model.

Republican ideology has not been the sole *determinant* of French immigration policy, but it has acted as a *constraint* on government actions. For example, French courts have ruled repeatedly that laws violating the civil liberties of immigrants are unconstitutional on the grounds that they are inconsistent with the country's republican values, which are derived from universal human rights. The government's anti-immigrant measures have also aroused large-scale public protests in an active civil society. As Hollifield argues, France and other liberal democratic states have certain built-in constraints that prevent them from crossing the "invisible line" and infringing on the basic civil liberties of citizens and denizens in violation of their founding principles.

For much of the postwar period, Britain was *not* a country of immigration, given that flows remained relatively modest compared with other labor-importing countries and that Britain succeeded, where other countries failed, in controlling immigration, matching outputs to outcomes. For this reason, Gary Freeman in earlier editions of this book referred to Britain as "the deviant case." Nevertheless, despite having a supposedly "zero-immigration" policy since the 1970s, immigration in Britain has been steadily rising in the past two decades. Randall Hansen in Chapter 6 sees this policy shift as a conscious choice made by Labour governments led by Tony Blair at the end of the twentieth century.

Thus, Britain reversed a trend toward increasingly restrictive immigration policies that had begun in 1962, when the country started to impose stringent controls on immigration from its colonies and the British Commonwealth. In the early 1970s, the government created a work permit system that generally did not allow family reunification or permanent residence. Additional restrictions, as well as a crackdown on visa overstayers, were implemented during the conservative governments of the 1970s and early 1980s. Britain further tightened its immigration system by adopting a narrower definition of British citizenship (the partiality rule), which denied most former British subjects the right to immigrate. And unlike other Western European countries, which granted free movement across borders to EU nationals under the Schengen Group protocols, Britain retained strict border controls. In 2004, however, Britain was one of the few EU member states to grant free movement immediately to the formerly communist states of East Central Europe when they acceded to EU membership, with the result that large numbers of workers from these states, especially Poland, came to Britain in search of work.

Hansen argues that the main driver of British immigration policy has been the demand (or lack thereof) for foreign labor. This is in contrast to the arguments advanced by Zig Layton-Henry in previous editions of this book. Layton-Henry attributed low levels of immigration to British racism and intolerance. Indeed, the British public and mass media have been hostile to large-scale immigration out of concern that it threatens the country's national character and overburdens the welfare system. Conservative and Labour governments once assumed that large numbers of racially and culturally different immigrants would cause a strong public backlash and lead to ethnic and racial conflict—hence Conservative politician Enoch Powell's comment in a 1968 speech that, if immigration were not controlled in Britain, there would be "rivers of blood." Immigration controls were viewed at that time as necessary not only for good race relations but also to reassure the public that immigration was being carefully managed to promote national economic interests. However, these policies of strict immigration control were reversed in the late 1990s and early 2000s by the "New Labour" governments of Tony Blair.

While historically Britain has had much more restrictive immigration policies than those of other countries of immigration, the gap between policy outputs and outcomes is no less prominent. Britain now has one of the largest ethnic minority populations in Western Europe. The government has had great difficulty in reducing the number of asylum seekers, resulting in greater politicization of immigration policy. Not surprisingly, Britain's reluctance to fully accept its status as a major country of immigration has made it less willing to adopt a proactive and coherent immigrant policy. This has forced local governments to bear most of the burden of providing basic human services to immigrants and asylum seekers. However, periodic race riots have vividly illustrated the uneven socioeconomic incorporation of immigrants, spurring the government to pay more attention to this issue.

The turn in the early 2000s toward more liberal admission of skilled immigrants—driven in part by a shortage of professional service workers—was accompanied by efforts to convince the public of the economic benefits of immigration. This policy was to some extent reversed by the Conservative-Liberal coalition government of David Cameron, who pledged in 2011 to cut the number of immigrants to 100,000 per year, raising the specter of a new gap between the supply of and demand for immigrant visas.

The Federal Republic of Germany, formerly the "*Gastarbeiter* (guest worker)" country par excellence, recoiled from the waves of foreigners that descended on it following the collapse of East European Communism in 1989. The arrival of 1 million foreigners in 1990 alone—including ethnic Germans relocating from the former Soviet Union and its satellites, relatives of immigrants already settled in Germany, applicants for political asylum, and legal and illegal foreign workers—made it by far the leading recipient of immigrants among OECD nations, even while German leaders declared that their country was "not, nor shall it become, a country of immigration, *Deutschland ist kein Einwanderungsland.*" It was not until January 2005 that Germany passed its first comprehensive immigration law covering issues of labor migration, family reunification, and integration.

In previous decades, as Philip Martin in Chapter 7 makes clear, Germany implemented a series of ad hoc immigration control policies, all of which went awry with major unintended consequences. In fact, the history of German immigration is one of huge gaps between policy outputs and outcomes. This is best illustrated by the country's guest worker programs, begun in the 1950s, which were intended to recruit foreign workers on a strict rotation basis. Although no numerical quota was set nor serious limits placed on foreign worker recruitment, a much larger number of guest workers migrated to Germany than expected, and a third of them settled there. Employers wanted them for longer periods, the workers prolonged their stays because of the high cost of living in Germany (which lengthened the time needed to accumulate savings), and many brought their dependents.

Germany's asylum policy follows a similar story line. Despite its generous and open-ended commitment to provide asylum to those fleeing political persecution—a legacy of World War II—the government clearly did not expect the huge flood of asylum applicants that it received beginning in the late 1980s, nor was it ready to accommodate them. The volume of illegal immigration has also been quite large; estimates of the stock of unauthorized workers vary widely between 150,000 and 1.5 million.

The government's attempts to assert control over immigration have met with limited success. While it was able to shut off guest worker recruitment in the early 1970s—owing mainly to the deep recession caused by the Arab oil embargo and the first oil shock—subsequent attempts to reduce the foreign worker population failed. Since the 1993 revision of Article 16 of the Basic Law, which stated broadly that "persons persecuted for political reasons shall enjoy the right of asylum," the government has been considerably more effective in reducing the flow of asylum seekers and convincing some of them to repatriate. However, attempts to control illegal immigration seem to have run into the same obstacles faced by other countries: insufficient resources for border control and internal enforcement, lack of political will due to opposition from employers and pro-immigrant NGOs, and concerns that stringent controls would be economically harmful to both Germany and immigrant-sending countries. According to Martin, Germany has been quite ambivalent in its efforts to socially integrate its unexpectedly large population of immigrants given that it has been simultaneously urging them to repatriate. Naturalization has been more difficult in Germany than in other liberal democracies, but in 1999 the red-green (SPD-Green) coalition government modified the *jus sanguinis* nationality law and accepted limited dual nationality.

Large gaps between policy outputs and outcomes inevitably created a popular perception that the German government had lost control over immigration, encouraging a public backlash led by right-wing extremists and nationalist politicians. Anti-immigrant actions (including violent attacks on foreigners) mushroomed in the 1990s, when the flood of asylum seekers was seen as an unacceptable economic burden in a context of high structural unemployment, especially in the former East Germany. In recent years labor-force participation among immigrants has dropped sharply, and their unemployment rate is twice that of natives, further reinforcing the public perception that they are an economic burden.

The government apparently has learned from its mistakes. Germany's new guest worker programs are very limited, project-specific, and carefully managed. Its so-called "green card" program, launched in 2001, is intended for highly skilled information technology professionals. In devising a new comprehensive immigration policy, Germany has looked to Canada and its points system, not to the United States. German governments apparently feel that, if immigrants are admitted based on a Canadian-style skills/qualifications test, and if efforts are made to reduce noneconomic, humanitarian migration, fiscal impacts will be reduced and anti-immigrant sentiment in the general public will deflate.

Although Germany has "converged" with the Canadian/Australian system, it remains to be seen whether it will be able to close the gap between policy outputs and outcomes as effectively as those two countries have. First, Germany has been unable thus far to attract the number of skilled immigrant workers it desires because the English-speaking, higher-paying United States, Canada, and Britain remain the favorite destinations of such workers. Second, pursuing a narrowly skills-based immigration policy in a country whose economy continues to demand large numbers of unskilled workers undoubtedly will produce a large gap between policy outputs and outcomes. Even so, Germany has bounced back strongly from the financial crisis of 2008 and the German economy has become once again a high-growth machine as well as a magnet for foreign workers.

At one time the Netherlands was a country of emigration, but it became a serious labor importer decades ago. Only in recent years, however, have some government officials begun to acknowledge that the Netherlands is, indeed, a country of immigration. This notion remains highly controversial, and as a result the country does not have a comprehensive policy based on an overall vision of itself as a country of immigration. Instead, it employs a series of ad hoc policies formulated in response to changing economic and social conditions.

Nevertheless, as Willem Maas in Chapter 8 argues, migration has been a central feature of Dutch political development going back to the founding of the Dutch state itself, and

Dutch society has been defined by core liberal values of pragmatism, tolerance, and humanism. These national values have prevented the government from veering too far toward a restrictionist immigration policy. Rather, Dutch policy has been a constant search for balance between pragmatic economic interests and humanitarian concerns. Responding to the economy's need for immigrant labor, the Netherlands operated a German-style guest worker program from the early 1960s to the mid-1970s. At the same time, because of its strong tradition of humanitarianism, it maintained a liberal asylum system, similar to Germany's pre-1993 regime, despite the importance of postcolonial migrations. In this respect the Netherlands is more similar to Britain than to Germany.

Immigration policymaking in the Netherlands has been a story of emerging gaps between policy outputs and outcomes, followed by attempts to close those gaps by tightening immigration controls. Virtually all of the country's immigration policies have produced serious unintended consequences. The guest worker program of the 1960s and early 1970s brought more immigrant workers to the Netherlands than initially anticipated, and they did not repatriate as expected. After the guest worker program was officially ended, recruitment of foreign workers was allowed to continue on a smaller scale. The generous Dutch asylum system was quickly overwhelmed as the country became one of the most attractive destinations for asylum seekers. The Dutch have been more lenient than the Germans and the British in allowing family reunification for asylum seekers, guest workers, and postcolonial immigrants, which has given employers "back-door" access to foreign-born labor. Like other immigrant-receiving countries, the Netherlands recently began to recruit temporary, highly skilled workers from abroad to meet the needs of its increasingly important knowledge-based industries. The Dutch immigration system has become a *gedoogbeleid* (a policy that unofficially tolerates what is officially prohibited), and the most densely populated country in Europe has experienced a large influx of immigrants from Islamic countries.

As the gap between policy outputs and outcomes grew and demographers predicted that the largest Dutch cities would have Muslim majorities within ten years, a serious public backlash developed. The initial lightning rod for anti-immigrant sentiment was Pim Fortuyn, a former Marxist academic turned populist-conservative who came close to being elected prime minister in 2002 by arguing that the Netherlands was "full up" and calling Islam a "backward religion." Fortuyn's ambitions were thwarted by a fanatic protester who assassinated him a few days before the election. His makeshift political party (Lijst Pym Fortuyn) has faded since then, but he succeeded in turning immigration and asylum seeking into issues that must be addressed by the "mainstream" Dutch parties.

Immigration politics in the Netherlands was further inflamed with the assassination in late 2004 of the controversial filmmaker Theo van Gogh, who was killed by a Muslim extremist. The mantle of anti-immigrant politics subsequently was taken up by Geert Wilders, the leader of the radical right People's Party for Freedom and Democracy, which had a minor role in the government following parliamentary elections in 2010. As Maas illustrates, the rise of anti-immigrant politics has had a profound effect on Dutch policies with respect to immigration, integration, and citizenship.

Attempts to narrow the gaps between immigration control policies and outcomes have included repeated, ultimately ineffective, efforts to limit family-reunification immigration, as well as numerous measures to discourage asylum seekers. None of these attempts have changed the Netherlands' image as a welcoming destination. In February 2004, the Dutch parliament voted to round up and expel up to 26,000 failed asylum seekers who had arrived in the Netherlands before April 2001—a harsher remedy than has been applied to asylum seekers in any other EU country. Legalization programs and stronger controls against clandestine immigration have also been attempted, but the latter have mainly had the effect of increasing migrants' reliance on professional people smugglers.

Meanwhile, Dutch integration policies remain generous and inclusive. Paradoxically, these policies are justified as efforts to prevent the establishment of "ethnic minorities" while allowing immigrants to maintain their cultural identities. Despite heated political battles, the system has been successful in terms of housing, education, and legal rights for immigrants and has produced high rates of naturalization. However, it has been less successful in promoting economic incorporation.

In Chapter 9, Grete Brochmann writes about the Scandinavian countries of Denmark, Norway, and Sweden, which since the 1960s have become countries of immigration. The Scandinavian case differs from others in that this subset of European countries operates according to the "Nordic model," whereby the social contract is assured by a comprehensive (cradle-to-grave) and universal welfare state. Guaranteeing the welfare of all citizens and legal residents is fundamental to the Nordic model of government, and for this reason it is impossible to talk about immigration or immigrant policies outside of the context of the welfare state. Moreover, immigration poses an acute dilemma for Scandinavia to the extent that it weakens social solidarity and undermines the welfare state (Freeman 1986; Crepaz 2008). This is similar but not identical to the "liberal paradox" described above.

Scandinavian countries have had fairly generous admission policies, especially for refugees and asylum seekers, but, as Brochmann notes, the emphasis on social solidarity and tight regulation of labor markets has made it more difficult for immigrants to integrate into the economy and society. Sweden has a longer history of immigration than Denmark or Norway, and its politics of immigration have been more liberal (open and tolerant), similar in some respects to that of Canada. Denmark has had the most restrictionist and, some would say, xenophobic politics, promoted by the Danish Peoples Party, and Norway is somewhere in the middle. Likewise, Sweden has embraced the more liberal Schengen system of free movement of persons and open borders (within the EU), while Denmark has opted out of many EU regulations with respect to migration and asylum seeking. Norway, on the other hand, while not a member of the EU, has adhered to its migration and asylum policies as well as the Schengen system. Overall, Brochmann argues, there are marked similarities in the "Nordic approach" to immigration control, characterized by careful admission policies and integration of immigrants via the welfare state. The Scandinavian welfare state serves paradoxically as a mechanism of strict immigration control and as a means of rapid integration for landed immigrants.

Finally, Switzerland, among the older countries of immigration, is a rather unique case, with a long and detailed history of immigration similar to that of France, dating back to the period of industrialization in the late nineteenth century. As Gianni d'Amato points out in Chapter 10, Switzerland is a confederal state with a multicultural society, located in the heart of Europe and always fearful of *Uberfremdung* (overforeignization) and of being overrun by more powerful neighbors, clinging to its tradition of strict neutrality. Yet despite the delicate nature of the Swiss constitution and Swiss society, the country has relied heavily on foreign labor to fuel economic growth throughout the twentieth century and into the twenty-first. During economic reconstruction in Europe after World War II, the foreign population increased steadily, but Switzerland maintained a rather strict guest worker, or rotation, policy that forced many foreign workers to return home following the economic downturns of the 1970s. D'Amato argues, however, that the politics of immigration shifted in the 1980s in favor of a more "rights-based" and integrationist policy that allowed foreigners to settle and obtain citizenship, even though the process of naturalization remains highly decentralized and depends almost entirely on the consent of the commune for accepting and naturalizing foreigners.

The confederal and consociational nature of the Swiss political system has made immigration policymaking difficult, with multiple actors and veto points leading to frequent referenda, usually framed in terms of overforeignization. As in other small European democracies (the Netherlands, Austria, and Denmark are good examples), the rise of right-wing populist parties has upset the delicate balance between the need for foreign/ immigrant labor, the need for maintaining social solidarity based on a strong welfare state, and the need to protect citizenship in increasingly multicultural societies. D'Amato argues that Switzerland is unlikely to embrace the more liberal approaches to immigration and citizenship characteristic of other EU countries, and that it will remain more parochial in its approach to migration management.

LATECOMERS TO IMMIGRATION

With rapid industrialization, economic growth, and democratization in Southern Europe and East Asia, a new group of nations has become a destination for immigrants. How have these countries managed this quick transition, and are they as welcoming of newcomers as settler nations? Latecomers to immigration are those countries that did not have notable immigration in the early decades of the post–World War II era (the 1950s through the 1970s) because labor demands could be successfully met by *internal* migration from poorer regions, increased utilization of previously untapped labor sources, and/or mechanization and rationalization of production.

In recent decades, however, these countries have begun to import large numbers of immigrants because of negative demographic trends (which are worse than in other countries), as well as structural economic and labor market needs mainly created by relatively recent economic growth (after the 1970s in some cases). However, the percentage of foreign-born residents remains quite low in most of these countries, which generally do not officially consider themselves to be countries, much less nations, of immigrants. In addition, all of these countries were prominent *exporters* of immigrant labor in the recent past, when they were less industrialized than other countries and going through rapid economic and social change with a concomitant rural exodus. As a result, they all made the transition from countries of emigration to countries of net immigration only in recent decades.

Among the latecomer immigration countries, Italy has the largest population of recently arrived, noncitizen residents, the vast majority of whom originated in Asia, the Middle East, and North and Sub-Saharan Africa. Here is a classic country of *emigration* for most of its history, but this trend reversed in the early 1980s. Although Italy (like Spain) was initially a way station for immigrants attempting to get to other European destinations through the "back door," it is now one of the major countries of immigration in Western Europe. In Chapter 11, Ted Perlmutter shows that Italy faces the same dilemmas of immigration control and integration as more advanced immigration countries as it attempts to negotiate a balance between strong demand for foreign labor, especially in the large informal sector of the Italian economy, and the need to maintain at least the appearance of immigration control. The need for control became more acute when Italy joined the Schengen Group in the 1990s, requiring various Italian governments to hastily construct highly ad hoc immigration policies to satisfy EU demands.

The reasons that Italy became dependent on foreign workers are common to most of today's major labor-importing countries. However, the demographic implosion—stagnant and declining birth rates—is more serious in Italy than in any other advanced industrial country. Italy has the world's lowest birthrate and the most rapidly aging population. Together with a native workforce that shuns arduous, low-wage jobs, the result has been a potentially crippling labor shortage. The strong demand for foreign labor also reflects a social welfare state that encourages underemployment and early retirement among native workers, as well as powerful labor unions that make cheap, undocumented foreign labor more attractive. As has been the case throughout its history, Italy has maintained a dual labor market, with a highly regulated formal sector and a largely unregulated informal, secondary labor sector.

Perlmutter argues that government interventions to control immigration are eventually overwhelmed by powerful market forces and by the extreme volatility of Italian politics, which saw fifteen different governments in the twenty-year period from 1990 to 2010. Mainstream political parties are whipsawed between xenophobic and nationalist forces of the Northern League on the one hand and fragile coalition politics on the other, making it extremely difficult to achieve consensus on the contentious issue of immigration control. Italian politicians find themselves making promises to the public about controlling immigration that they cannot possibly keep, enacting many laws and creating a tangled and ineffective control system. Substantial gaps between policies and outcomes are virtually guaranteed by quotas that are set too low and become de facto legalization programs for unauthorized immigrants already in the country; employer sanctions that are not enforced because of legal challenges by the courts and because of government confusion and division over policy implementation; a high percentage of illegal immigrants who work in the underground economy; and amnesty programs that fail because of the fiscal burdens that they impose on employers (a newer program based on legalization initiated by the immigrants themselves has been more successful).

Meanwhile, the stock of illegal immigrants has continued to rise, and pressure on Italy continues to mount from other EU members to improve its external border controls in order to reduce the influx of unauthorized migrants, especially from North Africa and the

Middle East. This pressure to control its porous border has become even more acute in the aftermath of the Arab Spring and the collapse of North African and Middle Eastern authoritarian regimes.

Italy's recent record on immigrant integration is mixed. The latest immigration law affirms labor rights for immigrants and provides access to basic human services. However, some provisions have been obstructed by local officials who fear a community backlash. Naturalization remains difficult, and multiculturalism has not been pursued as a social integration policy because of the widespread belief that African immigrant cultures threaten Italy's social cohesion and national identity.

Italian public opinion on immigration is highly polarized. Opinion surveys indicate that the Italian public is one of the most tolerant in Europe, but there is growing antagonism toward immigrants based on the belief that they threaten public safety, especially with the rise of terrorism during the 2000s. Right-wing political parties have made considerable headway in some parts of the country using anti-immigrant appeals. But anti-immigration political forces have been counterbalanced by a powerful coalition of pro-immigrant groups, including employers, labor unions, NGOs, and religious organizations that press the government for more open policies and measures to reduce the illegality and marginality of foreign workers. Italian labor unions, well entrenched in the formal economy and thus largely insulated from foreign worker competition, have been particularly strong supporters of rights for undocumented immigrants. As Perlmutter notes, however, because the hallmark of Italian immigration policy is extreme politicization and polarization, it is difficult for the country to settle on a coherent policy.

Like Italy's, Spain's experience with immigration is historically limited. Only since the mid-1980s have migrant workers, mostly from North and West Africa, replaced "sunbird" northern Europeans as Spain's most numerous foreign group. The foreign-born population grew rapidly in the 1990s, to nearly 1.7 million by the end of 2003, with most of it coming from non-EU countries. Although many foreign workers continue to pass through on their way to destinations in Northern Europe, Spain itself has become an important destination country for unauthorized migrants from Africa, Latin America, and East Asia. However, as Miryam Hazán notes at the beginning of Chapter 12, the economic collapse that began in 2008 and the resulting high levels of unemployment throughout the Spanish economy have stopped immigration in its tracks and shifted the dilemma from one of control to one of integrating a large, settled foreign population.

Until the economic depression of 2008, Spain was fairly typical of the latecomers to immigration, grappling with how to preserve legal access to the foreign labor on which major parts of the Spanish economy depended, especially its booming construction sector, while not allowing illegal immigration to get out of control and create opportunities for political extremists. As in Italy, most illegal immigrants in Spain worked in labor-intensive and service industries, such as construction, domestic service, restaurants and hotels, healthcare, and agriculture, which until 2008 were the most dynamic, labor-short sectors of the economy. As in Italy, the country's vast underground economy absorbed much of this foreign labor. With one of Europe's best-performing economies until 2008, a native-born workforce no longer willing to migrate internally for employment or settle for low-wage manual jobs, and a demographic profile that cried out for an expansionary immigration policy (rock-bottom fertility rates, rapid population aging), Spain was destined to be a large-scale importer of foreign workers in the twenty-first century. However, as Hazán notes, this changed dramatically in 2008.

Gaps between Spanish immigration control policies and their outcomes were and are quite large and growing. Attempts to crack down on migrant smuggling in the Strait of Gibraltar only shunted the traffic westward to the Canary Islands. None of the five different legalization programs (amnesties) carried out since 1986 reduced the stock of illegal immigrants, and a dysfunctional system of interlinked work and residence permits turned once legal foreign workers into *irregulares* with dismaying regularity. A quota system enabling employers to import foreign workers, mostly on short-term visas, fell far short of meeting demand. Moreover it was limited to nationals of five countries with which Spain had signed bilateral migrant labor agreements. Employer sanctions were inhibited by the high percentage of illegal workers in the underground economy and by the closeness of government-business ties.

As in Italy, in Spain high demand for foreign labor and a large informal economy combined to create high levels of illegal immigration, leading governments of the right and left to pursue amnesty, regularization, and legalization. Hazán explains that from the Plan GRECO, enacted by the right-of-center Aznar government in 2000, through the 2005 legalization put in place by the left-of-center socialist government under Zapatero, Spanish immigration policy emphasized quick and generous legalization of the large foreign work force to allow the foreign population to integrate as rapidly as possible. This approach to migration management, combined with a fairly decentralized policymaking process that relies on the autonomous regional governments to implement immigration policy, stymied xenophobic and populist parties. But, once again like Italy, Spain has been under pressure from the EU to control its borders and prevent African and Latin American migrants from transiting Spanish territory on their way to other EU destinations. Hazán concludes by pointing out that the severe economic crisis of the late 2000s has put pressure on native Spanish youth to emigrate in search of gainful employment, bringing Spain full circle: a sending country, to a receiving country, and once again a sending country.

Although past Japanese and Korean emigration was never on the scale of Italy's or Spain's, hundreds of thousands of Japanese did emigrate to the Americas from the late nineteenth century through the mid-twentieth century, creating large communities of Japanese descendants in the United States and Brazil. Koreans emigrated in large numbers to Japan, especially during the colonial period, and eventually many went to the United States as well. The economic and demographic factors that have turned Japan and Korea into countries of immigration are similar to those operating in Italy and Spain. However, unlike Italy and Spain, until recently Japan insisted on a closed-door immigration policy that prohibited unskilled migrant workers and permitted only highly skilled and professional workers. Korea, on the other hand, as Erin Chung in Chapter 13 notes, has taken a somewhat more liberal approach to immigrant settlement.

Both the Japanese and South Korean governments maintained a restrictive stance toward immigration through the high-growth periods of the 1980s (in the Japanese case) and the 1990s and 2000s (in the South Korean case). Both countries wanted to maintain their ethnic homogeneity and feared that large numbers of racially and culturally different immigrants would provoke social unrest. Japan's bureaucratic and centralized immigration policymaking regime made it relatively insensitive to lobbying by small and medium-sized employers and other pro-immigration groups. However, demographic decline has placed great pressure on Japan to open its economy and society to higher immigration levels, despite the so-called lost decades of slow economic growth in the 1990s and 2000s. The Japanese population has ceased to grow and is projected to decline by 22 million during the next fifty years, assuming current levels of fertility and immigration. Since 2001, Japanese aged 64 years and older outnumber those under age 15. A similar though less acute demographic force is at work in Korea, which has been much more economically dynamic than Japan.

As a result, the gaps between immigration policy and actual outcomes in Japan and South Korea are substantial. Despite attempts to exclude the importation of unskilled foreign workers, the two countries have become countries of immigration. Large economic disparities exist between Japan and South Korea on the one hand and South and Southeast Asia on the other; with high levels of growth in Japan in the 1980s and in South Korea over the last twenty years, foreign workers from the south have found ways to settle and integrate into both societies, although, as Chung argues, the mechanisms of settlement and the acquisition of rights have been quite different. Some immigrants to Japan were smuggled in clandestinely—most notoriously in the construction sector during the boom years of the 1980s and more recently in the home healthcare and sex industries—and many entered both Japan and South Korea on short-term visas and simply overstayed. Even after the bubble burst in the construction and housing sectors and after the financial collapse of the 1990s in Japan and the Asian financial crises of 1997–1998 that led to a sharp economic downturn in South Korea, neither state was able to crack down on illegal immigration because key sectors in both economies already were dependent on foreign labor and rights were accruing to foreigners in both societies. The Japanese and Korean governments seemed to recognize that employers were dependent on foreign labor and that a crackdown would further depress the economy. Meanwhile, both governments undermined otherwise restrictive policies by enabling large numbers of unskilled foreign workers to be imported through various "side-door" mechanisms: as company trainees, students, entertainers, and, in the case of Japan, ethnic Japanese return migrants from Brazil—the so-called *dekasegi*.

Japan's insistence on treating all foreign workers, except for ethnic Japanese returnees, as short-term "guests"—not potential permanent settlers—delayed explicit, national-level policies and programs to facilitate the social integration of settled immigrants. But, as Chung demonstrates, local governments and NGOs, as well as other actors in the civil society, provided basic social services and protections to foreign residents, creating a mechanism for integration that allowed foreigners to acquire rights. In the process, they transformed Japanese politics and society.

Thus far, the Japanese public—well known for its ethnic insularity—has shown surprising tolerance toward the immigrants arriving over the past decades, despite the long-running recession that followed the collapse of the "bubble economy" of the late 1980s. This relative tolerance is partly a function of the widely shared belief that foreign workers are alleviating Japan's labor shortage and thus contributing to the economy. But it also is indicative of the weakening of traditional conceptions of citizenship and nationhood, as Chung illustrates (see also Chung 2010).

Like Japan, Korea historically was a labor-exporting country that did not begin importing immigrants until the late 1980s. Also, like Japan's its foreign workers constitute only a small segment of the population, concentrated in the manufacturing and construction sectors with a growing presence in the service industries. Korea has traditionally denied that it is a country of immigration, officially forbidding the entry of unskilled immigrant labor and rejecting asylum seekers. But, as Chung shows, Korea, like Japan, has de facto side-door mechanisms through which significant numbers of unskilled foreign workers have been admitted, and the Korean state has taken an accommodating approach to integrating the foreign population.

Policy convergence between Korea and Japan, according to Chung, is partly due to strong local institutions and the willingness of civil society to incorporate de facto immigrants. Like Japan, Korea takes a monocultural approach to citizenship, even though it is more ethnically homogeneous. Both states still reject large-scale, permanent immigration, and they eschew multiculturalism. Nevertheless, Korean demand for immigrant labor has acquired a structural character because high levels of economic growth have been coupled with low fertility and population aging, a wealthy and highly educated native workforce that shuns unskilled jobs, and limited alternative sources of manpower. In addition, Korea has a Japanese-style, bureaucracy-dominated immigration policymaking system that has responded in similar fashion to the contradictory pressures of keeping the country immigrant-free and meeting domestic labor shortages. As a former Japanese colony, it inherited Japanese laws and subsequently imported many Japanese policies, copying wholesale several Japanese immigration control policies and programs. Nonetheless, as long as Korean and Japanese civil societies remain tolerant, these latecomers to immigration may converge toward the more "liberal" immigration policies of Euro-American countries, even though citizenship remains largely closed to foreigners.

THE FUTURE OF IMMIGRATION CONTROL

Barring a cataclysmic event like war or economic depression, international migration is likely to increase in the coming decades. Despite the 9/11 terrorist attacks on the United States and the great recession of 2008, liberal democracies have remained relatively open to immigrants. Global economic and demographic inequalities mean that supply-push forces remain strong, while at the same time demand-pull forces remain constant. Growing demand for highly skilled workers coupled with demographic decline in receiving countries has created economic opportunities for migrants in all of the countries studied here. Transnational networks have become more dense and efficient, linking sending and receiving societies. These networks help to lower the transaction costs of migration, making it easier for people to move across borders and over long distances. Moreover, when legal migration is not an option, migrants increasingly turn to professional smugglers. The result is a flourishing global industry of migrant smuggling—often with the involvement of organized crime.

But migration, like any transnational economic activity (such as trade and foreign direct investment), does not take place in a legal or institutional void. As the country studies presented in this volume illustrate, governments have been and still are deeply involved in organizing and regulating migration and the extension of rights to non-nationals has been an extremely important part of the story of immigration control in the post–World War II era. For the most part, rights that accrue to migrants come from the legal and constitutional protections guaranteed to all "members" of society. Thus, if an individual migrant is able to establish some claim to residence on the territory of a liberal state, his or her chances of being able to remain and settle increase. At the same time, developments in international human rights law have helped to solidify the position of individuals vis-à-vis the state, to the point that individuals (and certain groups) have acquired a sort of international legal personality, leading some to speculate that we are entering a postnational era characterized by "universal personhood" (Soysal 1994), the expansion of "rights across borders" (Jacobson 1996), and even "transnational citizenship" (Bauböck 1994).

Others have argued that migrants have become transnational because so many no longer reside exclusively on the territory of one state (Glick-Schiller 1999; Levitt 2001), opting to shuttle between a place of origin and a place of destination. This line of argument gives priority to agency as a defining feature of contemporary migrations, but it ignores the extent to which state policies continue to shape the choices that migrants make (Zolberg 1981, 1999; Waldinger and Fitzgerald 2004; Hollifield 2008). Regulating international migration requires liberal states to be attentive to the (human or civil) rights of the individual—if those rights are ignored or trampled on, the *liberal* state risks undermining its own legitimacy and *raison d'être* (Hollifield 1999). As international migration and transnationalism increase, pressures build on liberal states to find new and creative ways to cooperate, to manage flows. The country cases in this volume provide ample evidence that today's countries of immigration (official or de facto) are so integrated into a global labor market that few can afford to reduce immigration without major negative consequences for their economies. Virtually all of the countries under study in this volume, with the partial exception of Canada and the other nations of immigrants, would prefer to classify themselves as reluctant or unwilling importers of foreign labor.

In each of these cases, we can observe the interaction of four key trends: (1) high emigration from less developed countries, where economic and demographic push factors are strong and likely to remain so in the foreseeable future; (2) demographic profiles in the receiving countries that are changing in ways that inevitably increase the demand for foreign-born labor; (3) persistent demand in receiving-country economies for low-cost, flexible labor—a *structural* demand that has become decoupled from the business cycle— and for highly skilled workers who provide much-needed human capital in an increasingly competitive global market; and (4) frequent symbolic efforts by receiving-country governments to deter new immigration and discourage permanent settlement of immigrants and refugees, under pressure from hostile public opinion. In labor-importing country after labor-importing country, this confluence of trends produces deep ambivalence about immigration. There is grudging recognition of the economic and demographic need for it, but that recognition is coupled with keen sensitivity to the challenge of integrating ethnically and culturally diverse populations.

The cases that we examine in *Controlling Immigration* vividly illustrate the difficulties of intervening in the migration process to stop chain migration, break up migration networks, and roll back the rights of migrants, their families, and refugees. The historical record is littered with the wreckage of government interventions that appeared to work reasonably well at first but had little staying power, or that had long-term consequences exactly the opposite of initial intentions. These interventions rarely dry up "unwanted" migration flows or even significantly reduce them; more often, they simply rechannel the flows and create more opportunities for people smugglers to cash in on the traffic. Yet governments continue to tinker with the control measures to which they have committed themselves in order to improve their performance. Some have taken drastic and unprecedented steps to control immigrant and refugee flows (for example, the US experiment with "concentrated border enforcement operations" since 1993), and they continue to invest in such measures, even in the face of mounting evidence that they are not efficacious.

Why do failed immigration control policies persist in today's labor-importing countries, often long past the point when it becomes apparent that they are not working? Some political parties in labor-importing countries clearly see votes to be gained from advocating such measures (Perlmutter 1996; Arzheimer and Carter 2006). Governments with widely varying ideologies fine-tune their immigration policies and devise new ones because these measures are seen as useful in convincing the general public that the governments have not lost control. This political calculus has caused even liberal and moderate governments to crack down periodically on illegal immigration and "toughen" the political asylum process.

In Europe, as Geddes illustrates in Chapter 14, governments lend their support to ongoing regional efforts to "harmonize" immigration and asylum policies, to restrict labor mobility within an enlarged EU, and to forge new repatriation agreements with African and Asian sending countries. But meaningful, supranational immigration controls remain elusive, even in Europe, where these policies are the most advanced and global governance of migration is weak, with the partial exception of the international refugee regime (Hollifield 2000; Betts 2011). Nation-states retain their capacity to control immigration, but that capacity is limited by client politics (the privileged position of business in particular) and by rights-based politics at the domestic level (constitutional protections for migrants are strong in many of the countries under study here, especially those with active judiciaries) and at the international level in the form of human rights conventions. As a result, large gaps persist between policy outputs and outcomes because the number of domestic stakeholders in an expansionary (de facto) immigration policy is significant and likely to increase as demand-pull and supply-push factors intensify in the twenty-first century. Ineffective and "symbolic" immigration control measures are thus perpetuated because they reduce the potential for a broad public backlash.

One major question posed repeatedly here but not necessarily resolved, concerns the extent to which future governments in the labor-importing countries will succeed in rolling back the legal, political, and social rights of "within-country" immigrants that have made remaining easier for unauthorized immigrants who entered one of these countries in recent decades. Curtailing the rights of immigrants and asylum seekers is a tempting course for governments of labor-importing countries in the face of basic market and demographic forces that drive migration in both sending and receiving countries. This approach also avoids or mitigates most of the diplomatic costs associated with more stringent border enforcement or imposition of tough new visa restrictions on the nationals of high-emigration countries. However, a large body of research indicates that the curtailment of welfare rights is unlikely to appreciably stem the flow of new migrants because the availability of social services or entitlements is not a powerful magnet for would-be unauthorized entrants as compared with other demand-pull factors (Bommes and Geddes 2000). Moreover, migrant civil rights once extended have a very long half-life and it is exceedingly difficult for governments that operate under liberal constitutions with active judiciaries to simply roll them back (Hollifield 1999).

At what point in the future will the politics of appeasing anti-immigrant public opinion collide with the national interests of the receiving countries, defined in terms of economic growth and global competitiveness, along with individual citizens' desire to maintain lifestyles often made possible by immigrant service providers and producers of low-cost goods? When that point is reached, the goals of national immigration policy may have to be redefined in order to reduce the large and constantly widening gap between policy goals and outcomes. Redefining the goals of national immigration policies will compel reluctant countries of immigration, like Japan and Korea, to confront rather than ignore or downplay the trade-offs between more effective immigration control and other societal goals and principles.

What basic values and civil liberties, how much in tax revenues and future economic growth, will be sacrificed to gain greater control over unauthorized immigration and reduce the size of a foreign-born population? The outcomes of ongoing debates over these questions will determine whether persistently high levels of immigration—in whatever form—will be tolerated in the long term. Meanwhile, market forces and demography, along with transnational social networks, will be powerful drivers of international migration dynamics in the twenty-first century, like a powerful engine pulling a train down the tracks whose switches will be controlled by states, politicians, and policymakers. It is the switches that will determine whether the train continues along a safe course or plunges off a cliff (Hollifield 2008).

Some governments, as well as some international organizations, continue to hope for market-based/economic solutions to the problem of regulating international migration. It is hoped that trade and foreign direct investment—bringing capital and jobs to people through either private investment or official development assistance—will substitute for migration, alleviating both supply-push and demand-pull factors (Hollifield, Orrenius, and Osang 2006). Trade can lead to factor-price equalization in the long term, but, as we have seen in the case of the EU, in the short and medium term exposing developing countries to market forces often results in increased (rather than decreased) migration, as is evident with NAFTA and the US-Mexican relationship (Martin 1993). Likewise, trade in services can stimulate more "high-end" migration because these types of product often cannot be produced or sold without the movement of the individuals who make and market them (Ghosh 1997).

In short, the global integration of markets for goods, services, and capital entails higher levels of international migration; therefore, if states want to promote freer trade and investment, they must be prepared to manage higher migration levels (Bhagwati 1998). Many states (like Canada, Australia, and even Germany) are willing, if not eager, to sponsor high-end migration because the numbers are manageable and there is likely to be less political resistance to the importation of highly skilled individuals (Hainmueller and Hiscox 2010). However, mass migration of unskilled and less educated workers is likely to meet with greater political resistance, even in sectors like construction and healthcare, where there is high demand for this type of labor. In these instances, the tendency is for governments to go back to the old guest worker model in hopes of bringing in just enough temporary workers to fill gaps in the labor market but with strict contracts between these workers and their employers that limit the length of stay and prohibit settlement or family reunification. The alternative is illegal immigration and a growing black market for labor—a Hobson's choice, which is the dilemma facing the United States in the 2010s as the Obama administration searches for another grand bargain that will allow comprehensive immigration reform (Orrenius and Zavodny 2010; Hollifield 2010; see also Chapter 2).

CONCLUSION: SOLVING THE DILEMMA OF IMMIGRATION CONTROL

The nineteenth and twentieth centuries saw the rise of what Richard Rosecrance (1986) has labeled the *trading state*. The latter half of the twentieth century gave rise to the *migration state*. From a strategic, economic, and demographic standpoint, trade and migration go hand in hand because the wealth, power, and stability of the state are heavily dependent on its willingness to risk both trade and migration. As they have done in trade and finance, states must find ways to cooperate and use migration for strategic gains (Hollifield 2000, 2004). Likewise, international security and stability are dependent on the capacity of states to manage migration, but it is extremely difficult, if not impossible, for states to manage or control migration either unilaterally or bilaterally. Some type of global migration governance (Betts 2011) is required, similar to what the EU has achieved at the regional level for nationals of its member states. The EU model, as described by Geddes in Chapter 14, points the way to future migration control regimes because it is not based purely on *Homo economicus* but incorporates rights for individual migrants and even a rudimentary European citizenship that continue to evolve. Of course, the problem in this type of regional migration regime is how to deal with third-country nationals (TCNs). As the EU expands and borders are relaxed, the issue of TCNs, immigrants, and ethnic minorities becomes ever more pressing, and new institutions, laws, and regulations must be created to deal with it. In the end, the EU, by creating a regional migration regime and a kind of supranational authority to deal with migration and refugee issues, allows member states to finesse, if not escape, some of the dilemmas of immigration control described above, if not to solve the liberal paradox itself.

Regional integration reinforces the trading state and acts as midwife to the migration state (Hollifield 2004). As Geddes points out, in the EU migrants are gradually acquiring the rights that they need to live and work on member states' territories. Regional integration blurs the lines of territoriality, lessening problems of integration and national identity. The fact that there is an increasing disjuncture between people and place—which in the past might have provoked a crisis of national identity and undermined the legitimacy of the nation-state—is less of a problem when the state is embedded in a regional regime like the EU. This does not mean, of course, that there will be no resistance to freer trade and migration. Anti-globalization protests and nativist or xenophobic reactions against immigration have been on the rise throughout the OECD world (Joppke 1998). Nonetheless, regional integration—especially when it has a long history and is deeply institutionalized, as it is in Europe—makes it easier for states to open their economies and societies to immigration and trade, and for governments to construct the kinds of political coalitions that will be necessary to support and institutionalize greater openness.

The United States, in contrast, is reluctant to move rapidly on economic integration in North America, especially after the terrorist attacks of September 11, 2001, preferring instead to create new guest worker programs or continue with the current immigration system, which strictly limits the number of visas (and green cards) while tolerating high levels of unauthorized migration from Mexico and Central America. However, it is clear that North America is the region closest to taking steps toward an EU-style regional migration regime; meanwhile, the United States is facing the prospect of another legalization program similar to the 1986 Immigration Reform and Control Act (IRCA). In the long run, it is difficult for liberal states like the United States to sustain a large, illegal population, which undermines the rule of law and the social contract. For this reason, amnesties, legalizations, or regularizations have become a common feature of immigration policy throughout the OECD world.

Even though there are large numbers of economic migrants in Asia, this region remains divided into relatively closed and often authoritarian societies, with little prospect of rights for migrants and guest workers. The more liberal and democratic states, like Japan, Taiwan, and South Korea, are the exceptions; however, as Chung points out in Chapter 13, they have only just begun to grapple with immigration control and integration and on a relatively small scale. In Africa and the Middle East, which have high numbers of foreign workers and refugees, there is much political and social instability, and states are fluid with little institutional or legal capacity for dealing with international migration.

In conclusion, we see that migration is both a cause and a consequence of political and economic change. International migration, like trade and foreign direct investment, is a fundamental feature of the relatively liberal world in which we now live. Moreover, as states and societies become more liberal, more open, and more democratic, migration will increase. Will the increase be a virtuous or a vicious cycle? Will it be destabilizing, leading the international system into greater anarchy, disorder, and war? Or will it lead to greater openness, wealth, and human development? Much will depend on how migration is managed by the powerful liberal states because they will set the trend for the rest of the globe. To avoid a domestic political backlash against immigration, the rights of migrants must be respected and states must find ways to use migration for strategic gains; they must also cooperate in managing it. As states come together to manage this extraordinarily complex phenomenon, it may be possible to construct a truly international migration regime, under the auspices of the United Nations. But we are not sanguine about this possibility because the asymmetry of interests between the North and the South is too great. Even as states become more interdependent in an era of globalization, they are likely to remain trapped in a liberal paradox for decades to come.

REFERENCES

Arzheimer, Kai, and Elisabeth Carter. 2006. "Political Opportunity Structures and Right-Wing Extremist Party Success." *European Journal of Political Research* 45 (3): 419–43.

Bauböck, Rainer. 1994. *Transnational Citizenship: Membership and Rights in International Migration*. Aldershot, UK: Edward Elgar.

Benhabib, Seyla. 2004. *The Rights of Others: Aliens, Residents and Citizens*. Cambridge: Cambridge University Press.

Betts, Alexander. 2011. *Global Migration Governance*. Oxford: Oxford University Press.

Bhagwati, Jagdish. 1998. *A Stream of Windows: Unsettling Reflections on Trade, Immigration, and Democracy*. Cambridge, MA: MIT Press.

Bloemraad, Irene. 2006. *Becoming a Citizen: Incorporating Immigrants and Refugees in the United States and Canada*. Berkeley: University of California Press.

Bommes, Michael and Andrew Geddes. 2000. *Migration and the Welfare State in Contemporary Europe*. London: Routledge.

Brader, Ted, Nicholas A. Valentino, and Elizabeth Suhay. 2008. "What Triggers Public Opposition to Immigration? Anxiety, Group Cues, and Immigration Threat." *American Journal of Political Science* 52 (4): 959–78.

Brubaker, Rogers, ed. 1989. *Immigration and the Politics of Citizenship in Europe and North America*. Lanham, MD: University Press of America.

Carens, Joseph. 2000. *Culture, Citizenship, and Community: A Contextual Exploration of Justice as Evenhandedness*. New York: Oxford University Press.

Chiswick, Barry R., ed. 2011. *High-Skilled Immigration in a Global Labor Market*. Washington, DC: AEI Press.

Chung, Erin. 2010. *Immigration and Citizenship in Japan*. New York: Cambridge University Press.

Crepaz, Markus. 2008. *Trust beyond Borders: Immigration, the Welfare State, and Identity in Modern Societies*. Ann Arbor: University of Michigan Press.

Favell, Adrian. 1998. *Philosophies of Integration: Immigration and the Idea of Citizenship in France and Britain*. New York: St. Martin's Press.

Fetzer, Joel. 2000. *Public Attitudes toward Immigration in the United States, France, and Germany*. Cambridge: Cambridge University Press.

Freeman, Gary P. 1986. "Migration and the Political Economy of the Welfare State." *Annals of the American Academy of Political and Social Science* 485 (May): 51–63.

———. 1995. "Modes of Immigration Politics in Liberal Democratic States." *International Migration Review* 29 (4): 881–902.

Ghosh, Bimal. 1997. *Gains from Global Linkages: Trade in Services and Movement of Persons*. London: Macmillan.

Givens, Terri E. 2005. *Voting Radical Right in Western Europe*. Cambridge: Cambridge University Press.

Glick Schiller, Nina. 1999. "Transmigrants and Nation-States: Something Old and Something New in the U.S. Immigrant Experience." In *The Handbook of International Migration: The American Experience*, edited by Charles Hirschman, Philip Kasinitz, and Josh DeWind, 94–119. New York: Russell Sage.

Greenhill, Kelly M. 2010. *Weapons of Mass Migration: Forced Displacement, Coercion, and Foreign Policy*. Ithaca, NY: Cornell University Press.

Hainmueller, Jens, and Michael J. Hiscox. 2010. "Attitudes toward Highly Skilled and Low-Skilled Immigration: Evidence from a Survey Experiment." *American Political Science Review* 104: 61–84.

Hirsch, Harry N. 1992. *A Theory of Liberty: The Constitution and Minorities*. New York: Routledge.

Hollifield, James F. 1986. "Immigration Policy in France and Germany: Outputs vs. Outcomes." *Annals of the American Academy of Political and Social Science* 485 (May): 113–28.

———. 1992. *Immigrants, Markets and States: The Political Economy of Postwar Europe*. Cambridge, MA: Harvard University Press.

———. 1999. "Ideas, Institutions and Civil Society: On the Limits of Immigration Control in Liberal Democracies." *IMIS-Beiträge* 10 (January): 57–90.

———. 2000. "Migration and the 'New' International Order: The Missing Regime." In *Managing Migration: The Need for a New International Regime*, edited by Bimal Ghosh, 75–109. Oxford: Oxford University Press.

———. 2004. "The Emerging Migration State." *International Migration Review* 38: 885–912.

———. 2008. "The Politics of International Migration: How Can We 'Bring the State Back In?'" In *Migration Theory: Talking Across Disciplines*, edited by Caroline B. Brettell and James F. Hollifield, 183–237. New York: Routledge.

———. 2010. "American Immigration Policy and Politics: An Enduring Controversy." In *Developments in American Politics 6*, edited by Gillian Peele, Christopher J. Bailey, Bruce Cain, and B. Guy Peters, 256–81. New York: Palgrave Macmillan.

Hollifield, James F., Pia M. Orrenius, and Thomas Osang. 2006. *Migration, Trade and Development*. Dallas: Federal Reserve Bank of Dallas.

Hollifield, James F., and Carole J. Wilson. 2011. "Rights-Based Politics, Immigration, and the Business Cycle: 1890–2008." In *High-Skilled Immigration in a Global Labor Market*, edited by Barry R. Chiswick, 50–80. Washington, DC: AEI Press.

Hopkins, Daniel J. 2010. "Politicized Places: Explaining Where and When Immigrants Provoke Local Opposition." *American Political Science Review* 104: 40–60.

Huntington, Samuel P. 2004. *Who Are We? The Challenges to America's Identity*. New York: Simon & Schuster.

Jacobson, David. 1996. *Rights across Borders: Immigration and the Decline of Citizenship*. Baltimore: Johns Hopkins University Press.

Joppke, Christian, ed. 1998. *Challenge to the Nation-State: Immigration in Western Europe and the United States*. Oxford: Oxford University Press.

———. 2001. "The Legal-Domestic Sources of Immigrant Rights: The United States, Germany and the European Union." *Comparative Political Studies* 34 (4): 339–66.

Kepel, Gilles. 2012. *Banlieues de la République*. Paris: Gallimard.

King, Desmond. 2000. *Making Americans: Immigration, Race and the Diverse Democracy*. Cambridge, MA: Harvard University Press.

Kitschelt, Herbert. 1995. *The Radical Right in Western Europe*. Ann Arbor: University of Michigan Press.

Kymlicka, Will. 1995. *Multicultural Citizenship*. Oxford: Clarendon.

Lahav, Gallya. 2004. *Immigration and Politics in the New Europe*. Cambridge: Cambridge University Press.

Levitt, Peggy. 2001. *The Transnational Villagers*. Berkeley: University of California Press.

Lubbers, Marcel, Mérove Gijsberts, and Peer Scheepers. 2002. "Extreme Right-Wing Voting in Western Europe." *European Journal of Political Research* 41 (3): 345–78.

Martin, Philip L. 1993. *Trade and Migration: NAFTA and Agriculture*. Washington, DC: Institute for International Economics.

———. 2009. *Importing Poverty? Immigration and the Changing Face of Rural America*. New Haven, CT: Yale University Press.

Massey, Douglas S., Jorge Durand, and Nolan J. Malone. 2002. *Beyond Smoke and Mirrors: Mexican Immigration in an Era of Economic Integration*. New York: Russell Sage Foundation.

Messina, Anthony. 2007. *The Logic and Politics of Post-WWII Migration to Western Europe*. New York: Cambridge University Press.

Money, Jeannette. 1999. *Fences and Neighbors: The Geography of Immigration Control*. Ithaca, NY: Cornell University Press.

Mudde, Cas. 2007. *Populist Radical Right Parties in Europe*. Cambridge: Cambridge University Press.

Norris, Pippa. 2005. *Radical Right: Voters and Parties in the Electoral Market*. Cambridge: Cambridge University Press.

Orrenius, Pia, and Madeleine Zavodny. 2010. *Beside the Golden Door: US Immigration Reform in an Era of Globalization*. Washington, DC: AEI Press.

Perlmutter, Ted. 1996. "Bringing Parties Back In: Comments on 'Modes of Immigration Politics in Liberal Democratic Societies.'" *International Migration Review* 30: 375–88.

Ramakrishnan, Karthick. 2005. *Democracy in Immigrant America: Changing Demographics and Political Participation*. Stanford, CA: Stanford University Press.

Rawls, John. 1971. *A Theory of Justice*. Cambridge, MA: Harvard University Press.

Rosecrance, Richard. 1986. *The Rise of the Trading State*. New York: Basic Books.

Rudolph, Christopher. 2006. *National Security and Immigration: Policy Development in the United States and Western Europe since 1945*. Stanford, CA: Stanford University Press.

Ruhs, Martin, and Philip L. Martin. 2008. "Numbers vs. Rights: Trade-Offs and Guest Worker Programs." *International Migration Review* 42: 249–65.

Sassen, Saskia. 1988. *The Mobility of Capital and Labor*. Cambridge: Cambridge University Press.

Schain, Martin. 2012. *The Politics of Immigration in France, Britain, and the United States: A Comparative Study*. 2nd ed. New York: Palgrave Macmillan.

Schlesinger, Arthur, Jr. 1992. *The Disuniting of America*. New York: Norton.

Schuck, Peter H. 1998. *Citizens, Strangers and In-Betweens: Essays on Immigration and Citizenship*. Boulder, CO: Westview.

Sides, John, and Jack Citrin. 2007. "European Opinion about Immigration: The Role of Identities, Interests and Information." *British Journal of Political Science* 37 (3): 477.

Smith, Rogers. 1997. *Civic Ideals: Conflicting Visions of Citizenship in U.S. History*. New Haven, CT: Yale University Press.

Soysal, Yasemin N. 1994. *Limits of Citizenship: Migrants and Postnational Membership in Europe*. Chicago: University of Chicago Press.

Thielemann, Eiko. 2003. "European Burden-Sharing and Forced Migration." *Journal of Refugee Studies* 16 (3): 223–35.

Thränhardt, Dietrich, ed. 1996. *Europe: A New Immigration Continent*. Münster: LIT Verlag.

Tichenor, Daniel J. 2002. *The Politics of Immigration Control in America*. Princeton, NJ: Princeton University Press.

Waldinger, Roger, and David Fitzgerald. 2004. "Transnationalism in Question." *American Journal of Sociology* 109 (5): 1177–95.

Walzer, Michael. 1983. *Spheres of Justice: A Defense of Pluralism and Equality*. New York: Basic Books.

Weiner, Myron. 1995. *The Global Migration Crisis: Challenge to States and to Human Rights*. New York: HarperCollins.

Zolberg, Aristide R. 1981. "International Migration in Political Perspective." In *Global Trends in Migration: Theory and Research in International Population Movements*, edited by Mary M. Kritz, Charles B. Keely, and Silvano M. Tomasi, 3–27. New York: Center for Migration Studies.

———. 1999. "Matters of State: Theorizing Immigration Policy." In *Becoming American, American Becoming*, edited by Douglas Massey, 71–93. New York: Russell Sage Foundation.

Overcoming the Challenges of Immigration Control

Marc R. Rosenblum

This third edition of *Controlling Immigration* revisits the two most important arguments about immigration policy and policymaking from the last two decades of academic research on the subject: that the industrialized world is converging around a common set of immigration challenges and policy responses and that those responses are failing when it comes to effective migration control. As the contributors here point out, it is easy to marshal a certain amount of empirical evidence for both claims: migration inflows remain a source of controversy around the world, prompting the politicization of the issue; industrialized states rely on a similar set of enforcement tools at their borders and ports of entry, at work-sites, and in their communities; and yet in spite of ongoing control efforts since the 1980s, unauthorized immigrant populations reached all-time highs in most industrialized states during the first decade of the twentieth-first century.

These observations raise four questions. First, is the failure of immigration control in the four decades after 1970 a political or a practical problem? That is, is the "gap" between political demands and policy outputs or is it between policy outputs and migration outcomes? As the introduction argues, there is no shortage of arguments in the immigration literature about political obstacles to effective policies or why we would expect "image of control," rather than real enforcement, to be the goal. The authors review several of these arguments, including those focused on interest groups, international relations, and liberal political institutions.

Yet, after four decades of illegality and increased investment in migration control (regardless of its intention), this history creates powerful asymmetries that favor increased investment in migration enforcement over alternative immigration policies, such as legalization, new guest worker programs, or other types of visa reform.[1] Unauthorized immigrants are a visible and quantifiable reflection of flawed immigration policies, and tough enforcement offers a concrete and direct policy response: every alien detained and deported is one fewer unauthorized immigrant in the host state. Arguments about matching the supply and demand of labor through visa reform rely on sophisticated assumptions about complex social and economic systems. Similarly, unauthorized immigrants have made a choice that has resulted in their illegal status, and they bear some individual responsibility for that choice. There is no individual-level "blame" to be assigned for structural design flaws in the immigration system, however. For this reason, immigration enforcement is a "valence" issue: it is easy for politicians from all political backgrounds to support immigration controls, and difficult to defend a vote against enforcement or one in favor of additional visas or legalization. These dynamics create a ratchet effect with a progressive tightening of migration control measures over time.

In addition, the tacit acceptance of unauthorized immigration in most industrialized countries has relied on the *nonenforcement* of laws put in place beginning in the 1970s governing immigration controls at borders, at worksites, and within host-state communities. Thus, while legalization and visa reform require legislatures to pass new laws, in most states reducing immigration through tougher controls requires only that states "enforce the laws on the books"—laws that already permit fewer admissions and more deportations than now occur.

A final source of asymmetry relates to the political economy of migration enforcement. After decades of investment in migration control, key stakeholders in migrant-receiving states now have a financial interest in maintaining or expanding existing enforcement infrastructures, including detention facilities, border fencing and surveillance technology, and responsible law enforcement and civil service agencies. Turning Freeman's classic argument (1995) about the politics of immigration policy on its head, these actors derive concentrated benefits from enforcement while the direct costs of enforcement are borne by diffuse taxpayers through central governments and by unauthorized immigrants and their families—groups with little political power that face significant barriers to effective political organizing.

These asymmetries in the immigration debate exist in a context of persistently high unemployment; uneven integration by many immigrant groups; migration-related security concerns about terrorist attacks in the United States, England, and Spain; and the growing influence of anti-immigrant parties and movements in virtually every country considered here. Thus, the more pressing question is not about the politics of immigration policy but rather about why we continue to observe a gap between tough immigration policies—at least some of which are "sincere"—and inconsistent enforcement outcomes?

The answer to this question is that migration control is challenging not because it is a problem of enforcement but rather because it is a screening and filtering problem that requires the state to distinguish between citizens, diverse classes of legal immigrants, and unauthorized immigrants, and that requires enforcement of different sets of rules and protection of distinct rights and privileges for all of these groups. At and around borders, migration control policies must prevent illegal entries *while also* facilitating trade, tourism, and other legal flows. Moreover, within host states such policies seek to remove unauthorized immigrants and other deportable aliens *while also* promoting successful immigrant integration, avoiding undue enforcement against citizens and legal immigrants, and ensuring that even potentially deportable aliens are given the chance to petition for whatever forms of humanitarian relief they may be entitled to (including political asylum and judicial relief from deportation). More broadly, while host states seek to deter future illegal migration by denying unauthorized immigrants access to labor markets and certain social benefits, they must do so in a way that minimizes the burden on employers and on legitimate users of such benefits.

The fundamental challenge of migration control, then, is not about a philosophical tension between open markets and closed states. Indeed, in the two decades since Hollifield identified the "liberal paradox,"[2] courts, legislatures, and voters have repeatedly demonstrated their openness to rolling back the civil and even human rights of immigrants—including those of legal immigrants. Rather, the core barrier to successful enforcement is that there is no reliable way to limit the effects of enforcement to deportable aliens without imposing costs on legal immigrants and host-state citizens. In general, lawmakers must choose between erring on the side of underenforcement, permitting some illegal immigrants to remain within host states, or erring on the side of overenforcement, in which case some legal immigrants and citizens will be caught up in the enforcement process and all host state residents will suffer a range of potentially severe adverse effects. The complexity of immigration policy in most states and the strategic behavior of unauthorized immigrants and their supporters (including employers) exacerbate this tension.

The challenge of enforcement targeting, together with the long history of unintended consequences of immigration policy described in this introductory chapter, raises a third question: Can states resolve this dilemma through more and smarter investments in migration control technology, infrastructure, and personnel? Undoubtedly, the enforcement choices that states make matter. One set of choices concerns where enforcement occurs. As this chapter observes, in an era of globalization, lawmakers have a greater capacity to curtail rights within host states than to raise barriers to entry; they have even less capacity to alter the structural pushes, pulls, and social networks at the heart of most migration decision making. Yet the same hierarchy applies to the resulting adverse effects: "easy" enforcement tools that take away immigrant rights to services and access to the labor market impose the greatest costs on host-state citizens; more costly interventions at the border are better able to target legal and unauthorized immigrants; and efforts to reshape global migration pushes and pulls may require the greatest long-term investment and may be the least certain to achieve their desired effect but also the least likely to harm host-state residents.

A second set of choices concerns how and how much states invest in migration control. Even in an era of globalization and increased trade and tourism, states decide how much to spend on port infrastructure and inspections—investments that speed legal admissions while also increasing the capacity to detect contraband and illegal immigrants—versus how much to spend on surveillance and infrastructure between ports of entry. Individual host states choose between targeting immigrants for removal—through task forces and by erecting filters in the criminal justice system and at other points of contact—and how much to spend on deterrence by requiring employers and benefits providers to participate in the enforcement process.

Many migration control measures passed beginning in the 1980s may indeed have been largely "symbolic efforts" at control, as this introductory chapter asserts, and unauthorized immigrants have undoubtedly received a de facto message that once they make it into the host state they are relatively safe from deportation. But the cumulative effect of three decades of enforcement and new technologies may mean that policies on the ground have begun to catch up to and even exceed original enforcement goals. In the US case, for example, weak employer sanctions on the books since 1986 may be transformed into a real obstacle to unauthorized employment as a function of the growing E-Verify electronic eligibility verification system, which now screens one out of four new hires to prevent some types of document fraud; also, unauthorized employment may become far more difficult if E-Verify administrators work out a system to prevent identity fraud and the system becomes universally mandated. Employer screening was reinforced by high-profile worksite raids during the final years of the Bush administration and by thousands of employer audits under President Obama. The US Border Patrol has grown to 20,000 agents, supplemented by 650 miles of fencing and a sophisticated surveillance network of cameras, motion detectors, and unmanned aerial vehicles. Moreover, laws passed in 1996 to streamline the deportation process for many types of removable aliens have taken on far greater importance in the context of new screening programs and federal-state and federal-local partnerships that soon will allow immigration enforcement agents to review biometric records of every person arrested in the country. These control efforts have not come cheap; the enforcement agencies of the Department of Homeland Security spent $18 billion in 2012—an amount that does not begin to account for the indirect costs of enforcement to US businesses, immigrant communities, and citizens.

With these programs in place, the United States deported a record number of immigrants in twelve of the last thirteen years, including just under 800,000 during the first two years of the Obama administration, even as apprehensions of new unauthorized immigrants fell to a 40-year low.[3] Likewise, the estimated unauthorized population fell by about 1 million from its high point of about 12 million in 2007.[4] This chapter correctly observes that these numbers do not prove that "enforcement works," because they do not control for the economic downturn that has resulted in reduced migration pull factors—and it is especially important to distinguish between the effect of enforcement on new inflows and that of removal of long-time unauthorized immigrants.[5] It is equally true that poor job growth does not prove that enforcement has *not* contributed to these numbers, and it is a stretch to assume that enforcement has not been a factor in these unprecedented declines.

Thus, the final set of questions raised by this discussion regards how we weigh the costs and benefits of migration enforcement—that is, back to the politics of immigration policy—and the future of migration control. Will existing investments in migration enforcement at the border and within the United States continue to prevent growth in the unauthorized immigrant population even as a healthy level of employment creation resumes? Will European states converge around these more or less successful US enforcement tools if they do? Or, as the economy recovers and the natural generational process of immigrant integration unfolds, will the citizens of these host states come to view robust enforcement as too costly to maintain?

NOTES

1. See Marc R. Rosenblum, *US Immigration Policy since 9/11: Understanding the Stalemate over Comprehensive Immigration Reform* (Washington, DC: Migration Policy Institute, 2011).

2. James F. Hollifield, *Immigrants, Markets and States: The Political Economy of Postwar Europe* (Cambridge, MA: Harvard University Press, 1992).

3. US Department of Homeland Security, *Yearbook of Immigration Statistics* (Washington, DC: DHS, 2009), http://www.dhs.gov/files/statistics/publications/yearbook.shtm.

4. Jeffrey Passel and D'Vera Cohn, *U.S. Unauthorized Immigration Flows Are Down Sharply since Mid-Decade* (Washington, DC: Pew Hispanic Center, 2010), http://pewhispanic.org/reports/report.php?ReportID=126.

5. Although the question has not been examined thoroughly, research suggests that reductions in the US unauthorized population do not reflect a significant increase in return migration over historical levels, as for many years about half a million unauthorized immigrants annually have returned to their countries of origin. Rather, it reflects continuity in return flows combined with a sharp drop in new inflows.

REFERENCES

Freeman, Gary P. 1995. "Modes of Immigration Politics in Liberal Democratic States." *International Migration Review* 29 (4): 881–902.

Conceptual Challenges and Contemporary Trends in Immigration Control

Tom K. Wong

Immigration is one of the most prominent and enduring features of globalization. Since publication of the first edition of *Controlling Immigration* in 1994, the number of international migrants has increased by nearly 50 million,[1] so it is no wonder that the control and management of immigration continues to be one of the most pressing policy issues for the governments and legislatures of most advanced industrialized democracies. This introductory chapter asks how states have responded to increased large-scale immigration and how they have coped with the simultaneous and competing pressures for more openness to certain types of migration and tighter restrictiveness over others. Using a comparative research design unrivaled in its breadth of coverage and depth of analysis, this book answers these questions. It is organized around two central ideas: one, that there is convergence among immigrant-receiving democracies in the policy instruments used to control and manage international migration, as well as convergence in the efficacy and the effects of these policies; and, two, that the gap between immigration policy goals and outcomes has widened over time. While these two interrelated theses have served as the point of departure for much of the research that has followed since the first edition, they are also the source of continued scholarly debate.

CONCEPTUAL CHALLENGES

One question that *Controlling Immigration* raises centers on conceptualization: epistemologically prior to the analysis of immigration policies and their effectiveness is the question of what constitutes immigration control. Immigration control refers broadly to the policies and practices used to deter "unwanted" migration, meaning migration that is occurring despite and against the intentions of states (Joppke 2001). Substantial disagreement exists, however, over the depth of the deterrence objectives of immigration control. For example, one immigration policy priority in the United States is "operational control," which the Secure Fence Act of 2006, authorizing 700 miles of fencing along the US-Mexican border, defines as the "prevention of *all* unlawful US entries."[2] In contrast, the Customs and Border Patrol agency (CBP), which is at the front line of immigration control efforts, defines its mission not as preventing all unlawful entries but rather as establishing a "substantial probability" of apprehension.[3] Indeed, the meaning of immigration control is not just a subject of academic debate; definitional controversies exist even between policymakers and immigration enforcement bureaucrats within the same country.

Moreover, most of the work on immigration control has yet to deconstruct and analyze the components of the increasingly complex regimes in advanced industrialized democracies or the different venues that serve as the locus of control (e.g., interior efforts, including employer sanctions and the apprehension, detention, and deportation of unauthorized immigrants, as opposed to external efforts, including border enforcement and cooperation with third countries). This risks conflating disparate aspects of immigration control that may be governed by distinct factors and behavioral logics.

Questions about the conceptualization of immigration control feed into more substantive questions regarding the causes and the extent of policy gaps. The gap hypothesis assumes a central role in the literature, as it directs our attention to the contentious politics of immigration and challenges scholars to better understand the causes and implications of the gaps that exist between immigration control policies and outcomes. However, in disaggregating the mesh of policies and practices that constitute immigration control, it becomes necessary to question whether the causes of policy gaps are generalizable across this complex tangle and whether they monotonically increase in size across the different areas of immigration control. With respect to the former question, recent work on Germany and the United States shows that the same factors that encourage greater restrictiveness in the policy design stage of immigration control—namely, public opinion—work to produce less restrictive outcomes during policy implementation (Ellermann 2009). With respect to the latter question, emergent trends in immigration control suggest that policy gaps may, at least in some areas, be decreasing. For example, Figure 1.1 shows total deportations across Western immigrant-receiving democracies over the past decade. Since 2000, total deportations have increased by 43 percent. In 2000, the countries combined to account for approximately 460,000 deportations, and this number increased in 2009 to approximately 660,000. The figure also shows that the total number of deportations as a percentage of the foreign-born population increased across the sample.[4]

The US case is more striking. Figure 1.2 shows that deportations increased significantly in the first decade of the twenty-first century; from 2000 to 2009, they increased by 109 percent. In fact, we saw more deportations in the first year of the Obama administration than at any point in US history.

A look at other fundamental cogs in the machinery of immigration control suggests not just that policy gaps are deficits between policies and outcomes but that they also reflect the selectivity of immigration enforcement. Immigration detention in the United States provides one example of this. Figure 1.3 illustrates trends in immigration detention from 2005 to 2010. Since 2005, the total number of immigrants detained by Immigration and Customs Enforcement (ICE) increased by 64.3 percent. In 2005, 233,417 people were detained for immigration-related reasons, and by 2010 this number had increased to 383,615.

The period since 2005 is significant because it marks the start of the Secure Borders Initiative (SBI), a multiyear Department of Homeland Security (DHS) strategy that includes

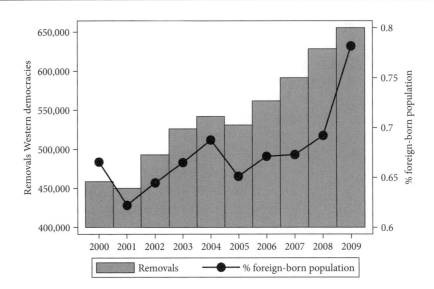

Figure 1.1   Total deportations and deportations as a percentage of the foreign-born population, Western immigrant-receiving democracies, 2000–2009. *Source:* Author's calculations taken from various national sources. See Tom K. Wong, *Human Rights, Deportation, and Detention in an Age of Immigration Control* (Stanford, CA: Stanford University
Press, forthcoming).

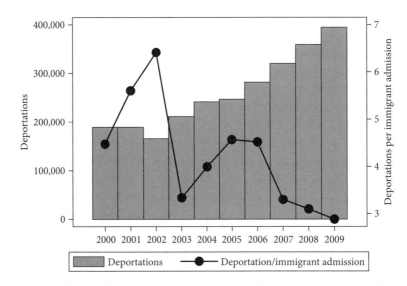

Figure 1.2   Total deportations and deportations per immigrant admission in the United
States, 2000–2009. *Source:* DHS, USCIS.

expanded immigration detention and removal capabilities.[5] In addition to expanding the
capabilities of enforcement agencies, the Obama administration has focused its efforts on
"criminal aliens" as opposed to low-priority cases.[6] Accordingly, in the first year of the
administration the detention of criminal aliens increased by 60 percent.[7] What this illus-

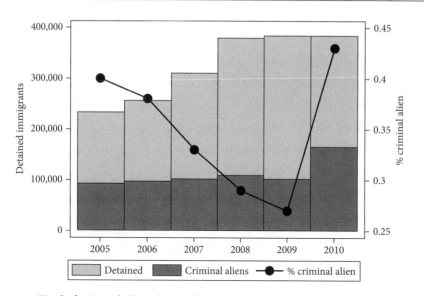

Figure 1.3 Total of criminal aliens detained in the United States, 2005–2010. *Source:* DHS, TRAC.

trates is purposiveness behind the selectivity of immigration enforcement priorities and how this results in certain categories of migrants becoming more or less subject to immigration control (the focus on low-priority cases recently evolved into administrative relief from deportation for some 800,000 undocumented youth). Such "on the ground" realities are not exclusive to the US case, but are reflective of the strategic logic of immigration control. Because it occupies the space between policies and outcomes, greater attention to this strategic logic would go far in improving our understanding of policy gaps.

Selectivity also becomes apparent when looking at asylum recognition rates. As Figure 1.4 shows, recognition rates for Western immigrant-receiving democracies have been steadily declining. In 2008, the combined rate for these countries was 15.8 percent. The commensurate rate for all other countries in the world during the same year was over double that, at 35.9 percent.

MOVING AHEAD

What does this all amount to? In turning back to initial questions about the meaning of immigration control and what it constitutes, we see that it is important to disaggregate the components of increasingly complex regimes, as doing so may reveal that the distinct mechanisms of immigration control exhibit opposite and competing trends over time. It may also reveal that the theorized determinants of immigration policy affect each of these cogs in different and sometimes unexpected ways.

Altogether, disassembling the machinery of immigration control not only provides another lens through which to analyze and investigate the empirical validity of the convergence and gap hypotheses; it also offers a way to build from the seminal ideas of this volume and, perhaps, chart new territory in the study of immigration control.

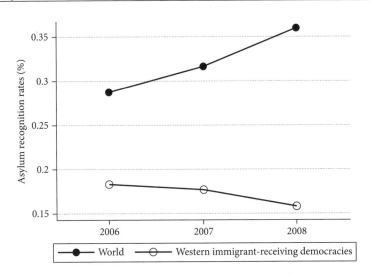

Figure 1.4 Asylum recognition rates in Western immigrant-receiving countries and the world, 2006–2008. *Source:* UNHCR.

NOTES

1. United Nations Population Division, Global Migration Database.

2. US Secure Fence Act of 2006, Pub. L. 109–367, 120 Stat. 2638–2640. Emphasis added.

3. US Homeland Security Council, *National Strategy for Homeland Security*, October 2007.

4. Though the trend was upward during the first decade of the twenty-first century, the annual number of deportations as a percentage of the foreign-born population was less than 1 percent in 2009.

5. The Department of Homeland Security (DHS) describes the Secure Borders Initiative (SBI) as a "comprehensive multi-year plan to secure America's borders and reduce illegal immigration" through infrastructure improvement, comprehensive and systemic upgrading of technology, more border patrol and immigration enforcement agents, and expanded detention and removal capabilities.

6. "Criminal alien" is a legal term that refers to noncitizens residing in the United States legally or illegally who are convicted of a crime.

7. These data should not be interpreted to suggest only that the administration's immigration enforcement strategy has been successful, as substantial controversy exists over how the administration has defined criminal aliens and how it has distinguished low-priority cases from others.

REFERENCES

Ellermann, Antje. 2009. *States against Migrants: Deportation in Germany and the United States*. Cambridge, MA: Cambridge University Press.

Joppke, Christian. 2001. "The Legal-Domestic Sources of Immigrant Rights: The United States, Germany and the European Union." *Comparative Political Studies* 34 (4): 339–66.

II NATIONS OF IMMIGRANTS

THE UNITED STATES

The Continuing Immigration Debate

Philip L. Martin

INTRODUCTION

The United States is a nation of immigrants. Under the motto "e pluribus unum" (from many one), US presidents frequently remind Americans that they share the experience of themselves or their forebears leaving another country to begin anew in the United States.[1] Immigration is viewed as serving the national interest; that is, immigrants can better themselves as they enrich the United States. However, there is an ever-wider gap between the goal of welcoming immigrants through established front-door channels and the presence of 11 to 12 million unauthorized foreigners. Closing this gap has been the major immigration debate of the past decade.

The US government began to record the arrival of immigrants in 1820 and, in the almost two centuries since, over 75 million arrived, including about 10 percent respectively from Mexico and Germany. Despite this immigration experience, there are still heated debates about the three major immigration questions: How many immigrants should the United States admit, who should have priority to enter, and how should immigration laws be enforced and the integration of immigrants promoted?

Over 100,000 foreigners enter the United States on a typical day. There are three major entry doors: a front door for immigrants, a side door for temporary visitors, and a back door for the unauthorized. About 3,100 foreigners a day receive immigrant visas that allow them to live and work in most private-sector jobs and become naturalized US citizens after five years. Over 95,000 tourist, business, and student visitors known as nonimmigrants arrive; some stay only a few days, while others stay for several years. Finally, 2,000 unauthorized foreigners a day were settling in the United States until the 2008–2009 recession reduced their number to less than 1,000 a day. Over half of the unauthorized eluded apprehension at the Mexican-US border, while the others entered legally but violated the terms of their visitor visas by going to work or not departing.[2]

The US immigration system recognizes 1.1 million foreigners a year as legal immigrants, admits 35 million tourists and other visitors a year, and has 300,000 to 400,000 unauthorized foreigners who settle each year. During the 1990s, there were often contentious debates about the relationship of immigrants and their children to the US educational, welfare, and political systems. More broadly, it was debated whether the immigration and integration system served US national interests. During the first decade of the twenty-first century, these debates have centered on how to prevent terrorism and what to do about unauthorized migration.

Public opinion polls find widespread dissatisfaction with the "broken" US immigration system, marked by debates over the proper mix of family and economic immigrants and a large number of unauthorized foreigners. Congress has debated immigration reforms for the past decade. The House approved an enforcement-only bill in 2005; the Senate approved a comprehensive bill in 2006 that included both enforcement and legalization. Nevertheless, Congress has been unable to agree on the three-pronged package embraced by President Obama: tougher enforcement against unauthorized migration, legalization of most unauthorized foreigners, and new and expanded guest worker programs. A three-pronged comprehensive immigration reform package was debated in summer 2013.

Two recent changes rekindled the immigration reform debate. The 2008-2009 recession, the worst in 50 years, exacerbated unemployment and reduced the entry of additional unauthorized foreigners. However, most of the unauthorized in the United States did not go home even if they lost their jobs, since there were also few jobs in their home countries.[3] The second stimulus for a renewed debate is the enactment of laws by states and cities to deal with unauthorized migration, including an Arizona law enacted in April 2010 that makes unauthorized presence in the state a crime. Arizona and a dozen other states require employers to use the federal government's electronic E-Verify system to check the legal status of new hires.

This chapter summarizes US migration patterns, puts the immigration and integration challenges facing the US in a global context, and reviews the evolution of US immigration and integration policy. Immigration brings newcomers from around the world, making the United States, in the words of former Census director Kenneth Prewitt, "the first country in world history which is literally made up of every part of the world"[4] (quoted in *Migration News* 2001).

IMMIGRATION, TEMPORARY VISITORS, AND THE UNAUTHORIZED

The United States had 39 million foreign-born residents in 2009; 11 million, almost 30 percent, were illegal. It has the most foreign-born residents of any country, three times more than number-two Russia, and more unauthorized residents than any other country. Generally, about 10 percent of the residents of major OECD countries are foreign born. The United States, with 13 percent foreign-born residents, has a higher share of immigrants among residents than most European countries but a lower share than Australia and Canada.[5]

There are three major types of foreigners in the United States: front-door immigrants, side-door temporary visitors, and back-door unauthorized. Immigrants are citizens of other countries who receive visas that allow them to settle in the United States. Immigrant visas today resemble credit cards, but they used to be printed on green paper, explaining why immigrants are sometimes referred to as green card holders.

Immigrants

The four major subcategories of immigrants reflect US immigration priorities. The largest subcategory is family unification, meaning that US citizens and immigrants settled in the United States ask the government to issue immigrant visas to their relatives. As Table 2.1 shows, about 500,000, or almost half of all immigrant visas in recent years, went to immediate relatives of US citizens, as when a US soldier abroad marries a local resident and wants to bring him or her into the United States, or when a newly naturalized US citizen requests visas for family members. The second part of the family unification category is for spouses and children of US immigrants and more distant relatives such as adult brothers and sisters; about 215,000 a year are admitted. There is no wait for visas for immediate relatives of US citizens, but families of immigrants and distant relatives of citizens sometimes wait a decade or more for visas.

The second largest immigrant category provides visas to foreigners requested or sponsored by US employers. There are several subcategories of employment-based visas, including one for foreigners with "extraordinary ability" in academia or the arts and another for foreigners who invest at least $500,000 in the United States to create or preserve at least 10 US jobs.[6] There are more extraordinary ability and investor visas available than are requested, but this is not the case for other employment-based visas, which require a US employer to show that a particular foreigner is uniquely qualified to fill a particular job. In many cases, the foreigner is already filling the job, and there can be waits of a year or more for an immigrant visa to become available.

TABLE 2.1

Entries into and out of the United States, FY 2004–2009

Category	2004	2005	2006	2007	2008	2009
Legal immigrants	957,883	1,122,373	1,266,129	1,052,415	1,107,126	1,130,818
Immediate relatives of US citizens	417,815	436,231	580,348	494,920	488,483	535,554
Other family-sponsored immigrants	214,355	212,970	222,229	194,900	227,761	211,859
Employment based	155,330	246,878	159,081	162,176	166,511	144,034
Refugees and asylees	78,351	150,677	216,454	136,125	166,392	177,368
Diversity and other immigrants	92,032	75,617	88,017	64,294	57,979	62,003
Estimated emigration	308,000	312,000	316,000	320,000	324,000	328,000
Legal temporary immigrants	30,781,330	32,003,435	33,667,328	37,149,651	39,381,925	36,231,554
Pleasure/business	27,395,91	28,510,34	29,928,57	32,905,01	35,045,86	32,190,95
Foreign students (F-1)	613,221	621,178	693,805	787,756	859,169	895,392
Temporary foreign workers	831,144	882,957	985,456	1,118,138	1,101,938	936,272
Illegal immigrants						
Apprehensions	1,264,232	1,291,142	1,206,457	960,756	791,568	613,003
Removals/deportations	240,665	246,431	280,974	319,382	358,886	393,289
Unauthorized foreigners	572,000	572,000	572,000	572,000	−650,000	−650,000

SOURCE: DHS Immigration Statistics Annual; unauthorized foreigners from Passel and Cohn (2011).

NOTE: The number of unauthorized foreigners rose from 8.4 million in 2000 to 12.4 million in 2007. In 2010, there were an estimated 11.2 million unauthorized foreigners.

The third immigrant subcategory is for refugees and asylees or applicants for asylum. Refugees are persons outside their country of citizenship who fear persecution at home because of race, religion, nationality, membership in a particular social group, or political opinion. Many leave their homes and live in neighboring countries of Africa, Asia, and Latin America, waiting for conditions at home to improve. The United States resettles about 70,000 refugees a year, two-thirds of them from Asia. Some people leave their countries for the United States and apply for asylum; that is, they ask to be recognized as refugees because they would face persecution at home. About 50,000 foreigners a year request asylum, and half are recognized as refugees, receiving immigrant visas that allow them to settle in the United States.

The fourth subgroup includes diversity immigrants. For the past two decades, the US government has made available 50,000 immigrant visas a year to nationals of countries that sent fewer than 50,000 immigrants during the previous five years. Yearly, about 15 million foreigners enter the lottery. Lottery winners must have completed secondary school and pass a background check to receive their visas.

Most immigrants are in the United States when their immigration visas become available. In recent years, 60 percent of all foreigners, and 90 percent of foreigners receiving employment-based visas, were already in the United States when their visas became available. This adjustment-of-status method of immigration marks a significant change from past patterns, when immigrants set off to begin anew in an unfamiliar place. Many immigrants-in-waiting are in the United States with some type of temporary visitor visa or are unauthorized foreigners.

The largest single source of immigrants is Mexico, which accounted for about 20 percent of immigrants in recent years. Countries that account for 5 to 10 percent of US immigrants include China, India, the Philippines, and the Dominican Republic. California attracts about a quarter of US immigrants, followed by New York with 15 percent and Florida with 10 percent.

Temporary Visitors

Over 35 million foreigners a year arrive as temporary visitors.[7] Most are welcomed. The US travel industry advertises overseas to encourage foreign tourists to visit, businesses invite foreign customers and suppliers, and US colleges and universities recruit foreign students. Most temporary visitors are from European and Asian countries whose citizens do not need visas to enter the United States. Nationals of 36 countries in 2011 were permitted to enter under the visa waiver program, which admits visitors for 90 days. The program is reciprocal; that is, Americans are allowed to visit these countries without visas for up to 90 days as well.

Other temporary visitors need visas to enter the United States, including foreign students and foreign workers. There are more than 25 types of visas for temporary visitors, from A-1 for ambassadors to F-1 for foreign students and H for foreign workers. L-1 visas are for intracompany transfers (workers employed by a multinational outside the United States who are transferred to the firm's US operations); P visas, for foreign athletes and entertainers; and TN visas, for Canadian and Mexican professionals admitted under the North American Free Trade Agreement.

Two types of temporary visitors are sometimes controversial: foreign students and guest workers. Between 1990 and 2000, the number of foreign students in the United States doubled to over 500,000 as economic growth in Asia made a US education more affordable. However, the fact that several of the September 11, 2001, terrorists who flew airplanes into the World Trade Center held student visas, including one who never showed up at the school that admitted him, led to new restrictions on students from some countries studying some sciences and to a new Student and Exchange Visitor Information System (SEVIS) to track foreign students while they are in the United States.

These restrictions and SEVIS led to a drop in the number of foreign students in the United States at mid-decade, but that number rose to a record of almost 700,000 in 2009–2010.[8] The leading countries of origin for foreign students are China, India, and South Korea; the US universities with the most foreign students (almost 45 percent are from these three countries)—more than 7,000 each—are the University of Southern California, the University of Illinois, and New York University. Almost 40 percent of foreign students in the United States study science and engineering, and another 20 percent are business majors.

Most foreign students in the United States are graduate students pursuing MS and PhD degrees. The fact that foreign students receive more than half of these degrees in engineering and many sciences has prompted a debate about why Americans are not flocking to these graduate programs. The National Science Board (2003) faulted math and science teaching in secondary school. Other observers, in explaining why Americans prefer to study business, law, and medicine to science and engineering, point to the fact that advanced degrees in engineering are not associated with higher salaries and that doctorates in science are often followed by lengthy low-paid postdoctoral apprenticeships (Teitelbaum 2003; Benderly 2010).

Many foreign students who graduate from US universities stay in the United States and work, highlighting the importance of temporary foreign workers. About a sixth of almost 155 million US workers were born outside the United States. They include about 15 million immigrants and naturalized citizens, eight million unauthorized foreigners, and up to two million temporary foreign workers. However, the temporary foreign workers garner much of the policy attention because the government permits employers hire them.

There are three major guest worker programs: H-1B, H-2A, and H-2B. Each is controversial, with the debate dominated by those who argue that foreign guest workers are essential to particular sectors of the US economy and those who argue that they distort the economy and hurt US workers.

The H-1B program was included in the Immigration Act of 1990 to help employers deal with what were perceived to be temporary labor market mismatches. During the 1980s, the US unemployment rate remained above 5 percent even as employers in fast-growing computer-related industries complained of labor shortages. The government had a twofold response. First, it launched programs to improve the education and skills of US workers in computer-related fields; second, the H-1B program gave employers easy access to foreign workers to fill jobs that "require theoretical and practical application of highly specialized knowledge to perform fully." In 1990, about 20,000 such workers a year were admitted, so the number of H-1B visas was capped at 65,000 yearly to allow employers to quickly get the workers they needed. The expectation was that the number requested would fall as US graduates appeared.

The early 1990s recession reduced employer requests for H-1B visas, but the IT boom in the late 1990s had employers asking for more than 65,000 H-1B visas a year. IT-related employers persuaded Congress to raise the annual cap several times, eventually to 195,000 a year, to add 20,000 visas for foreigners who earn MS and PhD degrees from US universities, and to exempt universities and nonprofit research labs from the H-1B cap.

Since H-1B visa holders can stay in the United States for up to six years, there were soon almost a million in the United States. Microsoft Chairman Bill Gates and other IT leaders argued that, because H-1B foreigners were essential to computer-related industries, the visa cap should be eliminated.[9] According to critics, the H-1B is about cheap labor because, they say, employers may lawfully lay off US workers to hire H-1B workers and because foreign workers who hope their US employer will sponsor them for immigrant visas are preferred for their "loyalty." The H-1B program differs from most guest worker programs in allowing employers to attest or assert that they have satisfied simple rules, mostly that they are paying H-1B workers at least the prevailing wage for the job; they are kept honest by inspections after complaints have been filed. The H-1B program has no requirement to advertise for US workers and give those who apply preference; some employers advertise for "H-1B visa holders only" and several have laid off US workers and replaced them with H-1B visa holders.

The H-2A and H-2B programs, which admit low-skilled foreign workers to fill seasonal jobs in agriculture and nonfarm industries such as landscaping, are different. Instead of the H-1B's easy-for-employers attestation procedure, H-2A and H-2B rely on a certification procedure that requires US employers to first recruit US workers to fill the jobs for which they are seeking permission to recruit and employ foreign workers. They are allowed to hire foreign workers only if this recruitment effort fails.

Certification provides more protection to US workers because employers must have recruitment ads for US workers checked and employers must record why US workers who applied were not hired. Also, the job offer or recruitment ad becomes a contract between the employer and US and foreign workers that the employees can sue to enforce. However, certification is considered "cumbersome," especially by farmers who grow perishable crops, since their job offers may have to be revised before they can begin recruiting first US and then foreign workers. Worker advocates, on the other hand, point to cases of abuse of low-skilled foreign workers with H-2 visas to assert that certification does not provide sufficient protection.

Other temporary visitor visas allow employers to hire foreigners without trying to recruit US workers first. Foreign students can work part time while they study and full time during school vacations, and they can remain in the United States for 12 months of work-and-learn optional practical training with a US employer after graduation.[10]

The J-1 exchange visitor program admitted over 400,000 foreigners in fiscal year 2009 for work-and-learn experiences as au pairs in private households or filling jobs in summer and winter resorts. The L-1 intracompany visa program allowed almost 335,000 foreigners in fiscal year 2009 to be transferred from foreign to US subsidiaries of the same multinational. Over 100,000 foreigners with O, P, Q, and R visas were admitted in fiscal year 2009 as temporary workers in arts and entertainment, sports, or religious activities, and 99,000 foreigners were admitted with TN visas that allow Canadian and Mexican professionals with US job offers to enter and work indefinitely.[11]

Foreign or guest worker programs are controversial, whether they admit skilled workers with university degrees or admit low-skilled workers who have not completed secondary school. Employers normally assert that they are in the best position to decide which worker is most qualified to fill a particular job, and they resent "government interference" when they decide that foreigners are most qualified and that attestation or certification places hurdles between employers and the workers they want. Employers prefer attestation, which allows them to effectively open border gates to foreigners with the government checking to ensure that employers are abiding by these promises, which explains why they resist making the H-1B a certification program and want to convert the H-2A and H-2B programs into attestation programs.

Unauthorized Foreigners

Unauthorized foreigners are often said to enter the United States via the back door, suggesting that they slip across the Mexican-US border as so-called entries without inspections. However, over 40 percent of unauthorized foreigners entered legally—as tourists or students, or with the border crossing cards available to Mexicans who want to shop in US border areas[12]—and then violated the terms of their legal entry by not departing or working illegally.

The United States has the largest number and share of unauthorized foreigners among the industrial democracies. In 2010, it had over 11 million unauthorized foreigners, meaning that over 25 percent of foreign-born residents were unauthorized and making the number of unauthorized about as large as the total foreign population of Russia, the second-leading country of immigration.

Most unauthorized foreigners are from Mexico, and most arrived recently. In 1970, when Mexico had about 50 million residents, there were fewer than 750,000 Mexican-born US residents. By 2000, Mexico's population had doubled to 100 million and the number of Mexican-born US residents had increased ten-fold to more than 8 million. Mexicans make up about 60 percent of unauthorized foreigners, followed by Central Americans (El Salvador, Guatemala, and Honduras) at about 15 percent. The other 25 percent of unauthorized foreigners are from other countries around the world.

Demographers have refined methods of estimating the number of unauthorized foreigners to converge on the estimate of 11 million in 2012, a sharp jump from the estimated 8 million in 2000 but down from a peak 12 million in 2007 (see Figure 2.1). About 8 million unauthorized foreigners are in the US work force, meaning that 5 percent of US workers are unauthorized. Their number surged during the housing boom of 2004–2007, as many unauthorized Mexican and Central American workers found jobs in residential building. The 2008–2009 recession appears to have reduced the number of unauthorized foreigners by about a million, reflecting the loss of 8 million US jobs in 2008–2009.[13]

There are several reasons for the rising back-door migration of the past decade and the recent drop. When the Immigration Reform and Control Act of 1986 was enacted, there were an estimated 4 million unauthorized foreigners in the United States. Almost 3 million

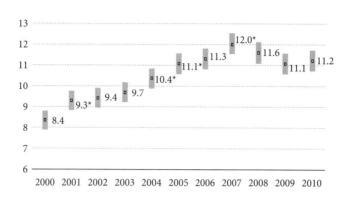

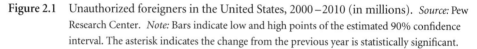

Figure 2.1 Unauthorized foreigners in the United States, 2000–2010 (in millions). *Source:* Pew Research Center. *Note:* Bars indicate low and high points of the estimated 90% confidence interval. The asterisk indicates the change from the previous year is statistically significant.

were legalized in 1987–1988, including 85 percent who were Mexicans. However, more arrived and there were still about 3 million by 1990. The number rose to 5 million in 1995, 8 million in 2000, and 11 million in 2005 as unauthorized foreigners spread from traditional immigration states such as California and New York to new destinations such as Georgia and North Carolina.

The US unemployment rate doubled between 2007 and 2009 to over 9 percent, and is projected to remain at historically high levels through 2015. If unemployment declines and there are no major changes in immigration policy, unauthorized migration is likely to pose a test of markets versus regulations. A resumption of construction activity as well as worker turnover in farm and service jobs is likely to create job openings that could be filled by newly arrived unauthorized foreigners. On the other hand, the number of US Border Patrol agents doubled to more than 21,000 between 2005 and 2010, a third of the 2,000 mile Mexican-US border has fences and vehicle barriers, and the Department of Homeland Security (DHS) is increasing audits of the I-9 forms that newly hired workers and employers complete to ensure that only legally authorized workers are hired.

If the unemployment rate drops toward 5 percent, employers are likely to complain of labor shortages, and migrants who elude the Border Patrol are likely to find vacant jobs. If hiring systems evolve to at least partially shield employers from fines for knowingly hiring unauthorized workers—such as intermediaries who serve as risk absorbers for major firms by providing temporary and seasonal workers—unauthorized migration may rise despite the new enforcement measures. On the other hand, increased smuggling costs and dangers, coupled with the lower wages often offered by intermediaries willing to risk fines, may discourage unauthorized entries if economic development is providing jobs at home.

IMMIGRATION HISTORY AND POLICY

Immigration to the United States occurred in four major waves. Large influxes of foreigners over several decades were followed by periods in which there was little immigration because of changes in immigration policy and economic conditions in the United States and abroad. The country is now in the midst of the fourth immigration wave and, because immigration policy today gives priority to relatives of US residents and because immigrants come from almost all countries, there is no "natural" end to the fourth wave in sight.

Four Waves of Immigrants

The first wave of US immigrants came before the United States was created. In the seventeenth and eighteenth centuries, English colonists established communities at Jamestown and Plymouth, seized control from the Dutch in New York, and overran various French and Spanish settlements. The English were 60 percent of the population in 1790, English became the most common language, and English common law became the basis for the US legal system.[14] The word "immigrant" emerged in the 1790s to mean a person who moves voluntarily from one established country to another.

The second wave of immigrants, between 1820 and 1860, accelerated the push westward. European peasants displaced from agriculture and artisans made jobless by the industrial revolution were eager to try their luck in the United States, and steamship and railroad companies advertised for passengers. New arrivals sent what came to be called "American letters" to Europe, encouraging friends and relatives to join them. About 40 percent of the 5 million second-wave immigrants were from Ireland, where an 1840s famine caused by potato blight encouraged emigration. Roman Catholics predominated in the second wave, and by 1850 the Roman Catholic Church was the largest denomination in the United States, although Protestants of various kinds outnumbered Catholics.

There was little immigration during reconstruction after the Civil War. It was not until 1880 that the third wave began, with almost 460,000 arrivals a year. The third wave ended in 1914, with 1.2 million arrivals on the eve of World War I—the highest rate of immigration in US history. During the third wave, over 20 million Southern and Eastern Europeans immigrated to the eastern and midwestern states and several hundred thousand Chinese, Japanese, and other Asians settled in the western states.

The American frontier was closed by 1890, and most newcomers found factory jobs in cities in the Northeast and Midwest. Immigrants represented over half of all operatives in steel and meat packing in 1910, and foreign-born men represented over half of the work force in cities such as New York, Chicago, and Detroit (Briggs 1992: 56–57).[15]

Immigration paused for the half-century between 1915 and 1964, largely because in the 1920s Congress enacted quotas that restricted the arrival of newcomers. The economic depression of the 1930s discouraged immigration, although after World War II almost 600,000 Europeans who had been displaced by the war were admitted. During the war the country began to admit Mexican Bracero guest workers; Bracero admissions peaked at 455,000 in the mid-1950s. During the 1950s, fewer than 250,000 immigrants a year were admitted.

Fourth-wave immigrants began arriving in the United States after 1965, when the national origins selection system, which favored immigrants from particular countries in Northern and Western Europe, changed to favoring immigrants with relatives already in the United States and those sponsored by US employers. This change, plus rapid economic growth in Europe, shifted the origins of most immigrants from Europe to Latin America and Asia. During the 1970s, the first decade that the family unification law was in effect, the United States accepted 4.2 million immigrants, including 825,000 Europeans and 621,000 Mexicans. By the 1980s, when immigration rose to 6.2 million, the number of Mexican immigrants, 1 million, topped the number of Europeans, 670,000, because recently arrived Mexicans sponsored family members still in Mexico.

There are many similarities between immigration at the end and that at beginning of the twentieth century. The number of immigrants arriving annually during the peak years—over 1 million—is about the same. Both waves brought people from countries that had not previously sent large numbers of immigrants, raising questions about language, religion, and culture and leading to efforts to fundamentally change immigration policy.

Immigration Policy: 1776–1980

During its first 200 years, US immigration policies went through three major phases: laissez-faire, qualitative restrictions, and quantitative restrictions. For the first 100 years, pretty much anyone who arrived was permitted to settle and naturalize. Many entities promoted immigration, including shipping companies looking for passengers, developers who had been granted land in exchange for building canals and railroads and needed laborers, and employers and others who wanted more people. Economic policies such as high tariffs on manufactured goods kept out lower-cost European goods and created a demand for workers in American factories, which encouraged immigration.

The first major backlash against this open-door policy was a reaction against Catholics arriving from Ireland and Germany in the 1840s. Protestant clergymen, journalists, and other opinion leaders formed the Order of the Star Spangled Banner, which urged restrictions on immigration from non-Anglo-Saxon countries. The order became the "Know Nothing" movement because members, when asked, were instructed to say "I know nothing." Adherents dominated the American Party, which won 70 House seats in the Congressional election of 1854. However, Congress did not enact their anti-immigrant agenda, and slavery soon replaced immigration as the major political issue of the day.

The door to some immigrants began to close in the 1870s, when immigration policy barred certain types of foreigners: convicts and prostitutes in 1875, followed by paupers and "mental defectives" in 1882. The Chinese Exclusion Act of 1882 for the first time barred immigration from a particular country, and this ban, enacted at the behest of California unions, was not lifted until 1943. In the 1880s, the importation of foreign workers who had contracts that required them to work for particular employers was banned.

During the third wave of immigration, between 1880 and 1914, restrictionists sought to add qualitative restrictions that would keep ill and illiterate immigrants out. Immigrants arriving at Ellis Island in New York harbor in 1900 were observed by doctors as they climbed the stairs, and could be ordered back to their countries of origin if they had contagious diseases.[16] Those who hoped to reduce immigration from Southern and Eastern Europe wanted a requirement that new arrivals must pass a literacy test so that only arrivals 17 years of age and older able to read in English or some other language would be admitted. Congress enacted three literacy tests that were subsequently vetoed, but President Wilson's veto of the 1917 Immigration Act was overridden, introducing another qualitative restriction on immigration.

There was little migration from Europe to the United States during World War I; however, when immigration resumed in the 1920s, restrictionists realized that the literacy test would not enough to stop immigration from Southern and Eastern Europe. The Congressional Dillingham Commission produced 41 volumes of reports on immigration in 1911 that concluded that immigrants from Southern and Eastern Europe had more "inborn socially inadequate qualities than northwestern Europeans" (quoted in Handlin 1952: 755).[17]

Congress used the Dillingham Commission report to impose quantitative limits on immigration in 1921, and revised these quotas in the Immigration Act of 1924 to cap the annual number of immigrants at 150,000, plus accompanying wives and children. The national origins formula made the maximum number of immigrants from any country in the Eastern Hemisphere "a number which bears the same ratio to 150,000 as the number of inhabitants in the United States in 1920 having that national origin bears to the number of white inhabitants of the United States" (House of Representatives 1952: 37).[18] Since there were more immigrants from Northern and Western than from Southern and Eastern Europe, over 80 percent of visas went to people from Northern and Western European countries from the 1920s to the 1960s.

After World War II, President Truman tried to abolish the national origins system. He failed, and the McCarran-Walter Immigration and Nationality Act of 1952 was approved despite his veto. President Kennedy made another attempt to eliminate the national origins selection system, and in 1965 the Immigration and Nationality Act was amended to institute the family unification and employer sponsor system as a replacement for the national origins system, which was abolished.

Immigration Policy: 1980–2010

For most of the past two centuries, US immigration policy changed once a generation, adding restrictions on how many immigrants and of what type could enter. These restrictions were in response to rising numbers of foreigners seeking admittance. Beginning in 1980, Congress enacted major immigration laws at least once a decade, but it remains divided on how to deal with unauthorized foreigners.

The major immigration laws enacted in the past three decades include the following:

- *The Refugee Act of 1980.* The United States adopted the UN definition of "refugee": a person outside his or her country of citizenship and unwilling to return because of a well-founded fear of persecution because of race, religion, nationality, membership in a particular social group, or political opinion.

- *The Immigration Reform and Control Act of 1986.* IRCA, which dealt with illegal migration, represented a grand bargain between restrictionists and admissionists. Restrictionists won federal penalties on employers who knowingly hire unauthorized workers (employer sanctions), while admissionists obtained immigrant status for unauthorized foreigners in the country since 1982 or employed in agriculture in 1985–1986 (amnesty or legalization).

- *The Immigration Act of 1990.* IMMACT, which dealt with legal immigration, raised the worldwide annual ceiling on immigration from 270,000 a year, plus immediate relatives of US citizens, to 675,000 a year, including relatives, and refugees. IMMACT more than doubled the number of employment-based immigration visas, from 54,000 to 140,000 a year, created the H-1B program, and created the diversity lottery immigrant visa program.

- *The Anti-Terrorism and Effective Death Penalty Act of 1996.* This law introduced expedited removal procedures for foreigners arriving at US ports of entry without proper documents and seek asylum but have no credible fear of persecution at home. It also expedited the removal of foreigners convicted of felony crimes in the United States. In many cases, foreign criminals move from state prisons to federal facilities while trying to convince a US immigration judge to allow them to stay in the country after they have served their sentence.

- *The Personal Responsibility and Work Opportunity Reconciliation Act of 1996.* This welfare reform law turned cash assistance for poor residents from an open-ended entitlement into a block grant to states, and gave states some discretion in deciding how to assist the poor. Most legal immigrants are not eligible for federal means-tested cash assistance until they naturalize after five years or work at least 10 years in the United States. Residents who sponsor their relatives for immigrant visas must provide an affidavit of support showing that they have incomes of at least 125 percent of the US poverty line for themselves and the immigrants they are sponsoring (at least $27,938 in 2011 for a couple sponsoring a set of parents, when the poverty line was $22,350 for a family of four).

- *The Illegal Immigration Reform and Immigrant Responsibility Act of 1996.* IIRIRA aimed to reduce illegal migration by doubling the number of Border Patrol agents to 10,000 by 2010 (subsequent laws increased that number to 21,000 in 2010). It also introduced several pilot employment verification programs, to prevent unauthorized foreigners from getting jobs, that have evolved into E-Verify, the Internet-based system under which employers submit data provided by newly hired workers to government databases to check their authorization to work.

- *The Enhanced Border Security and Visa Entry Reform Act of 2001.* EBSVERA was passed after the September 11, 2001, terrorist attacks to increase scrutiny of applicants for visas and to keep track of foreign students. In most cases, foreigners requiring visas to enter the United States must appear in person before a US consular officer in their country of citizenship; there are no detailed written requirements to obtain a visa and no appeals of denials. The student-tracking system became SEVIS, the Internet system by which universities report the progress of foreign students to DHS.

Congress debated what to do about rising unauthorized migration for the past decade, but no new laws were enacted. Unlike 1986, when restrictionists, who thought priority should be given to fines on employers who knowingly hired illegal workers, compromised with admissionists, who put priority on legalizing unauthorized foreigners.

The restrictionist approach was embodied in the Border Protection, Antiterrorism, and Illegal Immigration Control Act approved by the Republican-controlled House in December 2005. This enforcement-only bill would have added more fences and agents on the Mexican-US border and made "illegal presence" in the United States a felony, which complicated legalization because foreigners convicted of felonies are normally denied immigrant visas. The bill called on employers to screen newly hired as well as current employees to ensure that they are legally authorized to work.

Hispanic leaders condemned the House bill and organized demonstrations against it that culminated in a "day without immigrants" on May 1, 2006. Admissionists won provisions in the three-pronged Comprehensive Immigration Reform Act (CIRA) in May 2006 approved by the Democrat-controlled Senate. CIRA would have implemented many of the enforcement provisions in the House bill, including more secure work authorization documents, mandatory employer use of E-Verify, and more agents and fencing on the Mexican-US border. Also, it included a new guest worker program—a market-oriented H-2C visa program for employers who attested or asserted that they could not recruit US workers despite paying at least the minimum or prevailing wage. This program was considered market-oriented because the number of visas available could rise if employers requested all of them.[19] Finally, CIRA included several earned-legalization programs.[20] Unauthorized foreigners who satisfied eligibility requirements such as being in the United States at least five years or having worked in agriculture could become probationary immigrants. If they paid fines, learned English, and continued to work, they could become regular immigrants and eventually US citizens.

Elections in the fall of 2006 produced a Democratic Congress, and the Senate in 2007 debated a new version of a four-pronged Comprehensive Immigration Reform Act. As with earlier House and Senate bills, CIRA 2007 would have added fencing and Border Patrol agents on the Mexican-US border, created a mandatory E-Verify system that allowed employers to check the legal status of new hires, and required the Social Security Administration to develop fraud-resistant cards that newly hired workers would present to employers.

CIRA 2007 would also have provided a path to legalization for most unauthorized foreigners in the United States. They could apply for Z visas that gave them a temporary legal status, and then become regular immigrants by paying fines, undergoing background checks, and applying for immigrant visas in their country of origin—the so-called touch-back rule. There would have been separate legalization programs for farm workers and children brought to the United States before age 16.

CIRA 2007 would have created a new guest worker program that issued several hundred thousand Y- visas a year; the number of visas would have risen if employers requested all of them. Employers could hire Y-visa guest workers if the jobs they offered remained unfilled for at least 90 days and if they paid a guest worker impact fee of $500 to $1,250 depending on the firm's size.[21] Y-visa holders could have performed three two-year work stints in the United States, for a total of six years of US employment.

Finally, the US legal immigration system would have been modified with the introduction of a point system. Foreigners seeking to immigrate would have to earn at least 55 of the maximum 100 points, with up to 47 points available for employment (given for employer job offers and the age and work experience of the foreigner), up to 28 for education, up to 15 for knowledge of English and civics, and 10 points for having US relatives. Foreigners seeking visas to fill high-demand jobs, whether as janitors or engineers, would get up to 16 of the 47 employment points.[22]

Despite the active support of President Bush, the Senate failed to approve CIRA 2007. Unions that had supported comprehensive immigration reform withdrew their support because of the new guest worker programs; employers opposed the new E-Verify requirements and the H-1B program's new worker protections; and migrant advocates worried that the legalization touch-back requirement would deter unauthorized foreigners from seeking legal status.

During the 2008 presidential campaign, the major candidates, Senators John McCain (R-AZ) and Barack Obama (D-IL), supported comprehensive immigration reform—that is, more enforcement and legalization. McCain changed his emphasis during the campaign, calling for border security before legalization.[23] Obama stressed the need to enforce labor and immigration laws in the workplace to protect all workers, including the unauthorized.

The recession, healthcare, and financial regulation were the top domestic priorities of the Obama administration in 2009–2010. The worst recession in 50 years doubled the unemployment rate, reduced the entry of unauthorized foreigners, and made discussion of legalizing 11–12 million unauthorized foreigners difficult when 14–15 million workers were jobless. Legislative action shifted to the states, and Arizona enacted a law in April 2010 making unauthorized presence in it a crime. President Obama criticized the Arizona law, and the US Department of Justice obtained a court order to prevent it from going into effect as scheduled.

In 2011 and 2012, state and local governments enacted mostly restrictive laws to deal with unauthorized migration, in some cases to put pressure on the government to deal with illegal migration. However, a divided Congress did not tackle immigration reform because the Republican-controlled House refused to approve the type of legalization favored by the Democrat-controlled Senate. In summer 2013, the Senate approved the Border Security, Economic Opportunity, and Immigration Modernization Act of 2013 (S 744) negotiated by the so-called Gang of Eight: four Republican and four Democratic senators that embodies the three-pronged approach favored by President Obama—more enforcement to deter unauthorized entry and employment, a path to legal immigrant and eventual US citizen status for most of the 11 million unauthorized foreigners in the country, and new and expanded programs to admit more foreign workers. However, unlike the Senate's comprehensive approach that combined enforcement and legalization, the House considered a series of bills dealing with more enforcement and more guest workers, a piece meal approach that resulted in no major immigration reform in 2013.

IMMIGRATION'S IMPACTS

Immigration means change for the United States. The arrival of immigrants increases and changes the composition of the population, adds workers to the labor force, and can change political priorities and social norms. Most immigrants are from Latin America and Asia, and some of their children do not speak English well, raising questions about how best to teach English-language-learning children.

Immigration and Population

Immigration has a major effect on the size, distribution, and composition of the US population. As fertility fell from a peak of 3.7 children per woman in the late 1950s to the replacement level of 2.1 today, the contribution of immigration to population growth increased. Between 1990 and 2010, the number of foreign-born residents almost doubled from 20 million to 40 million, while the population rose from almost 250 million to 310 million. Thus, immigration constituted one-third of the population and, with the US-born children and grandchildren of immigrants, it represented one-half of the population's growth.

Immigrants are changing the composition of the US population. The population rose by over 100 million in the past 40 years and is projected to increase by almost 100 million by 2050. Immigrants and their US-born children contribute over half of US population growth. Since most immigrants are Hispanic and Asian, their share of the population is projected to increase from 7 percent in 1970 to 20 percent today and 35 percent in 2050.

In 1970, about 83 percent of the 203 million US residents were non-Hispanic whites and 6 percent were Hispanic or Asian. In 2010, when the United States had 308 million residents, two-thirds were non-Hispanic whites and 20 percent were Hispanic or Asian. If current trends continue,[24] the share of non-Hispanic whites in the population will fall from two-thirds in 2010 to just over half in 2050 (see Table 2.2).

Economic Impacts

Most immigrants come to the United States for economic opportunity. About half of immigrants and US-born persons are in the US labor force. A slightly higher share of foreign-born men are in the labor force, and a slightly lower share of foreign-born women. The share of US residents and US workers who were born outside the United States has almost doubled since a lows of 5 percent in 1970, but it is not yet at its historic peak. In 1910, about 15 percent of US residents were born abroad and 24 percent of US workers were foreign

TABLE 2.2
US population by race and ethnic group, 1970, 2010, 2050
(percentages)

US population by race/ethnicity	1970	2010	2050
White non-Hispanic	83	66	52
Black	11	13	13
Hispanic	5	16	29
Asian	1	4	6
Other	1	2	2
Totals[a]	101	101	102
Population (in millions)	203.3	307.9	398.5

SOURCE: US Census Projections with Constant Net International Migration. www.census.gov/population/www/projections/2009cnmsSumTabs.html.

[a]Totals may not add to 100 because of rounding.

TABLE 2.3
Foreign-born population and workforce shares,
1870–2010

Year	Population (%)	Labor force (%)
1870	14	22
1880	13	20
1890	15	26
1900	14	23
1910	15	24
1920	13	21
1930	12	17
1940	9	12
1950	7	9
1960	5	6
1970	5	5
1980	6	7
1990	8	9
2000	10	12
2010	13	16

SOURCE: US Census.

born. A century later, 13 percent of residents and 16 percent of workers were born abroad (see Table 2.3).

Immigration increases the number of US workers and increases the size of the US economy. Most working-age immigrants find jobs, earn and spend most of their wages, pay taxes, and consume public services. Immigration thus expands the economy and employment while slightly depressing wages or the growth in wages, especially for workers who are similar to immigrants. For example, almost half of adult workers who did not complete high school are immigrants. If they were not in the labor force, economic predictions are that wages for US-born high school dropouts would be higher.[25]

During the early 1990s, when many of the Mexicans who had been legalized under IRCA in 1987–1988 brought their families into the United States during a recession, several states sued the federal government, arguing that its failure to enforce immigration laws saddled them with education and other costs. California voters in 1994 approved Proposition 187, which would have required state-funded institutions, including K-12 schools, to verify the legal status of those seeking services.[26]

Proposition 187 was not implemented, but the debate it unleashed about the economic benefits and costs of immigration led to a major study that concluded that immigrants added a net $8 billion to the economy in 1996, when the GDP was about $8 trillion (Smith and Edmonston 1997). The economy was $200 billion larger because of immigration, according to the study, but $192 billion of this expansion went to immigrants in their wages. The presence of immigrants depressed wages by an estimated 3 percent and increased the *net* addition to the economy by one-tenth of 1 percent, or $8 billion.[27] Immigrants are a net benefit because the value of what they produce is more than that of the wages they are paid; thus, owners of capital and US workers who are made more productive by the presence of immigrants stand to gain.

As with most immigration-related studies, this study's results drew opposite reactions. Admissionists stressed immigration's net economic benefits to the economy, while restrictionists stressed that this net contribution was negligible. The then $8 trillion economy was expanding by 3 percent per year, or by $10 billion every two weeks.

Economic theory predicts that US workers who compete with immigrants will have lower wages and higher unemployment. The Economic Report of the President stated, "Although immigrant workers increase output, their addition to the supply of labor . . . [may cause] wage rates in the immediately affected market [to be] bid down. . . . Thus, native-born workers who compete with immigrants for jobs may experience reduced earnings or reduced employment" (Council of Economic Advisers 1986: 221). It has been very hard to find empirical evidence of these adverse effects by comparing cities with more and fewer immigrants. For example, in 1980 over 125,000 Cubans left for the United States via the Cuban port of Mariel. Many settled in Miami, increasing the labor force by 8 percent; however, the unemployment rate of African Americans in Miami in 1981 was lower than in cities, such as Atlanta, that did not receive Cuban immigrants (Card 1990). Other city comparison studies reached similar conclusions, prompting a leading student of immigration's economic effects to conclude that "modern econometrics cannot detect a single shred of evidence that immigrants have a sizable adverse impact on the earnings and employment opportunities of natives in the United States" (Borjas 1990: 81).

There are several explanations for the failure to find lower wages and higher unemployment rates in cities with more immigrants, including the possibility that immigrants do not adversely affect US workers because, for example, their presence encourages businesses to invest and create more jobs for both immigrants and the native born. However, the most common assumption is that there are adverse effects but they are hard to detect because US workers most similar to immigrants do not move to immigrant cities or move away from them.

Internal migration has changed how economists look for the impacts of immigrants on US workers. In the past decade, most economic studies grouped foreign-born and US-born workers by age and education to estimate how 20- to 25-year-old immigrants with less than a high school education affect similar US-born workers. However, these national studies reach different conclusions about immigrant impacts. Borjas assumed that foreign-born and US-born workers of the same age and with the same levels of education are substitutes, meaning that an employer considers them interchangeable, and found that the presence of immigrants depresses wages for similar US-born workers (Borjas 2003). Peri considered foreign-born and US-born workers in each age and experience cell to be complements, meaning that a 30-year-old US-born carpenter with a high school education is more productive because he has a foreign-born helper, and found that immigrants raise similar native-born workers' wages (Docquier, Ozden, and Peri 2010). Since impacts depend on assumptions about immigrant–US worker interactions, economic studies have not reached definitive conclusions (Lowenstein 2006).

The other major economic issue is immigrants' public-finance impact: Do they and their children pay more in taxes than they consume in tax-supported services? A major federally financed study concluded that they do: the average immigrant and his or her descendants was expected to pay $80,000 more in taxes (in 1996 dollars) than he or she would consume in tax-supported services.[28] Reaching this conclusion required "heroic assumptions" about the integration of immigrants, especially the children. The key assumption was that the children and grandchildren of immigrants would be average; that is, their earnings, taxes, and public service use would mirror those of Americans without immigrant parents and grandparents (Smith and Edmonston 1997). The study also assumed that the federal government would not allow federal debt to increase by raising taxes or reducing Social Security benefits.[29]

Studies of labor markets and public finance emphasize that the major economic impacts of immigration are distributional, meaning that some workers and entities are helped and others are hurt but the overall economic impact is small. In the case of taxes and public services, the distributional impact helps the federal government because most immigrants pay more in federal taxes, primarily social security taxes, than they receive in federally funded services. The reverse occurs for state and local governments, especially if immigrants have low levels of education, lower incomes, and larger families. For example, in 1996 households headed by Latin American immigrants in California consumed $5,000 more in state and local services than they paid in state and local taxes, which meant that the state's more numerous native-born households paid an additional $1,200 to cover the "immigrant deficit."

Most immigrants benefit economically by moving to the United States, and the US economy expands as a result. It has been hard to sort out the labor market effects of immigrants, which suggests that, whether they are positive or negative, wage and unemployment effects are small. It has also been hard to reach consensus on other economic effects of immigrants. Are they more entrepreneurial than US-born residents, as suggested by the large number of Silicon Valley tech firms with an immigrant co-founder, or does the fact that foreigners dominate graduate programs in science and engineering in US universities distort the incentives of able US-born students, who gravitate to business and law?

Economic studies agree on one key point. The government rations front-door visas, reserving two-thirds for family unification and one-sixth for employment. If the aim of US policy is maximizing the economic benefits of immigration to US residents, the government should admit more skilled and fewer lower-skilled foreigners. There are several ways to give priority to skilled immigrants, including a Canadian-style point system,[30] as was proposed in the Senate CIRA 2007 bill (Borjas 2001) and auctioning visas to the highest bidders, under the theory that the foreigners who will have the highest US earnings, or the employers who want to hire them, will be willing to pay the most for immigrant visas (Orrenius and Zavodny 2010).

IMMIGRATION AND POLITICS

Many immigrants become naturalized US citizens and vote; some hold political office, including ex-California Governor Arnold Schwarzenegger. The government encourages naturalization for legal immigrants who are at least 18 years of age, who have been in the United

States for at least five years, and who pass a test of English and civics, and there are often celebratory naturalization ceremonies on July 4 and other national holidays.

Almost 40 percent of foreign-born US residents (about 15 million out of 40 million) were naturalized citizens in 2010, (Passel and Cohn 2011: 9). Naturalization rates vary by country of origin. Immigrants from countries to which they do not expect to return are far more likely to naturalize than immigrants from countries to which they expect to return. Thus, naturalization rates are far higher for Cubans and Vietnamese than for Canadians and Mexicans.

Should the government make it easier for immigrants to naturalize? Australia, Canada, and New Zealand have shorter residency requirements, simpler naturalization tests, and lower fees, while most European countries have more difficult and expensive naturalization procedures. During the 1990s, there was a sharp upsurge in naturalizations, with the number topping a million in fiscal year 1996. There were several reasons for this upsurge: a green card replacement program that required legal immigrants to obtain new counterfeit-resistant cards;[31] welfare reform that limited legal immigrants' access to federal means-tested assistance; and the approval by migrant-sending countries, such as Mexico, of some form of dual nationality so that their citizens could become naturalized and still retain rights to vote in their country of origin.

Foreigners may not feel the need to naturalize if there are few distinctions between legal immigrants and naturalized citizens. Legal immigrants may live and work (except in some government jobs) where they please and buy houses, land, or businesses without restriction. Both legal and unauthorized immigrants have basic constitutional rights, including the right of free speech and the free exercise of religion. Non-US citizens can vote and hold office in US unions as well as in private organizations such as churches, foundations, and fraternal groups. Welfare reforms in 1996 introduced distinctions between immigrants and US citizens that may have contributed to the upsurge in naturalizations, raising questions about economic motivations.

Will immigration and naturalization reshape US voting patterns? Over half of US immigrants are from Latin America; they and their US-born children help to explain why there were almost 50 million Hispanics and 40 million African Americans in 2010. However, African Americans cast twice as many votes as Latinos in the 2010 elections, reflecting the fact that many Hispanics are children and others are not citizens.

Latinos are often called the "sleeping giant" of US politics, meaning that when they vote in large numbers, they can influence the outcome of federal, state, and local elections (DeSipio 1996). Most African Americans and Latinos vote for Democratic candidates, but in 2010 the Latino vote for president was much more evenly split between Democrats and Republicans than the African American vote was: 96 percent of African Americans versus 55 percent of Latinos voted for Obama.[32]

The United States has a *jus soli* principle of citizenship, which means that persons born in the country are citizens. This avoids the phenomenon of second- and third-generation foreigners seen in some European countries. The large number of unauthorized foreigners in the United States has made *jus soli* contentious. About 350,000 babies yearly are born in the United States to at least one unauthorized parent (70 percent of which are Mexican), and such children are 8 percent of 4.4 million births a year (Passel and Cohn 2011: 12).[33] Several bills have been introduced in Congress to overturn birthright citizenship, which was included in the Fourteenth amendment to the US Constitution in 1868 as a way to overturn the Supreme Court's 1857 Dred Scott decision, which held that African Americans could not be citizens. An October 2010 poll found registered voters split, with 46 favoring a constitutional amendment to end birthright citizenship and 46 favoring no change (Passel and Cohn 2011: 13).

IMMIGRANT INTEGRATION

Millions of Southern and Eastern Europeans arrived in the United States during third-wave wave of immigration early in the twentieth century, and the leading metaphor for their the fusion of Europeans and Americans was a "smelting pot" (Ralph Waldo Emerson), a "cauldron" (Henry James), or a "crucible" in which "immigrants were Americanized, liberated, and fused into a mixed race, English in neither nationality nor characteristics." (Turner 1920: 22–23). The hero of Israel Zangwill's popular 1980 play, *The Melting Pot*, proclaimed, "Germans and Frenchmen, Irishmen and Englishmen, Jews and Russians—into the Crucible with you all! God is making the American!"

Reality was more complex. There is always a tension between the desire of newcomers to retain their language and culture and the need and desire to adapt to their new country. The balance between retention and adaptation changed over time, but three principles have guided government policies. First, the United States was generally open to all immigrants—in the words of George Washington: "The bosom of America is open to receive not only the Opulent and respectable Stranger, but the oppressed and persecuted of all Nations and Religions; whom we shall welcome to a participation of all our rights and privileges." Second, US citizens were to act politically as individuals, not as members of officially defined ethnic groups. And third, a laissez-faire attitude toward old cultures. Newcomers could maintain their old culture with private support.

Scholars studying the integration of immigrants have suggested two opposing visions: integration and pluralism. Those favoring integration, or assimilation, emphasize the need for immigrants to become Americans, with an individual identity, while those favoring pluralism, or multiculturalism, aim to maintain cultures and distinct groups. Neither extreme characterizes immigration integration in the United States. The melting pot ignores the importance of the home culture and the fact that ethnic affiliation persists into the second and third generations, long after the language and knowledge of the "old country" has been lost.

Pluralism, on the other hand, can favor group loyalties over individual freedom, sometimes overlooking divisions among those from a particular country by allowing certain leaders to assert that they speak for all Mexican Americans or all Cuban Americans. Such group-based politics ignores the fluidity of people in the United States, where many immigrants work, make friends, and marry outside their ancestral communities.

Integration versus pluralism raises many practical questions. For example, should students in college dorms cluster by race and ethnicity, or should they be assigned to dorms with students from very different backgrounds? Should schoolchildren be taught in their home languages, or should they be brought together in English-language classes from the start? In the workplace, may employees talk to each other in languages other than English?

Historian John Higham proposed that the United States embrace what he called "pluralistic integration," the idea that there is a common US culture shared by all Americans alongside private efforts of minorities to preserve their own. Higham emphasized the danger of providing public support to maintain or promote differences between racial and ethnic groups: "No ethnic group under these terms may have the support of the general community in strengthening its boundaries." (Higham 1988: 244).

The use of public funds to support particular racial and ethnic groups is especially contentious in K–12 education. About 80 percent of Americans five years and older spoke English at home in 2007, which means that 55 million Americans spoke another language at home, usually Spanish (US Census Language Use 2010).[34] The issue for public policy is finding the best way to help school children who do not speak English well—so-called limited-English-proficient (LEP) pupils or English-language learners (ELLs).

In 1970, the federal government issued a memo to the 16,000 US school districts stating that if the "inability to speak and understand the English language excludes national origin-minority group children from effective participation in the educational program . . . the district must take affirmative steps to rectify the language deficiency in order to open its instructional program to these students" (www.ed.gov/about/offices/list/ocr/docs/lau1970.html). The United States had about 48 million K–12 pupils in public schools in 2008 and another 5 million in private schools: about 10 percent were English-language learners. The government did not prescribe the "affirmative steps" that school districts should take to help ELLs to learn, but many embraced bilingual education—that is, teaching children math and history in Spanish or other languages as well as English until they are ready to transition into a regular English-language classroom.

California, whose student population is about one-third ELL, embraced bilingual education, providing extra funds for instruction in native languages. Students were slow to move from native-language to English classrooms, prompting an effort to reform bilingual education.[35] When that failed, Proposition 227, the English for the Children initiative, was approved by California voters to speed the transition to English-only instruction by providing non-English speakers with a year of intensive English instruction. The results have generally been positive.[36]

Integrating immigrants has never been easy. In the past, US leaders sometimes rebuked their political opponents by slurring their national origins. In 1930, President Herbert Hoover did so with Representative Fiorella La Guardia (R-NY), later the mayor of New York City, by asserting that "the Italians are predominantly our murderers and bootleggers." He invited La Guardia and Italians who agreed with him to "go back to where you belong" because, "like a lot of other foreign spawn, you do not appreciate this country which supports you and tolerates you" (quoted in Baltzell 1964: 30). Presidents no longer use such language against their opponents with immigrant backgrounds.

Studies of immigrant integration paint a mixed picture. Most immigrants are finding the economic opportunity that they sought in the United States and their children are learning English; some of the children of Asian immigrants are among the top achievers in schools and universities. On the other hand, a significant number of children of Hispanic immigrants are not succeeding in US schools, which is likely to limit their economic mobility. Many of those who worry about such integration failures urge the government to fund programs that provide struggling immigrants with supplemental education, health, and other services (Fix 2006). The Commission on Immigration Reform (CIR) made similar recommendations: the government should do more to "Americanize immigrants" while expecting them "to obey our laws, pay our taxes, respect other cultures and ethnic groups."

MIGRANT NUMBERS VERSUS MIGRANT RIGHTS

US immigration and integration policy debates are increasingly framed by the extremes of no migrants and no borders. For example, the Federation for American Immigration Reform (FAIR) argues that "With more than a million legal and illegal immigrants settling in the United States each year . . . it is evident to most Americans that large-scale immigration is not serving the needs and interests of the country. FAIR advocates a temporary moratorium on all immigration except spouses and minor children of US citizens and a limited number of refugees."[37] At the no-borders extreme, the *Wall Street Journal* has twice advocated a five-word amendment to the US Constitution: "there shall be open borders" so that immigration can expand the labor force and the economy.[38]

During the 1950s, the United States admitted an average 250,000 immigrants a year. Admissions rose to an average 320,000 a year in the 1960s, to 425,000 a year in the 1970s, and to 625,000 a year in the 1980s; they have averaged over a million a year since the 1990s. The country is admitting ever more immigrants but restricting their rights to social services (Tichenor 2000).

Before welfare reforms were enacted in 1996, there was debate over migrant numbers and migrant rights: Should the number of needy immigrants be reduced but immigrant access to federal welfare assistance maintained, or should the number of needy immigrants remain high and their access to welfare assistance curtailed? President Clinton endorsed the recommendation of the Commission on Immigration Reform to favor migrant rights over migrant numbers—that is, to reduce admissions of needy immigrants but maintain immigrant access to welfare under the theory that immigrants are intending Americans. However, an unlikely coalition of business groups and migrant advocates blocked this recommendation in Congress, which in 1996 elected to allow numbers to remain high and instead restrict access to welfare benefits.

Figure 2.2 illustrates the debate. The United States in the mid-1990s was in the high numbers and high migrant rights cell of the table in A. The CIR recommended that immigration policy move toward B, reducing the number of needy migrants admitted but maintaining immigrant access to federal services. Instead, Congress moved policy from A to C,

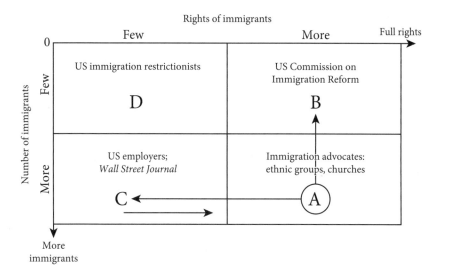

Figure 2.2   Migrant numbers versus migrant rights. *Note:* A. The United States in the mid-1990s was at A: a time of high and rising levels of immigration and full rights for legal immigrants. A was not stable. B. The US CIR recommended in 1995 moving toward B: reducing immigration, preserving full rights to welfare, etc. C. The United States in 1996 moved toward C: higher numbers, fewer rights. C was not stable; in 1997–1998, about half of welfare cuts were restored.

although the economic boom of the late 1990s prompted relaxation of some of the restrictions on immigrant access to means-tested welfare benefits.

GAPS AND CONVERGENCE?

There is a gap between the goals of US immigration policy—admit legal immigrants via the four major front-door channels, regulate the entry of side-door temporary visitors, and minimize back-door unauthorized entries—and its outcomes. Critics argue that front door immigration priorities should shift from family unification to employment considerations to maximize immigration's economic benefits, that side-door entries of students, guest workers, and others be made easier or more difficult, and that unauthorized migration be curbed. Narrowing the gaps between policy goals and outcomes is complicated by disagreement on both means and ends.

For example, there is widespread agreement on the need to reduce unauthorized migration, but there is also disagreement on the means to accomplish this goal. Border fences and more agents aim to raise the cost of illegal entry so as to discourage unauthorized migrants—a discouragement reinforced by more secure worker IDs, an efficient way to allow employers to verify the legal status of new hires, and enforcement to encourage worker and employer compliance with immigration laws. There is agreement that creating jobs abroad would make it easier to discourage illegal entries, but no agreement on exactly how the United States can help speed job creation in Mexico and other migrant-sending

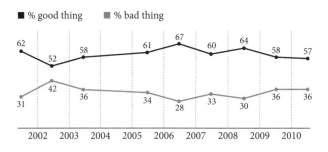

Figure 2.3 Responses to a 2012 Gallup Poll question: "On the whole, do you think immigration is a good thing or a bad thing for this country today?" *Source:* © 2012, Gallup, Inc.

countries. Similarly, discussions on secure IDs and improved workplace enforcement soon run into privacy and discrimination issues.

Opinion polls provide imperfect guidance on how to proceed. The Gallup poll finds that more Americans want immigration reduced than increased, with the gap growing especially wide during recessions (see Figure 2.3). In polls conducted in the aftermath of Arizona's enactment of Senate Bill 1070, the state law making illegal presence a felony and requiring police to ascertain the legal status of persons they encounter, half of respondents agreed that immigrants are mostly contributing to the United States, but most agreed with the Arizona law, even though they thought it would increase discrimination against Hispanics.[39] Two-thirds of respondents thought illegal immigration was a very serious problem, and 80 percent wanted the United States to do more on the borders to prevent it.

Americans are not alone in telling pollsters that their government is doing a poor job of managing migration, according to the 2010 Transatlantic Trends Immigration (TTI) survey (www.transatlantictrends.org). The share of respondents agreeing that their government was doing a "poor job" was 73 percent in the United States, 70 percent in the United Kingdom, and about 60 percent in Spain and France. Canada was the only country in which more respondents thought that their government was doing a good job of managing migration (48 percent) than thought it is doing a poor job (43 percent).

One theme of the Transatlantic Trends survey was that Canadians were the most satisfied with their country's immigration policy and US and UK residents were the least satisfied. Those polled who had recently lost jobs were the most likely to see immigrants as a labor market threat, especially in the United States and the United Kingdom. Employed residents of countries with segmented or insider-outsider labor markets, such as Italy, are least likely to see immigrants that way. Most Europeans, except for the British, supported giving legal and illegal foreigners access to social benefits such as healthcare, even though they agreed that immigrants are a burden because they receive more in social benefits than they pay in taxes.

Europeans expressed more concern about the integration of immigrants, especially Muslims, while Americans and Canadians were the most optimistic about immigrant integration, including Muslims. Spanish residents made the sharpest distinctions between the integration of immigrants generally, which most thought was going well, and the integration of Muslim immigrants, which most thought was going badly.

The gap between immigration goals and outcomes in industrial democracies might suggest a convergence in policy failure. In the past, industrial democracies faced with similar challenges often adopted similar responses despite differences in history, institutions, and political structures. For example, during the 1960s, when a central labor market challenge was how to manage the interaction of unionized workers and their employers in large factories, Canada, European countries, and the United States exchanged experiences in managing collective bargaining between professional managers and industrial unions and had some convergence in labor management policy (Dunlop et al. 1966). German, Dutch, and Scandinavian labor movements, which engaged in centralized bargaining with few strikes, contrasted sharply with strong unions and frequent strikes in the United Kingdom and weaker unions and more political strikes in France and Italy.

Migration policy may converge in a similar fashion. Industrial democracies already meet regularly to discuss migration issues of mutual interest, from how to deal with refugees and asylum seekers to creating systems for selecting immigrants desired for economic and employment reasons. Nonetheless, there are important transatlantic differences, especially in integration. The United States is unique among industrial democracies in not having a federal integration policy, leaving integration to immigrants, their US sponsors, employers, and state and local governments, including schools. European countries are more likely to have federal or state integration policies that, for example, require some knowledge of the local language and culture to enter or renew residence permits.

One reason for this transatlantic difference in policy may be that immigrants to the United States are generally allowed and encouraged to work but have restricted access to welfare benefits, while immigrants to European countries sometimes have easier access to welfare benefits than to labor markets. The US labor market makes it relatively easy for immigrants to get jobs, but these jobs do not ensure an above-poverty-level wage or access to health insurance and pensions. It is often harder for immigrants to get regular jobs in Europe but, if they do, they are generally assured decent incomes and access to more work-related benefits than are low-wage US workers, both native and immigrant.

CONCLUSIONS: WHITHER IMMIGRATION?

The United States is a nation of immigrants unsure about immigration and integration in the twenty-first century. There is widespread agreement that the immigration system is "broken" because a quarter of foreign-born residents are unauthorized. However, there is disagreement on how to fix it. What should the US government do to prevent illegal migration? What hurdles should unauthorized foreigners have to overcome before they can become legal? Should new guest worker programs make it easier for employers to hire migrant workers?

Interest groups, from the US Chamber of Commerce to the AFL-CIO, from La Raza to the Catholic Church, favor comprehensive immigration reform in a package that includes new enforcement efforts to reduce illegal entries and employment, a path to legal status for unauthorized foreigners in the United States, and new and revised guest worker programs. However, they disagree on vital details such as exactly how to keep unauthorized workers from getting jobs and how many additional guest workers should be admitted. States and cities are complicating matters by entering the fray. A few enact sanctuary laws that prohibit police from asking about immigration status, while others require police to check the immigration status of persons they encounter.

Meanwhile, the status quo of having 5 percent of US workers unauthorized, although generally deplored, continues in part because the economic actors most directly affected— unauthorized workers and their employers—are generally getting what they want. Migrant workers earn more than they could at home, and their employers pay lower wages than they would if immigration were more effectively controlled.

NOTES

1. The exceptions are American Indians who were already in what became the United States, slaves brought against their will, and people who became US citizens when the United States acquired the territory in which they were living.

2. DHS reported 1.1 million immigrants and 36.2 million nonimmigrants in FY09, excluding Canadian and Mexican border crossers. There were 556,000 apprehensions in FY09, almost all along the Mexican-US border.

3. The 2008–2009 recession resulted in the loss of 8 million jobs; civilian employment fell from 146 million at the end of 2007 to 138 million at the end of 2009. Job growth resumed in 2010 (http://data.bls.gov/cgi-bin/surveymost?bls). There was also stepped-up enforcement of immigration laws, especially after the US Senate's failure to approve a comprehensive immigration reform bill in 2007, including a proposal to require employers to fire employees whose names and social security data do not match (http://migration.ucdavis.edu/mn/more.php?id=3315_0_2_0).

There is agreement that the stock of unauthorized foreigners fell in 2008–2009 for the first time in two decades, but there is disagreement over why. Some studies stress the US recession, suggesting that the stock of unauthorized foreigners will increase with economic recovery and job growth. Others stress the effects of federal and state enforcement efforts to keep unauthorized workers out of US jobs. For a review of the debate, see http://migration.ucdavis.edu/mn/more.php?id=3433_0_2_0.

4. Quoted in Lizette Alvarez, "Census Director Marvels at the New Portrait of America," *New York Times*, January 1, 2001.

5. According to the United Nations, France had 11 percent migrants; the United Kingdom, 10 percent; Canada, 21 percent; Australia, 22 percent.

6. EB-5 investor visas are available to foreigners who invest at least $500,000 and create or preserve at least 10 full-time US jobs in areas with unemployment rates 1.5 times the US average. Most foreign investors invest their $500,000 via private and public agencies that recruit them to obtain funds for particular projects; that is, the foreigners generally do not actively manage their US investments. After two years and a check on the investment and jobs, foreign investors can convert probationary immigrant visas into regular immigrant visas.

7. DHS reported 163 million temporary visitors on nonimmigrant admissions in FY09, including Canadians who visit regularly or commute to US jobs and Mexicans with border-crossing cards that allow them to shop in US border areas. There were 36 million so-called I-94 admissions in FY09. These count events, not unique individuals, so a tourist who makes three visits in one year is counted three times.

8. IIE Open Doors 2010. www.iie.org/en/Research-and-Publications/Open-Doors. About 260,000 US students were enrolled in colleges and universities abroad in 2009–2010.

9. "Gates Urges Change in H-1B Visa Program," *Daily Labor Report*, March 8, 2007, A-8 (based on Gates's testimony before the House Committee on Science and Technology).

10. Foreign students who earn US degrees in science, technology, engineering, or mathematics (STEM) field may stay in the United States an additional 18 months, for a total of 30 months after graduation.

11. These admission data are from the 2009 DHS *Yearbook of Immigration Statistics*, Table 25.

12. Border-crossing cards are available to Mexicans from Mexican border areas who can visit the United States for up to 72 hours but must remain within 25 miles of the border.

13. US private-sector employment fell from 115 million in 2007 to 108 million in 2009; construction employment fell from 7.6 million to 6 million (Table B-46, Economic Report of the President 2011).

14. In addition to immigration and colonization, slavery brought Africans to the territory that became the United States. African slaves were 19 percent of the US population in 1790.

15. The 1910 Census found that foreign-born residents made up 15 percent of US residents and 24 percent of US workers. Archdeacon (1992: 548) emphasized that third-wave immigrants arrived in a largely rural America: only 35 percent of the 75 million Americans in 1900 were in urban areas. This meant that there could be a great deal of homogeneity in the small communities where most Americans lived, even though the country as a whole was becoming more diverse.

16. About 2 percent of the 12 million immigrants who arrived at Ellis Island were rejected for "physical or mental defects." The most common disease that prompted rejection was trachoma, a bacterial infection of the eye.

17. The Dillingham Commission was named for Senator William Dillingham (R-VT).

18. Each country was guaranteed at least 100 visas, so 154,477 visas were available annually.

19. Foreign workers would arrive with H-2C visas, and their employers could sponsor them for immigrant visas after a year of work.

20. The major legalization program was for foreigners in the United States for at least five years, who could become "probationary immigrants" by proving that they had worked illegally in the United States, had paid any back taxes and a $1,500 fee, and had passed English and background tests. At the end of six more years of US work and another $1,500 fee, these probationary immigrants could receive regular immigrant visas. Unauthorized foreigners in the United States for two to five years would have to satisfy the same requirements plus return to their countries of origin and re-enter the United States legally, while those in the United States less than two years were expected to depart as a result of stepped-up workplace enforcement.

There were separate legalization programs for farm workers under the Agricultural Job Opportunities, Benefits and Security Act; for unauthorized children brought to the United States before age 16, there was the Development, Relief and Education for Alien Minors.

21. The guest worker impact fee could be waived if the employer provided health insurance to employees.

22. For example, under this proposed point system, a 29-year-old Mexican who had worked six years as a Y-visa guest worker could achieve 61 points by having five years of US job experience in a high-demand occupation (healthcare aide), being young and knowing English, and having a US relative. However, a 45-year-old Indian IT worker with a PhD, a US job offer, but no US work experience would receive only 49 points, despite knowledge of English.

23. McCain stated that after "we have achieved our border-security goal, we must enact and implement the other parts of practical, fair and necessary immigration policy," including a temporary worker program and legalization. Obama repeated his support for CIRA, pledging to bring unauthorized foreigners "out of the shadows" and put them on the path to citizenship if they "pay a fine, learn English, not violate the law, and go to the back of the line for the opportunity to become citizens." Quoted in "Candidates, E-Verify, Visas," *Migration News* 15, no. 4 (October 2008), http://migration.ucdavis.edu/mn/more .php?id=3431_0_2_0.

24. These projections assume that net international migration will be 975,000 a year between 2010 and 2050 (www.census.gov/population/www/projections/2009cnmsSum Tabs.html).

25. In 2009, there were 12.1 million US workers aged 25 and older who did not complete high school; 48 percent were foreign born. The median weekly wages of the foreign-born dropouts were $415 in 2009 versus $500 for US-born dropouts ("BLS Labor Force Characteristics of Foreign-Born Workers," www.bls.gov/news.release/forbrn.toc.htm). Economic theory predicts that wages will rise for the US-born dropouts if there are fewer foreign-born dropouts.

26. "Prop. 187 Approved in California. 1994," *Migration News* 1, no. 11, http://migration .ucdavis.edu/mn/more.php?id=492_0_2_0.

27. The net gain from immigration is the size of the triangle in the US labor market due to the supply of labor-curve shifting to the right; the demand for labor is unchanged. The size of this triangle is half of (1) the share of GDP accruing to labor (70 percent) times (2) the percent of the labor force that is foreign born (10 percent in 1996) times (3) the decline in wages due to immigration (about 3 percent), or $0.5 \times 0.7 \times 0.1 \times -0.03 = 0.001$; that is, one-tenth of one percent of the $8 trillion GDP, or $8 billion.

The study assumed that the US economy had constant returns to scale (CRTS), which means that doubling the number of workers and the amount of capital doubles output. According to this assumption, immigration cannot increase the growth rate of wages.

28. However, immigrants arriving with less than a high school education received $89,000 in tax-supported benefits—more than they paid in taxes (1996 dollars), even if their children and grandchildren paid the same taxes and consumed the same benefits as children and grandchildren of US-born parents. Immigrants arriving with a high-school education or higher had a net fiscal present value of $105,000.

29. Immigrants cannot "save" Social Security unless their numbers rise each year. Social Security is a pay-as-you-go system, meaning that taxes paid by current workers support retirees. Immigrants earn benefits as they age, increasing the number of retirees who will receive Social Security benefits in the future.

30. Canada admits about 160,000 immigrants a year, including 60 percent via a points-selection system that awards points for youth, education, and knowledge of English or French. The Canadian point system ensures that immigrant adults have higher levels of education than Canada-born adults. In 2005, about 55 percent of Canadian immigrants had university degrees, compared with 35 percent of immigrants to the United States.

31. The then-INS cover letter noted that the fee for replacing green cards was $75, and that for $95 the foreigner could become a naturalized US citizen.

32. Non-Hispanic whites voted for McCain (53 percent) over Obama (43 percent) in 2010.

33. Among all children born between March 2009 and March 2010, 74 percent had US-born parents and 17 percent had legal immigrant parents.

34. Over half of those who spoke a language other than English at home (31 million) reported speaking English very well.

35. Surveys in 1998 found that only a third of California's ELL pupils were in either bilingual or English-immersion programs; that is, two-thirds received no special help. School districts had little incentive to reclassify ELL pupils as English-proficient, since because they received extra funds for these students and suffered no penalties if they did not reclassify. Ken Ellingwood, "Bilingual Classes a Knotty Issue," *Los Angeles Times*, May 18, 1998.

36. The former head of the California Association of Bilingual Educators changed his mind about English immersion classes. He said, "The kids began to learn—not pick up, but learn—formal English, oral and written, far more quickly than I ever thought they would. You read the research and they tell you it takes seven years. Here are kids, within nine months in the first year, and they literally learned to read." Jacques Steinberg, "Increase in Test Scores Counters Dire Forecasts for Bilingual Ban," *New York Times*, August 20, 2000.

37. FAIR's Purpose. http://www.fairus.org/html/fair.htm.

38. An editorial on July 3, 1986, first made this proposal, which was repeated in an editorial on July 3, 1990.

39. Randal Archibold and Megan Thee-Brenan, "Poll Shows Most in U.S. Want Overhaul of Immigration Laws," *New York Times*, May 3, 2010.

REFERENCES

Archdeacon, Thomas. 1992. "Reflections on Immigration to Europe in Light of US Immigration History." *International Migration Review* 26 (2): 525–48.

Baltzell, E. Digby. 1964. *The Protestant Establishment: Aristocracy and Caste in America.* New York: Vintage Books.

Benderly, Beryl Lieff. 2010. "The Real Science Gap." *Miller-McCune*, July–August. www .miller-mccune.com/science/the-real-science-gap-16191/#.

Borjas, George. 1990. *Friends or Strangers: The Impact of Immigrants on the US Economy*. New York. Basic Books.

———. 2001. *Heaven's Door: Immigration Policy and the American Economy*. Princeton, NJ: Princeton University Press.

Briggs, Vernon J. 1992. *Mass Immigration and the National Interest*. Armonk, NY: M. E. Sharpe.

Card, David. 1990. "The Impact of the Mariel Boatlift on the Miami Labor Market. *Industrial and Labor Relations Review* 43: 245–257.

"Census: Population and Foreign Born." 2001. *Migration News* 8 (2). http://migration .ucdavis.edu /mn /comments.php?id=2302_0_2_0.

Cornelius, Wayne A. 2001. "Death at the Border: Efficacy and Unintended Consequences of US Immigration Control Policy." *Population and Development Review* 27 (4): 661–85.

Council of Economic Advisers. 1986. *Economic Report of the President*. www.whitehouse .gov/cea/pubs.html.

Degler, Carl N. 1970. *Out of Our Past: The Forces That Shaped Modern America*. 2nd ed. New York. Harper & Row.

DeSipio, Louis. 1996. *Counting on the Latino Vote: Latinos as a New Electorate*. Charlottesville: University of Virginia Press.

Docquier, Frédéric, Çağlar Özden, and Giovanni Peri. 2010. "The Wage Effects of Immigration and Emigration." NBER Working Paper 16646. www.nber.org/papers/w16646.

Dunlop, John, Frederick Harbison, Charles Myers, and Clark Kerr. 1966. *Industrialism and Industrial Man: The Problems of Labor and Management in Economic Growth*. Oxford: Oxford University Press.

Fix, Michael, ed. 2006. *Securing the Future: US Immigrant Integration Policy: A Reader*. Washington, DC: Migration Policy Institute.

Handlin, Oscar. 1952. "Memorandum Concerning the Origins of the National Origin Quota System, Hearings Before the President's Commission on Immigration and Naturalization," 82nd Congress, 2nd Session. Washington, DC: US Government Printing Office.

Hanson, Gordon H., Raymond Robertson, and Antonio Spilimbergo. 1999. "Does Border Enforcement Protect U.S. Workers from Illegal Immigration?" Mimeo.

Higham, John. 1988. *Strangers in the Land: Patterns of American Nativism, 1860–1925*. New Brunswick, NJ: Rutgers University Press.

House of Representatives. 1952. Committee on the Judiciary, House Report 1365, 82nd Congress, 2nd Session, February 14.

Kramer, Roger. 2002. "Developments in International Migration to the United States: 2002: A Midyear Report." Mimeo.

Lebergott, Stanley. 1986. *The Americans: An Economic Record*. New York: Norton.

Lowenstein, Roger. 2006. "The Immigration Equation." *New York Times Magazine*, July 9. www.nytimes.com /2006/07/09/magazine/09IMM.html?pagewanted=all.

Martin, Philip L. 1994. "Good Intentions Gone Awry: IRCA and U.S. Agriculture." *Annals of the Academy of Political and Social Science* 534 (July): 44–57.

Martin, Philip L., and Elizabeth Midgley. 1999. "Immigration to the United States." *Population Bulletin* 54 (2). Washington, DC: Population Reference Bureau. http://www.prb.org.

McDonnell, Patrick J. 2002. "Wave of U.S. Immigration Likely to Survive Sept. 11." *Los Angeles Times*, January 10.

Mines, Richard, and Philip L. Martin. 1984. "Immigrant Workers and the California Citrus Industry." *Industrial Relations* 23 (1): 139–49.

National Science Board. 2003. "The Science and Engineering Workforce. Realizing America's Potential." NSB 03-69. nsf.gov/nsb/documents/2003/nsb0369/nsb0369.pdf.

Orrenius, Pia, and Madeline Zavodny. 2010. *Beside the Golden Door: U.S. Immigration Reform in a New Era of Globalization*. Washington, DC: American Enterprise Institute.

Passel, Jeffrey, and D'Vera Cohn. 2011. "Unauthorized Immigrant Population. National and State Trends, 2010." Pew Hispanic Center. http://pewhispanic.org/.

President's Council of Economic Advisers. 1986. *The Economic Effects of Immigration*. Washington, DC: Council of Economic Advisers.

Smith, James, and Barry Edmonston, eds. 1997. *The New Americans: Economic, Demographic, and Fiscal Effects of Immigration*. Washington, DC: National Research Council.

Teitelbaum, Michael. 2003. "Do We Need More Scientists?" *Public Interest*, no. 153: 40–53. www.nationalaffairs.com/public_interest/detail/do-we-need-more-scientists.

Tichenor, Daniel J. 2000. "Voters, Clients, and the Policy Process: Two Faces of Expansive Immigration Politics in America." Mimeo.

Turner, Frederick Jackson. 1920. *The Frontier in American History*. New York: Henry Holt.

US Commission on Immigration Reform. 1997. "Becoming an American: Immigration and Immigrant Policy." http://migration.ucdavis.edu/mn/cir/97Report1/titlepgs/titlepgs.htm.

US General Accounting Office. 2001. "INS' Southwest Border Strategy: Resource and Impact Issues Remain after Seven Years." GAO-01-842, US General Accounting Office, Washington, DC, August 2.

Crafting Policy in the National Interest:
The Benefits of High-Skilled Immigration

Pia M. Orrenius and Madeline Zavodny

INTRODUCTION

In his comprehensive overview, Phil Martin touches on the most important aspects of US immigration and related policies. He notes that massive unauthorized migration to the United States exemplifies the gap between policy intentions and immigration outcomes, and underlies the current political impasse over comprehensive immigration reform (CIR). This commentary complements Martin's chapter by discussing high-skilled and employment-based immigration in more detail. The emphasis on family ties over employment, the predominance of Latin American immigrants, and the fact that most of them have little education means that US immigration policy admits large numbers of immigrants with few skills. The impasse over CIR could possibly be broken by reforming policy to prioritize employment-based immigration, as this would increase the gains from immigration accruing to natives and better align US policy with the national interest.[1]

The main beneficiaries of immigration are the immigrants themselves; by migrating, they secure a better life for themselves and their descendants. Depending on the country of origin, the adjusted gains for a male with 9 to 12 years of schooling range from a two-fold (in the case of Mexico) to a twelve-fold (in the case of Nigeria) increase in annual income (Clemens, Montenegro, and Pritchett 2008). US natives also benefit from immigration, albeit on a much smaller scale. There are also the costs of low-wage immigration, which can harm low-skilled native workers while high-skilled native workers benefit. A shift to more employment-based immigration could increase immigration's net economic benefits while also reducing its distributional impact, and it may increase public support for immigration overall and immigration reform in particular.

A SYSTEM OF FAMILY-BASED IMMIGRATION

Existing immigration policy is largely rooted in the 1965 amendments to the Immigration and Nationality Act, which made family reunification the primary objective. The United States annually issues about 1.1 million green cards, which grant permanent legal residence. About 86 percent go to family members of US citizens or permanent legal residents, people

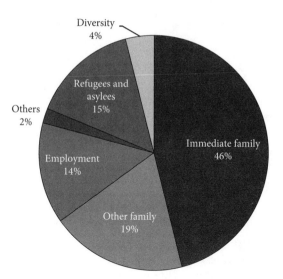

Figure 2.4   Share of legal permanent residents by admission class, 2006–2010. *Source:* Department of Homeland Security Yearbook of Immigrant Statistics. *Note:* Green cards go mostly to family and humanitarian immigrants.

seeking humanitarian refuge and "diversity immigrants," who come from countries with low rates of immigration to the United States (Figure 2.4).[2] The remaining 14 percent go to people who are immigrating for work and tend to be more highly skilled. Of that 14 percent, half go to workers' spouses and children, meaning that a mere 7 percent of green cards go to employment-based principal immigrants. No other major developed economy gives such a low priority to skill-based immigration. Canada, for example, allocates 67 percent of its permanent resident visas to skill-based immigrants (and their families) and only 21 percent to family-based immigrants.

BENEFITS OF HIGH-SKILLED IMMIGRATION

Family-based immigrants have significantly less education than employment-based immigrants, which has implications both for US workers and taxpayers. While immigration creates economic benefits for natives by boosting GDP and income per capita, the so-called *immigration surplus* can be outweighed by the fiscal impact of immigration, which, as Phil Martin reports, is negative for immigrants who do not have a high school diploma. Conversely, the fiscal impact of high-skilled immigrants is large and positive. A 2000 study showed that a selective immigration policy that admitted 1.6 million high-skilled immigrants aged 40 to 44 annually into a hypothetical economy with a 50 percent debt-to-GDP ratio would have balanced the budget within five years and eventually eliminated the national debt (Storesletten 2000). Balancing the budget via tax increases instead would have required a 4.4 percentage point increase in income tax rates, according to the study.

Immigration has distributional consequences that are more adverse in the case of low-skilled immigrants. While employers, investors, consumers and complementary workers benefit from immigration, substitutable workers may lose out. Losses are concentrated at the low-wage end of the labor market because so many immigrants are low-skilled and because foreign and native labor are more substitutable in manual-labor jobs than in occupations that require advanced language skills or institutional knowledge. While economists disagree about the direction and magnitude of immigration's effect on natives' wages, there is consensus that the large inflow of low-skilled immigrants since the 1980s has hurt low-skilled native workers (see Borjas 1999; Card 2005).[3]

The economic and fiscal impacts of high-skilled immigration enhance natives' gains, and this immigration surplus is larger if immigrants are complementary to natives and complementary to capital. This is more likely to occur if immigrants are highly skilled and attract capital and work in occupations where native-born labor is scarce. Research also suggests that high-skilled immigrants have positive, not negative, labor market effects on high-skilled native workers (Ottaviano and Peri 2008; Orrenius and Zavodny 2007).

If high-skilled immigrants are also more innovative and entrepreneurial, the economic impact is larger still. In this case, immigration can actually boost productivity growth, leading to a higher long-run rate of economic growth (Schumpeter 1934; Aghion and Howitt 1992). High-skilled immigrants play an important role in innovation and, in certain sectors, entrepreneurship, obtaining patents at more than twice the rate of highly educated natives. The difference has been linked to immigrants' overrepresentation in STEM (science, technology, engineering, and mathematics) fields and the growing number entering on employment-based and student visas (Hunt and Gauthier-Loiselle 2010; Kerr and Lincoln 2010; Hunt 2011; Chellaraj, Maskus, and Mattoo 2008). There may be positive spillovers for natives, meaning that immigrants not only raise innovation directly but also boost overall patent activity, perhaps by attracting additional resources and increasing specialization (Hunt and Gauthier-Loiselle 2010). High-skilled immigrants' entrepreneurial activities have been instrumental in the growth of the US high-tech sector (Saxenian 1999). Immigrants founded 25 percent of US high-tech startups between 1995 and 2005 (Wadhwa et al. 2007). They have much higher rates of business creation than natives and slightly higher self-employment rates.[4]

MORE TEMPORARY VISAS LED TO QUEUING

The United States has created several temporary visa programs to admit high-skilled workers. The best known is the H-1B program, which admits about 131,000 workers in a typical year, many of them Indians with university degrees who work in the information technology sector.[5] Another important temporary job–based measure is the Trade NAFTA (TN) visa, which brings in an additional 72,000 professionals, mostly from Canada. The L1 program admits multinational corporations' intracompany transferees (about 74,000 annually), while the O1 program provides visas for a small number of workers of "extraordinary ability."

In 1999 and 2001, the number of H-1B visas issued was increased, but not the number of permanent visas for foreigners sponsored by US employers. One result is an ever-lengthening queue of foreigners and their families already in the United States—over 1 million—awaiting permanent resident visas. Their applications have been approved, but their green cards won't be available for years because of numerical limits on employment-based permanent visas in most categories. There also are country of origin limits that restrict the number of immigrants from populous nations such as China and India.

EMPLOYMENT-BASED IMMIGRATION

Expanding employment-based immigration offers a host of benefits, including more high-skilled and procyclical immigration. Employment-based immigration is demand driven, which means that it declines when the US labor market weakens. The high-tech boom of the late 1990s and the housing and financial boom of the mid-2000s produced rapid expansion in temporary visas, while the 2001 recession, subsequent jobless recovery and the recession that began in late 2007 were all periods of decline. While temporary work-based visas respond to the business cycle, the total number of green cards issued does not. Issuance barely budged in 2008 and 2009, during the worst recession in 80 years, despite the loss of 8 million jobs and a steep rise in unemployment. Binding quotas that lead to lengthy queues have made permanent visas largely immune to the business cycle; while the number of new applications may fall during a recession, prospective immigrants whose applications were approved years ago are admitted regardless of current economic conditions.

CONCLUSION

Immigrants help fuel the US economy, representing about one in every six workers. Because of accelerated immigration and slowing US population growth, foreign-born workers have accounted for almost half of labor force growth since the mid-1990s. Both high- and low-skilled immigrants offer economic benefits. Both tend to complement the native workforce, bringing brains or brawn to locations and occupations where there is a need. The Hispanic immigrant population in Louisiana jumped nearly 20 percent following Hurricane Katrina, as foreign workers converged there to assist the cleanup and reconstruction. Nonetheless, the disproportionate number of low-skilled immigrants in recent decades has likely harmed competing native workers and imposed fiscal costs on taxpayers.

High-skilled workers come with more benefits and fewer costs than low-skilled workers. And their skills are important to the growth of some of the nation's most globally competitive industries and to research and development. In addition, many high-skilled immigrants work in industries that produce tradable goods or services, meaning that companies can employ their workers at home or abroad. Google can hire programmers to work in Mountain View, California, or in Guangzhou or Hyderabad or in any of the other 49 non-US cities in which it currently operates. If it cannot get visas for its workers, it can just employ them overseas (Richtel 2009). For all of these reasons, the United States has a lot to gain from rewriting its immigration policy to focus more on high-skilled and employment-based immigration.

NOTES

The views expressed here in no way reflect the views or position of the Federal Reserve Bank of Dallas or the Federal Reserve System. This commentary is based in part on an essay in the 2010 Federal Reserve Bank of Dallas Annual Report, Federal Reserve Bank of Dallas, 2011.

1. We use the terms *immigrant* and *foreign born* interchangeably to refer to individuals who reside in the United States but were born elsewhere to foreign parents. In contrast, Martin uses the term *immigrant* to refer to lawful permanent residents or holders of a green card.

2. Countries eligible for the diversity visa lottery include many in Africa and Europe. Applicants from Ghana, Bangladesh and Ethiopia were the top recipients of visas in the 2011 lottery.

3. Economists agree, however, that in the long run, wages are not affected by immigration. This is because the capital stock should adjust in the long run. If the number of workers increases as a result of immigration, wages initially fall and returns to capital increase. As the amount of capital increases in the long run in response to higher returns to capital, the returns to capital and labor revert to their initial levels.

4. Estimates suggest immigrants are 30 percent more likely to start a business. See Fairlie (2008). Immigrant self-employment rates are 11.3 percent versus 9.1 percent for natives (authors' calculations based on 2010 Current Population Survey data). This difference is driven by less-educated immigrants, perhaps because of their relatively poor labor market options.

5. Although the official H-1B cap is 85,000 visas (65,000 plus 20,000 for holders of US advanced degrees), the nonprofit sector is exempt from the cap.

REFERENCES

Aghion, Philippe, and Peter Howitt. 1992. "A Model of Growth through Creative Destruction." *Econometrica* 60 (2): 323–51.

Borjas, George. 1999. "The Economic Analysis of Immigration." *Handbook of Labor Economics* 3 (1): 1697–1760.

Card, David. 2005. "Is the New Immigration Really So Bad?" *Economic Journal* 115 (507): 300–323.

Chellaraj, Gnanaraj, Keith E. Maskus, and Aaditya Mattoo. 2008. "The Contribution of International Graduate Students to U.S. Innovation." *Review of International Economics* 16 (3): 444–62.

Clemens, Michael, Claudio Montenegro, and Lant Pritchett. 2008. "The Place Premium: Wage Differences for Identical Workers across the U.S. Border." Working Paper 148, Center for Global Development, Washington, DC. www.cgdev.org/content/publications/detail/16352.

Fairlie, Robert W. 2008. "Estimating the Contribution of Immigrant Business Owners to the United States Economy." Small Business Administration. Washington, DC: Government Printing Office.

Hunt, Jennifer. 2011. "Which Immigrants Are Most Innovative and Entrepreneurial? Distinctions by Entry Visa." *Journal of Labor Economics* 29 (July): 417–57.

Hunt, Jennifer, and Marjolaine Gauthier-Loiselle. 2010. "How Much Does Immigration Boost Innovation?" *American Economic Journal: Macroeconomics* 2 (2): 31–56.

Kerr, William R., and William F. Lincoln. 2010. "The Supply Side of Innovation: H-1B Visa Reforms and U.S. Ethnic Invention." *Journal of Labor Economics* 28 (July): 473–508.

Orrenius, Pia, and Madeline Zavodny. 2007. "Does Immigration Affect Wages? A Look at Occupation-Level Evidence." *Labour Economics* 14 (5): 757–73.

———. 2011. "From Brawn to Brains: How Immigration Works for America." In *2010 Annual Report*. Dallas: Federal Reserve Bank of Dallas.

Ottaviano, Gianmarco I. P., and Giovanni Peri. 2008. "Immigration and National Wages: Clarifying the Theory and the Empirics." Working Paper 14188, National Bureau of Economic Research, Cambridge, MA.

Richtel, Matt. 2009. "Tech Recruiting Clashes with Immigration Rules." *New York Times*, April 11.

Saxenian, AnnaLee. 1999. *Silicon Valley's New Immigrant Entrepreneurs*. San Francisco: Public Policy Institute of California.

Schumpeter, Joseph. 1934. *The Theory of Economic Development*. Cambridge, MA: Harvard University Press.

Storesletten, Kjetil. 2000. "Sustaining Fiscal Policy through Immigration." *Journal of Political Economy* 108 (2): 300–323.

Wadhwa, Vivek, AnnaLee Saxenian, Ben A. Rissing, and Gary Gereffi. 2007. "America's New Immigrant Entrepreneurs." Duke Science, Technology and Innovation Paper 23. http://people.ischool.berkeley.edu/~anno/Papers/Americas_new_immigrant_entrepreneurs_I.pdf.

COMMENTARY

Daniel J. Tichenor

One of the primary goals of this volume is to analyze the gulf between the official goals and the actual outcomes of national immigration policies. With this in mind, my comments focus on three gaps associated with US policymaking. The first addresses the straightforward "gap hypothesis" (or, more precisely, the empirical reality) at the heart of the book, highlighting the distance between US policy goals, tools, and outcomes. The second set of gaps that I quickly explore concern the shifting differences in preferences between elite policymakers and their grassroots constituents—an area that has proven quite fluid in recent years as both the salience and ideological content of American views on immigration have evolved. The third and final gap that I briefly consider lies in the divide between immigrant admissions and rights, which raises some useful questions about this volume's "convergence hypothesis."

Let us begin with the hypothesized gap between policy goals and results. I think we can gain some traction on this subject by breaking it down into two challenges facing US policymaking that regularly bedevil efforts to "control immigration." First is the fact that rather than a clear, consistent, and tight set of policy goals, immigration reform blueprints often stitch together varied and rival aims. Such are the realities of majority coalition building. This reminds us that before we take stock of the gap between policy aims and results, we first have to assess not only the clarity of those aims but also the political will to achieve them. A second challenge lies in the practical limitations of the policy tools most generally accepted for controlling immigration. Significantly, the gaps created by those limitations and the gaps and by rival policy goals are readily apparent when we consider four familiar ideas at the heart of contemporary US efforts to address unauthorized immigration: employer sanctions, border control, amnesty or legalization, and guest worker programs. Let us consider each of these in turn.

For more than half a century, policymakers, from Paul Douglass in the 1950s to Peter Rodino in the 1970s to Alan Simpson in the 1980s, have championed employer sanctions as serving two goals: weakening the magnet of jobs for unauthorized migrants and punishing unscrupulous employers. But sanctions always have inspired resistance by those with very different goals, such as guarding US businesses from new regulatory burdens and protecting civil liberties by opposing new ID systems to verify employee eligibility. Critically, fealty to regulatory relief among pro-business conservatives and civil liberties on both the American left and right has compromised the design and implementation of employer sanctions over time. Sanctions also have posed a variety of practical challenges. One of the most prominent is establishing a reliable means of checking the identity of workers, since the effectiveness of sanctions hinges on a secure system for verifying employee eligibility. Because they lacked such a system, the employer sanctions provisions of the Immigration Reform Act of 1986 were expected to be a "toothless tiger," and they lived up to their billing. Today, E-Verify is touted as the solution but former Labor Secretary Ray Marshall, the Migration Policy Institute, and others warn that it is deeply flawed and unreliable.

Effectiveness also depends on resources and desire to enforce, both of which have been in short supply since IRCA's passage. Amidst Tea Party and business demands for more limited government and fierce battles over spending cuts in Washington, the likelihood of a stricter enforcement regime seems highly improbable.

The fraught ideals and practical challenges associated with border control have been explored effectively in the rich scholarly literature on the subject. For our purposes, let me just highlight some of the most significant. Contradictory goals abound in the struggle over US border control efforts, providing an excellent illustration of what James Hollifield incisively describes as a "liberal paradox" for advanced industrial democracies that pits national sovereignty against the free flow of goods, ideas, and people across borders. At the southern border itself, these competing ends are readily evident in the clashes between humanitarian activists providing water stations to aid desperate border crossers and Minutemen vigilantes slashing bottles to discourage unauthorized flows. The practical limitations of border control policies are many, beginning with the enormous challenges of controlling a more than 2000-mile-long border with Mexico. Ironically, when we have been effective at border control, Doug Massey and his colleagues remind us, it has the unintended effect of encouraging unauthorized immigrants already here to stay rather than return home and face significant barriers to getting back in. In short, border control can freeze and expand the existing undocumented population.

Legalization programs—whether amnesty under IRCA or "earned citizenship" in contemporary proposals—routinely raise a variety of conflicting goals and ideals.

Rival notions of fairness abound on both sides of the legalization debate. So do competing ideas about how legalization relates to distributive justice, security, the rule of law, control, family values, and so forth. Legalization in the past served many goals well. IRCA's amnesty program and subsequent legalizations raised some controversy over implementation and charges of fraud, but they ultimately proved quite successful in bringing a subclass of almost 3 million undocumented immigrants "out of the shadows" and on a road to full membership. No significant gap between policy ends and results here. However, it is a different story if the primary goal is controlling immigration. Obviously legalization proposals in US reform packages are meant to complement effective control measures—hence the Alan Simpson declaration that legalization should be extended "one time only." I will leave it to others to assess the degree to which legalization spurs future undocumented flows, but its past success in regularizing undocumented immigrants places in bold relief the disappointments associated with expectations of greater control.

Guest worker proposals also evince conflicts over policy goals. These include tensions between work standards and access to cheap labor, streamlined versus regulated labor flows, and high-skill versus low-skill worker admissions. The outcomes of American guest worker programs over time also underscore a variety of practical challenges. As evidenced by the bracero program that brought more than 4 million Mexican *braceros* to the United States from the 1940s to the 1960s, guest worker programs raise the specter of abuse and exploitation of vulnerable laborers. Another practical challenge captured by post–World War II European programs is that guest workers are rarely as temporary as policy designers expect. These guests, European observers remind us, typically come to stay. A final practical challenge is that over the course of American history, large-scale guest worker programs have been accompanied by unanticipated illegal flows.

As we have seen, each of the four most prominent policy ideas or solutions associated with illegal immigration reform—employer sanctions, border control, legalization, and guest worker programs—manifest important gaps due to competing goals and important practical challenges. Another significant gap that merits analysis (and reappraisal) is the one that lies between elite policymakers and their grassroots constituents. Gary Freeman has been among the most incisive thinkers on this topic. His application of James Q. Wilson's policy typologies to immigration highlighted the late twentieth-century disconnect between largely pro-immigration elite decision makers (influenced by organized interests) and more restriction-minded ordinary citizens (removed from the policy process).

Over time, however, these dynamics have shifted. To borrow a tried and true concept developed by the legendary political scientist E. E. Schattschneider, the "scope of conflict" engendered by immigration has broadened significantly. The growing popular saliency of robust immigration and porous borders—indeed, public restiveness—was all too evident in the 1990s, from Pete Wilson's gubernatorial campaign to restricting immigrant access to welfare in 1996. Fast-forward to the present, and it is perhaps most precise to identify new interactions between elite policymakers and their grassroots constituents. The first is a general public that is profoundly dissatisfied with the immigration policy status quo but not squarely in favor immigration restriction. Most US citizens are not as predictably opposed to new immigration as they were in the past (Dr. Martin's essay captures this well). Indeed, whereas legalization in 1986 was deeply unpopular, earned citizenship proposals have drawn more popular support in the past decade than ever before. Yet Americans are decidedly cynical about the capacity or will of their government to control the nation's borders or immigrant numbers. This ambivalence, compared to earlier mass opinion, is a striking development. So is the fact that immigration reform is not nearly as insulated as it was with IRCA and the Immigration Act of 1990.

Second, there also is more convergence between US political leaders and their grassroots constituents in the base of each major party. Republican officeholders in recent election cycles have either curried favor or avoided offending a very restrictionist conservative base. Think about the symmetry between the hard-line bills of House Republicans in 2005–2006 and the anti-immigration mobilization of conservative activists at the grassroots that torpedoed a Kennedy-McCain-Bush bargain in the Senate during the summer of 2006. We remember well that McCain had to disentangle himself from immigration reform to survive the 2008 primaries.

We can discern a similar symmetry between liberal Congressional Democrats and a mobilized Latino and immigrant constituency that comports easily with its civil rights and labor base. Today, the widest gaps in US immigration preferences may have less to do with the distance between insulated policymakers and ordinary citizens and more to do with the disconnect between an ambivalent majority and the intense views held at the grassroots base of each party. And it is these mobilized grassroots that make Obama's promise to secure comprehensive immigration reform so daunting.

Let me close by offering some brief reflections about a third gap worth thinking about. For decades after nativists established draconian national origins quotas in the 1920s, both immigrant numbers and noncitizen rights were severely restricted. From the 1960s until the 1990s backlash symbolized by the 1994 passage of Proposition 187 in California, immigration opportunities and immigrant rights expanded together. The struggle over immigration and welfare policy in 1995–1996, however, brought a new slogan from free market conservatives like Dick Armey and Spencer Abraham: "Immigration yes, welfare no!" Today, welfare reform and get-tough immigration laws in states like Arizona and Georgia have contributed to a context of welcoming large-scale immigration but impoverishing noncitizen rights. It also is the best of all worlds for pro-immigration capitalists, feeding an insatiable appetite for migrant labor with little protection, economic security, health care, or safety net for these workers. To find a comparable time when we can discern such a gap between expansive immigrant numbers and limited immigrant rights, we may have to look to the nineteenth-century Gilded Age. This modern Gilded Age for US immigrants raises important nuances and questions for claims of cross-national convergence in immigration and integration policies.

3 | CANADA

New Initiatives and Approaches to Immigration and Nation Building

Jeffrey G. Reitz

Among the traditional "nations of immigration," Canada in recent decades has most consistently pursued a high-immigration policy directed at nation building. This policy emphasizes the recruitment of highly skilled workers and attempts to facilitate their integration into society though fast-track citizenship, language training and other settlement services, and a multiculturalism approach to encourage symbolic inclusion for ethnic and racial minorities in an increasingly diverse population. Although this policy has met with a considerable degree of success, as measured in relatively strong public support and a lack of controversy, it has not been without its problems, including lack of adequate recognition of immigrant skills in the labor market; an overall decline in immigrant employment success through successive cohorts; sporadic but continuing controversies about social problems and cultural practices in certain minority groups, particularly blacks and Muslims; and concerns about border control and possible abuses of process in reviewing refugee claims.

In this context, the government has quietly launched a series of initiatives, beginning in 2006 (following the election of the Conservative minority under Stephen Harper) and aimed at addressing these problems. While maintaining a strong emphasis on large-scale immigration based on economic needs, these initiatives have been directed at improving immigrant selection, integration, and border control. Changes in selection are by far the most noteworthy. They include an increase in the economic stream as opposed to family class, adjustments to the point system to emphasize knowledge of official languages and experience in specific labor-short occupations rather than general education; an increased role for the provinces in the selection process through "provincial nomination" schemes; and a substantial increase in temporary immigration. A new "Canada Experience Class" offers temporary immigrants, along with international students, the option of transition to permanent status after a period of continuing employment. Many of these changes are modeled on Australian immigration policy measures introduced by the Howard government about 10 years previously, for which successes had been claimed.

To speed integration, further efforts have been made to enhance immigrant skill utilization, but there have been as well measures to address the cultural side of integration, including a new citizenship handbook and test. All of these policies have been introduced, without much fanfare, in increments over time. As with most aspects of Canadian immigration policy, they have not generated a great deal of controversy. However, they are important departures from past practice, representing significant revisions to what has been regarded as the "Canadian model" for immigration, and their impact over time may be considerable.

Given the relative success of Canadian immigration, it may seem surprising that major new initiatives have been put in place. However, the significance of immigration in Canada is such that important problems may be expected to prompt major policy shifts. At the same time, it is far from clear that the new policy directions will actually improve the prospects for and impact of immigration. Information to assess them is not extensive, but, because of their significance, it is important to attempt to identify trends, note issues, and point toward a needed more comprehensive assessment.

CANADIAN IMMIGRATION POLICY: EVOLUTION AND CHANGE

The "Canadian Model" for Immigration and Nation Building

Canadian immigration policy has evolved in relation to three main goals: nation building and expansion of the economy and population; the needs of the contemporary labor market; and the long-term integration of immigrants. The number of immigrants sought has been large, almost amounting to "mass immigration." As a percentage of the resident population, Canadian immigration has been substantial for over a century. For the most recent 20 years, under both Liberal and Conservative governments, Canada has taken in between 200,000 and 250,000 immigrants a year, or roughly 0.8 percent of its population; in 2010, the number was 280,000 — the highest in decades (see Figure 3.1). The Canadian

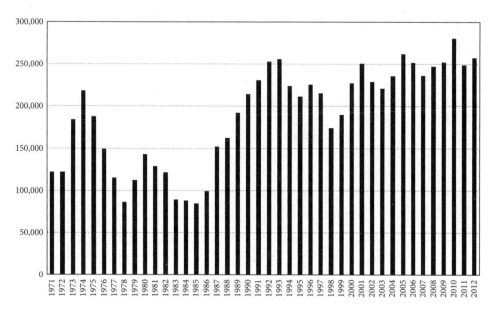

Figure 3.1 Numbers of immigrants to Canada, 1971–2012. *Source:* Citizenship and Immigration Canada.

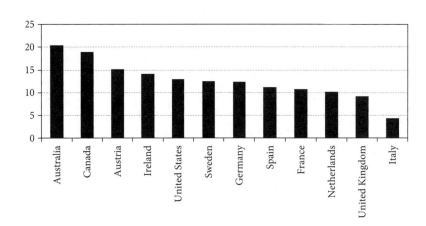

Figure 3.2 Percentage of foreign born among immigrant nations, 2005. *Source:* United
Nations, International Migration (2006).

program is roughly twice the size of its American counterpart, even including undocumented Mexican immigrants.

Despite a certain amount of emigration, or return migration, Canada has substantially
more foreign-born residents as a percentage of its population than the United States and
most European countries (see Figure 3.2). Immigration has contributed significantly to
Canada's population growth; and because of Canada's low birth rate, it is the primary source
of such growth.

When Canada removed country-of-origin barriers to immigration in the 1960s, immigrants' origins shifted to sources outside Europe. Immigration data by country of origin
over the period 1961–2010 (see Table 3.1) show that South Asia and China have been the
most important sources for more than thirty years. Moreover, by 2010, immigrants from
the Philippines had become as numerous as those from India or China. The impact of this
shift is reflected in Canadian census data on birthplace of immigrants (see Figure 3.3).

Since the 1970s, immigrants have settled primarily in Toronto, Montreal, and Vancouver, and the populations of these cities, which were virtually entirely of European origin in
1970, today include large non-European minorities (see Figure 3.4). These so-called "visible minorities" in Toronto and Vancouver are projected to become majorities by 2016 and
to reach 60 percent by 2031 (Statistics Canada 1994; Malenfant, Lebel, and Martel 2010).
Very recent trends show immigrant settlement becoming somewhat less concentrated in the
major cities. For example, Toronto received about 100,000 immigrants per year for many
years, but in each of the last two years it has received about 80,000.

Economic Class and the Points System for Immigrant Selection

Permanent immigrants to Canada are admitted in three main categories: economic,
family, and refugee, with a small group admitted on "humanitarian and compassionate"
grounds. As immigration numbers rose in the late 1980s and 1990s, the proportions of
economic immigrants remained fairly constant at about half (see Figure 3.5). Since the late
1990s, however, there has been a steady increase in economic migrants and a corresponding
decrease in the proportions of family class and refugee immigrants.

TABLE 3.1

Immigrants to Canada by origin (in thousands)

Origins	1961–1970 Number	1961–1970 Percentage	1971–1980 Number	1971–1980 Percentage	1981–1990 Number	1981–1990 Percentage	1991–2000 Number	1991–2000 Percentage	2001–2010 Number	2001–2010 Percentage
Africa and the Middle East	14.0	1.0	64.8	4.5	68.4	5.1	159.5	7.2	291.7	12.3
America (total)	246.8	17.5	401.7	27.9	280.4	21.1	294.3	13.3	323.6	13.7
Mexico	2.1	0.1	6.1	0.4	6.9	0.5	12.7	0.6	26.6	1.1
United States	161.6	11.4	178.6	12.4	75.7	5.7	60.6	2.7	85.5	3.6
Other North and Central America	6.2	0.4	2.5	0.2	40.8	3.1	43.6	2.0	14.7	0.6
Cuba	—	—	0.3	0.0	1.1	0.1	4.7	0.2	10.5	0.4
Other Caribbean	52.8	3.7	131.4	9.1	87.3	6.6	97.5	4.4	67.8	2.9
South America	24.1	1.7	82.8	5.7	68.6	5.2	75.1	3.4	118.4	5.0
Asia (total)	140.9	10.0	408.7	28.4	602.9	45.3	1313.6	59.5	1427.0	60.3
Hong Kong	36.5	2.6	83.9	5.8	129.3	9.7	240.5	10.9	14.0	0.6
Taiwan	—	—	9.0	0.6	14.3	1.1	79.6	3.6	27.2	1.1
China	1.4	0.1	10.6	0.7	36.2	2.7	181.2	8.2	337.3	14.2
Macao	—	—	—	0.3	2.0	0.2	4.1	0.2	0.3	0.0
Vietnam/Laos/Cambodia	—	—	66.2	4.6	100.6	7.6	47.6	2.2	24.9	1.0
Philippines	—	—	54.1	3.8	65.4	4.9	131.1	5.9	191.1	8.1
Japan	0.3	0.0	6.0	0.4	4.2	0.3	9.5	0.4	13.2	0.6
South Korea	—	—	16.0	1.1	16.5	1.2	43.2	2.0	65.8	2.8
South Asia	30.4	2.2	92.1	6.4	108.6	8.2	336.1	15.2	489.7	20.7
Other Asia	72.3	5.1	70.5	4.9	125.8	9.5	240.7	10.9	263.6	11.1
Oceania and Australia (total)	33.2	2.4	31.2	2.2	17.4	1.3	22.8	1.0	19.1	0.8
Australia	26.4	1.9	14.7	1.0	5.1	0.4	8.6	0.4	10.5	0.4
New Zealand	6.8	0.5	5.2	0.4	2.4	0.2	2.3	0.1	4.4	0.2
Other	—	—	11.3	0.8	9.9	0.7	11.8	0.5	4.2	0.2
United Kingdom	341.9	24.2	216.5	15.0	92.3	6.9	57.2	2.6	70.2	3.0
Other European countries	618.9	43.8	314.8	21.9	269.2	20.2	361.1	16.3	226.5	9.6
Unidentified countries	15.8	1.1	2.7	0.2	0.3	0.0	0.0	0.9	9.5	0.4
Total	1,411.5	100.0	1,440.4	100.0	1,330.9	100.0	2,208.5	100.0	2,367.58	100.0

SOURCE: Canada, Statistics Canada, Canada Year Book (1963–64, 203; 1967, 220; 1969, 208; 1970–71, 267; 1973, 235; 1975, 188; 1976–77, 212–13; 1978–79, 186); Canada, Employment and Immigration Canada (1986, 28–30; 1992, 34–36); Citizenship and Immigration Canada Statistics (1991, 26–31; 1992, 30–35; 1993, 32–39; 1994, 32–39; 1995, 32–39; 1996, 32–39; 1997–2000, Department of Citizenship and Immigration Canada); CIC Facts and Figures 2011.

NOTE: "Origins" is defined as country of last permanent residence.

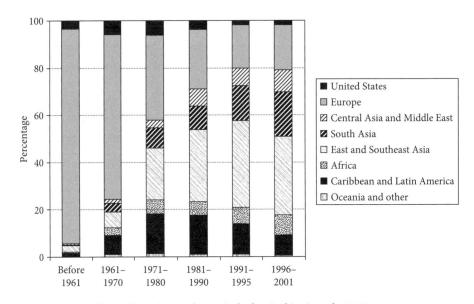

Figure 3.3   Birthplace of immigrants by period of arrival in Canada, 2001. *Source:* Statistics Canada, Census of Canada.

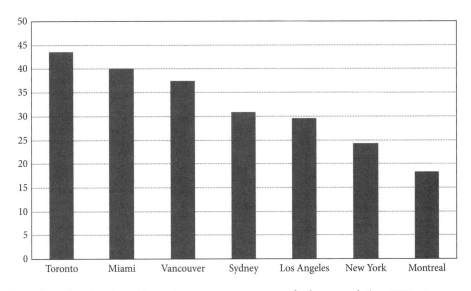

Figure 3.4   Immigration cities: migrants as a percentage of urban population, 2001. *Source:* Statistics Canada (2004).

There are several types of economic migrant. The largest category is skilled workers, who are selected in a points-based system that emphasizes employability criteria. Introduced in 1967, the points system has been effective in enhancing the employment potential of immigrants, which represents a significant benefit to the country. The criteria have changed over time. Initially, the emphasis was on experience in in-demand occupations. Over time,

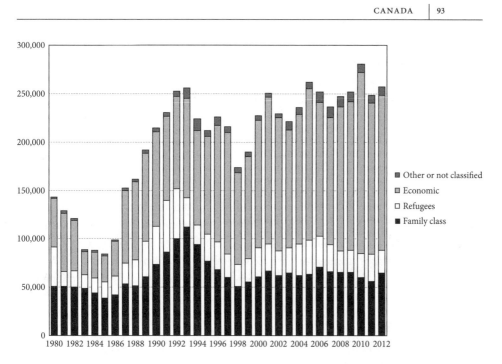

Figure 3.5   Immigration to Canada by class of entry, 1980–2012. *Source:* Statistics Canada (2004).

because of rapid labor market change, it shifted to formal education—human capital—to recruit immigrants thought most likely able to adapt. Other criteria include knowledge of one of the two official languages; work experience, particularly in in-demand occupations; having a job offer in hand; and other predictors of employment success. Since 1970, Quebec has maintained its own selection system, similar to that of the federal government but emphasizing distinct requirements for integration in a francophone environment (Young 1991). The points system applies only to "skilled workers" in the economic category, and then only to the principal applicants within a family. The economic class also includes special categories such as entrepreneurs, the self-employed, and investors. Each of these programs is based on criteria designed to ensure economic success.

The points system focuses on employability to enhance the economic impact of immigration, and it appears to have succeeded in this regard based on longitudinal analyses of immigrant earnings via tax records (Citizenship and Immigration Canada 1998). A points-based system can bring in larger numbers of immigrants, most of whom then find employment after arrival. However, there may be a trade-off between numbers and quality because a large intake may mean lower selection standards. Indeed, the essential idea of the points system is to reduce such trade-offs to a simple formula. Thus, the most points are given for high levels of education. However, without a university degree, sufficient points for admission may be obtained by other indicators of employability, such as an arranged job or relative youth. Canada wants immigrants with a four-year university degree, but, because of large numbers, over 20 percent of points-selected immigrants in 2005 did not have one.

Immigrant Integration Programs

Canadian immigration policy includes several programs that encourage effective integration in terms of settlement, language training, access to social services, and human rights and equality guarantees. Settlement and language training involve investments by both federal and provincial governments. Total federal expenditures for the Language Instruction for Newcomers to Canada (LINC) program were nearly C$100 million (according to an evaluation report dated 2009 and posted on the CIC website http://www.cic.gc.ca/english/resources/evaluation/linc/intro.asp).

Settlement itself consumes considerable resources. Settlement programs are local initiatives funded by a competitive grant process, and they are difficult to evaluate systematically. Government statistics indicate that each immigrant receives about $3,000 worth of settlement services, which implies a national budget of nearly $1 billion. Opposition critics say that the budget cuts for immigrant settlement total about $50 million, while the government maintains that it has increased settlement expenditures, especially for immigrants in "nontraditional" areas outside Toronto and Ontario.

Credential Recognition and Immigrant Skill Utilization

Along with immigrant employability, much attention has been given to the many barriers to employment success for immigrant professionals. Underutilization of immigrant skills reportedly costs the Canadian economy several billion dollars annually (Bloom and Grant 2001; Reitz 2001a), and it is one of the most important complaints expressed by immigrants about their experiences in Canada, according to the Longitudinal Survey of Immigrants to Canada (LSIC) (Statistics Canada 2005). Barriers to immigrant skill utilization include employers' lack of familiarity with foreign qualifications, professional licensing procedures set up with Canadian qualifications in mind, immigrants' lack of professional connections and their lack of familiarity with Canadian professional and business "lingo," and, of course, their lack of "Canadian experience." These employment problems are also reflected in the trend toward lower employment success for immigrants in successive arrival cohorts, despite rising selection standards.

Because of the significance of immigration in Canada, this problem has garnered public concern, and there have been many attempts to ameliorate it. There are government and business programs to help immigrants obtain jobs that use their skills, such as Ontario regulations that assure immigrants fair access to professional licensing. Many agencies provide credential assessment and recognition and bridge training programs to top up foreign-acquired skills and provide immigrants with work experience. And there are mentorship systems that help immigrants network with professionals in their field. This is to say nothing of the many websites crammed with helpful advice for newcomers. Still, circumstances vary greatly across occupations, and efforts to help immigrants have been uncoordinated and unevaluated. There is as yet no overall plan to address the problem, which may remain significant for many years.

Among the most noteworthy government initiatives is assessment of foreign credentials, which focuses on equivalencies between immigrants' training and training undergone by Canadian-educated professionals. Credential assessment services now exist in virtually every province in Canada. World Education Services, established in Ontario with a government mandate and a startup subsidy, now operates as an independent business, preparing 10,000 assessment reports annually. Quebec's provincial government provides assessment services, and the federal government has a multimillion-dollar program to develop the assessment concept further. The positive impact of credential assessment must be significant given that immigrants (at least in Ontario) are prepared to pay $115 for the most basic evaluation and more than double that for a more detailed evaluation.

Among community groups, one of the leaders in promoting immigrant skill utilization is the Toronto Region Immigrant Employment Council, known by its acronym TRIEC. TRIEC annual reports show the range of initiatives and provide some numerical impact assessment. In 2009, for example, it reported that its mentoring partnership program matched 5,000 skilled immigrants with Canadian professional mentors; Career Bridge internships, which TRIEC helped to initiate, provided 1,300 skilled immigrants with Canadian experience; 600 skilled immigrants made connections through TRIEC networking events. Buoyed by these successes, the TRIEC model has diffused across Canada.

There has been no effort to evaluate the impact of all these programs. At the same time, immigrant skill levels have risen significantly, magnifying the scale of the problem. If anything, the problem of immigrant employment in Canada has become more difficult over time, and more serious than when it was first identified in the 1990s (Reitz, Curtis, and Elrick 2014).

Linking Immigrant Selection to the Labor Market: Recent Policy Shifts

In recent years, there have been a number of policy initiatives aimed at linking immigration more closely to the labor market. Employers complain that the existing system does not enable them to use immigrants to fill jobs quickly. One problem is the application backlog, reported at one point to be in excess of 600,000. This problem is inherent in the selection system and is the direct result of more foreigners wanting to immigrate than there are visas for. It makes it difficult to use the traditional points-based immigration selection system to quickly fill short-term needs, especially because there is a significant demand for workers at skill levels too low to qualify under the points system.

There have been three main initiatives for dealing with the labor market–immigration linkage: (1) revisions to the selection criteria; (2) increased emphasis on provincial governments selecting immigrants (provincial nomination programs, or PNPs); and (3) increased use of temporary immigrant status, with the possibility of transition to permanent status in a new "Canada Experience Class," which includes similar opportunities for international students. The numerical impact of provincial selection and the Canada Experience Class is so far not large, but the numbers are growing (see Table 3.2). For example, PNP immigrants have tripled in the period 2006–2010; the number in 2010, 36,419, represented 13 percent of all immigrants, and Canada Experience Class numbers, less than 4,000 in 2010, are growing significantly as more temporary immigrants become eligible.

These initiatives have been implemented in phases over recent years, and an impact assessment at this stage can only be very preliminary. Some of the initiatives were modeled

TABLE 3.2
Permanent residents in Canada by category, 2006–2010

Category	2006	2007	2008	2009	2010[a]
Spouses and partners	45,305	44,912	44,209	43,901	40,755
Sons and daughters	3,191	3,338	3,254	3,025	2,953
Parents and grandparents	20,005	15,813	16,599	17,178	15,322
Others	2,016	2,179	1,519	1,100	1,177
Family class	70,517	66,242	65,581	65,204	60,207
Entrepreneurs: principal applicants	820	580	446	371	291
Entrepreneurs: spouses and dependents	2,273	1,577	1,255	945	795
Self-employed: principal applicants	320	204	164	180	174
Self-employed: spouses and dependents	632	375	341	358	326
Investors: principal applicants	2,201	2,025	2,832	2,872	3,223
Investors: spouses and dependents	5,830	5,420	7,370	7,434	8,492
Skilled workers: principal applicants	44,161	41,251	43,361	40,733	48,815
Skilled workers: spouses and dependents	61,783	56,601	60,373	55,220	70,524
Canadian Experience Class: applicants	0	0	0	1,775	2,532
Canadian Experience Class: spouses and dependents	0	0	0	770	1,384
Provincial/territorial nominees: Principal applicants	4,672	6,329	8,343	11,801	13,856
Provincial/territorial nominees: spouses and dependents	8,664	10,765	14,075	18,578	22,563
Live-in caregivers: principal applicants	3,547	3,433	6,157	6,273	7,661
Live-in caregivers: spouses and dependents	3,348	2,685	4,354	6,181	6,245
Economic immigrants	138,251	131,245	149,071	153,491	186,881
Government-assisted refugees	7,326	7,572	7,295	7,425	7,265
Privately sponsored refugees	3,337	3,588	3,512	5,036	4,833
Refugees landed in Canada	15,884	11,696	6,994	7,204	9,038
Refugee spouses and dependents	5,952	5,098	4,057	3,183	3,557
Refugees	32,499	27,954	21,858	22,848	24,693
DROC and PDRCC[b]	23	15	2	6	0
Temporary resident permit holders	136	107	113	106	109
H and C[c] cases	4,312	4,346	3,452	3,142	2,903
H and C cases outside the family class/public policy	5,902	6,844	7,168	7,374	5,836
Other immigrants	10,373	11,312	10,735	10,628	8,848
Category not stated	2	1	2	1	7
Total	251,642	236,754	247,247	252,172	280,636

SOURCE: Citizenship and Immigration Canada, RDM, Preliminary 2010 Data.

[a]Data for 2010 were preliminary and subject to change. For 2006–2009, these are updated numbers and may differ from those in Facts and Figures 2009.

[b]Deferred Removal Order Class and Post-Determination Refugee Claimants in Canada.

[c]Humanitarian and Compassionate. These are cases admitted at the discretion of the Minister of Citizenship and Immigration. http://www.cic.gc.ca/english/resources/statistics/facts2010-preliminary/01.asp.

after changes previously introduced in Australia and recommended for Canada in a comparative study by Hawthorne (2008), who argued that, based on Australian experience, the new Canadian policies would offer significant prospects for improved outcomes. However, the evidence for this recommendation was based primarily on short-term outcomes, and Australian census evidence does not suggest that the new policies produced any overall improvement (Reitz 2010). Indeed, the Australian government has greatly reduced visa opportunities for international students and is reviewing its selection policy more generally.

Revisions to Selection Criteria

The points grid has been revised to give more emphasis on official language knowledge, youth, and possession of a job offer, with experience reduced as a factor. These changes correspond with research indicating impact on labor market success.

Applicants without a Canadian job offer must have experience in a particular occupational category in current demand regardless of their points. The categories initially posted include twenty-nine specific occupations at various skill levels, from physicians, dentists, and architects to chefs, plumbers, electricians, welders, mechanics, crane operators, and workers in mining and oil and gas drilling. Many jobs in mining and oil and gas do not require a university education, which effectively lowers the educational standard for selection.

Unlike revisions to increase the emphasis on language knowledge and youth, there does not appear to be an explicit research basis for selection based on in-demand occupations. Canadian experience indicates that selecting immigrants based on such occupations is not always effective because demand changes so quickly. It was, in fact, because of this problem that selection emphasis shifted to formal education in the 1980s, since highly educated immigrants are thought to be better able to adapt to a changing labor market. A recent Statistics Canada study (Picot and Hou 2009) shows that the continuing decline in immigrant employment success in the period since 2001 is related to the so-called "IT bust"—that is, declining employment opportunity in information technology. In the late 1990s, when demand in this sector was strong, many urged Canada to use immigration to admit more IT workers, which the government did, and this may have aggravated current immigrant employment problems. To the extent that new selection criteria lower the educational levels of immigrants, longer-term immigrant integration may be threatened.

Provincial Nomination Programs

Another change allows provincial governments to play an increased role in selection. Quebec has selected all immigrants bound for that province for several decades; in the late 1990s, other provinces began to negotiate agreements with the federal government to nominate immigrants for permanent residence. The numbers mandated by the original agreements were not large, but provincial selection has grown modestly from 5 percent in 2006 to 13 percent in 2010.

The PNPs reflect the broader Canadian view of immigration as a huge economic boost. It represents a desire by areas of the country not now major destinations for immigrant settlement—places other than Toronto, Vancouver, and Montreal—to attract more immigrants. Not surprisingly, these areas include Alberta, a province where the oil industry during the economic boom created demand for workers of all kinds. Less obvious is the bid for immigrants by Atlantic Canada, where there are relatively few jobs and immigrants are sought as a way to create them.

Temporary Foreign Workers and the Canada Experience Class

Recently, the Temporary Foreign Worker Program (TFWP) expanded. This has implications for permanent migration to Canada (Sweetman and Warman 2010). When first introduced in 1973, the TFWP was relatively small and targeted at those with highly specialized skills, including academics, business executives, and engineers. There are programs for other categories, including seasonal agricultural workers and live-in caregivers, the latter allowing foreign caregivers to apply for permanent residence after two years. Employer demand for workers to perform jobs requiring lower skill levels prompted the federal government to introduce in July 2002 the Pilot Project for Hiring Foreign Workers in Occupations that Require Lower Levels of Formal Training, which has no limits on numbers (Nakache and Kinoshita 2010: 1–2).

Overall, the number of temporary immigrants entering the country each year has nearly doubled, from about 100,000 entrants in the 1990s to nearly 200,000 10 years later (see Figure 3.6), and the number of temporary immigrants has increased correspondingly. The data indicate that in 2011 those in the country with visas numbered more than 400,000. Although the data are incomplete, it appears that about half of the temporary foreign workers admitted to Canada in recent years have been at skill levels requiring secondary school training only, or below (Statistics Canada 2009).

A Canadian Experience Class introduced in 2008 provides new opportunities for temporary foreign workers (with at least two years of experience in a "skilled occupation") and for international students (who have graduated in Canada and have one year of experience). Foreign workers and students can apply for permanent residence from within Canada. This in effect extends opportunities, previously available only to live-in caregivers, to all qualifying temporary foreign workers regardless of their admission stream.

Under the rules of the Canadian Experience Class, eligible "skilled occupations" include not only management and professional occupations in which a university degree is normally required, but also occupations such as carpenter, plumber, bricklayer, and others in the construction trades, where much training may be based on apprenticeship. International students may qualify with university degrees or with degrees from any postsecondary institution. Hence, the educational levels of those qualifying for the Canadian Experience Class may vary considerably. The initial expectation was that the Canadian Experience Class would emerge as a numerically significant category, with 10,000 to 12,000

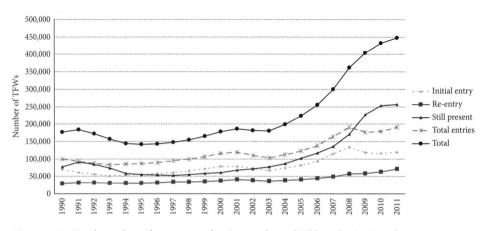

Figure 3.6 Total number of temporary foreign workers eligible to be in Canada. *Source:* Citizenship and Immigration Canada, Facts and Figures.

applicants in the first year (Citizenship and Immigration Canada 2008: 25). However, applications have been fewer, and expectations have been reduced (Citizenship and Immigration Canada 2010: 13).

The increased size of the TFWP, its administration, and its potential to adjust status has led to debates about the links between temporary and settlement immigration. The live-in caregiver program has been criticized as creating the potential for exploitation because of the power of the supervisor over the ultimate granting of a permanent resident visa. The same criticism has been raised about the Canadian Experience Class because employers must provide the evidence of employment required for a permanent visa to be granted. An enforcement problem arises whenever private citizens have a formal role in immigrant selection. The potential is there for both abuse and fraud (Reitz 2013).

Abuse arises if those with power over immigrant selection make unreasonable requests that prospective immigrants feel obliged to fulfill in order to maintain their status. Such situations have been reported, for example, in Toronto's construction industry, where temporary foreign workers hoping for permanent status are asked to work extra hours without pay. There may also be fraud because temporary workers must create a formal record of employment. In industries such as construction, where temporary immigrants are numerous, extensive and reliable record keeping is not the norm. Canadian Experience Class regulations may promote better record keeping, but this cannot be known without effective monitoring. According to a recent report of the auditor general (2009), there are significant problems with monitoring recent immigration initiatives to ensure that programs are operating as intended.

Temporary foreign workers who do not qualify for the Canadian Experience Class are expected to have even less education, and, although their formal opportunity to remain in Canada is limited, experience shows that many such workers may overstay their visas and in effect become permanently undocumented or "nonstatus." Enforcement efforts have proven ineffective, and, in the case of recent Canadian policy, there is little provision even to monitor the extent of visa compliance. Prospects for integration of low-skilled nonstatus immigrants are quite uncertain. The potential that they will increase as a result of increased temporary immigration is quite considerable. Figure 3.6 shows that more than 1.5 million temporary foreign workers have entered the country since 1990 and more than 100,000 enter each year. If half of Canada's temporary immigrants become permanent nonstatus residents, which may be a reasonable guess based on experience in other countries, the numbers on a per capita basis will be comparable to the numbers of undocumented immigrants settling in the United States from Mexico in a typical year. Based on international experience, Martin (2010) suggested that Canada be "cautious" in developing temporary worker programs.

PUBLIC OPINION ON IMMIGRATION AND POLITICS

Public Opinion

Canadian public opinion is generally supportive of immigration. Canada is clearly an exception to the prevailing pattern across most other industrial countries, where the majority

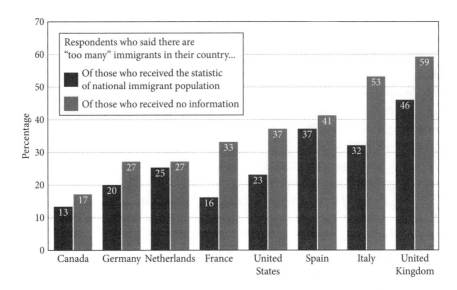

Figure 3.7 Public opinion concerning immigration levels in selected countries. *Source:* German Marshall Fund (2010: 7).

of residents want immigration reduced. This "Canadian exceptionalism" is shown most recently in a report from the German Marshall Fund (2010; see Figure 3.7), which indicated that Canadians also were more likely to see immigration as an opportunity rather than as a problem. In most countries, the reverse is true: there is less immigration, and the majority sees it as a problem and calls for reductions.

Canada's pro-immigration attitudes have been consistent for several decades. From 1975 to 2005, Gallup Canada frequently included the following question in nation surveys: "If it were your job to plan an immigration policy for Canada at this time, would you be inclined to increase immigration, decrease immigration, or keep the number of immigrants at about the current level?" The responses (see Figure 3.8) show that, in every year but 1982, a recession year, the majority endorsed either staying with existing immigration levels or increasing them. The highest level of support was found in the most recent year in the series, 2005, and the positive trend continued to 2010. This is according to poll results between 2004 and 2010 from EKOS Research Associates based on a similar question. In 2004, the proportion agreeing with current or higher levels was 63 percent compared to the 31 percent who thought there were too many immigrants. In 2010, the proportion agreeing with current or higher levels was 67 percent, compared to 23 percent who thought there were too many immigrants (see Figure 3.9).[1]

Of course, not all Canadians support present immigration policy. Despite the positive majority view, there is a degree of opposition—a distinct minority that does not command much space on the political stage. One commentator, Martin Collacott, argued in a Fraser Institute publication that opposition to immigration has become more significant and that majority support for it is a "myth" (Collacott 2002: 39), The same point is made on the website of the Centre for Immigration Policy Reform (www.immigrationreform.ca), with which Collacott is affiliated. However, as the previous discussion shows, majority support

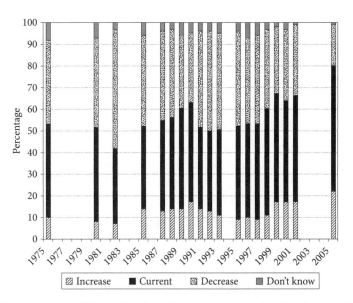

Figure 3.8   Responses to a Gallup Canada poll question concerning immigration levels: "If it were your job to plan an immigration policy for Canada at this time, would you be inclined to increase immigration, decrease immigration, or keep the number of immigrants at about the current level?" *Source:* Gallup Canada, Inc.

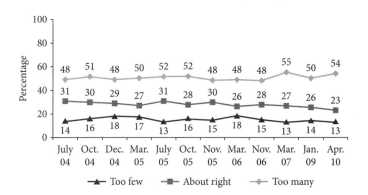

Figure 3.9   Responses to an Ekos Research 2010 poll question on immigration levels: "In your opinion, do you feel there are too many, too few, or about the right number of immigrants coming to Canada?" *Source:* Ekos Research (2010: 4). *Note: n* = 1530.

for immigration in Canada is indeed a fact, not a myth. Collacott based his claim on the argument that the proportion of Canadians supporting reduced immigration is larger than the proportion supporting its increase. This argument is clearly incorrect because it focuses only on those who want change and ignores the many who actually support the policy as it is, which is 50 to 60 percent in most opinion polls. Those who want to reduce immigration levels in Canada are very clearly the minority and have been for some time.[2]

The stability of Canadians' attitudes toward immigration may be explained by their multiple social and economic bases, as shown in analysis of a recent Environics "Focus Canada" national survey (Reitz 2011). Canadians are convinced of the positive economic benefits of immigration; they also accept multiculturalism as part of their national identity and accept continued immigration in support of it. These twin pillars of policy support provide a buffer against particular immigration-related issues arising from time to time that might otherwise raise questions about the policy.

On the economic side, Canadians tend to take an optimistic and expansionist view of their economic future, both at the national level and in terms of their own situation. Clear majorities of Canadians, 78.7 percent, believe immigration boosts the national economy, and only a small minority, 22.8 percent, believe immigrants take jobs from the native born. These views are common across the country, including regions such as Ontario and British Columbia, where labor demand is strong and immigrants are the most numerous, and other regions where the economy is weak. Thus, provincial government programs in places like Atlantic Canada that see immigrants as an economic stimulant are in accord with local public opinion. Although perceptions of immigrants' positive economic impact on the economy are strongest among those with jobs, among unemployed Canadians as well fully 68 percent see immigration as having a positive effect and only 36 percent believe that immigrants take jobs from other Canadians.

On the social and cultural side, support for multiculturalism appears to be a strong force supporting high levels of immigration in Canada. Focus Canada respondents were asked the question "How important is the following for the Canadian identity?" and were provided with a series of items, one of which was multiculturalism. Fully 85 percent felt that multiculturalism was either very important or at least somewhat important to the national identity and that, compared to other important national symbols, multiculturalism was in the top group behind healthcare, the flag, and the Charter of Rights and Freedoms but ahead of hockey, bilingualism, and the RCMP. Support for multiculturalism reinforces support for immigration. Those respondents who cited the importance of multiculturalism were significantly more likely to support immigration.

Support for multiculturalism does not mean that Canadians do not want immigrants to integrate fully into the mainstream of society. Majorities support multiculturalism, and they are concerned that too many immigrants are not adopting Canadian values and they worry about the implications (Angus Reid 2010). The Focus Canada survey showed that an overwhelming 80 percent of respondents agreed that "Ethnic groups should try as much as possible to blend into Canadian society and not form a separate community"; 51.3 percent "strongly" agreed. There are also strong concerns that immigrants are not in fact blending in. A majority of Canadians—nearly 70 percent—agreed that "there are too many immigrants coming into this country who are not adopting Canadian values"; over 40 percent of those "strongly" agreed. These views and others, such as dislike for racial minorities and concerns about so-called "bogus" refugee claims, do tend to be associated with less enthusiasm for immigration. Racial difference was also expressed as an issue, leading a small minority to object to immigration.

Concerns about questions of immigrant integration were clearly expressed in the Focus Canada survey, specifically regarding Muslims. When asked whether Muslims in Canada "want to adopt Canadian customs and way of life," most respondents felt Muslims "want to be distinct." When asked about the ban on the wearing of head scarves by Muslim women in public places, including schools, respondents were about equally divided, but a slightly greater proportion expressed the view that it was a good idea. The controversy regarding Muslims has been particularly prominent in Quebec and is reflected in the Focus Canada survey, particularly regarding the issue of head scarves.

Public emphasis on "blending" and the integration of immigrants is far from new. Although it is possible that these concerns may have intensified in recent years, with increased attention to Muslims, similar views have been found in many public opinion surveys throughout the period since the 1970s, when multiculturalism policy has been in place. For example, a poll conducted by Decima Research in 1989 showed substantial majorities of Canadians supporting the idea of immigrant "blending," more so in fact than respondents to a parallel poll in the United States (Reitz and Breton 1994: 27–28). Other evidence, such as a national survey conducted in 1976 (Berry, Kalin, and Taylor 1977), also shows that, while most Canadians accept cultural retention by minorities, most also favor immigrant integration into mainstream society (see the summary and discussion by Reitz 1980: 383–84).

Support for multiculturalism is related to a broader group of social attitudes, including support for the ban on capital punishment, for gun control legislation, for same-sex marriage, and for access to abortion. Together these attitudes are sometimes referred to as "social progressivism"; those not favoring these positions are often called "social conservatives." Support for the various items on the social progressive agenda tends to interrelate and extend to multiculturalism, and each item is associated with support for immigration. National pride is a part of this mix as well. All these progressive views are associated with pride in the Canadian lifestyle as superior to the American lifestyle, and this national pride also bolsters support for multiculturalism and thus for immigration (Reitz 2011).

The multiple sources of support for immigration may be an important reason for the stability of pro-immigration sentiment in Canada over time. Specific issues that might arise and possibly pose questions about immigration may not do so because of the persistence of other factors supporting it. For example, a prolonged recession; a visible sign of immigrants experiencing economic difficulty and requiring attention and possibly significant public expenditure; or a dramatic increase in illegal immigration—any of these could threaten pro-immigration sentiment by undermining the positive perceptions of immigration's economic value. In this context, however, the issue of culture and multiculturalism, and progressive social values generally, may help stabilize pro-immigration attitudes because they have been as important as the economic views. On the other hand, major developments such as social conflict or breakdown in immigrant minority communities that increases crime or possible terrorist activities might have the effect of eroding confidence in the belief that multiculturalism fosters Canadian unity. This could affect attitudes to immigration.

Political Parties and Immigration Politics

Immigration in Canada has been associated traditionally with the Liberal Party, but today all major Canadian political parties have pro-immigration policies. The Conservatives under Brian Mulroney (1984–1993) maintained high immigration numbers and introduced legislation in support of multiculturalism and employment equity. There is rarely any debate on immigration during Canadian election campaigns. Over the past decades, the word "immigration" has seldom if ever been mentioned in the nationally televised leaders' debates. In a debate preceding the May 2011 election, a question on immigration and multiculturalism was posed by a voter, and the four prime ministerial candidates competed to put forward the most pro-immigration position, defending the interests of immigrants and more accessible immigration.

In the Canadian context, even the immigration critics may be actually pro-immigration by international standards. For example, Daniel Stoffman, a critic of immigration, proposed reducing it to about 175,000 per year, representing 0.5 percent of the population—more on a per capita basis than advocated by immigration supporters in other countries (Stoffman 2002). Implementing Stoffman's proposal would still leave Canada as one of the world's leading immigration countries.

The Reform Party, which existed from 1987 to 2000 and was primarily an outgrowth of Western-based protest, had been seen as socially conservative and reluctant to support immigration. It merged with the Conservatives following their defeat in 1993. The minority Conservative government, elected in 2006, has maintained a strongly pro-immigration policy emphasizing its economic value, but has expressed less evident enthusiasm for multiculturalism as this concept is understood by many of its proponents. The Focus Canada survey showed that Conservative supporters are significantly less likely to support immigration, based on their socially conservative values (see Reitz 2011). The Conservatives have sought support among immigrants based on these values and, despite some success, have experienced difficulty because some of their related policies such as those on multiculturalism and citizenship (to be discussed later) portray immigrants as a threat to traditional Canadian values.

THE ECONOMIC ROLE AND IMPACT OF IMMIGRANTS

Immigrant Educational Levels and Labor Market Success

Canada's program of skilled immigration has meant that immigrants work in relatively highly skilled occupations. Unlike the less-skilled immigrants of the 1950s and 1960s, those arriving in Canada since 1970 have possessed relatively high educational levels (Reitz 2007a). Whereas earlier immigrants, particularly from Southern Europe, averaged eight years of education or fewer, more recent immigrant educational levels have been substantially higher. Over a number of years, and at least up to 2006, Canada significantly increased its emphasis on education in immigrant selection. The proportion of immigrants with bachelor's degrees more than doubled from just over 20 percent in the early 1980s to about 45 percent in the most recent period. Much of this increased has occurred since the mid-1990s, so that now the educational levels of immigrants exceed those of the native born.

Since the 1970s, the relative educational level of immigrants has changed in part because of changes in the educational levels of the native born. There have been two distinct periods. First, in the 1970s there were major investments in domestic education, creating a more competitive environment for new immigrants. Postsecondary educational participation rates have risen to meet or exceed levels previously seen only in the United States, so the competitive context for newly arriving immigrants has become more difficult. Immigrant educational levels still exceed those of the native born, but the gap has been reduced by the latter's gains. In fact, compared to their most likely native-born labor market competitors—namely, young people who are new to the labor market in Toronto and other major urban centers—immigrants in the 1980s and early 1990s were actually less educated.

In the early 1990s, there was a sharp increase in the significance of formal education in the points system. As a result, the proportion of immigrants with university degrees increased from about 30 percent to 45 percent by the end of the decade—a much more rapid increase than occurred in the native-born population. Since then, the relative educational levels of immigrants have continued to rise.

Declining Earnings and Increasing Poverty Rates

Despite fluctuations in immigrant educational levels relative to those of the native born, there has been a pervasive downward trend in employment rates and earnings of newly arrived immigrants over the entire period since the 1970s, among both men and women and in most origins groups. The most influential study of this phenomenon, by Frenette and Morissette (2003), shows that, despite substantial increases in immigrant educational levels, and taking account of business cycle fluctuations in labor demand, average entry-level earnings declined perhaps 20 percent for newly arriving immigrants, both men and women. Along with this, there has been a decline in employment rates (Reitz 2001b). Some evidence points to at least partial improvement for arrivals in the late 1990s, but the inter-cohort decline appears to have continued between 2001 and 2006 (Statistics Canada 2008).

High and increasing poverty levels are being reported for immigrants in recent studies, based on census data and on the longitudinal immigration database, or IMDB (Picot and Hou 2003; Picot, Hou, and Coulombe 2007; see also Kazemipur and Halli 2000 and the series on Toronto by Ornstein 1996, 2000, 2006). Some of the increase in poverty levels can be attributed to the business cycle and the difficulty in finding employment facing immigrants arriving during a recession. The recession of the early 1980s clearly created such difficulties, but there was an expected rebound for those arriving later in the decade. Weak employment demand reappeared in the early 1990s and created new employment difficulties, no doubt exacerbated by the large numbers of immigrants. The recession of the early 1990s was the first in which Canada kept immigration levels high, which made the numbers of immigrants affected correspondingly higher.

However, the continuing trend toward declining earnings extended across several business cycles and appears to have had its roots in more basic changes in the labor market that affected immigrants who had been in Canada for much longer periods of time and for whom the impact of business cycle factors at time of arrival had faded to insignificance (Reitz 2001b). Analyses of 2001 and 2006 census data confirm that the negative employment trend for immigrants continued during the relatively strong economy.

A number of reasons have been put forward for the downward trend in immigrant employment (Reitz 2007b). The shift in immigrant origins from Europe to Asia and the increase in racial minorities explain part of the decline, as there was a decline in employment opportunities for all new labor force entrants. Educational levels of the native-born workforce began rising more rapidly than those of immigrants, creating a competitive disadvantage. Many employers wanted evidence of formal education in the new "knowledge economy," which made it more difficult for immigrants with foreign-acquired credentials to get hired. Some analysts have noted a decline in return for foreign experience as well, although no explanation for this trend has been found. Finally, there was an overall increase in labor market inequality, which affects immigrants in a negative way because their employment was more often near the bottom of the earnings hierarchy.

Evidence on Improving Recognition of Foreign Qualifications

The effort to improve Canadian employers' recognition of foreign qualifications has received much media attention since the mid-1990s, but any effects are so far not visible in employment statistics. Overall, the educational level of Canada's immigrants has risen much more rapidly than that of the native born. However, despite having gained substantially in relative skill level since the mid-1990s as a group, the proportion of immigrants in the more highly paid occupations that use those skills, such as science, engineering, and nursing, is only marginally higher and these immigrants' relative earnings have remained unchanged.

A close look at trends between 1996 and 2006 also shows that the value of immigrant skills has not shown significant improvement over time (Reitz, Curtis, and Elrick 2014). In fact, there appears to have been a relative decline even in the most recent period, when one might have expected some immigration programs to begin to have an effect. Census data for 2006 show that immigrant skills in terms of both education and work experience have only about two-thirds of the value of corresponding skills held by native-born Canadians, and occupational underemployment is a significant reason for this imbalance.

Immigrants with university degrees might be expected to have benefited the most from the new immigration programs, but between 1996 and 2006 the proportion of recently arrived university-educated immigrants working in professional or semiprofessional fields actually declined, from 50.4 to 43.5 percent for men, with lower figures for women. At the same time, the proportion of highly skilled immigrants working in low-skilled occupations increased relative to their native-born counterparts. In 1996, the proportion was about 50 percent higher for skilled immigrants, but in 2001 it was 130 percent higher and in 2006 was almost 140 percent higher. So, despite attention to their plight, highly educated immigrants have been falling further behind.

There are many reasons that barriers persist, including their sheer complexity. Each Canadian professional group—doctors, engineers, accountants—has its own qualifications and evaluation procedures for persons trained abroad. Many occupations outside the regulated professions are seeking analytic and problem-solving skills, and it is in these that education plays an increasing role as a qualifying criterion. Such occupations include sales supervision, human resource management, and public relations, and in those occupations addressing barriers to foreign-acquired skills poses even greater challenges. Because of the relative lack of systematic standards in many unregulated fields, it is more difficult for immigrants to demonstrate the value of their specific skills. And while the economic loss for immigrants with professional qualifications is significant, it is actually even more so for immigrants with a bachelor's degree but without professional certification. Small or medium-sized firms, which represent the majority of employers in Canada, often lack formal human resources departments and may be less systematic in their approach to job applicants, and they may be less able to provide formal opportunities for immigrants to demonstrate their skills. Immigrants who fail to get the jobs for which they have specific qualifications may experience even more barriers at lower levels, often being dismissed as "overqualified," and can find themselves obliged to take jobs for which there are virtually no skill requirements whatever.

The Impact of Immigration on the Canadian Economy

Large-scale immigration has been justified and motivated by the prospect of economic gains and growth, as seen in public opinion data. Economic research has been guarded in assessing this impact, and most early accounts indicated immigration's small though positive effects (e.g., Economic Council of Canada 1991). Some studies have assessed the net impact of immigration on public finance as positive (Akbari 1995); others have cautioned against expectations that immigrants will support an aging population (Beaujot 1999). The geographer Richard Florida (2002) gained public prominence in Canada with his analysis indicating that immigrants are part of a "creative class" and stimulate economic growth. Because he based this analysis on theory and fairly simple interurban correlations, it has had limited influence with economic researchers who prefer more complex models and data analysis. However, a recent simulation study by Dungan, Gunderson, and Fang (2010) using a complex economic model indicates that the economic impacts of immigration depend significantly on how well immigrants are paid.

Immigrants may affect the distribution of earnings. In the United States, they are seen to increase overall income inequality. In Canada, however, comparative research by Aydemir and Borjas (2007) indicates that immigration may actually reduce income inequality. Immigrants compete for more highly skilled work in Canada, so the labor market impact is at levels of employment higher than the impact of relatively less-skilled immigrants in the United States.

SOCIAL ISSUES

Multiculturalism and Citizenship

In the popular view, support for multiculturalism, which was shown to be a factor in Canadians' positive attitude toward immigration, does not imply any desire for immigrants to remain separate from the mainstream. As was seen, the idea that immigrants should "blend in" is also a positive value, as is the acquisition of citizenship, participation in mainstream institutions, and, of course, learning at least one of the official languages. This integrationist intention may help explain why multiculturalism remains a positive value in Canada despite its rejection in much of Europe.

Canada's Debate over Multiculturalism

Even in Canada, however, there is a debate about multiculturalism, and fairly extreme views are heard on both sides. In the minds of some critics, almost anything that goes wrong in minority communities can be blamed on multiculturalism. They say that multicultural-ism, by celebrating diversity, not only encourages minorities to maintain possibly anti-democratic or sexist cultures and extraneous political agendas but also exempts them from criticism based on mainstream values. Incompetence is excused, crimes are condoned, and terrorist threats are ignored because multiculturalism makes people fear that criticism of minority groups, or even individual group members, will draw accusations of racism. In this vein, former British Columbia premier Ujjal Dosanjh recently blamed multiculturalism for helping promote Sikh extremism because it has been distorted to claim that "anything anyone believes—no matter how ridiculous and outrageous it might be, is okay and accept-able in the name of diversity."

For supporters, many of the positive indications of the impact of immigration can be cred-ited to multiculturalism, which they say promotes social inclusion and helps integrate minori-ties into the mainstream. For its supporters, multiculturalism helps minority businesses to be successful, helps minority kids to do well in school, and helped Ujjal Dosanjh to become Canada's first South Asian immigrant premier. Citing such positive experiences, the Canadian philosopher Will Kymlicka (1998) asserted that "the multiculturalism program is working."

There is little research to support either the critics or the supporters (for an extended dis-cussion, see Reitz 2014). The most useful compares countries with and without multicultural policies, and the few existing studies find little effect either way. One of them (Banting et al. 2006) showed that multiculturalism policies in twenty-one countries had little relation to the strength of the welfare state. This finding undermines the critics' claim of divisiveness, but does not support proponents' claims of enhanced cohesion. There are many reasons for Canada's relatively positive record on immigrant integration. For example, most analysts at-tribute its successful integration of immigrant minorities mainly to its skill-selective immigra-tion policy and not necessarily to multiculturalism.

Canadian multiculturalism is often compared to "assimilationist" policies in the United States, although official US policy is actually laissez-faire. The more negative status of mi-norities in the United States mostly has other reasons. The legacy of centuries of slavery can hardly be ended by adopting official multiculturalism any more than multiculturalism solves English–French relations in Canada. Nor can multiculturalism in the United States transform undocumented immigration from Mexico into a popular cause. Multicultural Canada is also averse to undocumented immigration, as illustrated by the strongly nega-tive reaction to a few Chinese people arriving off the coast of British Columbia in 1999. When "fair" comparisons are made between Canada and the United States., focusing on similar groups of immigrants—for instance, the highly educated from China, India, or the Caribbean—any differences due to Canadian multiculturalism appear quite small. More-over, rates of economic and social integration for comparable immigrants in the two coun-tries are virtually identical. Higher rates of intergroup marriage in Canada are sometimes cited as showing greater inclusiveness than exists in the United States, but recent studies reveal this difference to be more a result of demographics and opportunity than of prefer-ences arising from multiculturalism. The most convincing positive evidence comes from a study (Bloemraad 2006) showing that government funding of ethnic community organiza-tions produces higher citizenship acquisition rates in Canada.

Multicultural issues also resonate in debate over issues of immigrant religion and the status of women. This was reflected most prominently in Quebec, where controversies over "reasonable accommodation" of Muslims and other religious minorities led the Quebec government to commission a study (Bouchard and Taylor 2008). Because Quebec policy is symbolically different, possibly useful comparisons with the rest of Canada can be made. In Quebec, ambivalence toward multiculturalism has resulted in a provincial policy of *inter-culturalisme*, a difference that reflects the initial politics of multiculturalism. Re-emergence of national identity in Quebec during the 1960s raised issues of culture as well as language, eliminating traditional assimilationism as an option. Multiculturalism was chosen instead of biculturalism to accommodate immigrant groups, leaving many Quebeckers feeling that their interests had been downgraded.

Since much of the hypothesized impact of multiculturalism is at the symbolic level, does Quebec's use of a different word make any practical difference to immigrant integration? Results from Statistics Canada's 2002 Ethnic Diversity Survey suggest not. Immigrants in Quebec appear to be as well integrated into society as their counterparts in the rest of Canada, which apparently means that governments may usefully express support for diversity even without multiculturalism.

One aspect of the debate focuses on the social impact of immigrant enclaves. Findings on such enclaves suggest that they help immigrants feel at home but also tend to isolate them (Reitz et al. 2009). Persistent diversity both promotes and slows integration depending on its different aspects. This suggests that multiculturalism policy might consider ways to establish stronger exchanges among Canada's cultural communities.

Citizenship Issues

Citizenship for immigrants in Canada remains readily available, and permanent residents become eligible to apply after three years. Thus the rate of citizenship acquisition has been high relative to the US experience (Bloemraad 2006). Controversies exist over whether some immigrants acquire citizenship too easily or for reasons other than their commitment to the country or to residing in it. Large numbers of Canadian dual citizens live in their country of origin and retain full consular rights. The evacuation of 75,000 Canadian citizens from Lebanon during military activity there raised questions of whether Canada should create additional citizenship criteria.

Recently, the government introduced a new citizenship test and study materials that require immigrants to know more about Canada and to provide more information about Canadian values. The test generated controversy but may not represent a significant departure from past practice.

Racial Conflicts

Racial Disadvantages and Discrimination

The low earnings and high poverty rates for recent immigrants, discussed above, apply more specifically to so-called visible minorities. Ornstein's (2006) analysis for the 1996 Census showed high rates of poverty for racial minorities in Toronto. Poverty rates in certain visible minority groups were more than twice the rates for others—40.7 percent versus 19.8 percent—

and were particularly high among Ethiopians, Ghanaians, Afghans, and Somalis, who have poverty rates of 50 to 80 percent. Tamil, Pakistani, Bangladeshi, Central American, West Asian, and other African groups also have very high poverty rates (Ornstein 2000).

The reasons for these racial disadvantages, and particularly the significance of racial discrimination, are debated. Some point to evidence of racial discrimination in the workforce, such as has been evidenced in field trials involving actors from different racial groups presenting the same qualifications on job applications but receiving different responses from employers (Henry and Ginsberg 1985). Additional evidence of discrimination has been found in employer responses to applicant résumés with Asian and non-Asian names attached (Oreopolous 2009). Some suggest that immigrants from outside Europe may have qualifications representing lower levels of training or skill, at least partly accounting for their poorer showing in the Canadian labor markets.

There is a possibility that disadvantages for immigrant racial minorities net of measured qualifications can be explained by the poorer quality of those qualifications (and not by discriminatory treatment). This has been explored in studies focusing on racial minorities educated in Canada. An extensive study of the largest samples using census data, by Pendakur and Pendakur (2002), found that the racial disadvantage for racial minorities born in Canada is significant, although less so than for racial minority immigrants (see also Skuterud 2010; Li 2000).

The Canadian Human Rights Commission has found cases of racial discrimination. In 1997 such a case involved Health Canada, where minority qualifications were denigrated. The view that ethnic minorities may possess technical qualification but often lack "soft skills" such as communication and decision-making perspective was found to play a significant role in their low rates of promotion to management. In one tribunal, the commission decided that racial discrimination may be involved when a minority immigrant job candidate is rejected on the basis of being over-qualified. Immigrants encounter this complaint almost as often as the proverbial complaint about lacking "Canadian experience." Such rejections are sometimes defended as standard human resource practice, but the fact that immigrants are so often rejected for jobs for which they are qualified on paper means they must turn to lower-level jobs, where they are vulnerable to the complaint that they are overqualified. Because of this, a human rights tribunal found the practice of rejecting immigrants as over-qualified to be discriminatory.

Within minority groups, perceptions of significant racial discrimination in employment are quite widespread. For example, the 1992 Minority Survey in Toronto showed that 78 percent of blacks believed that they were being targeted for employment discrimination (Dion and Kawakami 1996). In a 1979 survey in Toronto, 57 percent of West Indian blacks stated that discrimination in employment was a "very serious" or "somewhat serious" problem (Breton 1990: 208). Among Chinese, 37 percent regarded employment discrimination as a "very serious" or "somewhat serious."

Although immigrant economic experiences do improve over time, and the children of immigrants have succeeded in attaining high levels of education and occupational, perceptions of discrimination are actually more widespread among immigrants who have been in the country for longer periods, and even more so for the children of immigrants. Evidence from the 2002 Ethnic Diversity Survey documents these trends and indicates that awareness of discrimination is one reason that, despite economic mobility, racial minority immigrants are slower to integrate socially into society than are European immigrants (Reitz and Banerjee 2007; Reitz et al. 2009).

THE IMPACTS OF RECENT POLICY CHANGES

Canada is likely to maintain its high levels of mostly skilled immigration and to continue multiculturalism, or, in Quebec, *interculturalisme*. However, a number of policy innovations to address some of the ongoing problems of immigration, although they offer promise, raise the possibility of new problems. For this reason, a key priority for the future may be timely evaluation to allow for assessment and, if required, adjustment or correction.

The "old problems" of Canadian immigration remain: the difficulties immigrants encounter in securing recognition for their foreign-acquired qualifications, the decline in the economic fortunes of successive cohorts of newly arriving immigrants, application backlogs which remain controversial, and issues of visa compliance and border control. And despite the popularity of multiculturalism, there are concerns about discrimination against immigrants and racial minorities in various areas of society, and questions about immigrants' social and cultural integration.

Each of the new initiatives carries the potential to lower educational standards for new immigrants, but it is not yet clear how this will work in practice; nor is the extent of any decline known. Formal requirements for the skilled immigrant category include an explicit shift away from formal education and general work experience toward youth and qualifications in specific occupations in current demand. The provincial nomination program seems likely to attract mainly applicants who do not qualify for admission under federal criteria, which may lower educational levels of newcomers. Permanent visas given to temporary foreign workers under the Canada Experience Class have been few, but the categories of eligibility include those who do not have postsecondary education. And, of course, those who become nonstatus permanent residents are likely to have low skill levels. However, the Australian experience is worth bearing in mind. Despite a number of policy changes that have been described as an abandonment of the human capital model, the educational levels of immigrants in Australia continue to rise.

A decline in the educational level of immigrants could have an impact on the long-term potential for successful integration. High levels of education have often been cited as a key factor in policy success. The assumption behind the new initiatives is that linking immigrants more firmly to the labor market from the outset may be more important in the long run. Which view is correct will have an important impact on the future of Canadian immigration.

The subtle move to soften multiculturalism is also difficult to assess in terms of impact. Criteria for attaining citizenship have been tweaked toward a greater emphasis on immigrants acquiring "Canadian values," and officials have openly speculated about the possible limitations of multiculturalism. However, the actual changes appear quite minor.

Evaluation, then, will be critical. In this regard, recent changes in the Canadian census may hamper assessment. Tracking immigrant progress has relied heavily on the "long-form" census questionnaire, administered to 20 percent of the population, which is being downgraded from mandatory to voluntary for the 2011 census. Many analysts believe that this will lead to under-representation of some of the most vulnerable groups in Canadian society, including recent immigrants encountering employment difficulty, and this will make assessing the impact of immigration policy changes difficult.

NOTES

1. A somewhat different, more negatively expressed question was asked by Environics Research Group over the period 1977–2010: "Do you strongly agree, somewhat agree, somewhat disagree, or strongly disagree with the following statement: Overall there is too much immigration to Canada." From the late 1970s to the early 1990s, majorities agreed, either strongly or at least somewhat, presumably indicating negative attitudes toward immigration. However, since the mid-1990s respondents have begun to disagree more strongly with the statement, and since 2000 clear majorities have disagreed. The poll in 2010 showed a slight upward trend in agreement that there is too much immigration, but a clear majority still disagreed that there were too many immigrants.

Since the mid-1990s, both series have shown majority support for immigration, which is remarkable since this is a period during which the highest immigration levels have been maintained. For the first portion of the period starting in 1975, the data show somewhat conflicting trends. The Gallup and EKOS polls also showed majority support during this time. The Environics polls showed lower levels of support, a discrepancy that may be related in part to the different wording of the questions in the Environics, Gallup, and EKOS polls. Gallup and EKOS presented respondents with a neutral choice between various options, whereas Environics requested agreement with a negative opinion (i.e., that there is "too much" immigration). One explanation is that a "positive response bias" might have been at work in the Environics interviews. This refers to the tendency of some survey respondents to agree with any statement offered by an interviewer as a simple gesture of politeness rather than an expression of a genuine opinion. If such a source of bias were discounted, it might be suggested that over the past three decades actual Canadian attitudes toward immigration have been more positive than the Environics poll data indicate. However, this would not explain why the Environics polls show significant change over time whereas the Gallup-EKOS series does not. In any case, there is agreement among all polls that Canadians have been generally positive on immigration for more than a decade, a period during which immigration has been maintained at quite high levels.

2. There is no basis for concluding that there has been a very recent turn away from support for immigration. Although the Environics series shows a slight downward trend in support, the EKOS series does not. In any case, both sources support the view that any recent negative trends are relatively small and have not affected majority support for high immigration levels.

REFERENCES

Akbari, A. H. 1995. "The Impact of Immigrants on Canada's Treasury, circa 1990." In *Diminishing Returns: The Economics of Canada's Recent Immigration Policy*, edited by D. DeVoretz, 113–27. Toronto: C. D. Howe Institute.

Angus Reid Inc. 2010. "Canadians Endorse Multiculturalism, but Pick Melting Pot over Mosaic." Poll released November 8. http://www.angus-reid.com/polls/43492/canadians-endorse-multiculturalism-but-pick-melting-pot-over-mosaic/.

Auditor General of Canada. 2009. *Report to Parliament,* chap. 2. Ottawa: Office of the Auditor General of Canada. http://www.oag-bvg.gc.ca/internet/English/parl_oag_200911_02_e_33203.html.

Aydemir, A., and G. J. Borjas. 2007. "Cross-Country Variation in the Impact of International Migration: Canada, Mexico, and the United States." *Journal of the European Economic Association* 5 (4): 663–708.

Banting, K., R. Johnston, W. Kymlicka, and S. Soroka. 2006. "Do Multiculturalism Policies Erode the Welfare State? An Empirical Analysis." In *Multiculturalism and the Welfare State: Recognition and Redistribution in Contemporary Democracies,* edited by K. Banting and W. Kymlicka, 49–91. New York: Oxford University Press.

Beaujot, R. P. 1999. "Immigration and Demographic Structures." In *Immigrant Canada: Demographic, Economic and Social Challenges,* edited by S. S. Halli and L. Driedger, 93–115. Toronto: University of Toronto Press.

Berry, J., R. Kalin, and D. M. Taylor. 1977. *Multiculturalism and Ethnic Attitudes in Canada.* Ottawa: Supply and Services Canada.

Bloemraad, I. 2006. *Becoming a Citizen: Incorporating Immigrants and Refugees in the United States and Canada.* Berkeley: University of California Press.

Bloom, M., and M. Grant. 2001. *Brain Gain: The Economic Benefits of Recognizing Learning and Learning Credentials in Canada.* Ottawa: Conference Board of Canada.

Bouchard, G., and C. Taylor. 2008. "Consultation Commission on Accommodation Practices Related to Cultural Differences." www.accommodements-quebec.ca/commission/index-en.html.

Breton, R. 1990. "The Ethnic Group as a Political Resource in Relation to Problems of Incorporation: Perceptions and Attitudes." In *Ethnic Identity and Equality: Varieties of Experience in a Canadian City,* edited by R. Breton, W. W. Isajiw, W. E. Kalbach, and J. G. Reitz, 196–255. Toronto: University of Toronto Press.

Citizenship and Immigration Canada. 1998. "The Economic Performance of Immigrants: Immigration Category Perspective." IMDB Profile Series, Citizenship and Immigration Canada, December.

———. 2008. *Annual Report to Parliament.* Ottawa: Minister of Public Works and Government Services Canada.

———. 2010. *Annual Report to Parliament.* Ottawa: Minister of Public Works and Government Services Canada.

Collacott, M. 2002. *Canada's Immigration Policy: The Need for Major Reform.* Vancouver: Fraser Institute.

Dion, K. L., and K. Kawakami. 1996. "Ethnicity and Perceived Discrimination in Toronto: Another Look at the Personal/Group Discrimination Discrepancy." *Canadian Journal of Behavioural Science* 28 (3): 203–13.

Dungan, P., M. Gunderson, and T. Fang. 2010. "Macroeconomic Impacts of Canadian Immigration: An Empirical Analysis Using the FOCUS Model." Presentation, CERIS seminar, October 10.

Economic Council of Canada. 1991. *Economic and Social Impacts of Immigration*. Ottawa: Supply and Services Canada.

EKOS Research Associates Inc. 2010. "Annual Tracking Survey—Winter 2010." Submitted to Citizenship and Immigration Canada, April.

Florida, R. 2002. *The Rise of the Creative Class: And How It's Transforming Work, Leisure, Community and Everyday Life*. New York: Basic Books.

Frenette, M., and R. Morissette. 2003. "Will They Ever Converge? Earnings of Immigrant and Canadian-Born Workers over the Last Two Decades." Analytical Studies Branch Research Paper Series, Statistics Canada, Ottawa. Catalogue no. 11F0019MIE—No. 215.

German Marshall Fund of the United States. 2011. *Transatlantic Trends: Immigration—Key Findings 2010*. Washington, DC: German Marshall Fund of the United States.

Hawthorne, L. 2008. "The Impact of Economic Selection Policy on Labour Market Outcomes for Degree-Qualified Migrants in Canada and Australia." *IRPP Choices* 14 (5): 1–47.

Henry, F., and E. Ginsberg. 1985. *Who Gets the Work? A Test of Racial Discrimination in Employment*. Toronto: Urban Alliance on Race Relations / Social Planning Council of Metropolitan Toronto.

Kazemipur, A., and S. S. Halli. 2000. *The New Poverty in Canada: Ethnic Groups and Ghetto Neighbourhoods*. Toronto: Thompson.

Kymlicka, W. 1998. *Finding Our Way: Rethinking Ethnocultural Relations in Canada*. Oxford: Oxford University Press.

Li, P. S. 2000. "Earnings Disparities between Immigrants and Native-Born Canadians." *Canadian Review of Sociology and Anthropology* 37 (3): 289–311.

Malenfant, É., A. Lebel, and L. Martel. 2010. "Projections of the Diversity of the Canadian Population: 2006 to 2031." Demography Division, Statistics Canada, Ottawa. Catalogue no. 91-551-X.

Martin, P. 2010. "Temporary Worker Programs: U.S. and Global Experiences." *Canadian Issues / Thèmes Canadiens* (Spring): 122–28.

Nakache, D., and P. J. Kinoshita. 2010. "The Canadian Temporary Foreign Worker Program: Do Short-Term Economic Needs Prevail over Human Rights Concerns?" IRPP Study 5, Institute for Research on Public Policy, Montreal, May.

Oreopoulos, P. 2009. "Why Do Skilled Immigrants Struggle in the Labour Market? A Field Experiment with Six Thousand Résumés." http://homes.chass.utoronto.ca/~oreo/research/compositions/why_do_skilled_immigrants_struggle_in_the_labour_market.pdf.

Ornstein, M. 1996. "Ethno-Racial Inequality in Metropolitan Toronto: Analysis of the 1991 Census." Institute for Social Research, York University, Toronto.

———. 2000. "Ethno-Racial Inequality in the City of Toronto: An Analysis of the 1996 Census." Access and Equity Centre, Toronto.

———. 2006. "Ethno-Racial Groups in Toronto, 1971–2001: A Demographic and Socio-Economic Profile." Institute for Social Research, York University, Toronto.

Pendakur, K., and R. Pendakur. 2002. "Colour My World: Has the Minority-Majority Earnings Gap Changed over Time?" *Canadian Public Policy* 28 (4): 489–512.

Picot, G., and F. Hou. 2003. "The Rise in Low-Income Rates among Immigrants in Canada." Analytical Studies Branch Research Paper Series, Business and Labour Market Analysis Division, Statistics Canada, Ottawa. Catalogue no. 11F0019MIE—No. 198.

———. 2009. "Immigrant Characteristics, the IT Bust, and Their Effect on Entry Earnings of Immigrants." Analytical Studies Branch Research Paper Series, Social Analysis
Division, Statistics Canada, Ottawa. Catalogue no. 11F0019M—No. 315.

Picot, G., F. Hou, and S. Coulombe. 2007. "Chronic Low Income and Low-Income
Dynamics among Recent Immigrants." Business and Labour Market Analysis, Statistics
Canada, Ottawa. Catalogue no. 11F0019MIE—No. 294.

Reitz, J. 1980. "Immigrants, Their Descendants, and the Cohesion of Canada." In *Cultural
Boundaries and the Cohesion of Canada*, edited by R. Breton, V. Valentine, and J. Reitz,
329–417. Montreal: Institute for Research on Public Policy.

Reitz, J. G. 2001a. "Immigrant Skill Utilization in the Canadian Labour Market: Implications of Human Capital Research." *Journal of International Migration and Integration* 2
(3): 347–78.

———. 2001b. "Immigrant Success in the Knowledge Economy: Institutional Change
and the Immigrant Experience in Canada, 1970–1995." *Journal of Social Issues* 57 (3):
579–613.

———. 2007a. "Immigrant Employment Success in Canada, Part I: Individual and Contextual Causes." *Journal of International Migration and Integration* 8 (1): 11–36.

———. 2007b. "Immigrant Employment Success in Canada, Part II: Understanding the
Decline." *Journal of International Migration and Integration* 8 (1): 37–62.

———. 2010. "Selecting Immigrants for the Short Term: Is It Smart in the Long Run?"
Policy Options 31 (7): 12–16.

———. 2011. "Pro-Immigration Canada: Social and Economic Roots of Popular Views."
IRPP Study 20, Institute for Research on Public Policy, Montreal.

———. 2013. "Closing the Gaps between Skilled Immigration and Canadian Labour
Markets." In *Wanted and Welcome? Policies for Highly Skilled Immigrants in Comparative Perspective*, edited by P. Triadafilopoulos, 147–63. New York: Springer.

———. 2014. "Multiculturalism Policies and Popular Multiculturalism in the Development of Canadian Immigration." In *The Multiculturalism Question: Debating Identity
in 21st Century Canada*, edited by J. Jedwab, 107–26. Kingston and Montreal: McGill-
Queen's University Press.

Reitz, J. G., and R. Banerjee. 2007. "Racial Inequality, Social Cohesion, and Policy Issues
in Canada." In *Diversity, Recognition and Shared Citizenship in Canada*, edited by
K. Banting, T. J. Courchene, and F. L. Seidle, 489–545. Montreal: Institute for Research on Public Policy.

Reitz, J. G., and R. Breton. 1994. *The Illusion of Difference: Realities of Ethnicity in Canada
and the United States*. Toronto: C. D. Howe Institute.

Reitz, J. G., R. Breton, K. K. Dion, and K. L. Dion. 2009. *Multiculturalism and Social Cohesion: Potentials and Challenges of Diversity*. New York: Springer.

Reitz, J. G., J. Curtis, and J. Elrick. 2014. "Immigrant Skill Utilization: Trends and Policy
Issues." *Journal of International Migration and Integration* 15 (1): 1–26.

Skuterud, M. 2010. "The Visible Minority Wage Gap across Generations of Canadians."
Canadian Journal of Economics 43 (3): 860–81.

Statistics Canada. 1994. *Population Projections for Canada, Provinces and Territories 1993–
2016*. Ottawa: Statistics Canada.

———. 2005. "Longitudinal Survey of Immigrants to Canada: A Portrait of Early Settlement Experiences." Special Surveys Division, Statistics Canada, Ottawa.

———. 2008. "Earnings and Incomes of Canadians over the Past Quarter Century, 2006 Census: Findings." Minister Responsible for Statistics Canada, Ottawa. Catalogue no. 97-563-X.

———. 2009. "Immigration Overview: Facts and Figures, 2009." Statistics Canada, Ottawa.

Stoffman, D. 2002. *Who Gets In: What's Wrong with Canada's Immigration Program—And How to Fix It*. Toronto: Macfarlane, Walter & Ross.

Sweetman, A., and C. Warman. 2010. "Canada's Temporary Foreign Workers Program." *Canadian Issues / Thèmes Canadiens* (Spring): 19–24.

———. 2006. *International Migration 2006*. New York: United Nations.

Young, M. 1991. "Immigration: The Canada-Quebec Accord." Law and Government Division, Library of Parliament, Ottawa.

COMMENTARY

Irene Bloemraad

The first edition of *Controlling Immigration* advanced two propositions: first, that highly industrialized countries were becoming more alike in their policies and public opinion regarding immigration (the "convergence hypothesis"); and, second, that a growing gap existed between policy goals and actual migration outcomes, which in turn fueled anti-immigrant sentiment among the public and politicians (the "gap hypothesis").

Canada does not fit this pattern, especially the gap hypothesis. Indeed, Canada is a striking outlier to the general trend toward greater immigrant restriction in policy and anti-immigrant attitudes in public opinion. As Reitz notes, Canadians are by far the most open to and optimistic about immigration compared to other developed immigrant-receiving countries. In one comparative poll, only 26 percent of Canadians agreed that immigration was more of a problem than an opportunity; the next closest percentage, in France, was much higher at 43 percent; and the highest percentage, 66 percent, came from the United Kingdom, where fully two thirds of respondents saw immigration as a problem.

Furthermore, these attitudes have absolutely no correlation to the underlying proportion of immigrants in the general population, or even to public perception of that proportion. Indeed, in the German Marshall Fund survey, Canada had by far the highest foreign-born percentage of residents, about six percentage points above the next highest, while the United Kingdom was among the countries with relatively few immigrants. As Reitz clearly shows, Canadian optimism regarding immigration exists in a context of high mass migration, especially if we consider the annual flows of migrants in relation to the total population.

Leslie Seidle's commentary further underscores the puzzling aspects of the Canadian case. Not only is the Canadian federal government bullish about migration—and has been for quite a while—but every Canadian province and two territories have struck agreements that allow them to bring migrants directly into their jurisdictions. To fully appreciate how strange this is, given the contemporary zeitgeist on immigration, we have only to look at various US states—Arizona, Utah, Georgia—that recently passed legislation explicitly about driving immigrants *out* of the state, not attracting additional newcomers.[1]

Why is Canada such an outlier when it comes to the "gap hypothesis"?

One of the key answers is the Canadian point-selection system, which selects immigrants based on their potential to join the labor force. Ideally, this is selection into well-paying employment, be it as a welder on Alberta's natural gas pipelines or as a doctor in a cancer hospital in Toronto. Of course, as Reitz makes clear, the points system is far from flawless: it has not always made it easy for oil companies to hire foreign welders, and far too many foreign doctors cannot practice their profession once they arrive in Canada. Nevertheless, the economic thrust of Canadian immigration policy presumably alleviates worries about immigration being a drain on the welfare state—as evident in various European countries—and it likely communicates a sense of control over immigration policy absent in places such as the United States, where just under a third of foreign-born residents do not have legal papers.

Indeed, as Reitz suggests, Canadians are not inoculated against fears of uninvited migrants. This becomes readily apparent in periodic public outcries after authorities stop a ship smuggling migrants into Canada. Importantly, Canada also has the benefit of geography: despite fears of "false" asylum seekers, it is relatively hard for undocumented migrants to get there. Unauthorized migration laps gently onto Canadian shores; it does not come in large waves that would cause politicians to speak of tsunamis swamping the country. In this context, Reitz usefully raises the danger that Canadian support for migration might decline if substantial numbers of temporary visa holders remain in Canada and become "irregular" migrants.

But are geography, economic selection, and relatively small populations of unauthorized migrants enough to explain the Canadian puzzle? The British Isles are geographically apart from the continent and share no border with a less developed country, but public opinion there is decidedly against further migration. In the United States, most migrants work, including the undocumented, and despite a miserly welfare state, Americans still link migration with perceptions of welfare abuse. Reitz raises the possibility that migration is troubling for some Americans because it increases inequality, but the link between migration and economic inequality is debated and, in the Canadian context, one can imagine a similar link but with migrants putting pressure on the top end of the income distribution. Indeed, the native born can easily resent rich, highly educated migrants, as seen most prominently in the Vancouver area, where residents regularly blame Chinese migrants for making it difficult for ordinary Canadians to enter the exorbitantly priced housing market.

I want to offer several additional arguments for Canadian exceptionalism, expanding on Reitz's observation that immigration in Canada is about nation building. This is a key insight, as it highlights some other critical, noneconomic aspects of the Canadian system. Immigration is about permanent settlement and integration into a diverse citizenry, where legal systems, public policy, and political structures encourage engagement and membership.

As a result, an apparent paradox—high support for immigration in a country with very high levels of new and existing migration—becomes an explanation. Immigrants to Canada generally feel welcomed; government policy promotes integration with community partners because it is presumed that both sides are together for the long-haul; and new citizens make it very hard for anti-immigrant politicians to gain a foothold. The remarkable transformation of the Reform Party is a striking case in point. At its founding, the Reform Party was highly antagonistic toward multiculturalism. In its current incarnation as the majority Conservative government, it actively sought out new Canadians in the May 2011 federal election. Let me elaborate briefly on some of these noneconomic features of Canadian policy.

PERMANENT IMMIGRATION AND SETTLEMENT

Canada has had modest and limited temporary migration programs. Unlike the Bracero program in the United States—arguably a catalyst to today's substantial undocumented population—or guest worker programs on the European continent, the vast majority of Canadian migration has been explicitly about permanent settlement. Two cases that can be seen as exceptions further prove the rule. In Canada, when refugee claims are accepted, asylum seekers immediately become permanent residents; in the United States, although refugees have residency guarantees, they must affirmatively apply for a "green card." Furthermore, temporary-labor programs such as that for domestic caregivers offer visa holders a pathway to permanent residence. Most analogous programs in other countries, from Japan to the United States, keep migrants temporary. One can well imagine that the native-born population has little incentive to see these foreigners as full members of their society, or for migrants to feel a sense of inclusion and investment in that society, when migration is supposed to be temporary rather than permanent. Looking to the future, the rapid—and largely hidden—increase in temporary foreign work visas may be a problem, as Reitz hints.

INTEGRATION INTO A DIVERSE CITIZENRY

Reitz suggests that the positive benefits of multiculturalism in Canada might be exaggerated. As evidence, he points to similarities in some integration outcomes in Canada and the United States or in Quebec and the rest of Canada; the overall modest investment in funding; the likely greater significance of economic factors; the evidence of racial inequalities in socioeconomic outcomes; and the more modest sense of belonging among "visible minorities" compared to those of European origins.

These are all valid points, and worries about unequal outcomes by race or national origin, in particular, should raise alarms. Indeed, some scholars and community groups have suggested that public multiculturalism has provided governments with a smoke screen to appear tolerant and inclusive without taking aggressive action on issues of racial discrimination. Unfortunately, the counterfactual to this argument is impossible to prove. Would the Canadian government and society have taken strong policy steps toward racial equality and seen better outcomes absent multiculturalism? To me, this argument seems difficult to uphold.

First, Canada—along with the United States—ranks as the country with the most developed anti-discrimination policies in MIPEX's survey of 31 countries. While the Canadian people and their governments could clearly do more to counter discrimination, they have done much. Second, multiculturalism has played an invaluable role in reorganizing the symbolic order of membership in Canada. The Bilingualism and Biculturalism Commission of the 1960s, which led to the eventual multiculturalism policy, still talked about the two "founding races" of Canada: the English (British) and the French. Given the stickiness of national ideologies—Brubaker (1992) famously argued that German and French citizenship policy rested on centuries of nation building—it is extraordinary that, within a generation, Canadians have shed these views and now support, at very high levels, the idea of a diverse citizenry. This shift has arguably gone further in English-speaking Canada than in Quebec, but even Quebecers' embrace of Michaëlle Jean—a Francophone Governor General who migrated from Haiti to Quebec at a young age—shows that traditional notions of the French Canadian nation have widened substantially.

LEGAL SYSTEMS, PUBLIC POLICY, AND POLITICAL STRUCTURES ENCOURAGE ENGAGED MEMBERSHIP

Permanent migration and ideologies around diversity probably would not matter as much if these notions of inclusive citizenship were not institutionalized as they are in contemporary Canada. I have already touched on Canada's relatively robust legal structure. The enshrinement of a Charter of Rights and Freedoms in 1982—one that outlaws discrimination, affirms equality guarantees, protects equity hiring, and even instructs justice to keep the multicultural heritage of Canada in mind when rendering decisions—has become, as Reitz notes, one of the top four things residents name as key parts of the Canadian identity.

Public policy around immigrant settlement, and probably also around general social policy such a universal healthcare, has also contributed to inclusion. As I have argued elsewhere, these policies generate feelings of attachment and membership among immigrants in Canada (Bloemraad 2006, 2011). Furthermore, the funding that government provides for these public initiatives is channeled into community-based organizations. As Seidle highlights, this is relatively rare. In other countries with integration policies, more of the work is done by public employees and state agencies. These public-private partnerships might also help explain part of the success of Canadian settlement policy. By contracting with community-based organizations, governments send a message that they want to work in partnership with immigrant communities and that they trust them with public funds. They also allow different migrant communities to offer language training, employment services, and similar programs in culturally appropriate ways and with variation depending on community needs, thereby avoiding some of the paternalism inherent in certain European integration programs. Finally, this funding provides resources that build up the political capacity of immigrant communities; it supports organizations and leaders that can speak up and mobilize community members around immigrant issues.

What evidence do we have that this matters? If we look at citizenship acquisition, we find that an astounding 85 percent of foreign-born individuals who had lived in Canada at least three years (the minimum residency requirement for citizenship) reported Canadian citizenship in the 2006 Census. They became citizens despite the fact that, as a matter of costs and benefits, the advantages of Canadian citizenship are modest: you do not need it for most jobs, you do not need it to access public health insurance, and you do not need it to sponsor your relatives into the country. In addition, despite concern in some Canadian corners that certain immigrants acquire citizenship as a passport of convenience, in a Focus Canada poll in 2010 almost four of five immigrants (78 percent) reported a stronger attachment to Canada than to their country of birth, and another 7 percent felt attached to both equally. Strikingly, immigrants' sense of belonging does not seem to undermine native-born Canadians' identity. Indeed, one recent paper found that those who expressed more patriotism were also more likely to support immigration—a correlation that went in the opposite direction in the United States.

Finally, I would argue that a notion of inclusive citizenry buttressed by policy and institutions has created feedback loops that make it difficult for Canadian anti-immigrant politicians to gain a foothold in the public space. There is no Canadian Geert Wilders or Pat Buchanan. As mentioned previously, the early Reform Party, the closest thing to anti-foreigner populism in contemporary Canadian politics, is now part of the governing Conservative Party, which actively sought out immigrants in the 2011 federal election. Indeed, their win came through their successful wooing of immigrant-origin voters in the greater Toronto area.

The full extent of immigrant inclusion in Canada is perhaps best illustrated by the fact that *all* of the federal political parties count at least one foreign-born member of Parliament among their ranks. Based on unofficial election results, 11 percent of MPs in the House of Commons are foreign born. The proportion of foreign-born MPs in each party ranges from 100 percent (the lone Green Party MP was born in the United States) to 9 percent for the right-wing Conservatives. Even the separatist Bloc Québécois (BQ) has a foreign-born MP (Maria Mourani, born in the Cote d'Ivoire of Lebanese parents), which means that a quarter of the BQ's representation is "immigrant."

In summary, while the apparent success of Canadian immigration policy—and its outlier status among other highly developed countries—may rest in part on the points system, this is far from the whole story. Immigration as nation building is as critical, and it relies on support for permanent immigration and settlement, inclusive ideologies of a diverse citizenry, and policies and institutions that make integration possible. Given the right tools, immigrants can become full and active citizens, fostering a virtuous immigration policy circle.

NOTES

1. Many of these laws target undocumented migration. It is, of course, possible for a state to be in favor of legal migration but opposed to unauthorized immigration, and the relative lack of undocumented migration in Canada undoubtedly plays a role in the country's unique stance. Nevertheless, political leaders and public opinion in states such as Arizona, Utah, or Georgia do not appear highly favorable to legal migration in the way that Manitoba has enthusiastically embraced the Provincial Nominee Program.

Immigrant Selection and Integration in Canada: The Intergovernmental Dimension

F. Leslie Seidle

Controlling immigration is closely linked to questions of national sovereignty such as border protection and, increasingly, security concerns. It is thus not surprising that, even in federal states, the selection of immigrants is the responsibility of the national government. Canada is an exception in this regard (under the Constitution, the federal and provincial governments have concurrent jurisdiction over immigration, with the federal government paramount). As Reitz explains, what was traditionally a function of the federal government has, over the past three decades, been shared with Quebec and subsequently with other provincial governments.

I explain the main changes in immigrant selection resulting from a series of bilateral agreements between the federal and provincial/territorial governments, then address the provision of settlement and integration services to newcomers, and explain how, again through intergovernmental agreements, a number of provincial governments have acquired a primary or expanded role. The result is a diffusion of government action in the immigration field. Although these developments can be seen as consistent with the dynamics of Canadian federalism, they raise some concerns about policy coherence.

Starting in the 1960s, Quebec's political leaders sought greater powers for their province, with its largely French-speaking population, on a range of matters. Policymakers, concerned about the province's slowing population growth, considered how to attract more immigrants. A key argument was that the Quebec government was better suited to select newcomers who could be expected to integrate into its society. The first of four immigration agreements with the federal government was signed in 1971. Its terms were modest: the Quebec government was authorized to post an immigration counselor in designated countries. The 1975 agreement gave Quebec a role in immigrant selection, which was enhanced in 1978.

A further step occurred in 1987, when the federal government and all provincial governments agreed on a set of constitutional amendments (the Meech Lake Accord) intended to recognize Quebec's distinctiveness. A new immigration agreement, known as the McDougall/Gagnon-Tremblay Accord enhanced powers for the province and came into effect when the Meech Lake amendments were proclaimed. When these failed to meet ratification requirements, McDougall/Gagnon-Tremblay was signed in 1991, giving the Quebec government the power to select all of its economic immigrants (the federal government can overrule candidates only for serious security or medical reasons).

Quebec selects economic immigrants using a points system based on the Federal Skilled Worker Program (FSWP), which assesses candidates' capacity in English or French. Because Quebec's grid places considerable emphasis on knowledge of French, its government can recruit a large share of immigrants from countries that are French speaking or where French is a second language. In 2009, the top three source countries for immigration to Quebec were (in descending order) Morocco, Algeria, and France (for the rest of Canada, the top three source countries that year were China, the Philippines, and India). Despite the aftermath of the recession that began in 2008, Quebec received 53,985 immigrants in 2010 — a record number and more than 10,000 above the 2005 level.

In the early 1990s, the three Prairie provinces and some of the Atlantic provinces began to express concern about not receiving a sufficient number of immigrants. Manitoba raised an additional issue: as a result of the selection criteria for economic immigrants, the province's need for workers in skilled and semi-skilled trades was not being met. The federal government, unwilling to copy its accord with Quebec, developed the Provincial Nominee Program (PNP), which allows each province or territory to identify a limited number of economic immigrants to meet specific regional needs and/or to receive priority attention for immigration processing. The PNP was intended to be modest: the 1996 target was 1,000 nominees.

Manitoba was the first province to take advantage of the PNP. Since its 1998 agreement with the federal government, it has used the program quite aggressively to attract more immigrants. All of the other provinces except Quebec have since signed agreements on provincial nominees, as have Yukon and the Northwest Territories. In 2008, the federal government removed the cap on provincial nominations, which grew further at the expense of federal government selection. In 2009, provincially selected (Quebec and PNP) immigrants accounted for 44 percent of the total permanent economic principal applicants admitted, whereas 38 percent were chosen through the FSWP.

Provincial governments have taken advantage of the flexibility they have been granted to set criteria for choosing nominees—for example, recruiting workers in trades (such as welding) that do not qualify under the FSWP. According to the 2009 report of the Auditor General, there were then more than 50 PNP categories. Some observers, including Reitz, have suggested that PNPs are being used mainly to recruit lower-skilled immigrants. In at least two provinces, this does not seem to be the case. An in-depth study of the Manitoba nominee program found that 58 percent of principal applicants who arrived between 2003 and 2008 had a bachelor's or higher degree (Carter, Pandey, and Townsend 2010: 21). In British Columbia (BC), 62 percent of principal applicants who arrived between 2004 and 2008 had at least one university degree (BC Ministry of Advanced Education and Labour Market Development 2009: 2). Although data are not available for the other provinces, it is probably not justifiable to look on the PNPs as primarily a channel for increased low-skilled migration. Rather, they allow provincial governments, through links with employers and other actors, to respond to particular labor market pressures. Ideally, PNPs and the FSWP should be complementary. Whether they are being managed in that optic is another matter, as discussed later.

As for settlement and integration services, as Reitz notes, there have been significant changes to what was once a solely federal responsibility. Although Quebec again acted as a catalyst, this led not to a shift to involvement on the part of all provincial governments but rather to asymmetric decentralization (see Banting 2011).

The Government of Canada began to fund settlement services in 1949 with a program to help refugees adjust to Canadian life. Settlement and integration programs grew considerably in subsequent decades. Unlike in many other immigrant-receiving countries, where these services are provided by public servants, in Canada they are principally delivered by a host of nongovernmental organizations—often referred to as service provider organizations (SPOs)—through quasi-contractual contribution agreements.

The budget for settlement/integration has risen significantly in recent years. The projected spending by Citizenship and Immigration Canada (CIC) for these programs (including transfers to the Quebec, British Columbia, and Manitoba governments) for 2010–2011 was almost $1.1 billion (in 2000–2001, its spending was just under $328 million) (for further details, see Seidle 2010: table 1). Until recently, most of the CIC's funding was allocated to three programs:

- *Immigrant Settlement and Adaptation Program (ISAP)*, which helps immigrants obtain services and integrate into their community; this includes reception and orientation services, translation and interpreting, employment assistance, and counseling.

- *Language Instruction for Newcomers to Canada (LINC)*, which provides instruction in either official language to adult immigrants for up to three years from the time they begin training.

- *Host Program*, which matches immigrants with established Canadians, who help them improve their language skills, learn about Canadian society, and develop networks.

In 2008, the CIC introduced a "modernized" approach to settlement programming that includes greater emphasis on outcomes.

Under the 1991 accord, the Quebec government assumed responsibility for all reception and integration services for new arrivals. To that end, the federal government provides the province with an annual grant, with each year's payment calculated according to an "escalation factor." The grant has grown from $76 million in 1991–1992 to $254 million for 2010–2011. In contrast to the situation in the other provinces, only a small proportion of language training and other settlement services is delivered by nongovernmental organizations (NGOs): in 2009–2010, NGOs received approximately 6 percent of the Quebec government's spending in this area (Reichhold 2011). This is distributed among more than 150 organizations, contributing to what one researcher has described as the underfunding of community organizations that work with immigrants (Chicha and Charest 2008: 20).

When the Quebec government took over reception and integration programs, other provincial governments did not call for similar treatment. Rather, the federal government opened the door to further change. As part of a program review (launched in 1994) intended to reduce the federal deficit, it offered to withdraw from managing settlement services in the other provinces. Only the Manitoba and BC governments accepted the offer, and settlement/integration services were devolved to these provinces in 1998.

In 2005, the federal and Ontario governments signed an agreement that provided for significantly enhanced spending on settlement/integration services in Ontario ($920 million in new investments over five years). Program administration remains in the hands of the CIC, but governance mechanisms have been established that allow the Ontario Ministry of Citizenship and Immigration to participate quite extensively in planning and ongoing assessment. An annex to the agreement provides for the involvement of the City of Toronto, in what is the only formal federal-provincial-municipal arrangement in this policy field.

Since the Manitoba, BC, and Ontario agreements were signed, language training has been expanded in each province and a number of innovations in programming have been launched. This heightened activity is entirely warranted. Research has underlined that language ability is a major influence on outcomes for Canadian immigrants, including whether they obtain employment in their field and, in some cases, whether they find work at all (at least during the initial period after their arrival). In all three provinces, in part because of the increase in federal funding after 2005, those who qualify (principally permanent residents) may now pursue language learning to a higher level than previously.

As for innovation, devolution has allowed the British Columbia and Manitoba governments to develop language programs that reflect their particular circumstances, such as the composition of immigration and the needs of recent arrivals. The BC Settlement and Adaptation Program, for example, includes language training that relies on flexible methods and informal settings to target newcomers who face multiple barriers to integration. A pilot initiative for immigrant seniors provides basic English-language training along with information on Canadian services, life, and culture, in small group settings. In Manitoba, there have been a number of innovations, including an initiative to provide English-language training in the workplace. This program, whose cost is shared with employers, is customized to meet client and employer language needs and accommodate work schedules.

A significant issue that has led to tensions between certain provincial governments and the CIC is eligibility for settlement services. The following do not qualify for settlement services funded by the federal government: refugee claimants (they become eligible if their claim is accepted), international students, recent arrivals who have become citizens, and temporary foreign workers. Some provincial governments do not have the same exclusions. For example, British Columbia has developed a series of Early Years Refugee Pilot projects, through which early childhood development and learning support is provided to refugee children and their families. In Ontario, the bulk of settlement services is still provided by federally funded SPOs, and the just noted criteria apply. However, the provincial government's own settlement programs can be accessed by all newcomers except temporary foreign workers.

Another issue that has been gaining attention in intergovernmental discussions is outcome measurement. Under the CIC's "modernized" approach, SPOs need to demonstrate how their projects contribute to one of five results, and they must report outcomes. There is a similar emphasis in the latest Canada-BC immigration agreement (signed in April 2010). In future annual reports to the CIC, the BC ministry will be required to provide data using five outcome indicators, including improved English ability, ability to pursue employment goals, and knowledge of Canadian systems and culture. Accountability for outcomes is also being addressed multilaterally. All governments (including Quebec's) have agreed to work toward developing a pan-Canadian settlement framework. As an initial step, a federal-provincial agreement on desired outcomes and indicators of success was reached in 2010.

This approach contrasts with the way agreements on provincial nominees and settlement services have been negotiated and are managed. For the most part, Ottawa has dealt with provincial governments on a bilateral basis—a dynamic that can be characterized as "spokes on a wheel." Annual meetings of the federal, provincial, and territorial ministers became the practice only in 2002. This is leading to a somewhat reactive way of managing immigration flows, and it raises questions about policy coherence.

On the first issue, the federal government's capacity to stay within the target for the country as a whole is being called into question. The Quebec government must inform Ottawa of its target for the coming year, but it seems that the target is accepted without much discussion and then factored into the level for the country as a whole. As noted, in 2010 Quebec accepted a record number of immigrants. In addition, during the past several years Manitoba and some other provinces have exerted pressure to be allowed to accept more provincial nominees. In 2008, the federal government removed the cap on provincial nominations. Selections through PNPs rose at the expense of those through the FSWP. The upward trend in provincial selections may partly explain why, in 2010, the numbers of immigrants admitted to Canada (280,636) exceeded by more than 15,000 the target for that year.

As for policy coherence, issues arise with regard to both selection and settlement services. On the first, provincial selection is leading to considerable variation in immigrant qualifications. Although Quebec's focus on French-language ability is wholly defensible, some observers are concerned that PNPs are diluting the emphasis on human capital (as reflected in relatively high education levels and presumed adaptability) in favor of responding to short-term labor market pressures. The data from Manitoba and British Columbia reported previously suggest that these fears may be somewhat overstated. There has nevertheless been a notable shift from a single Canadian program (with defined streams) to a mix of selection criteria and channels.

Asymmetry has also emerged in settlement services. Variation in services such as language training in the provinces to which settlement services have devolved may be seen as a satisfactory example of responsiveness to local conditions—one of the purported strengths of federalism. At the same time, some provinces have expanded their programming to offer settlement services to newcomers not eligible elsewhere, such as refugee claimants and their children. Such differences can give rise to a sense of inequity in what is a quite sensitive policy area. As governments in Canada face the future, it is important that immigrant selection and integration frameworks strike a balance between policy variation on the one hand and the need to maintain certain common principles and objectives for the whole country on the other.

REFERENCES

Banting, Keith. 2011. "Federalism and Immigrant Integration in Canada." Paper presented at the Forum of Federations Conference on Immigrant Integration and Canadian Federalism: Exploring the Issues, Toronto, January 28. http://www.forumfed.org/post/Banting_28_01_11.pdf.

British Columbia Ministry of Advanced Education and Labour Market Development. 2009. "Provincial Nominee Program Immigrants to British Columbia, 2004–2008." http://www.welcomebc.ca/local/wbc/docs/communities/nominee_program.pdf.

Carter, Tom, Manish Pandey, and James Townsend. 2010. "The Manitoba Provincial Nominee Program: Attraction, Integration and Retention of Immigrants." IRPP Study 10, Institute for Research on Public Policy, Montreal.

Chicha, Marie-Thérèse, and Éric Charest. 2008. "L'intégration des immigrés sur le marché de travail à Montréal." *Choix IRPP* 14 (2).

Reichhold, Stephan. 2011. "Quebec's Immigration Agreement and Settlement Services." Paper presented at the Forum of Federations Conference on Immigrant Integration and Canadian Federalism: Exploring the Issues, Toronto, January 28. http://www.forumfed.org/post/Reichhold_28_01_11.pdf.

Seidle, F. Leslie. 2010. *The Canada-Ontario Immigration Agreement: Assessment and Options for Renewal.* Toronto: Mowat Centre for Policy Innovation.

4 AUSTRALIA

A Classical Immigration Country in Transition

Stephen Castles, Ellie Vasta, and Derya Ozkul

INTRODUCTION

Planned mass immigration has been a key factor in transforming Australia from an insular society, looking mainly to Britain for its values and heritage, to a more populous and diverse society with people from around the world. About 25 percent of Australians are immigrants, and about another 20 percent have at least one immigrant parent. Since 1945, 7 million immigrants have come to Australia, including 700,000 refugees and displaced persons (DIAC 2010a). The population increased from 7.6 million in 1947 to 22.2 million in 2010 (DIAC 2010b). In addition, millions of people have come to Australia in recent years as temporary workers or students.

Despite this immigrant heritage, Australia's immigration and asylum policy is controversial and was an important issue in the 2001 and 2010 federal elections. Australia is a "classical immigration country" that historically based its nation-building strategy on settlers from Europe. Drivers and characteristics of migration to Australia have changed, but politicians and the public are often slow to come to terms with the transition.

Australians have always had mixed feelings about immigration, and many have seen newcomers as a threat to national identity and security. The indigenous inhabitants of Australia were overrun and dispossessed by immigrants—namely, British convicts and colonists, who arrived from 1788 onward. Ever since, white Australians have dreaded a similar fate. The Aboriginal and Torres Strait Islander peoples were decimated, with the number falling from 500,000 in 1788 to just 50,000 by the late nineteenth century. This near genocide was legitimated by the racist beliefs of the time (Reynolds 1987). As inhabitants of a "European outpost" on the rim of Asia, Australians have feared that they will in turn be colonized by people from the far more populous countries of the region. Opinions and policies on immigration have always had a subtext of concern about race.

Since colonial times, the Australian state has played a role in selecting (sometimes recruiting) immigrants and in social policy and service provision for immigrants. With the emergence of multiculturalism in the 1970s, the role of the state increased, although support for multiculturalism declined in the 1990s. Australia did not experience a serious recession during the Global Economic Crisis (GEC) of 2007–2009. As this chapter is being written, the resources sector (especially mining) is booming and employers are looking for more immigrant labor. Public debates on immigration, population, and multiculturalism are never far from the headlines, and some observers speak of an "immigration revolution" (Markus, Jupp, and McDonald 2009).

THE CHANGING GLOBAL CONTEXT

Australia's immigration policy is based on the principles of strict control of entries, predominance of permanent settlement, and the expectation that immigrants will quickly become Australian citizens. However, new means of transport and communication make border control much more difficult, and migrants can keep in contact with families and communities in the homeland or other countries, facilitating not only further mobility but also transnational links (i.e., regular cross-border relationships). Whether people move on temporary or permanent visas, a commitment to becoming permanent members and citizens of the new community cannot be taken for granted.

At the same time, there has been a widespread backlash against multiculturalism, especially since the events of 9/11 in the United States. In Australia, concerns about security often focus on Muslim migrant communities, and governments must negotiate between the desire for security and employers worried about shortages of labor and skills. Migration policies now emphasize securing marketable skills, while multicultural policies are being challenged by concerns about social cohesion. For Australia, the key event in changing attitudes on security and diversity was the Bali bombing of 2002, when attacks by the Islamist group Jemaah Islamiyah killed 202 people, including 88 Australians. Concerns about social cohesion led to the introduction of a citizenship test and a longer qualification period for citizenship.

Australians seem to see Asia as a great mass of people eager to come to their country for a better life, even though several Asian countries have become major industrial powers in their own right, often competing for both skilled and unskilled migrant workers. Asian migrants have more choices than in the past, so countries keen to attract them need to offer attractive wages, conditions, and lifestyles. Thus, Australia is not the only option but part of an increasingly competitive global migration market.

HISTORICAL BACKGROUND

Australia was first settled as a penal colony, but free settlement was encouraged as awareness of the continent's agricultural potential and mineral wealth grew. The population expanded in the 1850s following the discovery of gold, prompting employers to call for the recruitment of non-British labor to keep down wages and restrict the power of trade unions (de Lepervanche 1975). Organized labor was strongly opposed to such immigration, demanding wages "fit for white men," and racist propaganda accused the Chinese of undercutting wages, increasing crime, spreading disease and coveting white women. The colonial governments of Victoria, New South Wales (NSW) and South Australia introduced measures to exclude Chinese immigrants, leading to a close link between racism and the emerging feeling of Australian identity and nationhood (MacQueen 1970). The White Australia Policy was established by the Immigration Restriction Act—one of the first laws passed by the new Federal Parliament in 1901.

European immigration remained relatively low in the early twentieth century. However, the Second World War convinced policymakers that Australia needed a larger population and a stronger manufacturing sector to safeguard national sovereignty. A Department of Immigration was established to develop a national immigration policy, and it used the slogan "populate or perish" as well as a selection system meant to keep Australia white and British as a way to overcome resistance to newcomers. Labor demand quickly outstripped the availability of British migrants, and the Department of Immigration started recruiting displaced persons in European camps. Recruitment was soon extended to Italy, Greece, and Malta. Trade union opposition to non-British immigrants was overcome by promises that immigrants would be tied to unskilled jobs for two years and would not displace Australian workers.

The 1970s were an immigration watershed. The long boom was replaced by a more uncertain economic environment, prompting the Australian Labor Party (ALP) government of 1972–1975 to cut immigration sharply and to emphasize the need for skilled labor. The White Australia Policy was replaced by a nondiscriminatory selection system modeled on the Canadian points system. Successive governments also followed Canada in introducing multiculturalism as the basis for social policy toward immigrants. In the mid-1970s, Australia experienced the arrival of the first boat people since 1788, when Vietnamese refugees arrived on its northern shores. Despite public suspicion, the Liberal-National coalition government developed a resettlement program.

From the mid-1970s to the early 1990s, there was consensus between the major political forces on a nondiscriminatory immigration policy and multicultural policies toward ethnic communities. Immigration remained relatively high, with family reunion as the largest component of entries. The ALP government's 1989 *National Agenda for a Multicultural Australia* (OMA 1989) emphasized the need to recognize cultural diversity as a basis for Australian social policy, citizenship, and identity. However, anti-immigration and anti-minority sentiments were growing, exemplified by historian Geoffrey Blainey's 1984 warnings against what he called the "Asianization of Australia" (Blainey 1984; see also Castles et al. 1988: 16–38). In 1988, then opposition leader John Howard called for curbs on Asian immigration, but was forced to step down following accusations of racism.

Anti-immigration feeling continued to grow, and Howard was soon back as opposition leader. In 1996, he became prime minister, leading a coalition of the Liberal and National parties; Australian immigration policy entered a new era, with even stronger emphasis on recruitment of skilled immigrants, cuts in family reunion, draconian measures against asylum seekers, and a shift away from multiculturalism. An important new trend was the growth of temporary labor migration. The election of a federal ALP government in late 2007 saw the abandonment of some elements of the Howard government's asylum policy, but many of the key elements of migration policy generally, such as a preference for skilled over family migration and the growth of temporary migration, remained.

RECENT IMMIGRATION PATTERNS

Since 1947, Australia has had a planned intake of "permanent immigrants," or "settlers," who have the right to bring their families. For most of this period, the trend has been toward encouraging immigrants to become citizens, but this was reversed in the atmosphere of growing suspicion of foreigners after 9/11 and the Bali bombing. Australian immigration debates still focus mainly on permanent immigrants, but one of the most significant changes has been the exponential increase in temporary entries. Many temporary migrants leave after a few months or years, but temporary status sometimes serves as the first step toward permanent residency (Phillips, Klapdor, and Simon-Davies 2010: 13). At the same time, growing numbers of Australians live and work abroad.

Permanent Migration

Table 4.1 lists the outcomes of the Migration Program[1] and the Humanitarian Program, the two elements of planned permanent migration to Australia.[2] The number of visas provided for permanent migration to Australia has increased in the last decade, reaching a high of 171,318 in 2008–2009. The Humanitarian Program has been more stable, ranging

TABLE 4.1

Permanent migrants: Migration Program and Humanitarian Program visa grants since 1984–1985

Year	MIGRATION PROGRAM				Humanitarian Program
	Family	Skill	Special eligibility	Total	
1984–1985	44,200	10,100	200	54,500	14,207
1985–1986	63,400	16,200	400	80,000	11,700
1986–1987	72,600	28,500	600	101,700	11,291
1987–1988	79,500	42,000	600	122,100	11,392
1988–1989	72,700	51,200	800	124,700	11,309
1989–1990	66,600	52,700	900	120,200	12,415
1990–1991	61,300	49,800	1,200	112,200	11,284
1991–1992	55,900	41,400	1,700	98,900	12,009
1992–1993	43,500	21,300	1,400	67,900	11,845
1993–1994	43,200	18,300	1,300	62,800	14,070
1994–1995	44,500	30,400	1,600	76,500	14,858
1995–1996	56,700	24,100	1,700	82,500	16,252
1996–1997	44,580	27,550	1,730	73,900	11,902
1997–1998	31,310	34,670	1,110	67,100	12,055
1998–1999	32,040	35,000	890	67,900	11,356
1999–2000	32,000	35,330	2,850	70,200	15,860
2000–2001	33,470	44,730	2,420	80,610	13,733
2001–2002	38,090	53,520	1,480	93,080	12,349
2002–2003	40,790	66,050	1,230	108,070	12,525
2003–2004	42,230	71,240	890	114,360	13,823
2004–2005	41,740	77,880	450	120,060	13,178
2005–2006	45,290	97,340	310	142,930	14,144
2006–2007	50,080	97,920	200	148,200	13,017
2007–2008	49,870	108,540	220	158,630	13,014
2008–2009	56,366	114,777	175	171,318	13,507
2009–2010	60,254	107,868	501	168,623	13,770
2010–2011	54,553	113,725	417	168,685	13,799

SOURCE: DIAC (2012) and Phillips, Klapdor, and Simon-Davies (2010), where detailed sources are provided.

from 11,000 to 16,000 per year. Within the Migration Program, the various categories have shown rather different trends. The Family Stream has fluctuated between a low of 31,310 in 1997–1978 and a high of over 79,500 in 1987–1988. Recent years have seen fairly high levels of family migrants: about 50,000 to 60,000. In contrast, the Skill Stream has grown steadily from just 10,100 in 1984–1985 to a peak of 114,777 in 2008–2009—just before the effects of the economic crisis began to bite. The figure for 2010–2011, 113,725, is very close to the historical peak.

Temporary Migration

Long-term temporary migrants (overseas visitors allowed to stay for 12 months or more but not permanently) have increased and in 2000–2001 outnumbered permanent arrivals for the first time. The temporary residence program was originally designed to help Australia recruit skilled workers (such as managers, IT personnel, and technicians) from overseas on a temporary basis, including working holiday makers, entertainers, and sportspeople. The two main streams of temporary migrants in recent years have been skilled workers, entering under the 457 Temporary Business (long-stay) visa, and overseas students (DIAC 2010g). Table 4.2 shows a steady increase in both.

The number of 457 Visa holders has grown rapidly and now is nearly equal to the number of permanent skilled migrants. Many temporary migrants work in the fast-growing resources sector as mine workers, tradespeople, and technicians, while others are in the manufacturing and service industries.

Another source of migrant labor, especially for agriculture and tourism, is "working holiday makers"—students and other young people mainly from British Commonwealth countries and North America who work temporarily while visiting Australia. They are a crucial source of labor for seasonal harvesting of fruit and vegetables. The number of working holiday makers has steadily increased from 78,642 in 2000–2001 to 134,388 in 2007–2008

TABLE 4.2

Temporary migrants: Overseas student and Subclass 457
(business long-stay) visa grants since 1996

Year	Overseas students	457 visas
1996–1997	113,000	25,786
1997–1998	108,827	30,880
1998–1999	110,894	29,320
1999–2000	119,806	31,070
2000–2001	146,577	36,900
2001–2002	151,894	33,510
2002–2003	162,575	36,800
2003–2004	171,616	39,500
2004–2005	174,786	49,590
2005–2006	190,674	71,150
2006–2007	228,592	87,310
2007–2008	278,180	110,570
2008–2009	320,368	101,280

SOURCE: Phillips, Klapdor, and Simon-Davies (2010), where detailed sources are given.

(Tan et al. 2009: 4). In 2008, the government introduced the Pacific Seasonal Worker Pilot Scheme to admit seasonal farm workers from Vanuatu and other Pacific islands. The scheme offered 2,500 places over the initial three years, but as of March 2011 only 270 had been recruited (DIAC 2011b).

The number of overseas students entering Australia has grown even faster than the number of 457 Visa holders. Key policy changes in the skilled migration and overseas student programs from the late 1990s onward, including the introduction of bonus points for qualifications earned in Australia; the acceptance of onshore applications for permanent residency; and the inclusion of trades on the Migration Occupations in Demand List, led to a dramatic increase in overseas students. The number of student visas granted reached a peak of 320,368 in 2008–2009, making students the largest group of temporary visa holders. The main countries of origin were China, India, and South Korea (DIAC 2010h).

Overseas students became a major source of income for Australia's higher education sector, as parents in poorer countries like China and India paid high fees to get their children marketable degrees in an English-speaking country (Khadria 2008). Yet some colleges offered training in areas of limited occupational value, like cookery and hairdressing, attracting foreign students interested in permanent settlement. In addition, a series of attacks (often racially motivated) on Indian students around 2009 led to increasing concern on the part of students and their parents. Finally, appreciation of the Australian dollar made Australia a less viable destination for international students. In early 2010, following a number of reviews of international student education and student welfare, the government introduced significant changes that may decrease numbers.

Australia now has around 650,000 temporary migrants, most of whom make significant contributions to the labor force. Not included are New Zealanders, who have the right to free entry and are sometimes only temporary labor. This represents a significant shift in Australia's historical immigration model: people who enter with a temporary perspective are likely to have different ideas about settlement and citizenship compared to those who arrive with a more permanent perspective.

RECENT EMIGRATION PATTERNS

Emigration has increased in recent years, from around 88,000 in 1981–1982 to roughly 326,000 in 2008–2009 (Productivity Commission 2010: 36), as more Australians decide to live and work abroad. Many Australians go to the United Kingdom, the United States, and New Zealand, but they also depart for newer business centers such as Hong Kong, Singapore, Shanghai, and Mumbai. Of the 86,277 people who departed permanently in 2009–2010, 50.7 percent were born overseas (DIAC 2010c). These emigrants may return to their country of birth because of homesickness or insecurity, or they may return to retire. For Australia-born people, the decision to leave permanently is usually based on economic reasons, particularly employment. This trend is likely to continue as a result of the increasing internationalization of labor markets. On the other hand, because of the GEC and Australia's relatively strong economy, many Australians have decided to return to their homeland.

ENTRY CATEGORIES

Permanent immigration has two main components: the Migration Program, which includes the Family and Skill streams, and the Humanitarian Program, which serves refugees. Another category is New Zealanders, who can enter and remain freely on the basis of the 1973 Trans-Tasman Travel Agreement.

The Migration Program

Migration Program planning numbers have fluctuated according to government priorities and economic and political considerations: the 1969 planning figure was 185,000 while that for 1975 was 50,000. In 1988, there was a peak of 145,000 during the Hawke ALP government; this was followed by a decline to 80,000 in 1992–1993 (Spinks 2010: 2). After the Howard government came to power in 1996, following an initial dip there was a gradual increase in planned immigration intake, with immigration seen as closely tied to economic growth (see Table 4.3). This upward trend was initially continued under the Rudd ALP government to a record high of 190,300 in 2008–2009. However, as the GEC developed, the actual number of visas issued was kept at a lower level; the planned intake for 2009–2010 was reduced to 168,700 and was kept at this level during 2010–2011.

The early twentieth-first century saw a shift in the Migration Program away from the Family Stream in favor of the Skill Stream. In 1996–1997, skilled migration made up 37 percent of the program; by 2008–2009, it had increased to 67 percent (DIAC 2010i). It is important to note that figures for both the Skill and the Family streams include the primary applicant (the person who applied to migrate) and secondary applicants (the primary applicant's dependents). Thus, while the majority of places are allocated to the Skill Stream,

TABLE 4.3
*Migration Program planned intake and visas granted,
1996–2011*

Year	Planned intake	Visas
1996–1997	74,000	73,900
1997–1998	68,000	67,100
1998–1999	68,000	67,900
1999–2000	70,000	70,200
2000–2001	76,000	80,610
2001–2002	85,000	93,080
2002–2003	110,000	108,070
2003–2004	110,000	114,360
2004–2005	120,000	120,060
2005–2006	140,000	142,930
2006–2007	134,000–144,000	148,200
2007–2008	152,800	158,630
2008–2009	190,300[a]	171,318
2009–2010	168,700	168,623
2010–2011	168,700	168,625

SOURCE: DIAC (2012) and Spinks (2010), where detailed sources are given.

[a]This was decreased to 171,800 in March 2009.

many of those granted visas through it are in fact family members, not skilled migrants. In 2008–2009, 55 percent of visas granted through the Skill Stream were for dependents of the primary applicant (DIAC 2010i).

Four main categories exist under the Skill Stream: (1) General skilled, for skilled workers who do not have an employer sponsor; these migrants are selected (using a points test) according to their occupation, age, skills, qualifications, English-language ability, and employability; (2) Employer Nomination, for those who have an employer sponsor; (3) Business Skills, for those promising to develop new business opportunities; and (4) Distinguished Talent, for sportspeople, musicians, artists, designers, and the like. Since 2009, skilled migrants sponsored by an employer have been given higher processing priority than independent migrants (Spinks 2010: 3–5). The Migration Occupations in Demand List was replaced on July 1, 2010, with a new, much shorter Skilled Occupation List (SOL), designed to make the Skilled Migration Program demand-driven rather than supply-driven.

The Family Stream of the Migration Program also has four main categories: Partner, Child, Parent, and Other Family. The Partner category is the largest, with around 42,000 visas granted in 2008–2009. This compares to around 8,500 Parent visas, around 3,200 Child visas, and around 2,500 Other Family visas (DIAC 2010i). In 1996–1997, the majority of visas granted by the Migration Program were in the Family Stream, accounting for 50.5 percent. The planning level for the Family Stream in 2009–2010 was set at 60,300, which represented only 35.7 percent (DIAC 2010f; Spinks 2010: 6).

The Humanitarian Program

Australia has a voluntary resettlement program for refugees, yet its response to asylum seekers has become increasingly hostile. Asylum seekers who arrive from countries like Iraq, Afghanistan, and Sri Lanka on boats often provided by Indonesian people smugglers are detained for long periods in camps and are labeled as "queue jumpers" and "security threats" by politicians and the media. As ALP Prime Minister Julia Gillard noted, "Last year Australia received 0.6 percent of the world's asylum seekers. Refugees, including those referred for resettlement by the United Nations High Commission for Refugees, make up less than 8 percent of migrants accepted in Australia. Even if all those who arrived in unauthorized boats were found to be refugees, they would still be only 1.6 percent of all migrants to Australia" (Lowy Institute 2010).

The Humanitarian Program has an offshore and an onshore component. The majority of its visas are granted under the offshore component (Karlsen, Phillips, and Koleth 2010: 12). Onshore admissions are foreigners who apply for asylum after arrival in Australia. Despite a 16 percent increase in the number of unauthorized boat arrivals in 2008–2009, these accounted for 47 percent of onshore asylum seekers in that period (see Table 4.4). The majority of onshore asylum seekers arrive in Australia by air, with a valid visa, and apply for protection (Phillips and Spinks 2011). UNHCR statistics show that asylum applications in Australia increased to 8,250 claims in 2010, up 33 percent from 2009 (UNHCR 2011: 6). Although asylum seeker numbers in Australia are relatively low, their growth is politically controversial because it is seen as undermining the tradition of strict government control of entries.

TABLE 4.4
Number of visas granted for offshore, Special Humanitarian Program (SHP), and onshore categories

	1999–2000	2000–2001	2001–2002	2002–2003	2003–2004	2004–2005	2005–2006	2006–2007	2007–2008	2008–2009
Offshore	3,802	3,997	4,160	4,976	4,134	5,511	6,022	6,003	6,004	6,499
SHP	3,051	3,116	4,258	7,280	7,669	6,585	6,736	5,313	5,110	4,630
Onshore	2,458	5,741	3,891	869	2,020	1,082	1,386	1,701	1,900	2,378

SOURCE: DIAC (2010i) and Karlsen, Phillips, and Koleth (2010).

IMMIGRATION AND POPULATION

Australia's population has increased each year since the end of World War II. In 1901, 23 percent had been born overseas, but because of low immigration in the early part of the century, by 1947 the overseas-born proportion of the population had declined to 10 percent. It then began to increase, reaching 22 percent in 1977. From then until the early 2000s, it fluctuated between 21 and 23 percent. The high immigration rates of the late 2000s led to another increase: in 2008, the estimated number of overseas-born Australians was 5.5 million, representing just over one-quarter of the total population (see Figure 4.1).

The Migration Program has radically changed Australia's population. The 1947 Census counted 7.6 million people, of whom 90 percent had been born in Australia while most of the overseas born came from the United Kingdom and Ireland. In 1971, 85 percent of the immigrant population were from Europe, including half were from the United Kingdom. From the 1970s on, European immigration declined while entries from Asia, Oceania, and Latin America increased. In the early twenty-first century, these trends continued, while entries from Africa grew. By 2009, an estimated 73.5 percent of the total population were born in Australia, followed by 11 percent from Europe, Asia (8.5 percent), Oceania (3 percent), the Middle East and Northern Africa (1.5 percent), Sub-Saharan Africa (1.3 percent), and the Americas (1.1 percent).

Australia still has no predominant minority groups, like the 2 million or so Turks in Germany or the North Africans in France. Instead, there is an Anglo-Australian majority and

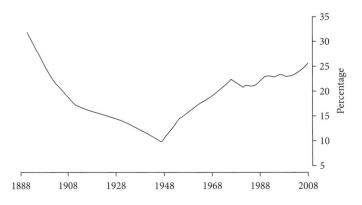

Figure 4.1   Foreign-born persons as a proportion of Australia's total population. *Source:* ABS (2010c). *Note:* Census years only until 1981. Post-1981 census data based on estimated resident population on June 30. Estimates for 2007–2008 are preliminary.

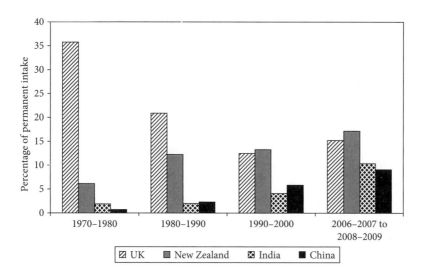

Figure 4.2 Countries of birth for settler arrivals—evolution over time. *Source:* DIAC (2010a); DIMIA (2001). *Note:* UK data for 1970–1980 includes immigrants from Ireland.

a large number of relatively small ethnic groups—variously estimated at between 100 and 200. However, diversity continues to increase—the 2006 Census indicated that 31.4 percent of the population of Sydney and 27.9 percent of the population of Melbourne spoke a language other than English at home, the most common being Arabic and Cantonese in Sydney and Italian and Greek in Melbourne (Markus, Jupp, and McDonald 2009: 7). Figure 4.2 gives an idea of the shifts in major immigrant groups' origins.

Demography has always been a highly political topic in Australia. In the early colonial period, governments encouraged high immigration in order to "people the empty spaces." Migration today is concerned primarily with economic goals, even though the population is about the same as that of metro Tokyo yet is dispersed over an area almost as large as the United States. However, much of Australia's interior is desert, so most people live in the coastal zones. Australian states experiencing negative net internal migration (notably South Australia) and with strong labor needs because of the resources boom (Western Australia and Queensland) are eager to attract immigrants, as are some rural and regional areas that lack workers and professionals (e.g., doctors).

On the other hand, the main components of population growth have altered over the years. Net overseas migration has become a greater factor than natural increase in population growth (ABS 2010a: 191). Also, aging and long-term population decline have emerged as significant demographic challenges. Whereas in 1988 the median age of the population was 31.6 years, in 2008 it reached 39.9 years (ABS 2010a: 192).

IMMIGRANTS AND THE ECONOMY

Australia's immigration policy in the 1950s aimed to recruit workers, many from rural areas of Southern Europe, for low-skilled jobs. Construction sites, mines, steelworks, and heavy industrial plants like the Snowy River Hydro-Electric Scheme served as entry points for successive waves of immigrants; few workers stayed because of hard working conditions and poor industrial relations (Collins 1991; Lever-Tracey and Quinlan 1988). Labor shortages during the boom years provided opportunities for upward mobility, including business start-ups (Collins et al. 1995). Since the 1970s, the characteristics of new immigrants have changed. Industrial restructuring reduced the need for unskilled labor, and the government aimed to attract skills in short supply in the domestic labor force.

Immigrant workers have made a crucial contribution to the growth and modernization of the Australian economy. Employers see immigration as essential for providing labor to sustain the resources boom—particularly in the export of minerals to China and Japan. Employment rates of present-day migrants can be observed through longitudinal surveys.[3] Immigrants who arrived in Australia between December 2004 and March 2005 had labor force participation rates that varied according to migration category (Skill, Family, and Humanitarian), and unemployment rates declined at considerably different speeds for each category as length of stay in Australia increased (DIAC 2010d). English-language skills have also been an important factor, with many immigrants experiencing upward mobility after they gain language proficiency and local knowledge.

However, data on employment rates may disguise significant differences between immigrant groups. Australians with ancestry linked to Lebanon, Vietnam, the Pacific Islands, and Africa had, in the past decade, much higher unemployment rates than immigrants of other ancestry, and high unemployment rates for Vietnamese and Lebanese have persisted for decades, suggesting structural rather than cyclical barriers to their employability (Collins 2010: 10). In 2006, unemployment rates for Muslim immigrants were much higher than for immigrants of other religious backgrounds (Collins 2010: 11). In comparison to the general population, recent migrants appear to be more affected by adverse conditions. For example, they were more affected by the mild economic downturn following the introduction of the Goods and Services Tax in 2000, and by the increase in unemployment during the global economic crisis.

THE IMMIGRATION POLICY REGIME

The importance of immigration is reflected in institutional structures. In 1945, the ALP government set up a Department of Immigration and there has been an immigration minister ever since. The department soon took on the additional function of providing "post-arrival services" for immigrants and became responsible for naturalization and citizenship. In the late 1960s, the Department of Immigration became the Department for Immigration and Ethnic Affairs (DIEA) to reflect emerging ethnic communities, while the 1972–1975 ALP government established a restructured Department of Immigration and Labor.

With the consolidation of multiculturalism in the late 1970s, the government restored the DIEA and included ethnic leaderships in the planning and delivery of social services; in 1987, it highlighted multicultural issues by setting up an Office of Multicultural Affairs (OMA) in the Department of the Prime Minister and Cabinet. The responsibility for immigration policy and service delivery remains in the (renamed) Department of Immigration, Local Government and Ethnic Affairs (DILGEA).

The Howard Liberal-National government abolished the OMA in 1996 and returned responsibility for multiculturalism to an again renamed Department of Immigration and Multicultural Affairs (DIMA). Philip Ruddock, immigration minister pursued a policy of increasing admissions of skilled immigrants and reducing family reunion, while cracking down on asylum seekers. In 2001, indigenous affairs was added to the (again renamed) Department of Immigration, Multicultural and Indigenous Affairs (DIMEA), much to the anger of Aboriginal leaders, who rejected the association with immigrant groups. Responsibility for indigenous affairs was moved to the Family portfolio in 2006, and in January 2007 yet another new name was announced: the Department of Immigration and Citizenship (DIAC)—the replacement of "Multicultural Affairs" with "Citizenship" was highly symbolic.

Despite the name changes, the main function of the department has remained to plan and manage the Immigration Program. The broad lines of policy are laid down by the prime minister and cabinet. Department officials draw up proposals for annual admission quotas in the various categories in consultation with interest groups and hold public hearings around Australia. Prospective immigrants (up to a million a year) apply to an Australian High Commission or Consulate, where they may be interviewed and given medical and occupational tests. Decisions are made by DIAC, which issues visas to successful applicants.

The Department is also responsible for issuing statistics and informing the public and has a small research section. Until 1996, Australia had a Bureau of Immigration, Multicultural and Population Research (BIMPR), with considerable autonomy to conduct independent peer-reviewed research. It was abolished by the Howard government in 1996, but one aspect of immigration research was maintained: the Longitudinal Survey of Immigrants to Australia (LSIA). DIAC still uses the results of these surveys and more recently initiated the Continuous Survey of Australia's Migrants (CSAM) to collect data on labor market outcomes of recent migrants from the Family and Skill streams (DIAC 2010g).

THE LEGAL FRAMEWORK

The main legislative basis for Australian immigration is the Migration Act of 1958, which mandates that all foreigners except citizens of New Zealand who wish to enter Australia must apply for visas in advance.[4] The procedure for obtaining tourist and short-stay business visas was simplified in the late 1990s so that in most cases they can now be obtained through travel agents when purchasing tickets. Despite the principle of comprehensive control, in 2010 there were estimated to be 53,900 overstayers (DIAC 2011a). Many work illegally, but DIAC seems to make little effort to detect and remove them, perhaps because so many are from the United Kingdom, the United States, and other developed countries. This is in sharp contrast with the treatment of boat people.

In the past, Australian immigration policy discriminated on the basis of race and national origins. Under the Immigration Restriction Act of 1901 (the White Australia Policy) non-Europeans were generally not admitted and certain Europeans were seen as less desirable than others. The White Australia Policy was watered down in the 1960s and finally abolished in 1972. Australia's immigration policy has since been nondiscriminatory (except for posi-tive discrimination in favor of New Zealanders).

The differences between the rights of citizens and those of lawful permanent residents are quite small (Rubinstein 1995). Immigrants enjoy a wide range of rights, including access to all employment-related, social security, and medical benefits. However, in January 1993 the ALP government decided to deny unemployment and sickness benefits to immigrants for their first six months after arrival. Fees were introduced for English-language courses for adult migrants (although refugees were exempted), and people sponsoring relatives as im-migrants had to promise to support them if they were unemployed or in need. In 1996, the Liberal-National government made further changes, increasing fees for visas and English-language courses and lengthening the waiting period for most welfare benefits to two years (Zappalà and Castles 2000).

The centerpiece of Australia's approach to incorporating immigrants has been easy ac-cess to citizenship. Australia has been considered an independent nation since 1901, but until 1949 all persons born, registered, or naturalized there were British subjects (Cronin 2001). The Nationality and Citizenship Act of 1948 defined Australians as British subjects, and naturalization required five years of residence (reduced to three years in 1973), an oath of loyalty to the British monarch, and evidence of cultural assimilation—all of which de-terred naturalization. As ethnic diversity increased, the pressure grew for a more inclusive notion of citizenship. In 1973 the law had been renamed the Australian Citizenship Act and by 1984 the waiting period had been reduced to two years and the English-language re-quirements had been relaxed. Dual citizenship was now permitted for immigrants seeking naturalization, and the oath of allegiance had become "Australia and its people" rather than to the British Queen (Castles and Davidson 2000: 165–68). In 2002, the law was further amended to allow Australians living abroad to take another citizenship without losing their Australian one, recognizing the emergence of the global Australian diaspora. The amend-ment also extended citizenship to allow a child born overseas to an Australian citizen to be eligible for registration as an Australian citizen by descent until the age of 25.

But the trend toward easier access was reversed by the Australian Citizenship Act of 2007, which introduced new provisions related to national security, extended the period of residency from two to four years for naturalization, and introduced a citizenship test. These changes followed years of debate about multiculturalism and "Australian values" that in-cluded questioning the commitment and loyalty of Australians of immigrant background, particularly given concerns about terrorism and the integration of Muslim Australians (Klapdor, Coombs, and Bohm 2009; Koleth 2010).

PUBLIC DEBATES ON IMMIGRATION

A number of groups have a special stake in immigration. For example, immigrant associa-tions want more family reunion, often for specific groups (Jupp 1993). International bodies have little influence on Australian policymaking, but sending countries have had some ef-fect when economic or financial issues are at stake. For example, when the One Nation Party unveiled an anti-Asian immigration platform, Asian media criticism influenced potential student decisions as well as investments. In 2009, protests by Indian international students in response to attacks received extensive media coverage and triggered significant public debate in India.

Business and employer groups take an active interest in immigration policy, seeing immigration as a way to strengthen the economy. The Business Council of Australia (BCA) advocates a "sustainable population strategy [with] population policies consistent with this growth path, that is, a rate of Net Overseas Migration that averages around 180,000 per annum and sustaining current fertility rates to support the natural increase of our population," with migration programs "predominantly focused on skilled migration" and "an effective temporary migration program" (BCA 2011).

Trade unions have influenced immigration policy significantly. From federation in 1901 up to the 1960s, unions largely supported the White Australia Policy. After 1947, they accepted the Migration Program only after receiving assurances that migrants would not take jobs from Australian workers. But as immigrant workers became concentrated in manufacturing, they formed an important segment of the rank and file, and trade union leaders in the 1960s and 1970s emphasized the importance of family reunion to their overseas-born members and supported the intake of refugees. Yet a certain ambivalence remained: trade unionists feared that immigration could increase unemployment, and they argued for improvements in vocational training as a substitute for skilled immigration. Trade unions have also advocated improvements in migrant workers' conditions. The president of the Australian Council of Trade Unions (ACTU) recently declared that "migration—including the humanitarian and refugee program—has played a great role in Australia's growth and prosperity and will continue to do so" and that "unions strongly reject any attempt to demonize asylum seekers for political gain" (ACTU 2010).

The environmental movement was strongly opposed to immigration in the past, but is more ambivalent today. Environmentalists opposed to immigration claim that Australia has a limited "carrying capacity" due to lack of water and thin and nutrient-poor soils (Jones 2001: 50–51). However, by 2010 Green Party policy had become much more favorable to asylum, family reunification, and multiculturalism.

PUBLIC OPINION

The 2010 Scanlon Foundation survey *Mapping Social Cohesion* examined issues related to immigration and population growth (Markus 2010). Fifty-one percent of respondents considered a projected population of 36 million in 2050 as "too high." This compares to the 42 percent who thought it "about right" or "too low." There was strong negative sentiment about the adequacy of government infrastructure for future population growth: 52 percent of respondents considered investments in infrastructure "poor" and 20 percent considered them "very poor." Only 5 percent responded negatively toward immigrants from English-speaking countries and Europe, but negative response toward immigrants from China and Vietnam was around 10 percent.

An April 2009 *Newspoll* survey found that 37 percent of voters believed that the government was doing a good job managing the asylum seeker issue, but only 36 percent believed that tougher policies would stop the flow of unauthorized boat arrivals (Phillips and Spinks 2011: 7). A survey conducted by Amnesty International in 2009 uncovered a great deal of misinformation concerning asylum seekers, with the majority of respondents believing that 80 percent of asylum seekers in Australia arrived by boat (Phillips and Spinks 2011: 7). Polling conducted by the Lowy Institute in 2010 found that 78 percent of Australians were either somewhat concerned or very concerned about asylum seekers coming to Australia by boat (Hanson 2010: 3–4; Phillips and Spinks 2011: 7).

The media have played a major role in turning public opinion against "boat people." Although Australia is a signatory to the UN Refugee Convention, boat people have been accused of being "queue jumpers" and of costing Australians billions of dollars. The idea of "queue jumpers" reveals a misleading discourse about the difference between onshore and offshore components of Australia's Humanitarian Program as well as a misunderstanding about the difference between an asylum seeker and a refugee. However, it is very difficult to evaluate public attitudes independent of political influences: government policies and political leadership do a lot to shape public opinion.

ETHNIC RIGHTS AND ANTI-RACISM

The late 1960s and early 1970s saw the beginning of major transformations in Australia as new movements challenged the social and political fabric of many Western democracies. The expansion of the welfare state was linked to the emergence of nongovernmental organizations (NGOs) and community activists that called for greater social equity and the inclusion of disadvantaged groups into society and polity via *rights* and *participation*. Both first- and second-generation immigrants became involved in the development and delivery of services at the community level.

Immigrant associations had been initially established in response to the cultural and social concerns of specific ethnic communities. However, the introduction of social policies aimed specifically at immigrants, first by the ALP and then by the coalition government, put a premium on ethnic mobilization and on formation of associations to speak in the name of immigrants (Vasta 1993). The emergence of multicultural policies and services became linked to the development of formal ethnic lobbying groups, including the state Ethnic Communities Councils (ECCs) and the Federation of Ethnic Communities Councils of Australia (FECCA).

Immigrants do not constitute a united political force, mainly because the differences among them are as great as those among the Anglo-Australian population (Jupp 1993: 220). Nevertheless, the sheer size of the migrant population in certain electorates generates an ethnic vote that politicians must heed. Migrant representation at state and federal levels is low but increasing. The ratio of ethnic and indigenous members to the total number of members of parliament is 20 to 135 in New South Wales; 24 to 150 in Commonwealth, and 27 to 128 in Victoria. However, the political influence of immigrants cannot be reduced to their role in formal institutions: community networks and associations acting as pressure groups mediate between individuals and those institutions. The growing relationship between government and ethnic communities was encouraged by the fact that many second-generation immigrants had become career public servants, making them both government officials and ethnic lobbyists.

The Howard government of 1996–2007 weakened the power of public institutions. For example, the Human Rights and Equal Opportunity Commission (HREOC) was weakened by reducing the number of commissioners. At the same time, the concern of many Australians about the recession of the early 1990s and the impact of globalization on their economic and social situation opened up the cultural and political space for resurgent anti-immigration sentiments, including the nationalistic One Nation Party (Vasta 1999). Furthermore, disaffection with multiculturalism was increased by fears and insecurities emanating from the aftermath of 9/11, the Bali bombings of 2002, and the invasion of Iraq in 2003. A major study undertaken by HREOC in 2004 revealed that Arab and Muslim Australians were experiencing heightened discrimination and vilification (HREOC 2004).

Issues of racism arose after the Cronulla riots of 2005, when groups of white "surfer" youths attacked youths "of Middle Eastern appearance" in a beachside suburb of Sydney, prompting hundreds of Lebanese-origin youths to retaliate. Right-wing talk radio hosts called on white youth to mobilize, and the results were civil disturbances and further isolation of Australia's Lebanese Muslims. Much research has been conducted on the Cronulla events (Collins 2010; Noble 2010; Wise and Velayutham 2009), but the issues have not been fully resolved and many Muslim Australians remain reluctant to visit Cronulla (Wise 2008). Such localized grievances have prompted much debate about Australian national identity and the role of nationalism and racism in Australia.

SOCIAL POLICY: FROM ASSIMILATION TO MULTICULTURALISM

Australia's postwar immigration policy was not intended to create a multicultural society. Instead, the goal was to maintain homogeneity. But without enough British immigrants, recruitment was broadened to other parts of Europe and assimilation was introduced to turn Dutch, Polish, Italian, and Greek immigrants into "New Australians." This was successful in some ways, as immigrants found work, settled, and became citizens, but it was also a failure because of labor market segmentation and residential segregation, inadequate schooling, and racism. As integration policy, assimilation did not work. This was the context for multiculturalism in the early 1970s. The aim was to redress class and ethnic minority disadvantages by improving educational facilities and social services. Recognition of cultural differences, and working with ethnic community associations, was vital to social reform. Successive governments continued these policies, although each gave them a new character to fit wider political agendas.

Australian multiculturalism has had two main aspects. The first is equality, to ensure immigrant participation in all societal institutions. The second is the principle that migrants have the right to pursue their own religion and languages and to establish communities. The Howard government (1996–2007) had strong reservations about multiculturalism. At first, Howard advocated a move back toward the assimilationism of the 1950s, a goal that Australia's culturally diverse society made unattainable. Subsequently, the government launched *A New Agenda for Multicultural Australia* (DIMA 1999), which largely endorsed the principles of the ALP's 1989 *National Agenda* (OMA 1989). The core values were reworked as "civic duty, cultural respect, social equity and productive diversity," and the *New Agenda* argued that multiculturalism must be an inclusive concept in terms of nationhood and identity "for all Australians." As Hage pointed out, this version of Australian multiculturalism corresponded with Howard's underlying belief in the essentially European nature of Australian society: "We are, as all of you know, a projection of Western civilization in this part of the world. We have inherited the great European values of liberal democracy" (Howard, quoted by Hage 2001).

The Howard government's next multicultural policy statement *United in Diversity* (Commonwealth of Australia 2003) was strategically framed in the context of concerns about terrorism and diversity. This was followed by the Citizenship Act of 2007, which introduced a citizenship test that asked new migrants about their knowledge of Australian history and culture. The booklet *Life in Australia*, provided by the Department of Immigration and Citizenship to potential immigrants, begins with an "Australian Value Statement" but "the supporting documents make no mention of multiculturalism as an Australian value or even a momentary dimension of Australian policy" (Jakubowicz 2009: 30). Similarly, in her analysis of the citizenship test, Tilbury found it to focus on homogeneity and suggested that it is mainly targeted at Muslims "who are seen to have values diametrically opposite to those of Australia" (Tilbury 2007). A review of the citizenship test found that it was "flawed, intimidating and discriminatory." In response, the new Rudd Labor government, in late 2007, pledged to change the test (Klapdor, Coombs, and Baum 2009: 19).

It was not until February 2011 that the ALP government announced its new multicultural policy. The policy's four principles focused on (1) cultural diversity for national unity, community harmony, and democratic values; (2) a just, inclusive, and socially cohesive society; (3) the economic benefits of a multicultural nation; (4) promoting understanding and acceptance while responding to expressions of intolerance and discrimination (DIAC 2011c: (5). Coalition leader Tony Abbott publicly (albeit hesitantly) called on the Liberal and National parties to affirm the principles of multiculturalism and a nondiscriminatory immigration policy, despite a strong right-wing polemic, particularly in the media, against multiculturalism (see Sheridan 2011).

THE NEW IMMIGRATION PANIC

Over the past sixty-five years, immigration has always been a political issue, yet in the past two decades migration and multiculturalism have become even more volatile. Before the March 1996 federal election, several Liberal and National candidates criticized the provision of special services for immigrants and Aboriginal people. Pauline Hanson, who was expelled from the Liberal party because of her extreme statements, won a seat as an Independent. Hanson attacked Aboriginal people, called for stopping immigration and abolishing multiculturalism, and warned of "the Asianization" of Australia. She went on to found the One Nation Party.

The situation was exacerbated by the increase in boat-people arrivals in Northern Australia starting in the mid-1990s. Numbers were not high by international standards—no more than 4,000 a year—but they provoked popular outrage very different from the reactions to boat-people arrivals from Southeast Asia in the 1970s, when the Fraser coalition government supported Vietnamese refugees (McMaster 2001: 54). In contrast, Philip Ruddock, the immigration minister, attacked the asylum seekers of the late 1990s as "queue jumpers," claiming that they took places from "genuine" refugees and were a threat to Australian sovereignty.

Matters came to a head in August 2001, when the Norwegian freighter *MV Tampa* picked up over 400 asylum seekers (mainly originating in Afghanistan and Iraq) from a sinking boat off Northern Australia, and the government refused to allow the ship to offload. Border control legislation passed in the aftermath of the *Tampa* incident called for the "excision" of Australian territories in the Indian ocean from Australia's migration zone and the establishment of offshore detention and processing facilities on Manus Island in Papua New Guinea (PNG) and Nauru (the "Pacific Solution"). Also included in the legislation were temporary protection visas (TPVs), which meant a denial of permanent residency for people attempting to enter Australia illegally, and refusal of refugee status for people who concealed their identity by destroying their documents. Through the Pacific Solution, Australia tried to export asylum seekers to its Pacific neighbors. Many asylum seekers (including children) languished for up to three years in camps (both in Australia and offshore), where hunger strikes, riots, self-inflicted injuries, and even suicide became commonplace. The government also introduced a series of legal measures to limit the right to judicial review in asylum matters (Crock and Saul 2002: chap. 5).

The Rudd Labor government introduced changes to asylum policy in 2007 that included abolishing TPVs and ending the Pacific Solution. However, it also retained some key elements, namely mandatory detention, the excision of certain Australian territories from the migration zone, and offshore processing on Christmas Island of asylum seekers arriving by boat (Karlsen, Phillips, and Koleth 2010). A significant increase in the number of unauthorized boat arrivals from 2008 to 2010 ensured that "border protection" was a central issue in the 2010 federal election. Both major parties treated boat arrivals as a threat to national sovereignty and security, and promised to strengthen border protection and anti-people-smuggling measures.

In early 2011, Prime Minister Gillard tried to persuade the government of East Timor to set up a detention and determination facility to which Australia could send asylum seekers. When East Timor refused, Gillard started negotiating with Malaysia to send asylum seekers for processing there, even though Malaysia is not a signatory to the UN Refugee Convention. This "solution" was prohibited by the High Court of Australia, which ruled that it contravened Australia's international obligations under the 1951 UN Refugee Convention. The ALP government then set up a small committee, led by former Air Force chief Angus Houston, to find a new policy that might gain support from all main parties. The Houston Committee reported in June 2012, proposing offshore processing on the islands of Nauru, PNG, and elsewhere, if the obstacles could be resolved. By late 2012, large numbers of refugees had been sent to Nauru and PNG, but boats full of asylum seekers were continuing to arrive on Australian shores. The government's hope of deterring boat arrivals by sending them offshore, detaining them under very basic conditions, and taking years to determine whether they will be granted refugee status, has clearly proved illusory. People fleeing persecution will come whatever the conditions they are exposed to, and the asylum debate remains very much alive. However, the public obsession with asylum had diverted attention from other major changes taking place at present, notably the growth of temporary migration.

CONCLUSION

Australia's immigration model since 1947 has been based on the assumptions of controllability of migration flows, the need to build up the population, the existence of large reserves of people with the right skills who want to come to Australia, and the desire of most immigrants to settle permanently and become Australian citizens. Since the 1970s, the White Australia Policy and its emphasis on European (especially British) immigration have been replaced by a worldwide intake that claims to be nondiscriminatory, with most new immigrants coming from Asia and Oceania. The principles of homogeneity and assimilation have been displaced by diverse urban populations and multiculturalism; moreover, the focus of immigration has shifted from population building to economic benefits.

These major transformations remain controversial. Australians are ambivalent: most people seem to support immigration and diversity, but are worried about changes in the composition of flows and in the characteristics of newcomers. Attitudes to migration vary according to social class: working and lower-middle-class groups that feel threatened by globalization and economic change often oppose immigration and multiculturalism. Views also vary according to location. Residents of cities that have historically attracted newcomers—especially Sydney and Melbourne—may blame housing shortages and traffic congestion on immigrants, yet they may also welcome cultural diversity. States with labor shortages—South Australia and Western Australia—and regional areas that need workers and professionals may seek to attract immigrants and yet worry about the effects of immigration on existing ways of life. Consistency of attitudes is often absent.

New transitions are taking place, often without much discussion or preparation. The shift from family to economic migration has been accompanied by rapid growth in temporary entries for work and study. Annual intakes of temporary entrants are now greater than those of permanent settlers. Temporary migrants often intend to leave after a few years—although unknown numbers end up staying on. The motivations of temporary migrants are varied, breaking the clear distinctions between temporary and permanent migration. The fluidity of relationships and the ease of transport and communication arising from global and regional integration processes are changing the meaning of international migration.

The meaning of citizenship is also changing, as temporary or circular migration grows and transnational linkages become more significant. Many people who migrate to Australia do not want to stay permanently. At the same time, the government, through the 2007 Citizenship Act, has made it harder for immigrants to become citizens; this could backfire because Australia's model of immigration and multiculturalism has been successful in large part because it offers strong rights and the chance of building a new life. Measures that encourage the growth of a mobile and unattached "guest worker" labor force may have negative social and cultural implications.

For a traditional country of immigration, understanding these transformations is crucial. The assimilation policies of the 1950s and 1960s failed—the result of labor market segmentation, residential segregation, and community formation. Australia moved to multiculturalism to recognize diversity and prevent social exclusion. Successive governments have endorsed multiculturalism—but increasingly reluctantly, and with a new emphasis on social cohesion. Still, the multicultural society of today is very different from that of 1973 or even 1989: diversity of origins, class, religion, and culture is much greater and aspirations have changed. Moreover, many people have life orientations that include strong linkages across borders, suggesting the need for a multicultural model that is open not only to ethnic identities but also to transnational relationships and, indeed, to multilevel attachments.

All of these changes are under-researched and poorly understood. The demolition of Australia's independent research capacity has led to a severe deficit in the capacity to analyze existing transformations and future trends. Australian leaders and the public seem inadequately prepared to rethink the meaning of the country's place in the region and the world, and the ways in which human mobility is changing.

NOTES

1. One limitation is the fact that the offshore visa recipients included in these numbers may not actually arrive and settle in the country in the year the visa was issued.

2. Note that Australian data are presented for financial years, which go from July 1 to June 30. The definitions and scope of the various programs will be discussed later on.

3. See below for more information on the longitudinal surveys.

4. The 1973 Trans-Tasman Agreement provides free movement for Australians and New Zealanders. In 1994, the Special Category Visa (SCV) was introduced for New Zealand citizens, but this had minimal practical impact: a SCV is electronically recorded and the passport stamped with a date of arrival in Australia. Statistically, New Zealanders are not counted as part of Australia's annual planned migration program, but their numbers are included in the Settler Arrivals reports and in total net overseas migration (when the intention is to stay for a 12-month period).

REFERENCES

ABS (Australian Bureau of Statistics). 2010a. *2009–2010 Yearbook*. Canberra: ABS.
———. 2010b. *3412.0 Migration Australia*. Canberra: ABS.
ACTU (Australian Council of Trade Unions). 2010. "Unions Call for Politicians to Stay Calm on Asylum Seekers and Maintain Humane Approach."
BCA (Business Council of Australia). 2011. *Submission on the Development of Australia's Sustainable Population Strategy*. Melbourne: BCA.
Blainey, G. 1984. *All for Australia*. Sydney: Methuen Haynes.
Castles, S., B. Cope, M. Kalantzis, and M. Morrissey. 1988. *Mistaken Identity— Multiculturalism and the Demise of Nationalism in Australia*. Sydney: Pluto Press.

Castles, S., and A. Davidson. 2000. *Citizenship and Migration: Globalisation and the Politics of Belonging*. London: Macmillan.

Collins, J. 1991. *Migrant Hands in a Distant Land: Australia's Post-War Immigration*. 2nd ed. Sydney: Pluto Press.

———. 2010. "Immigrants, Unemployment, Social Disadvantage and the Global Financial Crisis in Australia." Paper presented at the Immigration in Harder Times: The United States and Australia Workshop, Prato, Italy, May.

Collins, J., K. Gibson, C. Alcorso, S. Castles, and D. Tait. 1995. *A Shop Full of Dreams: Ethnic Small Business in Australia*. Sydney: Pluto Press.

Commonwealth of Australia. 2003. *Multicultural Australia: United in Diversity*. Canberra: Commonwealth of Australia.

Crock, M., and B. Saul. 2002. *Future Seekers: Refugees and the Law in Australia*. Sydney: Federation Press.

Cronin, K. 2001. "The Legal Status of Immigrants and Refugees." In *The Australian People: An Encyclopedia of the Nation, the People and Their Origins*, edited by J. Jupp, 792–95. Cambridge: Cambridge University Press.

de Lepervanche, M. 1975. "Australian Immigrants 1788–1940: Desired and Unwanted." In *Essays in the Political Economy of Australian Capitalism*, edited by E. L. Wheelwright and K. Buckley, 1: 72–104. Sydney: Australia & New Zealand Book Co.

DIAC (Department of Immigration and Citizenship). 2010a. "Fact Sheet 2: Key Facts in Immigration."

———. 2010b. "Fact Sheet 4: More Than 60 Years of Post-War Migration."

———. 2010c. "Fact Sheet 5: Emigration from Australia."

———. 2010d. "Fact Sheet 14: Migrant Labour Market Outcomes."

———. 2010e. "Fact Sheet 15: Population Projections."

———. 2010f. "Fact Sheet 29: Overview of Family Stream Migration."

———. 2010g. "Fact Sheet 47: Temporary Residence in Australia."

———. 2010h. "Fact Sheet 50: Overseas Students in Australia."

———. 2010i. *Population Flows: Immigration Aspects 2008–09 Edition*. Canberra: DIAC.

———. 2011a. "Fact Sheet 86: Overstayers and Other Unlawful Non-Citizens."

———. 2011b. "The Pacific Seasonal Worker Pilot Scheme Fact Sheet."

———. 2011c. "The People of Australia—Australia's Multicultural Policy."

———. 2012. *2010–11 Migration Program Report*. Canberra: DIAC. http://www.immi.gov.au/media/statistics/pdf/report-on-migration-program-2010-11.pdf.

DIMA (Department of Immigration and Multicultural Affairs). 1999. *A New Agenda for Multicultural Australia*. Canberra: DIMA.

Hanson, F. 2010. *Lowy Institute Poll 2010 Australia and the World: Public Opinion and Foreign Policy*. Sydney: Lowy Institute for International Policy.

HREOC (Australian Human Rights and Equal Opportunity Commission). 2004. *Isma–Listen: National Consultations on Eliminating Prejudice against Arab and Muslim Australians*. Sydney: HREOC.

Jakubowicz, A. 2009. "The Risk of Diversity." *Around the Globe* 6 (1): 25–33.

Jones, A. 2001. "The Business Council of Australia's Case for Population Growth: An Ecological Critique." *People and Place* 9 (2): 49–57.

Jupp, J. 1993. "The Ethnic Lobby and Immigration Policy." In *The Politics of Australian Immigration*, edited by J. Jupp and M. Kabala, 204–21. Canberra: Australian Government Publishing Service.

Karlsen, E., J. Phillips, and E. Koleth. 2010. "Seeking Asylum: Australia's Humanitarian Program." Background note, Australian Parliamentary Library, Canberra.

Khadria, B. 2008. "India: Skilled Migration to Developed Countries, Labour Migration to the Gulf." In *Migration and Development: Perspectives from the South*, edited by S. Castles and R. Delgado Wise, 79–112. Geneva: International Organization for Migration.

Klapdor, M., M. Coombs, and C. Bohm. 2009. "Australian Citizenship: A Chronology of Major Developments in Policy and Law." Background note, Australian Parliamentary Library, Canberra.

Koleth, E. 2010. "Overseas Students: Immigration Policy Changes 1997–May 2010." Background note, Australian Parliamentary Library, Canberra.

Lever-Tracey, C., and M. Quinlan. 1988. *A Divided Working Class*. London: Routledge & Kegan Paul.

Lowy Institute. 2010. "Moving Australia Forward." Speech by Julia Gillard to the Lowy Institute for International Policy.

MacQueen, H. 1970. *A New Britannia*. Victoria: Penguin.

Markus, A. 2010. *Mapping Social Cohesion 2010*. Victoria: Monash Institute for the Study of Global Movements.

Markus, A., J. Jupp, and P. McDonald. 2009. *Australia's Immigration Revolution*. Sydney: Allen & Unwin.

McMaster, D. 2001. *Asylum Seekers: Australia's Response to Refugees*. Melbourne: Melbourne University Press.

Noble, G., ed. 2010. *Lines in the Sand: The Cronulla Riots and the Limits of Australian Multiculturalism*. Sydney: Institute of Criminology Press.

OMA (Office of Multicultural Affairs). 1989. *National Agenda for a Multicultural Australia*. Canberra: Australian Government Publishing Service.

Phillips, J., M. Klapdor, and J. Simon-Davies. 2010. "Migration to Australia since Federation: A Guide to the Statistics." Background note, Australian Parliamentary Library, Canberra.

Phillips, J., and H. Spinks. 2011. "Boat Arrivals in Australia since 1976." Background note, Australian Parliamentary Library, Canberra.

Productivity Commission. 2010. *Population and Migration: Understanding the Numbers*. Melbourne: Productivity Commission.

Reynolds, H. 1987. *Frontier*. Sydney: Allen & Unwin.

Rubinstein, K. 1995. "Citizenship in Australia: Unscrambling Its Meaning." *Melbourne University Law Review* 20 (2): 503–27.

Sheridan, G. 2011. "How I Lost Faith in Multiculturalism." *Weekend Australian*, April 2–3.

Spinks, H. 2010. "Australia's Migration Program." Background note, Australian Parliamentary Library, Canberra.

Tan, Y., S. Richardson, L. Lester, T. Bai, and L. Sun. 2009. *Evaluation of Australia's Working Holiday Maker (WHM) Program*. Adelaide: National Institute of Labour Studies, Flinders University.

Tilbury, F. 2007. "The Retreat from Multiculturalism: The Australian Experience." Paper presented at the Third Global Conference on Pluralism, Inclusion and Citizenship, Salzburg.

UNHCR (United Nations High Commissioner for Refugees). 2011. *Asylum Levels and Trends in Industrialized Countries 2010.* Geneva: UNHCR.

Vasta, E. 1993. "Immigrant Women and the Politics of Resistance." *Australian Feminist Studies* 8 (18): 185–223.

———. 1999. "Multicultural Politics and Resistance: Migrants Unite?" In *The Future of Australian Multiculturalism*, edited by G. Hage and R. Couch, 133–42. Sydney: Research Institute for Humanities and Social Sciences, Sydney University.

Wise, A. 2008. *Engaging Muslim Communities: A Research Project on Community Based Strategies to Promote Engagement and Dialogue between Muslim and Non-Muslim Australians.* Canberra: Department of Immigration and Citizenship.

Wise, A., and S. Velayutham. 2009. *Everyday Multiculturalism.* Basingstoke, UK: Palgrave.

Zappalà, G., and S. Castles. 2000. "Citizenship and Immigration in Australia." In *From Migrants to Citizens: Membership in a Changing World*, edited by T. A. Aleinikoff and D. Klusmeyer, 32–81. Washington, DC: Carnegie Endowment for International Peace.

COMMENTARY

Gary Freeman

Castles, Vasta, and Ozkul authoritatively lay out both the historical and current characteristics of Australian immigration policy and the institutional structure of the various immigration regimes that have emerged in Australia from time to time. They carefully document the continuities and abrupt and not so abrupt changes in immigration and integration policy. Their overview raises interesting issues, not least of which is the causal argument that is implicit in their analysis.

The authors chart both the long history of immigration to Australia and its notable expansion in recent times. First, they point out its accelerated pace and scale, the appearance of asylum seekers arriving by ship, and the degree to which Australian governments seem either to have lost control or to have deliberately driven legal immigration into high gear— a transformation labeled an "immigration revolution" by some. They then conclude that it is to be expected that public debates on immigration, population, and multiculturalism are never far from the headlines.

This discussion usefully raises the question of whether there is a natural level of acceptance or rejection of immigration that we would expect to find wherever international migration takes place and be surprised only when in a particular country it is much lower or much higher than the norm. I do not mean something as formulaic as the "threshold of tolerance" enunciated in France in 1989. Instead, I refer to the common experience of receiving countries. Only Canada comes to mind as a traditional immigration country where there is a strong pro-immigration consensus in the face of a truly massive immigrant presence. Switzerland and Greece, on the other hand, may be examples of countries more unhappy with immigration than is normal among Western democracies. Locating what is a "normal" response to immigration is a serious matter because scholars tend to bring with them their expectations of appropriate behavior that may color their interpretations. Some immigration analysts are as "shocked, shocked" as Captain Renault in the movie *Casablanca* to find uneasiness about immigration, while others seem always to expect the worst.

At the risk of being counted in the latter category, I would put it this way: all known migrations in human history have brought in their train competition, displacement, and hostility; some more, some less. Australia has experienced both extremes: the near total extermination of the indigenous population and three-quarters of a century of the White Australia Policy. What is striking about the Australian case is the equanimity with which white Australians have in recent decades greeted peoples who were previously excluded but now arrive in numbers so large as to put in process the gradual transformation of white Australians into a minority. It is hardly surprising that European states, lacking the motivation of settling new and "unoccupied" territories, have been beset by hostile natives, individual acts of violence, and the emergence of extremist anti-immigrant movements and parties. What is surprising is how comparatively mild these sorts of reactions have been.

When I read this chapter as an analytical and explanatory essay, the lines of argument are provocative but not altogether clear. The contributors to this volume were not given a charge to develop a theoretical argument, but outlines of at least a causal pathway can be glimpsed in this chapter. The argument goes something like this.

Globalization (communications, travel, interdependence, transnational norms and institutions) is mostly composed of phenomena that emerge because of autarchic trends of a developing world economy. To the extent that they are the consequence of human artifice, they are more the result of private-sector initiatives than deliberate state actions. Confronted with these changes, states may either attempt to adapt or decide not to adapt. If they adapt, they adopt policies that take the global economy as given and open themselves to migration, creating a more welcoming society, building explicit multicultural institutions, and downgrading expectations of citizenship and permanent settlement and loyalty. States that do not adapt experience much the same outcomes—substantial migration, accelerating ethnic diversity, and multicultural institutions. In addition, however, because these outcomes are the result of failed controls, ineffective selection, and a less formally welcoming society, they get less well-integrated immigrants and more contentious ethnic diversity that in turn provokes heightened racism.

I realize that I am putting the case much more explicitly than Castles, Vasta, and Ozkul do or perhaps think fair. Their discussion is, nonetheless, a good vehicle for thinking about the options states have in this era of globalization. As I portray it, theirs is a strongly top-down model, suggesting that changes in the global context create conditions that states have little choice but to embrace. From this perspective, adaptation is the desired and rational course and failure to adapt a quixotic effort bound to fail.

The authors conclude, rightly in my view, that Australia has steered a kind of middle course as successive governments of both the left and the right have given immigration policy the appearance of one step forward, two steps back. Optimists like Castles, Vasta, and Ozkul advocate a more consistent adaptive policy in line with the realities of the global environment. They see that opposition to immigration and the expression of racism is "still" strong, but they give the impression that it is a puzzling but ultimately temporary recrudescence of outmoded, premodern impulses that cannot prevail in the end against the cosmopolitanism of the new world into which we are inevitably being thrown.

Australia has tried to adapt by eliminating racial and national discrimination in admissions, expanding temporary migration programs, self-consciously seeking to use liberal immigration policies to enhance its trading relationships with Asian neighbors, and encouraging the establishment of educational programs to attract skilled foreign labor. But these modern initiatives were merely grafted onto more traditional policies such as the large, politically potent family migration program. When uninvited asylum seekers began to arrive by boat on its northern shores, Australia responded with extraordinarily tough measures to discourage further arrivals. The larger part of Australian policy is still directed at annual admissions of selected and family-related immigrants seeking to settle permanently and become Australians. States like Australia that have followed a middle course either deliberately or by default now have an increasingly chaotic system looking more and more like the American model, which is no model at all. Anyone who offers the US immigration system as a standard to which the wise should repair, as General Washington hoped the Philadelphia constitution would be, has drunk the Kool-Aid of immigration enthusiasts. Certainly, US policy is not a model that our authors embrace.

Castles, Vasta, and Ozkul provide some intriguing evidence to account for the disarray of Australian policy. They note that the Australian state, for most of its history, has commonly directed immigration policy with something of an iron fist. They identify what seems these days to be an energized civil society that is able to constrain the immigration bureaucracy. They focus extensively on the important role of stakeholders, who turn out to be a large, rambunctious, and diverse set of interests that in their telling appears capable at times of overwhelming the government. The traditional story of state autonomy, punctuated occasionally by populist outbursts, seems to give way either to strong domestic interest groups that have fluctuating power depending on the government of the day—the domestic politics model—or to external pressures from the international system—the familiar globalization thesis model.

One question that the chapter prompts me to ask is whether in current circumstances the traditional countries of immigration for permanent settlement are moving willy-nilly toward regimes of temporary migration. Are traditional immigration countries a thing of the past? There has been a tendency for scholars to treat countries open to permanent immigration as better suited to the challenges of a globalizing world. European states that sought to construct a "Fortress Europe" were destined to pass up immigration's substantial economic and fiscal benefits. The Australian case, as described by Castles, Vasta, and Ozkul, is showing signs not of ending permanent settlement as a policy goal but of accepting, in addition, more temporary migrants selected for skill. In this way, Australia may hope to more efficiently extract the contribution migrants can make to the economy while avoiding housing them during their unproductive childhood and old age. Both the United States and Canada display the same recent inroads of expanding temporary migrant programs. I leave aside here reference to the massive literature showing that temporary or rotational migration schemes work only in authoritarian political systems. Disappointments are surely in store for those who design such schemes.

Migration for settlement was both sensible and inevitable when the New World had continents to people and travel across the seas was expensive and dangerous. These conditions have changed. Only Canada is still earnestly devoted to immigration as a means of national development, hoping to persuade millions to move to the icy north or the vacant prairies. Australia's commitment to settlement in its arid outback seems less firm and less credible than in the past. Other rich societies are unlikely either to try or to be able to follow in their paths. Immigration for permanent settlement was an endeavor suited to the unique period and circumstances associated with the founding of new states. It is not as obviously relevant to the postindustrial age we live in today.

III

COUNTRIES OF IMMIGRATION

5

FRANCE

Immigration and the Republican Tradition in France

James F. Hollifield

Unlike other European countries, France has a long history of immigration dating back to the middle of the nineteenth century, when industrialization began in earnest. France was not the only European country compelled to import labor to feed the fires of industrialization. British industry relied on Irish workers throughout the 1900s, while Germany brought in Poles and others from East Central Europe to work in mining and heavy industry in the *Ruhrgebiet*, especially during the period of intensive economic development in the 1880s and 1890s (Herbert 1986).

What distinguishes France from other European countries is its early willingness to accept foreigners as settlers, immigrants, and citizens. The acceptance of foreigners as potential citizens is part and parcel of a *republican* tradition, which stems from the French Revolution. Republicanism is strongly egalitarian, anti-clerical (*laïque*), and opposed to monarchy, instead stressing popular sovereignty, citizenship, and the rights of man. It can be nationalist and imperialist while at the same time promoting universal political values, such as equal protection of all individuals before the law. As an ideology and a form of government, republicanism was bitterly contested in France throughout the nineteenth and well into the twentieth century (Hoffmann 1963; Hollifield and Ross 1991; Lewis 2007).

Early in the twentieth century, the French state began to lay the legal foundations for nationality, which was to be based on the birthright principle of soil (*jus soli*) rather than blood (*jus sanguinis*) as in Germany (Brubaker 1992; Weil 2002; Noiriel 1988). Thus, the republican tradition found its expression in a more open and expansive notion of citizenship, similar (but not identical) to the birthright principle enunciated in the Fourteenth Amendment to the US Constitution ("All persons born or naturalized in the United States, and subject to the jurisdiction thereof, are citizens of the United States"); it is in stark contrast to the narrow, ethnocultural vision of citizenship that evolved in Germany of the Second Reich.

While Germany was struggling with the issues of national and territorial unification and would continue to do so, one could argue, until 1989–1990, France was becoming more comfortable with its revolutionary and republican heritage, as reflected in an expansive policy of immigration and naturalization. As I have argued elsewhere, the relationship between immigration and nation building is critical in enabling democratic states to man-age immigration and finesse the gap between policy outputs and outcomes (Hollifield 1986, 1997). Hence, a key argument in this chapter is that the more closely associated immigra-tion is with the political myths that legitimate and give life to the regime, the easier it is for governments to justify immigration and immigrant policies and to manage the ethnic and distributional conflicts that inevitably arise as a result of immigration.

As a cornerstone of French political and legal culture, republicanism has played a vital role in the country's history of immigration. Immigration accelerated in France during the latter decades of the nineteenth century. It was associated not only with the triumph of republicanism but also with industrialization, which was slow and late by comparison with Britain and even Germany. To sustain a surge in economic growth during *la belle époque*, French industry needed access to additional supplies of labor that they could not find at home. The reasons for labor shortages during this period were two-fold. Because of the revolutionary land settlement that gave French peasant-farmers legal control of their land, there was no large rural exodus in France in the nineteenth century comparable to what happened in Germany and Britain. Also, the labor shortage was compounded by anemic population growth due to the demographic transition that had occurred earlier in France than in any other society (Spengler 1938). Taken together, these two factors—a stagnant population and a weak rural exodus—set the stage for a rise in immigration in the latter half of the nineteenth century.

THE DEMOGRAPHIC AND REPUBLICAN NEXUS

Immigration started in earnest following the revolutions of 1848 and rose steadily dur-ing the Second Empire, intensifying during the early republican period (1870–1890) and lasting through *la belle époque* and the turn of the century. Without a strong rural exodus as occurred in Britain and Germany, French capitalists were forced to invent a working class largely through the private recruitment of foreign labor. Historically, it was left to the private sector to organize this recruitment, which accelerated to the point that the state was compelled to step in to try to regain control. Immigration during the early decades of the twentieth century was *organized but uncontrolled*, and the republican model served primarily to integrate newcomers, turning immigrant workers into French citizens, just as French peasants had been socialized into a modern, republican culture (via schools—*l'école laïque*—and the Army) two or three generations earlier (Berger 1972; Weber 1976).

During the First World War, the first steps were taken by the state to assert control over immigration, through the establishment of national identity cards. By imposing controls, the state created a national/legal identity for the population, native as well as foreign (Noir-iel 1988). After World War I, French industry was again faced with dramatic labor shortages because of the crippling effects of the war itself. In the early 1920s, two major interest groups emerged that would influence French immigration policy for decades to come. First were employers, who created the Société Générale d'Immigration (SGI)—a private organization that, with the blessings of the divided and stalemated governments of the 1920s, took as its mission the organization of recruitment and placement of immigrant labor (primarily

Italian and Polish). Second were the pronatalists of the Alliance Nationale Pour l'Accroissement de la Population Française, long active in Third Republic politics. Employers were interested in securing an unlimited supply of cheap, foreign labor; the pronatalists were inspired by a nationalist impulse to increase birth rates and grow the population.

The pronatalists were closely identified with the fascist Vichy regime, only to be rehabilitated and transformed into the *populationnistes* of the Fourth and Fifth Republics (Teitelbaum and Winter 1985). Beginning with the provisional Tripartite Government, the *populationnistes* took immigration as one of their primary concerns, providing a new rallying cry during the period 1945–1950, when population policies were still viewed with suspicion because of their association with eugenics, *Pétainisme*, and fascism. The thrust of the populationists' policies was outlined in the first issue of the French demographic journal *Population* in two articles by Alfred Sauvy (1950). He made the case for large-scale recruitment of Italian and Spanish immigrant workers and their families, arguing that such a strategy would give the French population (and by extension the economy) a fighting chance to catch up with more powerful European competitors, primarily Germany and Britain.

The *populationnistes* had a powerful ally in Charles de Gaulle, who helped them shape postwar French immigration policy. The thinking of the early Gaullist reformers, especially Jean Monnet, who was to head the newly created national planning agency—le Commissariat General du Plan—was that all necessary resources should be mobilized to modernize the economy. For the technocrats, modernization should be done quickly to take advantage of the political honeymoon between business and government after liberation. The political stalemate of the Third Republic was broken, and a new consensus in favor of immigration was emerging. Recruitment policies were supported by major segments of the republican right (especially the Gaullists), oriented to big business and rapid economic growth, and by segments of the old republican left (the radicals, socialists, and eventually the communists).

It is important to keep in mind that the emerging coalition for a new immigration policy, based on expansive (i.e. anti-Malthusian) demographic and economic principles, was firmly anchored in universalistic republican ideals. Republicanism in postwar France included respect for the civil and human rights of foreigners, especially refugees whose plight was easily recognizable following the devastation of the Second World War. France was quick to ratify the Geneva Convention, and the French left in particular was eager to return to the republican policies of the interwar period, when France was a reluctant host for those fleeing fascist persecution in Italy, Spain, Germany, and beyond (Schor 1985). As was the case in West Germany, adopting liberal refugee and asylum policies also was a way for the new French regime to atone for the crimes against humanity committed during the war and the Vichy period. One of the least noticed innovations of the tripartite government— and one of the great accomplishments of the early Gaullist reformers—was the creation of a full-blown welfare state, built on republican, mutual, and Catholic, rather than social democratic, traditions. New immigrant workers and their families benefited from the social rights associated with the construction of a welfare state (Ashford 1991).

If we combine the civil, human, and social rights of foreigners with the liberal naturalization and citizenship policies of the Fourth Republic, we can see the basis for an expansive immigration policy in the immediate postwar period, built on the pragmatic assessments of economic planners, the nationalist aspirations of the *populationnistes*, and the edifice of a revitalized republican synthesis.

The Ordonnances of 1945 laid down the basic outline of immigration and naturalization policy in postwar France, or what Patrick Weil (1991: 61) called *la règle du jeu*. The new law rejected the idea of selecting immigrants on the basis of ethnicity or national origins promoted by Georges Mauco, Alfred Sauvy (1950), and the *populationnistes*. French immigration policy since 1945 must be understood in terms of the demographic and republican nexus that helped to forge a consensus for foreign worker recruitment. But the crises and controversies over immigration *control*, from the 1960s to the present, stem in large part from the turbulence of decolonization and the dismantling of the French Empire, which was itself a creation of nationalist and republican aspirations. The liberal side of the history of immigration in postwar France cannot be told without reference to decolonization and the Algerian War, which created ethnic and racial fault lines in French society that persist today.

A look at the size and evolution of France's foreign and immigrant populations will help to round out the historical picture. From Figures 5.1 and 5.2 and Table 5.1, we see the changes in the foreign and immigrant populations from 1921 to 2008. By 1931, France was statistically a country of immigration—6.6 percent of the population was foreign (without French nationality), comparable to other immigrant-receiving countries. The foreign population dropped slightly during the war years and the early period of reconstruction (falling to 4.1 percent in 1954), but rose again with successive waves of immigration in the 1950s and 1960s (see Figure 5.1), reaching a high of 6.8 percent in 1982 before settling at around 5.8 percent in the first decade of the 2000s. Note, however, that the immigrant (foreign-born) population has been rising consistently throughout the postwar period, from 5.0 percent in 1946 and stabilizing at around 7.4 percent in the last decades of the twentieth century, before rising a full percentage point to 8.4 in the first decade of the twenty-first (see Figure 5.2). The first waves of immigration in the postwar period were made up of settlers (as opposed to temporary immigrants) with a heavy labor component. The more permanent nature of immigration during the *trente glorieuses* (thirty glorious years of economic growth from 1945 to 1975) and the weight of the colonial legacy make the French and German experiences quite different.

Looking only at the numbers, especially the size of the foreign population (stocks), the argument can be made that France has been a country of immigration since early in the twentieth century (Héran 2012). Yet despite its long and continuous history in modern France, immigration never achieved the legitimacy that it has enjoyed in the United States, Canada, or Australia—all *nations of immigrants*. Immigration was not a "founding myth" in any of France's various political regimes (republican or otherwise) in the nineteenth or twentieth century. Policies pursued by postwar French governments were designed to discourage settler immigration and encourage some nationalities, particularly North Africans, to return to their countries of origin. From the beginning of the postwar period, there was a sort of rotation logic embedded in French policy (similar to the German *Gastarbeiter* policy), which helps to explain why governments in 1974 and 1993 could seriously contemplate a halt to all immigration (the so-called zero immigration option). To understand the abrupt shift from recruitment to suspension in the 1970s to "zero immigration" in the

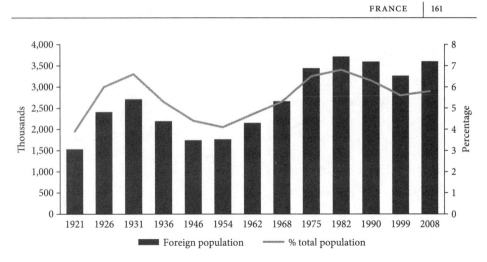

Figure 5.1 Foreign population of France, 1921–2008. *Source:* INSEE.

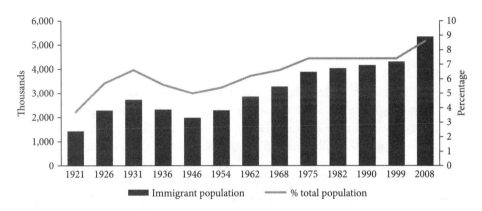

Figure 5.2 Immigrant population of France, 1921–2008. *Source:* INSEE.

1990s, to selective immigration (*l'immigration chosie et non subie*) in the 2000s, we must look at the origins of postwar immigration policy in the 1950s and 1960s. It was during this period that immigration control was defined in the highly statist terms of economic and demographic planning.

ECONOMIC PLANNING AND POPULATION POLICY

French postwar immigration control was created in a very short period of time after liberation. The two principal agencies for managing immigration and refugee flows, the Office National d'Immigration (ONI) and the Office Français pour la Protection des Réfugiés et Apatrides (OFPRA), were established in 1946, and population/family policies in general were given a boost by the creation of the Institut National d'Etudes Démographiques (INED). The ONI was touted (by Gaullists on the Right and Communists on the Left) as a model agency for the recruitment and placement of foreign workers in various sectors

TABLE 5.1

Foreign and immigrant populations, 1921–2008 (in thousands)

Year	Total population	FOREIGN POPULATION[a]		IMMIGRANT POPULATION[b]	
		Number	Percentage	Number	Percentage
1921	38,798	1,532	3.9	1,429	3.7
1926	40,228	2,409	6.0	2,288	5.7
1931	41,228	2,715	6.6	2,729	6.6
1936	41,183	2,193	5.3	2,326	5.6
1946	39,848	1,744	4.4	1,986	5.0
1954	42,781	1,765	4.1	2,293	5.4
1962	46,459	2,151	4.7	2,861	6.2
1968	49,655	2,664	5.3	3,281	6.6
1975	52,599	3,442	6.5	3,887	7.4
1982	54,296	3,714	6.8	4,037	7.4
1990	56,652	3,597	6.3	4,166	7.4
1999	58,521	3,263	5.6	4,309	7.4
2008	62,135	3,603	5.8	5,342	8.6

SOURCE: INSEE.

[a]Foreigners include all of those living in France who do not have French nationality.

[b]Immigrants include all of those who are foreign born living in France, including those (in the first generation) who have been naturalized. See Héran (2012: 30–31) and various SOPEMI reports, for example, Régnard (2006: 8–9), on how the French government measures foreign and immigrant populations.

of the French economy. Trade unions (the CGT and the CFTC) were especially pleased to have a "neutral" state agency to oversee foreign worker and immigration policy. They had lobbied hard to avoid a return to the interwar system of the SGI, where immigration was organized and controlled by business. Business associations, on the other hand, such as the Conseil National du Patronat Français (CNPF), were not yet sufficiently organized to have any formal influence on the creation of this system. They offered little resistance to the new directions in immigrant worker policy, except, ironically, to question the wisdom of importing large numbers of immigrant workers at a time of high unemployment, when many forced French laborers were returning from Germany (Hollifield 1992b; Schor 1985).

The two most influential groups in setting the agenda for postwar French immigration policy were economic planners on the one side and demographers on the other. Two individuals stand out among the policy elite during this period: Jean Monnet, who would coordinate economic policy as head of the Plan (CGP), and Alfred Sauvy, who was to become a principal spokesperson and advisor on economic and population issues for various Fourth Republic governments. Sauvy, unlike Monnet, was not a member of the Gaullist inner circle but was nonetheless closely connected to it through Robert and Michel Debré, two staunch pronatalists (Debré and Sauvy 1946). Other academics and public figures were influential in helping to shape French immigration policy, especially Georges Mauco and Alexandre Parodi, but *planning* was very much in the spirit of the age, and immigration came to be viewed in terms of input-output tables (Tapinos 1975; Weil 1991).

Throughout the period of the *trente glorieuses*, the economic plans published by the CGP contained specific targets for the importation of foreign labor, ranging from 430,000 in the First (Monnet) Plan of 1946–1947 to 325,000 in the Fifth Plan of 1966–1970. These figures, while not irrelevant, had little bearing on actual levels of immigration because the

TABLE 5.2
Immigrant population by country of origin, 1975–2008

Population	1975	1982	1990	2008
Immigrant	3,920,430	4,071,109	4,195,952	5,342,288
Percentage of total population	(7.5%)	(7.5%)	(7.4%)	(8.6%)
Spanish	609,605	485,764	412,785	257,315
Italian	714,650	606,972	523,080	317,260
Portuguese	659,800	644,428	605,986	580,598
Algerian	571,925	617,993	571,997	713,334
Moroccan	244,945	358,296	446,872	653,826
Tunisian	151,125	177,544	182,478	234,669
Turkish	59,515	108,708	158,907	238,862
Other African	—	171,884	275,182	669,401
Indochinese	—	124,420	158,075	162,684

SOURCE: INSEE.

system of immigration control during this period of high growth rates and rapid decolonization quickly slipped into private hands. The ONI became little more than a clearing house for employers, who went directly to the sending countries to find the labor they needed, brought the workers to France, integrated them into the workforce, and *then* sought an adjustment of status, or *régularisation*. This practice of bypassing the institutions created to manage immigration flows came to be known as immigration from within (*l'immigration interne*), and the legalization rate (*le taux de régularisation*) was the most important statistic for measuring the ability or inability of the state to control it. By the late 1960s, according to this measure, almost 90 percent of new immigrants were coming to France, finding a job, and then requesting an adjustment of status (Hollifield 1992b: 45–73). Italy had given way to Spain and Portugal, as well as former colonies, especially Algeria, as the principal recruiting ground for foreign workers (see Table 5.2).

It was also during this period that the confused and ambiguous status of immigrants from North and West Africa began to pose a problem. Following the Evian Agreements, which granted independence to Algeria in 1962, the status of these former "citizens" remained unchanged, and they had the right to move freely between France and their home countries. The continued arrival of hundreds of thousands of Algerians, which accelerated in the late1960s, led the French government to renegotiate the freedom of movement clause of the Evian Agreements. France was reluctant to unilaterally impose restrictions on the movement of Algerian nationals, but in 1968 the government of Georges Pompidou succeeded in convincing the Algerian authorities to give France greater control, provided there was no restriction on tourist visas for Algerians.

Morocco and Tunisia became major sending countries in the period 1968–1973, and they retained a privileged status as ex-colonies. The same was true for the states of West Africa, also known as the franc zone, even though the immigration rates of these nationalities (Senegalese, Ivorian, Cameroonian, and others) remained very low (until the late 1980s and 1990s, again (see Table 5.2) in comparison with the North Africans. In effect the process of decolonization created a special category of protected immigrants who were quasi-citizens of France. High rates of economic growth (demand-pull) combined with an open

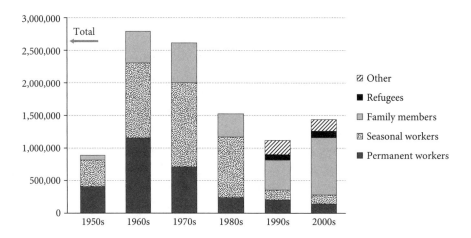

Figure 5.3 French migration flows, 1950s–2000s. *Source:* ONI/OMI and SOPEMI/OECD; 1946–1990 data is from Office des Migrations.

(rights-based) immigration regime made control difficult. The ambiguous status of North and West Africans played havoc with attempts by the French government to control immigration in the 1960s and 1970s because individuals in former African colonies who were born during the time of French rule had the legal right to ask for "reintegration" into French nationality. Thus, a cohort of former French nationals (most of them in their forties) constituted a latent reservoir of African immigration.

During the *trente glorieuses*, the French economy came to rely heavily on immigrant labor. By the early 1970s, foreign workers were to be found in substantial numbers in almost every economic sector (Hollifield 1992b). The rate of status adjustments declined slightly to 50 percent in 1972, but it rose to 60 percent the following year. Thus, the first real attempts by the French government to assert control over immigration (permanent workers, family members, seasonal workers, and the like; see Figure 5.3) ended in failure, unlike the German experience with *Gastarbeiter*, in which Turks were convinced to return home at the time of the first, shallow, postwar recession in 1967–1968 (see Chapter 7). The combination of high demand for labor, the ambiguous status of citizens of the former colonies (especially Algerians), and respect for the civil and human rights of foreigners, which was grounded in the republican tradition, helped to keep the immigration valve open in France right up to the first major economic recession of the postwar period.

STOPPING IMMIGRATION

The consensus for an open immigration regime held until 1973–1974, when the *trente glorieuses* abruptly ended as a result of the Yom Kippur War and the Arab oil embargo. However, stopping immigration (*l'arrêt de l'immigration*) would prove difficult because the mechanisms and instruments of control had not yet been developed by the French state, and cutting ties with former African colonies would not be easy. Reestablishing control over the flows of worker immigration (*travailleurs permanents*) would take many years

(Hollifield 1992b). Simply decreeing an end to immigration proved insufficient to master all the different flows (see Figure 5.3).

Apart from worker immigration, French authorities, like their German counterparts, struggled to deter family immigration, which remained at high levels (over 50,000 per year from 1974 to 1980) even after the immigration stop imposed in 1974 (see Figure 5.3). The mercantilist justification for stopping worker immigration was clear in both countries: with declining economic growth and rising unemployment—especially in France—employers were no longer allowed to recruit foreign labor, and the denial of visas (external control) and work permits (internal control) was seen as a necessary policy response to worsening economic conditions. The new control policies were also seen as a way to head off a rising tide of xenophobia, which was increasingly evident not only in France but also in neighboring countries like Switzerland and Belgium (Wihtol de Wenden 1988; Thränhardt 1997). This shift in policy reflected a widespread Malthusian and mercantilist impulse in Europe generally and in France in particular: if the receiving states could stop immigration, they could solve the problem of unemployment. The reasoning was that, because there were a limited number of jobs in each national economy, stopping immigration would create jobs and weaken xenophobic political movements.

One of the principal sending countries, Algeria, took steps in 1973 to prevent the free emigration of its nationals to the former *Métropole* because of the growing hostility toward Algerians in France. Yet immigration from Algeria and elsewhere continued throughout the 1970s, in large part because of increases in family reunification, which was much more difficult to control (see Table 5.2). The economic rationale for stopping worker immigration did not apply to family immigration, which was humanitarian in nature and constitutionally protected. Nevertheless, French and German authorities tried to impose internal (labor market) controls to slow the influx of family members by denying them work permits. In both instances, however, the courts ruled these policies to be unconstitutional (Weil 1991; Hollifield 1992b).

The French also had to cope with the continued inflow of seasonal workers, employed primarily in agriculture. From 1974 to 1987, the number of seasonal workers entering each year hovered around 60,000, with some coming from Spain and Portugal. The enlargement of the European Community and the extension of the Freedom of Movement clause in the Rome Treaty to cover Spanish and Portuguese nationals partially resolved the issue of seasonal migration (Tapinos 1975, 1982). In the late 1970s and early 1980s, Moroccans made up the bulk of seasonal flows, whereas in the 1990s North Africans were replaced by East Europeans, especially Poles (see Table 5.2).

During the presidency of Valéry Giscard d'Estaing (1974–1981), there was a radical shift away from the open immigration regime of the earlier Gaullist years toward a more closed regime. The methods used to stop immigration were heavy-handed and statist—consistent with the centralized Jacobin state—and they produced many unintended consequences (Hollifield 1992a). The most important of these—certainly not unique to France—was to freeze the foreign population in place. Simply by decreeing an immigration stop, France, like other West European states, inadvertently accelerated the processes of settlement and family reunification. Moreover, having raised expectations among the French public that the state could simply decree a halt to immigration, the government found that its hands were tied both by the law and by the uncontrollable effects of chain migration. The governments of Chirac (1974–1976) and Barre (1976–1981) tried to stop family reunification by denying visas and deporting family members. The Barre government also tried to encourage return migration by paying foreigners to leave (Hollifield 1992b; Weil 1991: 107ff.).

While the issue of immigration control continued to be hotly debated in France, the issue of integration (immigrant policy) surged onto the national agenda. Realizing that millions of Muslims were settling permanently in France, governments and political parties began to reconsider their approach to immigration and integration. Political parties, the party system, and the electorate were increasingly polarized on both issues. In 1981, the election of a socialist president, François Mitterrand, and the first left-wing government since the Popular Front of 1936 set the stage for some important policy shifts.

The socialists opted to maintain tight (external) control of borders and stepped up (internal) control of the labor market to inhibit the growth of a black market for undocumented workers (*travail au noir*). Labor market regulation was carried out by the *inspecteurs du travail*, who conducted surprise inspections and imposed sanctions on employers caught using undocumented workers (Marie 1992). At the same time, however, the new socialist government, led by Pierre Mauroy, offered a conditional amnesty to undocumented immigrants and longer (ten-year) residency and work permits for all immigrants. Anyone who had entered France prior to January 1, 1981, was eligible for a temporary residency permit valid for three months, which gave the immigrant time to complete an application for an adjustment of status (*régularisation exceptionnelle*). By the end of the amnesty period (1983), over 145,000 applications had been received (Weil 1991).

In a liberal and republican polity, strict control of entries together with amnesty for the undocumented came to be seen as a good way to integrate permanent resident aliens or, as Tomas Hammar (1990) called them, *denizens*. In addition to amnesty, to make foreigners residing in France more secure, the first socialist government under Mauroy (1981–1984) relaxed prohibitions against associational and political activities by foreigners. But no changes were made in the nationality law or in naturalization policy, leaving intact this key element of the republican tradition. Foreigners would be welcome within the strict guidelines of labor market rules and regulations; they would be integrated on the (republican) basis of respect for the separation between church and state (*laïcité*); and they were expected to assimilate quickly.

Having thus reaffirmed the previous governments' commitment to strict immigration control, and at the same time having taken steps to speed the integration of foreigners, it seemed that the socialists were forging a new consensus on the contentious immigration issue. In fact, however, the issue literally exploded onto the political scene in 1984 with the municipal elections in the city of Dreux, an industrial town just west of Paris. The Front National—a grouping of extreme right-wing movements under the charismatic and flamboyant leader Jean-Marie Le Pen—won control of the city on a platform calling for a complete halt to immigration and for the deportation of African immigrants. The electoral breakthrough of a neo-fascist, xenophobic, and racist movement profoundly changed the politics of immigration in France and throughout Western Europe (Betz 1994; Thränhardt

1997). For the first time since the end of the Second World War, an extremist party on the right was making itself heard and finding a new legitimacy, garnering support from large segments of the French electorate. Within a matter of years, the Front National would become, in the words of the political scientist Pascal Perrineau, "the largest working class party in France" (Perrineau 1995). From the beginning, the Front National was a single-issue party, taking a stand against immigration. Le Pen, its leader, called for a physical separation of the races in discourse that mixed xenophobia, nationalism (*La France aux français*), and anti-Semitism with appeals to the economic and physical insecurities of the French working class.

CRISES OF NATIONAL IDENTITY

The rise of the Front National contributed heavily to a sense of crisis in French politics, with immigrants at its center, from the immigrant suburbs (deemed *les banlieus de l'Islam*) to a veiled Marianne (*Marianne voilée*). Suddenly immigrants were seen as the cause of France's economic and cultural decline, provoking a loss of confidence in the republican model, especially on the right. Immigrants were accused of taking jobs away from French citizens and so contributing to high unemployment, and Muslims were deemed to be inassimilable and hostile to republican values. The socialist left, under President François Mitterrand, and the neo-Gaullist right (RPR-UDF), led by Jacques Chirac, had very different responses to the Front National's populist appeals to economic insecurity and xenophobia.

One of the first steps of the new government of cohabitation—a combination of neo-Gaullists (RPR) and liberals (UDF) under Prime Minister Jacques Chirac—was to reform immigration *and* naturalization policy. Chirac handed the dossier to the tough Corsican Minister of the Interior, Charles Pasqua, whose name would become synonymous with immigration reform. Pasqua's approach was quite different from that of any of his predecessors. He viewed control primarily as a police matter and moved quickly to reinforce border controls by giving sweeping new powers to the Police de l'Air et des Frontières (PAF) to detain and immediately deport anyone who did not have the proper papers. He also reinforced the power of the (internal) police forces to conduct "random" identity checks of any foreign or suspicious-looking individual. During this time (1986), a wave of terrorist bombings occurred in Paris, connected to the Middle East, specifically Iran. The violence helped further legitimize the new get-tough policy with respect to foreigners, and the immediate effect was to restrict the civil liberties of foreigners, specifically North Africans. These measures amounted to a psychological campaign against immigrants and immigration. They were explicitly designed to win back supporters of the Front National and prevent any further loss of votes on immigration to the extreme Right (Perrineau 1997). However, they also heightened the sense of crisis and contributed to the growing debate over insecurity and loss of national identity.

Still, if we look at the numbers (i.e., flows), what we find is considerable continuity. Immigration fluctuated between 200,000 and 100,000 persons annually throughout the 1980s (see Figure 5.3). The only noticeable increase, as in other European states, was in the number of asylum seekers, which peaked at 61,372 in 1989 (see Figure 5.4). With the end of the

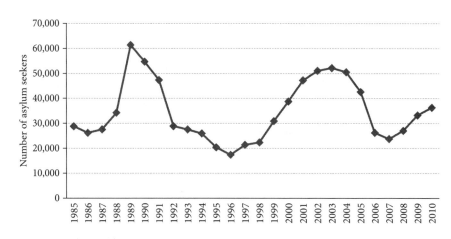

Figure 5.4 Asylum seekers in France. *Source:* Office Français de Protection des Réfugiés et Apartrides. *Note:* The measure of asylum seekers changed in 2004, making comparison of the series more difficult.

Cold War and the gradual implementation of the Schengen Agreement in the 1990s, the rate of asylum applicant rejection rose from 57 percent in 1985 to 84 percent in 1995, and the flows fell precipitously to below 20,000/year by the mid-1990s. So, if flows were not raging out of control, what was the purpose of the first Pasqua Law of 1986? The most controversial aspect of the Chirac administration's reforms was the attempt to weaken the birthright principle of *jus soli* by putting an end to the practice of "automatically" attributing citizenship at age 18 to children born in France of foreign parents. In actuality, this was a symbolic attempt to placate right-wing nationalists and win back Front National voters, but its effects were real (Perrineau 1995, 1997; Viard 1996). Any immigrant who had been sentenced to more than six months in prison was deemed excludable and would not be allowed to naturalize. West Africans were no longer allowed to naturalize under the streamlined procedure known as "reintegration into the French nation," and spouses of French nationals would have to wait two years (no longer one) before they could apply for naturalization.

The thrust of the proposed law was to require young foreigners to affirm their commitments to the republic by formally requesting French nationality and taking a loyalty oath. What effect such a change had on immigration flows was unclear, but the message was clear: French citizenship was a privilege, not a right, and it should be withheld from those who have not made a clear commitment to the French nation. The first Pasqua Law provoked a firestorm of protest, as various civil and immigrant rights organizations, such as La Ligue des Droits de l'Homme, GISTI, SOS Racisme, MRAP, and others, mobilized, leading Pasqua and Chirac eventually to withdraw it from consideration. The law did not affect second-generation Franco-Algerians in any case. Because they were born in France of parents who were born in Algeria prior to 1962—the year of Algerian independence— both parents and children were French by birth (double *jus soli*) and therefore eligible to naturalize (Weil 1991, 2002; Feldblum 1999; Schnapper 2000).

The withdrawal of the Pasqua bill was a major setback for the Chirac government, which had provided the increasingly active French civil rights movement with a new rallying cry:

"*Touche pas à mon pote!*" (Don't touch my buddy!). Thousands marched in Paris under this banner. In addition to altering the political landscape, launching a new debate about French citizenship and national identity, and creating political opportunities for the Left (Ireland 1994; Kastoryano 1997; Feldblum 1999), the attempted reform brought the power and prestige of the Council of State to bear. In ruling on the bill's legality and constitutionality, the council put the government on notice that the rights of individual foreigners and the republican tradition must be respected. This was a lesson in immigration politics and law that Pasqua would not soon forget. In 1993, he would have a much stronger hand to deal with the judiciary (to be discussed), but in this first round of reform the government was forced to compromise and the decision was made to appoint a special commission (Commission des Sages) to hold hearings on immigration and naturalization policy reform. This body was composed of political and intellectual elites and was chaired by Marceau Long, who, as vice president of the Council of State, had the moral and legal authority to tackle this difficult issue.

After hearing the testimony of many experts, the commission simply reaffirmed the importance of the republican tradition by defending the birthright principle of *jus soli*, at the same time stressing the importance of integrating foreigners into public and civic life (Long 1988). The whole episode of reform during the first government of cohabitation had little discernible impact on immigration flows, which remained well over 100,000 during the late 1980s and into the1990s (see Figure 5.3). The number of naturalizations remained in the 50,000 range during the same period (see Figure 5.5), but, if we look at changes in the ratio of naturalizations by decree (*par décret*) and attribution to those by declaration (*par déclaration*) or acquisition for the period 1984–2010, what we find is an upsurge in 1985–1986 and again in the late 1990s and early 2000s. This indicates that a larger number of individuals were filing for naturalization during the key years of the Pasqua reforms, while the number of those qualifying for "automatic" naturalization (by simple act of declaration /attribution) remained relatively constant. The exception is 1994, when the second

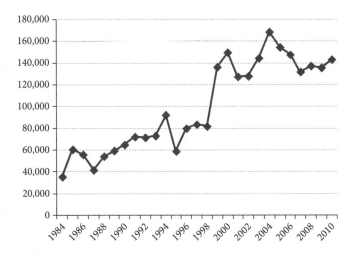

Figure 5.5 Naturalizations in France. *Source:* OECD, SOPEMI reports.

Pasqua Law (to be discussed) saw the number of those declaring themselves to be French shoot up to 43,035, twice the average of 19,911 for the period 1973–1992 (see Figure 5.5).

The big question—a difficult one to answer in France because of the lack of data (to be discussed; Tribalat 1996)—is what happens with the integration of the second generation. According to recent surveys, 11 percent of adults between the ages of 18 and 50, roughly 3.1 million people, have at least one immigrant parent. The percentage is larger for those under 18 and smaller for those over 50. It is estimated that 20 percent of the total French population is either an immigrant (first generation) or the child of an immigrant (second generation; see Héran 2012: 32–33).

The liberal and republican right (UDF and RPR) lost its battle to eliminate the Front National, and it also lost the elections of 1988. Jacques Chirac was defeated in his bid to unseat François Mitterrand, who won a second, seven-year, presidential term; moreover, the right also lost the legislative elections, as the socialists led by Michel Rocard regained control of the Assembly, albeit with the necessity of forming a minority government. With a score of 14.5 percent of the vote on the first round of presidential elections, Le Pen continued to cause problems for the Right. Because his party again exceeded 10 percent of the vote on the first round of the legislative elections but gained no seats in the Assembly, he claimed that the voices of a substantial segment of the French electorate were not being heard, specifically on the issue of immigration. In response, Charles Pasqua, now former Minister of the Interior, tried to reassure Front National supporters that the RPR shared many of their "concerns and values" with respect to immigration's impact on French national identity. Public opinion polls at the time (1988–1989) showed that approximately one-third of the electorate sympathized with the Front National's position (Perrineau 1995).

The new left-wing government, led by the two old socialist rivals Mitterrand and Rocard, essentially returned to the policies of the early 1980s, increasing regulation of the labor market, campaigning against illegal immigration, and taking steps to integrate immigrants. Rocard created the Haut Conseil à l'Intégration to study ways of speeding integration of the foreign population, which still constituted over 6 percent of the total population (Haut Conseil à l'Intégration 1991). For the period 1988–1993, socialist governments fell back on a "grand bargain" strategy of strictly controlling inflows in order to integrate foreigners already in the country. The hope was to depoliticize the whole issue and defuse the national identity crisis. But no sooner had the Left returned to power than it found itself confronting a highly symbolic controversy that struck at the heart of the republican tradition itself and risked splitting the Socialist Party into competing factions.

The controversy arose when three girls of Moroccan descent came to a public school wearing Islamic scarves (*foulards*), which was in violation of the separation of church and state (*laïcité*)—one of the core principles of the republican tradition. The event immediately became a *cause célèbre* for the anti-immigrant right as well as the republican left, with the more liberal (pluralist or multicultural) elements of the political and intellectual elite, including Prime Minister Rocard, caught in the middle. Allowing the girls to wear the scarves was bound to offend both the Left and the Right; but forcing them to remove them could open a new Pandora's box concerning the dividing line between the public and private spheres. Moreover, a ban would raise questions about the wearing of other religious symbols in the classroom, such as the crucifix or the Star of David.

The controversy heightened the sense of crisis with respect to immigration control because of widespread fears that the new immigrants from North Africa, especially the second generation, were prone to Islamic fundamentalism and therefore inassimilable in a secular, republican society in which the individual is to keep his or her private life and religious beliefs completely separate from the public sphere (Roy 1991; Schnapper 1990). One of the leaders of the Socialist Party who was most adamant in his opposition to such overt violations of the republican principle of *laïcité* was Jean-Pierre Chevènement, who held ministerial posts in various socialist governments.

Rocard and Lionel Jospin, his Minister of Education and future Prime Minister, took the decision to allow the girls to wear their scarves, so long as they agreed not to proselytize or in any way disrupt classes. As happens frequently with immigration and integration, when the rights of the individual vis-à-vis the state come into question, the Council of State (Conseil d'État) was invoked. In this case, the council simply ratified the Rocard compromise but this did little to allay growing public fears of Islamic fundamentalism.

The *foulards* affair, as it came to be known, raised a new specter of multiculturalism (*à l'américaine*), which was seen as yet another threat to French unity and national identity as exemplified by the "One and Indivisible Republic." *Le droit à la différence* (the right to be different) became the new rallying cry of those defending multiculturalism and the rights of immigrants (Roy 1991; Kastoryano 1997). A decade later, the 9/11 terrorist attacks would add a security dimension and new sense of urgency to these integration debates.

Despite the almost continuous atmosphere of crisis in French politics over immigration, integration, and national identity that dated back at least to the early 1980s, very little has changed, either in terms of policy outputs—controlling immigration—or policy outcomes—levels of immigration (Hollifield 1986, 1992a, 1997; Simon 2012). The first experience of *cohabitation* (1986–1988) did little to alter the republican model and the rules of the game as spelled out in the Ordonnances of 1945 (Weil 1991). Flows, which are the best measure of policy outcomes, continued at the level of 100,000 or more each year (see Figure 5.3), and the liberal nationality code allowed for the relatively quick naturalization of the foreign population (see Figure 5.5).

ZERO IMMIGRATION

When asked about immigration policy in 1991, President Mitterrand suggested that every society, including France, has a "threshold of tolerance" (*seuil de tolérance*) beyond which xenophobia and racism are likely to increase. But he did not say what that threshold might be in the case of France. Charles Pasqua, soon to be (for the second time in his career) Minister of the Interior, stated bluntly, "France has been an immigration country, but she wants to be no longer." Like any good nationalist and populist, Pasqua claimed to be speaking in the name of the French people, but, as a powerful member of the second government of *cohabitation*—elected by a landslide (the coalition of Gaullists and Liberals won over

80 percent of Assembly seats) in the Spring of 1993 — Pasqua made clear what the immigration policy of the new government would be: "the goal we set, given the seriousness of the economic situation, is to tend towards *zero immigration.*"

Faced with a badly weakened, divided, and demoralized socialist opposition, and having won an overwhelming majority in the National Assembly, the new right-wing government headed by Edouard Balladur had a virtually free hand to pursue draconian policies for (1) stopping all immigration, (2) reducing the number of asylum seekers to an absolute minimum, and (3) reforming the nationality code to block naturalization of as many resident foreigners as possible. What distinguishes this round of reform (in 1993) from earlier attempts to limit immigration (in 1974 or 1986, for example) is the clear focus on rolling back foreigners' rights. The second Pasqua Law presented a direct challenge to the republican model, as defined by the Ordonnances of 1945. Equal protection and due process (civil rights) were denied to foreigners by cutting off avenues of appeal for asylum seekers and giving the police much greater powers than ever before to detain and deport foreigners.

To constrain worker and family immigration in France, the second Pasqua Law (1994) required workers and foreign students to wait two years (rather than one) before bringing in any family members to join them. To inhibit permanent settlement of foreigners and to control illegal immigration, the law prohibited adjustments of status (*régularisation*) for any undocumented individual who married a French citizen, and mayors were given the authority to annul any suspected marriage of convenience (*mariage blanc*). In this case, the state inserted itself directly into the private lives of French citizens. Finally, under the second law, any foreigner expelled from France would be denied return to French territory for one year. All of these reforms indicate the lengths to which liberal states are willing to go in rolling back the rights of foreigners as a way to restrict immigration.

In France, as in other liberal states such as the United States and Germany, the courts play a crucial role in protecting immigrant rights. As it did with the first Pasqua Law of 1986, the Council of State—which functions in part as an institutional watchdog for any infringements of individual rights by the state—warned the Balladur government that some aspects of the proposed reform were illegal and possibly unconstitutional. It was especially concerned with the impact of the second Pasqua Law on the (constitutional) right of families to live together, and with the provisions of the law limiting the right of appeal for asylum seekers. Still, it has no real powers of judicial review; its opinions are only advisory, even though it is one of the most powerful *grands corps*—second only to the Inspection des Finances. The council has great moral, political, and legal authority, however, and governments ignore its views at their peril (Stirn 1991). Moreover, council decisions may presage a ruling by the Constitutional Council (Conseil Constitutionel), which does have powers of judicial review and may stop the implementation of any law deemed unconstitutional.

This is precisely what happened in August 1993 when the Constitutional Council ruled that certain provisions of the second Pasqua Law were unconstitutional. The judges rejected the one-year ban on reentry imposed on anyone deported from France. It also found to be unconstitutional provisions dealing with family immigration: (1) the longer waiting period imposed on foreign students and workers seeking to bring in immediate family members to join them and (2) restrictions imposed on marriages between French citizens and foreigners. In rendering these decisions, the Constitutional Council relied specifically on the Declaration of the Rights of Man and the Citizen, referring to the universalistic and egalitarian principles of this republican document, especially equal protection. Moreover, citing the Preamble to the 1946 Constitution—which requires that due process be accorded to all asylum seekers—it ruled that restrictions on the right of appeal and provisions for the automatic *refoulement* of refugees were unconstitutional. This ruling seemed to jeopardize France's participation in the Dublin Convention as well as the Schengen Agreement, both of which require European states that are parties to these agreements to refuse asylum to any individual who has passed through a safe third country.

The efforts of the Balladur government to move France to "zero immigration" did little to calm the national identity crisis. If anything, the second Pasqua Law heightened the sense of crisis and fanned the flames of xenophobia, leading to a full-blown constitutional debate. But one objective of the reforms seems to have been met: the average annual rate of immigration for the period 1993–1999 fell below 100,000 for the first time since the late 1940s and early 1950s (see Figure 5.3). As we will see in the crisis over the Debré Law in 1997, however, many of the heretofore legal flows were simply pushed underground, increasing the size of the undocumented (*sans papiers*) population and heightening the insecurity among the foreign population as a whole. The numbers of individuals caught trying to enter the country illegally (*refoulements à la frontière*) rose steadily from 1993 on, jumping from 8,700 in 1993 to 10,100 in 1995 and to over 12,000 in 1996, providing (indirect) evidence of increased illegal immigration.

THE LIMITS OF IMMIGRATION CONTROL

The election of Jacques Chirac as president of the republic in 1995 by a narrower than expected margin over the Left candidate, Lionel Jospin, did little to change French immigration policy, even though the Front National received 15 percent of the votes in the first round of the presidential elections. The new government, led by Chirac's lieutenant, Alain Juppé, had the support of the same large right-wing majority in the Assembly, the UDF and the RPR, which controlled 80 percent of the seats. But one big difference was the absence of Charles Pasqua from the government. Pasqua had supported Chirac's rival, the former Prime Minister Edouard Balladur, for the presidency. He was replaced as Minister of the Interior by Jean-Louis Debré, son of Michel Debré, the first Prime Minister of the Fifth Republic and author of the Constitution, as well as the grandson of the pronatalist politician Robert Debré. Debré *fils* would quickly make a name for himself by proposing further, draconian steps to limit the rights of foreigners in France and crack down on illegal immigration. The Debré Law of 1997 would test the limits of strategies for (internal) immigration control, leading to civil disobedience, more court rulings, new elections (thanks to the political blunders of Chirac and Juppé), and finally a resurgence of the republican left.

In the summer of 1996, the tough control policies described in the preceding section were challenged by a group of Africans, mostly from Mali, who were caught in the "Catch 22" of the second Pasqua Law (unable to obtain a residency permit even though they had resided in France for many years and could not be legally deported) and whose applications for political asylum had been rejected. The undocumented, or *sans papiers*, as they were called, occupied a church in Paris, demanding that they be given an adjustment of status (*régularisation*), and several of them launched a hunger strike. Apart from occasional acts of civil disobedience by these African *sans papiers*, which continued throughout 1995–1997, whether in the form of occupying churches or, in one case, occupying the offices of UNESCO, the civil war in Algeria also had an impact on French control policy. After the abrupt cancellation of the Algerian elections in 1992—which Islamic fundamentalists were poised to win—a civil war raged in the former French colony. It pitted Islamic radicals against the long-ruling FLN revolutionary party, which controls the military. The elections were canceled with the blessing of the French government, which made no attempt to hide its support for the Algerian military. France's involvement led to a number of terrorist attacks by Islamic militants against targets in France that forced the government of Alain Juppé to increase security throughout the country. The security sweeps by the police and the military, known as operation *vigipirate*, focused public attention on the Muslim (and African) communities in France, bringing the full power of the French state to bear in an effort to catch the perpetrators of these attacks.

As in the 1950s, French relations with former colonies, especially Algeria, were a driving factor in immigration and refugee policy. Various governments felt compelled to grant asylum (or at least temporary residence) to many members of the Algerian political and intellectual elite (from 1992 to 1997, over 400,000 upper-class and Francophone Algerians fled the civil war, most going to France or Canada). At the same time, they stepped up the pressure to keep other Algerians out and maintained a close watch on the established Algerian community. This atmosphere of crisis and public insecurity, together with continuing pressure from the Front National, led the Juppé government late in 1996 to propose a new (Debré) law designed to resolve the ambiguous status of some of the *sans papiers*, particularly French-born children of illegal immigrants and foreign spouses of French citizens. Under the proposed law, "foreign" children under 16 years of age would have to prove continuous residence in France for ten years and "foreign" spouses would have to have been married for two years to be eligible for a one-year residence permit.

The Debré Law had some liberal intent, it got much more publicity, and it became the focal point of controversy and protest because of a provision added to it by the conservative National Assembly. This provision required all private citizens to notify local authorities whenever they received in their homes any non-EU foreigner. Moreover, mayors would be given the authority to verify that a foreign visitor had left the private citizen's home once his or her visa had expired. What is most interesting about the Debré Law is not so much the effect (or lack thereof) that it had on immigration control but the response it received both from certain groups in civil society and from institutions of the liberal-republican state. Minister Debré, paraphrasing his predecessor Pasqua, stated: "I am for zero *illegal* immigration. . . . The State must be given the means to deter foreigners who want to enter France without resources, papers or jobs." The focus in this statement was on those clearly outside the law—that is, illegal immigrants—but public attention was focused on the effect that the law would have on private citizens, who would (by law) be compelled to inform on foreign visitors. Such an intrusion by the state into the private lives of individuals and families was deemed by many to have crossed the *invisible line* beyond which liberal states are not supposed to go. The Debré Law was denounced as an infringement of personal freedom and a threat to the basic civil liberties of all citizens. The European Parliament even went so far as to pass a resolution condemning it, equating it with Vichy-era laws that required French citizens to inform on their Jewish compatriots so that the Germans could deport these Jews to death camps.

Over the objections of the Council of State—which warned the government that requiring citizens to inform on foreigners might be unconstitutional—the Assembly approved the Debré Law but with some important modifications. Not only did judicial and other institutional checks come into play, but the reaction of certain elite groups in civil society was swift and severe, causing the government considerable embarrassment (Hollifield 1999). Fifty-nine film directors launched a campaign of civil disobedience by publishing an open letter in *Le Monde* declaring that "we are guilty, every one of us, of harboring illegal foreign residents . . . we ask therefore to be investigated and put on trial." A protest rally in Paris attracted 35,000 people, but the French public, according to polls published at the time, was heavily polarized, with a clear majority (59 percent) supporting the government's position.

It seemed that the Debré Law would be in violation of the liberal principle that an individual is innocent until proven guilty. For example, to renew their ten-year residence permits, foreigners would be required to prove that they were not a threat to public order and that they had maintained regular residency in France, thus shifting the burden of proof from the state to the individual. This provision, along with another that would give police access to the fingerprints of all asylum seekers, was subsequently struck down by the Constitutional Council, which, unlike the Council of State, has powers of judicial review. The final version of the law was passed by the French Parliament (Senate) in March 1996. Provisions concerning notification of the whereabouts of foreigners were watered down: the law required African visitors to prove that they had adequate accommodations and funds necessary to live in France during their stay and to return home afterwards.

Throughout this period of policy reform, a major concern of the French government was to devise a system for controlling entries by Africans (and other foreign visitors from developing countries) without imposing American-style quotas or overtly targeting specific ethnic or national groups. Resistance to quotas grew out of the republican desire to maintain an egalitarian approach to the issuing of visas—where all or most applicants coming from developing countries would be treated equally—as well as a desire to construct a system that would not overtly discriminate against individuals coming from former French colonies in West and North Africa. But regardless of intent, the effect of both the Pasqua (1993) and the Debré (1997) laws was to restrict the legal immigration of Africans to France.

A NEW "REPUBLICAN PACT"

To the surprise of many, President Chirac dissolved the National Assembly and called for early elections in May–June 1997. Having been elected on a promise to heal the *fracture sociale* and lower the record high levels of unemployment, which were running at 12–13 percent in 1996–1997, Chirac and Juppé found themselves caught in a political and economic bind, unable to stimulate the economy because of their commitments to the Economic and Monetary Union (EMU) but unwilling to abandon French workers to their fate in a more competitive European and international economy. As a result, Chirac decided to seek a new mandate for his government and his presidency—a huge political gamble that he lost. French socialists and their allies (a mixture of communists, radicals, and greens) won control of the National Assembly, launching the third period of cohabitation in a little over a decade. This time, however, the Right would control the presidency and the Left would control Parliament.

In the legislative elections of 1997, the Front National (FN) received about 15 percent of the vote in the first round but, thanks to the single-member, dual-ballot electoral system, only one seat in the Assembly, held by Jean-Marie Le Chevallier, the mayor of Toulon. What was different about this election was the refusal of the FN to cooperate with other parties on the Right (RPR and UDF) by withdrawing its candidates—who had received the constitutionally required 12.5 percent of registered voters on the first round—from the second round of voting. This set up over seventy *triangulaires* (three-way contests) in which the FN candidate essentially split the right-wing vote on the second round, thus helping to elect a candidate on the Left. In effect, the FN had a big hand in bringing down the Gaullist-liberal government and putting the socialist-communist-green left back in power.

The new left-wing government, headed by Lionel Jospin, took steps to return French immigration policy to its republican roots and to resolve the ambiguous status of the *sans papiers*. In his opening speech to the new Parliament on June 19, 1997, he announced that he would establish a "new republican pact" with the French people that would return to the "roots of the Republic" and at the same time strive to "modernize French democracy." He laid out a detailed republican vision of immigration policy, reminiscent of earlier periods in history, from the turn of the century, to the 1920s, to the Ordonnances of 1945, and finally to the early Mitterrand years in the 1980s. To quote Jospin,

> France, with its old republican traditions, was built in layers that flowed together into a melting pot, thus creating an alloy that is strong because of the diversity of its component parts. For this reason, birthright citizenship [*le droit du sol*] is inseparable from the French Nation [*consubstantiel à la nation française*]. We will reestablish this right. Nothing is more alien to France than xenophobia and racism. . . . Immigration is an economic, social and human reality which must be organized and controlled. France must define a firm, dignified immigration policy without renouncing its values or compromising its social balance.

To accomplish this goal, Jospin called for (1) a new republican integration policy that welcomes immigrants and respects their human rights but combats illegal immigration and black labor markets, thus returning to the "grand bargain" strategies of earlier socialist governments; (2) a new policy of cooperation with sending states to help control immigration at its source; and (3) a comprehensive review of immigration and nationality law (which was carried out by an interministerial task force chaired by the immigration scholar Patrick Weil (1997). During the campaign, Jospin had promised to repeal the Pasqua-Debré laws—a promise that would come back to haunt him (see below). His fourth reform called for a case-by-case review (*réexamen*) of the situation of all *sans papiers* caught in the maze of regulations and contradictions surrounding the laws. The government issued orders to the prefects to immediately begin reviewing as many as 40,000 cases. Foreigners who had waited months or years for their dossiers to be reviewed suddenly found a new willingness on the part of administrative authorities to help them by issuing temporary residence permits.

The Weil report, published in August 1997, contained 120 propositions for modifying immigration and nationality law. For the most part, like the bills that would be presented to Parliament later that year it tried to steer a middle course: reestablishing the centrality of the principle of *jus soli* in French nationality law and going back to the naturalization procedure that existed before the 1993 Pasqua Law, with a few modifications but not a blanket birthright citizenship, as exists in the United States; and reinforcing the rights of asylum seekers and the rights of family reunification but cracking down on illegal immigration—a position similar to the old socialist grand bargain. Finally, the report appealed to the republican tradition, linking immigration with an open, welcoming, but secular tradition in French law and history.

By giving such a high priority to immigration and nationality law reform, the Jospin government signaled its desire to confront the issue; by appealing to French republican values as a way of resolving the immigration crisis, it clearly hoped to return to the earlier "republican consensus," defuse the issue, and seize the political and moral high ground. Attempts were made by right-wing governments to "steal the thunder" from Le Pen and the Front National by cracking down on immigrants and thereby appeal to the insecurities and xenophobia of the electorate—what might be called the Pasqua-Debré approach to immigration policy—but this did little to reduce support for the FN (Perrineau 1997). Whether the socialists and communists could reconstruct the republican consensus would depend heavily on their ability to reach out to elements of the liberal and republican right. This was the strategy adopted in the Weil report (1997) and subsequently by the government itself.

Two bills were drafted and presented to the National Assembly late in 1997. The Guigou Law dealt with reform of the nationality code, whereas the Chevènement Law dealt with reform of immigration law. Both openly appealed to the republican tradition in an attempt to gain support from a broad spectrum of politicians on the Left and the Right. The Guigou Law was adopted in early December 1997 by a narrow margin (267 deputies for it and 246 against, with many communists and greens abstaining). The pro-immigrant left wanted to send a message to the government expressing its displeasure with the strategy of amending rather than repealing the Pasqua-Debré laws. This pink-green coalition was dubbed the "moral left," and it took a strong stand in favor of birthright citizenship, meaning an end to all restrictions on the naturalization of individuals born on French territory. Right-wing opposition denounced the reform as unnecessary and detrimental to the national interest. One UDF deputy, François Bayrou, following the lead of former president Valéry Giscard d'Estaing, called for a referendum on the issue. The sole representative of the National Front, Jean Marie Le Chevalier, called for the elimination of *jus soli* in favor of *jus sanguinis* as the organizing principle for French nationality law.

The Guigou Law in effect reinstated the principle of *jus soli* so that anyone born in France of foreign parents can acquire French nationality at the age of majority (18), as long as that individual can show continuous residence in France for at least five years after the age of 11.

Any minor born in France of foreign parents could request naturalization as early as age 13 if his or her parents give their consent and if he or she has resided in France for at least five years since the age of 8. To ensure that naturalization is voluntary, the law states that any young foreigner can refuse French citizenship in the six months before his/her eighteenth birthday or in the twelve months after. To avoid having individuals fall through the cracks of the law, as happened with the *sans papiers* under the Pasqua Law, the Guigou Law created a "republican identity card" (note the symbolism of the name!) to be given to every minor born in France of foreign parents. Finally, the law rolled back the waiting period for foreign spouses to request naturalization, from two to one year after the date of the marriage.

The Chevènement Law changed the Ordonnances of November 2, 1945, which govern the status of foreigners and which have been amended no less than twenty-five times, including five times in the last eleven years. For example, the Chevènement Law eliminated the "legal entry requirement" imposed by the Pasqua Law on any foreigner seeking to adjust his or her status. However, it kept the "threat to public order" as grounds for exclusion. Under the law, one-year residence permits were issued to (1) all minors entering under the auspices of family reunification, (2) all foreigners who entered France before the age of 10 and who reside in France, (3) any foreigners who can prove that they have resided in France for fifteen years, and (4) foreign spouses of French nationals as well as the foreign parents of French children. These changes were intended to emphasize the importance and the sanctity of the family under French law. The one-year permits are also issued to foreigners who are infirm. Special consideration in the issuance of residence and work permits also must be given to (1) foreign scholars and professors invited to work in France and (2) any foreigner who has a special personal or family situation. Foreigners who pose a threat to public order or who engage in polygamy are prohibited from receiving residence permits. A new, special residence permit for retired people, valid for ten years and renewable, also was created.

Apart from these broad changes in the issuing of residence permits, the Chevènement Law eliminated a number of conditions imposed on potential immigrants by the Pasqua Law, including the requirement that parents meet certain income criteria before bringing their children to France. They need wait only one year (instead of two) after establishing their residence in France to request reunification. Another important modification was the elimination of "housing certification," which had to be approved by the office of the mayor of a commune. This was replaced by a statement that the foreigner has a place to stay (*attestation d'accueil*). In a nod to the Right, however, the law limited appeals by foreigners denied a residence permit, keeping in place the *commission de séjour*, whose opinions in any given case would be only advisory. Likewise, the government would not be required to justify refusal of visas except in the case of family members. Criminal aliens are excludable, but the law requires the government to take into account the individual's personal and family situation, which is required by the European Human Rights Convention.

The Chevènement Law established two new forms of asylum for individuals persecuted because of their activities "on behalf of freedom." This is called "constitutional asylum." The Law created a French equivalent of the American "temporary protected status," which gives the French Minister of Justice (like the US Attorney General) the power to grant "territorial asylum" to individuals who would be in imminent, personal danger if they were returned to their country of origin. In another nod to the right, the length of administrative detention for irregular migrants was increased from ten to twelve days, but foreigners have additional time to appeal a deportation order.

The shift in policy toward greater external (border) controls seems to have had a discernible effect on flows, which already were rising from 95,757 in 1996 to 139,533 in 1998 and back down to 119,250 in 2000 (Lebon 2001; see Figure 5.3). These numbers are more in line with the annual averages of the 1980s and early 1990s (around 100,000; see Figure 5.3), and they reflect a partial amnesty of individuals with an irregular status. Over a three-year period (1997–2000), 76,300 individuals benefited from a review of their case (*réexamen*), which allowed them to obtain residence permits.

CHOOSING IMMIGRANTS

Following the victory of Jacques Chirac and the parties of the traditional republican right (rebaptized as the Union pour la Majorité Présidentielle, or UMP) in the presidential and legislative elections of May–June 2002, there was little immediate change in immigration policy, despite the fact that Jean-Marie Le Pen and the FN garnered 17 percent of the vote in the first round of presidential elections, eliminating Lionel Jospin (16 percent) and the fractured left from the second round of voting. Le Pen carried the banner of the extreme Right against Chirac and the UMP in the second round, improving his score slightly to 18 percent but handing Chirac the largest margin of victory (82 percent) in the history of presidential elections. In June 2002, the UMP won a crushing majority in the legislative elections, 399 out of 577 National Assembly seats. Thanks again to France's first-past-the-post, dual-ballot electoral system, Le Pen and the FN won no seats, thus weakening his claim to represent the one in five voters who, for whatever reason, supported him. He was successful in linking the old themes of insecurity and unemployment with illegal immigration, which helped him solidify the working class vote. Moreover, the terrorist attacks of September 11, 2001, further raised the specter of terrorism and radical Islam (Kepel 1991, 2012), which added fuel to the fire of anti-immigration politics. Immigration was now more than ever seen as a matter of national security.

The new government under Prime Minister Jean-Pierre Raffarin promised to crack down on crime and increase spending on public security; the new "law and order" Minister of the Interior, Nicolas Sarkozy, wasted little time in reframing the debate about immigration, vowing that France, as a sovereign nation, had the right to choose its immigrants rather than the immigrants choosing France. *L'immigration choisie, non subie* became the slogan and the cornerstone of French policy in the 2000s, a decade that saw the passage of no less than four new immigration laws. Although the thrust of these reforms was toward greater restriction—especially with respect to family immigration—the terms of the debate shifted from halting immigration (the so-called zero-immigration option; see above) to managing it in the "national interest." In practice, this meant limiting unskilled workers in favor of the highly skilled, further cracking down on illegal immigration, and requiring immigrants to demonstrate their willingness and ability to integrate, not only into the labor market (by finding employment) but also into society (by showing mastery of the French language and acceptance of "republican" values).

The debate over immigrant integration took on greater urgency as the so-called "war on terrorism" heated up. Terrorist attacks in Madrid (2004) and in London (2005) were followed in the fall of 2005 by riots and civil unrest across France, especially in the working-class and heavily immigrant suburbs (*les banlieus*) of Paris (Kepel 2012). The republican model appeared to be in crisis, as mostly second-generation (African) immigrants took to the streets to protest high unemployment, poor living conditions (in public housing projects, *habitations à loyer modéré*, or *HLM)*, and bleak prospects for future mobility in French society. The rioting continued off and on for almost one month, prompting President Chirac in November to declare a state of emergency and leading Interior Minister Sarkozy famously to declaim that the rioters were *des racailles* (scum) and that he would use a sort of steam cleaner (*Kärcher*) to cleanse the suburbs of these hoodlums (*des voyous*). By dialing up the rhetoric and vowing to rid the suburbs of these undesirable elements, Sarkozy placed himself at the center of debates over immigration and integration, and became the author of two new restrictive laws on immigration. Sarkozy I, passed in November 2003, strengthened the hand of administrative authorities to detain and deport undesirable or undocumented migrants, tightened restrictions on residency permits, especially for family members and spouses of French citizens, and linked residency to a willingness on the part of immigrants to demonstrate "republican integration." Three years later, near the end of the second Chirac administration, Sarkozy II, passed in 2006, again tried to tighten restrictions on family immigration by making it more difficult for immigrants to bring their relatives to join them and creating new administrative barriers to obtaining residency permits. As we can see from Figure 5.3, however, family immigration continued to increase in the 2000s, dominating immigration flows.

At roughly the same time (2005), the venerable Ordonnances of 1945, which had laid down the republican principles on which postwar immigration and naturalization policy was based, were replaced by a new code governing the admission and residence of foreigners and asylum seekers (Code d'Entrée et de Séjour des Étrangers et des Demandeurs d'Asile, or CESEDA). Also, in keeping with the idea that the French state should choose immigrants rather than immigrants choosing France, the making and implementation of immigration policy was centralized in the Ministry of the Interior. Somewhat ironically, at the same time the prefects (the direct arm of the administration in the provinces) were given new powers to make critical decisions about the conditions that immigrants would have to meet to obtain residency permits, marry, and reunify their families. The net result was to create greater bureaucratic obstacles for immigrants and strengthen the hands of the police and administrative authorities in "managing" migration vis-à-vis the courts and the Foreign Ministry.

The crackdown on family and worker migration was accompanied by a new quota system for highly skilled immigrants whereby the government would identify certain professions with skill shortages and facilitate the granting of visas to immigrants meeting critical labor market needs. But, just as in the 1970s, the government encountered opposition from the courts, specifically the Council of State, which ruled that the right of families to live together is protected both by the French Constitution and by European (and international) law. Thus, in 2007, with the parties of the Right firmly in control—Sarkozy easily defeated his socialist rival, Ségolène Royal, and his party (the UMP) gained a large working majority in the National Assembly—the government was frustrated in its efforts to limit immigrant rights, civil and otherwise, and to establish a more selective immigration policy. Nevertheless, two more immigration laws would be passed by the Sarkozy administration. The first, in 2007, was named for the new Minister of the Interior, Brice Hortefeux, and provoked a firestorm of controversy and intense opposition from civil liberties groups, like the GISTI and SOS Racisme. It required immigrants seeking family reunification to use expensive DNA tests to prove that those who were applying were blood relatives. Opponents argued that DNA testing was unethical and unconstitutional and that if immigrants refused to undergo or pay for the tests, their applications could more easily be rejected by administrative authorities on the grounds that they are fraudulent. Even though the law was upheld (with some reservations) by the Constitutional Council, the provision for DNA testing was never implemented. It would return in 2009, however, when Hortefeux's successor, Eric Besson, announced that he would open the way for the use of DNA tests.

A second law, named for Besson, was passed in 2011 and targeted illegal immigrants by increasing administrative detention and strengthening the hand of the police, particularly the border police (PAF). However, in France as in other major receiving countries, the majority of illegal immigrants are actually visa overstayers, and the legal and administrative difficulties associated with deportation are numerous. Over the past decade, deportation orders ranged from 50,000 to 80,000per year, with actual expulsions on the order of 10,000 to 20,000. In 2010, for example, 73,500 individuals were ordered to leave the country, but only 16,100 were actually deported (Régnard 2010; Breem 2011).

With all the twists and turns of immigration policy in the 2000s and the growing immigrant presence in France—from 7.4 to 8.6 percent of the total population (see Figure 5.2)—attention shifted from control of entries (admissions) to integration. Three of the four laws passed during the decade linked the granting of visas and residency permits to a willingness to integrate, and, in the case of Sarkozy II, potential immigrants were obliged to sign an "integration contract" (*contrat d'accueil et d'intégration*). The real issue, however (the proverbial elephant in the room), was the integration of a large and growing Muslim population and especially the fate of the 1.5 and second-generation immigrants (Tribalat 1996, 2011–2012).

Understanding integration requires knowledge of individuals' ethnicity, including religious practices and affiliations. Conducted in the early 1990s, the first survey to broach the issue of origins and ethnicity was highly controversial (Tribalat 1995, 1996) and provoked a bitter public debate within the scientific community over the appropriateness of collecting and analyzing information about ethnic origins (Le Bras 1998). This evolved into a general political and constitutional argument about so-called "ethnic statistics" (Simon 2003b, 2005), which eventually came before the Constitutional Council in 2007, at the same time as the controversy over DNA testing. The council ruled against the use of survey questions about ethnicity or religion on the grounds that such intrusive questions are a violation of Article 1 of the French Constitution, which states that "la France est une République indivisible, laïque, démocratique et sociale. Elle assure l'égalité devant la loi de tous les citoyens sans distinction d'origine, de race ou de religion" (France is a one and indivisible Republic, secular, democratic and social. Equality before the law is guaranteed for all citizens irrespective of national origin, race or religion).

The number of practicing Muslims in France is estimated to be 4 million, or 6 percent of the total population. This compares with a similar number in Germany, making up 5 percent of the population, and 2.4 million in the United Kingdom, which makes up 4 percent of the population (Tribalat 2011–2012). The preoccupation with assimilation of Muslim immigrants is not unique to France. Similar concerns about the effects of Islam on civic life have arisen across Europe, particularly in Britain, Germany, the Netherlands, and Switzerland (see Chapters 6, 7, 8, and 10). In France, highly symbolic measures, such as the deportation of several hundred Romanian gypsies in 2010 — the ban against women wearing the burqa in public in 2011, and the debate over halal meat stirred up by the Front National candidate Marine Le Pen in the presidential elections of 2012 — are symptomatic of the new identity politics.

As in previous periods (Hollifield 1986, 1992a), however, the effect of these immigration policy changes (outputs) on immigration flows and stocks (outcomes) is marginal at best. Flows recovered somewhat during the 2000s, stabilizing in the range of 120,000 to 130,000 per annum and trending upward (see Figure 5.3); this is despite the financial crisis of 2008–2009 and the deep recession that followed. In 2008, the immigrant (foreign-born) population in France reached a new high of 5.3 million, or 8.6 percent of the population as a whole (see Figure 5.2). France remains a highly open society—it is the number one destination for tourists in the world, welcoming over 80 million in an average year—and the "republican model," which, as with any national model, remains highly contested, is still operative. In spite of the increasing importance of the European Union (EU) in managing migration (Wihtol de Wenden 2001; see also Chapter 14), the republican model still frames debates about French immigration. The French society and economy are highly interdependent within Europe—migrants from EU member states have freedom of movement and, thus they are no longer counted in national immigration statistics. EU treaties, together with various EU directives on matters ranging from asylum, family reunification, and anti-discrimination measures for control of illegal immigration, to border control (FRONTEX) have led to increasing interdependence and some degree of policy harmonization. EU law has definitely acted as a constraint on French policy (Guiraudon 2010) and in some ways has challenged the republican model, compelling French authorities, for example, to set up procedures to combat racial and ethnic discrimination. Affirmation action or positive discrimination requires the state to single out specific racial and ethnic groups for special treatment, and such policies fly in the face of republican ideals (Schnapper 1990; Roy 1991; Bleich 2003; Simon 2003a).

The presidential elections of 2012 once again saw immigration taking center stage in French politics. The FN candidate, Marine Le Pen, received almost 18 percent of the vote in the first round, a score comparable to that of her father, Jean-Marie Le Pen, in 2002; however, it was not enough to get her to the second round. Her biggest impact on the election was to shift the debate about immigration to the right, and the incumbent president, Nicolas Sarkozy, chose to compete directly with her for the nativist vote, taking a hard line on immigration control and integration. During the campaign, Sarkozy criticized the EU for not being sufficiently Christian and promised that if re-elected he would renegotiate the Schengen Agreement and reimpose national border controls. As a result, Sarkozy lost many moderate voters in the center in the second round and so François Hollande, the socialist candidate, was elected with almost 52 percent of the vote. The socialists consolidated their power by winning a comfortable parliamentary majority in the legislative elections that followed.

The new government is likely to take a cautious approach to immigration reform in the hope of depoliticizing the issue; given the power of republican ideology, however, especially the principle of *laïcité*, it is likely that Hollande will adhere to the policies of previous socialist governments with something like the "grand bargain" strategies of the Mitterrand era—cracking down on illegal immigration to better legitimize legal immigration—and a return to the "republican pact" of the Jospin government in which immigration is seen as consubstantial with the republic.

CONCLUSION

Historically, immigration has had greater legitimacy in France than in the other major receiving countries of Western Europe. However, even though France became a country of immigration because of fundamental economic and demographic pressures, what is most important from the standpoint of the politics and policies of control is understanding how the early waves of immigration were legitimized. In this respect, France looks less like her European neighbors and more like the United States (Horowitz and Noiriel 1992)—in both cases, immigration was legitimized through an appeal to republican ideas and ideologies. From the very earliest days of the republic, politicians have appealed to republican ideals of universalism, egalitarianism, nationalism, and *laïcité* as a way of legitimizing immigration and integrating foreigners. Thus, it is not surprising to hear the former Prime Minister, Lionel Jospin, in 1997 calling for a new "republican pact" as a way of solving the social and economic crises associated with immigration.

Yet immigration, like republicanism, remains contested in France. It is not a "founding myth" of the French Republic, so we cannot say that France is, like the United States, Canada, and Australia, a *nation of immigrants*. Still, attacking immigrants and their rights is viewed by many as tantamount to attacking the republic. Conversely, one of the best ways for a government to defend immigrants is to cloak itself in the values and symbols of the republic. When Jacques Chirac sought to rally left- and right-wing voters to his side in the runoff with Jean-Marie Le Pen in the second round of the 2002 presidential elections, he appealed to all French voters to defend "the values of the Republic" by rejecting extremism.

Immigrants and immigration have come under attack in large part because of the shift in composition and ethnic mix of immigrant flows from predominantly Christian and European to Muslim and African. This shift was the result of two developments. First, decolonization in the 1960s contributed to an exodus of North and West Africans to France. Second, European integration gradually eliminated immigration from neighboring states, such as Italy, Spain, and eventually Portugal. In the early 1970s, the justification for stopping immigration was primarily economic. France had high levels of unemployment, so, consistent with a strong strand of Malthusian and mercantilist thinking, the reasoning went this way: if the state can stop immigration, this will solve the problems of unemployment. But this rationale for stopping immigration—although still present today—quickly gave way in the 1980s to the arguments advanced by Jean-Marie Le Pen and others: the French nation was being destroyed by an influx of unassimilable African immigrants. In this view, Muslims could never be good citizens of the republic because of their refusal to accept the secular principle of *laïcité* and to keep their private, religious views separate from their public life. Politicians began to play on these fears as a way of getting votes, and the republican argument (a double-edged sword) seemed to cut the other way. Throughout the 1980s and 1990s, the tactic of appealing to xenophobic fears and instincts led to further polarization of the electorate on immigration, and it contributed to the rise of the Front National (Perrineau 1997; Viard 1996; Thränhardt 1997). In the 2002 elections, which took place in the wake of the terrorist attacks in New York, Madrid, and London, immigration was linked to crime and national security. The same was true in the 2007 elections in the aftermath of the civil unrest (i.e., violence in the *banlieus*) that rocked France in 2005. It was again true in the 2012 elections, when the specter of an inassimilable, radicalized Muslim population seemed to haunt segments of the French electorate. Whether such fears are rational or irrational is open to debate, but there is no doubt that politicians have exploited them for political gain (or loss, as was the case for Nicolas Sarkozy in the 2012 presidential election).

By the mid-1990s, strategies for immigration control in France began to change dramatically. Instead of relying exclusively on the mechanism of external border controls—which were nonetheless being reinforced and further *externalized* and Europeanized through the Schengen and Dublin systems—or on the more classic mechanisms of internal regulation of the labor markets (such as employer sanctions), the first right-wing government of the 1990s began to roll back and limit the rights of immigrants by undercutting civil rights and liberties (due process and equal protection) and by going after certain social rights, specifically health care. Finally, political rights, naturalization, and citizenship were challenged through reform of the nationality code and erosion of the principle of *jus soli.*

We can see quite clearly the progression of control strategies: external controls (in the form of new visa regimes) in the early 1970s; restrictions on hiring foreign workers in 1974 coupled with return policies and employer sanctions; attempted rollbacks of family reunification "rights" in the late 1970s; increased labor market regulation during the socialist years of the 1980s (internal controls); a return to external control strategies with ratification of the Schengen and Dublin agreements; limits on social and civil rights (the first and second Pasqua laws, as well as the Debré Law); attempted limits on citizenship through changes in the nationality law (the first and second Pasqua laws); and a somewhat confused flurry of laws in the first decade of the twenty-first century, when immigration control strategies shifted again in favor of migration management and selection of immigrants on the basis of their potential contributions to the French economy. The policy of "choosing immigrants" for economic purposes, by focusing on discretionary flows of worker migration, was quickly overwhelmed by a crackdown on humanitarian (nondiscretionary) flows of family immigration, asylum seekers, and the like, putting the Sarkozy government at odds with the EU and domestic (constitutional) law. Whenever the state crossed the invisible line between controlling immigration and threatening civil society, thereby putting itself at odds with founding republican principles—institutional/constitutional, ideational, and societal— checks came into play (Hollifield 1997, 1999). As in other liberal republics, immigration control in France is not purely a function of markets, economic interests, or national security. Rather, it is heavily dependent on the interplay of ideas, institutions, and civil society.

REFERENCES

Ashford, Douglas E. 1991. "In Search of the Etat Providence." In *Searching for the New France*, edited by James F. Hollifield and George Ross, 151–72. New York: Routledge.

Berger, Suzanne. 1972. *Peasants against Politics*. Cambridge, MA: Harvard University Press.

Betz, Hans-Georg. 1994. *Radical Right-Wing Populism in Western Europe*. New York: St. Martin's Press.

Bleich, Erik. 2003. *Race Politics in Britain and France: Ideas and Policymaking since the 1960s*. Cambridge: Cambridge University Press.

Breem, Yves. 2011. *Rapport du SOPEMI pour la France*. Paris: Ministère de l'Intérieur.

Brubaker, Rogers. 1992. *Citizenship and Nationhood in France and Germany*. Cambridge, MA: Harvard University Press.

Debré, Robert, and Alfred Sauvy. 1946. *Des français pour la France, le problème de la population*. Paris: Gallimard.

Feldblum, Miriam. 1999. *Reconstructing Citizenship: The Politics of Immigration in Contemporary France*. New York: SUNY Press.

Guiraudon, Virginie. 2010. "Les effets de l'européanisation des politiques d'immigration et d'asile." *Politique Européenne* 31 (2): 7–32.

Hammar, Tomas. 1990. *Democracy and the Nation-State: Aliens, Denizens, and Citizens in a World of International Migration*. Aldershot, UK: Avebury.

Haut Conseil à l'Intégration. 1991. *La connaissance de l'immigration et de l'intégration*. Paris: Documentation Française.

Héran, François. 2012. *Parlons immigration en 30 questions*. Paris: Documentation Française.

Herbert, Ulrich. 1986. *Geschichte der Ausländerbeschäftigung in Deutschland 1880 bis 1980*. Bonn: Dietz.

Hoffmann, Stanley, ed. 1963. *In Search of France*. Cambridge, MA: Harvard University Press.

Hollifield, James F. 1986. "Immigration Policy in France and Germany: Outputs vs. Outcomes." *Annals of the American Academy of Political and Social Science* 485 (May): 113–28.

———. 1992a. "L'état français et l'immigration." *Revue Française de Science Politique* 42 (6): 943–63.

———. 1992b. *Immigrants, Markets, and States*. Cambridge, MA: Harvard University Press.

———. 1997. *L'immigration et l'état nation: À la recherche d'un modèle national*. Paris: Harmattan.

————. 1999. "Ideas, Institutions and Civil Society: On the Limits of Immigration Control in Liberal Democracies." *IMIS-Beiträge* 10 (January): 57–90.

Hollifield, James F., and George Ross, eds. 1991. *Searching for the New France*. New York: Routledge.

Horowitz, Donald L., and Gérard Noiriel, eds. 1992. *Immigrants in Two Democracies: French and American Experience*. New York: New York University Press.

Ireland, Patrick. 1994. *The Policy Challenge of Ethnic Diversity*. Cambridge, MA: Harvard University Press.

Kastoryano, Riva. 1997. *La France, l'Allemagne et leurs immigrés: Négocier l'identité*. Paris: Armand Colin.

Kepel, Gilles. 1991. *La revanche de dieu*. Paris: Seuil.

————. 2012. *Banlieues de la République*. Paris: Gallimard.

Lebon, André. 1988–2001. *Immigration et présence étrangère en France*. Paris: Documentation Française.

Le Bras, Hervé. 1998. *Le démon des origines*. Paris: Éditions de l'Aube.

Lewis, Mary Dewhurst. 2007. *The Boundaries of the Republic: Migrant Rights and the Limits of Universalism in France, 1918–1940*. Stanford, CA: Stanford University Press.

Long, Marceau. 1988. *Être français aujourd'hui et demain*. Paris: Documentation Française.

Marie, Claude Valentin. 1992. "Le travail clandestin." *Infostat Justice* 29 (September): 1–6.

Noiriel, Gérard. 1986. *Les ouvriers dans la société française*. Paris: Seuil.

————. 1988. *Le creuset français*. Paris: Seuil.

Perrineau, Pascal. 1995. *Le vote de crise*. Paris: Presses de la FNSP.

————. 1997. *Le symptôme Le Pen: Radiographie des électeurs du Front national*. Paris: Fayard.

Régnard, Corrine. 2003–2010. *Immigration et présence étrangère en France*. Paris: Documentation Française.

————. 2010. *Rapport du SOPEMI pour la France*. Paris: Ministère de l'Intérieur.

Roy, Olivier. 1991. "Ethnicité, bandes et communautarisme." *Esprit* (February): 37–48.

Sauvy, Alfred. 1950. "Besoins et possibilités de l'immigration en France." *Population* 2 (3): 209–34.

Schnapper, Dominique. 1990. *La France de l'intégration, sociologie de la nation*. Paris: Gallimard.

————. 2000. *Qu'est-ce que la citoyenneté?* Paris: Gallimard.

Schor, Ralph. 1985. *L'opinion français et les étrangers, 1919–1939*. Paris: Publications de la Sorbonne.

Simon, Patrick. 2003a. "Challenging the French Model of Integration: Discrimination and the Labor Market Case in France." *Studi Emigrazione* 152: 717–45.

————. 2003b. "Les sciences sociales françaises face aux catégories ethniques et raciales." *Annales de Démographie Historique: Politique des Recensements* 1: 111–30.

————. 2005. "The Measurement of Racial Discrimination: The Policy Use of Statistics." *International Journal of Social Science* 183: 9–25.

————. 2012. "Les revirements de la politique d'immigration." *Cahiers Français* 369: 86–91.

Spengler, Joseph J. 1938. *France Faces Depopulation*. Durham, NC: Duke University Press.

Stirn, Bernard. 1991. *Le Conseil d'État*. Paris: Hachette.

Tapinos, Georges. 1975. *L'immigration étrangère en France*. Paris: Presses Universitaires de France.

———. 1982. "European Migration Patterns; Economic Linkages and Policy Experiences." *Studi Emigrazione* 19: 339–57.

Teitelbaum, Michael S., and Jay M. Winter. 1985. *Fear of Population Decline*. Orlando, FL: Academic.

Thränhardt, Dietrich. 1997. "The Political Uses of Xenophobia in England, France, and Germany." In *Immigration into Western Societies: Problems and Policies*, edited by Emek Uçarer and Donald Puchala, 175–94. London: Pinter.

Tribalat, Michèle. 1995. *Faire France: Une enquête sur les immigrés et leurs enfants*. Paris: Découverte.

———. 1996. *De l'immigration à l'assimilation: Enquête sur les populations d'origine étrangère en France*. Paris: Découverte/INED.

———. 2011–2012. "Dynamique démographique des musulmans de France." *Commentaire* 136: 971–80.

Viard, Jean, ed. 1996. *Aux sources du populisme nationaliste*. Paris: Éditions de l'Aube.

Weber, Eugen. 1976. *Peasants into Frenchmen: The Modernization of Rural France, 1870–1914*. Stanford, CA: Stanford University Press.

Weil, Patrick. 1991. *La France et ses étrangers*. Paris: Calmann-Lévy.

———. 1997. *Mission d'étude des législations de la nationalité et de l'immigration*. Paris: Documentation Française.

———. 2002. *Qu'est ce qu'un Français?* Paris: Grasset.

Wihtol de Wenden, Catherine. 1988. *Les immigrés et la politique*. Paris: Presses de la FNSP.

———. 2001. *L'Europe des migrations*. Paris: Documentation Française.

COMMENTARY

Catherine Wihtol de Wenden

France is an old immigration country, the oldest in Europe. It is the first country to have introduced immigration a century before most of the other European states and the first to have shifted more than a century ago the right of blood citizenship introduced by Napoleon I in the conquered lands to an equilibrium between the right of the blood and the right of the soil (*jus sanguinis* and *jus soli*). Now it is the first country in Europe for the number of asylum seekers (over 50,000 in 2010), just after the United States in the world, and the first country in numbers of Muslims, roughly five million, mostly resulting from the country's colonial past.

In spite of its long tradition of immigration, France has never considered immigration a part of its founding national myth. Its republican model was built on a shared political consensus on the values of the French Revolution ("Freedom, Equality, and Fraternity") without reference to ethnic or regional origins. Immigration has been, for a long time, viewed as a provisional solution to labor shortages, the idea being that most immigrants would return to their country of origin rather than settle, even though citizenship was required to fill the need for soldiers and future citizens in periods of low population growth, such as during the nineteenth and early twentieth centuries. Thus, immigration has been more focused on control than on integration, which remains a *parent pauvre* (a despised part) of public and social policy.

Here I focus on the gap hypothesis in discussing the republican/liberal French paradox introduced by James Hollifield and the crisis of control and national identity. In my view, there are three main gaps in French immigration policy:

- The gap between the long history of immigration in Europe and in France in partic- ular and the reluctance to accept the reality of settlement
- The gap between the political desire to control immigration and the structural de- mand for labor
- The gap between policy outputs (laws) and outcomes

THE GAP BETWEEN IMMIGRATION HISTORY AND CURRENT REALITIES: THE MYTH OF AUTOCHTHONY

In spite of its republican tradition, historically France is a multicultural country. Before the French Revolution, provincial France was a patchwork of ethnicities and cultures. Monarchs of the *ancien régime* and the republican revolutions fought to suppress these multitude of identities in favor of a single national identity. No legal distinction was made between nationals and foreigners. During the revolution of 1789, some foreigners, such as Thomas Paine and Anacharsis Clootz, were granted the "status of citizens" because of their participation in the National Assembly. The presence of foreigners or immigrants was known only through police reports during the two revolutions of 1830 and 1848. Only in 1851 did France begin to count foreigners separately from French nationals and the census recorded 300,000 of them, then 1 million in 1900, 3 million in 1930—just on the eve of the law of 1932 that stopped immigration flows in the aftermath of the Great Depression. Since 1930, the number of immigrants has remained stable. In 2010, the census reported 3.6 million foreigners.

The unwillingness of the authorities to admit high levels of immigration and ethnic diversity of the French nation is linked to the founding national myth, which was mostly built on the heritage of the revolution and its republican ideals. When the Third Republic was born in 1875, it proclaimed its ambition to create public, compulsory, free-of-charge, and secularized primary education in a France made up of 80 percent peasants (the laws of 1882 and 1884). Teaching a common history to all citizens was a major part of the republican consensus. A main priority was the writing of a simplified history of France, taking into account the tragic memories of myriad struggles from the persecution and expulsion of Protestants following the revocation of the Edict of Nantes in 1685 to the massacre of the Vendéens by the armies of the republic in 1794.

Professor Ernest Lavisse, at the "College de France," was appointed to carry out this task. He created the citizen myth of the "Gaulois," ancestors of the French, and the image of an autochthonous French nation invaded by foreigners (the "Francs"), who developed a feudal society and started the line of Merovingian kings, princes, and nobles of the ancien régime. So, in spite of its high cultural and ethnic diversity, represented by division into two main parts—the countries of "langue d'oïl" in the north and "langue d'oc" in the south—France was described as an ethnically homogeneous and unified country thanks to the highly centralized state. The "peasant citizen" came to embody the myth of autochthony in his revolutionary struggle against a foreign monarchy. And in modern times this struggle came to be defined in terms of manual workers against cosmopolitan capitalism. This version of French history was supported by anti-Semites like Arthur de Gobineau.

Until the 1980s, there was no interest in immigration history, even though France had long relied on immigration for demographic, economic, and military reasons. The demographic decline that began at the end of the eighteenth century created labor shortages in a period of economic expansion during the Second Empire (1851–1870); the need for soldiers arose on the eve of the Franco-Prussian War of 1870 and again in 1914 at the outset of the Great War. These factors explain the "early willingness to accept foreigners as settlers, immigrants, and citizens," as James Hollifield accurately points out. Immigration in France was a necessity, and to enable it changes were made in the nationality code based on *jus sanguinis* (first promulgated in the civil code of 1804) to include elements of *jus soli* and "to turn foreigners automatically into Frenchmen." This was in accordance with laws passed in 1889, 1927, 1945, and 1973, until a legal and political balance was reached between *jus soli* (citizenship based on place of birth or soil) and *jus sanguinis* (citizenship based on blood or descent).

Newcomers other than full-time workers and soldiers were not seen as prospective citizens because of the transitory and seasonal nature of their work. Many Belgians and Germans were among the first immigrants to arrive at the end of the nineteenth century, along with the Swiss who came to work in the mines, in agriculture, and in industry. After the First World War, they were replaced by Italians (the first nationality to arrive in 1932), the Poles, and eventually the Algerians. The end of the great empires (Russia, Turkey, and Austria-Hungary), as well as the rise of authoritarian regimes, brought several waves of refugees (Armenians, White Russians, and minorities from Central Europe), followed by those from Italy, Spain, and Germany. The "thirty glorious years" (*trente glorieuses*) of economic growth (1945–1974) filled in this mosaic of immigrants with the Portuguese (the largest foreign group in the contemporary era) followed by the Spanish, then Moroccans, Tunisians, Turks, Yugoslavs, and Sub-Saharan Africans. Immigration from European countries dominated until 1982, becoming much more diverse thereafter. After the economic crisis of 1973–1974 immigration became more permanent with fewer return migrants.

THE GAP BETWEEN POLITICAL WILL TO CONTROL IMMIGRATION AND THE STRUCTURAL DEMAND FOR LABOR: THE LIBERAL PARADOX

The liberal paradox developed by James Hollifield particularly fits the French case. The history of immigration control in France can be summed up as a fight between the state and employers, who held the monopoly on recruitment until 1945. In that year, the National Office of Immigration (ONI) was created, but it progressively lost control of migration flows to employers, who needed more labor to feed the fires of economic growth during the *trente glorieuses*. Most of France's immigrants from the 1960s onward were from the Maghreb, which represented the majority of immigrants in France between 1945 and 1974.

Another political and economic conflict involved those who supported settler migration and those who wanted only guest workers. In 1945, supporters of selected immigration flows claimed a distinction between "good" immigrants, those ready and willing to assimilate, and those coming only to work. Georges Mauco, author of a pioneering book on migration, *Les étrangers en France* (1932), had already made a racial distinction between good and bad nationalities, those fit to be immigrants and those who should be kept out. In 1945, the demographer Alfred Sauvy argued for a selective immigration policy that distinguished those who promised to stay in France from those coming only to work. Two sociologists, Alain Girard and Jean Stoetzel, illustrated this idea with extensive field research, the results of which, published in 1953 and 1954, showed the capacities for assimilation among the different nationalities present in France at the time. They concluded that, because of the progressive failure of settlement policies (the exception being Italian farmers in the southwest of France in regions that had become depopulated), temporary or seasonal migration prevailed.

The immigration control debate saw the "liberal" trend represented by employers in opposition to the state, which wanted to control the flows in a period of public planning. But immigration was a topic of low politics decided by high civil servants such as Massenet, who in 1966 became the first Director of Population and Migration in the Ministry of Labor. Most decisions were adopted by decree (administrative rules), telephone calls, and telex: it was the reign of "infra law" carried out in a discretionary manner. Immigration was used to weaken the labor unions and fill labor shortages. The National Office of Immigration, once in charge of all recruitment, lost control, as previously mentioned, with only 18 percent of entries controlled by this office in 1968 (meaning that 82 percent were illegal, and legalized after entry). Efforts to manage immigration via policy failed, and this failure led to a halt in work-related immigration in 1974, in the aftermath of the 1973 oil crisis. In 1977, the Conseil d'État, the highest administrative court of France, condemned decisions prohibiting family reunification, which the government had tried to suppress in 1974, thus confirming the right of families to live together. A policy of return to countries of origin was promulgated by State Secretary Lionel Stoleru in 1977, but it also failed to achieve the objective of reducing immigration.

While no law on immigration control was enacted between 1945 and 1980, immigration became a theme of high politics and legislative activism propelled forward by the rise of the extreme Right after their electoral breakthrough in 1983. Thus, laws adopted between 1980 and 2011 followed an electoral cycle: in 1980, the Right made another attempt to reduce immigration (the Bonnet Law); in 1981, two socialist laws on entry, stay, and freedom of association were enacted, followed by others in 1983 dealing with entry, and in 1984 with stay (the ten-year residence card for those settled in France); with the return to power of the Right in 1986 (the first Pasqua Law on entry and stay); in 1989, another socialist law (the Joxe Law, on entry); in 1993, the Right returned (the second Pasqua Law on entry and stay and the first reform of the nationality code); in 1997, again the Right (the Debré Law, against illegal immigration); in 1998, the Left (the Chevènement Law on entry and stay and the Guigou Law reforming the nationality code); in 2002, the Right again (the Villepin Law on asylum), followed by others in 2003 (the first Sarkozy Law on entry and stay, named RESEDA), in 2004 (the law on secularism and prohibition of scarves at school), in 2006 (the second Sarkozy Law on "immigration choisie," named CESEDA), in 2007 (the Hortefeux Law on entry and stay), in 2010 (the law prohibiting the burqa in public spaces), and in 2011 (the Besson Law on entry and stay).

The ordinance of 1945, which spelled out the legal and constitutional status of foreigners, has been amended more than twenty times in sixty-five years. In the 1990s, the EU's rules were being incorporated into national laws, with the Schengen and Dublin agreements harmonizing border control and asylum at the European level. As a result, French immigration policy has become more dependent on EU politics and policy, which weakens the French republican tradition while reinforcing the separation of religion and politics.

The new cleavage is between an authoritarian and restrictionist approach to immigration policy and a more liberal admissionist approach, occasionally resulting in "strange bedfellows" of coalitions of Left and Right. For example right-wing employer unions (such as the MEDEF) have teamed up with the left-wing defenders of human rights, along with immigrant associations, and NGOs representing diaspora groups whose members look to stay close to their countries of origin. On the restrictionist side, the extreme Right and segments of the public fearing immigration for cultural or economic reasons have made common cause with republicans seeking to restore the authority of the national state in opposition to European rules and liberal policies that undermine assimilation. Trade unions also have joined these restrictionist coalitions in order to protect workers' interests.

THE GAP BETWEEN POLICY OUTPUTS AND OUTCOMES: THE VARIATIONS OF A SYMBOLIC AND DISCRETIONARY POLICY

The liberal paradox mostly covers the period from 1980 to 2011. The 1980s were characterized by a symbolic immigration policy geared more toward public opinion and designed to counter the rise of the National Front. The effectiveness of policy was more an afterthought. The National Front won only three to five seats in the National Assembly and in local and regional elections during this period and sometimes no seats at all. However, immigration control was the main issue for the extreme Right. For example, reform of the nationality code was first debated by a commission appointed in 1987 and its recommendations adopted in 1993; the reform tried to restrict French citizenship only to that acquired by birth. The nationality code was reformed again in 1998 to establish a balance between the principles of *jus soli* and *jus sanguinis*. Because of the electoral successes of the extreme Right, immigration is once again the subject of debate, this time focusing on dual citizenship and sometimes harking back to the dark days of Vichy and the 1940s, even to the point of denaturalization. As for entrance laws, in spite of their increasing emphasis on security, they have not been able to stop illegal migration flows, promote return to countries of origin, or convince elites to "help" their native countries with resettlement. This is despite the incorporation of these objectives in nearly all recent immigration laws. Most of these laws were adopted with some theater or *mise en scène* and largely designed to make headlines thereby giving the illusion that they emphasize extreme rightist claims with little thought to efficient outcomes. In spite of the general prohibition of mass amnesties, for example, most campaigns led by human rights groups have been followed by individual legalizations (*au fil de l'eau*, or case by case according to local bargains) or collective legalizations, such as in Cachan in 2007 on the eve of the presidential elections. The laws of the republic are rarely universally enforced on the territory. The intervention of the Ministry of the Interior also introduces some discretionary practices (*politiques du guichet*) at the local or regional level, giving some latitude to local authorities in policy implementation.

Another factor making implementation of laws difficult is the role of counter powers and pressure groups such as high courts of justice and civic associations. Some associations, such as Réseau Education sans Frontières (RESF) have been very successful in fighting repatriation of families with children at school, while the anti-discrimination associations like

SOS Racisme and France Plus (both founded in 1984) have succeeded in bringing more diversity in government and politics. Human rights associations such the League for Human Rights have strongly criticized national security policy for its repatriation quotas (between 25,000 and 30,000 per year since 2007).

Many high courts, such as the Conseil Constitutionnel, the guardian of the Constitution, the Conseil d'État, which has a strong judicial role, the European Court for Human Rights, and the Court of Justice of the European Union, show the power of judges, especially at the European level. The primary objective of French immigration policy is to give the illusion of sovereignty, but actual decisions are made elsewhere, in Brussels or in Luxembourg. One example is the critical approach of the European Commissioner of Justice, Viviane Redding, toward French policy regarding the Roma in the summer of 2010. Europe can also reinforce the trend toward security at the national level, which includes the directive on return adopted in June 2008 by the European Parliament, the adoption of the European Pact on Immigration and Asylum introduced by France at the European Commission in 2008, and the European Commission's acceptance of France's preventing 20,000 Tunisians from crossing the border between Italy and France in the spring of 2011, after the Tunisian and Libyan revolutions. The objective of these policies is to grab headlines and placate public opinion; they also encourage lawmakers to abdicate their responsibility to govern and solve problems of status and the rights of foreigners that have been debated for over thirty years with no action. An example would be the situation in Calais, where Afghans are still camping out before crossing the channel, in spite of many police operations to stop them. Such policies are disproportionate and ineffective and they do little to dissuade would-be immigrants. These policies are made purely to dissuade would-be immigrants and they result from short-term electoral calculations. The republican model is overwhelmed by anti-immigration politics.

The Republican Model: Myths of the Governance of Immigration and Integration

Patrick Simon

In his inspiring and wide-ranging history of recent French immigration policy, James Hollifield highlights the continuity of these policies over time, or at least the continuity of their principles. He relates this somewhat unexpected coherency against the background of several changes in political forces in office and the rise of anti-immigrant movements to the power of the republican framing and the role played by rights-based policies. The key assumption in this chapter is that a "republican consensus" on immigration and integration is prevailing beyond partisan cleavages between the progressive left and the conservative right, at least in the post–Second World War era. This consensus is said to rely partly on a "grand bargain" between strict controls of immigration to reduce the flows (and to select among immigrants) and a certain openness as well as proactive policies to enhance integration of immigrants and their descendants legally living in France. The trade-off can be discussed in its conception—why and how the reduction of immigration would have a positive effect on the integration prospects of the immigrants?—and in its implementation—do integration's prospects really improve when flows of immigration reach a low mark?

In the aftermath of this "grand bargain," the tone of the political debate on immigration and integration, and the different assessments that have been made of policy outcomes in these domains, prove that the bargain has not been successful. The same stances on the imperious necessity to downsize immigration flows have been repeated ad libitum by all governments in office since the end of the 1980s, whereas the beliefs in the efficiency of the republican model of integration have been seriously eroded, to the point that the model has been deemed to be in perpetual crisis. While Hollifield makes clear in his chapter that the "grand bargain" is mainly a cover to justify a succession of breaches in rights-based policies against migrants and to justify the discrepancy between the rationales of immigration and integration policies and their outcomes for both society at large and targeted groups (immigrants and their descendants), he argues that the state cannot "cross the invisible line between controlling immigration and threatening civil society." There is somehow a contradiction in these assertions: whether the state is forced by a "straitjacket" waved by human rights and cannot go as far as the political rhetoric claims to be able to, or the gradual diminution of the rights granted to migrants and foreigners have already reached a peak, which radically alters the notion of rights-based policies. The contradiction may be solved by defining a degree in the reduction of migrants' rights up to which the nature of immigration and integration policies shifts from coercive but still liberal to coercive and authoritarian, and even more xenophobic and racist.

Such a breakeven point is definitely not easy to draw, and much of the debate in French academic migration studies during the Sarkozy era (2007–2012) was devoted to this issue, and no consensus could be reached. Indeed, can the immigration policy implemented since 2002 be called a sharp break? The term has been used for each major modification of the 1945 immigration decree, making it hard to identify a specific turning point. Danièle Lochak uses the expression *engrenage* (which could be translated as path dependency) for the common inspiration behind the acts passed since 1974, although there have been notable differences in the style of regulation enforcement, particularly against undocumented migrants.

One may take the creation of the code for the entry and residence of foreigners and asylum seekers (Code d'Entrée et de Séjour des Étrangers et des Demandeurs d'Asile, or CESEDA) in March 2005 as the inflection point when immigration policy turned toward greater effectiveness in flow management and thus more active coercion against migrants and their families. This was made possible by an unprecedented administrative integration of the departments in charge of immigration management, with the creation of the Ministry of Immigration, Integration, National Identity and Co-Development in 2007. And yet the four immigration acts passed during this period did not really amount to a decisive break with previous practice. It did take longer to be granted a residence permit; residence permits were replaced by long-stay visas, there was wider use of short-stay documents to be renewed several times before a long-stay document could be obtained, and more requirements were imposed for family reunification and the entry of spouses of French nationals. However, more than a radical change of direction, this tightening-up may be seen as a significant reduction in opportunities to migrate to France and an increased burden on foreigners living in France and their relatives (including French citizens).

What lessons can be learned from Sarkozy's presidency? We know that, even if immigration had been at the center of political debates for at least three decades, Sarkozy brought the issue to its high ends by identifying himself as the champion of the restrictionists. There should be a political approach to immigration, he claimed, and the state should recover the full governance of migrations to France. The "grand bargain" then shifted to the "chosen migration" mantra—that is, the attempt to achieve what most immigration countries try to achieve: attracting high skilled migrants and rejecting others. The objective of increasing labor immigration from 10 percent of the total flow to 50 percent in five years was not met. In 2010, the last year for which data are available, the share of labor migration was still at the 10 percent level. Even worse, annual immigrant entries did not significantly decline under Sarkozy's presidency, but fluctuated around a medium level of 200,000 legal admissions. The emphasis placed on a strict policy of repatriation, with yearly numerical targets, has sent a signal to public opinion that the governance of migration was under control. The target was 28,000 in early 2008, and expulsions rose to nearly 30,000 by the end of the year, of which nearly 10,000 were counted as "voluntary returns" of Romanian and Bulgarian nationals. Being highly controversial, this stricter implementation did not lead to a reduction in the social visibility of undocumented migrants, however. As fully exemplified by the debate on immigration that took place during the 2012 presidential campaign, the voluntarism of the government on migration issues had failed to change significantly the coordinates of France's inevitable move toward a multicultural society.

As Hollifield reminds us, immigration in France has for a long time been "organized but uncontrolled." This may still be the case despite the tightening of rules and procedures that today condition the entry and the stay of foreigners. Looking at sixty years of migration flows, it seems that the decision to stop low-skill labor migration in 1974 is the only policy shock that can be identified in the statistical series. The high level of immigration in the 1960s and beginning of the 1970s was the result of economic pressures more than any governmental planning. The relative high level of the end of the 1990s and the 2000s took place despite the most proactive governance of migration aiming to cut down the flows. Even at its inception in the 1950s, French immigration policy failed to select among the origins of the migrants. Ethnic selection was not officially acknowledged, but there was a clear preference for Northern Europeans against Southern Europeans, and for Southern Europeans against North Africans.

The context of postwar transformations of the colonial empire jeopardized all efforts to filter the migration of undesirable Algerians. When an agreement was signed with Italy, foreseen to bring in 200,000 Italians for postwar reconstruction, only 20,000 finally came in, while 300,000 unexpected Algerians crossed the Mediterranean to settle in the *Metropole*. The *Noria* between Algeria and France quickly reached high peaks, with more than 350,000 entries and departures per year, until the Algerian war of independence broke out in 1954. At the same time, less than 20,000 labor migrants were legally introduced by the Office National d'Immigration (ONI).

There is a striking mismatch between discourses and policies on immigration and what migration statistics tell us. This enduring disconnection in a highly centralized and reputedly efficient state like France raises questions: How much do immigration policies influence the intensity and composition of flows?

The ability of the state to define and enforce its objectives is even more questionable in the case of integration policy. The republican model of integration is a trademark that no longer needs to be explained. Formulated as a tenet at the end of the 1980s, it has never really been translated into policy. Basically, what is called integration policy should better be called admission policy, since it mainly addresses the needs of migrants on their arrival and first years of stay: linguistic training and access to welfare and housing. Most of the policies labeled "integration" were indeed part of urban and social policies and did not target immigrants specifically. In any case, they addressed the main objective of the French model of integration: the transformation of immigrants into Frenchmen by rendering them invisible in social life and incorporating them in the polity through citizenship. This process of assimilation, strictly speaking, is achieved through the usual drivers: institutions, education being at the forefront, social interactions, political participation, and so forth. The invention of the "republican model of integration" in the 1980s was a direct response to the perception that the model was in crisis. The first "equality rallies" organized by second-generation Maghrebian and Portuguese in 1983 and 1984, respectively, and the simultaneous rise of the extreme Right were concrete cues that something was going wrong in the republic. Since then, the anxiety has risen and the revelation of ethnic and racial discrimination not only against immigrants but also against French citizens, has revealed powerful dynamics of ethnicization and racialization in social life. The fact that France's model of integration could not prevent the creation of quasi-ethnic minorities needs to be analyzed further; Hollifield acknowledges this dynamic but does not provide clues for interpreting recent developments.

Among the plethora of explanations that popped up to make sense of this failure, some incriminate the minorities themselves: in contrast with the Europeans who came before 1950, the new immigrants have distant cultures and religions that slow down their acculturation, or they are not playing by the rules, while institutions are weaker than they used to be. As a consequence, the political response to the crisis of the model has been to reinforce the coercive part of the "integration contract." In line with the wave of schemes promoting "civic integration" in several European countries (the Netherlands, the United Kingdom, Denmark, Germany), French integration policy is now emphasizing the adoption of "shared norms and values" and the creation of a common culture, which basically means assimilation into mainstream culture. The promises of equality of rights seem to have been postponed to an indefinite future, while the duties that immigrants and their descendants are asked to perform in exchange for acceptance in the French community tend to be more demanding.

Another line of interpretation sees resistance against the multicultural dimension of French society as a driver for discrimination and as representing lack of integration of the stigmatized minorities. One of the analytical keys to the rationalization of discrimination is the place given to what I call the "postcolonial narrative," by which I mean the tendency of analysis to give status to the fact that the main groups of postwar immigration have come from colonized and decolonized countries (with the notable exceptions of Portugal and Turkey), so that this immigration may be called "postcolonial migration." The category of "postcolonial immigrants" is defined as much by their shared experience of the colony (i.e., of its political and legal systems and its mental structures), as by their continued experience of prejudice and disadvantage in metropolitan France after decolonization. This may explain the discrepancy between the shift into invisibility of Polish, Italian, Spanish, and, more recently, Portuguese second generations and the enduring visibility of the descendants of Algerians, Moroccans, Tunisians, Sub-Saharan Africans, and those born in French overseas possessions. Why do second-generation Algerians still face discrimination while the Portuguese are protected against racism and unfair treatment? All indicators related to cultural integration show that second-generation Algerians are less involved in co-ethnic networks, cultural transmission, transnational ties, and so forth, than are second-generation Portuguese; thus, they are still perceived as not playing the integration game by the rules. It seems that, for Algerians and others, the bargain at the basis of the integration model is giving up specificities to merge into the mainstream as opposed to claiming the full panoply of rights to which they are entitled. Actually, the question is whether the bargain has ever been respected. Going back to the interwar period, when massive immigration from Poland and Italy was taking place, prospects for integration looked quite gloomy. The aftermath of the economic crisis stimulated a steady growth of xenophobia and racism, accompanied by massive repatriation of Polish workers. The most severe anti-immigrant law was passed just before the war as Spanish republicans and Jewish refugees from Germany and Eastern Europe were being held in detention camps. This dreadful trend culminated in World War II. The defeat of Nazism and reconstruction paved the way for a new republican pact, but the prospects for today's second generation of such a *tabula rasa* are bleak. Ultimately, there is no historical evidence that the French model of integration has performed well for the second generation in a time of peace.

6

GREAT BRITAIN

Paradigm and Policy Shifts:

British Immigration Policy, 1997–2011

Randall Hansen

Zig Layton-Henry's contribution to the first edition of *Controlling Immigration* character-ized the United Kingdom correctly as the world's only successful zero-immigration country. Whereas there was a substantial gap between restrictionist intentions and relatively expan-sive immigration outcomes in almost every other Western country, the United Kingdom had managed to restrict immigration to an absolute minimum. Before 1998, net migration was never above 80,000. Since that year, however, net migration has sharply increased and from 1998 on it was never below 140,000 (Migration Advisory Committee 2010: Foreword). Historically (for the United Kingdom) and comparatively (across Europe), this was an un-precedented policy reversal.

Migration is naturally made up of several components, and so was the post-1997 im-migration surge. One part was labor migration. The Labour Party increased the number of work permits issued and, by 2002, was issuing a record number: well over 100,000 each year from 2002 to 2006. Then, in 2004, the British government granted entry rights to hun-dreds of thousands of A8 nationals (those from the 2004 European Union [EU] accession countries minus Malta and Cyprus). The majority of these migrants were unskilled. By the middle of the 2000s, therefore, skilled and unskilled immigration was running at historical highs. During the Labour Party's tenure, 2.5 million foreign-born people were added to the population, and the United Kingdom's foreign-born workforce grew from 2 million to 3.5 million (Finch and Goodhart 2010).

Economic migration formed one pillar of the post-1997 immigration experience. Asy-lum seekers formed the second. In the 1980s, Britain received few asylum applications. Whereas Germany frequently had more than 100,000 applications, Britain had fewer than 20,000. This situation changed dramatically in the 1990s. Asylum seekers rose to 28,000 in 1993, and then tripled to 100,000 in 2000. For the first time ever, Britain overtook Germany as asylum seekers' main destination in Europe. All three migration streams converged to produce the largest migration in UK history.

These developments did not occur because the government, to paraphrase Saskia Sassen, lost control. Nor did a gap between policy intent and policy outcome emerge. Rather, the Labour government made four decisions that marked a fundamental break with previous

Conservative (and indeed 1970s Labour) practice: to increase sharply the number of work permits issued; to create new temporary labor migration schemes while expanding existing ones; to open Britain's borders to newly acceded EU member states; and to adopt an Australian-style points system. The search for skilled labor had its analogs in the European Union, but the United Kingdom was otherwise in a policy league of its own. For the purposes of this volume, the United Kingdom is once again a "deviant case," although this time deviant in its liberal openness to immigration rather than the opposite.

Policy toward asylum seekers was another matter entirely. As labor migration doors opened, asylum doors closed. Under Blair, Labour governments reduced entitlements, restricted asylum seekers' movement, and attempted to expand deportation. Egged on by the viciously anti-asylum tabloid press, the United Kingdom became one of the most restrictive countries in Europe in its policy toward refugees (though, it must be said, there is tough competition for the top spot).

By 2007, as Tony Blair resigned from the Labour Party, British immigration policy was based on the two pillars of a highly open migration toward economic migrants and an equally restrictive one toward asylum seekers. Then, in 2010, a new government knocked one of these pillars out. The Conservative-Liberal Democratic coalition formed in May 2010 agreed to a cap designed to reduce economic immigration radically, including, in theory at least, the skilled immigration that is widely viewed as economically beneficial.

Such was British immigration policy from 1997 onward. An account of it must explain three trends: (1) the expansive immigration policy from 1997 to 2010, (2) the restrictive asylum policy throughout this period, and (3) the 2010–present clampdown on immigration. An explanation requires that we conceive of immigration policy in Britain not as a separate field of inquiry but rather as a basic feature of *British* politics and, above all, of Labour party politics. The British story is not one of cross-European (or cross-OECD) policy convergence in response to common challenges (on this, see Hansen and Weil 2001: Introduction). Global international pressures in favor of skilled and unskilled immigration—business lobbying in favor of more liberal immigration policy, labor shortages in both high and low-skilled sectors, and massive supply pressures in the global South—bore down on all major receiving countries. Yet neither the United States nor any European country went as far as Britain in welcoming immigrants. The factor distinguishing Britain was the election of a Labour government that, first, defined immigration as basic to its modernizing project and, second, linked restrictions in asylum policy with liberalizations in policy toward unskilled migrants. These two developments made this unprecedented migration possible and opened the political space for the current (2011) Conservative policy reversal: Labour's liberalism allowed immigration to become a wedge issue, separating it from the opposition Conservative Party while alienating its own working-class base.

The rest of the chapter proceeds in five steps. First, it provides a brief overview of British immigration policy up to the 1990s. Second, it summarizes labor migration and asylum policies under Labour. Third, it offers an account of these policies located in British—and, above all, internal Labour, politics—one that highlights how expansion in unskilled migration was partly designed to reduce asylum pressures. Fourth, it examines current Conservative proposals and their prospects for success. Finally, it ends with a reflection on existing theoretical accounts of British immigration policy.

BRITISH IMMIGRATION POLICY: A BRIEF HISTORY

From 1905 until 1948, British policy distinguished two types of migrants: British subjects (who could enter the United Kingdom largely freely) and aliens (who could not). In 1905, it imposed the first class-based controls on the movements of aliens while British subjects continued to enjoy the right to enter. World War I led to the introduction of controls on movement across Europe, although low levels of economic growth during the interwar period meant that there was little migration to Britain. In 1948, in response to somewhat arcane constitutional concerns, the United Kingdom introduced an umbrella citizenship— citizenship of the United Kingdom and Colonies (CUKC)—for Britain and British colonial subjects. Until 1962, citizens of the United Kingdom and Colonies had full rights to move to and reside in the United Kingdom. The British government in no sense encouraged Commonwealth immigration; indeed, it very much wished to discourage it (Hansen 2000a). Rather, immigrants came to meet demands for postwar labor. Conservative governments tolerated them for a time because as much as they disliked immigrants they disliked the alternative—severing a symbolic link with the Commonwealth, particularly its old "White Dominions"—even more (Hansen 2000a; Joppke 1999; Wright 2010). In 1962, as numbers surged and domestic opposition grew, a Conservative government rather reluctantly placed controls on the movement of British subjects (both CUKCs from the colonies and citizens from Commonwealth Nations) to the United Kingdom.

From 1962 until 1971, British subjects enjoyed privileged access under a work permit scheme for the Commonwealth. From 1971, however, they were on the same legal footing as aliens, with a few exceptions, for purposes of migration. The Immigration Act of 1971 provided the legal framework for migration for the next three decades. Under it, individuals wishing to migrate to the United Kingdom could come only as a family member or with a work permit. Those with work permits had to have a job offer, and the company usually applied for work permits on their behalf. If granted, the permit allowed them to work in one position for up to four years. They could then apply for permanent residency. In 1973, in the same bill that ended British subjects' privileged access, European Economic Community workers were given the right to work in the United Kingdom. In 1981, the relic of imperial citizenship—CUKC—was replaced with British citizenship.

From the 1970s to the 1990s, there was very little primary immigration to the United Kingdom. Margaret Thatcher made her opposition to immigration clear in 1978, and, after she saw off the British National Policy in the following year, she maintained a tight immigration policy over the next decade. The government only begrudgingly issued work permits, and from the early 1970s until the mid-1980s (and in the early 1990s) there were few jobs for which people could migrate. From 1973 to 1989, 10,000 to 20,000 work permits were issued each year (Wright 2010: 149). Family migration continued, although the Conservatives limited it too through the primary purpose rule (spouses wishing to migrate had to prove that the "primary purpose" of marriage was not migration) and by ending the right to bring in foreign spouses. Asylum seekers were almost nonexistent. Throughout these years, governments were able to maintain the control regime partly because Ireland, then a net emigration country, constituted an ideal temporary labor supply: English-speaking workers who could easily travel to the United Kingdom and were more likely to return home if the economy soured.

Enter (New) Labour

The Labour Party came to power in 1997 armed with a massive majority and a modernizing agenda. The Party manifesto promised reforms to education, the health service, and the country's relationship with Europe, all packaged in Tory-imitating promises on crime (tough on it and on the causes too) and taxes (going nowhere). There was no mention of immigration (Wright 2010: 155), and immigration played no role in the campaign. Over the next decade, however, the government adopted a series of measures that led to a sharp increase in immigration (Wright 2010: 156).

- From 1997 to 2000, the government allowed the number of work permits issued under the 1971 legislation to expand rapidly in response to labor demand and company applications.

- In 2000, the government liberalized the work permit scheme. The requirement of a university degree *and* two years of work experience or five years' senior work experience was changed to a degree *or* three years of skilled work experience. The requirement to advertise locally was relaxed for "shortage" (for instance, IT) and "key" workers (where sectoral demand existed), and the maximum length of the work permit was extended from four years to five.

- Students graduating from undergraduate, MA, or PhD programs were given a one-year work permit.

- Chancellor of the Exchequer Gordon Brown raised the quota under the Season Agricultural Workers Scheme, from 10,000 in 1997 to 25,000 in 2002.

- In 2003, the government created the Sector-Based Scheme for the food and hospitality sectors, which provided 20,000 12-month work visas if companies could prove that they could not recruit low-skilled British workers.

- The Working Holiday workers scheme was transformed from a cultural exchange program to a labor market program. Both old and new Commonwealth citizens were given the right to work for two years in any sector. Significantly, working holiday-makers could transfer to a work permit after one year (Wright 2010: 158–61).

The government made two further changes, one for the skilled and one for the unskilled. For skilled workers, the government introduced, tentatively in 2002 and then fully in 2006, a points system allowing people with the right educational, linguistic, and professional skills to migrate. The points system is based on a five-tiered system: the first tier is for high-skilled migrants (the only group who do not need a job offer to qualify); the second tier covers skilled workers with job offers, as well as workers in occupations on the shortage occupation

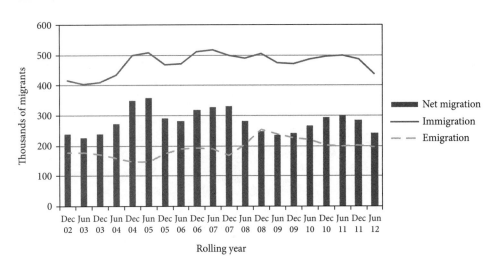

Figure 6.1 Net migration of non-British nationals. *Source: Migration Statistics Quarterly Report,* February 2013, Office for National Statistics.

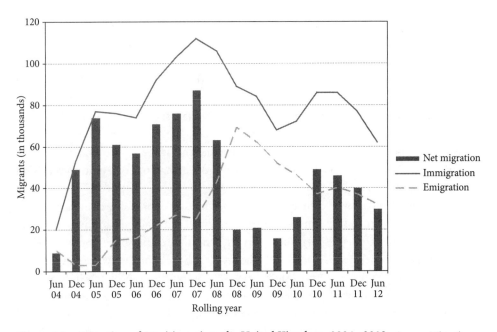

Figure 6.2 Migration of A8 citizens into the United Kingdom, 2004–2012. *Source: Migration Statistics Quarterly Report,* February 2013, Office for National Statistics.

lists; the third tier covers low-skill workers (applicants needing employer sponsors); the fourth tier is for students; and the fifth tier covers working holiday makers and professional athletes and creative temporary workers.

For unskilled workers, the British government was one of a handful in Europe that opened its doors to member states joining the EU in 2004. The effects of these changes were striking. Within a few years, net migration skyrocketed.

TABLE 6.1
Asylum seekers in the United Kingdom 1985, 1992–2010

Year	Asylum seekers	Year	Asylum seekers
1985	6,200	2001	91,600
1992	32,300	2002	103,100
1993	28,000	2003	60,100
1994	42,200	2004	40,600
1995	55,000	2005	30,500
1996	27,900	2006	28,000
1997	32,500	2007	23,600
1998	46,000	2008	23,400
1999	71,200	2009	24,000
2000	99,000	2010	17,800

SOURCE: 1985–2006 data from Salt (1999), European Commission (1998), and US Committee for Refugees (1999); 2007–2010 data from Binder (2011) and ICAR (2009).

NOTE: Numbers are rounded.

WHY?

In a commentary on Zig Layton-Henry's 2004 chapter in the second edition, I suggested that British immigration policy needed to be theorized in terms of markets rather than rights (Favell and Hansen 2004). That is, the key actors in immigration policy were neither activist courts nor pro-migrant civil society actors (both of whom rely on the language and the law of rights), but rather the double demand for migrants found at both the top and the bottom of the pay scale. Morgan Stanley and McDonald's, not judges and juries, drove immigration policy. Recent research suggests a more complicated picture: markets are certainly relevant because they generate the labor demand that is the basis of most migration movements, but the British state played the decisive role in making economic immigration possible (Wright 2010).

Westminster democracy of course places an inordinate amount of power in the hands of the government commanding a majority in Parliament (Lord Hailsham's famous "elective dictatorship"), but the Blair government further concentrated power in two ways. First, though the point is debated (Fawcett and Rhodes 2007), the cabinet saw its power transferred to the Prime Minister's Office (Hennessy 2003). Second, and absolutely indisputably, Gordon Brown, the Chancellor of the Exchequer emerged as the most powerful figure in the cabinet, close to, if not equal to, Tony Blair (Rawnsley 2010: 11–12). As Fawcett and Rhodes put it, under Blair, "we have a picture of a government in which barons vie for favour in the court of a would-be president as dependent on them for support as they are on him for favours. In addition, the greatest baron was Gordon Brown who constructed 'a command Chancellorship—not seen in Whitehall since Neville Chamberlain occupied Number 11 Downing Street….[T]he center of government was characterized, not by prime ministerial centralization, but by two men each presiding over their territory, which was ever more jealously guarded. Brown was 'immovable,' 'dominating his own territory' with 'jagged defenses designed to repel any invader, including the Prime Minister.'" (Fawcett and Rhodes 2007: 101–2).

Tony Blair himself unleashed the monster. As *Guardian* journalist Andrew Rawnsley puts it, "Blair allowed more latitude to Brown than any previous Prime Minister conceded to a Chancellor. . . . Blair surrendered "an unprecedented amount of prime ministerial authority to the Chancellor that went well beyond the normal and inevitably central position played by the Treasury in all administrations . . . it soon became known throughout Whitehall that . . . the Chancellor could defy the Prime Minister with impunity" (Rawnsley 2010: 62–63).

Formally, Brown's power expressed itself above all in the power of the purse: all bills requiring new spending needed his approval. But he went two steps further. First, the Treasury established a series of public service agreements (PSAs, specifying priorities) and efficiency targets that allowed Brown to influence directly not only how much but also *how* departments spent money (Fawcett and Rhodes 2007: 95). Second, the Treasury created no fewer than 42 spending and policy reviews (typically six or seven policy reviews for each spending review) along with multiple "independent" reviews commissioned by it (Fawcett and Rhodes 2007: 97–98). Backed up by a famously dour and truculent personality, what emerged was a "ruthless" chancellor who treated his ministerial colleagues with "more or less complete contempt" (Fawcett and Rhodes 2007: 98; Rawnsley 2010: 68–75). Such was Brown's power that, by 2005, Blair was unable to sack him despite the latter's open treachery and calls by the quality press to do so (Kavanagh 2007: 8).

The Chancellor was particularly interested in social policy but also turned his attention to immigration, as an early and fairly consistent advocate of increasing it. According to a highly detailed study of immigration policy under New Labour by Christopher Wright (Wright 2010: 162), the Treasury was the key actor, and Brown saw two advantages to an expanded policy. First, skilled immigration would increase the country's human capital, which in turn would improve the country's lagging productivity levels (Wright 2010: 162). Second, skilled immigrants would fill labor shortages which, if unfilled, would further inhibit productivity growth (Wright 2010: 162–63). Over the longer term, Labour's investment in education and training would provide the country with a permanent means of improving the country's skills, labor productivity, and international competitiveness (Wright 2010: 164).

Labour's new immigration policy was launched quickly and immediately. The Department of Education and Employment (DEE), which controlled the issuance of work permits until that power was transferred to the Home Office in 2001 (Spencer 2007: 350), streamlined application procedures and relaxed controls soon after the 1997 general election. The business community strongly supported the move, and the number of work permits issued rapidly increased (Spencer 2007: 349). As it required no legislation, or even a public announcement, and because the migrants were highly skilled, well paid, and easily incorporated into work, the move attracted little attention.

In 2001, following its decisive electoral victory, the Labour government decided it was time to attract more high-skilled immigrants. Two figures in particular were behind the push: Barbara Roche, Minister for Immigration, and Alan Johnson, Minister for Competitiveness. Carrying out a 1998 Department of Trade and Industry White Paper recommendation that barriers to skilled professionals be lowered, a July 25, 2000, DTI press release announced a pilot "innovators scheme" that would allow entrepreneurs with business experience and funding to enter the United Kingdom (Home Office 2000). After outing itself through the pilot scheme, the government decided to make a formal announcement of the new immigration policy. Barbara Roche, in a speech approved by the Treasury and the Prime Minister, announced the measures before the "progressive" Institute for Public Policy Research on September 11, 2000. The delivery was uninspiring, but the content was revolutionary: "The UK is in competition for the brightest and best talents—the entrepreneurs, the scientists, the high technology specialists who make the economy tick . . . [and] . . . we need to explore carefully their implications for immigration policy" (quoted in Somerville 2007: 30). Although Roche prudently limited herself to a call for a "British debate" on immigration, the message was clear. Delivered to a handpicked panel of academics ready to sing immigration's praises, the speech amounted to an official endorsement of skilled immigration. "I wanted," Roche later told Oxford University's Sarah Spencer, "to be the first Immigration Minister to say 'immigration is a good thing', that we are a nation of migrants. But it has to be legal, and it has to be well managed" (quoted in Spencer 2007: 350). The government had a secondary motivation, which was to increase migration to the point where the Conservatives would be unable to turn the clock back while increasing the pool of potential Labour voters.[1]

After testing the waters and finding them reasonably warm (there was no political blowback from the speech), the government waited until after the June 2001 election. Its only significant pre-election decision was an October 2000 reduction in the requirements for a work permit: from a job offer, a qualification, and two years of experience to simply a job offer and a qualification (Somerville 2007: 30). The government also waived the Resident Labour Market Test (RLMT) for certain professions (Somerville 2007: 30). The RLMT is an absurdly unenforceable rule maintained by all interior ministries that requires employers to prove that no worker in the country or, in the Britain's case, the EU, could do the job. Again, both decisions required a public announcement, and the subsequent increase in work permits excited no political controversy.

Following another decisive victory in the 2001 General Election, David Blunkett was moved from the Department of Education and Employment to the Home Office, taking with him responsibility for labor migration (DEE was split, with the "employment" portion moved to the Home Office) (Spencer 2007: 350). He announced the creation of a High Skilled Migrant Entry Programme (HSMP). Based on the points system invented by Canada in the 1960s (though the British gave Australia the credit out of a fear that Canadians appeared too soft on immigration), the HSMP assigns points for age, language, and education, but does not require a UK job offer. As everywhere, the idea is that such skills-rewarding migration systems will increase the country's human capital and therefore its competiveness. The scheme took effect in 2002.

Thus, by the early 2000s, the British government had successfully shifted both rhetoric and policy on immigration, and it had in place the policy levers for both demand-driven (the work permit scheme) and human capital migration (the HSMP). It was an utter reversal from 1992 policy, and, rather incredibly for a country not known for its warm welcome of migrants, it caused no political crisis. "Events," as Harold Macmillan put it, "are unpredictable in politics," and two crises—one unexpected and one generated—would wreck Labour's pursuit of a politically uncontentious immigration policy.

CAUGHT UNAWARES: ASYLUM POLICY

In the 1980s, Britain was a no-go zone for would-be refugees. Whereas Germany frequently received asylum applications from over 100,000 people, Britain peaked at 17,000 in 1989 (Gibney and Hansen 2003). From the mid-1990s, however, numbers shot up, peaking at 103,000 in 2002. There is some debate as to why asylum applications spiked. Many scholars cite push factors: instability and human rights abuses in the countries of origin (Castles and Loughna 2005). These no doubt drove asylum seekers, but the question is why they traveled to Britain rather than to other countries; asylum applications for Britain were growing faster than they were in any other European country. The Conservative opposition's answer was that Britain was a soft touch, but this was clearly untrue: Britain had among the most restrictive asylum policies in Europe (Hansen 2000b). The problem was rather that previous "soft touches," above all Germany, had become hard touches, as I argued in a 2004 commentary for *Controlling Immigration*.

It was not hard to see why (Britain had so few applications relative to Germany before 1993). At the time, migrants traveling to the United Kingdom were met with lower social entitlements, much stricter immigration control and a greater likelihood for deportation. As Freeman (1995), Joppke (1999) and others (including myself) pointed out, the United Kingdom simply had the world's most restrictive immigration regime. We also believed that it was the most effective. What seems now to be the case is that its effectiveness was a function of other countries' relative liberality. That is, if it were easier to obtain access to Germany, as it manifestly was pre-1993, then rational migrants would have little interest in traveling to the United Kingdom. Since then, the raft of restrictions instituted by Germany and all other European states have meant that the United Kingdom has lost its illiberal deterring effect. In other words, the success of UK immigration control depended on another sort of gap: *that between its restrictiveness and others' liberality*. Now that that gap has closed, the United Kingdom looks like any other nation in terms of unwanted immigration. Putting it another way, the convergence of asylum policy in Europe into a highly restrictive model exposed British deviancy as a chimera.

The political price paid for this exposure was immense. From the late 1990s, the tabloid press began an often hysterical campaign against asylum seekers, publishing predictably lurid stories about scrounging, crime, and welfare abuses. The Conservative opposition, desperate for an issue that would allow them to knock Tony Blair from his still dizzyingly high popularity ratings, seized on the issue. Ann Widdecombe, then Shadow Home Secretary, made the issue her own and bitterly denounced the government's supposed laxity over asylum (BBC News 2001). Possibly the most damaging development for the government was nightly pictures of asylum seekers escaping Calais's Sangatte refugee camp, scaling fences, and boarding trains bound for Dover in 2001 (Spencer 2007: 342). "By the end of 1992," a senior advisor remarked, "we were just getting slaughtered on asylum. It wasn't unusual for a there to be an asylum story on the front page of a tabloid every day of the week" (quoted in Spencer 2007: 342).

The story of how the Labour government acted is well known. The government passed a series of acts designed to make asylum seeking much more difficult. The first, passed just as the crisis was heating up, was the 1999 Immigration and Asylum Act, which had three key components:

1. *Carrier sanctions:* The law established fines for the operators of ships, vehicles, or aircraft transporting clandestine migrants who then applied for asylum. In most cases, transport was unknowing and unwilling (Part II, Sections 32 and 33).

2. *Rights of appeal:* The act empowered the Home Secretary to limit rights of appeal on grounds of national security (Part IV, Section 70), when the claim of human rights abuses is "manifestly unfounded" (Part IV, Section 72), and when the purpose of the appeal is to remain in the United Kingdom (Part IV, Section 73). All of these provisions extended immense powers of discretion to the Home Secretary.

3. *Social support and reception centers:* Part VI of the act empowered the Home Secretary to limit social support to a level he or she deems appropriate and to designate parts of the country as reception centers for asylum seekers.

The third set of provisions led to the most controversial measures: a voucher scheme replacing cash benefits and the dispersal of asylum seekers across the country. The government abandoned the former in the face of strong union opposition, while the latter crashed against the rocks of local government nimbyism (Spencer 2007: 343–47).

The 1999 act was followed by new legislation in 2002 and 2004. The 2002 legislation further expanded the Home Secretary's power to deport any asylum seeker whose case was "manifestly unfounded" (chiefly for nationals of A8 countries) and to limit social support (Spencer 2007: 344). Finally, legislation in 2004 further limited rights of appeal while excluding failed asylum seekers from secondary (that is, specialist) health care (Spencer 2007: 344).

What is less well known is the fact that the Labour government attempted to balance restrictions in the asylum sphere with liberalization in the migration sphere. Such a linking is by no means new. It was, after all, Harold Wilson's Labour government in the 1960s that sought to make restrictions on Commonwealth immigration more palatable by linking them with anti-discrimination rhetoric. As a young Roy Hattersley put it in 1965, "Integration without control is impossible, but control without integration is indefensible" (quoted in Layton-Henry 2004: 316). Labour's policy had both rhetorical and material aspects. Rhetorically, the asylum control measures were accompanied by official government speeches and papers that for the first time in decades (if not ever) emphasized immigration's positive benefits. With Tony Blair's backing (Wright 2010: 167; *Guardian* 2000), and with asylum applications at a new peak, Immigration Minister Barbara Roche spoke in 2000 of the benefits of "managed migration" and the importance of citizenship ceremonies in celebrating naturalization. Blair soon moved Roche out of the Home Office, but the Home Secretary himself, David Blunkett, picked up the theme and was by 2003 a public advocate of (skilled) immigration. Materially, the government, seizing on a theory that was being passed around seminar rooms at the time, decided that expanding unskilled immigration would take pressure off the asylum queues (Wright 2010: 170). As one Treasury official put it, "The idea was that you could be tougher on the asylum seekers if they had a legitimate route" (quoted in Wright 2010: 170).

The policy did not work for reasons that could have been predicted. The massive disparities in wealth, living standards, and quality of life between Britain and the major refugee-producing countries of Iraq, Afghanistan, and Zimbabwe meant and still mean that any opening of unskilled migration channels will be insufficient to meet demand. Allowing 20,000 food and hospitality workers, the most likely scheme under which asylum seekers could come, would not reduce the pressure of 100,000 asylum seekers, not least because language requirements made many of them unlikely waiters. The Foreign Secretary at the time, Jack Straw, recognized this fact,[2] but David Blunkett stubbornly refused to. As if one migration crisis were not enough, he generated another.

EU ENLARGEMENT

In 2004, the EU experienced the greatest enlargement in its history. Ten Eastern European countries, most of them poor, joined at once. Under the Accession Treaty, existing EU member states could restrict migration from the new states for up to seven years (Sriskandarajah 2004: 7). Austria, Germany, France, and most other EU members used these restrictions; only Ireland and Britain did not. The initial decision was uncontroversial, but as of May 1, 2004, the press began to run stories about Roma who were likely to opt for welfare rather than work (Spencer 2007: 352). Blunkett stood his ground, maintaining that there was demand for low-skilled workers and that such demand would otherwise be filled by illegal migrants (Spencer 2007: 352). Whitehall seemed largely to support the decision. Most departments had worked intensively with their opposite numbers in Eastern Europe, and there was a general feeling that Britain's strong rhetorical commitment to enlargement placed the country under a moral obligation to open its doors (Wright 2010: 173). The decisive argument was the cost-benefit calculation: the Home Office estimated that only some 5,000 to 13,000 would arrive per year, yet this small arrival would somehow generate great economic benefits. A wide range of academic studies supported both these conclusions (for a summary, see Sriskandarajah 2004: 12).

It did not turn out that way. After 2004, 700,000 to 1,000,000 Eastern European migrants arrived or legalized themselves in the United Kingdom (Galgóczi, Leschke, and Watt 2011), although as many as half may have returned (Pollard 2008). Rather ironically, the one organization that got the numbers right was the avowedly partisan and anti-immigration Migration Watch, whose analyses are frequently dismissed by scholars as alarmist. In 2004, it predicted a figure closer to 800,000 than the 13,000 projected by the government (Green 2004). Perhaps most damning for the government was a House of Lords report concluding that the migration's economic effects were small and that the most recent immigration wave had provided a small benefit to Britain's richest citizens while imposing a small cost on its poorest (House of Lords 2008). As both conclusions—that the costs or benefits of immigration were small and the overall effects distributional—were widely known to economists (Borjas 1999; Martin 2011), the conclusion should not have been greatly surprising. The problem was that, in its effort to attract support for immigration, the government had overreached: the Home Office claimed that the *annual* economic benefit of immigration to the United Kingdom was 6 billion pounds (Naughton 2007). This could hardly be taken seriously; a decade earlier, the most comprehensive study of the benefits and costs of immigration to the United States, a country six times larger than Britain, had placed the annual benefit at 10 billion dollars—almost exactly the same figure. Labour's overreach in turn set the stage for the Conservatives' counterattack.

THE CONSERVATIVES AND IMMIGRATION

As Ann Widdecombe's not terribly subtle interventions made clear, the Conservatives recognized immigration early on as an issue that they might exploit for electoral gain. That they did so is worthy of brief historical comment. From the 1970s, both major political parties had largely agreed not to make race and immigration a matter of electoral competition (Messina 1989). Why they did so is a matter of debate, but they likely concluded that it was one issue on which they could both lose simultaneously to the gain of the National Front (later the British National Party) and/or a divisive maverick such as Enoch Powell. By the late 1990s, the Conservatives had forgotten this agreement, decided to undermine it, or viewed asylum as a nonracial issue and therefore not subject to the agreement. In any case, in the early years of the millennium the Conservatives made consistent political capital out of asylum. During the 2005 election, the Conservative Party made immigration a central feature of its campaign. Its manifesto listed "Controlled Immigration" on its cover (more police, cleaner hospitals, lower taxes, school discipline, and accountability being the others) and devoted a section to "Secure Borders and Controlled Immigration," promising increased border surveillance and—most radically—a unilateral withdrawal from the 1951 UN Convention relating to the status of refugees and the creation of a cap on asylum applications. Positively, the manifesto also promised a points system (with the Australians again getting credit) that would shift immigration from unskilled to skilled.

According to both media reports and postelection academic analyses, immigration had at best a modest effect on the electoral outcome because anti-immigrant hostility was concentrated among those voters most likely to stay home—the young and uneducated (Ford 2006). These results were in some measure surprising, as the portion of voters who saw immigration as the most important issue had risen from below 10 percent in 2001 to over 30 percent four years later (Ford 2006). But the results were also consistent with past experience. In the early 1970s, at the Powellite height of anti-immigration sentiment in Britain, the anti-immigration vote at best affected the outcome in a small number of seats (Studlar 1978). Perhaps more important, the Conservatives overplayed their hand: by banging on endlessly about immigration, the Tories looked "opportunistic, monomaniac and unattractive to centrist and floating voters" (Rawnsley 2010: 306). And Labour was of course led in 2005 not by the charmless Brown but by Tony Blair, a politician who, though terribly weakened by the Iraqi disaster, retained rhetorical skills and political acumen that far outclassed his Conservative opponents. In a well-timed speech at Dover, he attacked the Tories for seeking to "exploit people's fears." Then, hovering over a wounded Michael Howard, he delivered the coup de grâce: "The Tory Party have gone from being a One Nation Party to being a one-issue party" (quoted in Rawnsley 2010: 306)." Far from securing electoral victory, the Conservatives' anti-immigration rhetoric in 2005 seemed only to confirm the widespread impression that they were a party of aging and somewhat demented soldiers fighting decades-old battles, nominally led by Colonel Howard but in fact taking orders from retired General Thatcher.

By 2010, the politics of immigration shifted in important ways. The number of voters ranking the issue as the most important rose some ten points to 40 percent (Carey and Geddes 2010: 854) and, as a result, the Labour Party became dangerously exposed on the issue. Its vulnerability was brutally revealed by one disagreeable woman who caught up with the prime minister on his way back from the shops.

On April 28, 2010, Gordon Brown was visiting Rochdale in Greater Manchester. A 65-year-old widow, Gillian Duffy, heckled him as he spoke. He ignored her, but then aides arranged a meeting in a hopeless effort to show his common touch. Duffy ranted about immigrants from "Eastern Europe," and then asked where they were "flocking in from" (a question she herself answered). Brown politely defended immigration and then thanked her. He had so far done rather well, but it soon went wrong. Back in his official car, with the microphone on, he spoke his mind: "She was just a sort of bigoted woman."

This was a more truthful and believable statement than were his many claims to have eliminated the business cycle: Duffy did walk and talk like a bigot. The press nonetheless had a field day. Journalists replayed Brown's remark for Duffy, who feigned the appropriate horror that anyone could think such a sweet lady bigoted. The nightly news replayed both to the nation, and Brown was forced into a series of humiliating apologies. The event was electorally important for two reasons. First, there was a widespread impression that Duffy was saying what many people were thinking: that Labour had allowed immigration to the United Kingdom, in the form of both asylum seekers and unskilled EU workers, to spin out of control. It was the fact that so many people shared her concerns that magnified the effects of what in other circumstances might have been an embarrassing but not fatal mistake. In this respect, the event was similar to a 2001 accosting of Tony Blair outside a hospital by Sharon Storer, a postmistress who berated him over the cancer care her friend was receiving. Brown's experience was, of course, worse because he said what he thought on air and because John Prescott failed to oblige him, as he had Blair, by distracting the press with a sharp left hook to a voter's jaw (on Blair, see Rawnsley 2010: 10).

Second, Duffy was herself working class, and therefore Labour's immigration policy was hurting the party by alienating working-class voters. Senior party leaders recognized this as they entered the election. In early 2009, Hazel Blears, a longstanding MP for the northern constituency of Salford and then Secretary of State for Communities and Local Government, released a report, based on interviews with residents at housing estates, suggesting that Labour's working-class supporters had been alienated by the party's stance on immigration (Summers 2009). She secured particularly strong support from the longstanding Labour MP Frank Field, who backed up her calls for the government to address white working-class fears of immigration (Summers 2009). In the same period, the Cabinet, in a split decision with Gordon Brown tipping the matter, agreed (1) that immigration was itself a major concern to voters and (2) that its policies therefore had to change (Cavanagh 2010: 31). The official position before that, one that sounded rather like a sociology seminar on the topic, was that housing, unemployment, and/or low wages were the real problem and were unrelated to immigration (Cavanagh 2010).

Since then, major figures in the Labour party have gone further still. In the run-up to the Labour leadership contest in 2010, Ed Miliband told the papers that Labour had been "wrong to allow so many eastern Europeans into Britain" as they undercut wages and worsened working conditions of poorer Britons (Balls 2010). Ten months later, the victor in the contest, Ed Miliband, who hails from the unionist left of the party, told the BBC that the Labour government "got it wrong," failing to see the impact that Labour would have on the wages of low-skilled British workers (Porter 2011). A left-wing MP from thoroughly working class Dagenham, Jon Cruddas, and *Guardian* contributor and Middlesex professor Jonathan Rutherford published the following in the *New Statesman*, a weekly tightly linked since its founding with the Labour Party:

> Labour's response was to prepare workers for the global market. It began to promote an entrepreneurial way of life and the aspiration of "earning and owning." The drive towards a more flexible labour market increased the use of short-term contracts, agency work, subcontracting and the hiring of those who were "self-employed." The model encouraged immigration into Britain, but left the British workforce one of the worst protected in Europe.
>
> The whirlwind of globalisation has destroyed working-class communities. In the most deprived areas, a culture of shame and failure has taken root. Children grow up expecting nothing and so give nothing in return. People fear that their identity and way of life are under threat; in consequence, they fear the stranger. This fear then spreads outward to the wider population, like ripples across a pond. (Cruddas and Rutherford 2010)

As this was going on, the Conservatives played their cards carefully. Opposition to immigration certainly presented them with an opportunity, but they needed to exploit it with caution. In the years preceding the election, they tried to shake the impression that they were what one senior Conservative called "the nasty party": harshly right-wing, uncaring, and beholden to extremists. That they had elected three of the most right-wing party leaders since Margaret Thatcher—William Haig (Thatcher's choice), Iain Duncan Smith (a hardened euroskeptic), and Michael Howard (a "hang them and flog them" Home Secretary)—certainly had not helped. The election of a young, urbane David Cameron in 2005 (a not very subtle imitation of Tony Blair) was designed in part to shake this image. Conscious that they consistently enjoyed a large advantage over Labour on the issue (Carey and Geddes 2010: 853), they made their position clear—a cap on immigrants—without actually talking that much about immigration (Carey and Geddes 2010). The strategy worked: although the election was fundamentally a referendum on Labour's management of the economy, voters concerned about immigration were more likely to vote Conservative (Ford and Somerville 2010).

THE IMMIGRATION CAP

During the campaign, the Conservatives promised repeatedly to reduce net annual immigration from hundreds of thousands to tens of thousands. Despite Liberal Democratic opposition, the immigration cap emerged intact following the coalition agreement. In July 2010, the government announced a temporary cap of Tier 2 visas at 24,100 and an increase in the points required under Tier 1 from 90 to 100. The cap was designed to avoid a last-minute upsurge in applicants. It is unclear whether there was personal or institutional memory of it, but this is exactly what the United Kingdom experienced in 1962, when it allowed six months before the announcement of immigration controls on the Commonwealth and their implementation (Hansen 2000a: chap. 2). Intensive business lobbying, backed up by Vince Cable of the Liberal Democrats, followed. Some companies threatened to move overseas.

In late October, the prime minister announced a significant concession: the cap would not apply to intracompany transfers, subject to a minimum salary of £40,000, a maximum stay of five years, and no right of settlement. In 2009, such transfers made up 40 percent of all Tier 1 and Tier 2 entrants (Migration Advisory Committee 2010: table 3.2) When the Home Secretary, Theresa May, announced the cap in April 2011, the global figure had not changed much—21,700—but the sorting had. Tier 1 (skilled without a job) was reduced to 1,000 (a fall of some 6,000 over the previous year), while Tier 2 (skilled with a job) was increased by a similar figure. In addition, high earners—those making over £150,000 per year—were exempted, as were a number of other special categories (ministers of religion and elite sports personalities) (Travis 2011a, 2011b). Finally, students entering under Tier 4 must prove proficiency in English, both through tests results and during an interview with UK Border Agency officials (de Lotbinière 2011). In addition, students at private colleges can no longer work part-time during their courses. These moves were motivated in part by the perception that those seeking to evade immigration controls use the colleges as a means to gain entry.

The obvious question is whether these efforts will work. According to the Migration Advisory Committee, a nonpartisan committee of experts created by Labour and maintained by the Conservative/Liberal Democratic government, some 15 percent of those who arrived in the United Kingdom in 2009 were British nationals (Migration Advisory Committee 2010: fig. 3.7). Another 30 percent were EU nationals whose entry could not be blocked. The rest—some 280,000 in gross terms—could be controlled (Migration Advisory Committee 2010: fig. 3.7). They break down into the following categories: Tier 1 (4 percent), Tier 2 (work permits, 8 percent), Tier 4 (students, 64 percent), and Tier 5 (working holiday makers, 4 percent) (Migration Advisory Committee 2010: fig. 3.14). Family and settlement categories make up another 11 percent (Migration Advisory Committee 2010: fig. 3.14).

Assuming a target figure of 50,000 per year (it could be 99,999 and still be within the government's promise), the British government would have to reduce yearly entry by some 120,000. In 2009, just over 55,000 Tier 1 and Tier 2 entries were granted (Migration Advisory Committee 2010: table 3.2). Once the exempt categories of investors (13,930), intracompany transfers (22,030), elite sports people (265), and ministers of religion (265) are subtracted, the figure becomes 18,570, *a figure lower than the current cap*.

The British government has effectively left skilled immigration alone. To achieve its aim, it will need to crack down radically on students while ending easy rights of settlement granted to those students who remain as well as those coming under Tier 5. Whether the English-language requirements and the restrictions on work will suffice remains to be seen.

CONCLUSION: THE *LONGUE DURÉE*: BRITISH IMMIGRATION POLICY AND THE STUDY OF BRITISH POLITICS

If the United Kingdom stands out among the countries examined in this volume, it is in its capacity for radical policy shifts: over seventeen years, the country went from a zero-immigration country, to a thoroughgoing country of immigration, to, once again, something approaching a zero- or little-immigration country. As I have elsewhere argued (Hansen 2000a), we need to focus on institutions to understand these shifts. The United Kingdom is the Weberian ideal of a powerful executive, and the Treasury is among the most powerful departments within it. This is always true, and it was particularly true under Gordon Brown and New Labour.

As this chapter has argued, the Labour Party, led by the Treasury and informed by a particular theory of migration's dynamizing effects, determined the sharp increase in skilled and unskilled labor migration, doing so in part to check the effects of unexpected and unwanted migration: asylum seekers. The surge in migration provided the Conservatives with a wedge issue on which they have acted since their election with an equally dramatic reversal of policy. It is worth reflecting on the theoretical implications. The broader question is how well existing theory accounts for these changes.

The answer is not very well. The earliest works on British immigration policy offered an essentially pluralist interpretation: the steady rise in nonwhite Commonwealth immigrants in the 1950s and the accelerated arrival in the early 1960s, led the Conservative government to end, reluctantly, the right of Commonwealth immigrants to enter (Deakin 1968, 1969; Rose 1969). Given general opposition to immigration control, however, pluralist accounts do well at explaining immigration policy restrictions but do less well at explaining policy expansion. Naturally, the business community and especially the City support immigration, but they always have, as the public has always opposed it. These factors are static; immigration policy is highly dynamic.

Other accounts do not get us much further. One early seminal work applied class analysis to the whole of Europe, including the United Kingdom (Castles and Kosack 1973; also see Miles 1982). According to Marxist-functionalist interpretations, immigrants responded to the needs of capitalism (namely a supply of cheap labor), cushioned its crisis tendencies (by bearing the brunt of unemployment), and delayed its inevitable collapse.[3] Closely related to this literature is a set of arguments that might be grouped under critical race theory (Carter, Harris, and Joshi 1987; Solomos 1993; Gilroy 1987). The title of Paul Gilroy's book, *There Ain't No Black in the Union Jack*, says it all. British immigration policies were determined to a superlative degree by racism, and British identity itself was race based (or "racialized"). Betraying their Marxist origins, under some versions of the thesis, the British working class was seen as enlightened and foreigner-friendly until being duped into racism by Labour and Conservative politicians (Foot 1965; Paul 1997).

Like many schools, both the Marxist functionalist and critical race approaches offer important insights. British immigration to the United Kingdom is largely market driven, and it is true that British politicians had a tendency to think that "race" rather than "racism" was the problem. But these approaches leave too much unexplained, both historically and today. In the former, opposition to immigration came too often from those with the greatest interest in capitalism (such as Margaret Thatcher) to accept the Marxist functionalist story as an explanation of policy (as distinct from an account of how markets move migrants). Similarly, the emphasis on racism could not explain why immigration policy stayed so liberal for so long (open borders until 1962 and easy movement until 1971); why there was never any serious effort to block family immigration; and why politicians such as Iain MacLeod (over the Kenyan Asians), Ted Heath (over the Ugandan Asians), Roy Jenkins (over anti-discrimination legislation), or David Blunkett and Gordon Brown (over A10 migrants) adopted bold, pro-migrant positions at variance with public opinion. The claim that the working class was a bastion of liberal opinion talked into racism cannot be taken seriously, as recent events have made abundantly clear. Finally, the most recent immigration debate focused as much on white (and Christian) immigrants from Eastern Europe as it did nonwhite ones from the Middle East or Africa.

The inadequacy of existing theories takes us back to the importance of institutions. From the 1990s, comparativists—mostly in political science but also in sociology—began to study the United Kingdom as one case among others in Europe. Two related trends stood out. First, British immigration policy had shifted from periods of great liberality (the 1950s and 1960s) to great restrictiveness (the 1970s to the mid-1990s), and back to (relative) liberality (the mid-1990s to the present). Numbers fluctuated accordingly: high in the 1960s to early 1970s; low in the 1980s; high again in the last decade. Second, rhetoric showed similar tendencies: periods of bipartisan consensus keeping immigration out of politics (the mid-1960s, much of the 1970s, the 1980s, and the early 1990s) were suddenly disrupted by periods of intense bipartisan competition. A number of authors (Freeman 1995; Joppke 1999; Hansen 2000a) explained these features with reference to British institutions. The absence of checks on the executive found in the United States or Germany means that the United Kingdom can maintain for relatively long periods policies that fly in the face of public opinion (open immigration). When governments do restrict, however, those same institutions also mean that they are able to achieve a very high degree of restrictiveness.

An institutional account also sheds light on the jarring shifts in rhetoric over immigration. Immigration is a highly divisive issue that tends to split parties—traditionally, the free trade/pro-European versus the protectionist/little Englander wings of the Conservative party and the working-class/liberal professional wings of Labour. It is also exceptionally hard to respect discourse constraints: as in Germany or the United States, debates over immigration often bring out nativist or xenophobic sentiment in both the parties and the public. For these reasons, the parties often agree informally to leave the issue alone. Yet, at the same time, Britain's system of adversarial government encourages competition over the issue, and both parties and individuals have an incentive to politicize it. This is particularly true when numbers are high and when there is little distance between the parties on economic issues (true of both the 1960s and the 2000s).

Framed in this way, an institutional account avoids the overdetermination of Marxist-functionalist or critical-race interpretations. Institutions encourage certain responses, but leave much room for agency. In the 1960s, Roy Jenkins articulated a vision of an inclusive, tolerant society (partly out of principle, partly because it did him a lot of good with the intellectual wing of the Labour party). In the 1980s, Thatcher (and some of her ministers, such as Kenneth Baker, Norman Tebbit, and Alan Clarke) was particularly hostile to immigration. Finally, in the 1990s Gordon Brown saw in immigration a partial solution to the United Kingdom's deficits in human capital and productivity. Nonetheless, in several of these cases politicians—Enoch Powell in the 1960s, Thatcher in the late 1970s (when she famously said that the British feared being "swamped" by people of a different culture), and the Conservatives under Hague, Howard, and Cameron—used immigration to create political distance between themselves and the opposition. Somewhat paradoxically, British institutions make UK immigration both excessively liberal and excessively illiberal.

NOTES

For research assistance, I am grateful to Alisa Gorokhova.

1. Implied by Andrew Neather (2009): "I remember coming away from some discussions with the clear sense that the policy was intended—even if this wasn't its main purpose—to rub the Right's nose in diversity and render their arguments out of date. That seemed to me to be a manoeuvre too far." This comment led to outrage among Conservatives and other anti-migration advocates and to strenuous denials on the part of senior Labour ministers. It is unclear why: the suggestion that the government would be sensitive to the broader social and implications of immigration, and the position of voters following it, is anodyne.

2. I put the question directly to the foreign secretary during an open debate in (I believe) early 2003.

3. Another important argument was offered in a book by Ira Katznelson (1973), who argued that Britain's integration policy reflected an adoption in the metropole of the colonial strategy of indirect rule: issues of immigration and race were shunted to the periphery (i.e., local government), where they were dealt with in cooperation with local elites.

REFERENCES

Balls, Ed. 2010. "We Were Wrong to Allow So Many Eastern Europeans into Britain." *Guardian*, June 6.

BBC News. 2001. "Tories Renew Asylum Attacks." April 25.

Borjas, George J. 1999. *Heaven's Door: Immigration Policy and the American Economy.* Princeton, NJ: Princeton University Press.

Carey, Sean, and Andrew Geddes. 2010. "Less Is More: Immigration and European Integration at the 2010 General Election." *Parliamentary Affairs* 63 (4): 849–65.

Carter, Bob, Clive Harris, and Shirley Joshi. 1987. "The 1951–55 Conservative Government and the Racialization of Black Immigration." In *Insider Babylon: The Caribbean Diaspora in Britain*, edited by Winston James and Clive Harris, 55–72. London: Verso.

Castles, Stephen, and Godula Kosack. 1973. *Immigrant Workers and Class Structure in Western Europe.* London: Oxford University Press.

Castles, Stephen, and Sean Loughna. 2005. "Trends in Asylum Migration to Industrialized Countries, 1900–2001." In *Poverty, International Migration and Asylum*, edited by George J. Borjas and Jeff Crisp, 39–69. Houndmills, UK: Palgrave.

Cavanagh, Matt. 2010. "Numbers Matter." In *Immigration under Labour*, edited by Tim Finch and David Goodhart, 30–34. London: IPPR/Prospect.

Cruddas, Jon, and Jonathan Rutherford. 2010. "See the Bigger Picture." *New Statesman*, May 31.

Deakin, Nicholas. 1968. "The Politics of the Commonwealth Immigrants Bill." *Political Quarterly* 39: 25–45.

———. 1969. "The British Nationality Act of 1968: A Brief Study in the Political Mythology of Race Relations." *Race and Class* 11 (1): 77–83.

De Lotbinère, Max. 2011. "UK Tells Foreign Students: 'Speak English or Stay Out.'" *Guardian*, April 12.

European Commission. 1998. RE Country Reports.

Favell, Adrian, and Randall Hansen. 2002. "Markets against Politics: Migration, EU Enlargement and the Idea of Europe." *Journal of Ethnic and Migration Studies* 28 (4): 581–601.

Fawcett, Paul, and R. Rhodes. 2007. "Central Government." In *Blair's Britain, 1997–2007*, edited by Anthony Sheldon, 79–103. Cambridge: Cambridge University Press.

Finch, Tim, and David Goodhart. 2010. "Introduction," In *Immigration under Labour*, edited by Tim Finch and David Goodhart, 3–9. London: IPPR/Prospect.

Foot, Paul. 1965. *Immigration and Race in British Politics*. Harmondsworth, UK: Penguin.

Ford, Robert. 2006. "An Iceberg Issue? Immigration at the 2005 British General Election." http://www.academia.edu/2783528/An_iceberg_issue_Immigration_at_the_2005_British_General_election.

Ford, Robert, and Will Somerville. 2010. "Immigration and the 2010 General Election: More Than Meets the Eye." In *Immigration under Labour*, edited by Tim Finch and David Goodhart, 10–14. London: IPPR/Prospect.

Freeman, Gary P. 1995. "Modes of Immigration Politics in Liberal Democratic States." *International Migration Review* 29 (4): 881–902.

Galgóczi, Béla, Janine Leschke, and Andrew Watt. 2011. "Intra-EU Labour Migration: Flows, Effects and Policy Responses." Working Paper 2009/3, European Trade Union Institute, Brussels. http://www.policypointers.org/Page/View/9398.

Gibney, Matthew J., and Randall Hansen. 2003. "Deportation and the Liberal State: The Forcible Return of Asylum Seekers and Unlawful Migrants in Canada, Germany and the United Kingdom." Working Paper 77, New Issues in Refugee Research Series, United Nations High Commissioner for Refugees (UNHCR), Geneva.

Gilroy, Paul. 1987. *There Ain't No Black in the Union Jack: The Cultural Politics of Race and Nation*. Chicago: University of Chicago Press.

Green, Sir Andrew. 2004. "Blunkett Has Failed to Wake Up to the Immigration Nightmare." *Daily Telegraph*, February 24.

Hansen, Randall. 2000a. *Citizenship and Immigration in Postwar Britain*. Oxford: Oxford University Press.

———. 2000b. "Asylum Policy in the European Union." *Georgetown Journal of Immigration Law* 14 (3): 779–800.

Hansen, Randall, and Patrick Weil. 2001. *Towards a European Nationality*. Houndmills, UK: Palgrave.

Hennessy, Peter. 2003. "The Blair Style and the Requirements of Twenty-First Century Premiership." *Political Quarterly* 74 (4): 386–95.

Home Office. 2000. "New Immigration Scheme to Attract Innovators." Press release. http://www.anglofil.com/en/?/archive/ukentryclearancevisas.

House of Lords Select Committee on Economic Affairs. 2008. *The Economic Impact of Immigration*. London: Stationery Office Limited.

ICAR (Information Centre about Asylum Seekers and Refugees). 2009. *Key Statistics about Asylum Seekers Applications in the UK*. London: ICAR.

Independent. 2010. "David Cameron Defends Immigration Cap." November 3.

Joppke, Christian. 1999. *Immigration and the Nation State: The United States, Germany, and Britain*. Oxford: Clarendon.

Katznelson, Ira. 1973. *Black Men, White Cities: Race, Politics, and Migration in the United States, 1900–30, and Britain, 1948–68*. London: Oxford University Press.

Kavanagh, Dennis. 2007. "The Blair Premiership." In *Blair's Britain, 1997–2007*, edited by Anthony Sheldon, 3–15. Cambridge: Cambridge University Press.

Layton-Henry, Zig. 1994. "Britain: The Would-Be Zero-Immigrant Country." In *Controlling Immigration: A Global Perspective*, edited by Wayne A. Cornelius, Philip Martin, and James Hollifield, 273–95. Stanford, CA: Stanford University Press.

———. 2004. "Britain from Immigration Control to Migration Management." In *Controlling Immigration: A Global Perspective*, edited by Wayne A. Cornelius, Takeyuki Tsuda, Philip Martin, and James Hollifield, 297–333. 2nd ed. Stanford, CA: Stanford University Press.

Martin, Philip. 2011. "Mexico-US Migration, NAFTA and CAFTA, and US Immigration Policy." In *Migration, Nation States and International Cooperation*, edited by Randall Hansen, Jeannette Money, and Jobst Koehler, 75–86. New York: Routledge.

Messina, Anthony M. 1989. *Race and Party Competition in Britain*. New York: Oxford University Press.

Migration Advisory Committee. 2010. *Limits on Immigration*. Croydon: Home Office.

Miles, Robert. 1982. *Racism and Migration Labour*. London: Routledge & Kegan Paul.

Naughton, Philippe. 2007. "Migrants Contribute 6 Billion to the UK Economy." *Times of London*, October 16.

Neather, Andrew. 2009. "Don't Listen to the Whingers: London Needs Immigrants." *Evening Standard*, October 23.

Paul, Kathleen. 1997. *Whitewashing Britain*. Ithaca, NY: Cornell University Press.

Pollard, Naomi. 2008. "Feeling the Pull of Home?" IPPR brief. http://www.ippr.org.uk/articles/?id=3125.

Porter, Andrew. 2011. "Ed Miliband: Immigration Lost Labour Votes." *Daily Telegraph*, April 20.

Rawnsley, Andrew. 2010. *The End of the Party: The Rise and Fall of New Labour*. London: Penguin.

Rose, E. J. B. 1969. *Colour and Citizenship: A Report on British Race Relations*. London: Oxford University Press.

Salt, John. 1999. *Current Trends in International Migrations in Europe*. Strasbourg: Council of Europe.

Solomos, John. 1993. *Race and Racism in Britain*. 2nd ed. New York: St. Martin's Press.

Somerville, Will. 2007. *Immigration under New Labour*. Bristol: Policy Press.

Spencer, Sarah. 2007. "Immigration." In *Blair's Britain, 1997–2007*, edited by Anthony Sheldon, 341–60. Cambridge: Cambridge University Press.

Sriskandarajah, Dhananjayan. 2004. *EU Enlargement and Labour Migration: An IPPR FactFile*. London: Institute for Public Policy Research.

Studlar, Donald T. 1978. "Policy Voting in Britain: The Coloured Issue in the 1964, 1966, and 1970 Elections." *American Political Science Review* 72 (1): 46–64.

Summers, Deborah. 2009. "White Working Class Feels Ignored over Immigration, Says Hazel Blears." *Guardian*, January 2.

Travis, Alan. 2011a. "Immigration Cap Exclusions Turn Policy into Gesture, Say Critics." *Guardian*, June 28.

———. 2011b. "High Earners Exempted from Immigration Cap." *Guardian*, February 15.

UN High Commissioner for Refugees (UNHCR). 1995. *The State of the World's Refugees 1995: A Humanitarian Agenda*. Oxford: Oxford University Press. http://www.unhcr.org/cgi-bin/texis/vtx/home/opendocPDFViewer.html?docid=3eedd83d2&query=state of the world's refugees.

———. 2000. "Global Refugee Trends: Analysis of the 2000 Provisional UNHCR Population Statistics, May 2000." http://www.unhcr.ch/statist/2000provisional/trends.pdf.

———. 2005. *Asylum Trends and Levels in Industrialized Countries 2005*. Geneva: UNHCR.

US Committee for Refugees. 1999. *World Refugee Survey 1999*. Washington, DC: US Committee for Refugees.

Wright, Chris. 2010. "Policy Legacies and the Politics of Labour Immigration Selection and Control." PhD dissertation, Cambridge University.

Contesting Hansen's Claim of Liberalism and Exceptionalism under New Labour

Alexander Betts

Randall Hansen's chapter sets out to characterize and explain British immigration policy in general but with a particular focus on the period of New Labour government between 1997 and 2011. While giving some credit to global conditions, developments in the EU, and national labor market conditions, Hansen argues that the most compelling explanation for the peculiarities of the British case lies in its unusual institutional framework, known as the Westminster system. This argument, which Hansen sees as a defining feature of postwar immigration policy in the United Kingdom, is suggested as the basis on which New Labour was able to derive the political freedom to chart a uniquely liberal immigration policy, relative to other industrialized migrant destination countries.

Hansen sees New Labour's policy as being based on a paradox of liberal immigration and illiberal asylum, in which the governments of Tony Blair and Gordon Brown pursued liberalization of legal immigration channels while tightening asylum legislation. Hansen suggests that in 2010, with the election of the Conservative Party, this period of liberalization ended, heralding an about-face on the prior period.

In line with his broader understanding of post-war immigration policy, Hansen explains this turnaround by strongly emphasizing the role of politics—suggesting that markets matter but only insofar as they are mediated through the specific institutional features of the British state. In particular, Hansen emphasizes how the concentration of power within Parliamentary democracy, accentuated by the centralization of power within the Labour cabinet structure, gave particular leeway to individual agency—allowing levels of policy change and liberalization that might be more constrained elsewhere.

This commentary engages Hansen's hypothesis on three levels. First, how can British immigration policy be characterized during the period addressed by this chapter? Second, how can that policy be explained? Third, why does the UK case (and particularly this chapter) matter for the volume as a whole?

To the first point, Hansen characterizes New Labour as having had a liberal immigration policy alongside an illiberal asylum policy between 1997 and 2010. This begs the question of how one judges what is a "liberal" or "illiberal" immigration or asylum policy and how one establishes benchmarks for these standards. Should we evaluate "liberalism" on the basis of numbers, rhetoric, policy, or legislation? The chapter provides compelling evidence for this characterization, but more nuance is required to highlight more precisely when and where the New Labour policy can be seen as a period of liberalization.

Temporally, the New Labour period was not equally liberal toward migration. Rather, it needs to be divided into periods. The 1997–2001 term was the most significant period of liberalization of labor immigration. Driven by a sizable parliamentary majority along with significant economic growth and recognition of demographic needs of an aging population, work permits were offered in shortage areas, for both low-skilled and high-skilled workers. However, while continuing to prioritize economic and demographic needs, policy liberalization arguably decreased. The events of September 11 brought a new Asylum and Immigration Act in 2002, in which the emphasis shifted from the economy to security. And while the numbers of migrants continued to rise, this was significantly attributable to the commitment, beginning in 2004, to freedom of movement for Central and Eastern Europeans, rather than further liberalization. Although Hansen sees this shift as policy liberalization—given that the United Kingdom could have opted out—the reality is that this decision was not based on a commitment to liberalize immigration policy but rather as part of a broader commitment to European integration. Had it opted out, The United Kingdom would have faced significant costs in areas other than migration.

The immigration/asylum division presented in this chapter risks overemphasizing New Labour's liberalism. The period from 1997 to 2011 was not a sea of openness coupled with a small, confined oasis of restriction in asylum. Rather, the so-called "asylum debate" represented something much bigger—the portrayal of irregular migration as a threat to security and the attempt to demonstrate authority over border management. These involved carrier sanctions, extended visa restrictions, growing cooperation on the external dimension of EU asylum and immigration, the use of detention centers, and an obsession with publishing deportation statistics. The introduction of these measures was ultimately a debate not about refugees but about proving to the public that Labour could manage who came in. "Asylum" became a catchall banner for the exclusion of immigrants that the United Kingdom wanted to keep out.

In relation to the second point, nuancing the characterization of the period is useful for recasting how best to explain the policy changes that took place. Hansen's explanatory argument is an institutional one: the nature of the British state gave New Labour enough power (and "wiggle room") to engage in liberalization. For Hansen, the British constitution gave particular individuals—including (in Hansen's words) "the charmless Mr. Brown" the agency to define Britain's immigration policy in a relatively insulated space.

This account risks underplaying significant structural variables—none of which are especially unique to Britain. Hansen suggests that Britain was deviant not in its understanding of the common challenges of mass migration but in the freedom enjoyed by its leaders to direct policy as they saw fit and the capacity they had to manipulate policy for partisan political purposes. His is clearly an inside-out model, and it rejects the outside-in framework that is common in the literature.

As with many of the chapters in the volume, the tendency is to look for explanations within a particular state when many policy changes can be explained by wider structural variables that lie beyond the state. First, demographic reality in the context of an "aging population" underlay liberalization in certain sectors. Second, the 9/11 terrorist attacks drove much of the focus toward irregular migration. Third, the wider institutional imperatives of the European Union gave the United Kingdom little choice but to open up to Central and Eastern Europeans after 2004. Fourth, changes in UK immigration policy mapped to cyclical fluctuations in the economy. In other words, demographic and economic changes—coupled with specific exogenous shocks (9/11 and 2004)—seem to play a strong explanatory role. This is not to say that they are not mediated through the intervening variable of British political institutions and personalities; however, Hansen's chapter arguably neglects wider structural trends that may make the United Kingdom appear more unique than it is.

Furthermore, as well as sidelining broader "exogenous" trends from the outside, applicable across states, Hansen's account also tends to ignore at least two domestic factors that may not necessarily be completely consistent with his argument. First, it leaves out any consideration of the role local governments played in the asylum saga. The centralized Westminster system could not make policy in disregard of the pushback from local governments whose citizens bore the brunt of the social and economic costs of large-scale asylum flows. The tussle between center and periphery over asylum has similarities with aspects of the struggle between Washington and local governments over unauthorized immigration in the United States. In both cases, the fiscal impact of migration provoked a version of a prairie revolt.

It is also surprising that Hansen gives so little attention to the security dimensions of the British debate. Admittedly, the immigration–terrorism connection can be overdone. Nonetheless, the 2005 London subway bombings, subsequent attacks abroad, and foiled operations in Britain were high-profile events that posed the question in many minds whether the immigrant population of mostly South Asian Muslims was a serious threat to British security. If, as Hansen notes, the tabloid press's exploitation of the asylum crisis got the government's attention, surely the uncovering of native-born Muslim extremist cells in the country should be given some credit (or discredit) for the heightened popular anxiety over immigration.

Finally, why does the case study matter here? It tells us something important and interesting about the conditions under which the liberal paradox set out by Jim Hollifield can and cannot be reconciled and with what consequences. During New Labour's term, the United Kingdom faced economic imperatives to liberalize and security imperatives to close. Hansen's account implicitly highlights how the United Kingdom created a legitimate political space in which to reconcile the paradox and engage in strategic liberalization.

New Labour used a number of mechanisms to reconcile anti-immigration public opinion with liberalization. For example, it created trade-offs across areas of migration. The scapegoating of asylum seekers and irregular migrants, for instance, was a means by which it attempted to create legitimacy for admitting "desirable" economic migrants. This type of rhetorical trade-off between different migrant categories also highlights features in some of the other chapters in this volume, with governments such as Australia similarly using arguments about "legitimate" and "illegitimate" ways to claim asylum as a means to justify migration control.

The government used mechanisms to reconcile the liberal paradox other than those addressed in Hansen's chapter. For example, an important feature of New Labour's immigration policy was its attempt to depoliticize the issue and make it appear technocratic by, for example, (1) outsourcing immigration control to private actors in areas from detention to refugee protection and (2) consistently highlighting the imperatives created by EU membership. However, a repeated problem with using these mechanisms to buy the political space necessary to liberalize migration has been their unintended consequences, both in terms of human rights and in the ultimate public backlash that, as Hansen shows, ultimately kicked in after 2010.

7

GERMANY

Managing Migration in the Twenty-First Century

Philip L. Martin

The Germans make everything difficult, both for themselves and for everyone else.
Goethe

INTRODUCTION

Germany was a reluctant country of immigration for most of the past half century. The government allowed employers to recruit guest workers, who were expected to rotate in and out. However, many settled in Germany with their families. Today, Turks and the children of other foreigners have high rates of unemployment and welfare dependency, prompting contentious debates over the best ways to ensure their economic and sociopolitical integration.

Germany became an acknowledged country of immigration in 2005, and a new gap has appeared: a policy to welcome highly skilled foreigners has attracted few. With the labor force projected to shrink, the major migration issues in Germany remain the integration of low-skilled foreigners and their children, attracting more skilled migrants, and reforming the social welfare system to care for an aging and shrinking population and at the same time promoting integration.

Since Germany finally acknowledged that it is a country of immigration, a variety of laws have shown policy convergence with the laws of other European countries. For example, a law giving Germany its first-ever regulated immigration system was passed in 2004 and came into effect in January 2005.[1] Similar to laws passed in Britain, France, and the Netherlands, this law not only included the development of new regulations on labor migration but also focused on cultural integration and family reunification with an emphasis on civic integration and language acquisition. Much of this convergence is due to the regulation of immigration policy at the European Union (EU) level, but policies in countries like Britain, the Netherlands, and France are also having a clear impact on Germany's approach to controlling immigration, particularly immigrant integration. Policies related to family reunification have had an important impact on reducing the number of unskilled immigrants into the country.

GERMANY AS AN IMMIGRATION COUNTRY

Germany is a country of immigration that regulates the residence and employment of foreigners through residence and work permits (see Table 7.1). It had 6.1 million foreign

TABLE 7.1

Foreign residents and employed foreigners, 1960–2012 (in thousands)

Year	Foreign residents	Foreigners employed	Percentage employed
1960	686	279	41
1968	1,924	1,015	53
1969	2,381	1,372	58
1970	2,977	1,839	62
1971	3,439	2,169	63
1972	3,527	2,317	66
1973	3,966	2,595	65
1974	4,127	2,151	52
1975	4,090	1,933	47
1976	3,948	1,874	47
1977	3,948	1,834	46
1978	3,981	1,862	47
1979	4,147	1,966	47
1980	4,453	1,926	43
1981	4,628	1,832	40
1982	4,667	1,710	37
1983	4,535	1,641	36
1984	4,364	1,553	36
1985	4,379	1,536	35
1986	4,513	1,545	34
1987	4,241	1,557	37
1988	4,846	1,607	33
1989	4,846	1,684	35
1990	5,343	1,793	34
1991	5,882	1,909	32
1992	6,496	2,120	33
1993	6,878	2,150	31
1994	6,991	2,110	30
1995	7,174	2,094	29
1996	7,314	2,051	28
1997	7,366	1,998	27
1998	7,320	2,024	28
1999	7,344	2,015	27
2000	7,297	2,008	28
2001	7,318	1,964	27
2002	7,347	1,960	27
2003	7,341	1,860	25
2004	7,288	1,796	25
2005	7,289	1,744	24
2006	7,256	1,782	25
2007	7,256	1,838	25
2008	7,186	1,901	26
2009	7,131	1,879	26
2010	7,199	1,925	27
2011	6,328	2,061	33
2012	6,628	2,233	34

SOURCES: 1960–2000, www.bundesauslaenderbeauftragte.de/; 2000–2012, *Statistiches Jahrbuch.*

NOTE: New methodology for counting foreign residents after 2011.

residents in 2013, making foreigners 7.6 percent of its 80 million German residents. The number of foreigners and German residents is smaller than some previous estimates because not all foreigners leaving Germany deregistered from local offices. Some 15 million German residents have a migrant background, meaning that they were born outside present-day German borders or have at least one parent born outside Germany.

A law giving Germany its first regulated immigration system was initially enacted in 2002, was re-enacted with modifications in 2004, and went into effect in 2005. The new law simplifies entries for skilled citizens of non-EU countries, including those with a job offer paying at least €66,000 ($93,600) in Germany, those who invest at least €250,000 and create at least five German jobs, and foreign student graduates of German universities, who can stay at least a year in order to get a job offer from a German employer. The 2005 law also aims to speed the integration of foreign residents by requiring those receiving unemployment or welfare benefits or deemed "in special need of integration" to participate in German-language and integration courses or risk reductions in their payments and possible nonrenewal of their residence permits. The SPD-Green government had already changed the nationality law in 1999. Since January 1, 2000, children born to legal foreign residents of Germany have been considered dual nationals until age 23, when they have the option to maintain German citizenship but must give up their other citizenship.

The road from guest workers to immigrants was long and twisting. Germany was primarily a country of emigration until the 1950s and was the major source of immigrants to the United States in the nineteenth century.[2] In the early 1900s, it was transformed from an agricultural into an industrial nation, and internal migration became more important than transatlantic migration. Most internal migration was from east to west, from Eastern Prussia to German cities such as Berlin, Leipzig, and Dresden, and later to the western German Rhine and Ruhr areas (Bade 1987: 62). "Ruhr Poles" were Prussian citizens who had a different language and religion, as were Italians who also worked in Ruhr-area mines and factories. Foreigners were 2 percent of the German population in the 1910 and the 1920 Census.

Migrant workers from further east replaced some of those moving west on Prussian estates. These migrant farm workers were supposed to return to their homes when their jobs ended, but many settled and were integrated. Some of the Poles who moved west within Germany integrated successfully, while others moved on to France and Belgium or returned to Poland (Bade 1984a, 1984b). This early German experience with foreign workers meant that "leakage into settlement" was not considered a serious consequence of migrant worker programs, but the successful integration of Ruhr Poles and Italians also did not lead to a feeling that immigrants enriched Germany.

During World War II, Germany used *Fremdarbeiter* from occupied nations in its factories. In August 1944, there were 7.5 million *Fremdarbeiter*, 2 million prisoners of war, and 5.7 million foreign civilian workers employed in German agriculture and factories, and foreign civilian workers were about one-third of the civilian labor force (Herbert 1997). World War II gave German employers experience dealing with foreign workers.

The Federal Republic of Germany was founded in 1949 amid massive unemployment. Currency reform, Marshall Plan aid, and the development of the "social market economy" put the republic on the path to sustained economic growth, but unemployment remained high as West Germany absorbed millions of ethnic and East Germans.[3] Germany signed a labor recruitment agreement with Italy in 1955 that permitted German farmers to hire Italian workers to harvest their crops. Italy wanted jobs for its unemployed workers, but insisted that they be recruited and employed under the terms of a bilateral labor agreement. It soon became apparent that the real need for additional labor was in German factories producing cars, machine tools, and consumer durables for booming export and domestic markets.[4]

GUEST WORKER RECRUITMENT: 1960–1973

In 1960, the number of job vacancies exceeded the number of registered unemployed, and German employers requested permission to recruit additional foreign workers. Hermann (1992: 7) concluded that there was "no noteworthy discussion" of alternatives to recruiting guest workers.

There were four major reasons that recruitment of guest workers seemed to be the best option (Bohning 1984; Krane 1975, 1979). First, the German labor force was shrinking in the early 1960s because of a delayed baby boom that limited female labor force participation, the greater availability of educational opportunities that kept more youth in school, and better pensions that prompted earlier retirements. Second, leaders who had experienced postwar privation were reluctant to risk what was still perceived to be a fragile economic recovery on uncertain mechanization and rationalization alternatives to foreign workers (Lutz 1963; Kindleberger 1967). Unions did not oppose recruiting foreign workers in this era of full employment, especially after the government and employers promised to ensure that they would be treated equally in wages and work benefits.

Third, a keystone of the European Community (EC) was worker freedom of movement, so recruiting guest workers allowed Germany to regulate the mobility expected to occur in any event after January 1, 1968.[5] Fourth, European currencies were undervalued in the early 1960s, which made Germany and other European nations magnets for foreign investment, which created jobs.[6] American multinationals poured so much investment into Europe that a French writer warned of *The American Challenge*.

Guest worker recruitment expanded faster than anticipated. In 1960, there were 329,000 foreign workers in Germany. After the Berlin Wall made east–west migration more difficult in 1961, Germany signed recruitment agreements with seven non-EC recruitment countries: Greece, Morocco, Portugal, Spain, Tunisia, Turkey, and Yugoslavia.[7] The number of guest workers employed in Germany first topped 1 million in 1964 and, after a dip during the 1966–1967 recession, climbed to a peak of 2.6 million in 1973, when they were 12 percent of wage and salary workers. Many guest workers were employed in agriculture in their countries of origin, although semi-skilled and skilled Turks and Yugoslavs moved to Germany to fill jobs in construction, mines, and factories, earning three to five times more than they could earn at home.

The German government required employers to recruit German workers before giving them permission to recruit foreigners. After receiving this permission, most used the public Employment Service (ES) to find migrant workers. The ES established offices abroad and selected workers from the lists of Turks and Yugoslavs who had registered to work in Germany. Guest workers could sometimes jump the queue by having family and friends already in Germany persuade German employers to recruit them by name, while others went to Germany as tourists and found employers to hire them. (Turks did not need visas to travel to Germany in the 1960s.)

Guest worker recruitment peaked between 1968 and 1973, when the migrant work force rose from 1 million to 2.6 million (Martin 1981). Two widely shared assumptions discouraged planning for the integration of guest workers and their families: rotation and return. The *Rotationsprinzip* assumed that, after completing a year of work and, for especially good workers, perhaps another two years, guest workers would return to their countries of origin with savings to finance upward mobility. If they were still needed, another Turk or Yugoslav would have the opportunity to earn higher wages in Germany.

The myth of return arose from surveys of migrants in the 1960s who said they planned to return to their families and communities. Most did return, but many stayed. Between 1960 and 1999, 70 percent of the 30 million foreigners who stayed in Germany for more than 90 days left, but 9 million, or 30 percent, did not.

MIGRANT SETTLEMENT: 1973–1980

Guest worker programs aim to add workers temporarily to the labor force, not settlers to the population. However, rotating guest workers through permanent jobs is often not in the interest of employers or migrants, leading to a gap between the goals and outcomes of guest worker policy.

Guest workers earned the higher wages they expected in Germany, but they soon realized that it would take longer to achieve savings targets because of high German living costs. Since migrants earned the right to unify their families in Germany after a year of work, some did so rather than return. German employers did not discourage family unification, since the wives of the guest workers could also work and bringing families in encouraged trained and experienced migrants to remain, saving employers the cost of recruiting and training new ones (Miller and Martin 1982; Castles 1989).

The desires of guest workers and their German employers meant that the rotation policy was not enforced. As the number of migrants and dependents swelled, the presence of migrant children in German schools made it apparent that some of the "guests" were settling in, but there was no unified integration response. Some schools taught migrant children in their parents' language to facilitate their return, while others taught in German to expedite integration.

Many Germans were aware of campaigns to expel foreigners in neighboring Switzerland, and the slogan "Foreigners out! Germany is for the Germans" became a rallying cry of fringe rightist and nationalist politicians. Most of the opposition to migrants came from the right and was based on fears that guest workers would change the culture. A few economists warned that Germany's famed industrial engine was becoming calcified because employers, with migrant labor readily available, did not aggressively develop labor-saving technologies. These Cassandras warned that the Japanese auto industry in the early 1970s was experimenting with robots for assembling cars after the Japanese government turned down their request to employ low-skill guest workers, while German employers hired Turks. However, mainstream politicians, employers, and unions defended the migrants, arguing that they preserved the *Wirtschaftswunder*.

By 1973, it was clear that many of the guests had become permanent residents; that is, the dynamics of guest worker migration had turned out differently than expected. Several events in 1973 stiffened the resolve of the government to slow and eventually stop recruitment, even though employers said that more guest workers were needed. In the spring of 1973, the employer-paid recruitment fee was raised from DM300 to DM1,000. Wildcat strikes involving migrants in the summer of 1973 convinced the government that it was losing control of foreign worker employment and settlement, and the October 1973 oil embargo threatened a recession that would eliminate the need for additional guest workers. On November 23, 1973, the German government announced a recruitment stop: no more unskilled foreign workers could be recruited for jobs in Germany that lasted more than 90 days. Employers, the labor ministry, and emigration countries expected that, with economy recovery, recruitment would resume in a year or two, albeit with tougher regulation.[8]

FROM GUEST WORKERS TO MINORITIES: 1980–1989

The failure of the *Rotationsprinzip* was the first significant migration policy–outcome gap. Several subsequent gaps compounded the sense that the German government could not manage guest worker migration. When the 1973 recruitment stop was announced, there were 2.6 million employed foreign workers among 4 million foreign residents (see Figure 7.1). Both numbers were expected to decrease as unemployment rose. However, while the number of employed foreigners fell as expected, the foreign population remained at 4 million because unemployed migrants who feared they could not return to Germany if they went home remained. Many unified their families, so the foreign population rose to 4.5 million in 1980 (Bade 1984a, 1984b).

The widening gap between the number of foreign residents and the number of employed foreigners led to policies aimed at slowing the unification of guest worker families.

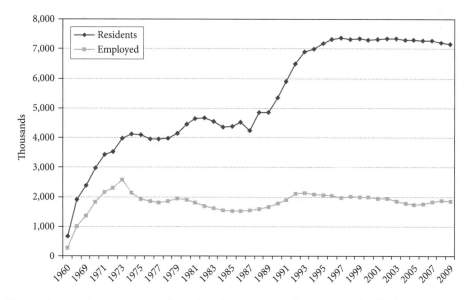

Figure 7.1 Foreign residents and employed foreigners in Germany, 1960–2009. *Source:* BAMF (2008).

To discourage family unification in the late 1970s, newly arrived spouses were not allowed to work for one to four years, which helps to explain why the ratio of nonworkers to workers among foreigners almost doubled. After 1975, full children's allowances—government payments to parents with children—were paid only if children were living in Germany, which encouraged some settled migrants to bring their children in. These hard-to-enforce measures did more to reduce the mobility and flexibility of guest workers than they did to prevent family unification.

The 1982 election was won by the conservatives—the Christian Democratic Party and the Christian Socialist Union—and they, along with their Free Democratic Party allies, promised to "do something" about migration. The government reduced the number of foreign residents temporarily by offering departure bonuses of up to $5,000 plus social security contributions to settled foreigners who gave up their work and residence permits, similar to a 1981 French departure bonuses program. Departure bonuses reduced the foreign population in Germany from 4.7 million in 1982 to 4.4 million in 1984–1985, but it rebounded to 4.5 million in 1986. Studies showed that most of the foreigners who took departure bonuses would have left in any event, so the scheme bunched normal emigration into the two years that bonuses were available (Hönekopp 1990).

The migration policy of the German government during the 1980s was clear: "The Federal Republic of Germany is not, nor shall it become, a country of immigration." This policy clearly failed: there were 4.6 million foreigners in Germany in 1981, when the statement was first made, and 5.8 million in 1991. German policy toward foreigners had three core elements: (1) promote the integration of legally resident foreigners and their families; (2) reduce non-EU immigration; and (3) encourage resident foreigners' voluntary return and reintegration into their home countries. The tension between promoting returns and fostering integration was reflected in the statement of then SPD Chancellor Helmut Schmidt after his October 1980 re-election. At a time when Germany had 62 million residents, Schmidt said that the country had to integrate the guest workers who made economic contributions during the 1960s, but he also said, "Four million is enough."[9]

Turks were never more than a third of the foreigners in Germany but, because they were the last nationality to arrive in large numbers and the most visible (because of women's head scarves), they came to mean "problem foreigners." Many Germans sympathized with the integration difficulties of Turks, emphasizing that many had little education, some brought with them Turkish cultural norms such as the different treatment of men and women, and some were caught up in the political divisions within Turkish society, such as that between Turks and Kurds. The Turkish government made demands on its nationals abroad, including children born to Turkish parents in Germany. For example, Turkish boys born abroad were required to perform 18 months of military service in Turkey or pay a fee equivalent to an average two years income in Turkey, which reduced the military obligation to two months.[10]

Turks played a special role in German migration policy during the 1980s because of several agreements signed during the guest worker era. The Ankara Association Agreement of 1963 and the Additional Protocol of 1973 promised Turkey a reciprocal lowering of tariff and migration barriers, including "free access" to the then EC labor market by December

1986. Turks did not gain free access to EC labor markets in 1986,[11] but Turkey applied to join the EC in 1987, when its economy was expanding rapidly as a result of an early 1980s switch from an inward-looking statist model to an outward-oriented market model. This change in economic policy increased EC investment in Turkey and Turkish trade with EC countries, but it did not quiet fears in Germany and elsewhere that Turkey's entry would unleash another wave of hard-to-integrate migrants, helping to explain why its application was rebuffed.

The German economy restructured in the decade after oil prices rose in 1973–1974. Before this restructuring, foreigners had a lower unemployment rate than Germans did. By the 1980s, the unemployment rate of foreigners was twice the rate of German unemployment, and unemployed Turks and other foreigners who had been recruited to work in factories found it hard to get new jobs. Foreign workers are generally more flexible than Germans, including more willing to work at night and on weekends, and some moved into low-level jobs that ranged from janitorial services to fast-food restaurants (over half of McDonald's employees in Germany are foreigners). Some foreigners became self-employed, opening travel agencies and restaurants to serve fellow foreigners and Germans, but most had few nonfamily employees.

There was an economic boom in Europe and Germany in the late 1980s associated with the lowering of economic barriers within the EC that increased the German demand for labor. The number of foreigners holding wage and salary jobs rose slightly, but the number of foreign residents rose even faster. Some of the foreigners who got jobs in Germany in the late 1980s were asylum seekers or nationals of Poland and other Eastern European countries who were finding it easier to travel west as tourists and work illegally in agriculture, restaurants, and other industries employing seasonal workers.

EAST GERMANS, ETHNIC GERMANS, ASYLUM: 1989–2000

There was east–west migration within Germany before and after the dissolution of East Germany. At the end of World War II, Germany was divided into four zones and occupied by troops from France, the United Kingdom, the United States, and the former Soviet Union. Some 730,000 Germans moved from the Soviet zone to the other zones in the late 1940s, and another 3.8 million moved from East Germany to West Germany between 1949 and the building of the Berlin wall in August 1961. Another 600,000 East Germans moved west between 1961 and 1988, including many pensioners who were permitted to leave. In a little noted migration, some 393,000 West Germans moved east during these years.

The fall of the Berlin Wall in November 1989 opened a new chapter in internal German migration. Migration hastened the demise of the communist regime in East Germany, and fears of "unification in West Germany" persuaded the government of Chancellor Helmut Kohl to undertake a costly economic stabilization program. Nonetheless, almost 800,000 people in the former East Germany moved to West Germany in 1989–1990, including many young people seeking jobs.

Germany's Persecuted and Refugee Law of 1953 (Bundesvertriebenen und Füchtlingsgesetz), enacted when borders to the east were largely closed, gives those born of German parents the right to citizenship if they suffered persecution after World War II because of their German heritage (those born after 1993 are no longer eligible for automatic citizenship). Some 4 million ethnic Germans moved to Germany between 1950 and 2000 in two distinct phases. The first, between 1950 and 1988, brought 1.4 million, mostly from Poland (62 percent) and Romania (15 percent). Many knew some German and maintained at least some of their German culture.

The second phase, from 1989 to 2000, brought about 2.6 million ethnic Germans, almost all from the former USSR, who knew less German and had only partly maintained German culture. These newcomers were a special strain on the local governments who provided them with housing and integration assistance. Many youthful arrivals from Russia considered themselves Russians rather than German, and some were reluctant to participate in German-language classes aimed at helping them find jobs. About three-fourths of those moving from the former Soviet Union were the (non-German) family members of ethnic Germans, prompting ever tighter tests to slow down entries.[12]

There was a related influx of Jews from the former USSR. In 1933, some 525,000 German citizens were Jews. By 1945, there were 15,000, and this number almost doubled to 29,000 by 1990. Germany opened the door to Jewish immigrants from the former Soviet Union in 1990, and about 137,000 came in the 1990s, although some moved on to Israel and the United States.[13] Local governments provide Jewish migrants with housing and integration services similar to those provided to ethnic Germans.

The influx of East Germans, ethnic Germans, and Jews in the early 1990s strained local governments and residents. The media sometimes emphasized that non-German speakers who had the opportunity to work in Germany were instead accepting welfare payments and spurning the language and other assistance offered to prepare them for jobs. In some cities, the so-called Russian mafia were accused of committing sometimes brutal crimes.

The challenge of integrating East Germans, ethnic Germans, and Jews into the labor market and into society was complicated by a fourth inflow in the early 1990s—asylum seekers. Because of the Nazi experience, in which Germans and others perished because other countries refused to provide asylum, the 1949 Basic Law includes an open-ended commitment to provide asylum to foreigners fleeing political persecution: According to Article 16, "Persons persecuted for political reasons shall enjoy the right of asylum." The 1951 Geneva Convention, signed by Germany, defines a refugee in need of protection as a person who, "owing to a well-founded fear of being persecuted for reasons of race, religion, nationality, membership in a particular social group, or political opinion, is outside the country of his nationality, and is unable to, or owing to such fear, is unwilling to avail himself of the protection of that country."

Germany received relatively few asylum applications until 1980,[14] when a military coup in Turkey and a realization that the recruitment stop would not soon be lifted prompted some Turks to fly to Germany, because visas were not required, and apply for asylum. After being denied, many appealed in order to work for the several years usually required for a final decision on their applications. Some Turkish newspapers reproduced Germany's asylum application form and provided suggestions on to complete it to maximize a legal stay in Germany. Turks were over half of Germany's 110,000 asylum applicants in 1980, and the government found a quick fix in requiring Turks to obtain visas and prohibiting asylum applicants from working for their first five years. The number of asylum applications dropped to less than 20,000 in 1983.[15]

This quick fix to the 1980 asylum crisis left Germany unprepared for the second flood of applications in the early 1990s, during the breakup of Yugoslavia. The number of applications, 103,000 in 1988, almost doubled in 1990 and peaked at 438,000 in 1992. After applying for asylum, foreigners were assigned to cities, where local governments were required to provide them with housing and food at a cost of about $10,000 per person per year while their applications and appeals were considered. Especially in areas with high unemployment in the former East Germany, foreigners living in asylum housing were attacked—in 1992 alone, there were almost 600 crimes of arson against them. Attackers did not distinguish between asylum seekers and other foreigners, prompting Japanese and other foreign investors to warn the German government that foreign investment was threatened by attacks on foreigners.

The major political parties could not agree on how to deal with the early 1990s upsurge in asylum applications. The rightist CDU-CSU-FDP coalition government wanted to amend the Basic Law to eliminate the open-ended right to asylum. The opposition SPD and Green parties strongly opposed this because of Nazi persecution and to pressure the government to develop an immigration system, using the argument that, if Germany opened more doors to immigrants, there would be fewer asylum seekers. A compromise preserved Article 16, but required asylum seekers to apply in the first "safe country" they reached after escaping persecution. With Germany surrounded by "safe countries," the hope was that foreigners would apply for asylum in Poland or Hungary rather than in Germany.

This compromise defused the asylum crisis. The number of asylum applications fell to less than 100,000 a year after 1998,[16] in part because of safe-first-country rules and because some Yugoslavs received Temporary Protected Status (TPS) (*Duldung*) rather than enter the asylum system. By 1995, fighting in the former Yugoslavia produced 3.5 million displaced persons and refugees, including 750,000 Bosnians, Serbs, and Croatians who moved to Germany and other European countries. German state governments, which spent $3 billion caring for foreigners with TPS status in 1996, showed considerable ingenuity in developing carrots and sticks to persuade Bosnians, Serbs, and others to return home.[17]

GUEST WORKERS, GREEN CARDS, UNAUTHORIZED

Poles and other Eastern Europeans began to work in Germany during their summer vacations in the late 1980s, often taking seasonal farm jobs. Strikes, the declaration of a state of emergency, and the partial opening of the Polish border encouraged Poles to seek work in Germany, and word soon spread among them that one could earn the equivalent of a year's wages at home by picking apples or wine grapes for one month in Germany. Hundreds of thousands of Poles and other Eastern European "tourists" soon arrived and found jobs.

The German government was reluctant to "re-create the Berlin Wall" on its eastern borders to stop this migration, but it was also unwilling to tolerate the widespread employment of unauthorized foreigners. The compromise was to launch several foreign worker programs in the early 1990s that permitted about 350,000 foreigners a year to work temporarily in Germany (Hönekopp 1997).[18]

These so-called new guest worker programs were different from those of the 1960s in several respects. First, in the 1990s programs some foreign workers were not considered German workers. For example, under the so-called project-tied program, German construction firms could subcontract with a Polish firm to erect a new office building. The Polish firm would provide both materials and workers to complete its contract, and the guest workers would remain Polish employees posted to a German worksite temporarily—not, as in the 1960s, Turkish employees of Opel or Volkswagen.

Second, the 1990s programs satisfied the 1973 recruitment stop by limiting foreigners considered German workers to a stay of less than 90 days. The so-called seasonal worker program has been the largest of the new programs, admitting over 300,000 mostly Polish workers per year to fill seasonal farm and service jobs. Employers usually specify by name the workers they want and spell out wages, housing arrangements, and other work-related benefits in bilingual contracts that must be approved by German and Polish (or other source country's), employment service.

Third, the 1990s programs included border-commuter and trainee programs that allowed the entry of Eastern European workers in ways that do not result in settlement. Czechs and Poles living within 50 kilometers of Germany's eastern borders, for example, could hold German jobs and stay overnight a maximum of two days a week. Up to 6,000 young Eastern Europeans could be recruited by German employers to participate in work-and-learn programs in factories and service-sector businesses.

The guest worker programs of the 1990s added some flexibility and mobility to the German labor market and likely reduced the employment of unauthorized migrants in fruit and vegetable agriculture and seasonal services. Most new guest workers complemented German workers; their negative effects, if any, fell mostly on settled foreign workers who were having trouble getting a foothold in the German labor market (Schulz 1999).

However, the program that received the most publicity was the "Green Card" program of 2000, which aimed to recruit non-EU foreigners to fill computer-related jobs. Modeled on the US H-1B visa but named after the US permanent resident card, the German Green Card program was a fallback migration proposal. In 2000, the German computer company association BITKOM argued that there were at least 75,000 unfilled IT jobs and that there were too few students graduating from German universities to fill them. The US government temporarily tripled the number of H-1B visas in 2000 from 65,000 per year to 195,000 per year, and there was talk of "war" between industrial countries seeking highly skilled foreigners. The German Green Card program offered five-year work and residence permits to non-EU IT specialists, who were paid at least $45,000 a year. The opposition CDU tried to block the Green Card program with the slogan "Kinder statt Inder" (children instead of Indians) in a May 2000 campaign in North Rhine-Westphalia, arguing that Germans should have more children and train them to be computer programmers instead of recruiting Indians. The CDU campaign failed, and about 14,000 green cards were issued in 2000 to non-EU foreigners, including one-quarter to Indians.

There was a major gap in the number of low-skilled and high-skilled foreigners arriving in Germany early in the twenty-first century, when there were more than 300,000 low-skilled foreign workers and fewer than 15,000 Green Card holders. That there were relatively few Green Cards issued was attributed to the fact that the United States was more attractive because US green cards are permanent visas that allow foreigners to live and work in most private-sector jobs and to become naturalized citizens after five years. H-1B visas permit six years of US work and allow employers to sponsor H-1B visa holders for permanent visas. The German Green Card program, by contrast, erected higher hurdles to employers and did not lay out an easy transition from Green Card to permanent resident status.

The Green Card program helped to break the mantra that Germany is not a country of immigration. The SPD-Green government appointed a commission chaired by a former prominent CDU member to propose a German immigration policy. The Suessmuth Commission report, issued on July 4, 2001, declared that "Germany is and should be a country of immigration." Noting that family unification brought in 75,000 newcomers, it recommended that Germany welcome an additional 50,000 foreign professionals selected under a Canadian-style points system and that the government do more to speed the integration of settled foreigners and their children.

The SPD-Green government introduced legislation that included many of the commission's recommendations to open Germany to "selective immigration" and develop carrots and sticks to promote the integration of foreigners. The Immigration Act was approved by the German Parliament in 2002, overturned because of procedural issues, and revised extensively before being approved again in 2004. The revised act, effective in 2005, acknowledges for the first time that Germany is a country of immigration that anticipates the arrival and settlement of foreigners

Lying at the center of Europe, Germany has millions of foreigners entering and exiting each year. There are no border controls with neighboring countries, so efforts to deter the entry and employment of unauthorized foreigners center on interior checks—primarily the requirement for residence permits, checks of public spaces such as railroad stations, and workplace inspections. It is not clear how effective these checks are: estimates of the number of unauthorized foreigners range from 150,000 to 1.5 million, with the number peaking in summer. Many are among the 43 million workers in the labor force.

Germany has separate systems to register residents and workers. The local Aliens Authority in each town and city reports to the state government and the federal Ministry of the Interior,[19] while the local work permits registry and labor inspectors are the responsibility of the state government and the federal Ministry of Labor. Computers cross-check these registers to flag suspicious individuals and their employers. Germany introduced fines on employers who hired unauthorized workers in 1972 and has increased them several times since.

The presence of unauthorized workers raises the question of whether the German labor market is too rigid or whether there is too little enforcement of immigration and labor laws. Some argue that generous unemployment and welfare benefits make jobless workers in Germany reluctant to accept low-wage jobs, which are then filled by flexible unauthorized workers. If unemployment and welfare benefits were lowered, this argument runs, jobless

German and resident foreign workers would fill these jobs and there would be fewer unauthorized foreigners. Others argue for more labor law enforcement to preserve good jobs in the high-wage, high-benefit labor market.

The German government followed both strategies, aiming to increase labor market flexibility and reduce the employment of unauthorized foreigners. The SPD-Green government in 2003 implemented an Agenda 2010 strategy to reduce unemployment, which seemed stuck at about 10 percent. Under the Hartz labor market and welfare reforms,[20] the duration of unemployment benefits changed from indefinite to between six and eighteen months, depending on a recipient's age and previous employment. The Hartz reforms also relaxed job protection laws and created "mini-jobs" with reduced payroll taxes on workers earning up to €400 a month and "one-Euro" public service jobs for those unemployed a year or more.[21] The government also stepped up the fight against illegal work with more inspectors, in an effort to detect unauthorized foreigners and Germans and resident foreigners who work for cash wages while collecting benefits.

NATURALIZATION 2000 AND IMMIGRATION 2005

Much of the debate over immigration until 1998, when the CDU-CSU-FDP government was replaced by an SPD-Green government, involved naturalization and its importance to integration. The SPD-Green government proposed to reform of the 1913 Reichs- und Staatsangehörigkeitsgesetz (RuStAG) to move the country from one of the most restrictive paths to naturalization to one of the most liberal in allowing dual nationality. The proposal to introduce birthright citizenship and permit dual nationality was routinely resisted, but in 2000 the 1913 law was amended to consider German citizens at birth those individuals born in Germany to at least one foreign parent who had been legally resident in Germany for at least eight years. These children have dual citizenship until age 23, when they must decide whether to retain German or their parents' citizenship. In practice, some of those electing German citizenship also keep their parents' citizenship as well.

For other foreigners, the question was how to ease the naturalization process. Germany has two types of naturalization: discretionary and by right (*Anspruch*). In the 1990s, most naturalization involved ethnic Germans who had a right to become citizens when they arrived in Germany from Poland, Russia, and elsewhere.[22] Foreigners seeking discretionary naturalization, by contrast, had to have lived in Germany at least fifteen years, show that they could support themselves, give up their current citizenship, and, in the words of CDU leader Erwin Marschewski, "show a credible integration into our social and state order." The sixteen German states test applicants for naturalization, so the test varied from state to state until federal legislation in 2007 made it more uniform.[23] German officials in the various states could deny discretionary applications on the grounds that naturalization is not in Germany's interest. Some migrant advocates complained that denying a naturalization application involved only one official, but approving an application required several.

Naturalization reform in 2000 reduced the period of legal residence before a foreigner could apply for asylum from fifteen to eight years, and led to a wave of naturalizations. Between 2002 and 2009, some 968,000 foreigners became naturalized, including 309,000

Turks, 62,000 Serbs, 46,000 Iranians, and 40,000 Poles. Naturalizations peaked at 187,000 in 2000, declined to less than 100,000 a year in 2008 and 2009, and rose to more than 100,000 a year between 2010 and 2012.

It proved much harder to enact a law admitting immigrants than to reform current naturalization laws, in part because of opposition from some government leaders. For example, SPD Interior Minister Otto Schily opposed an immigration law in 1999, saying, "There is no need for an immigration law because, if we had one, the quotas would be zero." Schily reflected public sentiment. A 2000 poll found that 66 percent of Germans thought immigration was "too high and has exceeded the limits of what is bearable," and 75 percent believed that Germany's asylum policies should limit the maximum stay of a refugee to nine months.

Schily appointed a commission that in 2001 recommended that Germany admit 50,000 more foreigners, including 20,000 foreign professionals per year selected on the basis of a points system, another 20,000 admitted temporarily with five-year permits, and 10,000 trainees and foreign graduates of German universities who had job offers from German employers. The commission's plan was to open six doors for labor market immigrants, including three for foreigners seeking entry on the basis of their personal qualifications such as entrepreneurs who wanted to establish businesses, young foreigners selected through a points system, and foreign students. Three other doors would open for foreigners sought by German employers, one for corporate managers and scientists, one for foreigners to fill vacant jobs (shortage workers), and one for trainees to fill vacant apprenticeship slots. shortage workers and trainees could apply for permanent residence through the points system while in Germany.

The key to successful integration, according to the commission, was knowledge of German. It reviewed proposed carrots and sticks to encourage immigrants to learn German and noted approvingly that the Dutch used "integration contracts" that offered a quicker path to an unlimited residence or work permit for those who could pass a language test and imposed penalties such as delayed family unification on those who failed it.

Schily included many of the commission's recommendations in a proposed immigration law in 2001 that was amended before the governing parties sought a compromise with the opposition parties. One goal of the major parties in formulating the law was to "keep immigration out of the 2002 election campaign"—that is, to prevent anti-migrant parties from gaining seats in the Bundestag by campaigning against foreigners. However, the effort to reach a compromise failed, largely because the opposition parties maintained that Germany could not enact an immigration law with 4 million unemployed workers. Nonetheless, the SPD-Green proposal was narrowly approved by the Bundestag in 2002,[24] but the procedure by which it was approved in the upper house was challenged in court.[25] The SPD-Green government was re-elected in 2002 with a reduced majority in the Bundestag, the Federal Constitutional Court struck down the 2002 migration law, and the government lost its majority in the upper house, forcing it to negotiate with the opposition on a revised immigration law that was finally approved in 2004 and took effect in 2005.

Germany's first Immigration Act aims to achieve two major goals: attracting skilled foreign immigrants and ensuring the integration of the mostly low-skilled foreigners and their children already living in the country. There is no limit on the number of immigrant visas available to non-EU foreigners who are under 45, invest at least €1 million (€250,000 and five jobs since 2009), and create at least ten jobs, or on scientists and professionals earning at least €84,000 a year in Germany (reduced to €66,000, or $93,000 a year in 2009). Students graduating from German universities can stay in Germany a year after graduation and, if they are offered a job, obtain residence and work permits. However, few scientists and professionals are arriving in Germany from outside the EU; there were fewer than 200 in 2010.[26]

The integration stick requires foreigners in Germany less than six years and receiving government assistance to enroll in German-language and culture classes or face potential problems renewing their work permits. This was prompted by the fact that less than 10 percent of German residents were foreigners in 2000 but non-German citizens were over 20 percent of those receiving cash assistance. Foreigners receiving assistance must participate in 600 hours of German-language courses and another 45 hours in German culture classes in order to renew their residence permits; an average of 120,000 foreign adults were enrolled in language and civics classes between 2005 and 2010. Since 2007, foreigners seeking to join family members settled in Germany have also been required to pass a German-language test.[27]

The immigration law also included provisions aimed at fostering integration and reducing the threat of terrorism. Some Turkish parents keep their children in Turkey as long as possible before bringing them to Germany so they are not "corrupted" by German society, but this means that the children arrive with little knowledge of German and have trouble finding jobs. The law lowered the maximum age at which children abroad can automatically join their parents to 12 and required those between 12 and 16 joining families to demonstrate knowledge of German before their arrival. It also made it easier to remove foreigners who are members or supporters of terrorist organizations, including "hate preachers" in mosques. The law was amended in 2007 to make it easier for foreign professionals to immigrate and harder for some foreigners to unify families.

INTEGRATION, TURKEY, AND THE EUROPEAN UNION

Elections in 2005 produced a grand coalition of the two major political parties, the CDU-CSU and the SPD, with the CDU's Angela Merkel becoming chancellor. In 2006, when foreigners were 8 percent of German residents, an opinion poll found that 61 percent of Germans agreed that "there are too many foreigners living in Germany."

Integrating foreigners who have settled in Germany continues to be a major issue. There is agreement that many second- and third-generation descendants of guest workers are having trouble climbing the German economic ladder, but disagreement on how to speed their integration. Merkel, who has held annual "integration summits" since 2006, emphasizes that there are more residents with migration backgrounds than foreigners living in Germany.

The integration debate is complicated by the fact that one-fourth of the foreigners in Germany are Turks.[28] Some fear that second- and third-generation Turks who cannot find good jobs will become an underclass attracted to terrorism. Unlike the United Kingdom and the Netherlands, Germany has had few terrorist incidents linked to Muslim immigrants, but there are often disputes over particular issues, such as efforts to build one of Germany's largest mosques near Cologne's Gothic cathedral, which prompted protests.[29] There are disputes over whether school teachers can wear head scarves and what to do about the poor performance of many children of 1960s guest workers in German schools.

Most foreigners arriving in Germany to settle do not speak German, which is why encouraging immigrants to learn the language has become a government priority. The 2005 immigration law included mandatory integration courses, including at least 600 hours of German-language instruction and 45 hours of culture instruction. These federally financed courses are a rare federal intrusion into integration policies, most of which are handled at the state and local level. Since 2007, foreigners arriving to settle with family members in Germany have had to pass a language test abroad to obtain a visa.

There continues to be disagreement about the meaning of integration. Integration commissioner Maria Böhmer, whose office produces an annual report on the integration of immigrants, noted in 2010 that eleven of the twenty-three players on the German national soccer team had migrant backgrounds, reflecting successful integration in sport. On the other hand, she acknowledged that the unemployment rate among non-German citizens was almost twice that of Germans—12.4 percent compared to 6.5 percent. In 2008, 13 percent of migrant youth did not graduate from secondary school compared to 7 percent of German youth. About 82 percent of Germans between the ages of 25 and 65 were in the labor force in 2008 compared to 75 percent of the foreign born, largely because foreign-born women are less likely to work or look for jobs.

Economist Thilo Sarrazin's best-selling 2010 book, *Germany Does Away with Itself* (*Deutschland schafft sich ab*), used these data to conclude that Muslims were not integrating. He asserted that Muslim immigrants are dependent "on the social welfare state" and are "connected to criminality" to argue that integration is becoming less successful over time, as the grandchildren of Turkish immigrants are less likely to become citizens than are their parents or grandparents. Migrant advocates disagreed with Sarrazin's interpretation of the data, arguing that the integration of foreigners lags because Germany for years denied that it was an immigration country. The lack of effective integration policies, combined with discrimination, they argued, explained lagging integration indicators.

Elections in 2009 returned Chancellor Merkel to power in coalition with the free-market-oriented FDP. There was little action on immigration, although the earnings requirement that foreigners must meet to get four-year Blue Card work and residence permits on arrival was reduced to €46,000 per year in 2012 (www.bluecard-eu.de). Still, during the first months that Blue Cards were available, fewer than seventy non-EU foreigners per month received them, including fifty-five who were already in Germany.

Merkel was re-elected in 2013 and will govern in coalition with the Social Democratic Party. In addition to Germany's first-ever national minimum wage of €8.50 in 2015, the coalition government promises to enact a law allowing children born to legal foreigners in Germany to keep both the citizenship of their parents and their German citizenship. In other words, the government will no longer force those born in Germany of dual citizenship who have reached age 23 to choose one or the other. Under the choose-one-citizenship model, 99 percent of foreign youth born in Germany chose German citizenship.

Merkel has been among the strongest European critics of multiculturalism, calling it a "total failure" in Germany, and Islam remains a flashpoint. Turkish Prime Minister Recep Tayyip Erdogan, during a 2011 visit to Germany, reignited the integration debate when he urged Turks living in Germany to teach their children Turkish first and German second. He said, "Our children must learn German, but first they must learn Turkish." Integration minister Böhmer immediately countered: "The German language takes precedence. Only those with good German have opportunities to advance in our country."

The uneven integration of Turks and potentially more Turkish migration if Turkey joins the EU remain contentious issues. Turkey applied to join what was then the EC in 1987, but its application was rebuffed. It applied for EU entry in 1997, and in December of 1999 EU leaders put Turkey on a list of countries eligible for future entry. Turkey reapplied, and accession negotiations began in 2005.

Turkey-EU accession negotiations have proceeded slowly. Since 2005, only a few of the 35 chapters of the EU *acquis* have been accepted by Turkey or accepted with exceptions agreed to by the EU.[30] Turkish Prime Minister Erdogan says that Turkey's goal is full membership, but the leaders of France, Germany, and some other EU member states argue that, rather than full membership, there should be some form of "special relationship" with Turkey. Support in Turkey for EU membership has been falling, from over 70 percent in 2005 to about 35 percent in 2013.

Turkish-EU labor migration has been on a declining trajectory for the past three decades. Turkey has been a net immigration country since the mid-1990s, but migrants transiting Turkey to EU countries from North Africa and the Middle East are an irritant when they cross illegally, via Turkey, into Greece. About 90 percent of the foreigners apprehended trying to enter the EU illegally in 2010 (128,000) were detected in Greece, and many were apprehended on the Turkey-Greece land border. Turkey allows Greece to return apprehended Turks and nationals of countries, such as Iranians, that have land borders with it, but it does not accept the return of nationals of Afghanistan, Pakistan, and North African countries. Turkey allows North Africans to enter without visas, which Greece says contributes to illegal migration.

Turkey and the EU signed an agreement in Fall 2013 under which the Turkish government agreed to accept the return of migrants who crossed Turkey before entering an EU country to apply for asylum and were rejected. In return, the EU promised to make it easier for Turks to obtain tourist visas to visit EU member states.

CONCLUSIONS

Until 2005, Germany was the major country admitting foreigners that did not have a formal immigration policy to (1) explain why foreigners were in the national interest, (2) establish priority for entry, and (3) lay out a clear path to integration. Politicians who wanted such an immigration policy were opposed by the generally conservative parties—the Christian Democratic Union and the Christian Social Union (CDU-CSU)—that dominated the government between 1982 and 1998. The Free Democratic Party[31] (part of the CDU-CSU coalition) as well as what was then the opposition SPD and the Green[32] parties wanted an immigration policy that welcomed immigrants and simplified naturalization (Hailbronner 1997a, 1997b).

Germany in the 1970s and 1980s pursued flawed policies that worked the first time they were tried. For example, the guest worker programs of the 1960s were based on the theory that workers would rotate in and out of Germany as needed. When rotation was tested during the recession of 1966–1967, it seemed to work because many foreign workers were newcomers.[33] Similarly, when Germany experienced a rush of asylum seekers in 1980, half of whom were Turks, the crisis was solved by imposing visa requirements. Neither rotating guest workers nor the use of visas to restrict the number of asylum applicants proved to be durable policies, but Germany did not have to look for durable policies when ad hoc policy changes solved immediate problems. This ad hoc approach to migration became more difficult in the twenty-first century.

Germany and the United States began from very different immigration and integration starting points, but they face similar migration questions today. How many foreigners should be admitted? From where should they come? In what status should they arrive? These questions are usually answered in an immigration policy that spells out which foreigners are welcomed to settle; regulations governing temporary visitors such as tourists, foreign students. and guest workers; and efforts to keep out and remove the unauthorized. Both Germany and the United States have had the highest number and percentage of foreigners and foreign-born residents in a century, and both are grappling with key integration issues, including the definition of successful integration.

There are still significant differences between Germany and the United States, as evidenced by the statements of political leaders. SPD Interior Minister Otto Schily in December 1998 said that Germany had

> . . . reached the limits, the point where we have to say we cannot bear any more. The majority of Germans agree with me: Zero immigration for now. The burden has become too great. I would not even dare publish the costs that stem from immigration. The Greens say we should take 200,000 more immigrants a year. But I say to them, show me the village, the town, the region that would take them. There are no such places.

Contrast this statement with that of President Clinton in June 1998:

> I believe new immigrants are good for America. They are revitalizing our cities. They are building our new economy. They are strengthening our ties to the global economy, just as earlier waves of immigrants settled the new frontier and powered the Industrial Revolution. They are energizing our culture and broadening our vision of the world. They are renewing our most basic values and reminding us all of what it truly means to be an American. [Americans] share a responsibility to welcome new immigrants, to ensure that they strengthen our nation, to give them their chance at the brass ring.

As Germany and other industrial democracies struggle to answer fundamental immigration questions of how many, from where, and in what status newcomers should arrive, it is important to keep three principles in mind. First, there are no magic bullets or quick-fix answers; managing migration was difficult in the past and is likely to remain one of the most challenging and contentious issues in the future. Second, immigration and integration policies must be flexible so they can be changed quickly, acknowledging the fact that the short-term consequences of immigration and integration policies may differ from their longer-term effects. Third, durable solutions to migration issues are more likely to be found nearer the middle than at the extremes of no borders and no migrants. In Europe and the United States, extreme voices often receive more attention than voices nearer the middle that urge the development and maintenance of managed migration.

APPENDIX: GERMAN IMMIGRATION CHRONOLOGY

Year	Event
1955	Recruitment agreement with Italy
1960	Recruitment agreement with Spain and Greece
1961	Recruitment agreement with Turkey
1963	Recruitment agreement with Morocco
1965	Recruitment agreement with Tunisia
1965	Foreigners Law: EC nationals have same labor market rights as Germans; non-EC foreigners to be rotated in and out of Germany
1968	Recruitment agreement with Yugoslavia
1973	Recruitment stop: no more unskilled non-EC foreign workers for German jobs lasting more than 90 days
1975	Only children living in Germany to get full allowance
1975–1977	Non-EC foreigners cannot move into "overburdened" cities with 12 percent or more foreigners
1977	Federal-state commission recommends foreigners policy
1978	New regulations: residence permit (*Aufenhaltserlaubnis*) after 5 years; residence right (*Berechtigung*) after 8 years
1979	Kühn memorandum calls for an integration policy for guest workers who settle in Germany
1981–1982	Migration goals: reduce non-EC immigration, promote voluntary returns, integrate foreigners who stay
1983–1984	Foreign worker departure bonus program
1989–1990	New "truly temporary" foreign worker programs launched
1990	Foreigners Law revised: more security for settled foreigners, but newly arrived find it harder to obtain secure residence rights
1993	Asylum law reform; 220,000 annual quota on persons recognized as ethnic Germans
1995	Schengen border-free agreement goes into effect between Belgium, France, Germany, Luxembourg, the Netherlands, Portugal, and Spain, March 26
1998	SPD-Green coalition replaces the CDU-CSU-FDP coalition government
1999	SPD-Green proposals for routine dual nationality are modified to allow children born in Germany to legal foreign resident parents to be German nationals; these "children of foreigners" lose German nationality if they do not give up their parents' nationality by age 23
2000	Kinder statt Inder (children instead of Indians) campaign fails; Germany begins issuing 20,000 "green cards" to non-EU foreigners earning at least DM100,000/year
2001	Independent commission declares Germany a country of immigration; recommends admission of up to 50,000 professionals a year; SPD-Green government introduces immigration law
2004	Germany enacts *Zuwanderungsgesetz*, the first ever regulated immigration system; to go into effect in 2005
2004	National Integration Plan, with new language and culture requirements for resident foreigners and family reunification immigrants; eases entry for highly skilled foreigners
2007	Labor Migration Control Act to ease the entry of highly skilled foreigners and increase controls against unauthorized employment
2009	Thilo Sarrazin, in *Deutschland schafft sich ab*, concludes that German integration policy is a failure and that Muslims in Germany were not integrating successfully
2010	Evaluations show that required language and culture training are helping low-skilled foreigners integrate in Germany
2011	Poles and other East Europeans can move to Germany and other "old" EU-15 member states and seek jobs on an equal basis with local workers; leads to increase in Polish and other workers posted by recruitment agencies in Germany

Year	Event
2012	German government launches a website to attract skilled foreigners (www.make-it-in-germany.com)
2013	Prime Minister Angela Merkel wins third term; coalition agreement with SPD includes Germany's first national minimum wage, €8.50, after 2015 and promise to allow children born to legal foreigners in Germany to keep both their German citizenship and their parents' citizenship

NOTES

1. A law was initially passed in 2002, but the manner in which it was approved in the upper house, by one disputed vote, led the constitutional court to declare it void in December 2002—the court did not rule on the substance of the law.

2. Between 1820 and 2010, the United States admitted 7.3 million immigrants from Germany and 7.8 million from Mexico.

3. The former West Germany absorbed large number of Germans (8 million) who moved west between 1944 and 1946. One writer called this westward movement "the greatest migratory movement of modern times." (Ardaugh 1987: 13). Estimates of the number of Germans who moved west between the end of World War II and the construction of the Berlin Wall in 1961 range from 9 to 13 million. Rainer Münz estimated in 1999 that there were 12 million east–west migrants and that 4.5 million were still alive in 1999.

4. Thirty countries expressed an interest in sending migrants to Germany, but German employers recruited mostly Europeans (the exception was a few hundred Koreans).

5. Freedom of movement within the European Economic Community (EEC) meant that a worker from any member state could enter another and remain for up to three months in search of a job. If the migrant found employment, the host country had to grant any necessary work and residence permits. Under EU freedom-of-movement rights, EU nationals do not need residence permits, although they can be required to register after stays of three months and show that they are enrolled in school, employed or self-employed, or have sufficient resources and health insurance to support themselves (or be a member of a family with someone who satisfies these study, work, and sufficient resources criteria).

6. If the exchange rate was $1 = DM4.2 when it "should" have been $1 = DM3, a $100 investment in Germany was worth DM420 to the investor rather than its "true" 300DM value.

7. Greece became a member of the EC in 1981, and Spain and Portugal became members in 1986. Greeks had to wait seven years, until 1988, for full-freedom-of-movement rights. Spain and Portugal, scheduled to have freedom-of-movement rights after seven years (in 1993), got freedom of movement a year early, in 1992.

8. Foreigners Commissioner Liselotte Funke said that employers and the labor ministry preferred to continue guest worker recruitment, but were willing to agree to tighter restrictions on family unification to avoid schooling and other integration issues (*Die Zeit*, February 17, 1989: 19).

9. In 1980, foreigners were 6 percent of the German population. Schmidt continues to be pessimistic about integrating foreigners. In a 2002 book, *Hand on Heart*, he wrote that Germany "brought in far too many foreigners as a result of idealistic thinking that

resulted from the experience of the Third Reich. We have seven million foreigners today who are not integrated, many of whom do not want to be integrated and who are also not helped to integrate. We Germans are unable to assimilate all seven million. The Germans also do not want to do this. They are to a large extent xenophobic."

10. The fee in the late 1980s was DM10,000. Turkish men who failed to perform military service or pay the fee could not get their Turkish passports renewed.

11. The European Communities were three international organizations governed by the same set of institutions: the European Coal and Steel Community (ECSC), the European Economic Community (EEC), and the European Atomic Energy Community (EAEC, or Euratom). In 1993, the EU replaced the EEC, which regulated economic affairs and migration, and the ECSC expired in 2002. Euratom continues to exist.

12. For example, after July 1, 1990, ethnic Germans had to fill out a lengthy questionnaire and be approved as such before departing for Germany; winning recognition as an ethnic German required passing a German test that a third of test takers failed (retakes are not permitted). After 1993, a quota of 220,000 ethnic Germans was approved per year.

13. Jewish law holds that religion comes from the mother, so many of those considered Jewish in the former USSR are not considered Jewish by Jewish religious authorities in Germany.

14. There were 1,737 asylum applications in 1967; 10,000 in 1970.

15. Germany was able to deal with other asylum surges in similar ad hoc ways. For example, it did not require foreign children under 16 to have visas, so some Sri Lankan Tamils and Iranians sent their children to Germany by air to request asylum. For example, 2,500 unaccompanied minors applied for asylum in 1988. Germany imposed fines on airlines carrying minors without documents, and began to require visas of unaccompanied foreign minors. Thus, the problem was solved.

16. The number of asylum applications was 78,600 in 2000 and 41,300 in 2010; the number of applications reached a low of less than 20,000 in 2007.

17. In one remarkable case, a German city of 90,000 that hosted 800 Bosnian Muslims built 61 moveable houses in Bosnia a few miles away from the Muslims' Serb-controlled village. If they are eventually permitted to return to their original village, their houses can be moved there. Each returning family also received DM2500 (Neil King, "Movable East German Mayor Finds Unusual Solution for Refugee Problem," *Wall Street Journal*, April 22, 1998).

18. Most of these "new guest workers" are employed less than a full year, so they add the equivalent of about 150,000 full-time equivalent workers to the German work force.

19. Germany has Ausländerbehörde (foreigners authorities) in most cities that issue Aufenthaltserlaubnisse (residence permits). Police in the late 1990s located 130,000 to 140,000 foreigners a year who were suspected of being unlawfully in Germany, such as by overstaying their visas (Beauftragte 2001: 72–73).

20. A fifteen-member commission chaired by Peter Hartz, then Volkswagen's personnel director, recommended these reforms, which took effect in 2003, 2004, and 2005. Hartz I allowed for private employment agencies (Personal-Service-Agenturen, or PSAs) and modified unemployment insurance; Hartz II allowed the creation of mini-jobs offering lower wages and benefit costs to employers and simplified self-employment (*Ich-AG*); Hartz I and II went into effect on January 1, 2003. Hartz III, in 2004, restructured the

German Employment Service, while Hartz IV, in 2005, combined long-term unemployment insurance benefits (*Arbeitslosenhilfe*) and welfare assistance (*Sozialhilfe*) benefits and reduced them to welfare assistance levels.

21. Employer payroll taxes are 23 percent of the wages paid in mini-jobs, much less than the 40 percent or more paid to higher-wage workers. Beginning on January 1, 2005, Germans who were unemployed more than a year received €345 ($450) a month plus money to cover their rent, and were required to take "one-Euro" public service jobs that paid €1.50 an hour for up to 20 hours a week.

22. Since 1993, foreigners aged 16 to 23 who have lived in Germany for at least eight years and have gone to school in Germany have a right to be naturalized if they apply.

23. For example, the state of Hesse developed a 100-question naturalization test in 2006 that was considered a model. The Baden-Württemberg test includes this question: "Some people consider the Jews responsible for all the evil in the world and even claim they are behind the Sept. 11 attack in New York. What do you think about such suggestions?" Naturalization can be revoked if an applicant hides her true feelings.

24. Immigration became a major issue in the 2002 election campaign, with the leader of the CDU-CSU coalition, Edmund Stoiber, asserting, "If you consider that almost half of Europe's immigrants end in Germany, it's very difficult to absorb them . . . and restrictions [on immigration] are highly advisable. . . . We have a serious burden . . . because we have too many foreign nationals who don't speak our language."

25. The bill was approved only when the state of Brandenburg, ruled by a coalition of Schröder's Social Democrats and conservative Christian Democrats, voted in favor. Conservatives claimed that the vote was invalid because state officials shouted both "yes" and "no" as the vote was taken. Article 51 of the German constitution requires states to cast a unanimous vote.

26. In the spring of 2011, Germany enacted a law aimed at speeding the recognition of foreign credentials. Germany has 350 regulated professions, and many of the 300,000 foreigners with qualifications earned outside the country cannot satisfy the rules to gain recognition. Under the new law, foreigners can apply to have their foreign-earned credentials recognized, and professional organizations are to complete their assessments within three months.

27. In 2006, some 50,300 foreigners arrived for family unification, including 14,000 who were foreign wives joining German husbands; 13,200 foreign wives joining non-EU husbands living in Germany; 10,800 children under 18 joining their families; and 3,700 foreign husbands joining foreign women who had settled.

28. At the end of 2009, there were 1.7 million Turks among the 6.7 million foreigners in Germany (25 percent).

29. In 2008, Germany had 2 million Muslim residents, 150 mosques, and 2,000 prayer rooms, many in cellars, warehouses, and other converted industrial spaces. At that time, over 90 percent of the imams serving in mosques were foreigners; many were Turkish civil servants posted to Germany for several years who did not speak German.

30. *The Economist*, in March 2011, reported that only one chapter dealing with science had been concluded and that there were no negotiations on eighteen chapters.

31. For example, the FDP proposed quota-based immigration in 1996 under which annual admissions would be based on economic indicators and graduates of "integration

courses" could receive unlimited work permits—that is, those issued without a labor market test. The FDP would have allowed foreigners born in Germany of legally resident parents to become dual nationals if they wished at age 18, and permitted foreigners to naturalize after eight years, down from fifteen years.

32. In 1997, the Greens proposed an immigration system that would make the maximum number of immigrants admitted the same as the number of ethnic Germans, then 220,000 a year, and grant German nationality to all babies born in Germany with at least one legal foreign parent. They also proposed that employers and governments share the cost of language and culture classes on a fifty-fifty basis. In 1997, the Social Democrats announced "principles" for reform of immigration and integration policies.

33. Between 1966 and 1967, for example, guest worker employment fell by 25 percent, while German employment fell by only 3 percent, suggesting that guest workers could be rotated in and out of the labor market as needed.

REFERENCES

Angenendt, Steffen, ed. 1997a. *Deutsche Migrationspolitik im neuen Europa*. Opladen: Leske & Budrich.

———, ed. 1997b. *Migration und Flucht: Aufgaben und Strategien für Deutschland, Europa und die Internationale Gemeinschaft Schriftenreihe*. Bonn: Bundeszentrale für politische Bildung.

Ardaugh, John. 1987. *Germany and the Germans*. London: Hamish Hamilton.

Bach, Hans-Uwe. 1987. "Entwicklung und Struktur der Ausländerarbeitslosigkeit in der Bundesrepublik Deutschland—Seit 1960." In *Aspekte der Ausländerbeschäftigung in der BRD*, edited by Elmar Hönekopp, 114: 144–78. Nuremberg: Bundesanstalt für Arbeit, Institut für Arbeitsmarkt und Berufsforschung.

Bade, Klaus J., ed. 1984a. *Auswanderer-Wanderarbeiter-Gastarbeiter: Bevolkerung, Arberitsmarket and Wanderung in Deutschland seit des 19. Jahrhunderts*. Ostfildern: Scripta Verlag.

———, ed. 1984b. *Das Manifest der 60: Deutschland und die Einwanderung*. Munich: Beck.

———, ed. 1987. *Population, Labor and Migration in 19th and 20th Century Germany*. New York: Berg.

———, ed. 1992. *Deutsche im Ausland—Fremde in Deutschland: Migration in Geschichte und Gegenwart*. Munich: Beck.

———. 1994a. *Ausländer-Aussiedler-Asyl: Eine Bestandsaufnahme*. Beck'sche Reihe Band 1072. Munich: Beck.

———. 1994b. *Der Manifest der 60: Deutschland und die Einwanderung*. Munich: Beck.

———, ed. 1996. *Die multikulturelle Herausforderung: Menschen über Grenzen—Grenzen über Menschen*. Beck'sche Reihe Band 1184. Munich: Beck.

———. 1997. "From Emigration to Immigration: The German Experience in the 19th and 20th Century." In *Migration Past, Migration Future: Germany and the US*, edited by Klaus J. Bade and Myron Wiener, 135–62. Providence, RI: Berg.

Barwig, Klaus, Gisbert Brinkmann, Bertold Huber, Klaus Lörcher, and Christoph Schumacher, eds. 1994. *Asyl nach der Änderung des Grundgesetzes: Entwicklungen in Deutschland und Europa: Hohenheimer Tage zum Ausländerrecht*. Baden-Baden: Nomos.

Beauftragte. 1999. "Daten und Fakten zur Ausländersituation." Beauftragte der Bundes-regierung für Ausländerfragen, Bonn, June.

———. 2001. "Migrationsbericht der Ausländerbeauftragten." Efms für Beauftragte der Bundesregierung für Ausländerfragen, Bonn, November. http://www.bundes auslaenderbeauftragte.de/.

Böhning, Wolf-Rüdiger. 1972. *The Migration of Workers in the United Kingdom and the European Community.* Oxford: Oxford University Press for the Institute of Race Relations.

———. 1984. *Studies in International Labor Migration.* London: Macmillan.

Böhning, Wolf-Rüdiger, and Jacques Werquin. 1990. *Some Economic, Social, and Human Rights Considerations Concerning the Future Status of Third-Country Nationals in the Single European Market.* Geneva: International Labor Office.

Bukow, Wolf-Dietrich, and Roberto Llaryora. 1993. *Mitbürger aus der Fremde: Soziogenese ethnischer Minoritäten.* Opladen: Westdeutscher Verlag.

Castles, Stephen. 1989. "Migrant Workers and the Transformation of Western Societies." Cornell Western Societies Program Paper 22, Cornell University, Ithaca, NY.

Cohn-Bendit, Daniel, and Thomas Schmidt. 1992. *Heimat Babylon: Das Wagnis der multi-kulturellen Demokratie.* Hamburg: Verlag Hoffmann & Campe.

Cornelius, Wayne A., Philip L. Martin, and James F. Hollifield, eds. 1994. *Controlling Immigration: A Global Perspective.* Stanford, CA: Stanford University Press.

Deutscher Bundestag. 1997. "Soziale Lage verschiedener Zuwanderergruppen in Deutsch-land unter besorderere Berücksichtigung von Flüchtlingen—Integrationsmöglich-keiten und -perspektiven." Uni Saarland für Enquete-Kommission Demographischer Wandel, Saarbrücken, August.

Dietz, Barbara. 1997. *Jugendliche Aussiedler: Ausreise, Aufnahme, Integration Schriftenreihe Aussiedlerintegration.* Vol. 7. Berlin: Berlin Verlag Arno Spitz.

Eckerle, K., D. Franzen, S. Rommerskirchen, K. Schilling, I. Weidig, C. Wirz-Bergmann, and H. Wolff. 1989. "The Development of the Labor Markets in the Single European Market Up to the Year 2000." Prognos, Basel, December. http://www.prognos.ch.

Faist, Thomas. 1995. *Social Citizenship for Whom? Young Turks in Germany and Mexican Americans in the United States.* Aldershot, UK: Avebury.

Frey, Martin, and Ulrich Mammey. 1996. *Impact of Migration in Receiving Countries: Germany.* Geneva: International Organization for Migration.

Gitmez, Ali. 1989. "Turkish Experience with Work Emigration." *Yapi Kredi Economic Review* 3 (4): 3–27.

Hailbronner, Kay. 1994. "Migration Policies, Third-Country Nationals and EC Law." In *Migration Policies: A Comparative Perspective*, edited by Friedrich Heckmann and Wolfgang Bosswick, 171–200. Stuttgart: Enke.

———. 1997a. "Der aufenthaltsrechtliche Status der verschiedenen Gruppen von Einwanderern in der Bundesrepublik Deutschland." In *Einwanderungsland Bundesre-publik Deutschland in der Europäischen Union*, edited by Albrecht Weber, 23–49. IMIS-Schriften 5. Osnabrück: Universitätsverlag Rasch.

———. 1997b. "Was kann ein Einwanderungsgesetz bewirken?" *Aus Politik und Zeitgeschichte* 46: 39–46.

Hailbronner, Kay, and Claus Thiery. 1997. "Schengen II und Dublin—Der zuständige Asylstaat in Europa." *Zeitschrift für Ausländerrecht und Ausländerpolitik* 2: 55–66.

Heckmann, Friedrich. 1981. *Die Bundesrepublik: Ein Einwanderungsland?* Stuttgart: Klett-Cotta.

Heilemann, Ullrich, and Hans Dietrich von Löffelholz. 1998. "Ökonomische und fiskalische Implikationen der Zuwanderung nach Deutschland." RWI-Papiere 52, Rheinisch-Westfälische Institut für Wirtschaftsforschung, Essen. www.rwi-essen.de/.

Herbert, Ulrich. 1997. *Hitler's Foreign Workers: Enforced Foreign Labor in Germany under the Third Reich.* New York: Cambridge University Press.

Hermann, Helga. 1992. "Ausländer: Von Gastarbeiter zum Wirtschaftsfaktor." Beiträge 173, Institut der deutschen Wirtschaft, Cologne.

Hof, Bernd. 1996. "Szenarien künftiger Zuwanderungen und ihre Auswirkungen auf Bevölkerungsstruktur, Arbeitsmarkt, und soziale Sicherung." Beiträge zur Wirtschaftsund Sozialpolitik, Institut der deutschen Wirtschaft, Cologne, February.

Hollifield, James. 1992. *Immigrants, Markets, and States: the Political Economy of Immigration in Postwar Europe and the U.S.* Cambridge, MA: Harvard University Press.

Hönekopp, Elmar. 1990. *Zur beruflichen und sozialen reintegration türkischer Arbeitsmigratiten in Zeitverlauf.* Nuremberg: Bundesanstalt für Arbeit, Institut für Arbeitsmarkt und Berufsforschung.

———. 1997. "The New Labor Migration as an Instrument of German Foreign Policy." In *Migrants, Refugees, and Foreign Policy: U.S. and German Policies toward Countries of Origin,* edited by Rainer Münz and Myron Weiner, 165–82. Providence, RI: Berghahn Books.

INS (Immigration and Naturalization Service). 1997. *Statistical Yearbook of the Immigration and Naturalization Service.* Washington, DC: INS.

Kindleberger, Charles 1967. *Europe's Postwar Growth: The Role of Labor Supply.* Cambridge, MA: Harvard University Press.

Krane, Ronald E. 1975. *Manpower Mobility across Cultural Boundaries: Social, Economic, and Legal Aspects: The Case of Turkey and West Germany.* Leiden: Brill.

———, ed. 1979. *International Migration in Europe.* New York: Praeger.

Kubat, Daniel, ed. 1979. *The Politics of Migration Policies.* New York: Center for Migration Studies.

Lederer, Harald W. 1997. *Migration und Integration in Zahlen: Ein Handbuch.* Bamberg: efms.

Lefringhausen, Klaus. 1971. "Wirtschafts-ethische Aspekte für lokale Actionen." In *Gastarbeiter-Mitburger,* edited by René Leudesdorff and Horst Zillessen. Gelnhausen: Burckhardthaus.

Lutz, Vera. 1963. "Foreign Workers and Domestic Wage Levels with an Illustration from the Swiss Case." *Banca Nazionale del Lauoro Quarterly Review* 16: 64–97.

Martin, Philip L. 1980. *Guestworker Programs: Lessons from Europe.* Washington, DC: U.S. Department of Labor, Bureau of International Labor Affairs.

———. 1981. "Germany's Guestworkers." *Challenge* 24 (3): 34–42.

———. 1991. *The Unfinished Story: Turkish Labor Migration to Western Europe, with Special Reference to the Federal Republic of Germany.* Geneva: International Labor Office.

———. 1993. *Trade and Migration: NAFTA and Agriculture.* Washington, DC: Institute for International Economics.

———. 1997. "Guest Worker Policies for the Twenty-First Century." *New Community* 23 (4): 483–94.

Martin, Philip L., and Mark J. Miller. 1980. "Guestworkers: Lessons from Western Europe." *Industrial and Labor Relations Review* 33 (April): 3.

Mehrländer, Ursula. 1974. *Soziale Aspekte der Ausländerbeschäftigung.* Bonn: Neue Gesellschaft.

———. 1987. *Aüslanderforschung 1965 bis 1980: Fragestellungen, theoretische Ansätze, empirische Ergebnisse.* Bonn: Neue Gesellschaft.

Mehrländer, Ursula, Carsten Ascheberg, and Jörg Ültzhöffer. 1997. *Situation der ausländischen Arbeitnehmer und ihrer Familienangehörigen in der Bundesrepublik Deutschland.* Bonn: Bundesministerium für Arbeit und Sozialordung Forschungsbericht.

Migration News. 1998. http://migration.ucdavis.edu.

Miller, Mark J., and Philip L. Martin. 1982. *Administering Foreign-Worker Programs: Lessons from Europe.* Lexington, MA: Lexington Books / D. C. Heath.

Münz, Rainer, Wolfgang Seifert, and Ralf Ulrich. 1997. *Zuwanderung nach Deutschland: Strukturen, Wirkungen, Perspektiven.* New York. Campus.

Schiller, Günter, Emmanuel Drettakis, and Roger Böhning. 1967. "Ausländische Arbeitnehmer und Arbeitsmarkt." Beitrag 7, Institut für Arbeitsmarkt- und Berufsforschung der Bundesanstalt für Arbeit, Nuremberg.

Schuck, Peter, and Rainer Münz, eds. 1998. *Paths to Inclusion: The Integration of Migrants in the United States and Germany.* Providence, RI: Berghahn Books.

Schulz, Erika. 1999. "Zuwanderung, temporäre Arbeitsmigranten und Ausländerbeschäftigung in Deutschland." *Vierteljahrshefte zur Wirtschaftsforschung* 3: 3–17.

Sen, Faruk, and Andreas Goldberg. 1994. *Türken in Deutschland: Leben zwischen zwei Kulturen.* Beck'sche Reihe Band 1075. Munich: Beck.

Servan-Schreiber, Jean Jacques. 1988. *The American Challenge.* New York: Atheneum. First published 1968.

Sessselmeier, Werner. 2002. "Immigration and the German Labor Market—The 1990s and the Near Future." Mimeo.

SOPEMI. 1997. *Trends in International Migration: 1996.* Paris: Organisation for Economic Co-operation and Development.

Steinmann, Gunter, and Ralf E. Ulrich, eds. 1994. *The Economic Consequences of Immigration to Germany.* Heidelberg: Physica-Verlag.

Straubhaar, Thomas. 1988. *On the Economics of International Labor Migration.* Bern: Haupt.

———. 1992. "Allocational and Distributional Aspects of Future Immigration to Western Europe." *International Migration Review* 26 (2): 462–83.

von Löffelholz, Hans Dietrich, and Günter Köpp. 1998. "Ökonomische Auswirkungen der Zuwanderungen nach Deutschland." RWI Heft 63, Rheinisch-Westfälisches Institut für Wirtschaftsforschung, Essen. www.rwi-essen.de/.

Weber, Albrecht, ed. 1997. *Einwanderungsland Bundesrepublik Deutschland in der Europäischen Union.* IMIS-Schriften 5. Osnabrück: Universitätsverlag Rasch.

Weidenfeld, Werner, ed. 1994. *Das Europäische Einwanderungskonzept.* Gütersloh: Bertelsmann Stiftung.

Werner, Heinz. 1985. "The Employment of Foreigners in Western European Industrial Countries." *Intereconomics* 1 (January–February): 10–15.

Werner, Jan. 1992. *Die Invasion der Armen: Asylanten und illegalle Einwanderer*. Mainz: Von Hase & Köhler Verlag.

Zank, Wolfgang. 1998. *The German Melting Pot: Multiculturality in Historical Perspective*. New York: St. Martin's Press.

Zimmermann, Klaus, Barry Chiswick, and Thomas Straubhaar. 1998. *Migration and Integration in Fortress Europe: A Policy Report*. London: Centre for Economic Policy Research.

COMMENTARY

Germany: From Ideological Battles to Integration Consensus

Dietrich Thränhardt

Phil Martin presents a detailed and exact description of German immigration history with all its contradictions and intricacies. Here, I make an attempt to sum up and synthesize, and link history to the new trends following the strong showing of the German economy in the aftermath of the 2008 economic crisis.

EUROPEAN PRIORITY

Since the first recruitment treaty with Italy in 1955, Germany's migration policy has been part and parcel of a deliberate policy to create a united and open Europe. Step by step, EU citizens have gotten more rights. As more and more countries joined the EU, their citizens could take advantage of open borders and equal rights. German guest worker recruitment began with Italians and went on with Spaniards, Greeks, Portuguese, and Turks. It ended with the oil crisis in 1973, but was followed by family reunification. After the opening of the Iron Curtain in 1989, the German government entered into seasonal work treaties with Poland and other neighboring countries to the east, to prepare for its accession to the EU and to soften migration pressure. In the 2011 debate over labor shortages, the federal government again discussed inviting Spaniards but not the Tunisians or Egyptians uprooted by the Arab Spring. Researchers often miss the European dimension of Germany's immigration policies, since for decades the uniting of Europe was considered "high politics" and immigration or "guest workers" were considered a less prominent social affair.

However, from the recruitment treaty of 1961 until today, there has been an ongoing debate over whether Turkey is a European country, whether Turkey should join the EU, and whether Turks or Muslims can be successfully integrated. In contrast to the United States, Canada, and Australia, Germany has never opened up to world-wide immigration, with the exception of small programs for intracompany transfers in 1998, IT specialists in 2000, big investors in 2005, and engineers and doctors in 2011.

AN OFFICIAL IMMIGRATION COUNTRY AT LAST

Germany accepted millions of immigrants, particularly between 1987 and 1995, even when the government proclaimed that it was "not an immigration country." The official position changed only with the Red-Green government, which came to power in 1998. They adopted a new naturalization law, including *jus soli*, in 1999, a recruitment program for IT specialists in 2000 (Kolb 2004), a federal immigration agency in 2004, and an immigration law in 2005. At the same time, however, immigration decreased and official net migration turned negative in 2008 and 2009 (BAMF 2011). In 2010, net migration was positive (+128,000) but did not outweigh the birth deficit, and the population shrank by 181,000.

The first reason for this puzzle is economic. Since the early 1970s, Germany has been a high-price country with a well-paid industrial workforce, not only in comparison to emerging countries like China but also relative to the new EU members next door. Germany deliberately shouldered financial burdens to foster a united and safe Europe.

The second reason is the end of the Cold War. With unification in 1990, inefficient industries in East Germany and subsidized industries in Berlin collapsed, and millions of people lost their jobs. In addition, ethnic Germans from Poland, Romania, and the former Soviet Union; asylum seekers; and other refugees took the chance to immigrate, but did not find work and became dependent on welfare. Following a conservative budget policy, Germany had low economic growth rates after reunification, counted up to 5 million unemployed in 2005, and tried to restrict further immigration.

Because of high unemployment, Germany's migration balance with most Western European countries turned negative in the early 2000s. Economically induced immigration started again in 2010, driven by a robust export industry and a growing labor shortage. As of June 2011, the government responded by opening the labor market to immigrants who are medical doctors and automotive and electrical engineers. Further steps toward opening up are expected.

The economic boom in Turkey has ended migration pressure from that country. In 2010, 5,862 more people went to Turkey than came to Germany. Only Switzerland received more migrants from Germany (-12,448) than vice versa. Immigration was highest from Romania (+25,717), Poland (+22,623), and Bulgaria (+15,602)—these are all new EU member states. Within Germany, people continue to move from the ex-Communist East to the dynamic regions in the South.

DIFFICULT ADAPTATION AFTER THE COLD WAR

Divided during the Cold War and remembering its totalitarian past, the Federal Republic introduced constitutional guarantees for special categories of immigrants in 1949: East Germans who enjoyed full rights to citizenship, individuals who had fled because of political and racist persecution by the Nazis, and political refugees. In 1953, full citizenship rights were extended to ethnic Germans in Communist countries. At this time, however, it was very difficult for them to leave. Up until the fall of the Berlin wall in 1989, every refugee from the East Germany was welcome and considered a demonstration of the superiority of the free world. The humanitarian impulse was strongly rooted in the constitution, in the traumatic memory of totalitarian dictatorship, and in public opinion. In spite of the collapse of East German industry, the newly elected, democratic East German government in 1990 invited Jews from the Soviet Union to immigrate, reacting to reports about anti-Semitism there. After unification, the Bundestag decided to continue this invitation in 1991 and to accept Jews from the Soviet Union as quota refugees. In 2003, Jewish immigration to Germany grew and eventually surpassed Jewish immigration to Israel.

All of these groups were entitled to welfare benefits upon entering Germany. Consequently, with the fall of the Berlin Wall and the end of Communist travel restrictions, millions of people arrived: ethnic Germans from Poland, Romania, and the former Soviet Union; Jewish immigrants from the former Soviet Union; and asylum seekers and war refugees, particularly from the Balkans.

Germany was slow to adapt to the post–Cold War environment. Only after a "state crisis" (chancellor Kohl), including arson murders of immigrants and demonstrations all over Germany against these atrocities (the *Lichterketten*, or light chains, in 1992 and 1993), were the constitution and several laws changed. Step by step, rights and privileges of ethnic Germans were taken away between 1990 and 2005 (Brubaker and Kim 2011). After an intervention by the Israeli ambassador with the Central Council of Jews in Germany, in 2005 Jewish immigration from the Soviet Union was reduced. Since 1993, individuals who have entered Germany through "safe countries" have been unable to claim asylum. Family immigration has required a language test since 2007. Thus noneconomic privileged immigration was reduced from a stream to a trickle, driven by the wish to curtail what Angela Merkel called "immigration into the welfare systems."

INTEGRATION AS A WELFARE STATE APPROACH

Since the start of recruitment, immigrants were included in the comprehensive German welfare state. In 1972, all foreign workers got voting rights in the influential works councils, bolstering employment stability even in crises. Healthcare, retirement, and unemployment insurance are now universal, giving immigrants important social rights and inducing them to stay.

To foster integration, the government introduced mandatory language and civic courses in 2005 for all newcomers except those from nations without German visa requirements. "Oldcomers" may also join in, and their participation is mandatory if they are unemployed. Thus, a new state-funded welfare program is created. This approach is in line with a general European trend (or Dutch model; Michalowski 2007) toward defining integration as a challenge that can be solved by active state intervention. Public discourse and many German researchers follow the same paradigm (Bommes 2010). In contrast, naturalization rates are comparatively low, even after the reform of 1999. German law does not allow dual citizenship, even if more than half of the applicants get exceptions (Böcker and Thränhardt 2008). Established denizens have largely the same rights as citizens, with the exception of voting rights and core state functions. For this reason, most of them do not feel pressured to naturalize. Typically, only refugees from oppressive countries like Iran naturalize as quickly as possible.

AN EMERGING POLITICAL CONSENSUS

Germany seems to have reached consensus regarding principles of integration and immigration. Chancellor Merkel has organized "integration summits" and institutionalized a "national integration plan." The minister of the interior has invited Muslim representatives for a "German Islam conference." Institutionalizing Islam with a status comparable to that of a Christian church is under discussion. Two German parties—the Liberals and the Greens—now have national chairmen with "migration backgrounds," one adopted as a boat-people child, the other born to Turkish parents in Germany. The government has set up working groups for the acknowledgment of foreign qualifications and certificates.

Labeling has become more general, embracing all immigrants irrespective of their background. In the past, refugees, asylum seekers, contingent refugees, guest workers, and foreigners had clearly separate statuses and legal rights, and were perceived as separate groups. Now there is a tendency to discuss immigrants in general terms: New terms such as *Zuwanderer* and "people with migration background" include all those with a foreign passport, a personal immigration history, or a parent born outside Germany. All of them are put together, and they have been granted new rights for welfare-state programs, particularly language and integration courses. With this new statistical basis, the public suddenly became aware that 19.7 percent of the German population has a "migration background," and 28.6 percent of those are under 25 years of age.

The underside of the integration discourse is a widespread characterization of immigrants, particularly Turks or Muslims, as welfare-dependent, low achieving, culturally different, and deficient—a far cry from the image of hard-working "guest workers" from the 1960s and 1970s. This sentiment was aggressively articulated by former Bundesbank board member Sarrazin, who sold 1.2 million copies of a resentful, xenophobic, and bizarre eugenic and anti-Islamic book in 2010. The book's success among the middle class can be seen as the German parallel to the success of aggressive xenophobic parties in most neighboring countries. However, sophisticated research has demonstrated that Germans are far more balanced and positive toward immigrants and that daily convivial contacts are intense (SVR 2011). In this sense, and contradicting Sarrazin, Federal President Wulff has said that "Islam is now also a part of Germany," along with Christianity and Judaism.

Martin and Givens have rightly portrayed Germany as a reluctant country of immigration. However, other researchers have been wrong to draw long lines of historic continuities in arguing that Germany necessarily had an "ethnic" understanding of citizenship or would be unable to introduce *jus soli*, as it did in 1999. Contingencies of the Cold War dominated decisions in a divided Germany as links to East Germany were cut and as both German states conducted their policies along prevalent lines of both world systems: West Germany by inviting migrants from the Mediterranean; East Germany, by inviting contract workers from Vietnam, Cuba, and Communist African countries. Because of Germany's and Europe's demographic deficit and industrial strength, Germany will need to develop more comprehensive immigration policies in the coming years.

REFERENCES

BAMF (Bundesamt für Migration und Flüchtlinge). 2011. *Migrationsbericht des Bundesamtes für Migration und Flüchtlinge im Auftrag der Bundesregierung: Migrationsbericht 2009*. Nuremberg: BAMF.

Böcker, Anita, and Dietrich Thränhardt. 2008. "Multiple Citizenship and Naturalization: An Evaluation of German and Dutch Policies." In *Of States, Rights, and Social Closures: Governing Migration and Citizenship*, edited by Oliver Schmidtke and Saime Ozcurumez, 135–56. New York: Palgrave Macmillan.

Bommes, Michael. 2010. "Migration Research in Germany: The Emergence of a Generalized Research Field in a Reluctant Immigration Country." In *National Paradigms of Migration Research*, edited by Dietrich Thränhardt and Michael Bommes, 127–85. Osnabrück: V & R Press.

Brubaker, Rogers, and Jaeeun Kim. 2011. "Transborder Membership Politics in Germany and Korea." *Archives Européennes des Sociologie* 52: 21–75.

Kolb, Holger. 2004. *Einwanderung zwischen wohlverstandenem Eigeninteresse und symbolischer Politik*. Münster: LIT Verlag.

Michalowski, Ines. 2007. *Integration als Staatsprogramm: Deutschland, die Niederlande und Frankreich im Vergleich: Das Beispiel der deutschen "Green Card."* Münster: LIT Verlag.

SVR (Sachverständigenrat deutscher Stiftungen für Integration und Migration). 2011. *Migrationsland 2011: Jahresgutachten mit Integrationsbarometer*. Berlin: SVR.

8 | THE NETHERLANDS

Consensus and Contention in a Migration State

Willem Maas

INTRODUCTION: THE NETHERLANDS AS A MIGRATION STATE

The Netherlands has always been a migration state.[1] Immigrants played crucial roles in the formation of the Dutch state and the subsequent Golden Age in the seventeenth century, when many were drawn to the country for its relative religious toleration. At least 150,000 people, primarily Calvinists and other Protestants—merchants, artists, and others—fled Flanders and Brabant during the war of independence from Spain (1568–1609) and settled in the northern Netherlands, where they constituted 10 percent of the new country's population (Maas 2013). The migrants settled chiefly in the cities, and the new Dutch Republic overtook northern Italy as Europe's most urbanized region.[2] Migrants from present-day Belgium and northern France were joined by Sephardic Jews from Portugal and Spain as well as Germans, Scandinavians, Scots, Ashkenazi Jews from central and eastern Europe, Huguenots from France, and others. They helped transform the Netherlands from a mostly rural and agricultural backwater into an urbanized society, a world center of economic, industrial, intellectual, financial, artistic, and scientific activity (*Algemene Geschiedenis Der Nederlanden* 1977).

Immigration continued more slowly in the eighteenth century (see Table 8.1) and then gradually decreased in the nineteenth century, increasing again in the twentieth century (Lucassen and Penninx 1997). Only recently has the proportion of immigrants in Dutch society approached the peak reached during the Golden Age: by 2010, foreign-born individuals accounted for just over 11 percent of the total resident population of the Netherlands (see Table 8.2). Immigrants and the children of immigrants accounted for one in five people in the Netherlands—just over 20 percent of the population—in 2010 (see Table 8.3).

At the same time, the twentieth and early twenty-first centuries were characterized by the emigration of large numbers of Dutch citizens. Over half a million persons born in the Netherlands—over 5 percent of the country's population—emigrated between 1946 and 1969, not counting the many who emigrated and subsequently returned (Elich 1983, 1987), encouraged by government emigration subsidies. Emigration of the Dutch-born population slowed slightly in the 1970s and 1980s, but then once again increased, driven by free

TABLE 8.1

Average annual migration to and from the Netherlands, 1796–2010

	Immigration	Emigration	Net	Immigration	Emigration	Net
	(IN THOUSANDS)			(PER 1,000 POPULATION)		
2000–2010	118.6	107.8	10.8	7.3	6.6	0.7
1975–1999	98.4	69.4	28.9	6.7	4.7	2.0
1950–1974	63.9	59.8	4.1	5.4	5.1	0.3
1925–1949	41.3	45.7	−4.5	4.8	5.3	−0.5
1900–1924	35.6	34.1	1.5	5.7	5.5	0.2
1865–1899	12.5	15.8	−3.3	2.9	3.7	−0.8
1796–1864	1.6	3.0	−1.4	0.6	1.1	−0.5

SOURCE: Data adapted from Nicolaas and Sprangers (2007), except for years 2000–2010, which were calculated from Statistics Netherlands figures.

TABLE 8.2

Foreign-born residents of the Netherlands by country of birth (in thousands)

Year	Germany	Indonesia	Suriname	Turkey	Morocco	Other countries	Total	Percentage of total population
2011	122.3	137.8	186.2	197.4	167.7	1,060.0	1,868.7	11.2
2010	120.5	140.6	186.8	196.7	167.4	1,020.5	1,832.5	11.1
2008	117.0	146.7	187.0	194.8	167.2	938.3	1,751.0	10.7
2007	116.4	149.6	187.8	195.4	168.0	915.2	1,732.4	10.6
2006	116.9	152.8	189.2	196.0	168.6	911.3	1,734.7	10.6
2005	117.7	155.9	190.1	195.9	168.5	907.9	1,736.1	10.6
2004	119.0	158.8	189.7	194.6	166.6	903.0	1,731.8	10.7
2003	120.6	161.4	189.0	190.5	163.4	889.2	1,714.2	10.6
2002	122.1	163.9	188.0	186.2	159.8	854.7	1,674.6	10.4
2001	123.1	165.8	186.5	181.9	155.8	802.3	1,615.4	10.1
2000	124.2	168.0	185.0	178.0	152.7	748.4	1,556.3	9.8
1999	125.5	170.3	184.2	175.5	149.6	708.8	1,513.9	9.6
1998	126.8	172.1	182.2	172.7	145.8	669.5	1,469.0	9.4
1997	128.0	174.8	181.6	169.3	142.7	637.3	1,433.6	9.2
1996	130.1	177.7	181.0	167.5	140.7	610.1	1,407.1	9.1
1971	128.9	204.4	29.0	28.2	20.9	194.9	606.3	4.6
1960	129.2	203.2	12.9	—	—	103.3	448.6	3.9
1947	135.5	79.9	—	—	—	76.6	292.0	3.0
1930	—	32.6	—	—	—	245.1	277.7	3.5

SOURCE: Calculated from Statistics Netherlands figures and Nicolaas and Sprangers (2007) for the years before 1996.

NOTE: "Indonesia" figures for 1930 and 1947 include Suriname and the Netherlands Antilles. After the five most important countries of birth, the next most important in 2011 were Netherlands Antilles/Aruba (89,429), Poland (66,634), former Yugoslavia (52,659), Belgium (49,957), United Kingdom (47,232), former Soviet Union (45,567), China (44,711), and Iraq (40,991).

movement within the European Union (EU), which allows individuals to more easily relocate to other EU countries. Belgium and Germany are particularly popular with the Dutch because of lower taxes and house prices, and there is also significant retirement migration to Southern Europe (Maas 2009). Between 1995 and 2009, there was net emigration of some 313,400 Dutch-born individuals (see Table 8.4), roughly the same number (averaging 20,000 annually) as during the postwar emigration boom. The postwar emigration of Dutch-born individuals was proportionately more significant, as the Dutch population has increased from approximately 10 million in 1950 to almost 17 million today. However,

TABLE 8.3

Number and background of allochtonen *in the Netherlands, 2010 (in thousands)*

			SECOND GENERATION				
Country	Total	First generation	Total	One parent	Two parents	Percentage of all *allochtonen*	Percentage of total population
Turkey	384.0	196.4	187.6	34.0	153.6	11.4	2.32
Indonesia	382.4	119.0	263.4	193.5	69.9	11.4	2.31
Germany	378.9	105.7	273.2	253.0	20.2	11.3	2.29
Morocco	349.0	167.3	181.7	25.5	156.2	10.4	2.11
Suriname	342.3	185.1	157.2	55.8	101.4	10.2	2.07
Antilles/Aruba	138.4	81.2	57.2	31.8	25.4	4.1	0.84
Belgium	113.0	37.6	75.4	69.7	5.8	3.4	0.68
Former Yugoslavia	79.1	52.7	26.4	10.8	15.5	2.4	0.48
United Kingdom	78.7	43.7	35.0	31.0	4.0	2.3	0.47
Poland	77.2	57.5	19.7	15.1	4.6	2.3	0.47
Former Soviet Union	55.9	41.8	14.1	8.5	5.6	1.7	0.34
China	53.3	37.2	16.2	2.8	13.3	1.6	0.32
Italy	39.4	19.3	20.1	17.5	2.6	1.2	0.24
Afghanistan	38.7	31.1	7.6	.3	7.3	1.2	0.23
France	37.2	19.3	17.8	15.6	2.2	1.1	0.22
Others	812.2	504.9	307.2	188.1	119.2	24.2	4.90
Total	3,359.6	1,699.8	1,659.9	952.9	707.0	100.0	20.27

SOURCE: Statistics Netherlands.

TABLE 8.4

Emigration of persons born in the Netherlands by destination, 1995–2009 (in thousands)

Destination	Emigration	Return	Net emigration	Net emigration percentage of subtotal
Belgium	102.5	50.3	52.2	23.6
Germany	80.8	44.8	36.0	16.3
Other Europe	82.8	48.3	34.6	15.6
United Kingdom	45.5	22.0	23.5	10.6
France	30.8	15.0	15.7	7.1
Spain	30.8	18.2	12.6	5.7
United States	37.4	25.9	11.6	5.2
Canada	13.1	5.2	7.9	3.6
Antilles/Aruba	35.4	27.7	7.7	3.5
Australia	17.0	9.3	7.7	3.5
Other	94.1	82.5	11.6	5.3
Subtotal	570.4	349.2	221.2	100.0
Unknown	92.2	0	92.2	
Total	662.6	349.2	313.4	

SOURCE: Calculated from Statistics Netherlands figures.

because of the significant increase in emigration (whether returning to countries of origin or moving elsewhere), there is now more emigration than ever before: 0.66 percent of the population, approximately one out of every 150 residents, emigrates every year.[3]

Immigration is even more significant than emigration, however, with annual inflows equivalent to 0.73 percent of the population. Immigration, particularly by those from non-

Western societies, has aroused a mixture of responses, and by the end of the twentieth century the Netherlands could be described—along with many other Western European states—as a reluctant immigration country (Entzinger 2004). The political situation in the Netherlands in the first decade of the twenty-first century has been challenging to immigration advocates, although policies and their implementation have not become as restrictionist as in some other European states.

Contrary to what some believe, Dutch public opinion is not more hostile to immigrants than public opinion in other European states, and the political salience of immigration in the Netherlands is *below* the EU average. The Dutch tradition of consensus building, a tradition in which all viewpoints are carefully considered and middle-of-the-road policies and bureaucratic inertia reign—reinforced by the extremely proportional electoral system—have allowed anti-immigrant parties not only to enter parliament but also to join the cabinet. Since the late 1990s, the essentially nondiscussion of immigration that had been the norm in the Netherlands was shattered by populist parties, most famously those led by Pim Fortuyn and Geert Wilders.

Tension between consensus building and contention currently characterizes Dutch migration politics and undermines a key assumption of the gap hypothesis. As discussed elsewhere in this book, this hypothesis holds that the gap between the goals of national immigration policy and actual policy outcomes is increasing. But this assumes that the goals of national immigration policy can be defined and are relatively fixed. The Netherlands currently provides a context in which this does not hold; aside from easy caricatures (e.g., uneducated and unemployable foreigners who have criminal backgrounds and no family ties, who cannot integrate, and who do not contribute to society should not be allowed to immigrate; highly educated and highly skilled foreign workers who already speak Dutch or will learn quickly and will immediately contribute to society should be welcomed), there is disagreement about almost every other aspect of migration politics and policies.

THE MIGRATION TRADITION

Whether caused by geography, political culture, economic links, or other factors, migration has been a central concern in the Netherlands since its foundation as a state. Like other colonial states, the Netherlands exported people abroad during the colonial period. But it also imported what today would be termed highly skilled immigrants. In the seventeenth-century Golden Age, the Netherlands was an economic and cultural magnet, with cities such as Amsterdam drawing the best and brightest. This changed during the eighteenth century, and during the nineteenth century the Netherlands was again a country of emigration.

In the first quarter of the twentieth century (1900–1924), the Netherlands became a net immigration country, drawing roughly the same proportion of immigrants as in the third quarter (1950–1974). Only from the late 1920s to the early 1960s was the Netherlands a net emigration country—until it briefly became an emigration country once again during a period of five years from 2003 to 2007—a situation unique in Western Europe until the economic crisis—as Ireland also once again became an emigration country.

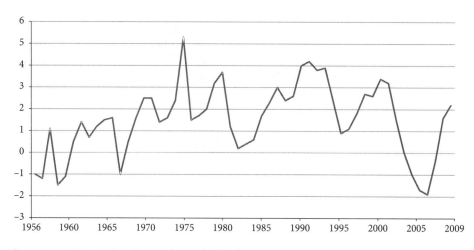

Figure 8.1   Net immigration to the Netherlands, per 1,000 population, 1956–2009.
Source: Statistics Netherlands.

Figure 8.1 shows net migration to the Netherlands between 1956 and 2009. Despite substantial postcolonial and labor immigration, the Netherlands was essentially an emigration country from the 1930s until the 1960s. The peak net immigration years included the 1970s (labor migration and the independence of Suriname), the late 1980s and early 1990s (asylum and family reunification), and the period around 2000.

POSTWAR EMIGRATION

In the immediate aftermath of the Second World War, the Dutch government started exploring the possibility of encouraging emigration. To build a welfare state, the government promoted industrialization and export industries and reduced reliance on farming. As a result, agricultural workers—who also had a very high birth rate—were considered surplus. In his New Year's address on January 1, 1950, Prime Minister Willem Drees famously announced that "part of our people should venture, as in previous centuries, to seek their future in larger realms than our own country."[4]

To encourage emigration, the government offered information and courses, facilitated transportation, signed international agreements such as the Netherlands Australia Migration Agreement (1951), and offered financial subsidies to those willing to leave. Farmers' associations, women's groups, and Protestant and Catholic emigrants' organizations assisted emigrants in their journey, and the government established a Netherlands Emigration Service.[5] From 1950 to 1959, roughly 350,000 Dutch emigrants settled in Canada (127,900), Australia (106,100), the United States (59,900), South Africa (29,100), New Zealand (19,900), and elsewhere. The peak year was 1952, when 52,000 Dutch emigrants left (Nicolaas and Sprangers 2007).

The war had devastated the country's infrastructure, and there were worries about the Cold War and insufficient work and food as well as a prevailing pessimism. A novelist captured the bleak mood: "The Netherlands is overpopulated. Every child that is born sets back civilization and makes us poorer. In ten years we will be bankrupt" (Hermans 1951; my translation). Severe storms on February 1, 1953, destroyed dykes and flooded large parts of Zeeland, South Holland, and North Brabant, leaving roughly 1,800 dead and causing the evacuation of approximately 72,000. The tragedy galvanized government spending on infrastructure and laid the groundwork for the so-called Deltaplan, intended to prevent future disasters. The rise of social programs introduced by the Social Democratic Drees government stabilized the situation. The standard of living started to rise and industrialization increased; the 1959 discovery of natural gas in Groningen added to the economic resurgence. Emigration slowed, and by the 1960s there were efforts to recruit workers, first from southern Europe (especially Italy, Spain, and Portugal) and then elsewhere (see the section on Labor Migration below).

POSTCOLONIAL IMMIGRATION

The Netherlands witnessed postcolonial immigration from three sources: Indonesia, Suriname, and the Netherlands Antilles.

Indonesia

The largest postwar immigration to the Netherlands was the movement of approximately 400,000 people from the former Dutch East Indies following the independence of Indonesia and its subsequent annexation of Netherlands New Guinea in 1945–1968. Many of these immigrants were among the roughly 300,000 people who had moved to Indonesia from the Netherlands between 1900 and 1940 (and thus were simply returning emigrants), but others were born in what became Indonesia (Beets, van Imhoff, and Huisman 2003). Indonesia-born immigrants quickly became the largest group of foreign-born residents.

Of particular note within the Indonesian-born population are the Moluccans, who are mostly Christian, Dutch-speaking, and part of the Dutch colonial elite.[6] In 1950, Moluccan soldiers who had served with the Royal Netherlands Indies Army declared an independent Republic of the South Moluccas (Republik Maluku Selatan, or RMS). Within six months, most RMS forces were defeated by the troops of the new Republic of Indonesia. The RMS leadership retreated to the Netherlands, where they established a government-in-exile, accompanied by some 12,500 soldiers and their families.

Initially housed in camps, many Moluccans never adopted Dutch citizenship, expecting that they would be able to return eventually to an independent South Moluccan state. By 2010, the Moluccan community numbered approximately 50,000 (Radio Netherlands Worldwide 2010).

The total number of Indonesia-born immigrants also remains significant: in 2010, over 140,000 people born in Indonesia resided in the Netherlands, although this population is aging fast. The second generation is much larger: by one estimate, in 2001 there were over 280,000 second-generation Indonesians (a person with at least one parent born in Indonesia) living in the Netherlands (Beets, van Imhoff, and Huisman 2003: 65). Subsequent estimates put that number at around 263,000 in 2010. Thus, the total number of first- and second-generation Indonesians is 382,400 (Table 8.3). Statistics Netherlands does not maintain statistics on individuals with foreign heritage beyond the second generation. It is clear, however, that many second-generation Indonesian immigrants now have children, grandchildren, and possibly great-grandchildren.[7]

Suriname

The other significant spurt of postcolonial migration occurred around the time of Suriname's independence in 1975. One of the Dutch government's motivations for granting independence (neighboring French Guiana was never granted independence and remains an overseas department of France) had been to reduce Surinamese immigration to the Netherlands (van Amersfoort 1999: 143). This plan backfired, however, as many Surinamese immigrated in anticipation of independence, fearing that it would have negative consequences and wanting to make use of their Dutch citizenship rather than lose it. Soon after independence, roughly one-third of Suriname's population had immigrated, rivaling the Indonesians as the largest group of foreign-born residents.

Suriname's population is ethnically diverse. The four largest groups are the Hindustani or East Indians (descendants of nineteenth-century contract workers from northern India), the Creoles (of mixed African and European, mostly Dutch, heritage), the Javanese (descendants of contract workers from the former Dutch East Indies), and the Maroons (descendants of West African slaves who escaped to the interior). Some estimates place the proportions at 37 percent Hindustani, 31 percent Creole, 15 percent Javanese, 10 percent Maroon, 2 percent Amerindian, 2 percent Chinese, 1 percent white, and 2 percent other.[8] Suriname's Chinese community has been growing, particularly since the 1990s (Tjon Sie Fat 2009).

The size of the Surinamese community resident in the Netherlands has also continued to grow, although more slowly after 1980, when visa restrictions were introduced. In 2010, there were approximately 187,000 Suriname-born residents in the Netherlands (Table 8.2) along with roughly 157,000 second-generation Surinamese (Table 8.3), for a total of over 340,000, compared with a total population in Suriname of around 490,000.

Netherlands Antilles

Dutch settlers colonized various islands in the Caribbean in the seventeenth century, trading and running slave plantations. After the 1814 Anglo-Dutch Treaty, the Dutch retained control of two sets of islands: Aruba, Bonaire, and Curaçao (off the Venezuelan coast) and Sint Eustatius, Saba, and Sint Maarten (in the Leeward Islands). Following postwar decolonization, the Netherlands Antilles became one of three constituent units of the Kingdom of the Netherlands (along with Suriname and the Netherlands). Aruba separated from the rest of the Netherlands Antilles in 1986, and Curaçao and Sint Maarten followed in 2010, when Bonaire, Sint Eustatius, and Saba became Dutch municipalities. The islands have a combined population of just over 300,000 (approximately 142,000 on Curaçao, 106,000 on Aruba, 37,500 on Sint Maarten, 13,400 on Bonaire, 2,900 on Sint Eustatius, and 1,700 on Saba).[9]

Antilleans hold Dutch citizenship, and their migration to the Netherlands is unrestricted; however, several islands limit migration from the Netherlands through residence permits and quotas. Migration from the Antilles to the Netherlands was for a long time chiefly temporary, as local youth sought opportunities for work or study in the Netherlands before returning. In the late 1990s, however, the economic situation in the Caribbean deteriorated, and many Antilleans immigrated; there was net migration of over 28,000 between 1997 and 2002, before the flow reversed. By 2010, an estimated 81,200 first-generation Antilleans resided in the Netherlands, alongside another 57,200 second-generation migrants (Table 8.3).

The increase in Antilleans and the fact that some Antillean youth became involved in criminal activities prompted the Dutch government in 2006, under immigration minister Rita Verdonk, to propose regulations allowing for repatriation of Antillean youth between the ages of 16 and 24 who were unemployed and whose employment prospects were few. Later proposals specified that only individuals who were convicted of a crime or who threatened national security could be repatriated. There were public discussions advocating restricting the migration rights of *all* Antilleans (Emmer 2007), but these ran into the problem that Dutch citizenship is supposedly unitary, with equal status and no distinctions between any of the Kingdom's constituent units. By 2010, the disjuncture between Antilles being able to limit migration from the Netherlands without the reverse had resulted in a draft law on free movement within the Kingdom.[10]

LABOR MIGRATION

In common with other Western European states such as Germany, the Netherlands in the 1960s signed several labor recruitment agreements with foreign countries intended to bring in immigrants who would work for some period of time and then return to their home countries. Such agreements were signed with Italy (1960), Spain (1961), Portugal (1963), Turkey (1964), Greece (1966), Morocco (1969), Tunisia (1970), and Yugoslavia (1970). Free movement within the European Community (EC) (Maas 2007) soon made obsolete the agreement with Italy and later those with Greece (which joined the EC in 1981) and Spain and Portugal (1986). The labor migration that resulted from these various agreements was at first mostly circulatory: the primarily young, male workers worked and indeed returned. Then the 1973 oil crisis significantly altered this pattern. Following the Egyptian and Syrian attack on Israel in October 1973 (the Yom Kippur War), the Organization of the Petroleum Exporting Countries (OPEC) first raised the price of oil and then set a total embargo on oil exports to the United States and the Netherlands, later extending it to other Western European states and Japan. The resulting crisis, coupled with a stock market crash and high inflation, resulted in recession across Europe and rising unemployment. Rather than returning home, however, many of the workers who had migrated to the Netherlands decided to stay.

During this time, the Netherlands had relatively liberal family reunification and formation policies that allowed labor migrants to bring in their families. For example, a comparison of the growth of Turkish populations in the Netherlands and Germany since the informal end of the guest worker system in 1974 shows that the Turkish population grew much faster in the Netherlands, mostly because of Germany's more restrictive family reunification and formation policies and its relative success during the 1980s at enticing unemployed Turkish workers to leave (Muus 2004: 269).

By 2010, as shown in Table 8.2, more residents of the Netherlands were born in Turkey (196,700) than in Suriname (186,800), followed closely by those born in Morocco (167,400) and ahead of those born in Indonesia (140,600). In other words, labor migration—primarily from Turkey and Morocco—coupled with liberal family reunification and formation policies, resulted in the population of labor migrants outnumbering that of postcolonial migrants. Of course this is partly a generational phenomenon: most immigrants from Indonesia arrived in the 1950s, while most labor migrants arrived thirty or more years later.

One way of examining the relative size of immigrant groups is to look at the statistics on immigrant backgrounds and those of their children. These statistics employ the Dutch concept of *allochtoon*, taken from the Greek roots *allos* (other) and *chthon* (land or earth), which is the opposite of the concept of *autochtoon* (in English autochthonous). Statistics Netherlands defines an *allochtoon* as someone born abroad with at least one parent who was born abroad (first-generation *allochtoon*) or someone born in the Netherlands who has at least one parent born abroad (second-generation *allochtoon*).[11]

Table 8.3 shows the top fifteen source countries for resident *allochtonen*. By 2010, one out of every five residents (20.3 percent) was *allochtoon*, roughly half first-generation and half second-generation, for a total of some 3.4 million people. More than half of this population originated in five countries of origin: Turkey, Indonesia, Germany, Morocco, and Suriname.

RECENT MIGRATION PATTERNS

Examining annual immigration and emigration statistics by the citizenship of migrants (Dutch or non-Dutch) shows stable immigration of Dutch citizens (return migration and immigration of those who acquired citizenship abroad, such as by marriage or birth to a Dutch citizen) from the 1970s to the 1990s and growing immigration of Dutch citizens since then. Emigration of Dutch citizens has grown, particularly after 2000. For non-Dutch citizens, the immigration trend is considerably more varied (with many ups and downs), while the emigration trend is stable and growing, particularly after 2002; in 2009, more than 57,000 non-Dutch citizens emigrated—the highest number ever.

Figure 8.2 shows net immigration not by citizenship status but by country of birth for the period 1972–2009. Suriname and the Antilles, which were the most important source of immigrants throughout the 1970s (postcolonial immigration) were joined by Turkey and then Morocco (labor immigration). Noteworthy is the ever growing importance of immigration from EU member states, particularly since the 2004 enlargement (most notably Poland) (Pool 2011).

Figure 8.3 shows annual net immigration by country of birth for the top eight source countries between 1995 and 2010 (ranked by total net immigration over the period, shown beside the country name). The next most important source countries are Suriname (18,161 net immigrants), the former Yugoslavia (17,511), Iran (13,697), Belgium (9,941), and the United States (8,126). Again, the most striking addition here is that of Poland, with growing numbers of Polish-born individuals settling permanently. Germany, the second EU country after Poland, appears ninth, while Belgium is thirteenth. Clearly, the numbers for net immigration mask the growing circular migration within the EU.

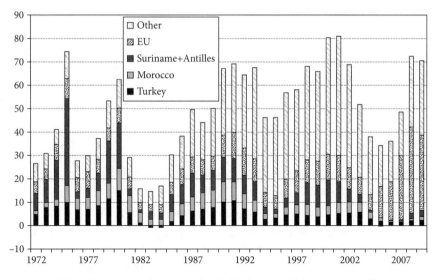

Figure 8.2   Net immigration to the Netherlands (in thousands) by country of birth, 1972–2009. *Source:* Statistics Netherlands.

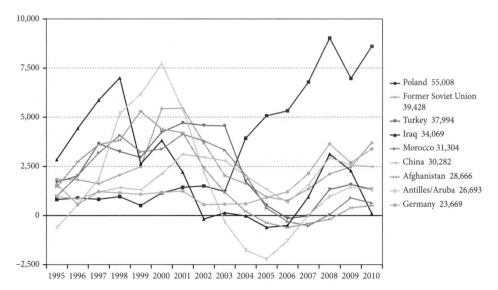

Figure 8.3   Net immigration to the Netherlands by country of birth—top countries, 1995–2010. *Source:* Statistics Netherlands.

Immigration by individuals born outside the Netherlands dipped in the middle of the first decade of the twenty-first century (especially 2002–2006) at the same time that emigration of those born in the Netherlands increased. Table 8.4 lists the most important destination countries of these Dutch-born emigrants. Evident is the significant "churn" in migration within the EU, caused by thousands of Dutch-born individuals both emigrating to and returning from other EU member states. The top five destinations of net emigration (emigrants minus immigrants) are all European, which contrasts with postwar emigration overseas. Indeed, net emigration to European destinations now accounts for almost four-fifths of all emigration.

CITIZENSHIP

In the wide range of citizenship and naturalization policies in Europe, the Netherlands has long been situated at one end. For example, a 1998 study of foreigners' rights in France, Germany, and the Netherlands found that the Netherlands provided foreigners the most rights because they could vote in local elections and their cultural rights were guaranteed under the minorities policy (Guiraudon 1998; 274). In addition, the Netherlands had the highest naturalization rate among European states.

Table 8.5 shows the percentage of residents who were born abroad and the percentage who had foreign nationality for nine European states in 1998, 2003, and 2007. The ratio is inexact because birth abroad does not necessarily mean foreign citizenship—for example, a child born abroad of citizen parents usually acquires citizenship through *jus sanguinis*, or acquisition by descent. However, the relative ratios are illustrative of the difference in naturalization rates.

In the Netherlands, the 1990s witnessed a debate over whether granting citizenship should be seen as a means of encouraging integration or rather as the statement of its successful conclusion. Political parties on the Left tended to promote the former view; those on the right, the latter, arguing that naturalization should be seen as the "crowning moment" at which a completely integrated person finally achieves complete legal equality. Those on the right also argued that granting citizenship too easily would cast doubt on the recipient's loyalty, while others argued that naturalization inherently provided a source of loyalty (Groenendijk 2005: 194).

Between 1992 and 1997, the view of the Leftist parties held sway: "Nationality is an expression of connection, not of indivisible loyalty. Because that connection can be of many

TABLE 8.5
Percentage of residents who are foreign born and who have foreign nationality

	1998			2003			2007		
Country	Foreign born	Foreign nationality	Ratio (%)	Foreign born	Foreign nationality	Ratio (%)	Foreign born	Foreign nationality	Ratio (%)
Netherlands	9.6	4.2	44	10.7	4.3	40	10.7	4.2	39
Sweden	11.0	5.6	51	12.0	5.3	44	13.4	5.7	43
United Kingdom	7.4	3.8	51	8.9	4.7	53	10.2	6.5	64
Germany	12.2	8.9	73	12.9	8.9	69	—	—	—
France	7.3	5.6	77	8.1	5.6	69	—	—	—
Belgium	10.0	8.7	87	11.4	8.3	73	13.0	9.1	70
Denmark	5.4	4.8	89	6.3	5.0	79	6.9	5.5	80
Switzerland	21.4	19.0	89	23.1	20.0	87	24.9	20.8	84
Spain	3.2	1.9	59	8.8	7.2	82	13.4	11.6	87

SOURCE: Calculated from OECD figures.

NOTE: Figures for France are for 1999 and 2005; for Germany, 1998 and 2005.

kinds, it is possible for an individual to have connections to more than one country. Nationality should therefore no longer be seen as an exclusive link with a single country; dual nationality is not a phenomenon that should automatically be opposed" (Driouichi 2007: 123; my translation). The complete toleration of dual nationality that resulted from this kind of argument resulted in large-scale naturalizations peaking at over 80,000 acquiring Dutch nationality in 1996 (see Figure 8.4).

Nevertheless, the openness toward dual nationality waned, and policies once again became more restrictionist (Penninx 2005). By 2007, the far Right politician Geert Wilders was proposing that dual citizens could not be cabinet ministers, a jab at two new cabinet members, one Turkish-Dutch and the other Moroccan-Dutch. His proposal was defeated, but the government did propose making it harder for those who naturalize at the age of 18 to retain their original nationality, and new laws make it easier to strip individuals of their Dutch citizenship.

Despite the perceived "restrictive turn in Dutch citizenship policy" (Van Oers 2008: 40), demographic data paint a more nuanced picture. As shown in Figure 8.5, the proportion of the Dutch population with a nationality other than Dutch has been growing, while the proportion of the population with only Dutch nationality has declined.

The most striking phenomenon is the growth of dual and multiple citizenship in the Netherlands. The number of resident individuals holding both Dutch and one other nationality increased from 402,088 (2.6 percent of the total population) in 1995 to 1,155,206 (7.0 percent of the total population) in 2010—a striking increase for such a short period of time. At the same time, both the number and proportion of residents of the Netherlands who do not hold Dutch nationality have been declining, from 749,061 (4.9 percent) in 1995 to 677,795 (4.1 percent) in 2007. The number is growing again, but has yet to reach previous levels. The story here is one of stability.

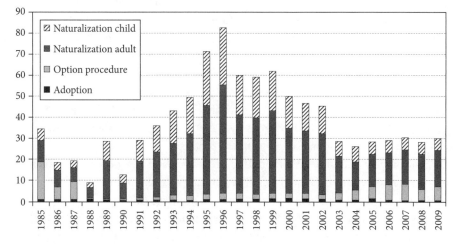

Figure 8.4 Acquisition of Dutch nationality (in thousands) by procedure, 1985–2009. *Source:* Statistics Netherlands. *Note:* Numbers for adoption include naturalization by recognition of paternity and by validation of marriage.

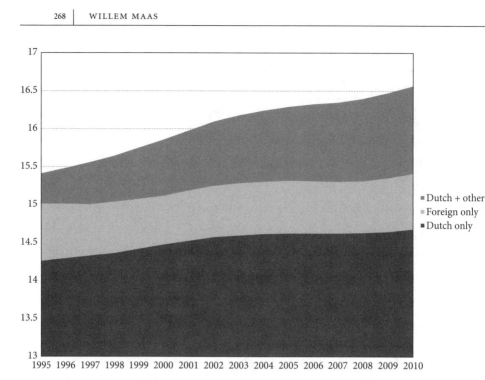

Figure 8.5 Residents of the Netherlands (in thousands) by nationality, 1995–2010.
Source: Statistics Netherlands.

Since all Dutch citizens can vote, the tripling of the number of citizens who hold another nationality—from around 400,000 (2.6 percent) in 1995 to almost 1.2 million (7.0 percent) today—can be expected to have electoral consequences. This is particularly true because of the proportional electoral system, in which 0.67 percent of the vote suffices to gain a seat in the lower chamber of Parliament. (Thus, for example, an animal rights party holds two of 150 seats). If there were a political party for dual citizenship and only those residents who hold more than one nationality voted for it, the party would win 11 seats (of 150) in parliament—not counting potential votes by Dutch citizens resident abroad, many of whom also hold dual citizenship.

Table 8.6 shows the twelve largest nationalities of residents of the Netherlands who do not hold Dutch nationality. The most striking change is the decline in the number of citizens of Morocco and Turkey, from over 250,000 (approximately 37 percent of all foreigners) in 1998 to under 170,000 (under 25 percent) ten years later. This change is presumably largely due to the naturalization of Turkish and Moroccan individuals, who thus no longer appear in these statistics. The contrast with the numbers of citizens of EU member states is stark: with some fluctuations, the numbers (and hence the proportions) of citizens of Germany, the United Kingdom, Belgium, Italy, Spain, France, Portugal, and so forth, are stable or increasing gradually. (Noteworthy here is the rise in the number of citizens of Poland living in the Netherlands.) These statistics include only legally resident individuals, and anecdotal evidence suggests that 26,200 is a significant undercount (see Pool 2011).

TABLE 8.6

Nationality of foreigners living in the Netherlands (in thousands) and percentage of total foreign population for twelve largest nationalities

	1998			2003			2008	
Nationality	Number	Percentage	Nationality	Number	Percentage	Nationality	Number	Percentage
Moroccan	135.7	20.0	Turkish	100.3	14.3	Turkish	93.7	13.6
Turkish	114.7	16.9	Moroccan	97.8	14.0	Moroccan	74.9	10.9
German	53.9	8.0	German	56.1	8.0	German	62.4	9.1
British	39.2	5.8	British	44.1	6.3	British	40.2	5.8
Belgian	24.4	3.6	Belgian	26.3	3.8	Belgian	26.2	3.8
Italian	17.4	2.6	Italian	18.7	2.7	Polish	26.2	3.8
Spanish	16.6	2.5	Spanish	17.5	2.5	Italian	19.0	2.8
Bosnian	14.6	2.2	American	15.4	2.2	Spanish	16.5	2.4
Somali	13.6	2.0	French	14.5	2.1	Chinese	16.2	2.4
Iraqi	13.0	1.9	Portuguese	11.3	1.6	French	15.1	2.2
American	13.0	1.9	Chinese	11.2	1.6	American	14.5	2.1
Surinamese	11.8	1.7	Indonesian	10.8	1.5	Portuguese	12.9	1.9

SOURCE: Calculated and compiled from Statistics Netherlands data.

NOTE: Individuals who hold two or more foreign nationalities are attributed to one based on a hierarchy: other EU state, other European state, other non-European state.

TABLE 8.7

Dutch citizens living in the Netherlands with dual nationality by country of second nationality, 2010 (in thousands)

Country	Number	Percentage
Turkey	284.8	24.6
Morocco	273.2	23.6
Germany	54.2	4.7
United Kingdom	44.3	3.8
Belgium	31.8	2.8
Italy	22.1	1.9
Poland	17.8	1.5
France	17.6	1.5
Spain	13.1	1.1
Other EU	42.0	3.6
Iran	17.3	1.5
Bosnia	16.7	1.4
Suriname	16.1	1.4
Egypt	14.1	1.2
United States	13.9	1.2
Vietnam	12.6	1.1
Other	190.0	16.4
Unknown	73.9	6.4
Total	1,155.4	100.0

SOURCE: Statistics Netherlands.

That the declining number of Dutch residents who are citizens of Turkey or Morocco but not citizens of the Netherlands is due to naturalization is evident from the data in Table 8.7, which disaggregates Dutch citizens in the Netherlands who hold dual citizenship with the country of their second nationality. Roughly half of all citizens of the Netherlands residing there who hold dual nationality—over 550,000 people—are Turkish or Moroccan citizens. Those who, besides Dutch nationality, hold an EU nationality account for roughly another quarter of all dual citizens.

IMMIGRANT INTEGRATION AND DUTCH NORMS AND VALUES

Immigrant integration in the Netherlands is coupled with the question of ethnic minorities. Dutch minorities policy became formalized with a parliamentary report drafted in 1981 and finalized in 1983, when it had become clear that both postcolonial migrants and labor migrants were going to remain in the Netherlands rather than return to their countries of origin. The report recognized that the Netherlands had become a "de facto immigration country" (Netherlands 1981, 1983). Since then, there have been a multitude of policies intended to promote the integration of ethnic minorities and immigrants. For example, in 1998 the Wet Samen (Wet Stimulering arbeidsdeelname minderheden), went into force. This was a law to stimulate the labor participation of minorities, which defines minorities as individuals who were born in, or who had at least one parent born in, Turkey, Morocco, Suriname, the Netherlands Antilles, Aruba, the former Yugoslavia, or any country in Africa, South or Central America, or Asia, except for Japan or Indonesia (which are considered Western countries for the purposes of Dutch minorities policy).[12]

Unlike citizenship, immigration is an area of policy where the will of the national government and the desires of municipalities and other decentralized authorities responsible for executing national policy do not always coincide. Consider the case of asylum. In the decade between 1992 and 2001, the Netherlands was the third largest recipient of asylum applications in Europe, behind Germany and the United Kingdom. Per capita, this made the country (along with Switzerland and Sweden) one of the most popular destinations in the 1990s in the world, at 2.27 applications per thousand inhabitants. (By comparison, the rate for the United States was 0.45; for Canada, 0.94.) By the end of the decade, however, asylum policy had become decidedly less welcoming (Van Selm 2000).

At least part of this change in attitude can be attributed to a former sociology professor who styled himself as the leading Dutch advocate of the "clash of civilizations" thesis, Pim Fortuyn. In his book *Against the Islamicization of Our Culture*, first published in 1997, Fortuyn warned that Muslims living in the Netherlands were a threat to traditional Dutch values: "Because of their advanced individualization, Dutch people are not aware of their own cultural identity and the rights they have gained: the separation of church and state, the position of women and of homosexuals. Their indifference makes the Dutch an easy and vulnerable prey" (Fortuyn 2002; my translation).

At first dismissed, then vilified, Fortuyn could no longer be ignored after his party won the March 2002 Rotterdam municipal elections. Nine days before the May 2002 national elections, he was assassinated by an ethnically Dutch environmental activist. The 2002 elections were among the most volatile in European history, leading commentators to argue that "after many years of stability and predictability, it is more important than ever to understand the nature of the increasing volatility of the Dutch electorate and the sudden changes in the Dutch political landscape" (van Holsteyn and Irwin 2003). Fortuyn's party won by a landslide, going from zero to 26 seats in the 150-seat lower house of parliament, becoming the second-largest party represented. The Lijst Pim Fortuyn (LPF) formed a governing coalition with the Christian Democrat CDA and the conservative VVD.

Without Fortuyn, however, the LPF imploded. An LPF deputy minister resigned within hours of being sworn in after it emerged that she had lied about her involvement in the Surinamese militia.[13] After further tensions within the party, the entire cabinet resigned within three months and new elections were called. The LPF dropped to eight seats in the January 2003 elections before disappearing.

Fortuyn's harsh line on immigration was later taken up by others, including Geert Wilders, a former protégé of conservative politician (later European Commissioner) Frits Bolkestein.[14] As VVD leader, Bolkestein had published a book in 1997 on Muslims in the Netherlands that advocated for cultural assimilation.[15] Wilders was a municipal councilor for the VVD in 1997 and then VVD member of parliament from 1998 until 2004, when he left the VVD and formed his own party, which won nine seats in the 2006 elections and twenty-four in the 2010 elections, becoming the third-largest party in the Netherlands.

After the 2010 elections, it looked unlikely that a government could be formed without the support of Wilders's party. The government formed after the 2010 elections was a coalition of the VVD (thirty-one seats) and CDA (twenty-one seats) which, because it lacked a majority of 75 or more seats, required the parliamentary support of Wilders's party. This arrangement, whereby the government depends on Wilders's support but does not include ministers from his party, was criticized for giving Wilders influence but no responsibility.[16]

The success of anti-immigration politicians has had its effects on policy. One observer noted that "the supposedly difference-friendly, multicultural Netherlands is currently urging migrants to accept 'Dutch norms and values' in the context of a policy of civic integration that is only an inch (but still an inch!) away from the cultural assimilation that had once been attributed to the French" (Joppke 2007: 2). Yet it would be a mistake to portray the change as a seismic shift. There were earlier examples of restrictionist policies and current examples of more open ones. For example, in mid-2007 the government granted amnesty to approximately 28,000 individuals who had been living in the Netherlands without authorization, and many mayors and town councils asked organizations working with illegal migrants to forward only those applicants who fulfill the requirements for a residence permit. Thus, the continued presence of "illegal" residents was tolerated.

One example of more stringent immigration policy is the new citizenship exam coupled with the requirement that applicants for a residence permit pass an integration test. The test is required of all applicants with the exception of citizens of Australia, Canada, Japan, Monaco, New Zealand, South Korea, Switzerland, the United States, and Vatican City. The United Nations Committee on the Elimination of Racial Discrimination warned the Netherlands that this is discriminatory.

Comparative public opinion data do not show that respondents in the Netherlands are more hostile to immigrants than are other Europeans. Indeed, they are significantly more likely than respondents from Germany, France, or the United Kingdom to claim that immigrants make the country a better place to live.

Similarly, the political salience of immigration is not extraordinarily high in the Netherlands, as demonstrated by comparative public opinion surveys that ask respondents to select the most important issues facing their country. Based on these surveys, it can be seen that immigration is much more politically salient in the United Kingdom, Spain, Denmark, Italy, and other countries not covered in this book; it is less salient in the Netherlands than the EU average.

CONCLUSION

The case of the Netherlands offers a possible corrective to the gap hypothesis. As discussed in this book, this hypothesis holds that the gap between the goals of national immigration policy and actual policy outcomes is increasing, thereby provoking greater public hostility toward immigrants in general and putting pressure on political parties and government officials to adopt more restrictions. For the gap hypothesis to operate it must first be clear what the goals of national immigration policy are. Such clarity is lacking in the case of the Netherlands, where both public opinion and the government's approach appear to be polarized and volatile.

The former governing coalition—which became a government only with the support of Geert Wilders's Freedom Party—was unstable. Several elements of the coalition agreement contravened EU treaties and legislation. Changing these treaties, laws, and policies would require agreement from some or all other EU member states and, in some cases, the European Parliament, and so it was infeasible. At the same time, declining relative net immigration from traditional source countries and their replacement with new source countries such as Poland and the former Soviet Union, coupled with the increasing emigration of Dutch-born citizens, particularly within the EU, changes the picture of both the immigrant and the emigrant.

NOTES

An earlier version of this chapter was presented at a workshop organized by the Tower Center at Southern Methodist University and the Federal Reserve Bank of Dallas. Some of the analysis also draws on Maas (2010). I am grateful to participants in the workshop and to the editors, particularly Pia Orrenius, for helpful comments.

1. The concept of the migration state is drawn from James Hollifield (2004), who uses it to mean a situation in which regulation of international migration is as important as providing for the security of the state and the economic well-being of its citizenry.

2. Amsterdam's population ballooned from 13,500 in 1514 to 104,900 in 1622 and to 200,000 in 1675; Leiden's grew from 14,300 in 1514 to 44,800 in 1622 and to 65,000 in 1675. In 1622, immigrants constituted 33 percent of the population of Amsterdam and Dordrecht, 38 percent of Gouda's, 40 percent of Rotterdam's, 51 percent of Haarlem's, 63 percent of Middelburg's, and 67 percent of Leiden's.

3. These numbers come from the residence statistics maintained by Dutch municipalities in the Gemeentelijke Basisadministratie persoonsgegevens (GBA), or municipal registry, known prior to 1994 as the bevolkingsregister. Every person residing in the Netherlands must register with a municipality and, once registered, is issued a citizen service number (burgerservicenummer, or BSN), which is necessary to access government and many private services. Those born in the Netherlands are registered at birth; those

taking up residence must register within five days of arrival; and those changing residence within the country must report their change. The GBA includes data on the following:

- Name, birthdate and place, and gender; parents' names with birthdates and places; current and former marriage(s) or registered partnership(s) with dates and places; divorce or separation with date and place; current and former spouse(s) or registered partner(s) with gender, birthdate, and place; children with birthdate and place; and death with date and place.
- Ward or legal guardianship status with details.
- Nationality or nationalities or a notation that nationality cannot be determined.
- For noncitizens, details of residence right.
- Date of registration in municipality with full address; date of residence application and name of former country of residence; for emigrants, address in country of destination.
- Administration numbers of applicant, parents, current and former spouse(s) or registered partner(s); children.
- BSN and date.
- BSN of parents, current and former spouse(s) or registered partner(s), and children.
- Name use and changes.

The use of and access to GBA data is subject to law and monitored by the data protection authority College Bescherming Persoonsgegevens (CBP).

4. "Een deel van ons volk moet het aandurven zoals in vroeger eeuwen zijn toekomst te zoeken in grotere gebieden dan eigen land."

5. http://www.nationaalarchief.nl/emigranten/nl/achtergrondinfo_2.1.asp.

6. Portugal controlled some of the islands in the fifteenth century, when Islam had only recently been introduced. Portuguese missionaries quickly set about to Christianize the population. When Spain took control, they were replaced by Spanish missionaries, including Francis Xavier, who later cofounded the Jesuits.

7. The child of an Indonesian immigrant (thus a second-generation immigrant) born in the Netherlands in 1946 could have had children in 1967 (at the age of 21), grandchildren in 1988, and great-grandchildren in 2009.

8. *CIA World Factbook*, https://www.cia.gov/library/publications/the-world-factbook/geos/ns.html.

9. Latest figures from Statistics Aruba (http://www.cbs.aw) and Statistics Netherlands Antilles (http://www.cbs.an/).

10. Rijkswet Personenverkeer.

11. It is sometimes remarked that most members of the royal family—including the current king and most people in the line of succession—are second-generation *allochtonen* (the king's father and grandfather were born in Germany; the queen, in Argentina).

12. Moluccans were included in the minority category, but others who were born or whose parent was born in Indonesia were not. http://www.eerstekamer.nl/wetsvoorstel/25369_wet_stimulering.

13. Philomena Bijlhout was elected LPF member of parliament in the May 2002 elections, then resigned to become deputy minister of emancipation and family affairs in the

cabinet sworn in on June 22, 2002. She resigned the same day when a TV station aired photos of her in the uniform of Surinamese military leader Dési Bouterse's militia. The photos were taken in 1983, after the December 1982 murders (in which fifteen prominent opponents of Bouterse's military regime, mostly journalists and lawyers, were shot dead); Bijlhout had earlier claimed she left the militia in 1981. She was replaced by LPF member Khee Liang Phoa.

14. Interestingly, both Bolkestein's and Wilders's mothers were of Indo (mixed European and indigenous Indonesian) ancestry, as was the mother of Eddie and Alex van Halen (of the band Van Halen), who emigrated from the Netherlands to California with their parents in 1962, as part of the postwar emigration discussed earlier.

15. The VVD grew from 31 seats in the 1994 elections to 38 seats in the May 1998 elections, but Bolkestein stepped down as party leader to become the European Commissioner for Internal Market and Services from 1999 to 2004. He lamented in 2010 that Wilders had become "completely radicalized."

16. Bolkestein, interviewed in *De Volkskrant*: "'Rutte is goud, Wilders is strovuur,'" March 5, 2011.

REFERENCES

Algemene Geschiedenis Der Nederlanden. 1977. Haarlem: Fibula–Van Dishoeck.

van Amersfoort, Hans. 1999. "Immigration Control and Minority Policy: The Case of the Netherlands." In *Mechanisms of Immigration Control: A Comparative Analysis of European Regulation Practices*, edited by Grete Brochmann and Tomas Hammar, 135–68. Oxford: Berg.

Beets, Gijs, Evert van Imhoff, and Corina Huisman. 2003. "Demografie van de Indische Nederlanders, 1930–2001." *Bevolkingstrends, 1e kwartaal 2003*. The Hague: Centraal Bureau voor de Statistiek. http://www.cbs.nl/NR/rdonlyres/482F9147-4512-4E9F -B8EF-BDD3E50607E9/0/2003k1b15p058art.pdf.

Driouichi, Fouzia. 2007. *De casus Inburgering en Nationaliteitswetgeving: Iconen van nationale identiteit: Een juridische analyse*. Amsterdam: Wetenschappelijke Raad voor het Regeringsbeleid.

Elich, J. H. 1983. *Emigreren*. Utrecht: Spectrum.

———. 1987. *Aan de ene kant, aan de andere kant: De emigratie van Nederlanders naar Australië 1946–1986*. Delft: Eburon.

Emmer, Piet. 2007. "Postkoloniale migratie: Stop de Antillianen." *NRC Handelsblad*. http://www.nrc.nl/nieuwsthema/antillen/article1890483.ece/Postkoloniale_migratie _Stop_de_Antillianen.

Entzinger, Han. 2004. "Commentary." In *Controlling Immigration: A Global Perspective*, edited by Wayne A. Cornelius, Takeyuki Tsuda, Philip L. Martin, and James F. Hollifield, 289–92. 2nd ed. Stanford, CA: Stanford University Press.

Fortuyn, Pim. 2002. rev. *De islamisering van onze cultuur: Nederlandse identiteit als fundament*. Uithoorn: Karakter.

Groenendijk, Cees A. 2005. "Het desintegratiebeleid van de kabinetten Balkenende." *Migrantenrecht*.

Guiraudon, Virginie. 1998. "Citizenship Rights for Non-Citizens: France, Germany, and The Netherlands." In *Challenge to the Nation-State: Immigration in Western Europe and the United States*, edited by Christian Joppke, 272–319. Oxford: Oxford University Press.

Hermans, Willem Frederik. 1951. *Ik heb altijd gelijk*. Amsterdam: Van Oorschot.

Hollifield, James F. 2004. "The Emerging Migration State." *International Migration Review* 38 (3): 885–912.

van Holsteyn, Joop J. M., and Galen A. Irwin. 2003. "Never a Dull Moment: Pim Fortuyn and the Dutch Parliamentary Election of 2002." *West European Politics* 26 (2): 41–67.

Joppke, Christian. 2007. "Transformation of Immigrant Integration: Civic Integration and Antidiscrimination in the Netherlands, France, and Germany." *World Politics* 59 (2): 243–73.

Lucassen, Jan, and Rinus Penninx. 1997. *Newcomers Immigrants and Their Descendants in the Netherlands 1550–1995*. Amsterdam: Het Spinhuis.

Maas, Willem. 2007. *Creating European Citizens*. Lanham, MD: Rowman & Littlefield.

———. 2009. "Unrespected, Unequal, Hollow? Contingent Citizenship and Reversible Rights in the European Union." *Columbia Journal of European Law* 15 (2): 265–80.

———. 2010. "Citizenship and Immigrant Integration in the Netherlands." In *Migrants and Minorities: The European Response*, edited by Adam Luedtke, 226–44. Newcastle upon Tyne: Cambridge Scholars.

———. 2013. "Immigrant Integration, Gender, and Citizenship in the Dutch Republic." *Politics, Groups, and Identities* 1 (4): 390–401.

Muus, Philip. 2004. "The Netherlands: A Pragmatic Approach." In *Controlling Immigration: A Global Perspective*, edited by Wayne A. Cornelius, Takeyuki Tsuda, Philip L. Martin, and James F. Hollifield, 263–88. 2nd ed. Stanford, CA: Stanford University Press.

Netherlands. 1981. "Ontwerp-minderhedennota."

———. 1983. "Minderhedennota."

Nicolaas, Han, and Arno Sprangers. 2007. "Buitenlandse migratie in Nederland, 1795–2006: De invloed op de bevolkingssamenstelling." *Bevolkingstrends, 4e kwartaal 2007*. The Hague: Centraal Bureau voor de Statistiek.

Penninx, Rinus. 2005. "Dutch Integration Policies after the Van Gogh Murder." Expert Panel on Social Integration of Immigrants, House of Commons, Ottawa.

Pool, Cathelijne. 2011. *Migratie van Polen naar Nederland in een tijd van versoepeling van migratieregels*. The Hague: Boom Juridische Uitgevers.

Radio Netherlands Worldwide. 2009. "Moluccan Exiles Will Settle for Autonomy." http://www.rnw.nl/english/article/moluccan-exiles-will-settle-autonomy.

———. 2010. "The Moluccan Dream—Still Alive at 60." http://www.rnw.nl/english/article/moluccan-dream-%E2%80%93-still-alive-60.

Tjon Sie Fat, Paul B. 2009. *Chinese New Migrants in Suriname: The Inevitability of Ethnic Performing*. Amsterdam: Amsterdam University Press.

Van Oers, Ricky. 2008. "From Liberal to Restrictive Citizenship Policies: The Case of the Netherlands." *International Journal on Multicultural Societies* 10 (1): 40–59.

Van Selm, Joanne. 2000. "Asylum in the Netherlands: A Hazy Shade of Purple." *Journal of Refugee Studies* 13 (1): 74–90.

A Restrictionist Shift That Matters

Irene Bloemraad

Willem Maas's chapter on the Netherlands provides an excellent introduction to the Dutch case. He underscores that immigration—and, at times, emigration—has been part and parcel of Dutch society from the sixteenth century to the present. And he carefully lays out three waves of post–World War II immigration: postcolonial, labor, and contemporary EU migration, helped along by EU citizens' mobility rights across member states. Finally, he touches on the three core policy questions: who gets in, what rights do migrants have once they arrive, and who has access to permanent membership through citizenship.

Maas also provides an informative overview of contemporary Dutch political debates. He argues that, while there has been a move from a relatively open, tolerant stance toward migrants to a more hostile one, the picture of Dutch immigration politics cannot be painted in black and white. Rather, there is no identifiable consensus position, which raises serious questions for the gap hypothesis because it presumes a relatively broad, stable agreement on policy goals. It is hard to assess the distance between immigration policy goals and outcomes, according to Maas, when Dutch public opinion and politicians seem so divided.

Maas is right to question any simple story of a Dutch "backlash" or 180-degree turn on immigration, but I suggest that a narrative of exclusion and assimilation is more dominant in 2012 than in the past, and that this has the potential to undermine two policy goals that most Dutch residents, of various political stripes, support: (1) successful integration of immigrants into the economic and social life of the Netherlands and (2) encouragement of high-skilled worker migration. Dutch residents debate *how* integration should be achieved, but largely agree on equality of opportunity in the labor market and education, as well as on the importance of harmonious intergroup relations. They also debate whether high-skilled migration should be the primary means of entry or is one stream in addition to family-sponsored migration and refugee admissions. However, given low fertility, an aging workforce, and an expensive social safety net, there is broad agreement that the Dutch economy needs to be at the forefront of the high-tech, financial, and scientific sectors—a goal that requires openness to migrants. The Dutch move to greater restriction, modest in policy terms but striking when it comes to public discourse, makes both of those goals harder to reach.

A SHIFT IN COURSE

The contradictory nature of the Dutch case can be summed up in a juxtaposition of two political moments. In 2002, Pim Fortuyn's party won the municipal elections in Rotterdam, campaigning on a strong anti-Muslim and anti-immigrant platform. The electoral manifestation of growing public anxiety over migration and the integration of residents of immigrant origin, especially young Muslim men, sent a shockwave through society. In 2008, Rotterdam made history again—but for a very different reason: Ahmed Aboutaleb, a Muslim, Moroccan-born politician in the Labour Party, was named the mayor of the city.[1]

Nevertheless, the Dutch case over the past ten years can be characterized as one of retrenchment from relatively open immigration and citizenship policy to greater exclusion and assimilation. It is important to underscore that actual policy has moved more slowly than has the shift in political rhetoric. Restrictionist politicians have proposed a wide range of laws, from modest changes in rules to highly symbolic moves such as calls to ban the burqa in public. However, the hue and cry is much more dramatic than are changes on the ground. For example, in its evaluation of migrant rights in seven policy areas, from long-term residence rights to labor market mobility, the Migrant Integration Policy Index (MIPEX) finds little change in Dutch policy from 2007 to 2010.[2]

The overall trend nevertheless is toward more restriction. In the area of immigration policy—who gets in—Dutch governments have tightened the rules for family-sponsored migration using two tactics. The first involves imposition of an integration test showing some knowledge of Dutch language and society *prior to* migration for the nationals of some countries, as well as the need to pass additional tests once in the Netherlands to keep a residence permit. The second tactic—struck down by the European Court of Justice but still on the table for new legislation—involves raising the minimum wage required to sponsor a spouse as well as the minimum age of the petitioner.[3] The government has also taken a "get tough" stance on would-be asylum seekers, although this has generated countermobilization.

In the area of rights and citizenship policy, we also find some retrenchment. The story from 1980 to 2000 was one of increasingly open access with emphasis on pluralism. In their analysis of group rights and civic citizenship, Koopmans and colleagues (2005) found that the Netherlands had moved from a moderate position on civic inclusion and cultural pluralism in 1980 to a position as the most open and multicultural among five countries studied in 2002.[4] A different analysis of twenty-one countries showed that, from 1980 to 2000, the Netherlands went from moderately supportive of group rights for immigrant-origin minorities to highly supportive, second only to Australia and Canada and tied with the United Kingdom.[5] Since then, however, the Netherlands has been one of only two countries to exhibit retrenchment in pluralism policy, a change that puts it back on par with the situation in 1980. Moreover, the procedures to become a citizen involve higher hurdles, including participation in integration classes and more demanding tests of language ability and knowledge of Dutch society and norms. Finally, as Maas highlights, some politicians have turned sharply against dual citizenship, a change from the gradual opening to multiple membership that occurred in the 1990s.

A SHIFT THAT MATTERS

The shift in course—and especially the shift in public debate—makes it harder for the Netherlands to succeed in integrating immigrants and their children, and it could make it harder to attract and retain high-skilled workers, a Dutch policy goal that has been emphasized increasingly since 2004. Maas highlights, quite correctly, that the Dutch public only expresses moderate concerns over immigration, and that worries over immigration are less salient than they are in many other European countries.[6] However, because of the proportional representation system based on a single, national electoral "district," a vocal minority can become much more politically prominent in the legislature than in the first-past-the-post, two-dominant-party systems in countries such as the United Kingdom, the United States, and Canada. Anti-immigrant rhetoric is thus amplified in the Dutch system beyond what public opinion would suggest. Furthermore, the critique of immigration and integration has come not just from the political Right but also from a vocal group on the Left. The latter argue for stronger assimilation policy to encourage labor market participation and advocate less immigration, because they worry that too much diversity will undermine support for the welfare state. For this reason, there are moments when many on the Right and some on the Left seem to agree that immigrants are a problem and that the solution should be fewer of them, especially from Muslim countries, and more coercive policies of integration. I believe that such political discourse matters.

The result could be two distinct policy gaps. Regarding the goal of integration, the divisive, aggressive debate may cause a backlash among Dutch-born minority youth, and it risks alienating migrants. Civic inclusion efforts, especially around language learning and labor-force inclusion, are not *prima facie* anti-immigrant, as the Canadian case suggests. However, the terms of the Dutch debate, which revolves around the superiority of Dutch secular and progressive culture, juxtaposed with the perceived backward views and habits of non-Western migrants, can be seen as paternalistic and as a new form of the cultural superiority inherent in prior colonial projects. The two-tiered nature of moral worth becomes especially evident in the statistical category of "non-Western," which includes Turks but excludes Japanese, and in policies requiring integration evaluations of some migrants but not others. As Maas notes, the fact that would-be Moroccan migrants need to take a test but Americans or Koreans do not has already raised flags for the UN Committee on the Elimination of Racial Discrimination.

The exceptions made for residents of rich countries are partially tied to a second migration goal, attracting high-skilled migrants, *kennismigranten*, who have quicker and easier access to residency permits, including the use of separate government offices for some of their paperwork. In addition, citizens of EU countries have free mobility rights—an opportunity that a growing number of EU residents have taken, as the statistics in Maas's chapter make clear. In some respects, however, these migrants show poor integration, especially in learning the Dutch language or sending their children to Dutch schools. A thriving set of international schools exists in places such as Amsterdam and the Hague that cater to the children of financial professionals, diplomats, lawyers, and other elite foreigners, but they generate no public outcry like that against "Muslim" schools or those set up for Hindu residents.

"Knowledge migrants" are rarely singled out as integration failures—further highlighting the two-tiered stratification of the "migrant problem"—but they can be alienated by the general tone of the anti-foreigner debate.[7] Given their human capital, however, high-skilled migrants face relatively low barriers in emigrating away from the Netherlands. If Dutch attempts to attract and keep these professionals are to succeed, the government and society need a pro-immigrant narrative. Such narratives help the United States, Canada, New Zealand, and Australia to retain these immigrants.

It would be possible for the Netherlands to shift the national discourse and build a narrative of immigration as a strength rather than a social problem. As Maas points out, religious tolerance for Protestants and Jews fleeing their homelands helped spur the economic, scientific, and cultural prominence of the Dutch Republic in the Golden Age. It is striking that calls for greater tolerance today are largely directed at immigrants and Dutch Muslims, with the curious result that being a good Dutch citizen requires embracing what Duyvendak, Pels, and Rijkschroeff (2009) call monoculturalism. Compared to those in North America, Dutch debates also need more vocal civil society actors who can speak out against discrimination and in favor of diversity and multiculturalism. In the current climate, anti-immigrant politicians such as Geert Wilders appeal to freedom of speech in order to say things that others consider hate speech. Lacking a strong countervoice, this speech seems to dominate the Dutch public space at times, even though Wilders and his party attracted fewer voters in the 2012 national elections than in 2010.

It is possible, in generating this alternative discourse, that the other side of the migration equation, emigrants, might have an important role to play. When the governing Conservative Party proposed eliminating dual citizenship, Dutch expats around the world became mobilized, petitioning the political parties and even spurring a US-based Dutch citizen to run for office in defense of multiple citizenship. Their claims that migration is a net positive and that multiple membership is not a sign of disloyalty might help open up the political space for immigrants and their descendants in the Netherlands as well.

NOTES

1. He was appointed in October 2008 and assumed office as Rotterdam's mayor in January 2009. In the Netherlands, mayors are appointed by the national cabinet, not elected by local residents.

2. For data and the methodology behind the Migrant Integration Policy Index. http://www.mipex.eu/netherlands.

3. Income restrictions were at the heart of the Chakroun case, on which the European Court of Justice rendered judgment in March 2010.

4. The other countries were the United Kingdom, France, Germany, and Switzerland.

5. Data are from the Multicultural Policy Index for immigrant minorities put together by Keith Banting and Will Kymlicka. The data and methodology are available at http://www.queensu.ca/mcp/immigrant.html.

6. For example, asked about immigrants in their country, only 27 percent of Dutch respondents felt there were too many, compared to 59 percent in the United Kingdom and

33 percent in France. The Dutch response was also more muted than in the United States, where 37 percent of those polled felt there were too many immigrants. For data and methods, see German Marshall Fund of the United States (2011), *Transatlantic Trends: Immigration, Key Findings 2010*, http://trends.gmfus.org/files/archived/immigration/doc/TTI2010_English_Top.pdf.

7. Not all EU migrants are accorded a similar welcome. In February 2012, Geert Wilder's Freedom Party generated significant criticism for setting up a website to collect complaints about Central and Eastern Europeans as a "general nuisance," generating pollution and displacing native Dutch workers. The European Parliament condemned the website in early March; later in the month, a similar statement of condemnation was released by the Dutch Lower House.

REFERENCES

Duyvendak, Jan Willem, Trees Pels, and Rally Rijkschroeff. 2009. "A Multicultural Paradise? The Cultural Factor in Dutch Integration Policy." In *Bringing Outsiders In: Transatlantic Perspectives on Immigrant Political Incorporation*, edited by Jennifer L. Hochschild and John H. Mollenkopf, 129–39. Ithaca, NY: Cornell University Press.

Koopmans, Ruud, Paul Statham, Marco Guigni, and Florence Passey. 2005. *Contested Citizenship: Immigration and Cultural Diversity in Europe*. Minneapolis: University of Minnesota Press.

9

SCANDINAVIA

Governing Immigration in Advanced Welfare States

Grete Brochmann

"America protects its welfare system from immigrants, but leaves its labor market open, while the EU protects its labor markets and leaves its welfare system open."[1] This contrast between the American and the European approach to modern immigration may have once captured some of the different dynamics across the Atlantic, but is less accurate today. Welfare systems have never been as open as some outsiders imagine, and most European governments have made their labor markets much more flexible.

However, it is more accurate to compare the US and Nordic[2] approaches to immigrant integration. The three Scandinavian states have historically combined strict regulation of labor immigration with equal treatment in access to welfare for legal residents. This chapter reviews the origins of the Nordic approach; the economic, political, and ideological factors that sustain it; and the institutional path dependencies that serve as obstacles to change and possible remedies.

THE HISTORICAL ACCOUNT

The three Scandinavian countries—Denmark, Norway, and Sweden—have received immigrants for centuries, but the so-called new immigrants from outside the Organisation for Economic Co-operation and Development (OECD) are mainly a post-1960s phenomenon.[3] Before the Second World War, most immigrants were labor migrants from neighboring Scandinavian countries. The first "new immigrants," in the 1960s, were labor migrants from Turkey, Yugoslavia, Morocco, and Pakistan. This labor immigration lasted only until the early to mid-1970s, when a new, strict regulation was introduced—the "immigration stops."[4] Labor migration became an issue again in the 2000s, particularly after 2004 when the European Union (EU) enlarged to include Central European countries.

The recruitment stops of the 1970s were a milestone in immigration policy in Scandinavia, introducing policy mechanisms with wide-reaching consequences. Their goal was to curtail unwanted, unskilled immigration while allowing the admission of skilled workers in demand, especially in Norway, where there was an oil boom in the early 1970s.[5] One legacy of the recruitment stops is a series of unforeseen consequences.

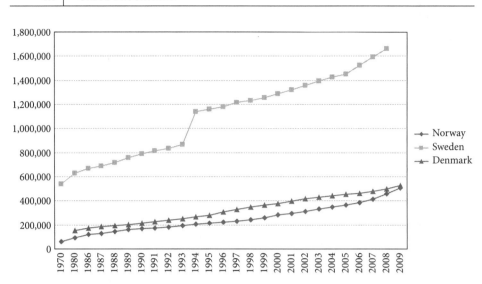

Figure 9.1 Number of immigrants and children of immigrants in Norway, Sweden, and Denmark, 1970–2009. *Source:* Based on Midtbøen (2008) (referred to in Brochmann and Hagelund 2012).

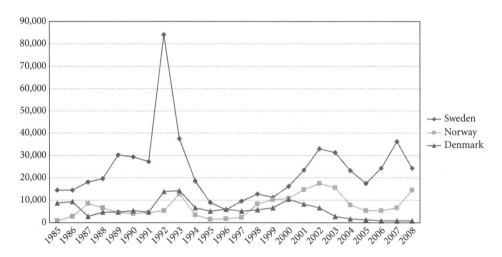

Figure 9.2 Asylum seekers in Norway, Sweden, and Denmark, 1985–2008. *Source:* Nordic Statistical Year Book (1995, 2005, 2007), Norwegian Directorate of Immigration (UDI), Statistics Denmark, and Statistics Sweden (referred to in Brochmann and Hagelund 2012).

As was the case in most receiving European countries, immigration changed character in the mid-1970s. When the legal channel was closed for low-skilled labor, foreigners arrived via other entry channels, as refugees/asylum seekers or as family members of already settled migrants.[6] The number of immigrants from non-OECD countries has increased because of international conventions and because of the general humanitarian platform of the Scandinavian social democracies.

The "Nordic welfare state," or the "Nordic model,"[7] is *comprehensive* regarding the kinds of social needs it tries to satisfy. It is *institutionalized* via social rights that give all citizens— in practice, all legal residents—a right to a decent standard of living. It is solidaristic and *universal* in the sense that welfare policy serves the entire population, not just particularly exposed groups.[8] The Nordic model turns many of life's risks over to the state, lightening the load of the family for care obligations.[9] It is service intensive, with local governments playing key roles in providing welfare services. Women's employment and social consumption are high, as is the level of taxation.

The Nordic welfare model is structurally linked to the highly centralized organization of working life. The regulation of the labor market via collective agreements, tripartite cooperation, an active labor market policy, and welfare security throughout life have contributed to productive economies with good flexibility and a high human capital. Working life and welfare represent mutual buffer functions, with a high rate of employment to finance welfare and reduce public spending.

Income security has been a fundamental pillar in this context, both in the form of social assistance and social insurance. The system, which was designed to constitute a basic safety net for all citizens from cradle to grave, has been remarkably generous and costly and has contributed to the three Scandinavian states having the world's most equal income distribution.[10] The state and the labor unions influence social change and development through an institutionalized system of industrial relations. State control and planning constitute major ingredients in the system, which is basically tax based.[11] Equal treatment is a key element, and the only criterion for accessing basic income security is legal residency.[12]

There are important structural, humanitarian, and ideological reasons for the setup of this model. The welfare state is basically an instrument to counteract socioeconomic marginalization. Humanitarian ideals, spelled out in terms of international solidarity in the wake of wartime devastation, and later on in the form of political radicalization in the 1960s and 1970s, also ideologically supported this policy. The Scandinavian approach has been labeled "something for nothing" as compared to the market logic "something for something,"[13] coupling benefits to contributions, as in other welfare state systems.[14]

In all three countries, the wide-ranging development of the welfare state was interconnected with nation building—the creation of nationhood and social cohesion based on historical myths and realities, facilitated by the oneness and homogeneity of the population. The welfare state project implied much more "than a mere upgrading of existing social policies,"[15] in the words of Gösta Esping-Andersen. Apart from economic redistribution, the welfare state was a moral construct, an entity for institutionalized solidarity and part of the nation building that took place after the Second World War. This essentially *political* project was necessary because a fully developed citizenship was seen as a precondition for stabilizing the vulnerable postwar democracy. The genesis of the Scandinavian welfare state has been described as a project of societal integration, with democracy, social citizenship, and modernization as its three basic ingredients.

A homogenization had taken place in the Scandinavian populations in the first half of the twentieth century, including a rather forceful streamlining of the few existing minorities in Sweden and Norway.[16] The new welfare state should be built by individuals liberated from old collectives and bonds and ready to accept a new and perhaps paradoxical fusion of modern individualism and a new sense of societal responsibility. This general homogenization— or assimilation—is usually seen as a precondition for the development of the specific Nordic brand of welfare state and for its continued support and legitimacy.[17] The fact that all three countries were *small* in terms of population most likely facilitated this process.

The "moral construct" of nation building relied on rights and duties[18] that forged a basic reciprocity between the individual and society through principles of solidarity. Historically, the two entities—*rights* and *duties*—have been closely intertwined, epitomized by the union slogan: "Do your duty, claim your rights!" (*gjør din plikt, krev din rett*). The collective imposes duties on the individual to strengthen the group, and the individual in turn is reaffirmed by the collective while strengthening his or her bonds to the group, with the possibility of acquiring goods—or rights—from it. This dynamic applies both to civil society and the state. In the Scandinavian context, the dialectic between rights and duties can be seen as the welfare state's core philosophy.

Folkhemmet—the People's Home—was a central concept of Swedish social democrats before the Second World War. It imagined a grand class alliance replacing the former class struggle that would steer society toward a socialist goal. "The integrative idea of the 'folkhemmet,' in which society was organized as a family, with the home as a metaphor, subordinated the class struggle to the national welfare."[19] This concept, appropriated from the conservatives, was used as an instrument for modernization after the war, with the solidaristic society as a building block.

In Denmark and Norway, similar tendencies were prevalent: The *folk* turned out to be a politically attractive concept in these countries as well: *Folkefællesskabet* (the people's community) in Denmark and *Hele folket i arbeid* (all the people to work) in Norway. Particularly in Norway and Sweden, the concept of *folk* was closely entwined with the concept of *nation*. Legitimacy for this broad plea for popular mobilization was, according to Bo Stråth, a combination of the national question and a specific protestant ethic prevailing among popular movements. This ethic was marked by pietistic value orientation, emphasizing individual freedom and radical claims of equality.[20] Pietism and duty often go hand in hand. Accordingly, the twin metaphors of home and people indicated, through their collective connotations, the sacrifices expected of the individual in return for social security.

Among these sacrifices, work holds a strategic position. Active labor market policies have been a basic characteristic of the Scandinavian welfare model from early on, bringing with them a duality. In Lundberg and Åmark's words: one side is "work for everyone; the other is that everyone has to work."[21] In other words, a high employment rate is a precondition for the necessary high taxation in the model. And, besides, having people work keeps them off the public budget: "In Scandinavia, according to Joakim Palme, labor market policy has been developed as a form of preventive social policy."[22]

All of these features—the (relative) homogeneity, the subtle balance between rights and duties, and the structure of the welfare model—potentially spell trouble when dealing with immigration.

INSTITUTIONAL PREREQUISITES FOR IMMIGRATION POLICY IN SCANDINAVIA

The Scandinavian welfare state has a tradition of regulation, large public sectors, economic transfers to weak groups, and equal treatment. This has two central implications for the "new immigration": control and integration.

First, controlling inflow has been seen as a prerequisite for maintaining the welfare system, which can be undermined by excessive burdens. This logic has been re-emphasized with the expansion of rights.[23] Social rights are a cornerstone of a modern welfare state, but the welfare state's need to control its geographical borders increases as new arrivals from the outside are awarded more rights, creating a fundamental tension between entry control and general living conditions for immigrants. The more rights, the more caution, as manifested in border control and categories of immigrants.[24] Different kinds of immigrants are given different residence statuses that activate different sets of rights and expenditures. The welfare state is to be universal—but only within its restrictively defined borders.

Second, the emphasis on equality and welfare rights has had a logical corollary in *integration* policy. If this policy framework is to be maintained, new, legally accepted inhabitants must be made a part of it. Good welfare states do not tolerate substantial numbers of persons or groups that live on the edge, disturb the regulated world of work, and burden social budgets—a Marshallian[25] recognition that a society cannot function smoothly if a large section of its population is marginalized and socially excluded. Organized labor plays a central part in politics and contributes to a regulated labor market, with specific consequences, because an orderly labor regime is one of the basic preconditions for the operation and maintenance of the system. Unions oppose a reserve army of cheap labor and favor the economic equality that is the basis for equal social citizenship as well as social cohesion and stability.

Integration and equality are closely intertwined, so that society starts with relatively small economic differences, achieved through economic redistribution, and social protection for all. This fully accomplished social citizenship is believed to engender freedom for the individual, freedom from dependence on kinfolk, freedom from anxiety over the provision of basic needs, and freedom to develop and prosper through education and good health. The grand task of the welfare state is to create the preconditions for this kind of citizenship.

Immigration and integration in this sense can contradict one another. At the outset, most immigrants are not desired, but if they nonetheless manage to enter, they have to be incorporated. The Good State must go further and lay the basis for successful integration, financed as it is through the income tax system, by instilling a positive attitude in the population toward immigrants. Consequently, there are important societal—or systemic—considerations behind Scandinavian integration policies in addition to liberal humanitarian principles.

The relation between immigration and the welfare state is thus tense and characterized by continuous two-way dynamics. The welfare state limits its immigration policies while it influences the behavior and actions of its immigrants, because they are both producers and consumers of welfare benefits. To the extent that immigrants represent cultural diversity or have special needs, they also challenge both the work forms of the welfare state and the legitimacy basis of the community. The Nordic countries—to differing degrees and partially in different ways—have had to face problems and dilemmas linked to increased immigration and the fact that they have become multicultural societies.

THEORETICAL APPROACHES TO THE WELFARE STATE—IMMIGRATION NEXUS

Is immigration a threat to welfare states? Gary Freeman presented the fundamental contradiction between inclusive welfare policies and comprehensive international migration, emphasizing that welfare states need to be closed to protect "the collective good component" from overexploitation from outsiders. He said that immigration has a tendency to erode the normative consensus on which generous welfare systems depend: "When the welfare state is seen as something for 'them' paid by 'us,' its days as a consensual solution to societal problems are numbered" (Freeman 1986: 62).

Today, there are four major arguments about immigration and welfare states. The first focuses on economic sustainability, in line with Freeman: generous welfare distribution depends on a restrictive selection of new members to avoid being overburdened. Michael Walzer, in *Spheres of Justice* (cited in Freeman's article), provided some basic philosophical premises for this position: "The idea of distributive justice presupposes a bounded world within which distributions take place: a group of people committed to dividing, exchanging and sharing social goods, first of all among themselves" (Walzer 1983: 31). Christian Joppke states this more bluntly: "Because rights are costly, they cannot be for everybody" (Joppke 1999: 6). Seyla Benhabib's (2002) concept, bounded universalism, pinpoints this logic, in which internal redistribution is combined with economically motivated access restrictions.

The second argument deals with the interconnection between boundaries and bonds—Freeman's "normative consensus": the popular support necessary to sustain the basic structure of a redistributive welfare state in democratic societies. This "social cohesion" asserts that increasing ethnic diversity weakens the normative consensus, gradually undermining the foundation of the welfare state (Alesina and Glaeser 2004; Goodhart 2004).

A third argument seeks to disprove the "social cohesion" argument. Banting and Kymlicka find no empirical proof for the cohesion hypothesis, and they argue that good welfare states can cushion the potential negative effects of immigration and diversity (Banting and Kymlicka 2006). Markus Crepaz (2008) takes this further, to argue that institutions shape the success of integration. In comparing the United States and Europe, he says that the United States was racially divided when it developed a welfare system, while in Europe institutionally strong welfare states were already in place when immigrants arrived. According to Crepaz, this fact has made the European welfare states more robust in withstanding pressure against generalized trust, as the ability to include newcomers as eligible for welfare and care was already established.

The fourth argument, stated by Ruud Koopmans (2010) holds that unfortunate combinations of welfare and multicultural policies are unsustainable. Where scholars such as Banting, Kymlicka, and Crepaz find evidence that generous and inclusive welfare states handle immigration better, Koopmans finds that immigrants fare worst in welfare states that combine generosity with multicultural policies "which do not provide strong incentives for host-country language acquisition and for interethnic contacts" (ibid.: 3). In this perspective, this type of welfare state is bad for the immigrants themselves as "it may lead to dependence on welfare-state arrangements and thereby to social and economic marginalization" (ibid.: 2). Koopmans claims that easy access to equal rights, when combined with a generous welfare state, leads to weak labor market participation and high levels of spatial segregation and overrepresentation in criminal statistics. Poor socioeconomic integration is thus blamed on the welfare state and multicultural policies. This argument makes welfare generosity toward newcomers not only bad for immigrants but also bad for society at large.

All four perspectives are present in current Scandinavian policymaking and public discourse on welfare and immigration. The Walzer-Joppke perspective is one of the constituting figures of the Scandinavian migration policy approach as such, and it premised the region's restrictive immigration regulations instituted in the early 1970s. Twisting Joppke's words: because rights are costly *but should be for all*, only a few select can be let in. Since the 1990s, both the authorities and the public have been increasingly concerned about the pressure of low-skilled immigration on welfare costs. A large proportion of these newcomers have proven difficult to integrate in the Scandinavian labor market, which is characterized by high demand for skills and a compressed wage structure that makes low-skilled labor comparatively expensive. The universalistic welfare approach—a generous inclusion of legal newcomers from day one in combination with a highly regulated and knowledge-intensive labor market—has made the three states particularly vulnerable to disincentive challenges concerning the absorption of immigrants in gainful work.

The Koopmans perspective has gained attention, particularly in Denmark. The OECD's annual report International Migration Outlook for 2007 (OECD 2007) reveals that the Scandinavian countries, along with the Netherlands, are at the very bottom of a scale that measures integration of immigrants in the labor market, with Sweden performing worst of all. Concurrently, the Migrant Integration Policy Index (British Council 2007) places Sweden at the very top among 28 European states in integration *policies*—due to the formal extension of rights to immigrants. Norway is eighth, and Denmark is at the bottom, joining the Eastern and Southern European states.[26] Seen together, these surveys leave the impression that the extension of rights to immigrants in the region has had a marginal impact on the ability of the states to include newcomers in productive work. There are definite weaknesses in both of these comparative exercises, yet the juxtaposition highlights the current political superstructure for retrenchment on rights—again, particularly in Denmark. The *causal link*—if it is the rights in question that serve to hinder immigrants to enter productive work—is not made clear by Koopmans or any others.

Social cohesion and its counterpart have become more important, particularly in Denmark but also in Norway, over the last decade. Cultural conflicts have been connected to welfare state sustainability and used as fuel for discussion of solidarity's limits. Public discourse has nonetheless been somewhat simplistic and polarized between the restrictionists, who want to keep immigrants out so as to sustain welfare and cohesion for the established citizens, and the admissionists, who want maximum inclusion and a generous access policy and disregard the cohesion problem as such. General support for the welfare state system is overwhelming in all three countries, yet policymaking on access and inclusion of immigrants increasingly differ among them. Broad political support of restrictions on family reunification and citizenship, as well as on welfare support for newcomers in Denmark are an example of Freeman's theorem: a majority not wanting a welfare system as something for "them" paid by "us." Sweden, on the other hand, exemplifies a Crepazian system, trying to use its institutional basis to withstand erosion of welfare state legitimacy for all it is worth.

THE "WELFARE CONTRACT" UNDER CHALLENGE

An awareness of the failure of immigrant inclusion, both in the labor market and more generally, has developed in Scandinavia since the 1990s. Multicultural immigration has "matured" as a policy field, with ever more conflicts and contradictions amid general structural and economic problems.

Economic crises hit all three countries in the 1980s and early 1990s (with different momentum and slightly different timing), making the Nordic model "sclerotic," with rigid obstacles to economic change and competitiveness. Generous income security was believed to create perverse incentives and cause a lack of response to new needs, thereby adding to inactivity. Sweden, Norway, and Denmark embarked on significant reforms, succeeding economically to the extent that, before the financial crisis hit in 2008, all three were rated as leading the world in terms of growth rates, economic efficiency—and equality (Dølvik 2008).

Despite the soundness of its economies, a relatively large share of the Scandinavian labor force has been out of work over the past several decades because of sick leave or rehabilitation and disability pensions. The immigrant population has been overrepresented in some of these welfare arrangements, and its unemployment rate has been roughly three times that of the native population, while the employment rate has been significantly lower (see Figure 9.3).[27] Correspondingly, consumption of welfare at this point is notably higher among the

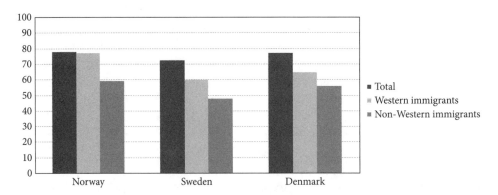

Figure 9.3   Percentage employment in Norway, Sweden, and Denmark, 2008. For the whole population and for Western and non-Western immigrants ages 16 to 64, 2000–2010. *Source:* Statistics Norway, Statistics Denmark, and Statistical Yearbook (SCB 2010) (referred to in Brochmann and Hagelund 2012).

immigrant population than among the population as a whole. In Norway, the likelihood of a non-Western immigrant receiving social assistance in 2003 was five times higher than that of the population at large. Adding housing support, the difference becomes eight times as high.[28]

Some argue that newcomers have been given residency on legitimate grounds and should be eligible for the support that the system offers. The moral touch of the resurrected ethics of duty nevertheless have affected immigrants more than others—at least in Denmark and Norway. The *duty* side in terms of labor and care feeds into an intentional double-talk that is inherent to the entire welfare system. Even though universality and solidarity have been pillars of the Scandinavian welfare state, legitimacy is a subtle underlying dimension in all welfare policy: Who deserves support and who should be able to care for themselves?

Welfare benefits to newcomers who have not contributed through work and taxes highlight the inherent tensions in the Scandinavian welfare system. Traditionally, there is considerable *shame* attached to receiving welfare benefits in Scandinavia, and one of the merits of the welfare state is that it diminishes this inferiority status among recipients. At the same time, the system has depended on a certain feeling of unease among potential beneficiaries over avoiding overtaxing or direct abuse of the system. There have been worries that immigrants not socialized into the subtleties of the welfare contract can more readily depend on transfers over time. Labor market participation and welfare dependency among immigrants is of course a complex issue, with elements of structural and discriminatory constraints, but the public's focus has been increasingly on the implicit constituents of *duty* attached to the principal of a generous welfare system. The most basic duty is obligatory solidarity—that is, the duty to support the institutionalized redistributive system. This is done in practical terms through work according to capacity and through paying taxes.

All three countries have realized the very basic challenge posed by the influx of low-qualified immigrants in a demanding labor market in terms of education and productivity. Like any other state, the Nordics want newcomers who can support themselves and contribute to diversity and innovation. Generous welfare rights and a compressed wage structure may defy this objective.

THREE APPROACHES TO THE IMMIGRATION CHALLENGE

The types of immigrants that have entered the Scandinavian countries since the 1970s are similar: labor migrants followed by relatively high proportions of humanitarian migrants after the introduction of "immigration stops" in the mid-1970s, followed by a new surge of labor migrants after the EU enlargement of 2004. The political mechanisms and measures implemented in the 1970s were similar but since 2000, there has been significant variation in immigration policies. Multiculturalism has been under attack, particularly in Denmark, and all three countries have lately embarked on different policies in relation to both immigration and integration. Sweden is referred to as the most multicultural country of the three,[29] whereas Denmark is moving in the opposite direction with its more majority-dominated policy, called assimilationist by many. Norway is somewhat in the middle, trying to muddle through by recognizing diversity and cultural traditions and emphasizing the need for "common values in society" as well as for the majority's value heritage.[30]

On the access side, all three states have wanted to restrain immigration considered a burden on welfare budgets and at the same time uphold their humanitarian responsibilities—that is, following the UN Refugee Convention and more generally international human rights. It is thus interesting that three basically very similar states, in terms of economic governance, welfare systems, and political traditions, in practice interpret the limits of these responsibilities differently.

In the following, the approaches to immigration taken by each country are delineated in relation to three policy fields: access (or immigration), integration, and naturalization.

Scandinavia—Similarities and Differences

Postwar immigration to Sweden started earlier than in neighboring countries and was far greater in scope: about twice what Denmark and Norway separately experienced. This explains Sweden's position as a pioneer in integration and its strong influence on the other two countries. Since 1980, this pattern has been much less clear because Denmark and Norway have gone their separate ways in a number of areas connected to immigration and integration.

When it comes to public debate, there have been large differences in Scandinavia. The focus on welfare state issues has been increasing when immigration is publicly discussed, notably in Denmark and Norway. In the early 1990s, a new concept was coined in Norway to this effect: *kindism*, or being kind to a fault.[31] A growing number of people used kindism to criticize the welfare-state rights policy for going too far; the wish to help weak groups in society was suppressing the necessity to make demands on newcomers. It took more or less another decade until this rhetoric had a serious impact on policymaking, although the 1990s can be characterized as a period of "preparation for change," when general retrenchments occurred in all three countries. The so-called Work-Line approach was reinvigorated despite political opposition.

In fact, the split question: "Is the welfare state too kind to immigrants, or is it not kind enough?" sums up the basic structure of the Nordic immigration debate and its policymaking since the 1990s, and it is a reminder of the key position held by welfare policy among the Nordics. Over the past years, the tone of Danish debate has hardened, with more immigration-critical voices making themselves heard. Danish policy has also become more restrictive when it comes to both immigration control and social policies. Something of the same development has been seen in Norway, although not to the same extent. As in Denmark, a critical searchlight has been focused on family immigration policy in the wake of debates about forced marriages and suppression of women. In addition, the authorities have signaled a tightening of the requirements for granting asylum, including possible cuts in support for asylum seekers. Norwegian changes to immigration legislation and the social rights of new arrivals have not, however, been as marked as in Denmark. Sweden has been the exception among the Nordic countries, more cautious about a comprehensive tightening of immigration policy, and more subdued in public debate, despite the fact that the country underwent considerable general welfare retrenchment in the early 1990s because of a serious economic crisis. So, on a "kindness" continuum, Sweden has often been at one extreme and Denmark at the other, with Norway in the middle.

The EU has a significant, and increasingly important position with regard to control policy in Scandinavia. Since the 1990s, internationalization in general and EU politics more specifically have contributed to reducing the elbow room for control by member countries. All EU countries have come to depend on each other in terms of external control of migration as a result of the gradual establishment of institutions and harmonization among member states. For the time being, the welfare state is the domain of each member state, but coordination of social security rights and harmonization in other areas (e.g., control policy) provide an important premise for national freedom of action in social policy.[32] Especially after EU expansion eastward in 2004, EU/EEA[33] membership has implied considerable labor immigration.

The Scandinavian states have chosen different forms of affiliation to the European Union. Sweden has full EU membership (with the exception of the currency union); Denmark has the longest membership, but negotiated an opt-out position for itself regarding common immigration policy (justice, freedom, and security), and it too remains outside the currency union. Norway has decided to stay outside the union, but it is fully incorporated into the Single Market regime through its EEA membership and is part of the Schengen area.[34] Ironically, Norway—the only nonmember of the EU proper—is the most strongly affected by labor immigration from the EU member countries that joined in 2004.

Access Policy

All three states have, as we have seen, the same basic structure in their interconnections between external control and welfare-state integration policy: A restrictive front and an inclusive inside in order to protect the welfare/labor market model. Until the early 2000s, their concrete policies were also by and large similar although with some detailed differences.

The legacy of the stop policy of the 1970s was the entire control/integration nexus in the decades that followed. Ideally, very few people should have access because of costly welfare and challenging labor conditions. Nevertheless, the humanitarian principles have tied access policies in all three states to a fairly liberal approach to refugees/asylum seekers and family migrants, thus creating self-reinforcing mechanisms that have spurred further humanitarian immigration. However, it was not until the late 1980s that the governments in the region started discussing (to different degrees) how to restrict these channels of access. The legitimacy discourse on asylum seekers in this respect became a tool. Since not all immigrants could claim a need for protection according to the UN Refugee Convention, restrictions were legitimized. The impact of the more meticulous examinations is hard to estimate; regardless, the number of asylum seekers was still rising, although with some fluctuations during the 1990s. Sweden continued to be the grand magnet in Scandinavia.

As the problems attached to productive incorporation of newcomers in the labor market (and the concomitantly growing burdens on welfare) gradually developed into a great worry during the same decade, and there was a push for better control. The nature of refugee immigration, however, made it difficult to impose restrictions. *Family* immigration thus materialized as a better target for retrenchment. This kind of immigration had not been a topic of public discourse nearly to the same extent as asylum seekers, and the incorporation of families into work and civil society was not widely investigated despite the magnitude of the inflow. During the 1990s, this category of immigrants came to the fore, through a focus on *transnational marriages*, much more than did family reunification proper. Issues such as forced and arranged marriages, as well as honor-based family violence, became targets for heated discussions in the public and revealed a complicated interplay between immigration control, integration endeavors, human rights, and family relations.

Denmark reformed large parts of its immigration policy as a result of the change in government in 2001. The new Center-Right coalition modified control and access policies, including the elimination of the *de facto refugee* category so that protection would be granted only to refugees under the 1951 Geneva Convention. In addition, to be able to marry a foreigner, both partners had to be 24 years of age and their combined attachment to Denmark had to be stronger than to the country of origin. The reforms also added requirements for applicants' economic capacity to support themselves with a decent standard of housing, as well as a bank guarantee of 50,000 kr. to cover any public assistance needed for the foreign spouse. Sweden and Norway have so far not followed Denmark in these specific reforms, although the general tendency has been more restrictive. In the last few years both Sweden and Norway introduced requirements for documented economic support capacity in applications for family immigration. All three countries have stepped up their policy for return of asylum seekers whose cases have been declined.

These major retrenchments concerning "unwanted" immigrants came around the turn of the century—at the same time that a shift in paradigm related to "wanted" immigration took place. As for several other European states, shortages of skilled labor prompted a more liberal approach to high-skilled immigration. During a short period of time, the focus on immigrants as *consumers* of welfare changed into an emphasis on the need for more *producers* from the outside, to stem the demographic tide and maintain economic growth and the level of welfare. The result was a dual policy approach in which further restrictions were initiated for the humanitarian categories, joined by stimulating regulations for attractive immigrants. Sweden walked alone on one important point: in 2008, it introduced a liberalized labor immigration policy for the entire world. It is demand-side driven, and employers are the ones to decide the need. Denmark and Norway have judged the EU extension eastward as a sufficient supply base for the years to come.

Integration Policy

Sweden was the pioneer in the region (and in Europe as a whole) in formulating an *integration* approach: people should have access to equal rights, at the same time retaining freedom of choice as to cultural adjustment. In other words, social citizenship should be possible without identification with the majority nation. Sweden went even further, committing itself to protect minority cultures from being eroded.[35] Freedom of choice was not a prominent characteristic of the social-democratic welfare state in Scandinavia during its "Golden Age" (1945–1970),[36] and Sweden probably occupied the extreme end of the scale with regard to central planning and governing zeal. Given a choice between freedom and equality, equality was unerringly chosen. Standard solutions of high quality had become a distinguishing characteristic of the Swedish welfare state, made possible in a country whose citizens gave massive support to centrally prescribed models based on the belief that only a strong and centralized state could provide guarantees for the equality and fairness desired, through universal solutions financed by taxation. This project to establish equality concerned not only rights and economic redistribution; the governing ardor of the Swedish state touched even the private sphere—far beyond what was perceived as legitimate or desirable in other Western European countries.

Sweden became world famous for its social engineering. Norway and Denmark have been somewhat less zealous than Sweden in this respect, although control through social policies is also a prominent feature in these countries. What is notable is that Sweden, where social engineering had proceeded the farthest, also became a pioneer country with regard to multicultural liberalism—in that immigrants could choose, so to speak, to retain their culture and their private sphere undisturbed.

How this has turned out in practice is a recurring topic of debate in all three countries, but early on Sweden was definitely the ideological trendsetter during Nordic integration policymaking. In the early 1970s, when the new immigration was starting to make itself felt in Denmark and Norway, Sweden had already had multicultural immigration for several years.

Considering the historical context, integration policy, through its concept of freedom of choice, inevitably achieved the character of *exception* for a distinctive group—the immigrants. Thus, even if it was argued along equality lines—that newcomers should be provided with real opportunities to preserve their language and culture in the same manner as the majority population—it was hard to escape deviance. Freedom of choice was a concession to people who were so different that they could not be expected to adapt to the universal solutions; this in turn emphasized their position as outsiders.[37]

This apparent oxymoron was accepted as a formative premise by the other states, and it still (although less dogmatically) constitutes the nerve center of Scandinavian integration policy: How should the welfare state's requirement for universal solutions and equal treatment be reconciled with minority rights and cultural diversity?

Since the initial phase of the integration approach (in the 1970s and early 1980s), all three states have adjusted their inclusion policies, and, since the late 1980s, the differences between the countries have been more marked. For a long time, internal variation in Scandinavia appeared as a "difference in degree" in the same basic concepts. Looking back in 2011, it is nevertheless possible to trace early signs of today's distinctions. Even though Sweden, Denmark, and Norway have been influenced by multicultural thinking, the Danish *national* approach was already significantly present in the 1970s (Jønsson and Petersen 2010). Partly following from this, Denmark has emphasized the *duties* of newcomers more clearly from an early stage, whereas both Sweden and Norway were for long time more inclined to let rights suffice. Even so, the duty side, in terms of work-line policies, has been accentuated more energetically in all three states in the last decade or so. Denmark has again been at the forefront in reforming important parts of its labor activation policies, and—more strikingly—introduced a two-tier policy for social security as a way to spur employment among immigrants. Permanent residency was only given after seven years (a change from the previous three-year requirement), conditioned on knowledge of Danish and a clean police record. Social assistance was differently distributed, and full rights were not given before seven years of residency. This striking breach of the universalistic Nordic welfare approach was nevertheless rolled back when the Social Democratic Thorning-Schmidt government took over in 2011. Sweden and Norway have so far refrained from similar adjustments, and, in particular, Swedish authorities have vigorously criticized the Danish path. Among the three states, Sweden has most strongly retained freedom of choice in its integration policy, whereas Denmark has taken the lead when it comes to social engineering. Consequently, the two states have, historically speaking, exchanged roles.

NATURALIZATION

The welfare state has, as we have seen, been the prime motor of integration among the Nordics, through social engineering and the extension of rights. As concerns social cohesion, however—the "normative consensus" for shared values as a way to sustain the welfare model—the instruments have been less clear cut. How are Sweden, Denmark, and Norway to forge a new or renewed societal foundation for upholding treasured liberal democratic values, universal welfare, and possibly a sense of bounded belonging in a context increasingly characterized by diverse loyalties and lifestyle preferences?

States have a limited number of options to deal with this complicated and nebulous challenge. Naturalization policies have since the 1990s been revitalized as one tool for integration, being located at the intersection between the cultural (nationhood) and sociopolitical field (the right to vote and the full range of citizenship rights). Although the connection between citizenship legislation and questions of cohesion, identity, and belonging is indistinct and controversial—"identity cannot be legislated" (Joppke 2008: 536)—a number of states in practice act as if it is worthwhile to give it a try. A perceptible dividing line between policy approaches to this legislation is its relationship to integration: whether citizenship for newcomers should serve as a tool in the inclusion process or, the opposite, as a reward for the effort. The three Scandinavian states lie along a scale signified by the traditional *ethnos/demos* division, in terms of what it takes to become a national and conceptions of national identity. Of all immigration-related policy areas in today's Scandinavia, naturalization stands out as the one with the most internal disparity. Similar problem definitions have generated different conclusions. This is even more interesting considering the very close cooperation that existed among the three countries in forging national citizenship legislation from 1880 until 1979.[38]

Swedish authorities explicitly use access to citizenship as a means of integration. The dual citizenship policy—five years of legal residence and no language or skills requirement—is seen as a part of this thinking. Yet Denmark, too, with its much more demanding naturalization requirements, sees its policy as part of integration. In 2002, a nine-year residency requirement replaced the seven-year one. Also, Denmark refuses dual citizenship and has introduced a fairly demanding language/skills test to qualify. This legislation should contribute to a situation in which it becomes more attractive (or absolutely necessary) to attain the needed qualifications to become a citizen. Norway has again placed itself somewhere in the middle, retaining a single-citizenship policy that requires seven years of residence. It has also introduced a very mild language rule. On the other hand, this policy has served to liberalize naturalization to a certain extent: citizenship is now obtained solely by law, which means that an applicant fulfilling certain criteria has a *right* to citizenship—no additional juridical assessments of the application are made.

It seems right to interpret the move away from coordinated policymaking in the Nordic countries as an upgrade of their citizenship laws. National interests are apparently conceived as so important in this area that no one wants any longer to be subordinated to a possible Nordic norm. In other words, the weight of national sovereignty has been reinforced; that is, national vested interests have increased in line with more differentiated Scandinavian immigration policymaking over the last decades. Thus, in this apparently homogeneous region, in terms of both culture and polity, differences in recent citizenship laws most likely reflect a divergence in national approaches to immigration. And this divergence most likely reflects basically different viewpoints when it comes to conceptions of the nation, which for a while was subdued in the spirit of postwar cooperation, as well as in response to economic interests in stimulating intra-Nordic migration.

Denmark has, as we have seen, parted from the neighboring countries in formulating a more restrictive immigration policy—in terms of both access control and welfare policy. The adoption of a liberal Swedish citizenship model would not match their overall response to the immigration challenge. Sweden, on the other hand, having pushed its humanitarian ideology somewhat further than most other nations, would have problems harmonizing its citizenship law with Denmark's. Instead, Denmark has served as a negative sounding board in public discourse on immigration and plural society. Norway, in the middle, wants to reinforce nationhood as well as retain a humanitarian image. Politically, the government is strongly pressured from both sides on immigration matters and tends to go for compromises whenever possible.

Overall, Sweden, Denmark, and Norway want to *integrate* their immigrant population in functional terms: They want their immigrants to be working, to be good parents, and to be participating members of society. It seems that eventually they also want them to be *citizens*, although what that takes differs significantly. The rationale of the instruments varies as well. Social cohesion is necessarily a concern in all three countries, but it is spelled out differently.

Which tools related to citizenship are needed to forge "societal glue" and "generalized trust"? Most important, as long as the denizenship concept takes care of most substantial social rights for legal newcomers, legal citizenship will be of political and symbolic significance. Naturalization as a means to build trust—in the Swedish case as a stimulus for immigrants in the process of integration while in the Danish and Norwegian cases naturalization reinforces a national "we feeling." Trust is built through slow and complex processes. Naturalization policy may play a part in trust building under specific political circumstances, and the respective Scandinavian governments have achieved their individual understanding of this connection under current conditions. The more material aspects of citizenship have not been decided once and for all. The relative importance of legal citizenship may increase in the years to come if rights attached to denizenship are rolled back.

There is no doubt, however, that Danish public discourse has been quite rough during the last decade, bringing with it negative *culturalizing*, particularly in relation to Muslims. The idea of the "Danish nation" has held a much more central position in both discourse

TABLE 9.1

Citizenship and residence requirements for permanent residence in Sweden, Norway, and Denmark

Requirements	Sweden	Norway	Denmark
Acceptance of double citizenship	Yes	No	No
Language acquisition	No	Indirectly	Yes
Knowledge of society	No	Indirectly	Yes
Economic self-sufficiency	No	No	Yes
Citizenship ceremony	Voluntary	Voluntary	Voluntary
Oath of allegiance	No	Compulsory if there is an official ceremony	Compulsory
Right to citizenship when conditions are fulfilled	Several groups but not all	Yes	Only second-generation Nordic citizens

SOURCE: Based on Midtbøen (2008), referred to in Brochmann and Hagelund (2012).

and policymaking in Denmark than equivalent concepts have held in Sweden and in Norway. Whereas introductory programs for newcomers in Denmark aim to give immigrants an understanding of "Danish values and norms," Swedish equivalents underline respect for democratic, not Swedish, values. And whereas Swedish and Norwegian public documents communicate a positive attitude toward cultural, religious, and value diversity, such signals have disappeared from Danish documents. On the other hand, Danish policymakers have a tendency to consider *demos* values as part of the Danish *ethnos*; these are values that are held by the Danish majority in contrast to minority groups—first and foremost Muslims (Mouritsen 2006). Consequently, pressuring newcomers to acquire "Danish" liberal, democratic values is necessary to protect the polity for future generations.

Regardless of possible dialectical twists in the *ethnos-demos* landscape, substantial differences remain in all three policy areas (see Table 9.1). By way of conclusion, then, what can possibly explain the current distinctions among Scandinavian immigration policies? And how equipped are Sweden, Denmark, and Norway to handle the challenges imposed by multicultural immigration?

CONCLUDING REMARKS

Roughly 40 years have passed since the initiation of multicultural immigration in Scandinavia. Sweden was the pioneer with its multicultural integration policy in the early 1970s, and it has stayed with this basic approach ever since. Swedish ideology and policymaking served as beacons for Denmark and, particularly, Norway. The Danish state nevertheless took a stronger stand on nationhood from early on and was more hesitant to adopt multiculturalism. The initial Swedish position needs closer study, yet there are suggestions that point in the direction of ideology and politics.[39] The international role that Sweden energetically established for itself after the Second World War as a "humanitarian superpower" (Borevi 2010) provided a foundation for the handling of immigrants at home. Finnish immigration actually dominated the inflow to Sweden prior to the 1970s, and this group of "equals" had a strong impact on the way other immigrants could be handled later.

Much of the difference in policy in Scandinavia after the initial phase is most likely explained by constellations in party politics. The parties on the Right have been differently composed and have had diverse positions on immigration. The Danish Progress Party (Fremskridspartiet), which is to the right of the Conservatives, as early as the 1970s criticized immigration. Their successor—the Danish Peoples Party—was very important, particularly after the 2001 election, as a supporter of the Center-Right coalition government. It has strongly influenced the reform policy that the coalition government introduced. Moreover, the Social Democrats have been split on the issue, contributing to a stronger politicization of immigration policy at an earlier stage than occurred in Sweden and Norway. In Norway, the Progress Party (Frp) (inspired by the Danish equivalent) was established in the 1970s, yet it did not become a recognized anti-immigration party until the late 1980s. The Frp has been extremely influential in public discourse since the 1980s, as none of the other parties have considered immigration a winning theme. Because of increasing support by the Frp (since 2000 it has occasionally been the country's biggest party), other parties have been pressured toward a more restrictive line. Sweden has also faced notable opposition to immigration in parts of its population; however, there was never a significant party that capitalized on immigration in parliament. This changed in the 2010 election, when the Sweden Democrats gained 5.7 percent of the votes and 20 seats.

As this analysis has revealed, the baseline of the political approach—a dual policy of external restrictions and internal welfare inclusion—was initially shared by Sweden, Denmark, and Norway, and is in fact still the overarching approach in the region. However, the tightness of access control and the generosity of welfare inclusion have become more diverse.

All three states, despite their political distinctions, are today faced with an immigration policy squeeze: The Nordic model depends on a high employment rate and high standards of working life to sustain generous and universal welfare. On the other hand, universal welfare, generous social security, and a compressed wage structure (high salaries for low-qualified labor) have a tendency to attract—and hold—immigrants who have problems satisfying these very preconditions.

Given the welfare state's structure and international humanitarian responsibilities, its policy options are not plentiful. All three states have increasingly tried to constrict the access channel. Moreover, in practice they have—to different degrees and in varied combinations—opted for a Crepazian approach. The solution is refinement of welfare state instruments through long-term investment in human resources as well as enhanced emphasis on individual duties—participation through work. The welfare state is both the problem and the solution.

NOTES

I am particularly indebted to Anniken Hagelund, coauthor of *The Boundaries of Welfare: Immigration Policy and the Welfare State in Scandinavia 1945–2010*. London: Palgrave.

  1. Migration Policy Institute, Washington, DC.

2. In this context "Nordic" and "Scandinavian" are used synonymously, even though the Nordics formally include Finland and Iceland.

3. There is internal variation in Scandinavia. Sweden was the first to recruit foreign labor. It was not occupied by the German Nazi regime, as Denmark and Norway were, and its economy expanded more quickly.

4. The immigration stops were introduced in Denmark in 1973 and Norway in 1975. In Sweden, a stricter regulation was gradually developed starting in the late 1960s.

5. Norway in fact had an opposite business cycle compared to the rest of Western Europe at the time. The main reason for curtailing the immigration of low-skilled labor in the early 1970s elsewhere was the so-called oil crisis with its substantial increase in oil prices.

6. Sweden has all along received more immigrants than the other two countries have. In 2008, the percentage of foreign-born persons in Denmark was 7.3; in Norway, 10.3; and in Sweden, 13.9. In Norway, the immigrant population has increased seven times since 1970 (see www.ssb.no).

7. See, for example, Kauto et al. (1999) and Kildal and Kuhnle (2005).

8. Esping-Andersen and Korpi (1987).

9. Sejersted (2005).

10. Barth, Moene, and Wallerstein (2003).

11. See Esping-Andersen (1990), Kauto et al. (1999), and Kangas and Palme (2005).

12. Qualification periods are, however, necessary for some of the other benefits.

13. Petersen (2007).

14. Korpi and Palme (1998), quoted in Hansen (2001: 101).

15. Esping-Andersen (1996: 2)

16. The politics of "Norwegianization," as it was actually called in Norway, included cultural, linguistic, educational, and religious "normalization," particularly of the Sami minority.

17. Löfgren (1999: 54).

18. This theme is further developed in Hagelund and Brochmann (2009).

19. Stråth (2005: 35).

20. Ibid.

21. Lundberg and Åmark (2001: 176).

22. Palme (1999: 41).

23. Again, there has been internal variation over the years in the three countries as to the strictness of access control. Sweden is generally the most liberal.

24. See Brochmann and Kjeldstadli (2008) for the historical account and Brochmann and Hagelund (2012) for more details.

25. Marshall (1965).

26. http://www.integrationindex.eu/.

27. In 2009, 23 percentage points lower in Sweden; 22 and 20 percentage points, respectively, in Denmark and Norway (NOU 2011).

28. St. meld. nr 9 (2006–2007). It should be added that there is significant variation among different immigrant groups and that their situation improves over time.

29. Langvasbråten (2008).

30. See Brochmann (2007) for a more elaborate discussion of the Norwegian approach.

31. Gerhardsen (1991).

32. Regulation 1408/71.

33. The European Economic Area (EEA) covers all EU countries as well as Norway, Iceland, and Lichtenstein, and grants access to the Internal Market; however, it has as yet no position in the EU political structure.

34. The only areas of exemption are agriculture and fisheries.

35. There are in fact several examples, particularly in Swedish and Norwegian public documents, of concern that encounters with majority institutions will threaten minority cultures. See Björkman et al. (2005).

36. Esping-Andersen (1990).

37. Gür (1996) and Borevi (2002).

38. See Brochmann and Seland (2010) for closer scrutiny of citizenship policies in Scandinavia.

39. See Borevi (2010) and Björkman et al. (2005).

REFERENCES

Alesina, Alberto, and Edward L. Glaeser. 2004. *Fighting Poverty in the US and Europe: A World of Difference.* Oxford: Oxford University Press.

Banting, Keith, and Will Kymlicka, eds. 2006. *Multiculturalism and the Welfare State: Recognition and Redistribution in Contemporary Democracies.* Oxford: Oxford University Press.

Barth, Erling, Kalle Moene, and Michael Wallerstein. 2003. *Likhet under press: Utfordringer for den skandinaviske fordelingsmodellen.* Oslo: Gyldendal Norsk Forlag.

Benhabib, Seyla. 2002. "Transformations of Citizenship: The Case of Contemporary Europe." *Government and Opposition* 37 (4): 439–65.

Björkman, Ingrid, Jan Elfverson, Åke Wedin, and Jonathan Friedman. 2005. *Exit Folkhemssverige: En samhällsmodells sönderfall.* Torsby: Förlag Cruz del Sur.

Borevi, Karin. 2002. *Välfärdsstaten i det mångkulturella samhället.* Skrifter utgivna av Statsvetenskapliga föreningen i Uppsala 151. Uppsala: Acta Universitatis Upsaliensis.

———. 2010. "Sverige: Mångkulturalismens flaggskepp i Norden." In *Velferdens grenser,* edited by Grete Brochmann and Anniken Hagelund, 41–131. Oslo: Universitetsforlaget.

British Council. 2007. http://www.integrationindex.eu/.

Brochmann, Grete. 2007. "Til Dovre faller: A bli norsk—å være norsk—troskapsløfte og statsborgerskap i den foranderlige nasjonen." In *Migration och tillhörighet: Inklusions- och exklusionsprocesser i Skandinavien,* edited by Gunnar Alsmark, Tina Kallehave, and Bolette Moldenhawer. Göteborg: Makadam Förlag.

Brochmann, Grete, and Anniken Hagelund. 2005. *Innvandringens velferdspolitiske konsekvenser—Nordisk kunnskapsstatus.* Copenhagen: Nordisk Ministerråd.

———. 2012. *The Boundaries of Welfare: Immigration Policy and the Welfare State in Scandinavia 1945–2010.* London: Palgrave.

Brochmann, Grete, and Knut Kjeldstadli. 2008. *A History of Immigration: The Case of Norway 900–2000*. Oslo: Universitetsforlaget.

Brochmann, Grete, and Idunn Seland. 2010. "Citizenship Policies and Ideas of Nationhood in Scandinavia." *Citizenship Studies* 14 (4): 429–45.

Crepaz, Markus M. 2008. *Trust beyond Borders: Immigration, the Welfare State, and Identity in Modern Societies*. Ann Arbor: University of Michigan Press.

Dølvik, Jon Erik. 2008. "The Negotiated Nordic Labour Markets: From Bust to Boom." Paper presented at the Conference on Nordic Models: Solutions to Continental Europe's Problems? Center for European Studies, Harvard University, May 9–10.

Esping-Andersen, Gösta. 1990. *The Three Worlds of Welfare Capitalism*. Cambridge: Polity Press.

———. 1996. "After the Golden Age? Welfare State Dilemmas in a Global Economy." In *Welfare States in Transition: National Adaptations in Global Economies*, edited by Gösta Esping-Andersen, 37–53. London: Sage.

Esping-Andersen, Gösta, and Walter Korpi. 1987. "From Poor Relief to Institutional Welfare States: The Development of Scandinavian Social Policy." In *The Scandinavian Model: Welfare States and Welfare Research*, edited by Robert Erikson, Erik Jørgen Hanson, Stein Ringe, and Hannu Uusitalo, 112–45. New York: M. E. Sharpe.

Freeman, Gary. 1986. "Migration and the Political Economy of the Welfare State." *Annals of the American Academy of Political and Social Science* 485 (May): 51–63.

Gerhardsen, Rune. 1991. *Snillisme på norsk*. Oslo: Schibsted.

Goodhart, David. 2004. "Too Diverse? Is Britain Becoming Too Diverse to Sustain the Mutual Obligations behind Good Society and the Welfare State?" *Prospect* 95 (February).

Gür, Thomas. 1996. *Staten och nykomlingarna: En studie av den svenska invandrarpolitikens ideer*. Stockholm: City University Press.

Hagelund, Anniken, and Grete Brochmann. 2009. "From Rights to Duties? Welfare and Citizenship for Immigrants and Refugees in Scandinavia." In *Conflict, Citizenship and Civil Society*, edited by Patrick Baert, Sokratis M. Koniordos, Giovanna Procacci, and Carlo Ruzza, 141–61. London: Routledge.

Hansen, Lars-Erik. 2001. *Jämlikhet och valfrihet: En studie av den svenska invandrarpolitikens framväxt*. Acta Universitatis Stockholmensis. Stockholm: Almqvist & Wiksell International.

Jönsson, Heidi Vad, and Klaus Petersen. 2010. "Danmark: Den nationale velfærdsstat møder verden." In *Velferdens grenser*, edited by Grete Brochmann and Anniken Hagelund, 131–211. Oslo: Universitetsforlaget.

Joppke, Christian. 1999. *Immigration and the Nation-State*. Oxford: Oxford University Press.

———. 2004. "The Retreat of Multiculturalism in the Liberal State: Theory and Policy." *British Journal of Sociology* 55 (2): 237–57.

———. 2008. "Immigration and the Identity of Citizenship: The Paradox of Universalism." *Citizenship Studies* 12 (6): 533–46.

Kangas, Olli, and Joakim Palme, eds. 2005. *Social Policy and Economic Development in the Nordic Countries*. New York: Palgrave Macmillan.

Kauto, Mikko, Matti Heikkilä, Bjørn Hvinden, Staffan Marklund, and Niels Ploug. 1999. "Introduction: The Nordic Welfare States in the 1990s." In *Nordic Social Policy: Chang-*

ing Welfare States, edited by Mikko Kauto, Matti Heikkilä, Bjørn Hvinden, Staffan Marklund, and Niels Ploug, 67–84. London: Routledge.

Kildal, Nanna, and Stein Kuhnle, eds. 2005. *Normative Foundations of the Welfare State: The Nordic Perspective*. London: Routledge.

Koopmans, Ruud. 2010. "Trade-Offs between Equality and Difference: Immigrant Integration, Multiculturalism and the Welfare State in Cross-National Perspective." *Journal of Ethnic and Migration Studies* 36 (1): 1–26.

Korpi, Walter, and Joakim Palme. 1998. "The Paradox of Redistribution and Strategies of Equality: Welfare State Institutions, Inequality and Poverty in the Western Countries." *American Sociological Review* 63 (5): 661–87.

Langvasbråten, Trude. 2008. "A Scandinavian Model? Gender Equality Discourses on Multiculturalism." *Social Politics: International Studies in Gender, State and Society* 15 (1): 32–52.

Löfgren, Orvar. 1999. "Nationella arenor." In *Försvenskningen av Sverige*, edited by Billy Ehn, Jonas Frykman, and Orvar Löfgren, 29–42. Stockholm: Natur & Kultur.

Lundberg, Urban, and Klas Åmark. 2001. "Social Rights and Social Security: The Swedish Welfare State 1900–2000." *Scandinavian Journal of History* 26 (3): 157–76.

Marshall, Thomas H. 1965. *Class, Citizenship and Social Development*. New York: Anchor.

Midtbøen, Arnfinn Haagensen. 2008. *Innvandringens ideologiske konsekvenser: Årsaker til og implikasjoner av statsborgerrettslig divergens i de skandinaviske landene*. Master's thesis, Department of Sociology and Human Geography, University of Oslo.

Mouritsen, Per. 2006. "Fælles værdier, statsreligion og islam i dansk politisk kultur: Det nordiske medborgerskabs specifikke universalitet." In *Bortom stereotyperna? Innvandrare och intergration i Danmark och Sverige*, edited by Ulf Hedetoft, Bo Petterson, and Lina Sturfelt, 109–48. Göteborg: Makadam Förlag.

Palme, Joakim. 1999. *The Nordic Model and the Modernisation of Social Protection in Europe*. Copenhagen: Nordic Council of Ministers.

Petersen, Klaus. 2007. "(U)rettfærdigt! Og hvad det så kommer velfærdsstaten ved?" In *13 værdier bag den danske velfærdsstat*, edited by Jørn Henrik Petersen, Lis Holm Petersen, and Klaus Petersen, 172–94. Odense: Syddansk Universitetsforlag.

Sejersted, Francis. 2005. *Sosialdemokratiets tidsalder: Norge og Sverige i det 20. århundre*. Oslo: Pax.

St. meld. nr. 9. 2006–2007. *Arbeid, velferd og inkludering*. Oslo: Arbeids og inkluderingsdepartementet.

Stråth, Bo. 2005. "The Normative Foundations of the Scandinavian Welfare States in Historical Perspective." In *Normative Foundations of the Welfare State: The Nordic Perspective*, edited by Nanna Kildal and Stein Kuhnle, 143–56. London: Routledge.

Walzer, Michael. 1983. *Spheres of Justice: A Defence of Pluralism and Equality*. New York: Basic Books.

Sweden and Scandinavia

Eskil Wadensjö

The Scandinavian countries resemble each other in many respects: they are advanced welfare states with high average incomes and small income differences; high labor force participation among both men and women; and many immigrants. But there are also important differences in immigration and integration history and policy, some of which I underline here.

IMMIGRATION HISTORY UP TO THE EARLY 1970S

Sweden became a net migration country in the 1930s, but this represented mainly return migration from the United States and a few refugees.[1] During World War II, Sweden received large numbers of refugees because it was one of few countries in Europe not at war. Many came from Denmark and Norway, and most immediately found work because the Swedish male population was mobilized during the war and there were many job vacancies. Some refugees remained in Sweden after the war—for example, those from Estonia—but most returned to their home countries.

After the war, there was a strong demand for labor in Swedish industry that was met in part by the recruitment of workers in other countries. Some arrived via the Labor Market Board, while others went directly to Sweden. The Common Nordic Labor Market (formally declared in 1954 but in practice in the 1940s by unilateral Swedish decisions) reinforced a very liberal granting of work permits for those coming from other countries.

The 1960s, especially, was a period of high economic growth in Sweden. The major source of migrants was Finland, but others arrived from Denmark, Germany, and Norway. From the mid-1960s on, labor migration from the Mediterranean countries also became important (Greece, Italy, Turkey, and Yugoslavia were the main source countries), and labor migration spread to Denmark and Norway.

Brochmann emphasizes the "immigration" stops introduced in Sweden in 1972, in Denmark 1973, and in Norway in 1975.[2] However, labor immigration was already becoming more regulated in Sweden by 1966, a year of very low unemployment, when blue-collar trade unions closely related to the Social Democratic government began to narrow entry doors in 1966, 1967, and 1968. The business boom in 1970 led to a record level of immigration from Finland, a member of the Common Nordic Labor Market. There were no changes in Swedish immigration policy in 1972, but in that year immigration went into a steep decline because of a recession.

IMMIGRATION HISTORY UP TO 2012

In the mid-1970s, all three Scandinavian countries had restrictive immigration policies, so that most newcomers were refugees and family relations. Labor migrants came predominately from other Nordic countries, but there were some specialist migrants from elsewhere. Denmark became a member of the EU in 1973, and in that way became part of the Common European Labor Market. Norway and Sweden entered the Common European Labor Market through membership in the European Economic Area in 1994.

The EU expanded in 2004 and 2007, adding twelve new member countries. Sweden was the only country not implementing any transitional rules. Denmark introduced rules that made it more difficult for citizens of the new member countries to immigrate, but abolished them when the transitional period (which cannot be longer than seven years) ran out.[3] Sweden also opened up for new labor migration from outside the EU starting on December 15, 2008. In practice, the only requirements for Swedish immigration are that the applicant have a job offer and that the wage be decided through collective agreement or at a level corresponding to collective agreement in the industry, which allows low-skilled labor immigration in a manner similar to that of the mass labor immigration in the 1960s, but without trade union involvement to the same extent.

In 2011, 14,722 citizens from countries outside the EU were granted work permits. Half of them were highly educated specialists, mainly in information technology and civil engineering. However, most of the other half were low-skilled jobs—for example, as cleaners, restaurant workers, and seasonal workers in agriculture.[4] The three largest source countries were Thailand (mainly seasonal workers in agriculture), India (mainly IT specialists), and China (both IT specialists and restaurant workers). Currently, most permits are granted for work in the three big-city counties, especially Stockholm County, and short-term work permits are granted in the agricultural sector in the summer. Denmark and Norway, on the other hand, are trying to restrict labor immigration to high-skilled workers. Denmark has introduced a minimum yearly income from labor as a method of regulation.

For the development of migration to and from Denmark, Norway, and Sweden since 2000, see Table 9.2. The yearly immigration to Sweden corresponds to approximately 1 percent of the Swedish population. In relation to population size, immigration is larger in Denmark and especially Norway, but because Sweden has had large-scale immigration for more years, the foreign-born share of its population is larger than that of the other two countries.

INTEGRATION POLICY, THE WELFARE STATE, AND THE WORK PRINCIPLE

The Scandinavian welfare states are based on high workforce participation combined with generous compensation for those out of work. Thus, a broad tax base and high taxes are

TABLE 9.2

Migration to and from Denmark, Norway, and Sweden, 2000–2011

	IMMIGRATION			EMIGRATION		
Year	Denmark	Norway	Sweden	Denmark	Norway	Sweden
2000	52,915	36,542	58,659	43,417	26,854	34,091
2001	55,984	34,264	60,795	43,980	26,309	32,141
2002	52,778	40,122	64,087	43,481	22,948	33,009
2003	49,754	35,957	63,795	43,466	24,672	35,023
2004	49,860	36,482	62,028	45,017	23,271	36,586
2005	52,458	40,148	65,229	45,869	21,709	38,118
2006	56,750	45,776	95,750	46,786	22,053	44,908
2007	64,656	61,774	99,485	41,566	22,122	45,418
2008	72,749	66,961	101,171	43,490	23,615	45,294
2009	67,161	65,186	102,280	44,874	26,549	39,240
2010	68,282	73,852	98,801	45,882	31,506	48,853
2011	69,298	79,498	96,467	46,684	32,466	51,179

SOURCE: Statistics Denmark, Statistics Norway, and Statistics Sweden.

necessary to finance them. In Sweden, the work principle was established after a debate during World War I resulted in public work for the unemployed rather than state-subsidized unemployment insurance. Public work and other active labor market programs were also the policy chosen in the depression in the 1930s; the Rehn-Meidner model—including a restrictive fiscal and monetary policy, a solidaristic wage policy, and an active labor market policy—became government policy starting in the late 1950s.

In Sweden, the work principle governed immigration, including that of refugees. The Labor Market Administration was in charge of refugees in World War II, and its role continued until 1985, when a special authority, *Invandrarverket*, and the municipalities were given that responsibility. At that time, more emphasis was placed on learning the Swedish language. Since December 1, 2010, the Labor Market Administration has again been responsible for refugees, with the goal of improving labor market integration. Denmark and Norway also give priority to work in their integration policies. However, immigrant employment is lower than native employment in all three countries.

Integration policy differs. Danish policy expects refugees and family-related immigrants to take part in integration programs to receive income transfers or to enter the country (in the case of family-based immigrants). In Norway, participation in these programs is both a right and a duty; in Sweden, participation is a right, encouraged by economic incentives.

NATIONALIZATION POLICY

Policy regarding nationalization also differs. Sweden is the most liberal country, with a short and recently shortened qualification period and no test of language proficiency or knowledge of Swedish history and society.[5] Table 9.3 outlines the development of naturalization in Denmark, Finland, Norway, and Sweden in 2001–2011. The Swedish increase in 2005 and 2006 is explained by a shortening of the qualification period for non-Nordic citizens. Denmark has introduced a long qualification period as well as a test for proficiency in the

TABLE 9.3

*Number of foreign-born residents granted citizenship in Denmark,
Finland, Norway, and Sweden, 2001–2011*

Year	Denmark	Finland	Norway	Sweden
2001	11,892	2,720	10,838	36,399
2002	16,662	3,049	9,041	37,792
2003	6,583	4,526	7,867	33,222
2004	14,976	6,880	8,154	28,893
2005	10,197	4,433	12,655	39,573
2006	7,961	4,433	11,955	51,239
2007	3,648	4,824	14,877	33,629
2008	5,772	6,682	10,312	30,461
2009	6,537	3,413	11,442	29,525
2010	3,006	4,334	11,903	32,457
2011	3,991	4,558	14,286	36,634

SOURCE: Statistics Denmark, Statistics Finland, Statistics Norway, and Statistics Sweden.

Danish language and knowledge of Danish history and society. This explains the decline in the number of immigrants who obtain citizenship. The number of citizenships granted in Denmark is now lower than that not only in Norway and Sweden but also in Finland, which has many fewer noncitizens than Denmark has.

IMMIGRATION, ITS ECONOMIC EFFECTS AND SUPPORT FOR THE WELFARE STATE

Economic research shows that the economic effects of immigration are rather small. Its impact on wages and unemployment is not large (although it varies across studies). Of more relevance are the effects on public-sector finances, on which labor migration has positive effects (more taxes paid than tax-supported benefits consumed) and refugee migration has negative effects.[6] The total effect is not large as a percentage of GDP. The costs for refugees are most likely less than the expenditure on foreign aid, and the motivation for those expenditures is more or less the same: to help people who are in a difficult position. The explanation for resistance to immigration probably has to be found elsewhere.

WHY SUCH DIFFERENT IMMIGRATION AND INTEGRATION POLICIES IN THE THREE COUNTRIES?

Scandinavian immigration policies that were similar in the 1990s are diverging, especially with Danish policy after 2001 turning in a more restrictive direction while Swedish policy is opening up for labor immigration from non-EU countries. There are several reasons for the differences in attitudes and policies, including

1. Sweden has never been occupied and has not been at war since 1815. Norway was first part of the Danish Kingdom (up to 1814) and then part of the Swedish Kingdom (up to 1905), and was occupied during World War II. Denmark lost two wars

TABLE 9.4

Fifteen largest groups of foreign born in Denmark (January 1, 2012), Norway (January 1, 2012), and Sweden (December 31, 2011)

DENMARK		NORWAY		SWEDEN	
Country of origin	Number	Country of origin	Number	Country of origin	Number
Turkey	32,379	Poland	67,565	Finland	166,723
Germany	28,584	Sweden	46,968	Iraq	125,499
Poland	28,043	Germany	27,292	Poland	72,865
Iraq	21,197	Denmark	23,260	Yugoslavia	70,050
Bosnia-Herzegovina	17,580	Lithuania	22,707	Iran	63,828
Norway	14,882	Iraq	21,959	Bosnia-Herzegovina	56,290
Sweden	13,079	Somalia	20,658	Germany	48,422
Iran	12,883	United Kingdom	18,058	Denmark	44,951
United Kingdom	12,229	Pakistan	18,043	Turkey	43,909
Pakistan	12,078	United States	16,558	Norway	43,058
Yugoslavia	12,028	Philippines	16,301	Somalia	40,165
Lebanon	12,012	Russia	15,312	Thailand	33,613
Afghanistan	11,134	Thailand	15,190	Chile	28,385
Romania	10,135	Iran	14,374	China	25,657
Somalia	9,951	Vietnam	13,297	Lebanon	24,394

SOURCE: Statistics Denmark, Statistics Norway, and Statistics Sweden.

NOTE: Yugoslavia stands both for Yugoslavia before it broke up into separate republics in 1991 and for Yugoslavia before Serbia and Montenegro became two separate republics.

against Prussia in the nineteenth century and was occupied during World War II. This may explain why Denmark and Norway are more nationalistic than Sweden and less prone to accept immigrants and multiculturalism. For example, Denmark and Norway, but not Sweden, still have Lutheran state churches.

2. Sweden has a longer recent history of immigration, which means that people are more accustomed to the presence of immigrants. Large-scale immigration started with refugees during the war and continued afterward in the form of labor immigration. Large-scale immigration to Denmark and Norway began in the late 1960s.

3. The composition of the immigrant population differs in the three countries. Immigrants from Finland are the largest group in Sweden (see Table 9.4). That so many immigrants are from a neighboring country with which Sweden has a long common history may have been a factor in Swedish attitudes toward immigration.

NOTES

I would like to thank Christer Gerdes and Philip Martin for helpful comments on an earlier version of this commentary.

1. Sweden has had net migration in all years since 1930 except 1972 and 1973; it was in recession in this two-year period, and immigration declined at the same time that many immigrants from Finland who had arrived in 1969–1971 returned to their home country.

2. See Boguslaw (2012).

3. See Doyle, Hughes, and Wadensjö (2006) and Gerdes and Wadensjö (2008).

4. This information is from Migrationsverket (Migration Authority), which is in charge of implementing migration regulations.

5. See Boguslaw (2012).

6. See Gerdes, Schultz-Nielsen, and Wadensjö (2011).

REFERENCES

Boguslaw, Julia. 2012. *Invandringspolitikens långa historia*. Lund: Studentlitteratur.

Doyle, Nicola, Gerry Hughes, and Eskil Wadensjö. 2006. *Freedom of Movement for Workers from Central and Eastern Europe: Experiences in Ireland and Sweden*. Stockholm: Swedish Institute for European Policy Studies.

Gerdes, Christer, Marie Louise Schultz-Nielsen, and Eskil Wadensjö. 2011. *The Significance of Immigration for Public Finances in Denmark*. Odense: University Press of Southern Denmark.

Gerdes, Christer, and Eskil Wadensjö. 2008. *Immigrants from the New EU Member States and the Swedish Welfare State*. Stockholm: Swedish Institute for European Policy Studies.

10

SWITZERLAND

Immigration and Integration in Switzerland: Shifting Evolutions in a Multicultural Republic

Gianni D'Amato

INTRODUCTION

As a small country located at the crossroads of Northern and Southern Europe, Switzerland is widely known for its neutrality and peaceful attitudes, its ethnic and linguistic diversity—German, French, Italian, and Reto-Romansch[1] are all national languages—and a decentralized government that makes most of its laws at the canton (or state) level.[2] There is a good reason that control and integration policies figure largely in a federalist country that was challenged since its birth—in the aftermath of the successful liberal revolution of 1848—by centrifugal forces on the religious, regional, political, social, and ideological levels. Certain foreign scholars, puzzled by Switzerland's apparent enduring stability (and overlooking the history of violent and disruptive conflicts from the civil war of 1847 until the social unrest of the 1930s), detect the source of this solidity in the clever management of a multicultural country through its federal institutions (Schnapper 1997). Others see Switzerland as a "paradigmatic case of political integration" as a result of the subsidiary structure of the Swiss state, which supports both the strong municipal autonomy and the comparatively high participation rate of the (male) constituency in the polity (Deutsch 1976). Still others see the source of the country's stability in the successful creation of a strong national identity, which helped overcome the social distrust that arose during rapid industrialization and which was based on the country's small size and the idea that it was under permanent threat from strong neighboring countries (*Uberfremdung*) (Kohler 1994; Tanner 1998).

Notwithstanding this fear of being demographically and culturally overrun by foreigners, Switzerland had one of the highest immigration rates on the continent during the twentieth century. According to the 2000 census, 22.4 percent of the total population of 7.4 million was foreign born and 20.5 percent, or nearly 1.5 million, was foreign (defined here as persons with a foreign nationality). In relative numbers this is twice as high as the number of foreigners in the United States and considerably higher than the number of foreigners in Canada—both of which are classic countries of immigration. In contrast to its internal pluralistic character, however, Switzerland does not consider itself a country of immigration—in fact, it has denied the existence of an immigrant policy at the federal level before the nineties (Mahnig and Wimmer 2003). This policy of prevention influenced the country's decision not to admit any Jewish refugees after 1933, and it affected the implementation of a "guest worker" rotation model after the oil crises of 1973.

Another paradox concerns the handling of admission and integration issues at the political level. Just after World War II, Switzerland was a popular destination for "guest workers" from France, Germany, and Italy. In the second half of the twentieth century, however, it became home to Eastern European dissidents, Yugoslavian refugees, and asylum seekers from the Middle East, Asia, and Africa. During the entire century, and in the complete absence of the social hardships encountered in neighboring countries (high unemployment rates among migrants, ethnic and social segregation, social unrest, etc.), the immigration issue grew contentious, especially in the period after the 1960s, winning priority on the Swiss political agenda at certain times.

This inconsistent situation must be explained by a careful analysis of how immigration and integration policies evolved in Switzerland. In the next section, I describe immigration and integration during the twentieth century by way of a brief historical overview, and present some demographic data. In the following section, I emphasize the importance of various stakeholders who influence migration policies at the different state levels, and devote attention to external factors, which may have had an effect on their creation. I show that the political opportunity structures in Switzerland—influenced by its federalism, municipal autonomy, and a consensus-oriented political culture—had an impact on the formulation of immigration policy as well—just as much as various external challenges (foreign governments, the European Union [EU]) did. In my conclusion, I discuss the factors that may have influenced Switzerland's particular immigration and integration policy outcomes.

IMMIGRATION AND IMMIGRANT POLICIES IN HISTORICAL PERSPECTIVE

Switzerland's reputation as an ideal place for exiles dates back to the sixteenth century, when the Huguenots of France were welcomed as religious refugees and found their place in the Swiss cultural, political, and entrepreneurial elite. But the modern transformation of Switzerland into a country of immigration—as it is known today—took place during its accelerated industrial take-off in the second half of the nineteenth century (Holmes 1988; Romano 1996). In contrast to its rural image, the Swiss Confederation is a European forerunner in various modern mechanical and chemical industries and has had an enormous need to invest in knowledge and infrastructures. While many rural inhabitants were leaving the country to make their living as peasants in the New World, many German intellectuals fleeing the failed liberal revolutions of 1848–1849 found their place in the local universities. Italian craftsmen and workers also were recruited at the end of the nineteenth and the early twentieth century, mainly in construction and the railroad sector.

During the late nineteenth and the early twentieth century, the size of the foreign population in Swiss cities increased: 41 percent in Geneva, 28 percent in Basel, and 29 percent in Zurich were foreign born. Nationwide, the Germans outnumbered the Italians and French (Efionayi-Mäder, Niederberger, and Wanner 2005). Moreover, the proportion of foreigners in the total population increased from 3 percent in 1850 to 14.7 percent at the eve of World War I, with most of them coming from neighboring countries. During the two world wars, however, the foreign population decreased significantly. By 1941, it had dropped to 5.2 percent (Arlettaz 1985).

In the liberal period preceding World War I, immigration was largely the responsibility of the cantons, whose laws had to conform to bilateral agreements signed between Switzerland and other European states. Like other agreements from this period concerning free circulation in Europe, these were open toward immigrants because they needed to ensure that Swiss citizens could easily emigrate if they needed to find work. However, after a first campaign against aliens during World War I, a new article in the Constitution appeared in 1925, giving the federal government the power to address immigration issues at the national level, which provided the legal basis for the creation of the federal aliens police (*Fremdenpolizei*) and the enactment of the Law on Residence and Settlement of Foreigners, which came into force in 1931 (Garrido 1990). This law allowed the new federal aliens police to implement immigration policy at discretion, although at the time their aim was to maintain national identity rather than to regulate migration. Essentially, the authorities had to consider the country's moral and economic interests and the "degree of overforeignization" (*Grad der Überfremdung*) that would affect their decisions. The nationwide political consensus on ensuring cultural purity prevented the enactment of any consistent immigrant policy until very recently. Foreigners, in principle, had to leave the country and were not allowed to settle permanently.

Postwar Labor Migration

Shortly after World War II, the economic demands of neighboring countries engaged in economic recovery stimulated the rapid growth of the Swiss economy. In the context of the postwar economic boom, Switzerland signed an agreement with the Italian government in 1948 to recruit Italian guest workers. These workers were mainly employed in the construction sector but also in textile and machine factories. Afterward, a steady flow of foreign workers immigrated to Switzerland. Their number increased from 285,000 in 1950 (6.1 percent of the total population) to 585,000 (10.8 percent) in 1960 and to 1,080,000 (17.2) in 1970. Predominantly Italian during the 1950s, their composition diversified in the 1960s: while over 50 percent were still Italians in 1970, about 20 percent were German, French, and Austrian; 10 percent were Spaniards; and 4 percent were Yugoslavs, Portuguese, and Turks (Mahnig and Piguet 2003). Initially, they were entitled to stay for one year, although their contracts could be prolonged, which frequently happened. A similar agreement with Spain was signed in 1961.

To ensure that the workers did not settle permanently and could be sent home, the period required for obtaining a permanent residence permit was increased from five to ten years, and restrictive conditions on family reunion were adopted. This policy was called the "rotation model" because it meant that new workers could be brought in as others returned home. As the economic boom continued throughout the 1960s, the Swiss government's guest worker system became less tightly controlled. As the country faced increasing pressure from Italy to introduce more generous family reunification laws, the number of Italian workers willing to come to Switzerland decreased as other destinations, such as

Germany, became more attractive after the signing of the Treaty of Rome in 1957; also, the internal economic boom and development started a wave of internal migration, particularly to destinations in Northern Italy.

It was also at this time that the Organisation for European Economic Co-operation (OEEC) introduced standards for family reunification. Other international lawmaking bodies, such as the International Labor Organization (ILO), also pressured the Swiss government into making its family reunification policies more "humane." In response, the government started to replace its rotation system with an *integration-oriented* scheme that facilitated family reunification, made foreign workers more eligible for promotions, and attempted to end labor market segmentation (Niederberger 2004).

Following the oil crisis in 1973, many workers became unneeded and had to leave the country because they did not have adequate unemployment insurance. This allowed Switzerland to "export" its unemployed guest workers without renewing their resident permits (Katzenstein 1987). The total percentage of the foreign population fell from 17.2 in 1970 to 14.8 in 1980. But as the economy recovered, new guest workers arrived not only from Italy but also from Spain, Portugal, and Turkey. Their percentage of the population increased from 14.8 (945,000) in 1980 to 18.1 (1,245,000) in 1990 and to 22.4 in 2000 (nearly 1.5 million people) (Mahnig and Piguet 2003).

In the late 1970s, the government gave seasonal workers many of the same rights as guest workers who came on longer contracts—namely, the ability to transform their seasonal permits into permanent residence permits and to bring their families. Since the number of issued seasonal permits did not decrease—they numbered on average 130,000 per year between 1985 and 1995—they became a gateway for permanent immigration and a means for supplying cheap-labor sectors of the economy, which would otherwise not have been able to survive given Switzerland's high wages. In 1982, a reform of the alien's law was meant to regulate the transformation of permits heuristically and give permanent residents a firm incentive to stay in the country. But the successful referendum of a radical right-wing fringe party, the Swiss Democrats, accepted by a slight majority of the population, put an end to the reform of all immigration and migrant settlement laws. Therefore, seasonal permits were still available until 2002.

By the time the worldwide recession of the early 1990s reached Switzerland, unskilled and aging guest workers were suffering high rates of unemployment and found it very difficult to find new jobs. This situation led to unprecedented structural unemployment and poverty, which Switzerland had not experienced in prior decades. The larger cities, which, according to the subsidiary logic of the Swiss federal system, had to cover welfare expenses, urged the federal government to act and support expanded integration requirements toward immigrant workers (D'Amato and Gerber 2005). A new admission policy, which has yet to be formulated, should combine the evolving needs of a new economy with those of migration control. Before we turn our attention to the policymaking process, however, the most important actors in Swiss migration policy must be discussed.

Asylum Policy

After World War II, the Swiss government recognized that its authorities had been responsible for denying admission to many Jewish refugees. The government stressed its willingness to uphold the humanitarian tradition of the country and in 1955 signed the Geneva Convention Relating to the Status of Refugees of 1951. During the next two decades, the country adopted a liberal policy, offering asylum to refugees from communist countries in Eastern Europe. In 1956, 14,000 Hungarians were allowed to settle permanently after the uprising in their country against Soviet troops, and, in 1968, 12,000 Czechoslovakian nationals arrived (Efionayi-Mäder 2003).

These people, who were often well educated, had little difficulty in obtaining refugee status. The government and the public gave them a warm welcome, which is not surprising given the strong anti-communist sentiments at this time. In the mid-1970s, the arrival of a few hundred Chilean dissidents fleeing Pinochet's regime ignited controversial debates about their asylum eligibility. Between 1979 and 1982, Switzerland offered protection to approximately 8,000 Vietnamese and Cambodian boat people, who were accepted on the basis of yearly quotas. The subsequent integration of these refugees was more difficult than that of any previous refugee group (Parini and Gianni 1997, 2005).

All these events prompted the creation of a new federal asylum policy in 1981, which codified the country's relatively generous practices. It defined the rules of the refugee status determination procedure and gave the Confederation policymaking power, while clearly giving the cantons the responsibility of policy implementation. In domains such as welfare, education, and repatriation, the power of the cantons in making refugee-related decisions was significant. As a result, there were major policy differences between cantons.

After 1981, two trends emerged. First, the number of applications, which had been steady at about 1,000 per year during the 1970s, increased exponentially. Second, most refugees—except for a large number of Polish refugees in 1982—came from other parts of the world: Turkey, Sri Lanka, the Middle East, Africa, and Asia. Unlike the anti-communist dissidents, they were not always professionals or university graduates. Some came from rural areas, some had not even finished primary school, and others had university degrees that were not recognized in Europe. In addition, a weak economy made it difficult for these non-Europeans to find work.

As more people from outside Europe filed applications, asylum became a sensitive subject, particularly in the mid-1980s. In public debates, refugees were called "asylum seekers" or even the derogatory "asylants" to indicate that they did not deserve refugee status. After the 1981 law's revisions created stricter procedures, the government gradually started granting a decreasing number of asylum requests, even from people fleeing civil wars and violence. As a rough indicator of this trend, the share of accepted applications averaged 86 percent between 1975 and 1979. This number dropped to an average of 47 percent between 1980 and 1984 and dropped again to an average of 6 percent between 1985 and 1990 (Efionayi-Mäder, Niederberger, and Wanner 2005).

IMMIGRATION POLICIES AND POLICYMAKING

Because immigration and integration policies in Switzerland are intrinsically bound, this section first presents the main actors in policymaking and then discusses the recent changes in admission, asylum, integration, and naturalization policies.

The Actors in Policymaking

Until recently, two federal offices within the Federal Department of Justice and Police dealt with "foreigners" living in Switzerland: the Federal Office for Refugees (FOR) and the Federal Office for Immigration, Integration and Emigration (IMES). The first was introduced in 1991 in reaction to the influx of asylum seekers since the 80s. The second was introduced in 2000, but had predecessors dating back to the Law on Residence and Settlement of Foreigners of 1931. Its main task was to prevent "overforeignization" and enforce integration of foreigners. FOR and IMES were merged into one entity, the Federal Office for Migration (FOM) on January 1, 2005. One of FOM's branches continues to be responsible for implementing Swiss asylum policy. Another continues to administer admission policy as IMES did, including enforcing laws governing residence in Switzerland (immigration and residence section); it also assesses labor market needs (labor market section). The changes in the organization of the federal office reflect the desire to implement a coherent policy on foreigners dealing with admission, stay, and integration (see Efionayi-Mäder et al. 2003).

The State Secretariat for Economic Affairs (SECO), which is a part of the Federal Department of Economic Affairs (DEA), is the agency responsible for economics and labor issues. SECO has influenced Swiss labor migration policy since 1945 by determining the qualitative and quantitative needs of the country's labor market.

At the federal level, there are three important permanent commissions: the already mentioned Federal Commission for Foreigners (FCF), the Federal Commission against Racism (CFR), and the Federal Commission for Refugees (EKF). The FCF was made up of experts from the Federal Council in 1970; it reports directly to the Federal Department of Justice and Police.

The central concern of the FCF is the integration of foreigners. Since 2001, its funds have been available for projects that promote integration. At present, the FCF is made up of 28 members, two of whom have the status of observers. Members are representatives of various foreigners' organizations, municipalities, communities, cantons, employers and employees, and churches, or they have a professional background in integration policy. The FCF assists in the creation of educational and vocational opportunities for foreigners and in the recognition of professional training in cooperation with the relevant cantonal authorities; participates in the international exchange of views and experience; mediates between organizations that are active in the field and federal authorities; publishes opinions and recommendations regarding general issues of migration; and consults on migration questions during legislative proceedings.

The Federal Commission on Foreigners, the Federal Commission for Refugees, and the Federal Commission against Racism hold meetings on a quarterly basis, and they organize joint events, such as the national conference on the revision of naturalization law. The Federal Commission Against Racism is part of the Federal Department of Home Affairs (DHA). Within the DHA, there is a branch that coordinates the various actors participating in the fight against racism. Among other activities, the DHA administers a fund for anti-racism projects. The Federal Commission for Refugees advises the government and relevant ministries on refugee issues.

All of these bodies form an important interest group in the promulgation of new laws, insofar as a significant part of decision making in Switzerland is left to the institutions of direct democracy. Particularly in the migration policy, political processes and policymaking are dominated by pre-parliamentarian negotiations and direct democracy, with Parliament playing a secondary role (Mahnig 1996). Significantly, the two levels of policymaking and the political process are also characterized by different political styles (Neidhart 1970). In pre-parliamentarian negotiations compromise is the final objective of the consultation process, in which expert commissions play a decisive role, the arena of direct democracy is mainly characterized by confrontational attitudes and divisive outcomes.

At the federal level, the most important political parties in Switzerland are the centrist bloc, composed of the Christian Democrats (CVP), the Swiss People's Party (SVP), and the liberal Radical Party (FDP), and the left-wing bloc, composed of the Social Democrats (SPS) and the Green Party (GP). With the exception of the Green Party, all parties are members of the government. The Swiss People's Party is an important stakeholder in debates on migration and asylum policy. Formerly the party of artisans and peasants, it became a modern radical populist party when Christoph Blocher, a charismatic lawyer and entrepreneur, took over its Zurich branch in the late 1970s. The SVP supported a popular initiative aiming to reduce the number of illegal residents in Switzerland and was in charge of the initiative "against asylum abuse." In Zurich, the party has launched an initiative demanding that all requests for naturalization be subject to popular referendum.

Trade unions and employers also play a role in the formulation of immigration policy. They exert their influence both in a formal manner (in the consultation procedure) and in an informal manner (in determining the quota of foreigners allowed into Switzerland). Because of the federal structure of the Swiss state, the cantons are also very influential in the formulation of governmental policies. Their sphere of authority includes the alien police and determination of labor market needs. Furthermore, the cantons are responsible for the implementation of integration measures. As the confederation does not have a police force, the cantons are responsible for maintaining public order and enforcing decisions involving repatriation. Thus, it is through their competence and experience in implementing asylum measures that they contribute significantly to policymaking in this area. The Conference of Cantonal Ministers of Justice and Police (CCMJP) has become increasingly vocal on questions of asylum and interior security (i.e., crimes committed by foreigners).

Cooperation with municipalities is important because the municipalities are responsible for accommodating asylum seekers and refugees and must pay the costs of providing social services for regular immigrants. Their standard point of view is that their concerns are not sufficiently taken into consideration in asylum and immigration policymaking and implementation. Larger cities, especially Zurich, have launched spontaneous initiatives on asylum that have caused a major debate. Smaller municipalities have also been in the headlines: recently one refused to accommodate the requested number of asylum seekers, and others have banned them from public areas such as schools, playgrounds, and soccer fields.

NGOs play a part in the implementation of Swiss asylum policy. They offer social counseling and legal advice to asylum seekers. For example, The Swiss Refugee Aid, an umbrella organization of Swiss asylum groups, seeks to exert influence on political decision making by publishing position papers on various asylum-related questions.

Other NGOs in the asylum field include the charity organizations Caritas and HEKS and the Swiss Red Cross. In March 2001, the Swiss Forum for the Integration of Migrants (FIMM) was created. Composed of 330 representatives, it is the umbrella organization of all foreigners' associations. FIMM organizes public debates on issues concerning foreigners (e.g., the Schengen Agreement), collaborates with the federal authorities (IMES, FCF), and participates in the consultation procedure. It is partially financed by the Federal Commission for Foreigners.

Recent Changes in Immigration Policies

The way in which the different interest groups consult with the federal administration, with Parliament during the policymaking process, and, not least, through direct democracy, is the subject of the following paragraphs.

Regarding regular immigration, there have been two major changes in the last few years: first, in June 2002, the Bilateral Agreement on the Free Movement of Persons between Switzerland and the EU member states was enacted. Second, the admission policy applicable to third-country nationals is more restrictive than the policy that Switzerland has pursued so far. "Only urgently required qualified workers" will be admitted from outside the EU/ EFTA (European Free Trade Agreement) area. Work permits will be issued only to executives, specialists, and other highly qualified workers from outside this area if no Swiss or EU national meets these requirements. Further, when issuing residence permits, the authorities will take into consideration candidates' professional qualifications, ability to adapt to professional requirements, language skills, and age. If a person meets the criteria, she or he should be able to achieve sustainable integration into the Swiss labor market and society (Efionayi-Mäder et al. 2003).

The draft of a new immigration law was under discussion in 2005 in both chambers of Parliament and was passed at the end of 2006 despite the introduction of referendum to prevent a "two-class" admission system between EU and non-EU immigrants. During hearings, it became evident that this bill would cause sharp and polarized campaigns, not to mention that the last attempt to reform the alien's law in 1982 had been doomed to failure. The reform proposal was supported only by the Christian Democrats (CVP) and the Radical Liberal Party (FDP); the Swiss People's Party (SVP) did not want any improvements for non-EU nationals, thus denying them the opportunity for family reunification. The political Left, particularly the Social Democratic Party (SPS), the Green Party (GP), and the unions, criticized the discriminatory partitioning of foreigners into two categories, which for them strongly evoked the memory of old initiatives that had been rejected by voters. When the bill finally was presented at Parliament, it was challenged by the Left and the Right for different reasons: the Left asked for equal treatment of all foreigners; the Right, for a more effective means of combating abuse of foreigners' laws, and the cancelation of any possibility of reunification of families.

A few representatives of the political right were especially irritated that the National Council had passed a special regulation concerning the *sans-papiers* (migrants without papers who have resided illegally in the country for more than four years), giving them, for humanitarian reasons, the right to request authorization for legal residence in the near future. Curiously enough, there was no protest over the motion of a SVP MP, submitted at the same time (but not passed in the final parliamentarian vote), that would have allowed the hiring of unqualified third-country nationals as seasonal workers in farming, tourism, and construction. From then on, the allocation of residence permits would be connected to completion of integration courses subsidized (against the will of the SVP) by the federal government. The National Chamber also passed articles against migrants marrying for convenience as well as against smugglers and illegal migrants. It also introduced carrier sanctions at Swiss airports for all airlines responsible for the transport of passengers without valid papers.

This bill was ratified by the national chamber with the support of the Christian Democrats and the Radical Party. The Social Democrats (SPS) also approved it, largely in order not to hinder further negotiations and to prevent a more restrictive interpretation. The Green Party and the SVP refused to support the law for opposite reasons: the former because of human rights concerns; the latter because the bill was not strict enough against abuse by foreigners. Thus, in December 2003 the new Federal Council elected a member to be responsible for migration issues. This was Minister of Justice Christoph Blocher (SVP), who announced a more restrictive version of the bill to be presented in the second chamber, the Council of States (i.e., representatives of the cantons).

The second chamber of Parliament, the Council of States, which is led by a CVP-FDP majority, voted for a more severe interpretation, that would cancel all automatic rights in the foreigner's law: for example, persons with a residence permit would not be allowed to reunite with their families automatically but only at the discretion of the cantons. A special regulation concerning *sans-papiers* was also abolished because Christoph Blocher argued that, with the exception of those showing hardship, all illegal immigrants should leave the country. Thus, both laws regarding the reunification of families and the regularization of *sans-papiers* were impeded: to facilitate the integration of young persons from reunified families, the age at which a permanent residence permit could be applied for was lowered from 14 to 12 years of age.

In the second reading, the National Council joined the Council of States in abolishing the article that would allow a limited number of unqualified persons to enter the country. The SPS and the Greens announced a referendum against the bill, and they were supported by migrant associations, particularly the umbrella organization FIMM (Forum pour l'intégration des migrantes et des migrants). Even the Federal Commission on Foreigners published a report in which they expressed concern about severe interpretation of integration measures. The bill was resubmitted, together with the revised asylum law, to a referendum that was won by the government in September 2006. Thus, the more restrictive law passed all procedures.

In quantitative terms, the new bill (like the old law) lays the foundation for authorities to pursue a more permissive or a more restrictive admission policy as necessary. For the authorities, the decisive factors in determining the number of people to be admitted from outside the EU/EFTA are the economic situation in Switzerland and the needs of certain segments of the labor market. They will continue to have the right to adopt a quota solution for nationals of third countries (*Kontingentierung*).

The basic policy principle in the current law is that admissions must be in the interest of the entire economy and not that of particular segments of it; rather, professional quali-fications and the ability to integrate should play a decisive part. In addition, admission has to take the social and demographic needs of Switzerland into consideration. In contrast to today's regulations, a controlled opening of the market to the self-employed is foreseen in the law if they are "likely to stimulate competition." Increased competition should pro-mote efficiency and, in the long run, guarantee the international competitiveness of Swiss companies. Assessment of labor market needs was revised in the 1990s in recognition that postwar migration policy was one of the main reasons for reduced investments and the decline of Swiss competitiveness in different, new industries (Blattner and Sheldon 1989; Sheldon 1998).

On the one hand, the new immigration law constructs a higher barrier to admission for nationals of non-EU/EFTA states. On the other hand, the situation for foreigners who lawfully and permanently reside in Switzerland is improved through more opportunities to change their occupation, job, and canton. The immigration of families of short-term resi-dents and students is also permitted, provided that residential and financial requirements are satisfied. These measures facilitate integration, simplify procedures for employers and authorities, and ensure a uniform application of the law. In the areas mentioned above, the law aims to harmonize the rules applicable to third-country nationals with those applicable to EU/EFTA nationals (Efionayi-Mäder et al. 2003).

Recent Changes in Asylum Policy

As elsewhere in Western Europe, asylum migration gained in importance during the 1980s. It overtook labor migration as an issue for public discourse because of its manifold moral, political, and judicial implications. Although asylum recognition rates decreased in the 1990s, many asylum seekers were able to remain in Switzerland under subsidiary protec-tion or for humanitarian reasons. Although their rights were restricted for a period of time regulated by the cantons—for example, their access to the labor market and to welfare was limited and family reunification was forbidden—most of those who were granted protec-tion were later able to settle permanently.

In the 1990s, war in the former Yugoslavia prompted a massive influx of asylum seekers from Bosnia and Kosovo, many of whom had family ties in Switzerland because of the labor migration that started in the 1960s. Between 1990 and 2002, Switzerland received a total of 146,587 asylum applications from the war-torn Balkans. According to the Swiss Federal Of-fice for Migration, about 10,000 people were granted asylum and 62,000 received temporary or subsidiary protection over the course of several years (Kaya 2005).

The Swiss public had become concerned about the increasing number of asylum ap-plications, largely because the economy was in recession and unemployment was rising. The federal government adopted administrative and legal measures to speed up applica-tion processing and decision implementation. But after numerous partial revisions, a com-pletely revised asylum law came into force in 1999. Among the many changes that made it more restrictive, the law introduced new grounds for nonadmission to the regular asylum procedure. This means that applicants who stayed in the country illegally prior to their request or who did not submit travel or identity documents are generally refused asylum. Nevertheless, as a concession to humanitarian arguments, the law now allows for the collective temporary protection of war refugees. Although the government has never used this provision, Kosovars and Bosnians were given temporary admission.

Most of the asylum seekers from Bosnia and Kosovo had to leave Switzerland after the conflicts ended in 1995 and 1999, respectively. Those who returned home, including those who had waited several years to do so, benefited from a return program offering financial support, construction materials, and support for their home communities. An estimated 40,000 to 60,000 people from Bosnia and Serbia-Montenegro returned home, with or without aid from the Swiss government, while approximately 10,000 with refugee status from the former Yugoslavia stayed. There are no reliable figures for how many asylum seekers from Bosnia and Kosovo remained in the country illegally (Efionayi-Mäder, Niederberger, and Wanner 2005).

Despite the continuing decrease in asylum requests—in 2003, the number fell by around 20 percent (20,806 in absolute numbers) as compared with the year before—the SVP continued its battle to restrict asylum inflows. Because its initiative against asylum abuses did not pass in 2002 (it received one-tenth of 1 percent of the vote), the party searched for new fields of operation. As a "moral winner," it demanded a new asylum initiative in June 2003 because it did not expect any revolutionary improvements from the parliamentarian revisions. Provoked by SVP chairman Christoph Blocher's demand (Blocher was still MP at this time), the other parties condemned it as a form of "blackmailing" and as pure electioneering, and they reacted with a revision of the asylum law. Although an exact wording was still missing at this time, control over asylum matters would be completely transferred to the federal level at a future date. Another idea was to block uncooperative and liable asylum seekers, as well as those who were in the country illegally, from beginning the asylum application process. Instead, they would face prison or expulsion (*NZZ* [*Neue Zürcher Zeitung*], June 11, 2003, September 15, 2003).

In reaction to the unexpected success of the SVP with its initiative against abuses, the National Council's standing committee on political institutions decided not to revise the foreigner's law first and the asylum law second, as had been originally intended, but to take both revisions to a vote simultaneously. Meanwhile, the SVP's plans to bring forward its own revision of the law had no success. (*NZZ*, January 10, 2003).

The government realistically interpreted the population's skeptical attitude toward its asylum policy, even though the decreasing number of asylum requests no longer supported this interpretation *de facto*. Its hopes to regain support from the people thus had to be realized through a new asylum law. Asylum seekers whose requests could not be accommodated in the future would now be treated as illegal foreigners without any rights to social welfare benefits. They were left with the less attractive, but still constitutionally protected, emergency aid, which is subject to administrative controls.

The government expected this change to produce not only annual savings of approximately 77 million Swiss francs (CHF) but also fewer repatriations and a lowering of Switzerland's attractiveness as country of destination. However, only a few years before the cantons and cities had refused to support a similar measure because they feared the impact on housing costs (cantons and municipalities are responsible for emergency aid) (*NZZ*, February 13, 2003, February 14, 2003, April 5, 2003). Still, given the electoral success of the SVP, the mood in Parliament was shifting toward a more restrictive policy.

The National Council affirmed the third-state regulations with a strong majority and support from the center-right parties. Consequently, Switzerland would in the future stop accepting requests for asylum if applicants had already received a negative response from an EU or EES country. At the same time, it approved humanitarian admission. However, neither the SVP proposal favoring stricter admission requirements nor the proposals of the Social Democrats and the Greens for less constraint, were taken into account. Thus, the humanitarian admission program would be granted only if expulsion was not allowed for humanitarian reasons and the applicant was in a state of serious need. The admission program foresaw the right to reunify families under certain conditions and granted facilitated access to the labor market.

In the final vote, the National Council accepted the revision of the asylum law 98 to 49 with 30 abstentions. The CVP and the FDP favored the bill with no exceptions; the Greens were just as opposed to it. Two-thirds of the Social Democratic council members were in favor of the revision. The majority of the SVP was against it, and most of the abstentions came from its members (*NZZ*, August 31, 2004; on the position of Federal Council member Christoph Blocher, see *Der Bund*, April 7, 2004).

However, Christoph Blocher, now a federal councilor, was not satisfied with the changes approved by the National Council and requested modifications with regard to the consultation of the *Ständerat*. The Minister of Justice pleaded for a further tightening of the deportation rules, the expansion of territorial bans, the introduction of short-term arrests, the tightening of decisions with regard to *sans-papiers*, the abolishment of humanitarian admissions, and the introduction of fees to be collected from asylum seekers if they withdrew their admission requests. In a consultation, the cantons welcomed these innovations, in particular the coercive measures. However, they agreed less with the financial consequences of a system change, especially those associated with humanitarian assistance.

While welfare organizations, the UNHCR, the churches, the Social Democratic Party, the Greens, and five cantons expressed fundamental doubts about the revision, the FDP and the CVP largely supported it, even though they had reservations about some paragraphs. The SVP supported the suggestions of its Minister of Justice with no sign of flinching, at the same time wishing for even stricter measures. At the end of August, the Federal Council endorsed the revisions put forward by Christoph Blocher in toto, but refused to support the expansion of deportation orders and the cancelation of humanitarian admission (*NZZ*, July 1, 2004, July 21, 2004 [churches]; *NZZ*, July 28, 2004 [UNHCR]; *NZZ*, July 22, 2004 [local authorities association]; *NZZ*, August 6, 2004 [cantons]; see also *Tages-Anzeiger*, August 8, 2004).

The *Ständerat* did not disappoint the expectations of the Federal Council and the cantons when it came to its turn to speak for a more severe asylum law during debates in the 2005 spring session (*NZZ*, March 18, 2005). However, considerable resentment prevailed over the fact that Minister Blocher proposed his amendments in accelerated proceedings. Although it did not stand a chance, a request was made by Simonetta Sommaruga (Social Democrat member of the Upper House) for an examination of the conformity of the amendments with the Constitution and international law. In response, Christoph Blocher stated that none of his suggestions had so far been rejected, either by the Federal Council or by internal experts, on the grounds that they were offensive to international law.

Finally, the decision of the Political Institutions Committee of the Upper House corresponded to the desires of the cantons in opting for a stricter interpretation of the asylum law. Its members asked for consideration of coercive detention, which could be expanded up to a period of two years. Moreover, it was the only governing body in Europe to reject the new status of humanitarian admission, because of the automatic family reunification program it originally included in the revised proposal. For cases of hardship, the *Ständerat* wanted to apply the instrument of provisional admission. Thus, the cantons could grant access to the labor market to immigrants whose return was inadmissible, unreasonable, or impossible, and who were socially integrated. However, requests for asylum would no longer be considered if, at the beginning of the asylum process, no passport or identity card was submitted to authorities but only such documents as birth certificates or driver licenses. If persecution in the country of origin could be proven, the asylum proceeding would remain open.

It was this last point that was criticized by the political Left and some members of the Center-Right as being disproportionate and unconstitutional. The Left also resisted, in vain, the freezing of social welfare assistance to rejected asylum seekers, as the new law foresaw only emergency support for this group, which could be denied to uncooperative asylum-seekers (*NZZ*, March 18, 2005).

The argument of Federal Councilor Christoph Blocher passed the *Ständerat* and the second reading in the *Nationalrat* with a large majority. The *NZZ* took note with astonishment how unanimously all center-right parties stood behind Blocher and expressed its surprise that no further suggestions were introduced in the formulation of future migration policy. This seemed to prove

> ... how much the mood had changed after Christoph Blocher had taken over the justice department. Today bills are passed with large majorities whereas a few years ago they would have caused even doubt and refusal in the political center-right camp. The Left, the charitable organizations and the churches have not reacted to these changes and, furthermore, practically oppose all changes in the whole country instead of focusing on some really problematic reinforcement of the law. (*NZZ*, September 28, 2005)

Together with the foreigner's law, the asylum law was submitted to a popular referendum and passed by a 3–1 vote in September 2006.

Recent Changes in Integration Policies

When the Swiss government dropped its rotation policy in the early 1960s, it recognized that the alternative could only be a policy of integration. The belief—both then and now—however, is that integration takes place naturally in the labor market and in schools, as well as in associations, labor unions, clubs, churches, neighborhoods, and other informal networks (Niederberger 2004). Since the 1970s, the Confederation's main integration policy has been to improve the legal status of immigrants, reuniting families more quickly and granting immigrants a more secure status. To facilitate integration and to respond to public concerns about foreigners, the government established the Federal Commission for Foreigners (FCF) in 1970 (see above), the purpose of which is to promote the coexistence of foreign and native populations and to bring together municipalities, communities, cantons, foreigners' organizations, employers and employees, and churches. The FCF cooperates with cantonal and communal authorities, immigrant services, and immigration actors such as charities and economic associations. It also publishes opinions and recommendations on migration issues and gives testimony in migration-related policy debates.

After the strong lobbying of the cities during the economic crisis of the 1990s, Swiss policy on foreigners adapted to the new reality, considering the integration of foreigners a prerequisite for achieving politically and socially sustainable immigration. "Integration" refers to the participation of foreigners in Swiss economic, social, and cultural life. The integration article in the old alien law, passed in 1999, paved the way for a more proactive federal integration policy; it also strengthened the FCF's role. Since 2001, the government has spent between 10 and 12 million Swiss francs (€6 million and €7 million) yearly to support integration projects, including language and integration courses and training for integration leaders. Cantons and larger municipalities have their own committees and offices for integration and intercultural cooperation, which also offer courses in language and integration. In many communities, foreigners are members of school boards and, in some cases, participate in municipal government. With the support of consulates and local education departments, larger communities offer courses in immigrant children's native languages and cultures. Churches were early promoters of the coexistence of the Swiss and the foreign population. Other nongovernmental organizations have also become more interested in coexistence.

The new immigration law foresees that immigration candidates will have to fulfill certain criteria to facilitate their integration. This restrictive component corresponds to the criterion of "qualitatively high standard immigration." The level of education and professional qualifications should improve the integration of foreigners and guarantee their vocational reintegration in the case of unemployment. The restriction aims at avoiding the errors that were committed in the past involving the granting of temporary work permits to low-skilled seasonal workers. As a corrective, the new immigration law abolishes the status of seasonal workers. Furthermore, it explicitly states that it is the immigrant's duty to make every effort to facilitate his or her integration. Permanent residents and their families are required to integrate on both the professional and the social level (Efionayi-Mäder et al. 2003).

The government has a budget available to fund projects that promote integration. New instruments have been adopted to coordinate measures at the federal and cantonal levels. Cantons have had to establish integration offices and launch projects that promote linguistic, professional, and other forms of integration. A first round of projects to promote integration has already been implemented.

Recent Changes in Naturalization Policies

People who have resided in Switzerland for twelve years (the years spent between the completed tenth and twentieth years are counted double for this purpose) may apply for naturalization. The Federal Office for Migration examines whether applicants are integrated into the Swiss way of life, whether they are familiar with Swiss customs and traditions, and whether they comply with Swiss laws and do not endanger internal or external security. In particular, this examination is based on cantonal and communal reports. If the requirements of the federal law are satisfied, applicants are entitled to obtain a federal naturalization permit from the Federal Aliens Office (Wanner and D'Amato 2003).

Because naturalization proceeds in three stages, the federal naturalization permit constitutes only the green light for acquiring Swiss nationality. The cantons and communities have their own, additional residence requirements that applicants have to satisfy after the federal preconditions are met. Once they have obtained the federal naturalization permit, only those applicants who have also been naturalized by their communities and cantons become Swiss citizens. As a general rule, there is no legally protected right to naturalization by a community and a canton. The cantons' criteria, as well as the way in which they decide who gets citizenship, vary greatly. For example, in the canton of Nidwalden, applicants must have spent their entire 12 years of residence there. In Geneva, two years of residence are sufficient; candidates who have moved from other cantons fulfill the federal preconditions. The requirements at the communal level can vary greatly as well.

In three referendums that were passed over the last twenty years (1983, 1994, and 2004), Swiss voters have rejected laws that would have made it easier for the children of immigrants to become naturalized. Indeed, the 2004 referendum would have allowed the Swiss-born grandchild of a foreign resident to automatically gain Swiss citizenship at birth. The main reason for this new provision was that an "automatic" naturalization would have eliminated the community's decision-making role, which many Swiss consider an important step in the political process. Over the last forty to fifty years, naturalization rates have been lower than desired by federal authorities because many immigrants decide to return to their home countries after working in Switzerland.

In 1992, it was decided to allow dual citizenship. Between 1991 and 2001, the number of naturalizations increased from 8,757 to 37,070. Nationals from the former Yugoslavia, mostly from Kosovo and Bosnia, have been the quickest to naturalize—they have little interest in returning "home" because of the unstable political situation there. Also, having Swiss citizenship means that they can never be forced to return. Citizenship is not always necessary for voting in local elections, however. In several cantons in the French-speaking part of Switzerland, foreigners who have lived in the area for many years have the right to vote on the municipal level and, in a few cantons, even on cantonal matters. The introduction of such a legal innovation in 2004 led to controversy over the significance of citizenship.

As already mentioned, in 2002 the Swiss Parliament debated the revision of the citizenship law for a third time. In the detailed consultation process, suggestions for shortening the minimum residence requirements presented by the Federal Council and the Christian Democratic CVP were violently criticized. The Social Democrats and the Greens wanted a reduction of six years; the SVP and a majority of the FDP wanted to maintain the original twelve years. Concerning the regulations on facilitating naturalization of the second generation, the SVP demanded more severe legislation. It expressed the opinion that only those born in the country should profit from an easier access to citizenship, as opposed to young people who have only spent little over half of their school life in the country. The National Council rejected this proposal. The Social Democratic Party, the liberal FDP, the Christian Democratic CVP, and the Green Party all supported facilitated naturalization; only the SVP rejected it.

However, when the debate shifted to a discussion of whether citizenship should automatically be given to children of the third generation (introducing the principle of *jus soli*), it became heavily polarized. This legal innovation was categorically rejected by the SVP. On the other hand, the CVP and the FDP were reluctant to limit the rights of the parents in this manner. Thus, the FDP wished to make the right of naturalization dependent on the parents' request. In the end, the CVP's proposal found a lot of support with the argument that parents could renounce the citizenship of their child at birth, and that the child was free to revoke his or her decision at the age of majority. Against the acrimonious resistance of the SVP, the National Council also approved the right to complain for those whose request was rejected in municipalities without reason. At the end of the consultations, the SVP announced that it wished to initiate a referendum against this revision (*NZZ*, September 17, 2002).

Shortly after this debate, the discussion about granting easier access to citizenship was influenced by a decision of the Federal Supreme Court in Lausanne. The judges decided that granting citizenship for reasons of origin or religion was unconstitutional because it violated the principal of nondiscrimination. The judges ordered that municipalities adopt a procedure that did not offend the Constitution and in their written justification declared that no immigrant had an automatic right to be naturalized, but that in certain municipalities voting on applicants was an administrative function since it entailed a decision on the status of inhabitants. This function would require the authorities and the population to respect the prohibition of discrimination (*NZZ*, July 10, 2003, July 25, 2003).

Many experts as well as the political Left gave their support to this judgment. The political center reacted with consternation at such a verdict coming only a few weeks before the general elections. The SVP protested vociferously against the limitation of sovereignty and municipal autonomy, which in their eyes gave the impression of a partisan political decision. This question became one of the major topics in the SVP's 2003 election campaign, which criticized the judges who had acted against the will of the people. A party convention held a few days before the elections launched a political initiative that demanded that naturalizations be granted at the people's discretion. In the SVP's opinion, naturalizations were political, not administrative, acts.

Both chambers of Parliament passed the bill with practically no alterations. Only the SVP voted unanimously against it, disapproving of easier access for the second generation, the *jus soli* for the third generation, and the right to appeal for those rejected by the people. On the last point, the SVP was supported by a large minority of the radical FDP.

On September 26, 2004, the referendum took place. Advocates of the change—the Christian Democrats, the Social Democrats, and the liberal FDP—gave little propaganda support, underestimating its importance of the referendum for the SVP campaign. Polling analysis allowed the center-left parties to presume that they would win the referendum, but the winds changed just days before the vote. The support of the employers' association and the unions was not powerful enough. Newly elected Federal Councilor Christoph Blocher should have supported the bill since it came from his ministry, but for obvious reasons his campaign only imparted technical information about the new provisions to a restricted audience.

With a rather high voter turnout (54 percent), the majority of the people and the cantons refused to reform the citizenship law. Facilitated naturalization was rejected by a majority of 57 percent; the automatic naturalization of the third generation at birth was also rejected, by a majority of 51.6 percent. Interestingly, the rollback closely compared to the referendum of 1994: with the exception of the canton of Basel City, all other Swiss-German cantons that had approved a more liberal application of the naturalization law ten years earlier had now switched to the other camp (*NZZ*, September 27, 2004).

There are two explanations for this shift: the parties that had favored it in Parliament (SPS, CVP, and FDP) would not commit when it came to defending facilitated access to citizenship during the campaign. Spellbound by promising polls, they were surprised at how easily and successfully the SVP, in the last weeks before the voting, was able to mobilize fears of granting valued citizenship to nondeserving young immigrants. The SVP had defined automatic nationality as a devaluation of Swiss citizenship and objected to the weakening of local popular sovereignty that it implied (Kaya 2005). And this time the reform law was not backed by the Federal Department of Justice and Police, which had originally envisioned this change.

Interests and Orientations

As discussed in the previous section, integration has been the object of political contention in Switzerland. In this respect, different comparative studies have confirmed the perseverance of interests and orientations in discourses on migration politics (Brubaker 1992; Hollifield 1992; Ireland 1994). In the case of Switzerland, it has been shown that migration politics is shaped by three major arguments (see Mahnig 1996). The liberal position argues that the free market is the ideal regime of migration regulation. According to this position, migration is not to be prevented or restricted but handled in a fashion similar to the handling of the free trade of capital and goods. Any state intervention is seen, economically, as highly ineffective, unless it is meant to reduce immigration control or adapt immigration rates to business demands.

The internationalist position also takes a critical stand toward national immigration control, but for different reasons. The argument here is based on the proliferation of international human rights calls for global standardization of legal and social equality for individuals. In this view, migration policy is seen as an instrument of social compensation between rich and poor countries.

Finally, the nationalist position seeks to defend Swiss national interests against the interests of immigrants. These interests have economic and labor market dimensions (e.g., protection of certain economic sectors and the local workforce), and they are oriented toward defense of a national identity that seems constantly threatened.

It appears that, at the beginning of the 1990s—through changes due to both internal (comprehensive citizenship reform, prolonged economic crisis) and external (the end of the Cold War, the integration process, changes in naturalization laws all over Europe) factors—government policymakers were forced to redirect their orientation from nationalist-liberal to more liberal-internationalist (Jacobson 1996; Soysal 1994). Adjustments in the EU, acceptance of dual citizenship, attempts to reform citizenship laws, and protection of cultural rights through the recently created Federal Commission against Racism—these are all indications of this process of adjustment to the new political environment. The clear shift in matters of immigration, citizenship, and cultural rights also represents new challenges for actors that were always present on the Swiss political scene, and it opens for them a new space of contention: the right-wing populist parties, which are discussed in the next section.

The way in which interests and orientations contend on social cohesion and, in particular, the outcomes of these contentions, can only be understood if the Swiss institutional context of policymaking is considered. Three areas are relevant for the study of Switzerland: its federalism and its consociational and direct democracy.

THE SWISS POLICYMAKING PROCESS

In order to understand Swiss policymaking, three distinct features of the national polity have to be taken into consideration: the federal structure of the state, the financial and political autonomy of the municipalities, and the tool of intervention employed in the consociatonal negotiations of interest groups and in the participation of the people through direct democracy.

Federalism

As mentioned before, it is primarily through the institutions of federalism that Switzerland succeeded in accommodating its cultural and religious diversity. The country is a confederation of 23 cantons, which have a large measure of autonomy in making education, public safety, and taxation policy. According to this principle, the Swiss Parliament functions on two levels: the National Council (*Nationalrat*, which represents the people) and the State Council (*Ständerat*, which represents the cantons). New laws have to pass both chambers, but can be immediately vetoed by a popular referendum with 50,000 signatures.

The mechanisms of decision making in Switzerland are complex. The Swiss population does not elect members of the Federal Council directly, as it does at the cantonal level. That is the prerogative of Parliament, which elects the seven members of the Federal Council for four-year terms. In the Swiss political system, Parliament cannot vote confidence or no confidence on actions of the Federal Council, which gives the latter a certain amount of autonomy. However, this autonomy is restricted by the two instruments of Swiss direct democracy: the referendum and the popular initiative. The popular initiative gives citizens the right to seek a decision on an amendment they want to integrate into the Constitution. For such an initiative to be organized, the signatures of 100,000 voters must be collected within 18 months. Federal laws are subject to an optional referendum: in this case, a popular ballot is held if the signatures of 50,000 citizens are obtained. Signatures must be collected within 100 days of the publication of a decree. The referendum is similar to a veto. For such a plebiscite to pass, a majority of the popular vote and of the vote of the nine cantons is required. At the cantonal and municipal level, voters can also launch an initiative. Cantonal laws are subject to the optional referendum.

With regard to the admission and integration of migrants, federalism plays an important role in many domains, among them education, which is presented here as a paradigmatic case (religion or political rights could also have been used for this purpose). In Switzerland, the educational system is organized by the cantons, which, as we have seen, want immigrants to adopt cantonal language and culture. During the 1970s, cantonal education systems experienced difficulties in accommodating the different social (and cultural) situations of immigrants, and they could not guarantee equal educational opportunities (Schuh 1987). Problems of school segregation still persist at the curriculum level, even if the federal education authorities (*Schweizerische Erziehungsdirektorenkonferenz*, or EDK) regularly publish recommendations for better integration of immigrant children (Schweizerische Konferenz der kantonalen Erziehungsdirektoren 1972, 1976, 1982, 1985, 1991, 1993, 1995a, 1995b, 2003). Some cantons give more support to immigrant children and promote their integration in school by providing schools more resources and by introducing institutional changes, such as team teaching and an intercultural program that promotes the integration of children with migrant backgrounds (Truniger 2002b).

However, not all cantons implement such recommendations; in fact, several favor discriminatory practices. Differing cantonal responses roughly correspond to linguistic and political cleavages. In German-speaking cantons, one generally observes a tendency to set up specific institutions for immigrant children (the exception here is German-speaking urban cantons that have the tools to support their schools without enforcing segregation (Truniger 2002a). In contrast, French- and Italian-speaking cantons integrate all children into mainstream institutions.

Switzerland has a highly federalized institutional system characterized by vertical segmentation and horizontal fragmentation. This allows both the federal government and cantonal authorities a high degree of organizational and political autonomy, with special attention given to the cantons. As in the case of voting, the cantons can use their autonomy to experiment with various approaches in migrant-related political fields and to influence federal decision making. The cantonal *Ständerat* makes it necessary for federal authorities to secure the loyalty of the cantons and to make sure that strong cantonal political entrepreneurs do not upset the consensus. Thus, if the cantons hold fast to a change, the federal level has to adapt. However, because the general mood has become anti-immigrant, the example of the autonomous educational system makes it clear that cantons have enough space to maneuver and do not have to share a common approach to immigrant admission and integration.

Municipal Autonomy

Strong trade ties among cities and political fragmentation explain why Switzerland has a relatively solid urban network. Moreover, municipal autonomy is a key factor when it comes to citizenship and, paradoxically, nationhood. As already mentioned, there are three stages in the naturalization process, citizenship of the municipality, then citizenship in the canton, and finally citizenship in the nation.

There is much variety in naturalization at the local level, particularly between the German- and French-speaking cantons. While the French cantons have more formalized procedures, many German cantons hold to the romantic principle of adherence and political participation. The question of who is allowed to apply for citizenship can easily be turned into accusations of preferential treatment and prejudice. Newspaper stories have reported that, in several small towns in the German part of Switzerland, Eastern European or Asian origins have been used as negative markers in granting naturalization (Ehrenzeller and Good 2003; Leuthold and Aeberhard 2002). Therefore, even if the country was founded on the idea of political contract, naturalization is, to a large extent, based on local ethnicity.

Furthermore, since the decision by the Federal Supreme Court on July 9, 2003 (1P.228-2000), which declared unconstitutional public votes on naturalization in certain municipalities, a new debate has emerged on the role of judicial authority in naturalization matters. This is largely a debate between those who favor the rule of law and those who interpret the granting of access to citizenship as a political and sovereign right of the citizenry. The *Ständerat's* Political Institutions Committee argued in favor of the right of municipalities to hold votes on individual naturalization applications; nevertheless, it asked localities to provide a justification for refusing an applicant, even if the decision would have been taken by ballot. For this reason, the Court's action is an indicator of the tension between Supreme Court and conservative parts of the Parliament and between the opportunities and limits of the rule of law and of direct democracy.

Consociational and Direct Democracy

Consociational and direct democracy, two aspects of the Swiss political system, are more important for understanding integration *politics* than for understanding integration *policies*. However, as Hans Mahnig and Andreas Wimmer stated in a lucid article, they are responsible for the high politicization of migration in Switzerland and for the exclusion of migrants from political participation (Mahnig and Wimmer 2003).

Consociational democracy refers to the proportional representation of minorities (linguistic, political, and religious) in federal institutions and the search for compromise between political forces that goes beyond simple majorities (Linder 1998). All members of the government as well as members of the higher administration are chosen in proportion to their party affiliation (the "magic formula") and their linguistic and regional origins. Swiss politics is characterized by a permanent process of compromise building between these groups.

The *consultation procedure* is another important way to influence political decision making. This is the phase in the preparation of legislation when draft acts introduced by the Confederation are evaluated by cantons, political parties, associations, and sometimes other interested groups to ascertain their potential for acceptance and implementation. Persons who are not invited to take part in the consultation procedure can still state their views on a proposal. The views and possible objections of all stakeholders are evaluated for their potential power to veto a reform. The Federal Council then passes the main points of its proposal on to Parliament. Finally, the council debates the draft legal act in light of the outcome of the consultation.

Direct democracy gives social groups some opportunities to participate directly in the political process through the already mentioned popular initiative and referendum, which are operative at the federal as well as the local level. According to some observers, the instruments of direct democracy created the consociational system because all laws voted in Parliament can be submitted to a referendum; therefore, they need the support of large alliances within the political elite (Neidhart 1970). In the domain of immigrant policy, these two main instruments of Swiss direct democracy have provoked not only the politicization of immigration issues but also the exclusion of immigrants from political participation (Mahnig and Wimmer 2003).

First, because of its long decision-making process, a consociational democracy requires that a compromise be negotiated, which for immigration issues has led to long periods of indecision because the interests involved are too divergent to reach agreement easily. Second, the instruments of direct democracy have forced the political elite to negotiate on "overforeignization" with populist challengers. Immigration policies that had once permitted the various actors to come to agreement on the economic needs of the country became contested and controversial from the 1960s, when radical right-wing populist parties started to gain public support in claiming that Switzerland was becoming "overforeignized" by ever-increasing numbers of immigrants. Using the tools of direct democracy, these xenophobic movements succeeded in vetoing liberal government reforms and put their parties under pressure by launching eight popular initiatives and several referendums asking for a curb on foreigners. Although none of these initiatives passed, they still consistently influence Swiss migration policy and public opinion on immigration by urging the government to make admission more restrictive (Niederberger 2004).

Very recently, one political entrepreneur with a known anti-immigrant agenda successfully entered the federal government through a political campaign focused on the costs of immigration control, security, and restriction: this was the platform of the right-wing populist Swiss Peoples Party (SVP), which had won the biggest share of parliamentary votes in the 2003 general elections. The SVP's victory upset the traditional consociational system that since 1959 had seen the even distribution of power among the four leading political parties. Following his election, the leader of the SVP, Christoph Blocher, became Minister of Justice and Police in December 2003, which put him in charge of migration and asylum. Thus far, the government has approved several of the minister's proposals for dealing with illegal migration, undocumented workers, and asylum law abuses, as well unsatisfactory international cooperation on the issue of readmission of rejected asylum seekers.

Because of the direct character of Swiss democracy, the anti-immigrant political parties that successfully enter (cantonal) governments are in a strategic no-lose situation: through their agenda setting, they may influence parliamentary debate and veto any controversial reform if they do not achieve their goals. Direct democracy has been proven to have a strong impact on political rights: controversial questions can never be restricted to parliament alone. A "behind closed doors" strategy is impossible in Switzerland, however crucial it might be in extending political and social rights to migrants in other parts of Europe (Guiraudon 2000).

CONCLUDING REMARKS

For a long time—from World War II until the late 1990s—the economic needs of the labor market influenced Switzerland's immigrant admission policy without taking integration into account. Admissions during this time were based on a rotation model that fueled the economy with labor without necessarily introducing any integration provisions for the migrants who came to stay. This was because immigrants were not conceived as a potential part of the population. A utilitarian policy seemed to fit best with the need to keep the country free of foreign cultural influences, as was laid down in the alien's law of 1931—a law that reflected the xenophobic spirit of the 1920s.

Since the 1970s, immigrants' length of stay, changing attitudes, and changing expectations, as well as the evolving needs of the economy and the school system, have made a more inclusive Swiss migration policy inevitable. But the alliance between the government, regional economies, and supranational human rights interests (that labored for inclusion of foreign workers through legislative reforms) was continuously forced to deal with a radical, xenophobic movement that, while politically isolated, used the opportunity structures to leverage the government's decision making through a referendum. This type of policy referendum was generally favored by a minimal welfare state that, until the 1970s, excluded migrants from solidarity networks and thus exposed them to the social risks of returning home.

A paradigm shift occurred in the 1980s, after the oil crisis, when it became clear that many migrants were not returning to their home country and staying in Switzerland. The introduction of unemployment insurance and the inauguration of a larger welfare system also gave protection to labor migrants and introduced them to social citizenship. However, the 1980s were also when the asylum issue emerged as a metaphor for unwanted immigration. The government reacted to this new challenge with a two-tiered approach: first, a new severity on the asylum issue and enforcement of a policy that deterred illegitimate immigration; second, legislative reforms that favored the integration of wanted labor migrants.

The paradigm shift seems to have culminated in the new aliens and asylum law that was very recently passed. Both were always contested by radical right-wing challengers and thus had to go through the referendum process.

Federalism, municipal autonomy, and consociational and direct democracy offer a framework within which many actors and stakeholders attempt to influence policymaking. This is a form of multilevel governance that for a long time has prevented Switzerland from matching its immigration policy to European standards of inclusive social rights (and to its new economic needs). Still, in recent years Switzerland's guiding principles have been converging with those of its important European partners. The obvious points of similarity in immigration and migration policy between Switzerland and the EU since the signing of the Bilateral Agreement will no doubt become more numerous in the future. Still, the specter of "overforeignization" will probably prevent Switzerland (at least at the federal level) from adopting the liberal citizenship policy shared by its European partners. Switzerland's cultural inhibitions are too strong for it to open its symbolically highly valued citizenship institutions to "undeserving" immigrants. Who is to say, however, that in the evolution of human things latecomers will not one day become one-time European forerunners, especially in the volatile field of migration and citizenship?

NOTES

1. The cultural minority who speak different dialects of this Romance language consists of around 50,000 people who live in the canton of Graubünden in the eastern part of Switzerland.

2. Indeed, migration and integration policies are matters of cantonal sovereignty to a certain degree.

REFERENCES

Arlettaz, Gérald. 1985. "Démographie et identité nationale (1850–1914): La Suisse et 'La question des étrangers.'" *Etudes et Sources* 11: 83–174.

Blattner, Niklaus, and George Sheldon. 1989. "Foreign Labour, Growth and Productivity: The Case of Switzerland." In *European Factor Mobility: Trends and Consequences: Proceedings of the Conference of the Confederation of European Economic Associations, (. . .)*, edited by Ian Gordon and Anthony Philip Thirlwall, 148–65. Houndmills, UK: Macmillan.

Brubaker, Rogers. 1992.*Citizenship and Nationhood in France and Germany*. Cambridge, MA: Harvard University Press.

D'Amato, Gianni, and Brigitta Gerber, eds. 2005. *Herausforderung Integration: Städtische Migrationspolitik in der Schweiz und in Europa*. Zurich: Seismo.

Deutsch, Karl W. 1976. *Die Schweiz als ein paradigmatischer Fall politischer Integration*. Bern: Haupt.

Efionayi-Mäder, Denise. 2003. "Asylpolitik der Schweiz 1950–2000." *Asyl* 18 (3): 3–9.

Efionayi-Mäder, Denise, Sandra Lavenex, Martin Niederberger, Philippe Wanner, and Nicole Wichmann. 2003. "Switzerland." In *EU and US Approaches to the Management of Immigration: Comparative Perspectives*, edited by Jan Niessen and Yongmi Schibel, 491–519. Brussels: Migration Policy Group.

Efionayi-Mäder, Denise, Josef Martin Niederberger, and Philippe Wanner. 2005. "Switzerland Faces Common European Challenges." *Migration Information Source*. New York: Migration Policy Institute.

Ehrenzeller, Bernhard, and Paul-Lukas Good. 2003. *Rechtsgutachten zu Handen des Gemeinderates von Emmen betreffend das Einbürgerungsverfahren in der Gemeinde Emmen*. [St. Gallen?]: [s.n.].

Garrido, Angela. 1990. "Les années vingt et la première initiative xénophobe en Suisse." In *Racisme et xénophobies: Colloque à l'Université de Lausanne, 24–25 novembre 1988*, edited by Hans Ulrich Jost, 37–45. Lausanne: Université de Lausanne.

Guiraudon, Virginie. 2000. *Les politiques d'immigration en Europe: Allemagne, France, Pays-Bas*. Paris: Harmattan.

Hollifield, James F. 1992. *Immigrants, Markets, and States: The Political Economy of Postwar Europe*. Cambridge, MA: Harvard University Press.

Holmes, Madelyn. 1988. *Forgotten Migrants: Foreign Workers in Switzerland before World War I*. Rutherford, NJ: Fairleigh Dickinson University Press.

Ireland, Patrick. 1994. *The Policy Challenge of Ethnic Diversity: Immigrant Politics in France and Switzerland*. Cambridge, MA: Harvard University Press.

Jacobson, David. 1996. *Rights across Borders: Immigration and the Decline of Citizenship*. Baltimore: Johns Hopkins University Press.

Katzenstein, Peter J. 1987. *Corporatism and Change: Austria, Switzerland and the Politics of Industry*. Ithaca, NY: Cornell University Press.

Kaya, Bülent. 2005. "Switzerland." In *Current Immigration Debates in Europe: A Publication of the European Migration Dialogue*, edited by Jan Niessen, Yongmi Schibel, and Cressida Thompson, 383–98. Brussels: Migration Policy Group.

Kohler, Georg. 1994. "Demokratie, Integration, Gemeinschaft: Thesen im Vorfeld einer Einwanderungsgesetzdiskussion." In *Migration: Und wo bleibt das Ethische?* 17–34. Zurich: Schweizerischer Arbeitskreis für ethische Forschung.

Leuthold, Ruedi, and Christian Aeberhard. 2002. "Der Fall Emmen." *Das Magazin* 20: 18–31.

Linder, Wolf. 1998. *Swiss Democracy: Possible Solutions to Conflict in Multicultural Societies*. Houndmills, UK: Macmillan.

Mahnig, Hans. 1996. "Das migrationspolitische Feld der Schweiz: Eine politikwissenschaftliche Analyse der Vernehmlassung zum Arbenzbericht. Neuchâtel: Forum Suisse pour l'étude des migrations.

Mahnig, Hans, and Etienne Piguet. 2003. "La politique suisse d'immigration de 1948 à 1998: Évolution et effets." In *Les migrations et la Suisse: Résultats du Programme national de recherche "Migrations et relations interculturelles,"* edited by Hans-Rudolf Wicker, Rosita Fibbi, and Werner Haug, 63–103. Zurich: Seismo.

Mahnig, Hans, and Andreas Wimmer. 2003. "Integration without Immigrant Policy: The Case of Switzerland." In *The Integration of Immigrants in European Societies: National Differences and Trends of Convergence*, edited by Friedrich Heckmann and Dominique Schnapper, 135–64. Stuttgart: Lucius & Lucius.

Neidhart, Leonhard. 1970. *Plebiszit und pluralitäre Demokratie: Eine Analyse der Funktion des schweizerischen Gesetzesreferendums*. Bern: Francke.

Niederberger, Josef Martin. 2004. *Ausgrenzen, Assimilieren, Integrieren: Die Entwicklung einer schweizerischen Integrationspolitik*. Zurich: Seismo.

Parini, Lorena, and Matteo Gianni. 1997. "La tension entre précarité et intégration: Politique à l'égard des migrants en Suisse." In *A paraître dans: Politiques publiques et droit / Françoise Lorcerie Paris: Ed. LGDJ, 1997/98 (Droit et société)*.

———. 2005. "Enjeux et modifications de la politique d'asile en Suisse de 1956 à nos jours." In *Histoire de la politique de migration, d'asile et d'intégration en Suisse depuis 1948*, edited by Hans Mahnig, 189–252. Zurich: Seismo.

Romano, Gaetano. 1996. "Zeit der Krise—Krise der Zeit: Identität, Überfremdung und verschlüsselte Zeitstrukturen." In *Die neue Schweiz? Eine Gesellschaft zwischen Integration und Polarisierung (1910–1930)*, edited by Andreas Ernst and Erich Wigger, 41–77. Zurich: Chronos.

Schnapper, Dominique. 1997. "Citoyenneté et reconnaissance des hommes et des cultures." In *Dire les autres: Réflexions et pratiques ethnologiques: Textes offerts à Pierre Centlivres*, edited by Jacques Hainard and Roland Kaehr, 139–48. Lausanne: Payot.

Schuh, Sibilla. 1987. "Luciano und die Höhle der Elefanten—Selektionsdruck im Spannungsfeld zwischen zwei Welten." In *Fremde Heimat: Soziokulturelle und sprachliche Probleme von Fremdarbeiterkindern*, edited by Armin Gretler, Ruth Gurny, Anne-Nelly Perret-Clermont, and Edo Poglia, 223–39. Cousset: Delval.

Schweizerische Konferenz der kantonalen Erziehungsdirektoren. 1972. *Grundsätze zur Schulung der Gastarbeiterkinder, vom 2. November 1972*. Bern: Schweizerische Konferenz der kantonalen Erziehungsdirektoren.

———. 1976. *Grundsätze zur Schulung der Gastarbeiterkinder: Ergänzung vom 14. Mai 1976*. Bern: Schweizerische Konferenz der kantonalen Erziehungsdirektoren.

———. 1982. *Ausländerkinder in unseren Schulen: Nach wie vor ein Problem?* Geneva: Sekretariat EDK.

———. 1985. *Empfehlungen zur Schulung der fremdsprachigen Kinder, vom 24. Oktober 1985*. Bern: Schweizerische Konferenz der kantonalen Erziehungsdirektoren.

———. 1991. *Empfehlungen zur Schulung der fremdsprachigen Kinder, vom 24./25. Oktober 1991*. Bern: Schweizerische Konferenz der kantonalen Erziehungsdirektoren.

———. 1993. *Interkulturelle Pädagogik in der Schweiz: Sonderfall oder Schulalltag?: Zusammenstellung der Tagungsbeiträge: EDK-Convegno, Emmetten, 1992*. Bern: Schweizerische Konferenz der kantonalen Erziehungsdirektoren.

———. 1995a. *Empfehlungen und Beschlüsse*. Bern: Schweizerische Konferenz der kantonalen Erziehungsdirektoren.

———. 1995b. *Erklärung zur Förderung des zweisprachigen Unterrichts in der Schweiz, vom 2. März 1995*. Bern: Schweizerische Konferenz der kantonalen Erziehungsdirektoren.

———. 2003. *Aktionsplan "PISA 2000"—Folgemassnahmen*. Bern: Schweizerische Konferenz der kantonalen Erziehungsdirektoren.

Sheldon, George. 1998. *The Effect of Foreign Labor on Relative Wages and Growth in Switzerland*. [Basel?]: Labor Market and Industrial Organization Research Unit (FAI).

Soysal, Yasemin N. *Limits of Citizenship*: Migrants and Postnational Membership in Europe. Chicago: University of Chicago Press.

Tanner, Jakob. 1998. "Nationalmythos, Überfremdungsängste und Minderheitenpolitik in der Schweiz." In *Blickwechsel: Die multikulturelle Schweiz an der Schwelle zum 21. Jahrhundert*, edited by Simone Prodolliet, 83–94. Lucerne: Caritas-Verlag.

Truniger, Markus. 2002a. *Qualität in multikulturellen Schulen, QUIMS: Schlussbericht der Projektleitung über die zweite Phase (1999 bis 2001)*. [S.l.]: [s.n.].

———. 2002b. *Schulung der fremdprachigen Kinder und interkulturelle Pädagogik: Überprüfung der Umsetzung der Empfehlungen (Schuljahre 1999/2000 und 2000/01): Bericht zuhanden des Bildungsrats*. [Zurich?]: [s.n.].

Wanner, Philippe, and Gianni D'Amato. 2003. *Naturalisation en Suisse: Le rôle des changements législatifs sur la demande de naturalisation: Rapport*. Zurich: Avenir Suisse.

COMMENTARY

Switzerland's Troublesome Success

Dietrich Thränhardt

Switzerland is the most successful immigration country in Europe. It does what other countries aspire to do: recruit large numbers of qualified immigrants (e.g., doctors, businesspeople, and STEM specialists), staff the headquarters of its multinational companies, and attract new holdings and other enterprises with its low taxes and excellent business climate. From 2003 to 2009, 269 international companies moved their headquarters to Switzerland; this represents 27 percent of all international assets managed there. Of the world's billionaires, 10 percent live in Switzerland (*Avenir Suisse* 2011: 7–10). 86 percent of Switzerland's foreigners are Europeans—two-thirds from EU or EFTA countries, and 56 percent have an academic diploma (*Avenir Suisse* 2011: 16).

Even though Switzerland is a small country, immigration makes all types of labor available. Immigrants have a reputation for working hard, and many speak one of the official languages and come from a neighboring country. Even refugee groups from countries far away, such as Tamils from Sri Lanka, have become well integrated and accepted because they are viewed as embodying the Swiss value of hard work (Moret, Efionayi-Mäder, and Stants 2007).

Immigrants balance the Swiss birth deficit, as the country reproduces only two-thirds of its population. Because of full employment and a functioning vocational-training system, the second generation ("Secondos" and "Secondas") is well integrated into the economy. Immigrants are also important contributors to the Swiss social security systems, paying much more than they extract. From the commencement of the free migration system in the EU from 2007 to 2010, Switzerland has had a net immigration of 330,000 people, or 4 percent of its population (Table 10.1).

In a recent interview with the Zurich city president, the first question was why "the city is so good" (*NZZ Online* 2011). On the day of the interview, at a reception the city president told 700 elderly immigrants from Italy and Spain: "We eat better, we dress better, spend more time outside, we are more creative and have learnt to enjoy parties. Zürich has become a livelier city since you have come here" (Hotz 2011; my translation).

Yet Switzerland is also a forerunner in creative xenophobic campaigns. It gained a worldwide reputation for its minaret initiative, which violated basic liberal principles of religious

TABLE 10.1

Foreign resident population by nationality at year end (in thousands)

	2008	2009	2010	2011	2012
Total	1,669.7	1,714.0	1,766.3	1,816.0	1,870.0
EU-27/EFTA countries	1,037.1	1,077.6	1,101.5	1,145.0	1,191.9
Germany	234.6	251.9	263.3	275.3	284.2
France	87.4	92.5	95.6	99.9	104.0
Italy	291.6	290.6	287.1	288.0	291.8
Austria	35.7	36.7	37.0	37.9	38.8
Portugal	196.8	206.0	212.6	223.7	237.9
Spain	65.2	65.0	64.1	65.8	69.4
Other European	406.8	402.2	403.4	400.8	399.8
Serbia and Montenegro	184.4	181.3	—	—	—
Serbia	—	—	121.9	109.3	98.7
Turkey	72.2	71.6	71.8	71.4	70.8
Africa	54.8	57.7	71.5	74.8	78.2
America	69.8	72.7	74.5	76.6	77.7
Asia	96.9	99.3	110.5	113.6	117.2
Australia/Oceania	3.8	4.0	4.0	4.1	4.1
Stateless, unknown nationality (or not stated)	0.5	0.6	0.8	1.1	6.0

SOURCE: ESPOP, Annual Population Statistics.

freedom and equality. Working for the Swiss People's Party (SVP), a German immigrant produced one emotional poster after the other with openly racist messages—black hands grabbing the cherished Swiss passports (very few Africans live in Switzerland), criminal immigrants, and minarets identified with missiles. In 2011, a SVP poster asked whether Germans are a "race" different from the Swiss.

Such campaigns are often successful in plebiscites, the exception being a referendum on the reintroduction of controls at borders with EU member states. Different from the traditional Swiss style of low-key local and personal campaigning, the SVP's campaigns are extremely well funded and organized in an aggressive commercial style. Also different from the Swiss tradition of factual discussion and serious argument, they are extremely emotional, comparable to campaigns in California. The SVP is often surprising and entertaining. The racist posters were followed by the appearance of a black-skinned party member at a party conference, telling his listeners that he felt "terribly angry [literally, I am so angry that I became black] because of so many naturalizations with unpronounceable names in my home community" (*NZZ* 2011).

Until the 1990s, such tactics kept the SVP a small middle-class group representing farmers and craftsmen. Now it is the largest Swiss party, carrying 27 percent of the vote in 2011. Xenophobia of all sorts, anti-EU rhetoric, populist sentiment against "the Left and the nice," and Swiss nationalism are its issues. In an unregulated campaign finance system, the SVP spends more than do all of its competitors together—15 against 7.1 million CHF combined for the other three main parties (Schweizer Fernsehen 2010). Big business does not spend much in campaigns, and it declined to finance one against the extradition initiative in 2010 because it did not seem relevant economically (Gernet 2011: 24). This contrasts with the spending of Swiss companies in American campaigns.

Unlike populist leaders in countries like Holland, Austria, France, and Italy, SVP leader Christoph Blocher is a patriarchal self-made multimillionaire who carries an aura of traditional Swiss solidity and old-fashioned values (for a comparison with populism in consociational countries, see Thränhardt 2008). In the spring of 2011, the immigration issue was number two on the political agenda, right behind Fukushima-related environmental problems. Even the quality paper, *Neue Zürcher Zeitung*, published an emotional article about the overcrowding of Switzerland, with stereotypes of crowded trains, wealthy immigrants pushing Swiss people out from city centers, unqualified immigrants lacking education, and too much family immigration (Mijuk and Furger 2011). By 2011, immigration numbers had fallen, but the national elections were coming.

Switzerland has an old and intense history of immigration and emigration. In past centuries, emigration in many cases had a professional character. Even today, the Swiss Guard protects the pope, and "Schweizer" is still a label for a milk and cheese specialist (http://de.wikipedia.org/wiki/Schweizer_%28Beruf%29) in the German language. *Die fünfte Schweiz, la Cinquième Suisse*, or "fifth Switzerland" is a common term for Swiss citizens in foreign countries and their wish to participate in decision making (Schönenberger et al. 2010). Even today, more Swiss citizens emigrate than immigrate because of intensifying relations with the outside world, the worldwide expansion of Swiss companies, and a feeling of narrowness in a small and well-regulated country. In 2009, 26,800 Swiss citizens left the country, and 22,400 came back (Carrel 2011). Switzerland's development as a competitive economy is closely related to immigrants like the German Heinrich/Henri Nestlé, the founders of Brown, Boveri & Co., or the thirty liberal German professors who were invited to found the University of Zürich in 1830.

Whereas Switzerland was on the same developmental level as its neighbors until 1914, with open migration in and out, this changed after 1914. Despite the European catastrophes of World War I and World War II, Switzerland remained a rich island in a destroyed continent. Thus, it became a safe haven for some of Europe's riches and a limited number of political refugees, and a comfortable place for business. Against the aggressive posturing of the totalitarian powers in Germany and Italy, Switzerland highlighted its traditions, proclaiming "geistige Landesverteidigung" (mental defense). In that time, a strong myth of specialness became prominent (*Sonderfall Schweiz*), contrasting Switzerland with its neighbors and consequently immigrants. It also began to cultivate its image as a peaceful country and the seat of many international institutions, from the International Red Cross to the International Soccer Federation. In contrast to Sweden, it was able to uphold its economic advantage and is still the country with the highest per capita income in Europe.

Whereas the borders were open until World War I, more and more controls, fences, and walls were introduced to protect the wealthy island in a devastated Europe after 1945. Swiss immigration policy reacted with a system of rotational labor recruitment, first from Italy and later from other Southern European countries, which made settlement difficult. *Fremdarbeiter* (strange workers), as they were called (even in the title of a leading sociological book by Hans-Joachim Hoffmann-Nowotny; see Hoffmann-Nowotny 1973), could stay just as long as they were working or if they were there for seasonal work; and there were regional and other restrictions as well. Only after long years could they bring their families.

It took time, competition for workers with less restrictive countries like Germany, pressure from the Italian government, and criticism from civil society to change the system. In the end, Switzerland opened up to the system of free movement in the European Community, including the new member countries from May 1, 2011, on and Romania and Bulgaria later. Swiss author Max Frisch condenses the situation of the 1960s into the sentence: "Wir riefen Arbeitskräfte, und es kamen Menschen" (We called for workforce, and human beings came).

The uneasiness in the Swiss public today can be explained in the following ways:

- Whereas traditionally immigration was strictly controlled and limited to working people with limited rights, now EU citizens are free to move in and out, and they have full rights, including unemployment benefits if they have paid contributions. Again and again, taking advantage of unemployment benefits is criticized because the public is not used to it.

- Since EU citizens are free to look for a job in Switzerland, the government can no longer tell the public that it restricts immigration. Numerical limits have always been symbolically important. In the past, two initiatives for restriction were defeated in plebiscites, one for a 10 percent limit in 1970 and another for an 18 percent limit in 2000. The SVP proposed a new one in 2011. Switzerland now has a quota for citizens from Estonia, Latvia, Lithuania, Poland, Slovakia, Slovenia, the Czech Republic, and Hungary (as of May 2012). The caps were extended in 2013 to 17 other European countries (the rest of the EU; http://www.bbc.co.uk/news/world-europe-22285886).

- Switzerland's political system produces rational discourse and inter-party cooperation over time, interrupted by occasional explosive turmoil in referenda. The system has been characterized as people's sovereignty (in contrast to constitutional sovereignty in the United States and Germany and parliamentary sovereignty in Britain; Abromeit 1995). Thus, there are few limitations on the will of the people and a strong aversion to outside interference (e.g., from European or international courts). The referendum against minarets has a historical precedent (the hundred-year ban on Jesuits from 1874 to1973) as defending liberal democracy. As in the United States, there is a powerful myth of the common people defending themselves against outside powers. Every Swiss child learns about the William Tell story in school—a father defending his son and his country against a cruel and repressive imperial bailiff, or *Landvogt*. This is the dominant national narrative, and the public is upset when historians prove it to be a myth.

- Today's immigrants are not just doing the unwanted jobs but are present everywhere, including in prominent positions, For example, many Germans hold university chairs, which is reminiscent of the pre-1914 situation, and standard German is once again spoken in public places, and some circles react with strong anti-German and anti-immigrant sentiment and try to reaffirm the specialness of Switzerland (Helbling 2011). Globalization and nativism sometimes contrast in a rather comical way. One example is the introduction of early English instruction for all children from the second grade on in Canton Zürich, before they learn French in the fifth grade. This was followed by a successful referendum in May 2011 prohibiting teachers from speaking standard German in kindergartens and instead sticking to the local dialect. This is quite complicated since many German kindergarten teachers do not speak the dialect and so standard German will be lost between the dialect and English. Still, the initiative demonstrates the desperate wish to keep Swiss identity.

• Despite its wealth, stability, and growth rates, even Switzerland had to undergo some shocks in the last years, among them various American rulings against Swiss banks and insurance companies and the collapse of Swissair, the national airline.

• Traditionally, Switzerland had a low naturalization rate. This has changed since the acceptance of multiple citizenship. At the same time, the Swiss Federal Court has challenged the traditional sovereign right of Swiss municipalities to decide on the naturalization of immigrants, in some smaller places through referenda or in the public municipal assembly. This challenge is well founded because of factual discrimination against certain nationalities, but it goes against the traditional Swiss idea of the people's sovereignty and is a cause of resentment. Such a conflict is an interesting illustration of the problems with Communitarian philosophy.

REFERENCES

Abromeit, Heidrun. 1995. "Volkssouveränität, Parlamentssouveränität, Verfassungssouveränität: Drei Realmodelle der Legitimation staatlichen Handelns." *Politische Vierteljahresschrift* 36: 49–66.

Avenir Suisse. 2011. "Magnet Schweiz: Die Schweiz Im Internationalen Standortwettbewerb."

Carrel, Noemi. 2011. "Niemand weiss genau, wer die Schweiz verlässt." *Terra Cognita* 18 (Spring): 26–30.

Gernet, Hilmar. 2011. *(Un-)heimliches Geld: Parteienfinanzierung in der Schweiz*. Zurich: NZZ.

Helbling, Marc. 2011. *Why Swiss-Germans Dislike Germans: On Negative Attitudes towards a Culturally and Socially Similar Group*. Berlin: WZB.

Hoffmann-Nowotny, Hans-Joachim. 1973. *Soziologie des Fremdarbeiterproblems: Eine theoretische und empirische Analyse am Beispiel der Schweiz*. Stuttgart: Enke.

Hotz, Stefan. 2011. "'Siamo tutti zurighesi': Zürich dankt den italienischen und spanischen Einwanderern der ersten Stunde." *NZZ Online*, May 23.

Mijuk, Gordana, and Michael Furger. 2011. "Es wird eng: Bald leben zwei Millionen Ausländer in der Schweiz." *NZZ Online*, April 18.

Moret, Joelle, Denise Efionayi-Mäder, and Fabienne Stants. 2007. *Die srilankische Diaspora in der Schweiz*. Bern: Bundesamt für Migration.

NZZ (Neue Zürcher Zeitung). 2011. "Die SVP nimmt die Personenfreizügigkeit ins Visier: Delegierte lancieren Volksinitiative zur Einführung von Zuwanderungs-Kontingenten." May 28.

NZZ Online. 2011. "'Zürich kann durchaus noch wachsen': Stadtpräsidentin Corine Mauch (SP) erklärt, was das Wachstum für Zürich bedeutet." May 22.

Schönenberger, Silvia, et al. 2010. *Die Fünfte Schweiz: Auswanderung und Auslandschweizergemeinschaft.* Neuchâtel: Swiss Forum for Migration and Population Studies.

Schweizer Fernsehen. 2010. *Wahlkampfkässeli sind unterschiedlich prall gefüllt. 27 December.* http://www.tagesschau.sf.tv/Nachrichten/Archiv/2010/12/27/Schweiz/.

Thränhardt, Dietrich. 2008. "Xenophobic Populism and the Crisis of Consociational Democracy: Austria, Switzerland and the Netherlands." In *Migratierecht en Rechtssociologie / Migration Law and Sociology of Law: Liber Amicorum C. A. Groenendijk,* edited by Anita Böcker et al., 281–94. Nijmegen: Centrum voor Migratierecht.

"'Zürich kann durchaus noch wachsen': Stadtpräsidentin Corine Mauch (SP) erklärt, was das Wachstum für Zürich bedeutet." 2011. *NZZ Online,* May 22.

IV

LATECOMERS TO IMMIGRATION

11

ITALY

Political Parties and Italian Policy, 1990–2009

Ted Perlmutter

Italy is one of the European countries where immigration has most recently become an issue. It was not until 1990, when the Legge Martelli (law n. 39/90), the first effort at comprehensive immigration legislation, was passed. In the intervening twenty years, there have been dramatic changes in Italian immigration, legislation and the party system. The analytic elements this chapter emphasizes include the effects of political parties on immigration policy regarding the contested issues of planned entry, amnesties, and enforcement policies, particularly those related to expulsions.[1] On planned entry and enforcement in particular, the original Martelli legislation was underdeveloped—and dealing with the lacuna in policy would be the challenge for subsequent legislation. The Martelli law's efforts at regularization were partially successful, but did not encourage as many people to apply as had been hoped for.

The critical components of the recent Italian immigrant experience are these:

- A continued acceleration in the level of immigration and an ongoing demographic and labor market need for high levels of immigration.

- A difficulty in elaborating and developing the ideas in the Martelli legislation, particularly those regarding planned labor supply, which has meant a frequent recourse to forms of regularization (legalization) of unauthorized immigrants already living in Italy.

- A new political party system, inaugurated in 1994, has produced alternating governments of the Left and the Right, but has lacked stability and produced fragmented alliances, particularly on the Right, that have struggled to create coherent and effective policy.

- The contested efforts to produce an effective removal policy and to develop temporary protection centers to house those to be deported.

This chapter provides first a description of the Italian labor market and the demographics of immigration; then a description of the oscillations in the planning process as they regard the issues of planned inflows, regularization, and expulsions that emphasize the ways in which political parties have shaped these policy proposals and outcomes; and finally reflections on the effects of the party system on policy and possible innovative ways of handling labor market planning, given the constraints of the party system.

DEMOGRAPHY / LABOR MARKET

The most striking characteristics of Italian economic development are the differences between north and south and the large underground or shadow economy. Since the founding of the country in 1861, there has also been a profound difference between an industrial north and an agricultural south. The resulting "southern question" has preoccupied economic planners in Italy ever since.

Indeed, Italy was the only country in Europe that industrialized during the 1960s and 1970s, drawing on its own internal labor reserves. The factories of the industrial triangle of the North—Turin, Milan, and Genoa—drew on rural workers, first in the northeast of the country and then later on, and to much greater effect, workers from the South. Italy continues to have the largest regional difference in income in the European Union (EU).

The other striking characteristic of the Italian economy is the large underground or unregulated sector, which encompasses about 13 percent of the workforce. It is also estimated that about 18 percent of Italian income escapes taxation. This underground economy predates the rise of unauthorized migration and has been widely condoned by the Italian polity. It facilitates unauthorized migration by providing accessible employment opportunities for workers lacking documentation.[2]

Unauthorized migration has permeated all of the low-skill sectors of the Italian economy, including manufacturing. However, it is particularly noticeable in "domestic services, agriculture, cleaning services, social and personal services, retail and wholesale trade, hotels and catering, construction" (Reyneri 2007: 3–4).

Another critical determinant is Italy's demography. It has one of the lowest birth rates in Europe—at present an average of 1.5 children per mother—well below the 2.1-children replacement level but well above its nadir of 1.14 children in 1995. Castiglioni and Dalla Zuanna (2009: 25) illustrate the problem quite succinctly. They point out that while the native population declined by 700,000 between 1999 and 2006, overall population for those eight years show a growth rate of 2.1 million; the difference is immigrants and their children.

The authors estimate that, for 2006, there were 300,000 new immigrants to Italy, both legal and illegal, along with 50,000 children whose parents were both immigrants. They also estimate that to keep the working-age population (those ages 20 to 59) constant in Italy for the twenty-year period between 2007 and 2026, a similar level of migration—around 300,000 per year—will be required.[3]

The most striking aspect of Italian migration is its changing velocity. Since the early 1990s, the pace of immigration has increased four-fold. The average yearly increase rose from 50,000 to 70,000 in the early 1990s, to 156,000 in the late 1990s, reaching 236,000 for the first half of the last decade (Istat 2007).

The recent effects of this acceleration can be seen in Figure 11.1 (Zincone 2009).

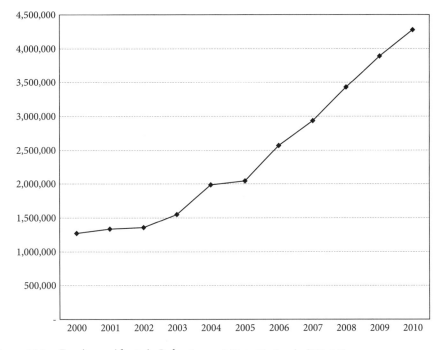

Figure 11.1   Foreign residents in Italy. *Source:* Istituto Nazionale di Statistica.

T A B L E 11.1
Immigrants to Italy by major nationalities

Country of origin	Regularized immigrants (1986–2002)	Foreign population (January 1, 2007)
Morocco	181,311	343,288
Romania	168,726	342,200
Albania	118,251	375,947
Ukraine	102,140	120,070
China	77,649	144,855
Philippines	59,592	101,377
Senegal	56,865	59,857
Tunisia	55,034	88,932
Ecuador	41,571	68,880

S O U R C E : Finotelli (2007).

There is a wide range of countries from which Italian immigrants arrive, with countries from Africa, Southeastern and Central Europe, Asia, and Latin America in the top ten (see Table 11.1). It is also evident that, for most of these countries, at least 50 percent and in some cases substantially larger percentages first came to the country without authorization and were only later regularized.

In the initial stages of immigration into Italy, there was a remarkable breadth to the number of sending countries. The numbers are becoming more concentrated in terms of individual countries, a trend that the Interior Ministry (2007) sees as indicative of greater chain migration (see Table 11.2).

TABLE 11.2
*Top 10 nationalities' share of total
immigration*

Year	Percentage
1970	13
1980	19
1990	40
2000	50
2005	57

SOURCE: Ministero dell'Interno (2007).

There has recently been a change in the areas of migration, with immigrants from South-eastern Europe and particularly the countries into which the EU has recently expanded assuming a greater presence at the expense of Africa (Cvajner and Sciortino 2009).[4]

IMMIGRATION LEGISLATION REGIMES

By exploring the oscillations in policy between Left and Right regimes, and by noting the internal power struggles over policymaking, it is possible to better understanding both the coherence of Italian immigration policy and the role that political parties play in its construction. By using the original Martelli legislation as the starting point, we get a sense of both the original cultural matrix and the challenges that it left behind.

Legge Martelli (the Five-Party Coalition)

By the late 1980s, the need for new immigration legislation was clear to all parties concerned with the issue. Since at least the late 1970s, Italy had been a country of net immigration. The immigrant population, documented and undocumented, was estimated at between 750,000 and 1,250,000, approximately 2 percent of Italy's population as a whole. Immigrants entering Italy in the late 1980s were faced with a regulatory system that had only recently been amended and that offered partial and inadequate coverage.

Before 1986, when law n. 943/1986 was passed, there was no substantial body of law covering immigration, which left the rules governing entry to the fascist decrees of June 18, 1931, and May 6, 1940. The 1986 legislation regulated the entry of migrants seeking work and provided regularization for those living in Italy who could prove they had a job. The regularization provisions proved to be less than successful. Despite three successive decrees extending the deadline until September 30, 1988, a disappointing percentage of immigrants legalized their status. The legislation also suffered from a limitation in its coverage, one that reflected a lack of understanding of the immigrant labor market at the time, since it did not apply to the self-employed, a category that encompassed a substantial component of Italian immigrants at that time.

As political actors became aware of the limited coverage and efficacy of the 1986 law and the costs of not having comprehensive legislation, recognition of the need for a new law grew. In addition, there was pressure from the European Commission to bring Italian immigration and refugee provisions into accord with the Schengen Agreement.

Immigration Politics in the First Republic

In what has come to be known as the First Republic, the Italian party system was character-ized by a high degree of political fragmentation. In the 1980s and early 1990s, when the first immigration legislation was passed, Italy was governed by five-party (*pentapartito*) coali-tions dominated by the Christian Democrats (DC), a highly factionalized mass party with a substantial working-class constituency in addition to its traditional Catholic base.

Of the four minor parties in the alliance, the Republican Party (PRI) and particularly the Socialist Party (PSI) were the most visible and powerful. The PSI and the PRI took the most outspoken stands in the immigration debates. They positioned themselves to the left of the DC, occupied similar electoral terrain, and sought to mobilize similar constituencies among newly emergent professional and managerial classes. Competition made for tense and combative relations between these members of the government (Pridham 1988: 168, 327). The system of governing coalitions was premised on the exclusion of the Communist Party, even though it represented a substantial part of the nation's working class and re-ceived between one-quarter and one-third of the vote. This pattern of nonalternation made for fragile, litigious governments.

The small parties clearly staked out more decisive positions than the mass parties—the Christian Democrats and the Communists. The latter supported moderately open immi-gration policies but primarily in closed forums. Even though they provided crucial support for the Martelli legislation in parliament, they were rarely heard from during the critical months of public discussion.

Claudio Martelli, a Socialist leader who was the vice president of the Council of Min-isters, proposed new open immigration legislation. Within the government, his proposals met with widespread although not unanimous support. Martelli sought out the support of the Left, including the unions and the Catholic voluntary sector, and made clear to the public that he was doing so. The task was difficult since these actors initially opposed practi-cally all regulation or restriction. In opening to the Left, he dismissed the concerns of con-servatives within his own government who were much more concerned with the Schengen Agreement and the need for restrictionist policies. The original intention was to pass a comprehensive legislative package regulating health services and access to high schools and universities. However, after bitter internal battles in late December, the governing coalition decided on a narrowly focused emergency decree (*decreto-legge*). The most disputed clauses concerned regularization for all foreigners who could demonstrate their presence before a certain date, and a procedure to plan annually the flow of immigrants who could enter the country.

The PRI strongly opposed this decree, declaring that it was "offended" by the lack of "collegiality" in the way the government overruled the party's objections. The PRI's rancor-ous protests provoked deep rifts in the governing coalition, with frequent demands that the PRI either support the government's position or go into opposition. The Socialists charged that the Republican Party was fishing for votes to its right. Even during the earliest policy debates, the accusations were harsh and direct. Claudio Martelli asserted that "in its desire to compete with the Lega Nord and the MSI [the neo-fascist party], the PRI is offering a political vehicle for the insidious racism that is spreading throughout Italy, as it is throughout European civilization." Martelli added that the PRI's behavior "resembled the sorcerer's apprentice, who speculated on the real problems—the enormous difficulties that accompanied the process of integration, on the frustrations, moods, and diffuse resentments toward the new arrivals, foreigners and blacks" (*Le Sole/24 Ore*, February 13, 1989).

Denying the charge of racism, the PRI claimed it was the ill-thought-out policy that had driven them to opposition. The party employed its traditional language of critiquing the laxity of the government and the need for greater rigor in restricting immigration. More surprising than its obstructionist legislative tactics was the PRI's willingness to use its opposition to the legislation as an issue in the upcoming administrative elections. The conflict between the PSI and the PRI, with the other parties standing aside or excluded by media bias, defined the debate over the Martelli legislation. The nonmainstream parties played no role in the public debates. This is particularly striking in the case of the far-right MSI, whose objections to the legislation were even more fundamental and whose obstructionist tactics even more unforgiving than the PRI's.

By all accounts, there was substantial gap between the law's intention and its accomplishments in three critical areas. One, the planned inflows (*programmazioni dei flussi*) did not achieve the desired goals. The bureaucratic challenges to hiring through this channel were so great as to discourage employers from using them. In addition, the numbers allowed were too few, never based on a realistic assessment of the Italian labor market, and rarely produced in a timely manner. Two, the regularization provisions legalized 235,000, but this was far less than the estimated numbers of those illegally in Italy at the time. Three, the expulsion procedures were deeply problematic. As described by Finotelli and Sciortino:

> Act 39/90 helped however to strengthen the control apparatus. . . . The number of expulsions started slowly to increase though enforced expulsions remained a small percentage of the overall expulsion orders. The difficulty to enforce them was partly due to the absence of detention centers for irregular immigrants who had to be expelled. Police forces, moreover, often did not have the administrative resources needed to carry out successfully the implementation of expulsion orders. In addition, the expulsion procedure was too long and bureaucratic, because expulsions could not be enforced without the *nihil obstat* of the competent judge. (2009: 13)

The Political Interim: 1991–1995

If during the next five years, little was done to transform the legislative landscape; it was not due to a lack of pressing items on the political agenda. Indeed, at the time, it seemed as though it would be a propitious period for immigration legislation, particularly of a restrictive nature. From 1991 to 1995, overall Italian employment figures dropped considerably (Reyneri 2004: 73) and unemployment rose from 8.6 percent in 1991 to 11.2 percent in 1995—representing almost the highest levels of unemployment since World War II. There was also the rise of the Lega Nord, a xenophobic party that often played on anti-immigrant themes, although it opted not to push on immigration issues during this period.

The Immigration Policy Debates, 1992–1993

Absent a strong xenophobic mobilization, the policy debates were framed by the conflicts between the left and the center, and the issue was contested in parliament, largely outside the scope of public debate. The lacunae in the 1990 Martelli legislation and the problems with its enforcement would provide the terrain for subsequent legislative conflicts. Although the legislation had provided for broad regularization, many immigrants could not or would not legalize their status. The accompanying legislation originally envisioned as necessary to complete the process, particularly to regulate seasonal labor, never passed. A further gap in the legislation was the difficulty of deporting those in the country illegally, and consequently, there remained a large number of undocumented foreigners, primarily in the South, whom Italy could neither legalize *nor* expel.

As the political class came under greater assault, the two governments of the eleventh legislature became increasingly technical, and the direct control that parties had maintained over the forming of governments became more attenuated. In the first government, Giuliano Amato was chosen as prime minister. The Amato government's most significant immigration initiative was the July reissuing of the Boniver decree (named after the previous immigration minister), which had first been submitted shortly before the 1992 elections. Virtually all immigrant advocacy groups opposed this because it restricted the rights of immigrants facing deportation. An alliance of pro-immigrant lobbying groups called the Anti-Racist Pact and a pro-immigrant lawyer's organization, the Association for Juridical Studies on Immigration, lobbied successfully to defeat the bill.

The Anti-Racist Pact's most daring proposal was to regularize undocumented immigrants through an amendment to the general employment legislation (D.L. 57, March 10) that would regulate seasonal labor and provide regularization for all illegal immigrants. This amendment had strong support in the public and private works committee but was ruled nongermane by the chair. After the President of the Chamber of Deputies overturned this decision, a large majority passed the amendments on April 21, 1993. They never came to a vote in the Senate because of the fall of the Amato government.

The Anti-Racist Pact (the pact) sought to convince the next technical government, led by Carlo Azeglio Ciampi, to support its proposal. Despite the pact's public demonstrations and private meetings, it failed to persuade the new labor minister, Gino Giugni, to include its amendments in the reissued employment decree (D.L. 148, May 20). Ministerial testimony at subsequent hearings would reveal the grounds for the government's reservations about the pacts proposals. The minister of social affairs, Fernanda Contri, claimed that it was a surreptitious general regularization and would jeopardize relations with European neighbors that were concerned with tightening border controls. The Ciampi government addressed seasonal labor in a new decree law (D.L. 200, June 22), which the pact saw as inadequate and which led its members to propose an amendment to the employment legislation that was similar to the one submitted with the spring employment legislation. After the Senate Labor Committee approved this amendment by a large majority, it appeared likely that the entire Senate would do the same, but the amendment was derailed when the government called for a vote of confidence on the employment legislation, a tactic that eliminated all amendments. The pact then sought to insert this amendment into the seasonal labor decree. When it appeared as though this strategy would succeed, the government withdrew its decree and set up a commission to produce a comprehensive bipartisan program.

The Change in Electoral System and the Rise of the Center-Right

The idea behind the electoral reforms of the early 1990s was to produce a system that would guarantee strong parties and an alternation between Left and Right. While alternation was achieved, the compromises necessary for it involved maintaining a low (4 percent) threshold for election to parliament, which allowed small parties to continue to play a role in the broader center-right and center-left coalitions.[5] It produced a system described by Ilvo Diamanti "as a fragmented and unstable bipolarism, which works for winning elections, but becomes a setback when governing or organizing the opposition in parliament" (2007). The smaller parties had diverse effects on the coalition. In the case of the center-left, they tended to the more radical side and caused the most conflict in resistance to increased efforts to enhance border controls or deport immigrants. On the center-right, the most significant were the small Catholic parties, which tended to be more sympathetic to solidaristic immigration policies and wanted to put a stop to the more restrictionist policies of the AN and the Northern League.

The center-right coalition would prove to be a dominant force in Italian politics (in power in 1994, from 2001 to 2006, and since 2008). It did not, however, have a compact ideology on the broader questions of social policy, much less on immigration. The Northern League was aligned with the interests of the northern regions, particularly Lombardy and the Venetian region. It sought to loosen the national government's hold on their regions, sometimes by separatist claims, at others by federalist claims. League members were often xenophobic and extremist in their rhetoric, even if, as will be seen, they were willing to compromise. The National Alliance (AN) was largely a party of the South and Center of the country, building from its neo-fascist roots to encompass a broader range of support as the Christian Democrat party dissolved. Its members tended to favor a strong national identity and were often at odds with the anti-state components of the Lega's ideology.

The leading party, Forza Italia (FI), represented business interests and was opposed to the most restrictive policies favored by the Northern League and the National Alliance. In subsequent administrations, it would be joined by groupings of small Catholic parties that were more sympathetic to immigrants and equally opposed to the more conservative members of the coalition.

The Failure of the Center-Right on Immigration Politics

The likelihood of restrictive legislation appeared to increase substantially after the national elections in March 1994, when an unwieldy coalition of the center-right, led by Silvio Berlusconi of Forza Italia (FI) won by constructing an alliance in the North with the Lega and in the South with the Alleanza Nazionale (National Alliance, or AN). However, the government did not confront the issue of immigration until the fall.[6] Initially reluctant, it responded to popular concern over prostitution and boats of illegal immigrants landing on Italian shores (Balbo 1994). Both the Lega Nord and the National Alliance proposed restrictive legislation, but of different degrees of strictness. The proposals of the National Alliance were consistently restrictive, whereas the Lega Nord presented an ambiguous policy posture. On the one hand, the proposed legislation from the Lega Nord highlighted the long list of crimes for which immigrants should be immediately expelled, thereby emphasizing public order, but it was silent on provisions for integrating those already in Italy. On the other hand, Roberto Maroni, the interior minister from the Lega Nord, testified before Parliament that immigrants already working in Italy who lacked only a piece of paper should be entitled to legalize their status.

The politics within the government reflected the parties' interests. When the issue reemerged in the fall, the responsibility was placed into the hands of the Ministry for Family and Social Affairs, headed by Antonio Guidi, a prominent union supporter in Forza Italia. The immigration stance of this ministry was less restrictionist than that of either the Ministry of the Interior or the Ministry of Justice. The political conflicts were resolved in interministerial negotiations, which directly involved prominent party leaders. Undersecretary Maurizio Gasparri (AN) represented the justice ministry and Undersecretary Mariø Borghezio (Lega Nord) represented the interior ministry. This agreement would never be submitted to the cabinet for further discussion. However, the original proposals, were circulated and then leaked to the newspaper *Il Manifesto*.

The public writings of Guido Bolaffi, the author of the government proposals, make it possible to analyze the political compromises involved in the attempted legislation. Bolaffi sought to depoliticize the issue by taking it out of the hands of the parties and making it an administrative question. In the journal *Il Mulino*, Bolaffi explicitly took to task the "paladins of the ultra-right" (with whom he was now negotiating) and "the ideologues of the most extreme left" (by which he meant the Anti- Racist Pact) for politically exploiting the issue (Bolaffi 1996: 1055). In ministerial meetings, Bolaffi represented the more moderate political interests of Forza Italia. He succeeded in limiting deportations to illegal entrants and excluding legal entrants who overstayed their visas. The proposal that emerged can be read as a compromise between the more open politics of Forza Italia and the restrictive politics of the National Alliance and the Lega Nord.

Dini Decree (Technical Government)

In the fall of 1995, when the Dini government sought to develop a legislative agenda on immigration, the Lega Nord was willing to cooperate. In exchange for policies that would facilitate expulsions, the Lega Nord made concessions on a wide range of more integrative policies. These included increased medical care, education of minor children, general social welfare policies, and increased visa opportunities for family reunification and seasonal work (Einaudi 2007: 198–99). Most important was a new regularization that would eventually encompass 256,000 applicants, of whom 238,000 were accepted. Intended to narrowly focus on workers who could prove stable employment, the decree eventually broadened out, as would subsequent regularizations, to include other forms of work as well. Applicants had to demonstrate residence in Italy, employment during the past six months or a job offer from an employer, and payment of three months of social security (Reyneri 2001).

This proposed decree produced considerable controversy within the Left, splitting the PDS from the associations that had supported the Anti-Racist Pact and the Refounded Communist Party. Nevertheless, since any effort to amend the decree before the government approved it would have resulted in a Lega Nord veto of the budget, the compromise was accepted. The government was not able to pass the decree into law within the required sixty days. The decree would instead be reiterated two more times before the elections, on January 18, 1996, (law n. 22) and once again on May 18 (law n. 269) after the 1996 elections, when a center-left government came to power (Bonetti 1996: 190). This compromise—the trade-off of regularization for easier forms of expulsion—would be the legislative cornerstone until the Turco-Napolitano law of 1998, and would crop up again during discussions by the center-right leading up to the Bossi-Fini law of 2002 (law n. 189/2002).

In terms of politics, the lessons of this interim period were that the Lega Nord would be both more flexible and less consequential on immigration than its early critics had imagined. In the 1992–1993 period, in which political parties were reshaping themselves and a viable coalition was difficult to form, it was interest groups that occupied this political space on immigration. In 1994, the sharp divisions within the center-right coalition, and the centrality of those divisions to the policy proposals that emerged, were quite clear.

In terms of policy, the cost of this phase of weak party politics was that the obvious lacunae in the Martelli legislation could not be resolved and an organic effort to put forward comprehensive legislation would have to await the arrival of a center-left government.

1998 Turco-Napolitano Act (Center-Left)

When the Left came to power, it had an intellectual patrimony of ideas relating to immigration policy. The legislative proposals it put forward drew heavily on the analytic work of experts developed over a number of years. The Turco committee, appointed by the Prodi government in 1996, drew heavily on the work of the Contri Commission in 1994 and to a large extent on the same team of experts. Efforts were made to absorb lessons from other countries and from local experience as well (Zincone 2006b: 354).

The underlying approach to immigration policy was to draw on a solidaristic and multicultural set of ideas that emphasized the need to make immigrants' rights as equivalent to Italians' rights as possible. One of the critical components of the legislation would be to guarantee access to education and emergency healthcare.

In terms of labor inflows, a high priority was the development of more rigorous and effective procedures that would go beyond this need for regularizations of unauthorized immigrants. Secretary of the Interior Giorgio Napolitano said:

> There is no doubt that we share the need to get beyond "emergency" approaches, whose effects are difficult to see and to pin down, and inevitably create diffuse situations of illegality. As a result, there are the amnesties regarding which there are justly many concerns; we want to put an end to this practice. (Einaudi 2007: 244)

This planning for employment quotas was made mandatory and was based on a three-year planning document with an extraordinarily wide-ranging consultation process that involved local associations concerned with integration, employer associations, organizations of regional and provincial governments, and national ministries and parliamentary committees. The legislation, which had to be approved by parliament and signed off by the executive, had an equally broad mandate to deal with permanent and temporary workers and entrepreneurs, as well as to assess the impact on the labor market of family reunification and temporary protection policies.

The slots available under the employment quotas grew from 20,000 in 1997 to 58,000 in 1998, and eventually to 89,400 in 2002—an increase of almost 450 percent in five years.

A striking example of policy innovation was the expansion of who could sponsor immigrants. Previously only employers with a job to offer could be sponsors, but this proposed legislation added Italian citizens and resident foreigners, regions, local authorities, professional associations and unions, and voluntary organizations.[7]

This rigorous approach to planning labor flows would eventually give way to pressures from others within Prodi's own coalition and from civil society, and there would be a substantial regularization (for those could show an opportunity to work, housing, and a clean criminal record). This regularization would receive 308,000 applications, of which 192,300 would be approved.

Another significant cause for the passage of the Turco-Napolitano Act was to ensure Italy's entry into the Schengen Accords, itself a measure of Italy living up to European standards and requirements (Zincone 2006a: 26). Interior Minister Giorgio Napolitano captured this partisan satisfaction with his country's success: "It put the lie to many forecasts that had been made, such as those that say Italy is a sieve, that it is the soft underbelly of Europe, and so forth, continuing that national self-defeating attitude, promoted by the intemperate statements of the opposition."

Temporary Detention Centers

To live up to European immigration standards required a more effective expulsion regime. The main proposal to accomplish this was temporary detention centers (*Centri di Permanenza Temporanea*, or CPT) in which foreigners who had illegally entered or were without documents could be held to determine their identity and facilitate their expulsion.

In addition to the CPTs, there were a number of other enhancements to the control regime. The new law would permit forced expulsion for reasons of public order. It would allow police to treat immigrants found within six months of illegal entry as similar to those who had been refused entry. It would increase penalties for smuggling. Also, Italy would sign bilateral accords with various countries, granting higher annual quotas in exchange for facilitating deportations.

This set of policies proved highly divisive and was sharply contested by the Left, causing the smaller, more radical parties—the Greens and the Rifondazione Comunista (Communist Refoundation, or RC)—to threaten not to support the overall legislation. Their support was eventually obtained with an agreement to modify some of the law's more onerous provisions (Zincone 2006b: 355).

The rationalization of the work-based quota system, as well as the increase in applications allowed, would be a lasting achievement of this government, as would prevailing against the Left's internal opposition to the detention centers, which would make possible a more functional expulsion system. Even with such a fundamentally solidaristic agenda, the center-left did not face concerted opposition from the center-right. Only the Lega Nord was a consistent and obstructionist critic. The government could even count on the support of Catholic parties of the center-right for quorum calls.

2002 Bossi-Fini (Center-Right)

Following a long electoral season, from 1999 to 2001, in which immigration was a critical and explosive issue, the center-right set out immediately to develop a new set of immigration policies that would mark a profound rupture from the past. The coalition showed a much greater sense of urgency than it had the last time it was in power in 1994, when it waited five months before proposing legislation. As Giovane Zincone described it, the campaign had produced an "electoral bill of exchange that centrist parties were obliged to honour" (2006a: 30). Pressing forward on the issue would also have the benefit of unifying the coalition by pushing on an issue that both the National Alliance and the Northern League, often at odds, could collaborate on as a critical part of their governing agenda.[8]

The issues that had been advanced during the campaign included:

- Greater severity in combating migrants' clandestine status, particularly as it is often seen as a cause of crime.

- Reduction of long-term entries based on the inflow planning process and policies enacted to instead re-equilibrate labor markets by bringing southern workers north and northern employers south.

- Re-emphasis on temporary worker policies by decreasing possibilities for migrants to become long-term residents and citizens, and by lessening the emphasis on integration, which was increasingly seen as impossible for Muslims (Einaudi 2007: 308)

Going from election campaign rhetoric to legislation would not be an easy process. Unlike the center-left five years previously, the center-right did not have a well-articulated body of policy analysis and reflection on which to build. The legislation would draw on two proposals, written while the center-right was in opposition. One was the Bossi-Berlusconi bill, which emphasized that the only reason for coming to Italy was to work and proposed to make it much more difficult for workers to become members of the Italian polity. The other was the AN Landi-Fini bill, which criminalized illegal migration, calling for immediate arrest, trial, and deportation for those found guilty. The original legislative proposal that was put forward on the basis of these and other ideas had a rushed and provisional quality to it (Colombo and Sciortino 2003: 305). The hard core of these proposals was criminalizing illegal entry and making deportation easier, restricting immigrant flows, and rejection of any regularization.

These proposals would most effectively be resisted from within the coalition by the small Catholic parties, the CCD and the CDU, which would merge into the UDC—L'Unione dei demoratici cristiani del centro (Union of Christian Democrats of the Center) in 2002. The Catholic parties pushed for regularization and resisted the more radically repressive proposals of AN and the Lega on criminalization (on the question of entry quotas, they did not play a significant role).

The government's proposals in the summer of 2001 envisioned a much more stringent illegal immigration regime. They included the criminalization of illegal entry or undocumented presence, leading to immediate deportation of those found guilty, and allowed for indefinite stays in a detention center rather than the three months permitted under previous legislation. However, these proposals were killed largely as a result of opposition by the UDC.

Some of the policies that passed increased the penalties for crimes committed by unauthorized immigrants, but the Constitutional Court of Italy turned a skeptical eye toward a number of these new policies. Indeed, in 2003 fully 56.3 percent of the cases that arrived on the docket of the constitutional court concerned immigration law (Einaudi 2007: 322), and two of the more far-reaching and controversial proposals of law n. 189/2002 were rejected. Refusing to leave the country after being found without a residency permit or with an expired one was ruled to be insufficient grounds for mandatory imprisonment. Similarly, an arrest and an immediate escort to the border for expulsion on the basis of the decision of an individual judge without right of appeal was deemed unconstitutional (Zincone 2006a: 367).

THE NEW QUOTA PROCESS

After failing in its initial efforts to abolish the three-year planning process for determining employment quotas, the conservative actors in the coalition sought to channel the flows in the ways they wanted: away from long-term permits, which were seen as more likely to lead to settlement, and toward seasonal permits, which struck its critics as headed in the direction of a guest worker policy. Although there was support for a more open policy on the part of Forza Italia and the CCD, these parties had relatively little effect on this policy decision, which was largely managed by Interior Minister Roberto Maroni, a leader of the Northern League.

The 2002 decree, the first after the Bossi-Fini law took effect, decreased the overall number of employment quota positions by almost 10,000, from 89,400 to 79,500. Far more striking was the dramatic increase in seasonal permits at the expense of the long-term permits. In 2001, there were 50,000 long-term permits, approximately 54 percent of the overall pool. In 2002, there were only 19,500, or 20 percent of the pool, and by 2003 that number had fallen to 11,000, or 12 percent of the pool, representing the lowest number of long-term permits since the inflow process had begun in 1991 (see Table 11.3).

The government also eliminated the proposals of the previous legislation that allowed a much wider range of sponsorship of immigrants looking for work. These proposals were considered to be insufficiently tied to labor markets, potential contributors to chain migration, and in general too difficult to control. The government brought back the requirement that employers show that no Italians were available to take the job and gave preference to workers abroad who could show Italian heritage.

TABLE 11.3
Summary of legal entries for work in Italy, 1991–2006

Year	Entry authorization for work	Work authorization[a]	Entry authorization for nonseasonal work	Entry authorization for seasonal work	Entry authorization for domestic work	Quota for new EU community members	Demand from new EU community members
1991	6,000	—	6,000	—	—		
1992	31,630	—	29,971	1,659	21,828		
1993	23,088	—	20,300	2,788	14,555		
1994	22,474	—	16,697	5,777	12,420		
1995	25,000	25,000	17,413	7,587	6,183		
1996	23,000	23,000	14,120	8,880	6,795		
1997	20,000	20,000	11,551	8,449	—		
1998	27,303	58,000	10,743	16,560	—		
1999	36,454	58,000	16,074	20,380	—		
2000	83,000	83,000	41,944	41,056	—		
2001	89,400	89,400	50,000	39,400	—		
2002	79,500	79,500	19,500	60,000	—		
2003	79,500	79,500	11,000	68,500	—	TRANSITIONAL PERIOD	
2004	79,500	79,500	29,500	50,000	—	36,000	26,000
2005	99,500	99,500	54,500	45,000	—	79,500	57,000
2006	170,000	550,000	120,000	50,000	—	170,000	79,500

SOURCE: Ministero dell'Interno (2007).
[a]Since 1995; quotas from inflow decrees, including seasonal and nonseasonal work.

However, the number of long-term permits would subsequently rebound, to the point where, by 2006, they were roughly similar to the center-left's quotas of about 90,000. Indeed, the effective numbers were higher because they would be supplemented by the visas allocated to the countries in Southeastern Europe that had recently been included in the EU's "transitional quotas," having become members in the latest round of expansion. Those quotas would be 36,000 in 2004, 79,500 in 2005, and 170,000 in 2006.[9]

This reversal was caused by a range of factors, both internal and external. Eastern European enlargement (and Germany's open visa policy) increased the flows. EU sentiment was opposed to mass regularization, and there was a need to maintain relations with sending countries and to accept the increasing role of foreign labor in Italy (Finotelli and Sciortino 2008: 8).

In many ways, the most surprising result of the center-right's policy initiative was the large number of regularizations that Italy went through. The process by which it came about is indicative of the forces in play.

The Catholic parties made their greatest effort to change the immigration law to introduce regularization. Originally, their efforts were rejected, but their demands were accepted in an incremental process over the opposition of the Northern League and the more restrictionist element of the National Alliance. First, there was an acceptance of a new category of *badanti* (care providers). Acceptance was then extended to all domestic service workers and, after complaints by employers that they were being discriminated against, all workers.

There was a trade-off between regularization and more control-oriented measures in two senses: first, because it was a part of the coalition's general balancing act; second, and more critically, because passing measures that would ease expulsions without ensuring the status of workers who were integrated but lacked proper papers risked indiscriminate harm.

For the Northern League to save face with its electoral base, regularization was submitted as a separate decree. It would be far and away the largest regularization in Italian history—634,700 of the 700,000 who applied were accepted. Of these 700,000 applications, 372,000 were "general" employees, 190,000 were domestic workers, and 140,000 were care providers.

Most commentators at the time saw this period as a failed effort at restrictionism. This was particularly true for those who based their assessments on electoral rhetoric and legislative proposals developed when the center-right parties were in opposition. They emphasized the role of the Christian Democratic Party as resisting the more draconian measures proposed by the Lega Nord and the National Alliance on criminalization of immigration.

However, it is possible to regard this as a first step, with the subsequent security decrees of the next center-right government, in a more profound attack on the center-left framework.

2007 Amato-Ferrero Proposal (Center-Left)

When the center-left returned to power in 2006 with the election of Romano Prodi as Prime Minister, it put forward wide-ranging proposals under the name of the Amato-Ferrero law. Because of the government's thin parliamentary majority (sustained in fact by the electorate of Italian citizens living abroad), ongoing internal conflicts between the center and left parts of the coalition, and the coalition's short lifespan, it was unable to pass these reforms.

Nonetheless, these reform proposals provide a useful guide as to the policy goals of the center-left coalition of the time. In general, they favored more open policies toward entrance and more solidaristic policies toward immigrants, oriented towards facilitating long-term settlement.[10]

The quota requests were reported to be 200,000, a figure substantially higher than in previous years. There was also a provision that would have allowed housekeepers and caregivers, two of the largest groups, to be excluded from these ceilings (Reyneri 2007: 26). There was also to be a reversion back to the Turco-Napolitano provisions allowing a variety of entities to sponsor immigrants, provisions that had been struck down by the center-right government. Finally, the permits for foreigners seeking jobs and for employment would be greatly extended and made easier to access, thereby facilitating a greater likelihood of immigrants' finding and keeping work.

The one element that was enacted, largely because it could be done by decree and did not require an extended legislative process, was the regularization decree. According to Reyneri (2007):

> In late 2006 the newly appointed government decided to accept all the applications exceeding the yearly quota forecast by the previous government. Over 350,000 unauthorized migrant workers were in practice regularized, but the procedure, although time consuming and very cumbersome, avoided the usual pull effect as well as the criticism by public opinion.[11]

On questions of immigration control, the proposals were nuanced, but largely in favor of reducing the weight of more repressive control mechanisms. On the one hand, the government wanted to close down or at least radically reduce the role of detention centers (CPT), which had been a cornerstone of Italian expulsion strategies since they were first implemented under the center-left Turco-Napolitano law in 1998. The CPTs had been particularly contested by the more radical members of this coalition, both during debates about creating them and subsequently in 2004 when condemning reports by human rights organizations, particularly Doctors without Borders, surfaced (Einaudi 2007: 338). However, it is not clear that EU law would have allowed their closure or radical restructuring. In a highly unusual practice, the Vice-President of the European Commission responsible for Freedom, Security and Justice publicly commented to the effect that these changes would be incompatible with EU norms (Pastore 2007: 5).

On the other hand, in 2007 the government presented a decree that would allow the police to deport EU citizens and their family members from Italy if they were considered a threat to public order. The decree (D.L. 181/2007) was a response to a savage murder of an Italian woman by a Romanian citizen.

While the legislative process did not move far enough along to make possible a systematic comparison with the practices of the center-right government or to judge how much rupture or continuity would have been involved, one does see both a commitment to higher quotas and to a more elastic set of definitions regarding who can "invite" than the center-right would have wanted. Additionally, one sees an effort to reconfigure the cornerstone of the control mechanisms, the CPTs, whose salience the center-right had been emphasizing and would continue efforts to increase.

2008–2009 Security Legislation (Center-Right)

In the 2008 elections, won overwhelmingly by the center-right coalition, the Northern League successfully mobilized around issues of criminality and illegal immigration. The candidate of the Left also emphasized the need for public order. The center-right coalition, with core members Forza Italia, AN, and the Lega Nord, won so convincingly that it did not need the support of the small Catholic Party, the UDC, which had played such a critical role in constraining previous administrations.

The center-right quickly sought to redeem its electoral promise to deal with immigration as a security issue (Finotelli and Sciortino 2008) by passing a security package (law no. 125/2008).[12] In so doing, it left the previous immigration framework intact, even as it increased the control powers of the state, radically changed legislation criminalizing immigrants, (a long-held theme of the Right), and passed new proposals impinging on the social rights of immigrants by cracking down on landlords who rented to immigrants and requiring public officials to report the status of any unauthorized immigrants.[13] This law also amended the penal code to enable deportation of a foreigner or removal of an EU citizen if convicted of a crime with a sentence greater than two years.

Law no. 94/2009, also known as the Security Package, criminalized illegal entry or presence, establishing a fine of 5,000 to 10,000 euros for those convicted. It also required all state officials, except healthcare workers, to report irregular status.[14] It is difficult to foresee whether the law will run afoul of EU norms, the Italian courts, or the limit on available resources that frequently undermines this type of legislation.

On the questions of inflow quotas, the center-right coalition put forward proposals that were substantially less than the demand. In 2005, there were 210,000 applications; in 2006, 480,000; and in 2007, over 700,000. The government adopted a ceiling of 150,000 in 2008 and in 2009 decided to provide entrance only to temporary workers, citing the economic recession.

On the question of regularization, the government had none in 2008 and offered it only to domestic workers and care providers (*badanti*) in 2009 (law n. 102/2009) with a ceiling of 300,000. By September 30, 180,408 domestic workers and 114,336 healthcare assistants had applied.

CONCLUSION

This section addresses the issues raised in the introduction regarding how conditions have changed since the 1990 Legge Martelli (law n. 39/90) regarding parties, policies, and proposals for managing future employment-based quotas.

Deciphering the role of political parties is important because it shapes one's understanding of the coherence of Italian immigration policy and forms the basis on which one can judge whether there has been a gap between intentions and outcomes. Italy has had a tumultuous twenty years of political party development and oscillation, with fifteen different governments and seven changes in the form of government since 1990. This has also been the era in which comprehensive immigration legislation has been developed.

Broadly speaking, the Left has set the framework and wrote most of the legislation of the first eight years, whereas the Right has had greater legislative impact in the last twelve.

The first effort at comprehensive regulation was the Martelli law, which, even though the government that wrote it was dominated by Christian Democrats, represented a policy outreach on the part of the Socialist Martelli to the Italian Communist Party (PCI) and to social organizations sympathetic to solidaristic policy and willing to alienate the more conservative parties in the government. The first truly comprehensive legislation was the Turco-Napolitano law in 1998. After that, however, the main policy thrusts have come from the right—first with the Bossi-Fini law in 2002 and then with the security package laws in 2008 and 2009.

Judging the coherence of Italian immigration policy requires some assessment of whether there is policy convergence in immigration control, regularization, and employment quotas. The more systematic assessments made in the immediate aftermath of the last center-right government in 2006 emphasized, with some variation, the extent to which there was a degree of settled policy.[15] The policies of the last eight years, with the failure of the center-left to enact more solidaristic policies in 2006–2007, and Berlusconi's People of Freedom (PdL) administration's focus on redefining immigration as a security issue from 2007 to 2013, has seen policy move in a more restrictive, if not repressive, direction and has raised the question of how much underlying agreement actually exists.

In judging the coherence of Italy's immigration policies, one also needs to pay attention to the internal coherence of the coalitions themselves, particularly given the electoral system, which tends to privilege disparate, fragmented party groupings and give substantial weight to the small parties within them. This has been particularly true for the center-right, which in 1994 developed out of the marriage of convenience of three political traditions. Even though it had more numerous parties and less identifiable and powerful leadership, the center-left coalition, was more ideologically compact. This difference was accentuated with immigration, where there was much more of a governance-based approach on the Left and much more of an electorally driven one on the right (Zincone 2006a).

One last factor that needs to be accounted for is the role of Italy's domestic courts and of the EU. The center-left coalition was pushed to more effective control mechanisms by the EU's desire for less porous borders, particularly in the run-up to the Schengen Agreement in 1998. The center-right coalition faced opposition to its overreaching on expulsion measures and criminalization of illegal entry from the constitutional court, and increasing attention from the EU and other actors in the international community for its treatment of asylum seekers.

Criminalization of Immigration and Expulsions

Debates over the construction of a new control regime centered on the need to effectively expel those found guilty of violating Italian laws. This in turn has devolved into a discussion of detention centers. To evaluate the CPTs' effectiveness requires analyzing the data given in Table 11.4.

If one accepts estimates that only 10 to 20 percent of the expulsion orders before the 1998 Turco-Napolitano law were carried out (Reyneri 2001: 22; Einaudi 2007), one can see

TABLE 11.4
Expulsions and readmissions in Italy, 1991–2006

Year	Ordered expulsions	Enforced expulsions	Readmitted according to readmission agreements	Total deported (enforced expulsions and readmitted)
1991	28,733	—	—	—
1992	35,120	—	—	—
1993	52,918	—	—	—
1994	61,627	—	—	—
1995	58,894	—	—	—
1996	37,362	—	—	—
1997	52,111	—	—	—
1998	44,121	—	—	—
1999	40,489	12,556	11,399	23,955
2000	64,734	15,398	8,438	23,836
2001	58,171	21,639	12,751	34,390
2002	53,125	25,226	17,019	42,245
2003	9,378	19,729	9,901	29,630
2004	9,524	17,200	7,996	25,196
2005	4,514	16,690	10,295	26,985
2006	4,065	13,397	8,293	21,690

SOURCE: Ministero dell'Interno (2007).

that the regime of the CPTs was successful, even if there were persistent complaints about the management and treatment of those detained. While originally a proponent of CPTs, the center-left has become increasingly critical; in 2007, the Amato-Ferrero law called for a serious rethinking of their use.

Readmission agreements with foreign governments also contributed to a more effective deportation policy that was eventually accepted on both sides of the Italian political divide.[16]

A related issue, over which there had always been animated debate between the Left and Right, is the criminalization of illegal entry or presence. The parties of the Right, the National Alliance and the Northern League, had often pushed for making illegal entry or presence a crime that would result in immediate expulsion, with minimal rights to juridical appeal. The center-left, as well more moderate elements within the center-right coalition, had always resisted this. Only in the most recent security package was illegal entry made a crime, but it was punishable by a substantial fine, not immediate deportation.

Toward an Active Labor Recruitment Policy?

Unlike most countries in Europe, Italy has, in law and in self-conception, accepted the need for labor recruitment from outside its borders and, in particular, from outside the EU. That said, from 1990 to 2010, it did not develop and apply policy instruments that would keep up with labor demand and channel it in an effective manner. Indeed, as Francesco Ciafaloni has noted, the practice was more often than not to legalize those who were already present in Italian territory.

> It has been noted, but must be remembered, that to understand the mechanisms and the conflicts, that the only immigration policy that has really been followed by Italian governments—of the old five party system, technical government, or those of the Right or the Left . . . , has been to tolerate unregulated entry and the presence of those without adequate documents and to give them amnesty every four or five years. (Ciafaloni 2004: 138)

Indeed, the five regularizations that occurred from 1986 on totaled 1,419,600 people plus the 300,000 applicants from the 2009 process which were pending. (See Table 11.5.)

Every major change in Italian immigration law was accompanied by a regularization. Particularly in the more recent episodes, regularizations tended to start with a narrow category of applicants and then expand. They were increasingly regarded as a necessary evil, with each government stressing that they were not an amnesty since they involved only

TABLE 11.5
Numbers of migrants regularized in Italy, 1986–2002

Year	Applicants	Regularized
1986–1987	Not known	118,700
1990	Not known	235,000
1995–1996	256,000	238,000
1998–1999	308,000	193,200
2002	700,000	634,700

SOURCE: Levinson (2005).

those who had jobs. The extent to which this process of bringing people out of the shadows had become suspect can be seen in the decision of 2006 to use a quota to accomplish the same goal, even though it would be slower and more convoluted.

While the idea of a quota regime is firmly in place, its uses clearly cover a wide range of possibilities. The center-left generally supported larger quotas with an easier path to long-term residency, while the center-right, at least during the early years of the second Berlusconi regime in 2001, favored programs that were closer to guest worker policies. Indeed, one way to explore the question of convergence would be to sketch out two different sets of policies and reflect on the political likelihood that there could be some form of agreement on them between the center-left and the center-right.

As argued by Christian Joppke (2002), there is a considerable difference between regulating existing flows ("stemming") and actively seeking new ones ("soliciting"). The Italian employment quota policy as of 2010 was one that in principle accepted the possibility of actively "soliciting," but was in reality more comfortable with "stemming"—that is, regularizing the flows of those already in the country illegally.[17]

The first policy alternative, which will be called "planning from above," would be to take seriously the idea of employment quotas based on centrally determined labor needs along the lines suggested by Sciortino (2009), who acknowledges the challenges as follows:

> The government is then called to assume responsibility for uncertainties linked to the process of establishing a quota and the future impact of the flows. In other words, governments undertaking an active immigration policy must define as certain what is unknown, knowing perfectly well that this will imply both a restriction of the future room for maneuver and the assumption of responsibility for the policy outcomes.

Sciortino further notes that engaging in such a process, regardless of the numbers arrived at, could be seen as encouraging increased immigration flows. To make this policy work would require, either explicitly or implicitly, agreement across the political spectrum. One proposal is to adopt the American idea of a bipartisan commission to assess labor market needs.[18] It is, however, difficult to imagine this working in the Italian context, even though there likely are business interests in the center-right coalition who would support it, because it would require the Northern League and the National Alliance to limit their use of immigration issues in electoral campaigns. The Northern League in particular uses immigration as an electoral issue to maintain its stance as the party that defends the interests of its northern constituencies against the despised "Roman" government—but is part of the state at the same time and thus in many ways both an anti- and a pro-system party (Sartori 1976).[19]

The second idea—allowing groups other than employers to bring in prospective workers and giving them more flexibility in seeking work—can be seen as a form of "planning from below" because it allows individuals to seek out on their own the employment possibilities that are available. Again, it is not clear a priori why business interests represented by the center-right coalition would necessarily be opposed to this, although there are reasonable concerns that this type of recruitment might be driven more by chain migration than by labor market needs. What is clear is that this has been defined as a partisan issue—with the center-left inserting it into the legislation in 1998, the center-right removing it in 2002, and the center-left again proposing it in 2006. It is unlikely that one will see progress on the consistent development of this as a part of an Italian employment quota system.

This idea of looking at planning from above and below emphasizes the extent to which partisanship is likely to inhibit future innovation in managing employment quotas. As this is one of the critical elements of immigration policy, it does give one pause—as do the obvious and apparently growing differences between Left and Right over detention and criminalization—as to whether there is a coherent set of intentions against which results can be judged.

NOTES

1. This choice of issues tends to emphasize the contrast between political parties. If one were to choose social rights of immigrants, one would find little contestation between center-left and center-right on access to health and educational services. Focusing on asylum and temporary protection issues would likely be a middle case, with some slight difference between the coalitions in 2009 when the Berlusconi government's treatment of potential asylum seekers from Libya, along with other issues, aroused the ire of the European Commission and the United Nations High Commission for Refugees.

2. For a description of sources regarding illegal migration, see Fasani (2009).

3. This estimate of 300,000 was also made by Golini (2001). For an elaboration of the issues, and projections of future growth rates given different immigration scenarios, see Einaudi (2007: 51–83) and Bonifazi (2007).

4. Pastore (2007), concerned about the costs of neglecting Africa as a source of immigration and as a potential partner in development, expresses concern as to whether Europe will continue to be an adequate source of future immigrant flows.

5. This quota would, in subsequent changes to the electoral law, be lowered to 2 percent.

6. This section draws heavily on Perlmutter (2002).

7. This sponsorship would consist of assisting the applicant in gaining access to the labor market and housing and medical services.

8. This account draws primarily on Einaudi (2007). For a comprehensive version in English that focuses on party dynamics, see Geddes (2008).

9. The number of those who actually came was substantially lower.

10. This interpretation was reconstructed from three sources: Pastore (2007), Einaudi (2007), and EMN (2008).

11. This approach also avoided the criticism of the EU, which had become increasingly skeptical of mass regularizations and was encouraging countries to do them only on a case-by-case basis.

12. Since the Left had not been in power long enough to pass any legislation, there was nothing to reverse regarding the CPT and planning quotas, as had been in the case for the most recent government.

13. One cannot but be struck by the convergence of Italian policy with the efforts of American states over the past five years, and particularly recent legislative initiatives, such as SB 1070 in Arizona. If this trend were to continue, it would mark a fundamental change

with previous policy by center-right governments, which had generally refrained from restricting the social rights of illegal immigrants.

14. Some of these initiatives look very similar to US state legislation passed, in particular SB 1070 in Arizona.

15. Zincone (2006a, 2006b) tends to emphasize convergence; whereas Einaudi (2007), who gives greater weight to the specifics of the quota-planning debates, sees greater distance between the center-right and the center-left. Finotelli and Sciortino (2008) occupy a position somewhere in the middle.

16. Einaudi argues that these were weakened by the three years in which the center-right drastically reduced nonseasonal admissions. The decline in ordered expulsions after 2002 can be seen as a result of the expansion of the EU to encompass Romania and Bulgaria, as well of the readmission agreements. Decreased funding for expulsions is also seen as a factor in explaining their decline (Finotelli and Sciortino 2008: 8).

17. Reyneri (2007) argues that reducing the underground economy and the role of immigrants in it would be good for immigrants as well as the Italian economy as a whole. A large underground economy weakens the case for immigration by inflating the unemployment rate and thus minimizing the apparent need for immigrants. It obscures immigrant contributions to the economy and to the welfare state and thus their case for being allowed a more permanent status. Finally, by making immigrants appear part of illicit enterprise, illegal status makes it easier to define them as extraneous to Italian society.

18. The idea was recently associated with Ray Marshall, Labor Secretary in the Carter administration (*Los Angeles Times*, March 29, 2009), and elaborated in AFL-CIO and Change to Win (2009), although similar ideas had been articulated in discussions held by the Migration Policy Institute.

19. For an elaboration of the place of the Lega Nord and similar populist parties on a political spectrum, see the argument in Perlmutter (1996b), which draws on the framework of Sartori (1976).

REFERENCES

Adinolfi, Adelina. 1992. *I lavoratori extracomunitari: Norme interne e internazionali.* Bologna: Il Mulino.

AFL-CIO and Change to Win. 2009. "The Labor Movement's Framework for Comprehensive Immigration Reform." April.

Afsana, Francesco. 2009. "Undocumented Migration: Counting the Uncountable. Data and Trends across Europe." Clandestino Project.

Balbo, Laura. 1994. "Passagio di fase [a partire dagli immigrati]." *Politica ed Economia* 4 (5–6): 20–21.

Barbagli, Marzio. 2004. "Regolarizzazioni, espulsioni e reati degli immigrati in Italia (1990–2004)." In *I sommersi e i sanati: Le regolarizzazioni degli immigrati in Italia*, edited by Marzio Barbagli, Asher Colombo, and Giuseppe Sciortino, 201–22. Bologna: Il Mulino.

Barbagli, Marzio, Asher Colombo, and Giuseppe Sciortino, eds. 2004. *I sommersi e i sanati: Le regolarizzazioni degli immigrati in Italia.* Bologna: Il Mulino.

Bolaffi, Guido. 1996. *Una politica per gli immigrati*. Bologna: Il Mulino.

Bonetti, Paolo. 1996. "Note sugli aspetti costituzionali e legislativi delle prospettive delle politiche migratorie italiane." *Rivista Internazionale dei Diritti dell'Uomo* 9: 8–53.

Bonifazi, Corrado. 2005. "Accettazione e rifiuto nelle opinioni degli italiani." *Quaderno Cesifin* 20: 87–117.

———. 2007. *L'immigrazione straniera in Italia*. Bologna: Il Mulino.

Castiglioni, Maria, and Gianperra dalla Zuanna. 2009. "La bassa fecondità italiana: Cause, consequenze e politiche." In *La fatica da cambiare: Rapporto sulla società italiana*, edited by Rainaldo Catanzaro and Giuseppe Sciortino, 17–32. Bologna: Il Mulino.

Ciafaloni, Francesco. 2004. "I meccanismi dell'emergenza." In *I sommersi e i sanati: Le regolarizzazioni degli immigrati in Italia*, edited by Marzio Barbagli, Asher Colombo, and Giuseppe Sciortino, 187–200. Bologna: Il Mulino.

Colombo, Asher, and Giuseppe Sciortino. 2003. "La legge Bossi-Fini: Estremismi gridati, moderazioni implicite e frutti avvelenati." In *Politica in Italia 2003*, edited by Jean Blondel and Paolo Segatti, 195–215. Bologna: Il Mulino.

Cornelius, Wayne, Philip Martin, and James Hollifield. 1994. *Controlling Immigration: A Global Perspective*. Stanford, CA: Stanford University Press.

Cvajner, Martina, and Giuseppe Sciortino. 2009. "Dal Mediterraneo al Baltico? Il cambiamento nei systema migratori italiani." In *La fatica da cambiare: Rapporto sulla società italiana*, edited by Rainaldo Catanzaro and Giuseppe Sciortino, 33–54. Bologna: Il Mulino.

Diamanti, Ilvo. 2007. "The Italian Centre-Right and Centre-Left: Between Parties and 'the Party.'" *West European Politics* 30 (4): 733–62.

Einaudi, Luca. 2007. *Le politiche dell'immigrazione in Italia dall'unità a oggi*. Bari: Laterza.

———. 2008. "Il rompicapo dei nuovi flussi di lavoratori immigrati." www.nelmerito .com.

EMN (European Migration Network). 2007. *The Organization of Asylum and Migration Policies in Italy*. Rome: Idos.

———. 2008. *ITALIA: Rapporto annuale sulle politiche 2007*. Rome: Idos.

———. 2009. *ITALIA: Rapporto annuale sulle politiche 2008*. Rome: Idos.

Fasani, Francesco. 2009. "Undocumented Migration: Counting the Uncountable. Data and Trends across Europe." Clandestino Report.

Finotelli, Claudia. 2007. *Illegale Einwanderung, Flüchtlingsmigration und das Ende des Nord-Süd-Mythos: Zur funktionalen Äquivalenz des deutschen und des italienischen Einwanderungsregimes*. Münster: LIT Verlag.

Finotelli, Claudia, and Giuseppe Sciortino. 2008. "New Trends in Italian Immigration Policies: 'To change everything in order to keep everything the same.'" ARI 161/2008, Real Instituto Elanco, September 12.

———. 2009. "The Importance of Being Southern: The Making of Policies of Immigration Control in Italy." *European Journal of Migration and Law* 11: 119–38.

Freeman, Gary. 1995. "Modes of Immigration Politics in Liberal Democratic States." *International Migration Review* 29 (4): 881–913.

Geddes, Andrew. 2008. "Il Rombo dei Cannoni? Immigration and the Centre-Right in Italy." *Journal of European Public Policy* 15 (3): 349–66.

Golini, Antonio. 2001. *L'emigrazione italiana all'estero e la demografia dell'immigrazione straniera in Italia*. Bologna: Il Mulino.

Istat. 2005. *Gli stranieri in Italia: Analisi dei dati censuari. 14° Censimento generale della popolazione e delle abitazioni*. Rome: Istat.

———. 2007. *La presenza straniera in Italia: Caratteristiche socio-demografiche*. Rome: Istat.

Joppke, Christian. 2002. "European Immigration Policies at the Crossroads." In *Developments in West European Politics*, edited by Paul Heywod, Erik Jones, and Martin Rhodes, 259–76. New York: Palgrave.

Levinson, Amanda. 2005. *The Regularisation of Unauthorised Migrants: Literature Survey and Country Case Studies*. Center on Migration, Policy and Society, University of Oxford.

Ministero dell'Interno. 2007. *Primo rapporto sugli immigrati in Italia*. Rome: Ministero dell'Interno.

Papademetriou, Demetrios G. 2005. "The 'Regularization' Option in Managing Illegal Migration More Effectively: A Comparative Perspective." Task Force Policy Brief 4, Migration Policy Institute, Washington, DC.

Pastore, Ferruccio. 2007. "La politica migratoria italiana a una svolta: ostacoli immediati e dilemmi strategici." http://www.cespi.it/PDF/Pastore-POL-MIG-IT-07.pdf.

Perlmutter, Ted. 1996a. "Immigration Policy Italian-Style." *South European Society and Politics* 1 (2): 229–52.

———. 1996b. "Bringing Parties Back In: Comments on 'Modes of Immigration Politics in Liberal Democratic Societies.'" *International Migration Review* 30: 375–88.

———. 2000. "Political Parties and Interest Groups in Italy, 1990–1994." Paper presented at the International Conference on Explaining Changes in Migration Policy: Debates from Different Perspectives, University of Geneva, Geneva, October 27–28.

———. 2002. "The Politics of Restriction: The Effect of Xenophobic Parties on Italian Immigration Policy and German Asylum Policy." In *Shadows over Europe: The Development and Impact of the Extreme Right in Western Europe*, edited by Martin Schain, Aristide Zolberg, and Patrick Hossay, 269–98. London: Palgrave.

Pridham, Geoffrey. 1988. *Political Parties and Coalitional Behavior in Italy*. London: Routledge.

Pugliese, Enrico. 2006. *L'Italia tra migrazioni internazionali e migrazioni interne*. Bologna: Il Mulino.

Reyneri, Emilio. 2001. "Migrants' Involvement in Irregular Employment in the Mediterranean Countries of the European Union." International Labour Organization, Geneva. www.ilo.org/public/english/protection/migrant/download/imp/imp41.pdf.

———. 2004. "Immigrants in a Segmented and Often Undeclared Labour Market." *Journal of Modern Italian Studies* 9 (1): 71–93.

———. 2007. "Immigration in Italy: Trends and Perspectives." IOM, Argo.

Sarti, Raffaella. 2006. "Domestic Service and European Identity." In *Proceedings of the "Servant Project,"* edited by Suzy Pasleau and Isabelle Schopp, 5: 195–284. Liège: Presses Universitaires de Liège.

Sartori, Giovanni. 1976. *Parties and Party Systems: A Framework for Analysis*. Cambridge: Cambridge University Press.

Schain, Martin, Aristide Zolberg, and Patrick Hossay, eds. 2002. *Shadows over Europe: The Development and Impact of the Extreme Right in Western Europe.* London: Palgrave.

Sciortino, Giuseppe. 2009. "Fortunes and Miseries of Italian Labour Migration Policy." Politiche Migratorie e Modelli di Società, Centro Studi di Politica Internazionale (CeSPI), Rome.

Veikou, Mariangela, and Anna Triandafyllidou. 2000. "Immigration Policy and Its Implementation in Italy: A Report on the State of the Art." European University Institute. http://www.mmo.gr/pdf/library/Italy/triandaf.pdf.

Zaslove, Andrei. 2006. "The Politics of Immigration: A New Electoral Dilemma for the Right and the Left?" *Review of European and Russian Affairs* 2 (3): 10–35.

Zincone, Giovanna. 1998. "Illegality, Enlightenment and Ambiguity: A Hot Italian Recipe." *South European Society and Politics* 3 (3): 43–82.

———. 2006a. "The Making of Policies. Immigration and Immigrants in Italy." *Journal of Ethnic and Migration Studies* 32 (3): 347–75.

———. 2006b. "Italian Immigrants and Immigration Policy Making: Structures, Actors, Practices." Paper presented at the IMISCOE Conference on the Making of Migratory Policies in Europe, University of Turin, Turin, May 19–20.

———. 2009. "Citizenship Policy Making in Mediterranean EU States: Italy." European University Institute, Florence Robert Schuman Centre for Advanced Studies, and EUDO Citizenship Observatory.

Zolberg, Aristide. 1987. "Wanted but Not Welcome: Alien Labor in Western Development." In *Population in an Interacting World*, edited by William Alonso, 36–73. Cambridge, MA: Harvard University Press.

COMMENTARY

Giuseppe Sciortino

Over the last few decades, Italy—once the quintessential European emigration country—has become one of the strongest immigration magnets in the world. At the beginning of 2011, more than 4,500,000 foreign nationals were registered as regular residents, making up 7.5 percent of the population. This population, to whom a few hundred thousand irregular migrants must be added, has more than tripled in less than ten years. Even in recent times, despite the serious economic crisis, the flow of foreign workers has continued, at a slower but far from negligible pace. In a short span of time, virtually all Italian institutions—from schools to prisons, from firms to malls, from churches to TV shows—have had to deal with the impact of this change. Unsurprisingly, the phenomenon of immigration is one of the most active and controversial topics in Italian public and political debates.

Italian immigration policies enjoy a widespread—in fact, nearly universal—bad reputation. In European and international public opinion and policy circles, the country is perceived as being particularly weak in preventing unwanted entries, as well as extremely lenient in its subsequent treatment of irregular migrants. Television images of overcrowded boats with immigrants landing on the shores of the tiny island of Lampedusa seem to confirm that the country's control of its borders is precarious. The ways in which such landings are handled appear to blatantly disregard international conventions and EU directives. The size of the resident undocumented foreign population—as well as the many hundreds of thousands of irregular migrants who have acquired legal status through the frequent amnesty programs launched in the last twenty-five years—are taken as equally convincing evidence both of the lack of effective internal controls and of widespread tolerance.

Italian policies are supposedly farfetched and erratic, with their implementation fragmented and often random. If the harsh, often openly xenophobic, statements of many Italian politicians and pundits are added to the recipe, it is easy to conclude that the situation is increasingly critical, if not crossing into the realm of out of control.

Ted Perlmutter provides a convincing portrait of such a reality and offers an original explanation for its causes: in order to understand why Italian immigration policies do not work, it is necessary to enter the byzantine world of Italian party politics, a field where most observers, including a large number of Italians, fear to tread. Perlmutter has a remarkable capacity for introducing the reader to this peculiar world, and he argues that a sequence of loose and unstable party coalitions, whatever their composition, has prevented the country from developing a stable policy framework to deal with the issue of immigration.

Perlmutter explains the special nature of the Italian case by painting the country as a land of weak controls, ineffective policies, and strange politicians. This is an assessment, it should be noted, that most of the very same politicians would be happy to confirm (claiming, of course, that it only applies to their adversaries). As for Italian public opinion, it is enough to mention that the *Transatlantic Trends* survey of 2010 has shown that Italy is the only country where half of the interviewees would be more than happy to transfer key decisions concerning immigration policy to Brussels, far away from their own national government.

The problem is that, as social scientists often conclude, a diffuse and popular account is not necessarily correct. Doxa is not necessarily episteme. What if this popular vision of Mediterranean exceptionalism (or Orientalism?) does not fit with the available empirical evidence? What if, as turns out to be the case, a large number of the alleged peculiarities of the Italian case are actually not quite so peculiar?

In fact, the evolution of Italian immigration policies—as well as their levels of efficiency and effectiveness—is more a variant of the European pattern than an exotic anomaly. A few well-established facts are worth mentioning. Although the economic burden of European control policies falls disproportionately (and unfairly) on the countries bordering non-EU territories, over the last two decades Italy has invested quite substantially in personnel and technologies directed at border control and has assigned immigration control a significant priority in its diplomatic strategies. The results are easily documented. One of the largest and most complex irregular migration flows active in the 1990s (that between Albania and the Southern Italian coast) was effectively halted by Italian authorities. Before the recent Libyan conflict, the same could be said about the sea crossings through the Mediterranean, as demonstrated by the diminishing number of arrivals and a steep increase in the prices demanded by smugglers. From the end of the 1990s, as a matter of fact, sea landings have been increasingly reserved for refugees, whose entry is not a matter of ineffective controls but, more simply, of the legal protection guaranteed by the non-refoulement principle of international refugee laws. Most irregular migrants arrive in Italy—as in any other European country—not by violating the border through clandestine crossings but with duly issued tourist visas, often given by German or French embassies, which, as statistics reveal, are markedly more liberal than Italian ones in granting Schengen-wide visas. Italian external controls certainly have their weaknesses (and they are expensive ones), but they do not seem to be in a state of structural crisis.

A similar consideration applies to the country's internal controls. As Asher Colombo, using the best available data, argues in *Fuori Controllo? Realtà e miti dell'immigrazione in Italia*, there is no evidence that the size of the irregular foreign population in Italy is extraordinary in comparison to other Western European countries. The rate of detected irregular migrants is also in line with other European countries, and the rate of actual deportations is not markedly different.

A spell of irregular residence, before acquiring permission to stay through an amnesty, has been nearly universal in the biographies of immigrants to Italy. In recent years, however, the eastern enlargement of the EU, the growing importance of family reunification, and the (slowly) improving effectiveness of Italian labor migration policies have markedly increased the percentage of recent immigrants entering legally. Even amnesties are far from being a Mediterranean anomaly: it is not necessary to be a historian to remember that endemic postentry regularizations were quite common in the early decades of the recent migration history of many European countries. If Italian control policies have problems, they are surely not so different from those that all other European countries have had or have to deal with.

If the outcomes of Italian control policies are not structurally different from those of other European countries, the same applies to the mechanisms and processes that make sense of them. In terms of the European labor market, one must mention first the combined impact of an aging population and conservative welfare arrangements that trigger a large demand for affordable domestic service workers; one must then acknowledge the transition to a post-Fordist economy, which triggers, among many other things, a substantial demand for low-skilled (or, in any case, low-paid) work in the construction and service sectors. To these economic factors, operating across the continent, Italy adds a particularly extensive shadow economy, which contributed, at its historic *low* in 2006, 16 percent to the GDP while employing approximately 12 percent of the country's workers. Because shadow employment is largely concentrated in agriculture, construction, and household services, it is not surprising that these are also the sectors where a large number of irregular foreign workers are concentrated. The presence of such a large shadow economy surely magnifies the problem, but these structural strains are far from being solely an Italian phenomenon.

The same applies to the contextual constraints that contribute to explaining why the Italian state, very often against the preferences of its own citizens (and the rhetoric of its rulers), tolerates unwanted migration. First, Italy has a highly independent judiciary, whose public image has been enhanced by the tribute of blood paid in fighting terrorism and organized crime (and, more recently, by its endemic conflict with former Prime Minister Silvio Berlusconi). Unsurprisingly, a large number of the most repressive measures approved by center-right cabinets (and quite a few of those approved by the center-left when in power) were quickly struck down by the courts. The importance of judicial review, moreover, is likely to become stronger in the future, given the new spaces opened to the European Court of Justice by the Treaty of Lisbon. Another important factor is the existence of a wide and ramified humanitarian infrastructure committed to an ethic of principles rather than consequences. Such an infrastructure, often linked to the Catholic Church and not infrequently state financed, enjoys a high level of prestige and provides immigrants, regardless of their legal status, with a key set of resources. Both the judiciary and the humanitarian infrastructure are indeed heavy constraints on the restrictive practices of the Italian state, but it would be difficult to claim that their force is significant only along the EU's southern rim.

A final set of constraints originates within the state itself, for immigration policy is always implemented (if at all) in the context of other policies embedded in a myriad of bureaucratic interests. It is undoubtedly true that immigration policy, spanning a large number of bureaucratic domains, is likely to trigger endemic turf wars. This was frequently witnessed in the history of Italian immigration policy, rooted since the beginning in competition between the labor and interior ministries, with the Ministry of Foreign Affairs trying at times to become the *tertius gaudens*. It is possible that these turf wars have been particularly acrimonious in Italy and (given the poor quality of Italian public administration) have resulted in greater unintended consequences. Notwithstanding, they are surely not unheard of in the other countries covered by this book. Moreover, bureaucratic turf wars seem to have been settled effectively lately, though perhaps not optimally, by the clear-cut victory of the Interior Ministry, which in the past decade—and this seems likely to last—established itself as the dominant player in Italian immigration policy. Another important constraint is that each state operates within a web of interdependent interests vested in other EU-member states as well as in other sending and transit countries. In managing such a web of interests, effective immigration control often becomes one goal among many others. But in the Italian case, the record seems actually *more* focused on immigration control than it is in most other EU countries. For example, quite a number of substantial problems in the Italian tourist industry were created by Italy's exacting visa policy.

In short, the outcomes of Italian immigration policy are far from being as disastrous as they are often claimed to be. They are, in fact, as is shown by the available evidence, quite similar to what they appear to be across the EU. The policies' limitations and failures, moreover, appear to be caused by the very same set of mechanisms that *Controlling Migration* identified in 1994 and has chronicled since.

If Italy is simply a variant of the European pattern, and if the actual content of its control policy actually has been quite stable over the last decade, what should we think of the heated political conflicts so carefully chronicled by Perlmutter? To be sure, Perlmutter is correct in pointing out that immigration is a deeply divisive issue in Italian political *communication*. It is also true that Italian center-right parties use a language that would otherwise be considered inappropriate, even by the standards of Northern European populist parties. Islamophobic claims have circulated widely, being sometimes popular in leftist circles and the highbrow press. At the same time, however, a close reading of actual texts and administrative dispositions shows that, behind this strongly polarized political rhetoric, there is an equally strong, indeed impressive, policy continuity.

The two coalitions (namely, the center-right and the center-left) exhibit significant contrasts over the issue of integrating the growing number of long-term foreign residents. The center-right is openly in favor of a restrictive approach to the granting of any rights, although even this sentiment manifests itself more through tardy and underfinanced practices than through full-fledged opposition. The center-left timidly endorses a more inclusive approach but without the energy necessary to strongly campaign for it. (It should not be forgotten that both the Left and the Right voted in favor of the highly restrictive 1992 citizenship law.) This is no small problem in a country where more than half of non-EU immigrants are now long-term residents and where a fifth of the foreign population is made up of minors growing up without stable legal status. The integration of long-term residents and the structural consequences of a large and ramified shadow economy are, however, precisely the issues that have been effectively sealed off from political debate through mutual agreement on low-profile fudging and procrastination.

As for control policy, on the other hand, sharply polarized rhetoric characterizes the minor extent of actual divergence in policy action. It is no secret that some of the largest amnesties have been carried out by center-right cabinets and that some of the readmission agreements with undemocratic sending countries have been promoted or even signed by center-left ministers. The actual policy spectrum is definitely smaller than is generally claimed, and the policy choices are fewer than they are made to appear during electoral campaigns. *Sous la plage, le pavé.*

12 | SPAIN

The Uneasy Transition from Labor Exporter to Labor Importer and the New Emigration Challenge

Miryam Hazán

INTRODUCTION

At the end of 2011, under a seemingly endless economic recession, and with an unemployment rate around 23 percent for the general population and over 40 percent for people ages 15 to 24, Spain faced a new, if once familiar, potential reality: becoming an exporter of labor as it had been from the mid-1950s until the early 1970s when close to 1.5 million Spaniards left to work in other western European countries. This time around, however, the problem was not so much the number of emigrants as the fact that most of them were young and educated.[1] Spain was losing the very people it needed to restructure its economy from one highly dependent on construction and services to one more diversified and more dependent on research and development and industrial innovation in fields in which Spain already had a competitive advantage (e.g., renewable energy, biotechnology, and transportation). Between January and September of 2011, 50,521 Spaniards left the country— 36 percent more than had left in the same period one year earlier.[2] Germany's Federal Statistics Office reported that, during the first half of 2011, Germany took in around 2,440 Spanish immigrants, a 40 percent increase from the previous year.[3] These were not just any kind of migrants but recent university graduates with a variety of language and technological skills. Such Spaniards sought new opportunities in other countries as well—primarily the United Kingdom, France, the United States and in Latin America.[4]

Parallel to this new phenomenon, government data showed that migration to Spain from countries outside the European Union (EU) had stopped, while the number of immigrants already in the country had actually diminished. For the past two decades, immigrants from these countries had helped satisfy labor market demand for low-skilled workers in a context of demographic stagnation among the native born. The economic downturn that officially started in January 2008 changed this trend. According to government data, in 2010, the number of non-EU immigrants legally in the country decreased by 37,056—a 1.45 percent decline—to a total of 2,524,976.[5] Although the number of all immigrants legally in the country remained almost unchanged from 2009, at 4,926,608 people, this was the result of an increase of 172,432 in the number of EU residents, whose reasons for migrating were not closely related to business-cycle dynamics.[6]

If the lack of growth in non-EU migration was caused by market events, it was also the result of immigration policies adopted since 2005, which aligned immigration flows from non-EU countries to labor market needs such that, in the absence of new jobs, flows would be curtailed.

This combination of business-cycle shock and policy-imposed incentives presented Spain with challenges that would have seemed unlikely a few years earlier: how to integrate the massive number of immigrants already settled in the country when unemployment was high; whether and how the emergence of xenophobic sentiment might be contained so as not to polarize the political landscape, especially in the context of economic decline; and how to deal with the secular trend of falling population that immigration had in recent years ameliorated or obscured. Although the birth rate increased from 1999 to 2009 thanks to immigration, it declined in 2010.[7] In some regions of the country, depopulation has been sharp enough to make economic recovery particularly difficult. The loss of immigrants also raises the question of how Spain will fill, from the ranks of its prospective highly educated young workforce, the nearly 2 million low-skilled positions now held by aging Spaniards.[8] Wanted are immigrants to fill these low-skilled positions and the young native workforce to fill skilled positions. What the country faces instead is a shortage of low-skilled workers and large-scale emigration among those trained for better jobs.

SPAIN'S DILEMMAS

Spain's transformation from major exporter to major importer of low-skilled labor happened over a relatively short time. It started in the 1980s when the country's economic prospects were improving via consolidation of its young democratic system and entry into the European Community (EC); it accelerated in the late 1990s as a result of an economic expansion generated by membership in the European Monetary Union and the associated real estate boom. When the country entered economic recession in 2007, that transformation was perhaps complete. Today, the country must somehow deal with the immigrant population that settled in the country during the period of economic expansion, while at the same time discouraging the emigration of its young population.

While notably sharp in the Spanish case, the dilemmas presented by this transformation are not unique to it. Like other economically advanced countries, Spain faces both an imperative to expand its population of recent immigrants and an imperative to restrict it. The need to expand its labor supply and the size of its domestic market, to finance its welfare system, and to address its demographic imbalances pushed Spain to implement policies that facilitated the arrival of newcomers. At the same time, the need to protect its native population from job displacement and wage depression and its welfare system from a fiscal burden; to avoid the emergence of xenophobic sentiment; to maintain the balance of its national and cultural composition; and to fulfill its commitments to the EU on immigration control, have compelled the country to restrict newcomers' entrance. All of these competing factors led the government to enact a series of immigration reforms starting in the mid-1980s that were more or less restrictive depending on evolving political and economic dynamics. These reforms included periodic regularizations to incorporate unauthorized newcomers into the formal economy and make them contributors to the welfare system; but they also included policies to order and control migratory flows, such as guest worker agreements, visa requirements, and greater collaboration with African countries to contain irregular migration.

The basic dilemma transcends immigration policy narrowly defined as the question of whom to allow to enter or to stay. It also appears in the field of citizenship and integration policy: how to accelerate the integration of newcomers without altering too much the country's cultural and national balance. This question has led to a variety of policy responses at the national and subnational levels. On the one hand, the national government maintained citizenship policies derived from its authoritarian past that primarily benefited immigrant groups perceived as closer to the idea of a cultural *Iberoamerican* nation—specifically, those from Latin America—and made entrance into the polity more difficult for all other national groups. Somewhat in contrast to this policy, Spain has also embraced the ethnic and cultural diversity brought by new immigrant groups and has followed an "intercultural" approach toward integration. As described by Spanish officials, interculturalism attempts to encourage a mutual exchange between natives and newcomers in a way that is supposed to transform both into a new and better national whole. This policy is supposed to be different from other European models (French assimilationism and Dutch multiculturalism), which Spanish elites portray as failing to acknowledge the value of difference or as promoting political fragmentation.[9] In practice, however, the Spanish model has amounted to the implementation of social and educational policies that have attempted to facilitate the co-existence of natives and newcomers, and to smooth the assimilation of immigrant groups deemed to have values different from those of Spaniards, especially those of Muslim/African origin.

With respect to this last group, elite and institutional responses have been ambiguous. On the one hand, they have emphasized the value of cultural and religious diversity and tolerance. On the other, they have argued that immigrants should share Spain's democratic values, including that of gender equality, and avoid non-Western practices such as female circumcision, or ablation. This discourse reached its climax in 2008 when Mariano Rajoy, then the Popular Party (PP) presidential candidate, proposed that immigrants sign an "integration contract" after one year in Spain that would commit them to respect the country's laws, including the prohibition of ablation.[10] This proposal copied a French law implemented by President Nicolas Sarkozy in 2004.

In addition, in the context of an expansionary economic period, Spain implemented an ambitious experimental policy to link newcomers to the development of their country of origin as a way to facilitate their integration into Spanish society. This policy has been termed "codevelopment." Although it may not survive the economic downturn unchanged, it has helped to create an entire institutional infrastructure that engages local and regional institutions with immigrants and with the realities of their places of origin.

Given high degrees of decentralization and linguistic and cultural variation, regional and local governments have an important responsibility in immigrant integration, and have pursued different approaches. While in some of them the approach chosen has been closer to the interculturalist idea promoted by the national government, in others, especially those that define themselves as culturally or linguistically different (e.g., Catalonia and the Basque Country), the approach adopted seems to be more assimilationist, even if the term *interculturalism* has been officially adopted. As we will see, integrating in Catalonia has not been the same as integrating in Madrid.

A third, more recent dilemma relates to high-skill emigration. Here Spain's major test is to implement policies that reduce the chances of a major brain drain because of high levels of unemployment among its young population.

In this chapter, I discuss Spain's evolution from an emigration to an immigration country and analyze the different dilemmas it has confronted as a result. I also consider the possibility that Spain will become an exporter of high-skilled labor.

I argue that Spain's rapid evolution from an emigration to an immigration country is a product of a combination of demographic deficits and the development model the country has pursued in recent times, both of which encouraged the arrival of massive numbers of low-skilled migrants. The prospect of Spain becoming an exporter of high-skilled labor in the context of a deep economic crisis is also a consequence of the economic model pursued for the past few decades. On the one hand, economic growth became highly dependent on sectors of the economy that required low-skilled rather than high-skilled, formally trained and recognized labor. On the other hand, the existence of a labor market that protects seniority made it difficult for young and educated Spaniards to integrate themselves into the labor force.

I also want to understand how Spain has chosen its immigration and integration policy responses to the basic dilemma. The Spanish state's policy in this area, I argue, is the result of three factors. First, the country's historical legacies, including: (1) its experiences as an emigration country, and (2) its national, cultural, and linguistic diversity, which has forced its elites and state institutions to deal with the problem of difference and become more tolerant than other European countries toward the presence of "others." Second, its institutional arrangements, including the corporatist patterns of its representation of socioeconomic interests, which have granted a predominant voice in the immigration field to three main actors at different stages: the government, with its varying perspectives depending on the governing party coalition, the unions, and the business community. Another institutional arrangement is its highly decentralized political system, which has allowed subnational governments to have significant leverage in defining the integration of newcomers. Third, membership in the EU, which at different times has exerted pressure on Spanish elites to become more proactive in securing the country's borders as Europe's southernmost point.

FROM AN EMIGRATION TO AN IMMIGRATION COUNTRY

When Spain Was an Emigration Country

From the mid-1850s until 1979, Spain was primarily a country of emigration. Through the 1920s, Spaniards migrated primarily to Latin America, with which Spain had had continuous, very intense, contact since Columbus. Although migration flows to this region were briefly arrested by its movements for national independence, emigration from Spain re-emerged at mid-century, when restrictions on immigration in most of Latin America were lifted. Migrants went primarily to Argentina, Cuba, Brazil, and, to a lesser extent, Uruguay and Mexico. Like most migrants from Europe to the Americas at the time, Spaniards were looking for economic opportunities promised by the newly created countries' low population density, abundant natural resources, and general sense of infinite possibility. It is estimated that between 3 and 4 million Spaniards migrated to the Americas between 1882 and 1930.[11] The late nineteenth century also witnessed Spanish migration to North Africa (Morocco, Algeria) and less to Equatorial Guinea.

Emigration for economic reasons ground to a halt around 1930, as Latin American countries introduced immigration controls, following the example of the US Immigration Act of 1924, which dramatically reduced immigration from Southern and Eastern Europe.

Spanish emigration re-emerged quickly, however, driven now by the flight of Socialist, Communist, and other Republican exiles from General Franco as his control of the country reached its peak in 1939. Around half a million Spaniards left for France and Mexico, but significant numbers headed for the Soviet Union or Algeria and others still for the Americas and other European countries. Many among the exiles were highly educated, making their migration a brain drain for Spain and a brain gain for receiving countries—most notably, perhaps, Mexico, which took in many public intellectuals, scientists, and artists.

Although emigration of political exiles abated for a time, in part because of exit controls instituted by the Franco regime, a new emigration wave arose in the mid-1950s, when these controls were lifted. This wave, which lasted into the early 1970s, landed largely in western Europe—with particularly large numbers received by France, Germany, Switzerland, and the United Kingdom. These most recent immigrants resembled the standard migrants of today from developing to developed countries. Economic modernization in Spain, after the failure of an autarkic economic model originally implemented by the Franco regime, produced major economic and regional imbalances. In the countryside, mechanization of agriculture during the 1950s generated worker displacement in the poorest areas of the country, especially in Extremadura, Andalucía, and Castilla-La Mancha. Workers migrated to big cities such as Barcelona, Madrid, and the Basque Country as industrial production in these cities gradually expanded with some government support. National industry, however, did not provide jobs to all of these internally displaced workers, or to the growing urban labor force more generally; conditions thus favored emigration to other European countries, facilitated and actually encouraged by the Franco regime, which, in a full policy reversal, eliminated the previously imposed emigration restrictions and created the National Institute for Emigration (NIE) in 1956. The NIE was in charge of channeling migratory flows in a way that would be the most profitable to the country. With that goal in mind, it negotiated guest worker agreements with Belgium (1956), Germany (1960), France, Switzerland, the Netherlands (1961), and Austria (1966).[12] The NIE monopolized information on job offers coming from these countries, and it was also responsible for recruiting suitable workers for these positions. Generally, poorly educated workers from areas of the country with high unemployment rates were the ones selected. Emigration was thus explicitly used as a safety valve in easing the country's economic adjustment and modernization and in containing social instability.[13] A new economic stabilization plan implemented in 1959, the National Stabilization Plan, which also liberalized the economy, produced additional economic displacement due to salary freezes, reduced investment and consumption, and higher unemployment rates—all of which created additional incentives to emigrate. Because of the many bureaucratic hurdles that would-be migrants had to clear in order to qualify for positions offered abroad, around 50 percent of them left the country without authorization. It is estimated that around 1.5 million Spaniards went to work abroad between 1960 and the early 1970s, although many of them repatriated themselves thereafter.[14]

Becoming an Immigration Country

Restrictions on emigration imposed by receiving countries as a result of the economic crisis of the 1970s, along with improving economic conditions in Spain, finally brought the mid-century migratory wave to a halt. A few years later, by the 1980s, the country gradually became a country of immigration. By the mid 1980s, Spain was receiving substantial numbers of immigrants attracted by the beginnings of the economic boom that coincided with its entry into the EC (see Table 12.1).

Through the 1990s, however, the immigrant population grew at a relatively slow pace. In 1981, there were 233,000 immigrants, representing 0.6 percent of the population. As Table 12.1 shows, in 1998 there were 637,085, or 1.6 percent of the population. Immigration accelerated dramatically as the 1990s came to a close, and the acceleration continued into the 2000s. According to government numbers, between 1998 and 2007, Spain received around 500,000 immigrants each year.[15] In the peak year of 2007 alone, it received 957,000.[16]

TABLE 12.1
Immigration trends in Spain since the 1980s

Year	Foreigners registered	Percentage of total population
1981	198,042	0.52
1986	241,971	0.63
1991	360,655	0.91
1996	542,314	1.37
1998	637,085	1.60
2000	923,879	2.28
2001	1,370,657	3.33
2002	1,977,946	4.73
2003	2,664,168	6.24
2004	3,034,326	7.02
2005	3,730,610	8.46
2006	4,144,166	9.27
2007	4,519,554	10.0
2008	5,220,600	11.3
2009	5,598,691	12.0
2010	5,747,734	12.2
2011	5,730,667	12.2

SOURCE: National Institute of Statistics (INE).

Although this rate of growth diminished in the ensuing years as a result of the acute economic crisis in Spain, by 2009, when the growth of the immigrant population finally stabilized,[17] there were 5.6 million immigrants,[18] representing 12.2 percent of the population. As a result of this growth, which was exceptional in the European context, Spain became the third largest recipient of immigrants in the world in absolute numbers after the United States and the Russian Federation.[19]

Apart from Europeans and other immigrants who qualify for admission under the "communitarian regime,"[20] Spain has received a large number of migrants from many parts of the world. These are the ones of particular interest for this chapter because, while communitarian migrants can enter, work, and reside on Spanish territory with few restrictions, and because of the Spanish Government's limited capacity to do anything about them, noncommunitarian immigrants face many restrictions and are the natural targets of new policy initiatives.[21]

The 1980s and 1990s witnessed a surge of immigrants from North Africa and eastern Europe. In the boom years of this century, the country also attracted large numbers of immigrants from Latin America, especially former Spanish colonies that in those years were confronting major economic crises. These included Ecuador, Colombia, Peru, and Bolivia, which together surpassed Morocco as the source of the largest immigrant contingent after 2000, and to a lesser extent Argentina, the Dominican Republic, and Paraguay. Still, Moroccans remained the largest noncommunitarian national immigrant group after the Romanians, who today are the largest group, qualified for the communitarian regime following Romania's accession to EU membership in 2007 (see Table 12.2).

A large number of immigrants who have arrived in Spain in the last few decades have done so as tourists or in other legal ways, generally reaching Spanish territory by air or land; very few arrive clandestinely by sea. This has forced Spain to require visas, especially from countries that have provided large numbers of immigrants, such as Morocco, and, more recently, Ecuador, Colombia, Peru, and Bolivia.

The rapid growth of the immigrant population is tightly linked to economic developments that took place in Spain during the 1990s and 2000s. After a recessionary economic period during the early 1990s, Spain entered a period of economic expansion that lasted from 1994 to 2007, during which the economy grew at an average of 3.5 percent per year. This growth encouraged a notable rate of expansion of the money supply. The standard policy response would have been to raise interest rates, with the goal of lowering inflation and forcing people and companies to save and discouraging new debt facilitated by cheap credit. In Spain, however, this response proved impossible. Complying with the 1992 Maastricht Agreement establishing the European Monetary and Economic Union, Spain *lowered* interest rates in pursuit of equalization with the more sluggish economies of the EMU, most notably France and Germany. Interest rates fell even further when the peseta stopped circulating in 2002, with foreign investors showing great trust in Spain as a eurozone economy.

With greater access to credit for the Spanish population and investment coming from abroad, the economy continued growing. Most of this growth was sustained, however, by investments in real estate and in tourism-related industries, which in turn spurred the expansion of the construction sector to build new properties and tourist infrastructure.

TABLE 12.2
Ranking of immigrant nationalities in Spain

Rank	Country	2001	2006	2011	Percent change, 2001–2011
1	Romania	31,641	407,159	864,278	2,632
2	Morocco	233,415	563,012	769,920	230
3	United Kingdom	107,326	274,722	390,880	264
4	Ecuador	139,022	461,310	359,076	158
5	Colombia	87,209	265,141	271,773	212
6	Bolivia	6,619	139,802	197,895	2,890
7	Germany	99,217	150,490	195,842	97
8	Italy	34,689	115,791	187,847	442
9	Bulgaria	12,035	101,617	172,634	1,334
10	China	27,574	104,681	166,223	503
11	Portugal	47,064	80,635	140,706	199
12	Peru	30,574	124,681	131,886	331
13	France	51,582	90,021	122,385	137
14	Argentina	32,429	150,252	120,012	270
15	Brazil	17,078	72,441	106,908	526
16	Dominican Republic	31,153	61,071	90,612	191
17	Paraguay	928	28,587	87,406	9,319
18	Ukraine	10,318	69,893	85,913	733
19	Poland	13,469	45,797	85,862	537
20	Pakistan	8,274	42,138	69,841	744
21	Senegal	10,627	35,079	63,248	333
22	Algeria	18,265	47,079	60,538	231
23	Venezuela	16,549	51,261	59,453	259
24	Netherlands	23,146	39,484	54,424	135
25	Cuba	24,534	44,739	54,406	122
26	Russia	10,047	39,904	52,832	426
27	Nigeria	7,598	31,588	44,870	491
28	Uruguay	6,828	45,508	42,581	524
29	Chile	11,674	39,704	41,712	257
30	Belgium	19,869	29,526	35,876	81
	Total	1,370,657	4,144,166	5,730,667	318

SOURCE: National Institute of Statistics (INE).

Construction and tourism had already become important sectors of the Spanish economy starting in the 1960s, when the country urbanized and opened up to the world. These sectors, however, acquired even greater relevance when the country entered a period of deindustrialization, especially after having joined the EU. Thus, the high unemployment rates Spain experienced during the 1990s were related to employment losses in the industrial sector,[22] and Spain's employment and growth prospects thereafter became more dependent on construction, tourism, and finance.[23]

Construction and tourism generated strong demand for low-skilled workers. Stagnant population growth due to low birth rates (1.3 today but 1.2 during much of the construction boom years), combined with ever higher average education levels of the native-born population, ensured that only immigration would provide a labor pool adequate to meet demand in these fields.[24] Immigrants responded to these demand-side incentives, with immigration peaking alongside the real estate bubble in 1998. The combination of these factors clearly attracted massive numbers of immigrants. From this perspective, im-

TABLE 12.3

Distribution of legal immigrant workers in Spain by sector, 2009

Sector	Number of workers
Primary	275,252
Industry	125,619
Construction	163,808
Services	1,050,502
Autonomous workers	196,698
(most in construction and services)	
Total	1,811,879

SOURCE: Spanish Ministry of Employment and Social Security (2011).

migration can be seen as a cause and a consequence of Spain's bubble era of economic expansion.

However, immigrants were not only employed in construction and similar industries linked to the real estate bubble. They also responded to Spain's broader demographic and economic dynamics. As the economy grew and unemployment decreased, more women joined the labor force. As a result, many immigrants, especially women, were employed in domestic services. They were also employed in dependent care jobs, which have gained in importance as Spanish society ages. Finally, immigrants also worked in intensive agriculture and other areas of the primary sector (see Table 12.3 for a breakdown of immigrant employment by economic sector).

Of the close to 7 million jobs that the Spanish economy created between 1998 and 2007, half were filled by immigrants. The developmental model pursued in the last few decades—highly dependent on construction and services along with demographic factors, including a declining fertility rate and the growing participation of women in the labor market—helps explain Spain's transformation into a country that imports labor, primarily low-skilled workers. So it is that less educated workers account for roughly one in seven among native workers age 16 and older, but close to one in four of immigrant workers age 16 and older.[25]

The Demographic and Economic Transformation

Immigration has undoubtedly contributed to the country's demographic well-being: it is behind the extraordinary population growth that Spain experienced in little more than a decade, from 39.8 million in 1998 to 47 million in 2010.[26] Apart from the large number of newcomers, immigrants also contributed to this growth because they were over-represented in the young adult population, especially the cohort of those 30 to 34 years of age, and because of the high fertility rates of immigrant women compared to those of native women (1.33 children for natives versus 1.67 children for immigrants in 2009).[27] Immigrants have thus been playing an increasingly important role in population replacement. Indeed, 24.1 percent of the children born in 2009 had immigrant parents.[28]

Immigrants have also contributed to the country's economic development. Newcomers played an important role in reinvigorating the labor market by helping to reduce imbalances between demand and supply and by providing flexibility and geographical mobility. According to the Spanish government, more than 50 percent of GDP growth from 2000 to 2005 can be attributed to the arrival of foreign workers. Without them, GDP would have grown significantly slower than the 2.6 percent increase during those years.[29] Furthermore, immigration helped reduce structural unemployment between 1996 and 2005 because of the flexibility it introduced in the labor market (which, for example, allowed more women to enter the workforce) and because it helped increase national demand for goods and services.[30] Finally, immigrants helped expand the tax base and, because of their underrepresentation in the population of those over 50 years of age, were net contributors to, rather than claimants on, the social security system.

SPAIN'S IMMIGRATION AND INTEGRATION DILEMMAS: THE POLICY RESPONSES

The rapid and somewhat unexpected growth of the immigrant population starting in the 1980s and accelerating during the late 1990s forced the Spanish government to implement a variety of immigration and integration policies to balance the country's demographic and economic needs with its political imperatives. These policies have been guided primarily by the country's historical legacies; by the evolving dynamics among the government, unions, and the private sector as part of its representation of socioeconomic interests; and by the influence of the EU on the country's decision making.

Historical Legacies

Spain's experience as an emigration country, the persistence of strong internal divisions along linguistic/cultural lines, and its experience as an empire and nation that forged itself in its fight against Islam, from which it inherited a strong cultural legacy, have been important factors in shaping the country's responses to immigration.

Although Spain experienced minimal immigration for close to five centuries following unification under its Catholic kings after the Conquest of Granada in 1492, it has a long and rich history of linguistic and cultural differences that at times have challenged its very survival as an integral political entity. During the Franco regime, such cultural and linguistic differences were suppressed through political repression. However, conflicts re-emerged under democratic rule. The Constitution of 1978 tried to address the differences by allowing regional decentralization of state functions. It also granted autonomy to the different nationalities and regions, which became political and territorial entities known as autonomous communities. Still, conflict remained over issues related to fiscal solidarity and the competencies that autonomous communities should have. The need to deal continually with political difference and the presence of "others" means, at least in theory, that elites and institutions are more practiced in and comfortable with the arrival and integration of newcomers than their long isolation from transnational immigration should have made them.

A similar effect can perhaps be attributed to Spain's experience as an emigration country. Spanish elites continually refer to the Spanish emigration experience as a reason for accepting and integrating newcomers and regularly refer to it as an antidote to racism and xenophobia.[31] On an abstract level, Spaniards seem to have more positive views on immigration than other Europeans, linking the immigrants among them with stories of ancestors forced to emigrate. In a 2010 national poll,[32] for example, when the country was already in a recessionary period, 59 percent of respondents stated that when they think about immigration, they think about the "need to come and find a job," "an analogy to the Spanish emigration experience," "poverty and inequality," "feelings of empathy and solidarity," and the "*Pateras.*"[33] In contrast, only 20 percent associated immigration with ills such as "excessive increase of immigrants," "illegality and irregularity," "social privileges vis-à-vis Spaniards," "crime and insecurity," "negative impact in the labor market," and "problems of integration and co-existence."

At the same time, however, prevailing notions of nationhood based on Spain's imperial past have created a dual system of access to membership in the polity, which means that the country is more welcoming toward some immigrant groups than toward others. Immigrants from former Spanish colonies or from countries linked to Spain through historical connections identified as belonging to an Iberoamerican cultural idea are granted citizenship in two years. These include newcomers from Latin America (including Brazil), Portugal, the Philippines, Andorra, and Equatorial Guinea. For this reason, immigrants from Latin America, who arrived in massive numbers in recent years, have been the primary recipients of most citizenship petitions Spain has granted in the past decade, even while immigrants from Morocco, for example, have been in the country for a longer time (see Figure 12.1).

In 1982, the Spanish government modified Article 22 of its civic code to extend the two-year citizenship benefit to Sephardic Jews. This legal change was an official recognition

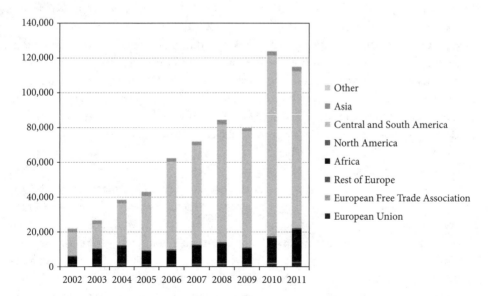

Figure 12.1 Evolution of Spanish nationality per origin, 2002–2011. *Source:* Spanish Ministry of Employment and Social Security (2011).

that Jews had been unfairly expelled from Spain in 1492. Immigrants from Morocco have expressed dissatisfaction with the fact that they did not obtain a similar benefit, claiming that they also have had a historical connection to Spain after many centuries of Moorish presence.[34] The national perception of Moroccans and other immigrants from Africa, however, is more ambiguous. While it is still politically incorrect in Spain to warn darkly of the continent's impending "Islamization" or "Africanization," there also has been skepticism about the country's capacity to absorb large numbers of Muslim and African migrants. When asked in the national poll mentioned earlier, "How important is it for you that immigrants to Spain come from countries with a Christian tradition?" only 7.7 percent of respondents answered that it was very important. This was in contrast to the 33.9 percent who declared it very important that those who come to the country have labor qualifications the country needs, the 20.9 percent who answered that immigrants should have a good educational level, and the 23 percent who said that immigrants should speak Spanish or the language of the autonomous community where they reside.[35] Furthermore, though Spaniards tend to express a preference for Latin American and European immigrants over other groups, the most disliked are not Moroccans or others from Africa but Gypsies (and by extension Romanians, notwithstanding differences between Romanian and Roma), who are popularly associated with high levels of criminality.[36] Around 700,000 Gypsies in Spain have Spanish nationality, and they are the most frequent targets of racism, although there have been incidents of racist hostility directed against Muslims[37] and other groups.[38] A standard position taken on Muslims is that they should be accepted provided they accept Western values, including those related to gender equality and the rejection of practices such as ablation. This view was dramatically advanced by the president of government Mariano Rajoy when he proposed during his unsuccessful 2008 presidential bid that immigrants should sign an "integration agreement" like that employed in France, a proposal clearly targeted toward Muslim immigrants. Though it went nowhere at the time, probably because Latin Americans were taking over as a larger immigrant contingent, the proposal reflected Spain's complex relationship with Islam. The country's identity was forged in its great victory for Christendom, but the long history of Muslim settlement (between two and eight centuries prior to the *Reconquista*, depending on the region, and with many Muslims remaining after Muslim dominion had been broken) as well as the sheer proximity to North Africa, has meant a richness of exchange unparalleled elsewhere in the West.

The lack of fast-track access to citizenship for immigrants from African and other non-EU countries outside Latin America has meant that these immigrants are more likely to fall into irregularity. As we will see, over the past two decades, Spain implemented a number of regularizations, but they were for temporary, not permanent, residence. This is not a minor issue. Spain has a complex system of short-term labor contracts, work permits, and residence permits, all mutually contingent. An immigrant can obtain a residence permit lasting from ninety days to a maximum of five years. To obtain permanent residence, immigrants must have lived legally in the country for at least five years. This means that an immigrant who benefited from regularization with a permit that lasts less than five years, cannot renew it and unless he has access to citizenship in two years, can fall back into irregularity very easily. The impact of this situation obviously increases during an economic downturn, when many immigrants are not able to renew their work permits, which are necessary to maintain legal status. Although the number of irregular migrants arriving in Spain decreased as a result of the economic crisis that started in 2008, estimates based on government data show that by the third trimester of 2009, 500,000 immigrants who had once enjoyed legal residency had fallen back into illegality.[39]

National Institutional Arrangements

Spain's responses to immigration and integration policies have also been shaped by the country's institutional arrangements, including its representation of socioeconomic interests. Particularly important in this respect is the high degree of decentralization that has granted a very important role to regional and municipal institutions in the integration of newcomers.

The Role of Socioeconomic Actors

Spain has a concentration of socioeconomic actors in two main unions, the General Workers Union, or Union General de Trabajadores (UGT), and the Workers Commissions, or Comisiones Obreras (CCOO), which represent most of the working class, along with one business association, the Spanish Confederation of Business Organizations, or Confederación Española de Organizaciones Empresariales, which represents most of the business class. This grouping of interests has been institutionalized over the years by national legislation that has granted a privileged role in decision making to institutions considered the most representative of the population, to the extent that it is possible to argue that, in the policymaking on social and economic issues, Spain operates in a corporatist fashion. This has certainly been the case in the immigration and integration arenas, where the majority of decisions have been made by the competing interests of the unions and the business community, especially during the first decade of this century, when immigration to the country accelerated dramatically and these actors had greater stakes in influencing the national immigration debate. The capacity of such corporate actors to exercise influence, however, has been greatly determined by their level of access to a political party or a political coalition in power or their ability to challenge the dominant power structure. In general, unions have shown a greater capacity to influence immigration decision making when the PSOE has been in power, while the business community has had more influence during PP administrations.

Decentralization

Regional and municipal authorities play a very important role in the integration of newcomers. Municipal governments are the first institutions with which immigrants come into contact once they arrive and settle in Spain. To receive any kind of services, including health and education, they are required by law to register with the municipalities where they reside regardless of their legal status. Some services are provided by autonomous communities, including health and education, while municipal governments provide social aid and housing subsidies, among other services. All such points of interaction help define the integration path immigrants will pursue. In 2005, the government implemented for the first time an integration program known as Strategic Plan for Citizenship and Integration 2005–2008 (which would be followed by a new version for 2009–2012). After the plan's implementation, the government created a national fund to supplement the costs associated with the integration of newcomers, which a 2008 decree stipulated should be shared among autonomous communities, municipal governments, immigrant-oriented NGOs, and immigrant associations. The goals of this fund are to guarantee social cohesion and to help equalize the rights and obligations of the immigrant community with those of the autochthonous community.[40] The fund reached a peak of 200 million euros in 2008. However, as a result of the economic crisis, it fell to 100 million in 2009, 70 million in 2010, and 66.6 million in 2011. Such a dramatic decline speaks to a real crisis, given that immigrant integration has become a national priority.

Even with reduced resources, all regional and local entities that receive large numbers of immigrants currently have in place specific integration policies. In places where a language other than Castilian Spanish predominates, such as Catalonia, the main priority is to facilitate the cultural and linguistic immersion of newcomers. Here the goal is not only to facilitate adaptation but also to diminish the threat that newcomers represent to local power arrangements. The influx of residents more likely to speak Spanish than Catalan, as is overwhelmingly the case for Latin American immigrants, threatens political marginalization of Catalan speakers. Thus, in Catalonia there have been more pressures from the right to require immigrants to integrate by forcing them to sign an "integration contract" that commits them to having at least a working knowledge of Spanish and Catalan, as well as an "adequate knowledge of Catalan civil life."[41]

Probably because of the political challenge newcomers represent to local power arrangements, anti-immigrant and xenophobic sentiment has been more prominent in Catalonia than in other parts of Spain. A prominent example is the Municipality of Vic, which suffered an important shift in its population structure during the past decade after the arrival of large number of immigrants primarily from Morocco. In 2010, Vic authorities announced that they would not register any more newcomers unable to prove legal residence, thus denying them basic services such as health and education.[42] Vic is the home of Josep Anglada, the founder and president of Platforma per Catalunya (PpC), a Catalonian political party whose main platform is opposition to massive immigration, with a xenophobic plank targeted especially against Muslims. The PpC, which represents Spain's most xenophobic political expression so far, is particularly influential in Vic and in neighboring Vendrell, Manlleu, and Manresa, all of which are industrial cities with high levels of immigration and native unemployment.[43] At the regional level, it won 2.4 percent of electoral votes in the 2011 municipal elections, its highest ever, although it was unable to attain parliamentary representation in Catalonia. Anglada's xenophobic agenda has not been implemented, but in 2010 the Parliament of Catalonia took direct steps to force immigrants to learn Catalan, requiring them to speak the language in order to regularize their immigration status or to obtain resident permits.[44]

In other places, such as the autonomous community of Madrid, where language assimilation is less of an issue, the emphasis has been on reducing the marginalization and segregation of newcomers, the idea being to prevent immigrants becoming a major social problem, as they are in countries like France, through a policy of intercultural exchange in which natives and newcomers learn to co-exist.[45]

The Role of the European Union

Since Spain joined the EU, its responses to immigration have been influenced by EU immigration prerogatives. Faced with immigration challenges from the east and south, the EU's main priority has been to control its borders by imposing restrictions on immigration. Spain has been crucial in this regard because of its strategic location as Europe's southernmost country. Spain's preferred strategy from the very beginning has been to avoid being cast in the role of "policeman of Southern Europe," keeping the Third World hordes at bay. Instead, it has attempted to persuade its fellow EU members to step up development assistance to the labor-exporting countries of North Africa. However, Spain's capacity for persuasion has been dependent on its influence vis-à-vis other countries, which in turn has depended on its economic development. As we will see, in the beginning Spain had no choice but to follow the dictates of the EC, which were reflected in its first immigration law enacted under democratic rule. During the economic boom of the late 1990s and early 2000s, the country acquired a greater capacity to decide its own policies, as seen in a 2005 regularization that was implemented despite strong opposition from EU member countries, which then pushed to impose the requirement that EU member states consult each other before implementing any massive regularization.[46]

By this time, the pendulum was swinging again, helped by a widely held perception that immigrant numbers had surpassed the point at which liberal accommodationist policies no longer made sense, and Spain was forced to step up its immigration control efforts through the gradual imposition of visas and more control at the borders. An additional mechanism of immigration control has been *Plan Africa*, now in its second version (2009–2012), which at the discourse level privileges Spain's preferred strategy of providing development assistance to sending African countries. In practice, however, most of the aid provided has been devoted to projects intended to manage migratory flows, as reflected in a thorough analysis of the destination of assistance funds.[47]

In the face of a new economic downturn, with strong dependence on EU support to recover from it and with a large immigrant population to integrate, Spain's focus will be to strengthen its borders further even while the pressures of immigration flows have diminished in the ongoing economic downturn.

Stages in Spanish Immigration

Considering the factors that have shaped Spanish immigration and integration policies, we can identify three distinct stages of immigration.[48]

In a first stage that lasted roughly from 1985 to 2005, the guiding factors were to satisfy the immigration imperatives of the EU as well as the needs of the business sector. During the early 1980s, the main national goal had been to modernize the country and to become part of the EC. In this context, the administration of then president Felipe González produced in 1985 the first law on the Rights and Liberties of Foreigners in Spain, which attempted to satisfy the security requirements of the EC. Popularly known as the Ley de Extranjería (Law on Foreigners), it focused more on restrictions than on defending the rights of immigrants, even though it was implemented by the Labor Ministry rather than the Interior Ministry. Over the years, these two ministries have competed intensely over setting the immigration agenda.

The main goal of the Law on Foreigners was to control immigrant access to the labor market, which made stable residency very difficult. Newcomers could obtain residency permits only once they had a job offer, and they could only renew them after meeting numerous requirements.

Because of these limitations, many immigrants ended up with an irregular status. Furthermore, in contrast to the United States, where family reunification had been the guiding principle of immigration law since 1965, the Spanish law made family reunification very difficult, a situation that was corrected only in 1996 when an amendment to the law was introduced that acknowledged immigration as a structural phenomenon and recognized that newcomers' rights included the right to reunify their families.

As compensation for the many limitations it imposed, the foreigners law considered the possibility of regularization but, as noted above, only under temporary conditions. Immigrants could attain regular status by applying on an individual basis or through their employers; they had three months to present the necessary documents. Because the foreign population in Spain was still relatively small, regularization was not significant in terms of numbers—only 38,131 benefited from it—and it did not require the involvement of major societal actors such as the unions and the business community.

Because of the harsh immigration policies introduced in 1985, many immigrants were left without the possibility of securing the documentation necessary to attain legal status. This situation left the door open for further regularizations, in 1991 and 1996, still under the government of Felipe González, although the 1996 regularization was designed but not implemented by the socialists because the PP took control of the national government that year.

In 2000 and 2001, the PP was forced to implement yet two more amnesties because the flaws in the 1985 law, despite the 1996 reforms, were still making it very difficult for foreigners to attain legal status. As the migratory flows into the country were becoming larger, however, so were the numbers of those affected by the regularizations. This, in turn, magnified political and social tensions. Labor unions began to perceive these amnesties as counter to their interests—as a means of expanding the pool of legal workers and thus pushing wages down. In contrast, the business sector not only did not suffer real sanctions for hiring unauthorized immigrants but also was not forced to register workers in the social security system. Because the amnesties only required immigrants to have a job offer (and on many occasions even this was not necessary) rather than an employment *contract*, in many cases they had offers but maintained their irregular status in the labor market.

The tensions created by the amnesties were reflected in a conflict between the PP government of José María Aznar and the opposition when a new foreigners law was being negotiated. In January 1998, the opposition—including IU, the Catalan Nationalist Party Convergencia I Unió, and Grupo Mixto—introduced an initiative to create a new foreigners law, which was finally approved on January 12, 2000, with a broad political consensus;

all political parties voted in favor, including the PSOE and the PP—however, the PP did so only because it did not have an absolute majority in Parliament; indeed, the new law was against its interests.

The Law on the Rights and Freedoms of Foreigners in Spain and their Integration—technically Organic Law 4/2000—marked a drastic shift in Spanish immigration policy that would have repercussions in the future, especially in 2005. Until 2000, the main function of Spanish immigration law had been immigration control rather than promoting integration. The new law would grant more rights to immigrants regardless of their legal status, including the right to associate, to rally, and to unionize. (The right to unionize was a triumph for UGT and CCOO, the main Spanish unions.) It also recognized the immigration phenomenon as global and permanent and accordingly emphasized the importance of incorporating newcomers into the labor market. In addition, it introduced for the first time in Spanish legislation the notion of co-development—the idea that, to control its migratory flows, Spain had a responsibility to help in the economic and social development of sending areas. This policy was supported by local and regional governments, some of which were already implementing pioneering policies in this field, drawing on their previous support of cooperation in development of the third world and inspired by the work of Sami Nair, a French political scientist and official of Algerian origin who first articulated the potential benefits of such cooperation.

After the March 2000 elections, the PP recovered its absolute majority in Parliament and just a few months later passed Organic Law 8/2000 to amend the previous legislation. This law was less generous than Organic Law 4/2000. Among other things, it granted the rights of association, rallying, and unionizing only to legal immigrants.[49] Nonetheless, it kept integration as a key to Spanish immigration policy. Organic Law 8/2000 was the basis for what became known as Plan GRECO—a program for presenting immigration as a desirable phenomenon that argued for seeing foreigners as active contributors to Spain's economic development. However, the PP argued that Spain should follow the principles of the EU, including the emphasis on security. On those grounds, the regulatory functions concerning immigration were passed from the Labor Ministry, where they had been until passage of Organic Law 8/2000, to the Interior Ministry.

An important contribution of Plan GRECO was its recognition of the vital role of regional governments in the integration of newcomers; this recognition would become very important in government integration policies implemented thereafter. In addition, as part of a broad policy on immigration designed by the PP, Spain concluded guest worker agreements with sending countries. After the first such agreement was signed with Morocco in 1997, Spain concluded similar agreements with Romania and Bulgaria. These countries had not yet joined the EU and so sent many undocumented immigrants to Spain. A few years later, Spain also signed similar agreements with Senegal and Ecuador, Colombia, and Peru. An interesting aspect of these programs is that they provided workers access to Spanish citizenship after a certain period of time if they returned to their countries of origin when their contract agreements ended. If a worker duly returned to her home country, she was allowed to come back to Spain the following year, subject to agreement with her Spanish employer.

The guest worker programs were important because they showed the business sector a pool of workers they could hire without running afoul of the law. This facilitated the support of the business sector in 2005 for an ambitious regularization system that would be in stark contrast to previous ones. It would be implemented by the incoming Socialist government after Zapatero's victory in the 2004 elections.

While previous regularizations had been carried out on an individual basis and, for the most part, without regard to the immigrant's job prospects, the 2005 regularization was clearly undertaken with labor market needs in mind. Only immigrants who had a work contract could be regularized, and the onus of regularization was not on immigrants but on employers, who became responsible for regularizing their workforce within a specified period of time to avoid sanctions. Immigrants benefited from this because they were directly integrated into the welfare system, becoming beneficiaries of as well as contributors to it.

The 2005 regularization marked a second stage in Spain's immigration history, one characterized by a broad consensus among business and labor at a time when large migrant contingents were arriving in the country and immigration was being recast as necessary to address labor shortages and demographic needs. It benefited 577,923 people and was enacted with little public debate and in closed-door meetings between the government, the UGT and CCOO, and the CEOE.

Parallel to the 2005 regularization, two extraordinary amnesties were created to facilitate the regularization of those who did not qualify for legal status and those who arrived after the regularization was implemented. The first is known as social attachment, or *arraigo social*, whereby an immigrant could qualify for legal residency if she had been in the country for a period of at least three years (a fact that could be confirmed simply by registering on arrival with the municipality in which she was settling), did not have a criminal record in Spain or in her country of origin, had a work contract of at least one year, and could prove some social links to the community where she would be residing in Spain.

The second mechanism is known as labor attachment, or *arraigo laboral*, whereby an immigrant could attain legal permanent residency if he could prove that he had been in Spain for a period of at least three years, had a labor relation with an employer (proved by bringing the employer into court), and had no criminal record in Spain or in his country of origin.

The new amnesties were implemented in an atmosphere uncommonly favorable to immigration experimentation: the Socialists had just assumed power, after eight years in opposition, with high legitimacy and public support. Also, Spain's strong economic growth underpinned arguments for amnesty based on the demand for immigrant labor. Furthermore, Socialist governments s were less interested than in the past in following the dictates of the EU because Spain was by then sufficiently powerful and institutionalized, and had been accepted as a member of the union, which had confidence in its independent political judgment.

The new socialist president, Jose Luis Rodriguez Zapatero, had won the 2004 legislative elections against Mariano Rajoy, who had been selected by outgoing president Jose Maria Aznar to replace him as PP leader. The dramatic events immediately preceding the 2004 elections are worth recalling. Aznar blamed the separatist ETA (Euskadi Ta Askatusuna) for the terrorist attacks that took place in Madrid three days before the election, even though the ETA denied responsibility. These attacks killed 191 people—almost a third of them recent immigrants to Spain on their way to work—when a series of bombs exploded in trains approaching Madrid's Atocha Central Train Station. The public was angered by Aznar's hasty, unfounded, and false accusation of ETA and punished the PP by giving an unexpected victory to the PSOE. In fact, investigations already becoming public suggested that Muslim extremists from Morocco were the authors of the attacks. Thus, disgust with the PP government's cynical handling of the nation's trauma fed into pre-existing public animosity over its support of the US war in Iraq, producing a sharp electoral repudiation.[50] Zapatero responded by immediately setting out to govern from the left, in pointed contrast to the markedly right Aznar administration.

The Iraq War, the Madrid bombings, and the politics of immigration came together as the Zapatero government was quickly distancing itself from xenophobic stances toward Muslims and immigrants. This position taking was reinforced by the government's transferring of most immigration policy jurisdiction from Interior back to Labor and Social Affairs. In both rhetorical and practical terms, transferral reframed immigration as an economic and labor issue. As part of this process, Zapatero created a new secretariat in the Labor Ministry focused on immigration and emigration. Four years later, right after the legislative elections of March 2008 confirmed the results of 2004, a further emboldened Zapatero changed the name of the Ministry of Labor to Ministry of Labor and Immigration, thus consolidating the perception of immigration as a matter of labor and welfare.

In line with these administrative changes, immigrant integration became a major goal of the Spanish state. Starting in 1994, during the Gonzalez administration, the Council of Ministers approved the Plan for the Social Integration of Immigrants, the goal of which was to aid the settlement of newcomers. Although many of the plan's objectives were never fully realized, two major instruments that emerged from it not only survived but actually set the parameters of future integration policy. These were the Forum for the Integration of New Immigrants and the Permanent Observatory of Immigration to Spain. The first had the goal of promoting immigrants' civic participation and representation by allowing them to elect representatives to the forum, which plays an advisory role. The second produced research on immigration and integration for use in policymaking. Both were emulated at the subnational level in most Spanish autonomies and cities where large numbers of immigrants had settled, including those controlled by the PP, which, as noted earlier, in the Plan GRECO also emphasized the important role of local governments in immigrant integration. In 2007, a year before the transformation of the Labor Ministry, the Zapatero administration presented the Strategic Plan on Citizenship and Integration, the goal of which was the promotion of social cohesion in the country through policies granting equal rights to newcomers. Working with this same logic, in July 2008 the socialist government proposed to grant the right to vote to non-EU citizens in local elections, conditioned on the principle of reciprocity established by the Spanish Constitution. By this time, however, the country was immersed in a major economic crisis, signaling a new stage in Spanish immigration history.

The third stage, which started in 2008, has been characterized by greater alignment with the restrictive policies of the EU, including those that emphasize return migration and, at the same time, immigrant integration. Also in 2008, the government of Zapatero restricted access to family reunification by excluding the parents and the in-laws of naturalized immigrants and immigrants with permanent residence on the grounds that they would burden the welfare system as likely dependents of productive laborers. The administration also increased inspections of employment sites[51] and offered incentives for legal residents without employment to return to their countries of origin. These incentives included immediately paying them 40 percent of their unemployment benefits and the rest on their return to their home countries, in exchange for forfeiting residence rights and promising not to return to Spain for at least three years. This program had little success, but immigrants nonetheless started to leave the country as the economic crisis deepened, as reflected in a 2010 drop in incoming immigration flows.

Since immigration policy has been aligned with labor market needs, the government has also followed a policy of zero hiring in source countries. The result has been a freeze on new immigration from non-EU countries. On the integration front, however, the Zapatero administration introduced, a few months before leaving office, a new form to regularize newcomers who were settling in the country, even as many others were joining the ranks of the undocumented as they lost their jobs and with them their working permits to be in the country legally. This new instrument is called Arraigo Familiar (Family Attachment), and its goals are to regularize the parents of Spanish-born minor children and so avoid their effective orphaning caused by their parents' deportation. Women able to prove domestic abuse will also be able to obtain residence on their own account.

These measures, together with the Arraigo Laboral and the Arraigo Social introduced earlier, are addressing the situation of many immigrants who have fallen into illegality during the current economic crisis. However, the ascension of Mariano Rajoy to the presidency may change the immigration power structure once again. Just a month after Rajoy took office, his government announced that it would tighten immigration law by applying Angela Merkel's model. That is, it will allow entrance only to those immigrants who obtain a work contract and will deport all those who have lost their jobs. In addition, the Rajoy government will eliminate the social attachment mechanism that was widely used to regularize newcomers, and that helped to keep the numbers of irregular migrants down since its implementation.[52] If Rajoy's measures are implemented, Spain will have traveled full circle in its treatment of immigration, once again privileging the dictates of the EU and the needs of the business community with little consideration of the unions and other social sectors.

THE EMERGING EMIGRATION CHALLENGE

At the end of 2011, a new trend was emerging in Spain: the emigration of its young and educated. With youth unemployment rates nearing 50 percent, Spain has seen emigration increase. The census of Spaniards residing abroad shows that 300,000 have settled in other countries since the crisis began. This situation threatens to undermine the restructuring of the Spanish economy so that it is more diversified and dependent on technological advances through research and development. And it represents a major challenge with which Spain will have to deal in its near future if it wants to address its longstanding deficit of competitiveness and its long-running demographic challenges.[53]

NOTES

1. See "América Latina es el segundo destino de los nuevos emigrantes españoles," Infobae.com, December 26, 2011, http://america.infobae.com /notas /40842-America -Latina-es-el-segundo-destino-de-los-nuevos-emigrantes-espanoles.

2. See Charo Nogueira, "La salida de españoles se dispara un 36.6% este año por la crisis," *El País*, December 25, 2011.

3. See, among others, "La 'miserable' situación económica de España obliga a los jóvenes a emigrar a Alemania," *ABP Noticias*, January 2, 2012, http://www.abpnoticias .com /index.php?option=com_k2&view=item&id=1281:la-miserable-situaci%C3%B3n -econ%C3%B3mica-de-espa%C3%B1a-obliga-a-los-j%C3%B3venes-a-emigrar-a -alemania&Itemid=73. See also "Angela Merkel: 'Vente a Alemania Pepe' version 2.1," *Revista Berlín*, February 2, 2011, http://revistaberlin.com /angela-merkel-vente-a -alemania-pepe-version-2-1/.

4. See Nogeuira, "La salida de españoles."

5. The immigrant groups showing the largest decreases were primarily those from Latin America, including Ecuador (10.78 percent), Argentina (9.3 percent), Colombia (7.73 percent), and Peru (5.51 percent). See Ministerio de Trabajo e Inmigración, *La cifra de extranjeros residentes se estabiliza en 2010* (Madrid: Ministerio de Trabajo e Inmigración, 2011). See also "El número de inmigrantes en España cae por primera vez desde el 2010 hasta los 2.5 millones," *El Periódico*, March 1, 2011, http://www.elperiodico.com / es /noticias /sociedad /20110301/numero-inmigrantes-espana-cae-por-primera-vez-desde -2010-hasta-los-millones /910128.shtml.

6. Ibid.

7. See "Cae la tasa de natalidad por primera vez en 10 años," *America Economía*, July 22, 2010, http://www.americaeconomia.com /politica-sociedad /sociedad /cae-la-tasa-de -natalidad-en-espana-por-primera-vez-en-10-anos.

8. See Florentino Felgueroso and Pablo Vázquez, "Immigración y crisis: Aciertos, desaciertos y políticas complementarias," in *La crisis de la economía española: Lecciones y propuestas* (Madrid: Sociedad Abierta & FEDEA, 2009), http://www.crisis09.es /ebook / inmigracion-y-crisis.html.

9. The Minister of Immigration in 2002 said publicly that multiculturalism is "unacceptable" for Spain. At most, he argued, Spain might become a "multi-ethnic society." Quoted in Amnesty International, "Spain: Crisis of Identity," www.amnesty.org, April 16, 2002, p. 6.

10. See Tomás Bárbulo and Josep Garriga, "Rajoy quiere obligar a los inmigrantes a firmar 'un contrato de integración,'" *El País*, February 7, 2008, http://elpais.com / diario /2008/02/07/espana /1202338806_850215.html.

11. See Alicia Alted, ed., *De la España que emigra a la España que acoge*, catalog to the exhibition "Madrid, Círculo de Bellas Artes" (Madrid: Fundación F. Largo Caballero y Obra Social Caja Duero, 2006), 33.

12. Ibid.

13. See Gobierno de España, Ministerio de Educación, Cultura y Deporte, *Cúales fueron las causas de la emigración*, auce.pntic.mec.es /jotero /Emigra3/causas.htm.

14. Until early 1992, the immigration office in the Ministry of Labor was anachronistically called the "Spanish Institute of Emigration." For the number of emigrants during that period, see Valeriano Gómez, "Crisis, inmigración y política de empleo: Una visión de conjunto," in *Inmigración y crisis económica, impactos y perspectivas de futuro*, ed. Eliseo Aja, Joaquín Arango, and Josep Oliver Alonso (Barcelona: CIDOB, Diputació Barcelona, Fundación Acsar, Centro de Estuidos Andaluces & Unicaja, 2010), 112.

15. See Secretaria de Estado de Inmigración y Emigración, "II Plan Estratégico de Ciudadanía e Integración," 26–27.

16. See Joaquín Arango, "Después del gran boom: La inmigración en la bisagra del cambio," in *La inmigración en tiempos de crisis: Anuario de la inmigración en España*, ed. Eliseo Aja, Joaquín Arango, and Josep Oliver Alonso (Barcelona: Fundación CIDOB & Diputació Barcelona, 2009), 54.

17. During 2008, immigration flows were not directly affected by the economic crisis, as immigrants still retained their jobs at even higher rates than the native population. By mid-2009, however, these flows had finally slowed down as unemployment among the immigrant population increased. See Eliseo Aja, Joaquín Arango, and Josep Oliver Alonso, "Bajo el influjo de la crisis," in *La inmigración en tiempos de crisis: Anuario de la inmigración en España*, ed. Eliseo Aja, Joaquín Arango, and Josep Oliver Alonso (Barcelona: Fundación CIDOB & Diputació Barcelona, 2009), 11.

18. These numbers come from the National Institute of Statistics, which totals all of the immigrants registered by Spanish local governments. It includes the unauthorized population, since to receive health and education services immigrants have to register with local authorities regardless of their status. It is important to point out, however, that there can be unauthorized migrants who have not registered, which may add to the size of the total immigrant population. The number used by the NIS differs from the number used by the Labor Minister for Immigration and Emigration, which counts only legal immigration.

19. See Arango, "Después del gran boom," 54.

20. The "communitarian regime," or *régimen comunitario*, is the legal framework that regulates the entrance of citizens from EU countries and those from countries in the European Free Trade Association (EFTA). It grants entrance to family members of EU citizens and family members of Spanish citizens regardless of their nationality. The legal framework that oversees entrance of all other nationalities is the "general regime," or *régimen general*.

21. Romanian immigrants, and especially Gypsies, present a more complex situation, however, since they do shape many perceptions about immigration and have been a major concern of the Spanish state both before and after they became communitarian immigrants. The complexity of their case deserves a more profound analysis. For this reason it is not be considered here.

22. Gómez, "Crisis, inmigración y política de empleo," 109.

23. Although there are various explanations for the Spanish real estate boom, experts now agree on its fundamental reliance on expansionary monetary policy. See Juan Ramón Rallo, *Los precios de la vivienda y la burbuja inmobiliairia en España* (Madrid: Observatorio de Coyuntura Económica, Instituto Juan de Mariana, 2008), http://www.juandemariana .org/pdf/080304burbuja.pdf.

24. As Valeriano Gómez demonstrates, of the five largest European economies (Germany, France, Spain, Italy, and the United Kingdom), Spain had become the largest employer in the construction industry by 2007. This situation was abnormal given that, being the smallest economy of the five, it should have been the one that employed the fewest workers. For this very reason, 50 percent of job losses during the economic crisis that officially began in January 2008 have been in this sector. See Gómez, "Crisis, inmigración y política de empleo," 109–10.

25. See Ruth Ferrero Turión, "Migration and Migrants in Spain: After the Bust," in *Migration and Immigration Two Years after the Financial Collapse: Where Do We Stand?* ed. Demetrios Papademetriou, Madeleaine Sumption, and Aaron Terrazas (Washington, DC: Migration Policy Institute & BBC World Service, 2011), 105.

26. Ibid., 27.

27. Ibid.

28. Ibid., 28.

29. Ibid., 45.

30. Ibid.

31. Interestingly, the current institution in charge of newcomer integration, the State Secretary of Immigration and Emigration, in the Ministry of Labor and Immigration, evolved from the former Spanish Institute of Emigration. This secretariat has assumed a very active role in newcomer integration in the same way that the SIE once assumed an active role in regulating emigration and protecting emigrants.

32. See CIS (Centro de Investigaciones Sociológicas), *Distribuciones marginales, actitudes hacia la inmigración (IV)*, Estudio 2.846, September–October 2010, http://www.cis .es/cis/export/sites/default/-Archivos/Marginales/2840_2859/2846/Es2846.pdf. The center has conducted polls over the years that show the prevalence of similar perceptions.

33. The boats in which immigrants from Africa cross the Mediterranean into Spain; they are generally associated with the suffering that the immigration experience entails.

34. This, for example, was expressed in interviews with leaders of immigrant organizations from Morocco in 2007.

35. See CIS, *Distribuciones marginales*, 10.

36. Ibid.

37. One of the most publicized cases was that of a Muslim student forbidden to attend school wearing a veil. See "El Ayuntamiento contra el velo de Najwa," *ABC.es*, April 18, 2010, http://www.abc.es/20100418/madrid-madrid/ayuntamiento-contra-velo-najwa -20100418.html.

38. See Amnistía Internacional, "España: Entre la desgana y la invisibilidad, politicas del estado español en la lucha contra el racismo," April 10, 2008, http://www.es.amnesty .org/uploads/media/Datos_y_Cifras_Racismo_Espana.pdf.

39. Cristina Manzanedo and Raúl Gonzáez Fabre, "Impacto de la crisis económica sobre los inmigrantes irregulares en España," Contribución de Pueblos Unidos a PICUM como parte del Input para un reporte del Committee on Migration, Refugees and Population de la Asamblea Parlamentaria del Consejo de Europa.

40. "El gobierno dota al Fondo de Integración de Inmigrantes con 66 millones de euros, un mínimo histórico," *El Día*, April 29, 2011, http://www.eldia.es/2011-03-11/

sociedad/23-Gobierno-dota-Fondo-Integracion-Inmigrantes-millones-euros-minimo-historico.htm.

41. "Cataluña: Partido de derecha exige el contrato de integración a los inmigrantes," *LibreRed*, April 26, 2011, http://www.librered.net/?p=6760.

42. To understand the demographic transformations that Vic has undergone as a result of immigration, see Lucía González Rodríguez, "El impacto sociodemográfico de la inmigración extranjera en Vic," *Cuadernos Geográficos* 36, no. 1 (2005): 451–63, http://www.ugr.es/~cuadgeo/docs/articulos/036/036-027.pdf.

43. See "La ultraderechista Plataforma per Catalunya irrumpe con fuerza en muchos municipios catalanes," *20Minutos.es*, May 22, 2011, http://www.20minutos.es/noticia/1059736/7/ultraderechista/pxc/catalanes/.

44. "La Generalitat considerará determinante el dominio del Catalán para otorgar la residencia," *Latinoamérica Exterior*, March 16, 2011, http://www.latinoamericaexterior.com/region/106-CATALUNYA/noticia/171679-La_Generalitat_considerara_determinante_el_dominio_del_catalan_para_otorgar_la_residencia.

45. Comunidad de Madrid, *Plan de integración 2009–2012 de la Comunidad de Madrid*, http://www.campusepic.org/file.php/1/PLAN_INTEGRACION.pdf.

46. See "UE analiza sistema para informar sobre regularización," *El Universo*, February 25, 2005, http://www.eluniverso.com/2005/02/21/0001/626/4C96D296076D4474A6C6FAAAFD827F50.html.

47. See Nerea Azkona, *Políticas de control migratorio y de cooperación al desarrollo entre España y Africa Occidental durante la ejecución del primer Plan Africa* (Bilbao: Alboan & Entreculturas, 2011), http://www.entreculturas.org/files/documentos/estudios_e_informes/InformeControlMigratorioyAOD_2011.pdf?download.

48. This section is partly based on Miryam Hazán, "Políticas de inmigración y regularización en los Estados Unidos y España: Una perspectiva comparada," in *Estudios sobre la integración de los inmigrantes*, ed. Enrique Alvarez Conde and Ana María Salazar de la Guerra (Madrid: Universidad Rey Juan Carlos & Consejería de Inmigración y Cooperación, Comunidad de Madrid, 2010), 107–36.

49. In 2007, the Constitutional Court declared that the limits introduced by Organic Law 8/2000 on the rights of association, rallying, and unionizing were unconstitutional.

50. According to polls, more than 95 percent of the Spanish population was against Spain's involvement in the war. Even most right-wingers were against the official policy of the Spanish government on Iraq.

51. Tomás Bárbulo, "El cambiazo en inmigración," *El País*, July 20, 2008, http://elpais.com/diario/2008/07/20/espana/1216504803_850215.html.

52. "El gobierno de Rajoy exigirá contrato a los inmigrantes," *Periodista Latino*, January 29, 2012.

53. "Los jóvenes emigran de España en busca de empleo," *La Voz de Rusia*, February 6, 2012, http://spanish.ruvr.ru/2012/02/06/65432018.html.

COMMENTARY

Rut Bermejo Casado

Most observers would agree with the idea that less than three decades is an extremely limited period of time to allow for characterizing and classifying Spanish immigration policy. Some analysts, including Hazán, portray this policy and its practice as stable and continuous. Thus, some patterns are overemphasized: first, the attempt to regulate labor migration in order to fulfill the need for workers, particularly the low-skilled, and close the gaps in the labor market; second, the fight against illegal immigration.

These two priorities, shared by most receiving countries, can also be analyzed from the point of view of reactionary rather than continuous policy. A whole range of conclusions can always be drawn from a given economic, social, and political landscape. Preconditions such as historical legacies, institutional arrangements, or international obligations, as Hazán's excellent analysis shows, open up a range of political options to be considered. This focus on change instead of continuity shifts attention from institutions to actors in the political arena.

A good example illustrating this point is Spain's membership in the EU. The development of treaties and immigration policies can be presented as an institutional scenario in which member states have very limited scope in following their own policies. Nevertheless, sometimes EU membership has been used by different Spanish governments to press Brussels for aid and funds in order to attain their domestic policy goals. At times, European institutions have been used as scapegoats for policy failures. As a result of national strategies, common European responses to border control and, in general, progress toward European solutions have been slow. As Schain discovered some years ago, international relations and institutions have become the context in which the enhanced ability of states to control immigration can be understood (Schain 2009).

Spain is among receiving countries that try to intervene in migration and to restrict, select, or at least channel and manage the arrival of immigrants. In this way, it confronts the "gap hypothesis"—that is, the gap between the goals and outcomes of immigration policies. In this context, the focus on politics and the party in government raises some relevant questions: (1) Have different political parties followed the same discourse and policy principles?

(2) What are their differences in policy formulation and instruments? (3) How are conflicting interests dealt with? The analysis of these questions is the main task of this commentary.

In Spain, two main political parties compete to win elections every four years: the conservative Partido Popular (PP) and the social-democratic Partido Socialista Obrero Español (PSOE). Both have enjoyed several periods in government since the first immigration law was enacted in 1986. The PSOE was in power from 1982 to 1996 and from 2004 to 2011; the PP, from 1996 to 2004 and from 2011 onward.

Immigration issues did not generally give rise to intense political controversy in Spain, but this changed from time to time during pre-election periods. The electoral campaign of 2000 was the first in which immigration was publicly debated. This was due to a serious outbreak of anti-immigrant violence in El Egido (on the southwest coast). The PP party was against the recently enacted law on immigration and saw the violence as a good opportunity to publicize its ideas. As a consequence, 2000 can be singled out as the year in which each political party publicly defined its immigration discourse and strategy. The PP party decided to introduce immigration into the electoral debate to mobilize support. Its stance on legislative changes identified some priorities: (1) enhancing control of migration flow, (2) being tough on illegal immigrants, and (3) cooperating with sending countries to reduce and channel migration flows. These priorities were a consequence of the party's opinion that a call for strict border controls and for accepting only those legal immigrants needed in the labor market was the best policy for the country.

Upon its introduction to the electoral debate, the PP advocated the adaptation of immigrants to a minimum standard of values and customs. Their consideration of this issue included the idea of a "threshold of tolerance" in the sense that Spain could not absorb everyone. As a consequence, the ideas of improved controls and the fight against illegal immigration were compelling. They were complemented by the concept of "easiness to integrate," which referred to immigrants who had close or similar values to those of Spaniards. This concept led the government to prioritize the hiring of South American workers through bilateral agreements so that only those needed in the labor market could enter and, among those, especially those who were easier to integrate.

All of these ideas and priorities were required to close the gap between the Popular Party's restrictive policy goals and their outcomes. This gap was highlighted by the mass media's yearly summer coverage of *pateras* (little rowing boats) arriving at southern coastal borders and by some EU countries pointing out Spain for not doing its homework and failing to properly control the union's external border. Cooperation with sending countries was primarily the forging of new repatriation agreements with African countries and the improvement of patrols to stop immigrants at the beginning of their journey, thus preventing them from entering Spanish territory.

The Center-Left Spanish Socialist Party (PSOE) was known for its low-profile immigration policy until 1996 (Cornelius 2004). At the beginning, both political parties agreed on the reform of the 1986 law; then the PP party opened and hardened its stance on immigration during the electoral campaign of 2000. The PSOE actively opposed the PP's rhetorical "hard line" and the priority it placed on control over individual rights.

The PSOE's ascension to power in 2004 meant a new rhetoric. The idea of control was presented as an old paradigm insofar as globalization made it impossible to pursue because it was formulated a century before. A new discourse was structured around the idea of managing the flow of people as a wider policy towards migrants. Stopping flows was not possible, so the public perceived a continuous policy failure, one that was desirable neither in political nor in economic terms. For the PSOE, border control was just a small part of the policy, not the central idea. The principal goal was to better regulate those entering so as to increase the number of legal entries and decrease the use of irregular channels, while reducing the number of irregular migrants through different means (including general and individual regularizations). No distinction for nationality, religion, or ethnic origin was made in the area of incorporation.

Just as both political parties differ about the way to cope with the immigration, so their approach to immigration and the organization of immigration policy are different. For each party, instruments to implement their ideas became crucial in achieving their goals. The years between 1996 and 2004 were ones of improvement in the means available to control immigration. Between 1996 and 2004, the Interior Ministry was in charge of designing immigration policy, and its strategy was to find ways to better control immigrant flows. The SIVE (Integrated Surveillance System for the Strait of Gibraltar) is considered a major improvement in technological terms, but there is also reliance on visas, bilateral agreements with sending countries, policing, and recruitment agreements to channel offers of employment to foreign workers. It is surprising that, despite the emphasis on curtailing irregular immigration, internal controls in workplaces were not improved.

The 2004 electoral campaign was again used by the PP to publicly debate immigration. As Hazán notes, the PP's candidate, Mariano Rajoy, promised a contract of integration that was to be signed by all would-be immigrants before coming to Spain. However, the PSOE's return to power in 2004 meant a relaxation of attempts to control immigration while an inclusive attitude toward immigrants was declared and a long-term immigration policy was established. There was a change in the ministry in charge of immigration policy, from Interior to Labor, and an appointment of a deputy minister for immigration (Secretaria de Estado) for the first time in Spain's history. Regularizations and rights were again a central part of the PSOE's attempts to improve and redesign such tools as bilateral agreements with sending countries. These agreements now incorporated cooperation in development initiatives to benefit sending countries and to contribute to their growth as a way to avoid both a future brain drain and the need for would-be migrants to leave their countries of origin.

Taking into account the development of different tools that make up immigration policy in Spain, it can be concluded that these measures (e.g., radar, bilateral agreements, regularization, immigrant centers) have evolved since Spain's original policy as a result of having to adjust to policy failures as well as to each government's ideas and principles on how to cope with immigration and immigrants themselves. Ideology has had an important role in the recent formulation of Spanish immigration policy.

Economic crisis and elections in November 2011 have brought the Popular Party to government again. Although no statements on immigration were made during the electoral period, some measures to reduce the welfare state have been formulated. These involve immigrants as residents—for example, increased controls at workplaces; however, some are directly related to irregular immigrants—for example, the intensification of street searches for documents and the end of health assistance. New measures—such as "pay to go" schemes that encourage unemployed migrants to return home and improved methods of increasing temporary migration—try to adapt the flows of immigrant workers to a contracting economy.

The third consideration relates to the accommodation of conflicting interests in the political arena regarding immigration policy. I disagree with Hazán's statement that one of the variables explaining the legacy of Spanish policy is the "corporatist patterns of its representation of socioeconomic interests." It is true that labor issues are commonly agreed on by the unions and the Confederation of Business Organizations, but such agreements have to conform to the government's will and ideology. Unions and employers can agree on reforms but if a government has a majority in Parliament, it can break negotiations if they do not progress as expected. This has happened several times in recent years. The will of politicians has also been evident at certain stages of immigration policymaking; for example, the participation of unions in the 2005 regularization of immigrants was closely related to the failure of previous processes and to the unionist past of the Deputy Minister for Immigration.

This commentary, focused as it is on political ideologies and their dependence on tools, gives a slightly different insight into Spanish immigration policy from Hazán's. Internal factors, and particularly party politics, are significant variables influencing policymaking in addition to the economic and institutional layout.

REFERENCES

Cornelius, Wayne A. 2004. "Spain: The Uneasy Transition from Labor Exporter to Labor Importer." In *Controlling Immigration: A Global Perspective*, edited by Wayne A. Cornelius, Takeyuki Tsuda, Philip L. Martin, and James F. Hollifield, 387–429. 2nd ed. Stanford, CA: Stanford University Press.

Schain, Martin A. 2009. "The State Strikes Back: Immigration Policy in the European Union." *European Journal of International Law* 20 (1): 93–109.

13 | JAPAN AND SOUTH KOREA

Immigration Control and Immigrant Incorporation

Erin Aeran Chung

INTRODUCTION

A common approach to analyzing immigration politics and policy in Japan and South Korea (hereafter Korea) is to start with the premise that recent immigration has posed serious challenges to social and political stability in otherwise ethnically homogeneous societies. In Japan, the foreign population more than doubled from 850,000 in 1985 to over 2 million in 2011 (see Table 13.1). Korea's foreign population has grown more than four-fold in less than a decade, from approximately 210,000 in 2000 to almost 1 million in 2011 (see Table 13.2), plus another 412,000 unregistered foreigners (Korea Immigration Service 2011).

Although Korea and Japan are projected to have declining working-age populations, both countries kept their borders closed to unskilled workers and met labor demands through de facto guest worker programs and preferential policies for co-ethnic immigrants from the mid-1980s to the early 2000s. Despite closed-door policies, the number of unauthorized foreigners rose, reaching a peak of over 300,000 in both countries, first in Japan in 1993 and in Korea in 2002. In Japan, this number was reduced by half by the early 2000s in large part because of the institutionalization of strict border controls, severe penalties for employers knowingly hiring undocumented immigrants, and intensified crackdowns on undocumented workers. Korea also reduced its undocumented migrant workers from 90 percent to less than 20 percent of all immigrants by enacting similar, but less severe, measures.

While the problem of illegal immigration was an unintended consequence of restrictive immigration policies coupled with domestic demand for labor, it was not entirely unanticipated. What came as a surprise in both countries, however, was the *response* to growing immigrant populations—both documented and undocumented—by a significant cross-section of civil society groups. The growth of foreign populations in Japan and Korea not only immersed both societies in debates about border control, national identity, and social order; it mobilized a range of state and nonstate actors to advocate for migrant labor rights, established a wide array of services and programs for immigrant integration, and worked with immigrants to create a vision for a multicultural society.

TABLE 13.1

Registered foreign residents in Japan by nationality

Year	North and South Korea	China	Philippines	United States	Brazil	Peru	Other[a]	Total	Percentage[b]
1985	683,313	74,924	12,261	29,044	1,955	N/A	49,115	850,612	0.7
1986	677,959	84,397	18,897	30,695	2,135	553	54,736	867,237	0.71
1987	673,687	95,477	25,017	30,836	2,250	615	58,393	884,025	0.72
1988	677,140	129,269	32,185	32,766	4,159	864	68,781	941,005	0.76
1989	681,838	137,499	38,925	34,900	14,528	4,121	72,644	984,455	0.8
1990	687,940	150,339	49,092	38,364	56,429	10,279	82,874	1,075,317	0.87
1991	693,050	171,071	61,837	42,498	119,333	26,281	104,821	1,218,891	0.98
1992	688,144	195,334	62,218	42,482	147,803	31,051	114,612	1,281,644	1.03
1993	682,276	210,138	73,057	42,639	154,650	33,169	124,819	1,320,748	1.06
1994	676,793	218,585	85,968	43,320	159,619	35,382	134,344	1,354,011	1.08
1995	666,376	222,991	74,297	43,198	176,440	36,269	142,800	1,362,371	1.08
1996	657,159	234,264	84,509	44,168	201,795	37,099	156,142	1,415,136	1.12
1997	645,373	252,164	93,265	43,690	233,254	40,394	174,567	1,482,707	1.17
1998	638,828	272,230	105,308	42,774	222,217	41,317	189,442	1,512,116	1.19
1999	636,548	294,201	115,685	42,802	224,299	42,773	199,805	1,556,113	1.23
2000	635,269	335,575	144,871	44,856	254,394	46,171	225,308	1,686,444	1.33
2001	632,405	381,225	156,667	46,244	265,962	50,052	245,907	1,778,462	1.4
2002	625,422	424,282	169,359	47,970	268,332	51,772	264,621	1,851,758	1.46
2003	613,791	462,396	185,237	47,836	274,700	53,649	277,421	1,915,030	1.5
2004	607,419	487,570	199,394	48,844	286,557	55,750	288,213	1,973,747	1.55
2005	598,687	519,561	187,261	49,390	302,080	57,728	296,848	2,011,555	1.57
2006	598,219	560,741	193,488	51,321	312,979	58,721	309,450	2,084,919	1.63
2007	593,489	606,889	202,592	51,851	316,967	59,696	321,489	2,152,973	1.69
2008	589,239	655,377	210,617	52,683	312,582	59,723	337,205	2,217,426	1.74
2009	578,495	680,518	211,716	52,149	267,456	57,464	338,323	2,186,121	1.71
2010	565,989	687,156	210,181	50,667	230,552	54,636	334,970	2,134,151	1.67
2011	545,397	674,871	209,373	49,815	210,032	52,842	336,150	2,078,480	1.63

SOURCE: Ministry of Justice statistics 2003–2012; Japan Statistical Yearbook (2006).

[a]"Other" includes nationals of more than 180 countries on every continent. Among the largest numbers of foreign residents in this category are nationals of Thailand, Vietnam, Indonesia, the United Kingdom, India, Canada, Australia, and Bangladesh.

[b]Percentage of the total Japanese population.

Korea and Japan's restrictive immigration policies overlapped until the mid-2000s, but the ways in which each society attempted to incorporate immigrant populations diverged significantly. In Korea, the arrival of migrant labor generated centralized rights-based movements and eventually national rights-based legislation. In 2004, Korea opened its borders to unskilled workers through the Employment Permit System (EPS), which gave these workers the same protections and rights as Korean workers. In 2006, Korea became the first Asian country to grant local voting rights to foreign residents, a measure that has been under debate in Japan for almost a decade. The Korean government launched the Korea Immigration Service (KIS) in 2007 to consolidate the management of policies regarding immigration, naturalization, and immigrant integration; moreover, between 2006 and 2010, Korea's National Assembly passed a series of bills pertaining to noncitizen human rights, immigrant integration, and, most recently, dual nationality.

None of these developments occurred in Japan. Instead, decentralized grassroots movements and partnerships between local governments and civil society organizations

TABLE 13.2

Registered foreign residents in Korea by nationality

Year	China	Vietnam	Philippines	United States	Indonesia	Taiwan	Other[a]	Total[b]	Percentage[c]
2000	58,984	15,624	15,961	22,778	16,700	23,026	57,176	210,249	0.4
2001	73,567	16,048	16,361	22,018	15,617	22,791	63,246	229,648	0.5
2002	84,590	16,951	17,296	22,849	17,140	22,710	70,921	252,457	0.6
2003	185,485	23,315	27,562	23,208	28,349	22,585	127,450	437,954	1.0
2004	208,323	26,053	27,934	22,566	26,063	22,285	135,652	468,876	1
2005	217,002	35,514	30,649	23,476	22,572	22,178	134,753	486,144	1.1
2006	311,823	52,157	40,246	24,998	23,715	22,118	156,162	631,219	1.4
2007	421,493	67,197	42,939	26,673	23,698	22,047	161,699	765,746	1.7
2008	484,674	79,848	39,372	28,853	27,394	21,789	172,077	854,007	1.80
2009	488,651	86,166	38,423	31,379	25,937	21,698	178,382	870,636	1.9
2010	486,083	86,806	38,822	30,941	26,076	21,609	228,580	918,917	2.0
2011	536,699	110,564	38,366	26,466	29,573	21,381	219,412	982,461	2.0

SOURCE: KIS (2011) and SOPEMI (2012).

[a]"Other" includes nationals of more than 50 countries on every continent. Among the largest numbers of foreign residents in this category are nationals of Thailand, Mongolia, Japan, Uzbekistan, Sri Lanka, Cambodia, Pakistan, Canada, Bangladesh, and India.

[b]The ROK government publishes statistics for unregistered foreigners in Korea. In 2011, they numbered 412,616, making the total number of foreigners in Korea 1,395,077.

[c]Percentage of total Korean population.

generated an assortment of local services and programs for foreign residents that ranged from Japanese-language classes, multilingual information distribution, and cultural exchange programs, to consultation services, housing and employment assistance, and foreign-resident assemblies. The first national attempt to establish a comprehensive framework for immigrant incorporation came in the form of a "multicultural coexistence promotion" plan announced in 2006 by the Ministry of Internal Affairs and Communications (MIC), which proposed to coordinate programs that local governments had already developed. Although few structural reforms followed the arrival of recent immigrants, social welfare provisions for foreign residents already settled in Japan were among the most generous of those in industrial democracies as early as the mid-1980s.

How do we explain divergent policies for incorporating immigrants in Korea and Japan given the similarities between each country's immigration and citizenship policies, which are marked by assumptions of ethnocultural homogeneity, overlapping immigrant populations largely from neighboring Asian countries (with the exception of Latin American immigrants in Japan), and common dilemmas of accommodating social diversity while adhering to liberal democratic principles? If East Asian democracies adhere to an exclusionary model of immigrant incorporation, how do we account for their relatively generous provisions of alien rights?

Rather than begin with the assumption that recent immigration has challenged ethnically homogeneous societies in East Asia or with the assumption of a particular immigrant incorporation regime, I identify patterns of interaction between recent immigration and existing institutions that have shaped relationships between state and nonstate actors, dominant populations and minority communities, and national and local institutions. Because Korea and Japan maintained official closed-door policies throughout the 1980s and

1990s, immigrants within their borders were, for the most part, populations to be returned or expelled, not incorporated. Patterns of immigrant incorporation until the early 2000s, therefore, were not the products of deliberate decision making by either state to manage the permanent settlement of immigrants. Rather, civil society actors and local governments drew on existing strategies for incorporating historically marginalized groups to confront the challenges of immigrant incorporation in the *absence* of official immigrant incorporation programs at the national level.

In contrast to the conventional approach to understanding immigrant incorporation as a two-way relationship between the state and individual immigrants, the Japan and Korea cases point to the significance of the role played by intermediary organizations in shaping paths for immigrant incorporation and political empowerment. This chapter defines "immigrant incorporation" as the process by which immigrants and their descendants become permanent members and recognized political actors of their receiving societies (see Messina 2007: 233). Although I use the term "immigrants" to refer primarily to the first-generation, "immigrant incorporation" can refer to policies and practices pertaining to multiple generations of foreign residents. Incorporation, as understood this way, is equivalent neither to full legal membership as national citizens nor to sociocultural assimilation (see Chung 2010b: 677).

After a brief discussion of immigration patterns in Japan and Korea in the post–World War II era, I discuss the ways in which the Japanese and Korean governments attempted to maintain official closed borders while meeting domestic demands for labor through unofficial "side-door" policies and practices through the 1990s. I then analyze how grassroots movements established the blueprint for distinct patterns of immigrant incorporation in each country. Next, I examine areas where immigrant policies have diverged in Korea and Japan since 2000, focusing on each country's first comprehensive proposals for immigrant incorporation. Finally, I discuss how these patterns are reflected in naturalization and permanent residency rates as well as their potential problems for permanent settlement of immigrants.

CONVERGENCE THROUGH THE 1990S: CLOSED BORDERS AND SIDE DOORS

Resisting Immigration

Both Japan and Korea are traditional "sending" countries that, until recently, had emigrant populations well exceeding their immigrant populations. By the 1960s, over 2 million Japanese migrants had settled in North and South America and, to a lesser extent, in Japan's former colonies in Asia. Indeed, it was not until 1973 that the Japanese government ceased official emigration programs to Latin America (Chung and Kim 2012). In Korea's case, over 5 million emigrants to North America, China, Japan, Australia, and the former Soviet Union, among other countries, continue to outnumber immigrants to Korea. Although more than half of the country's emigrant population are descendants of those who emigrated from the Korean peninsula prior to the establishment of the Republic of Korea in 1948, South Korean government statistics estimate that there are approximately 2.87 million South Korean nationals living abroad, with the vast majority residing in the United States, Japan, and China. In Japan and Korea, the net migration rate as of 2011 remained at zero.[1]

Japan and Korea were, moreover, late developers that underwent rapid economic growth in their recent histories, transforming them, respectively, into the third (formerly second) and thirteenth largest economies in the world. Capitalist development and immigration patterns in both countries are, further, intricately tied together in Japan's colonization of Korea (1910–1945). As one of Japan's most important colonies, Korea supplied rice from the South and a much needed industrial base with its cheap labor and abundant supply of cheap hydroelectric power in the North. As an imperial power, Japan underwrote the expansion of Korea's infrastructure, the commercialization of its agriculture, and the beginnings of its modern capitalist enterprises, albeit in an uneven and dependent relationship. Both countries' immigration histories, therefore, are closely connected to the stages of their political economic development as well as to their shared colonial history.

Japan's immigration history can be divided broadly into three categories: (1) colonial migration from the early twentieth century to the immediate post–World War II period; (2) refugee and "skilled" migration in the late 1970s to early 1980s; and (3) unskilled labor migration from Asia and Latin America from the late 1980s to the present. Large-scale immigration to South Korea, in contrast, did not begin until the late 1980s, especially after the 1988 Seoul Summer Olympics. The only significant foreign population settled in Korea until this time comprised Taiwanese nationals known as *hwagyo* (or *huaqiao* in Chinese) whose roots in Korea date back to 1882, when Korea and China signed a trade agreement permitting Chinese merchants to own and lease land in Korea's treaty ports (Lee 2002).

Although Japanese employers and officials played important roles in recruiting immigrants—forcibly for a subset of colonial migrants from 1939—Japan's borders were officially open only for the first wave of immigration, when Japan was a colonial power with territories that included Formosa, Korea, southern Sakhalin Island, the Kwantung Leased Territory on the Liaotung peninsula, and the mandate islands of Micronesia (Chen 1984: 241). By the end of World War II, more than 2 million colonial subjects primarily from the Korean peninsula and Formosa were residing in Japan (see Caprio 2009). Approximately two-thirds of this population were repatriated during decolonization and, by the end of the American occupation of Japan in 1952, Japan implemented strict immigration and border controls to prevent the mass influx of former colonial subjects. However, with unstable conditions in the Korean peninsula following Korea's liberation from Japan in 1945 and escalation to the Korean War in 1950, illegal immigration to Japan largely by former repatriates to the Korean peninsula became a formidable problem during this period, as documented by Tessa Morris-Suzuki's (2010) in her path-breaking study of this first wave of immigration. Nevertheless, less than 700,000 foreigners resided in Japan by the end of the Occupation.

Although Japan experienced labor shortages in the 1960s similar to those in other industrialized countries, Japanese officials and corporations did not import foreign labor, opting instead to automate production, shift production abroad, and tap into alternative sources of domestic labor such as women, students, the elderly, and rural migrants (Chung 2010a: 149). Japan's high-growth period in the 1960s coincided with the country's greatest rural-urban exodus, as 4 million farmers migrated to urban areas annually (Lie 2001: 9; Mori 1997: 55–57).

The second wave of immigration in the 1970s to early 1980s did not therefore represent responses to labor shortages. Rather, it was made up largely of three unrelated groups. The first and largest group consisted primarily of women from the Philippines, Thailand, South Korea, and Taiwan who were recruited to Japan as "skilled" workers to fill the demand in the so-called entertainment industry. By 1987, the number of immigrants from Asian countries with "entertainer" visas surpassed 40,000. By 1991, that number jumped to over 64,000 (Ministry of Justice, Japan, 1989). Until recently, most "entertainers" were recruited to work as hostesses in the industry known in Japan as *mizu shōbai* (water trade, in reference to bars, cabarets, restaurants, and so forth) and as prostitutes (Sellek 2001: 37–38, 160–61).[2] Other "skilled" workers residing in Japan during this period were generally white-collar professionals, many of them from the United States and Europe.

The children and grandchildren of Japanese citizens who remained in Japan's former colonies, mostly China, made up the second group. Although ethnically Japanese, and recognized as Japanese nationals, this relatively small group of "returnees" encountered significant problems of adjustment and discrimination, similar to those experienced by non-Japanese immigrants.

Finally, refugees from Indochina made up the third group, with more than 10,000 entering Japan with temporary visas between 1979 and 1999. It should be noted, however, that the Ministry of Justice recognized only a total of 315 refugees out of 3,118 applications between 1981, when Japan ratified the United Nations Convention Relating to the Status of Refugees, and 2004 (Flowers 2008: 340).

Japan's labor shortage in the 1980s could not be met with the same tools that had been employed in the 1960s. Internal sources of labor by this time were depleted, and rising land prices in urban centers triggered a reverse migration to surrounding areas. Starting in the late 1980s, large numbers of foreign workers entered Japan with tourist visas and overstayed their three-month limit, thus establishing a formidable undocumented immigrant population that reached a high of 300,000 in 1993 (SOPEMI 2007).

It was during this same period that Korea also began to experience its most significant labor shortages following two decades of rapid economic growth in which per capita GNP went from approximately US$100 in 1963 to over US$5,000 in 1989 (and to over US$27,000 in 2010). To meet short-term demands for labor, especially in the manufacturing, production, and service industries, Korean government officials turned a blind eye to companies that recruited foreign workers who entered the country with tourist visas and overstayed, in what Timothy Lim (2003) calls a "wink-and-nod" approach. What began as an unofficial practice of importing migrant labor on an as-needed basis quickly became a de facto guest worker program that generated a serious illegal immigration problem. By 1991, more than 45,000 migrant workers from China, South Asia, and Southeast Asia had entered Korea to fill labor shortages in low-skilled jobs; among them, over 90 percent were undocumented (Lim 2006: 244; Seol 2000: 8).

Opening the Doors to Unofficial Immigration

In an effort to combat illegal immigration and, at the same time, meet labor demands, both Japan and Korea instituted two key legal loopholes to allow entry of unskilled migrant workers and at the same time maintain official closed-door policies: (1) preferential policies for co-ethnic immigrants and (2) "industrial trainee" programs. First, co-ethnic immigration policies created a relatively large pool of unskilled workers who would presumably pose a minimal threat to each society's stability and ethnic homogeneity. The Japanese government revised the Immigration Control and Refugee Recognition Act in 1990 to impose criminal penalties on employers knowingly hiring undocumented workers.[3] At the same time, this revision granted *Nikkei* (ethnic Japanese) immigrants and their descendants (up to the third generation) long-term residency visas that gave them unrestricted entrance and employment rights in Japan.[4] Despite the stated purpose of inviting ethnic Japanese to learn the Japanese language, explore their cultural heritage, and visit their relatives, the vast majority of *Nikkei* with long-term visas after 1990 were Brazilian and Peruvian nationals who were recruited to work in the construction and manufacturing sectors (Tsuda 2003).

Although Korea did not create a corresponding visa category for co-ethnic immigrants, ethnic Koreans were given preferential treatment in the industrial trainee system and, later, the EPS (Skrentny et al. 2007: 799). Korea also passed the Overseas Korean Act in 1999 that created an "Overseas Korean" (F-4) visa category that gave eligible co-ethnic immigrants access to health insurance, pensions, property rights, unrestricted economic activity, and broad employment opportunities (Park and Chang 2005). Until 2003, however, ethnic Koreans from China (*Chosŏnjok*)—who make up the largest immigrant population of ethnic Koreans in Korea—and from the former Soviet Union (*Koryŏin*) were excluded from this status based on the provision that only those who left the Korean peninsula after the founding of the Republic of Korea in 1948 were eligible.[5] Unlike many industrialized democracies with descent-based citizenship policies, neither Japan nor Korea grants co-ethnic immigrants automatic, or even simplified, access to formal citizenship.[6]

Second, the industrial trainee programs, established first in Japan and adopted in toto by Korea in 1991, served as de facto guest worker programs in which foreign workers were initially granted one-year visas to acquire technical skills. Because "trainees" were not officially recognized as workers, they received only "trainee allowances" and were not protected by labor laws in either country, making them vulnerable to industrial accidents, unpaid wages, and employer abuse. As Seol Dong-Hoon (2000: 7) points out, they were also denied three basic labor rights: "unionizing, collective bargaining and collective action." Despite several revisions to better regulate these programs—extensions to trainee visas; government guidelines prohibiting abusive employer practices; and landmark court decisions from 1993 on that affirmed foreign workers' rights to industrial accident compensation, back wages, and severance pay—many trainees continued to experience poor working conditions, overstayed their visas, and/or sought employment in higher-paying jobs.

Japan and Korea thus shared analogous immigration policies and exclusionary practices directed at migrant workers until the early 2000s. Both countries kept their borders closed to unskilled workers despite labor shortages; instead, they used "side doors" to meet labor demands. Although both countries' official and unofficial immigration policies and practices did not produce the intended effect of eliminating illegal immigration, they added resiliency to official claims that Japan and Korea were not countries of immigration even as both experienced acute labor shortages.

THE UNINTENDED CONSEQUENCES OF CONTROL: ADVOCACY FOR IMMIGRANTS

The more significant unintended and unanticipated consequences of Japanese and Korean policies and practices came not from immigrants but from the native population within each country's borders. Whereas large-scale immigration to Western European countries mobilized restrictionist movements *against* immigration, large-scale immigration, combined with already restrictive national immigration policies, spurred unprecedented *advocacy for* immigrants by civil society actors

The Push for Migrant Workers' Rights in Korea

Less than five years after nationwide anti-government protests by a wide segment of Korean civil society toppled Chun Doo Hwan's (Chŏn Tu-hwan) authoritarian regime and led to the June 29, 1987 announcement of Roh Tae Woo's (No T'ae-u) eight-point program of democratic reforms, the Roh administration enacted plans to deport undocumented workers and import additional, legal migrant workers. Although there were fewer than 50,000 undocumented migrant workers in Korea at the time, the government's attempt to "dispose" of them caught the attention of a small number of religious and labor organizations who proceeded to campaign for basic workers' rights alongside migrant workers in a series of high-profile nonviolent protests from 1994 to 1995. These protests—including the 1995 protests by thirteen Nepalese workers staged in front of the Myongdong Cathedral in Seoul—described by Katharine Moon (2000: 155) as the "traditional stage and refuge of antigovernment protestors in the era of military rule"—garnered the support of human rights groups. Not only did the mistreatment of migrant workers and police crackdowns of undocumented migrants seem to the protesters strikingly similar to the abusive practices and political repression of Korea's past authoritarian regimes; the language and tactics adopted by migrant workers and their advocates were almost identical to those of the labor movements in Korea's recent past. Slogans such as "We are human, not animals" and "We are not slaves" came to epitomize the migrant workers' movements, much as "We are not machines" represented the Korean workers' movements of the 1970s and 1980s.

What is most significant about Korea's pro-immigrant advocacy organizations is their position within Korea's democratization movement and post-1987 democratic consolidation. As Joon Kim (2003: 253) describes, these groups represent a cross-section of Korea's civil society that includes moderate and radical labor organizations, Protestant, Catholic, and Buddhist groups, women's organizations, and a range of progressive citizen groups that either have a long history within the democratization movement or emerged after 1987 amid the expansion of intermediate, voluntary associations in Korean civil society. For example, the NGO that organized the 1994 rallies for undocumented migrant workers, the Citizens' Coalition for Economic Justice (CCEJ), was established in 1989 by approximately 500 individuals representing various walks of life—"economics professors and other specialists, lawyers, housewives, students, young adults and business people"—as the first civic organization "in pursuit of economic justice" in Korea (*Han'gyŏre sinmun*, November 2, 2009). The coalition members' strong tradition of activism, coupled with the reconfiguration of political power in the late 1990s—starting with the inauguration of the first opposition president, Kim Dae Jung (Kim Tae-chung), in 1998 and that of a former human rights activist and labor lawyer, Roh Moo Hyun (No Mu-hyŭn), in 2003—lent the struggle for migrant labor rights significant potency and magnitude in Korean society. By employing the tactics, symbols, and language of the democratization movement, foreign workers and their advocates reframed the debate away from the dangers that migrant workers posed for Korean society and toward the threat that an exploitative industrial trainee system posed for the hard-fought rights of Korean workers in Korea (see Lim 2010). How could a pro-labor government condone exploitative practices toward migrant laborers that many in the administration, including the president himself, had struggled against for decades?

As early as 1996, the Joint Committee for Migrant Workers in Korea (JCMK), an umbrella organization for migrant advocacy groups, drafted a bill to legalize the status of migrant workers, which was submitted to the National Assembly in 1997 with the support of the Ministry of Labor and the ruling party. Although the assembly did not pass the bill that year because of strong opposition from key ministries, opposition parties, and the Korean Federation of Small and Medium Businesses (KFSB), the government introduced a modified version of it whereby trainees could become legal workers after a two-year training period (Lee and Park 2005). Korea eventually terminated its trainee system in 2007 and replaced it with an official guest worker program, the EPS, which had been introduced in 2004. The new system treats foreign workers as Korean workers by guaranteeing their protection under labor laws such as the Labor Standards Act, the Minimum Wage Act, and the Industrial Safety and Health Act (SOPEMI 2008). It also provides foreign workers with three-year visas that can be renewed for an additional two years.[7] While the EPS is limited to guest workers from countries that have signed bilateral agreements with Korea, Korea has now opened its borders, if only slightly, to unskilled immigration.

As partnerships between Korean state officials and human rights activists paved the way for ground-breaking legislation on migrant workers' rights from the late 1990s onward, another group of immigrants began to grow precipitously: marriage migrants. Between 2000 and 2004, when the EPS was announced, the number of marriage migrants in Korea grew from approximately 25,000 to over 57,000 and reached more than 125,000 in 2009 (KIS 2009b). Their arrival during a critical period of cooperation between the central government and civil society organizations proved momentous for them. Pro-immigrant NGOs offered social and legal support, activists and the media publicized cases of domestic violence and human trafficking, and the Ministry of Gender Equality established a women's hotline and changed its name to the Ministry of Gender Equality and Family in order to expand its services to marriage migrants (see Lee 2008). In 2006, the government announced a "grand plan" for integrating marriage migrants, and in the following year the National

Assembly passed two related bills: the Plan for Social Integration of Mixed-bloods and Migrants and the Plan for Social Integration of Marriage Immigrants.

Two significant developments altered the course of immigrant incorporation patterns in Korea such that the spotlight shifted from migrant workers to marriage migrants. Prior to the establishment of the EPS in 2004, the government announced plans to deport all undocumented workers so that the program could be implemented with a "clean slate." Not surprisingly, this was met with vehement protests by pro-immigrant activists. Although the government eventually conceded with a proposal to grant amnesty and a one-year visa to undocumented workers who agreed to leave Korea within a year, the movement for legalization continued. Unlike earlier movements, however, the renewed push for legalization lacked both state and public support. Having abolished the despised industrial trainee system, the government could now gain political capital by concentrating on the much less volatile issue of integrating marriage migrants into Korean society.

Second, the heyday of progressive administrations in Korea ended with the inauguration of Lee Myung-bak (Yi Myŏng-pak) as president in 2008. Whereas some pro-immigrant activists had access to the highest echelons of previous administrations, they had few political allies within the conservative Lee administration. The honeymoon period between pro-immigrant activists and the Korean government had come to an end. As one activist explains,

> We used to meet regularly with top officials. Four-star generals have visited my [migrant] center and have shared a meal with migrant workers. . . . The government now doesn't even invite us to participate in their committees and conferences on migrant issues. Instead, they consult with scholars who don't have any experience with migrants to create new programs. . . . We are simply trying to survive now. (Personal interview, June 1, 2010, Seoul, Korea)

Local "Multicultural Community Building" in Japan

Japan's industrial trainee system generated many of the same problems that arose in Korea: exploitation by employers and a rapidly growing population of undocumented workers among trainees. Rather than abolish the system, however, Japan established the Technical Intern Training Program (TITP) in 1993, which allows foreign workers with an employment contract to stay in Japan for up to three years and explicitly prohibits exploitative practices. Although liberal and conservative lawmakers alike have criticized the trainee system—among them Kōno Tarō of the Liberal Democratic Party, who deemed it a "failure" (lecture, Waseda University, April 14, 2010, Tokyo, Japan)—there have been no legislative moves for its abolition.

Similar to Korea, hundreds of civil society organizations have played key roles in providing services and advocacy for foreign trainees (see Shipper 2008). Additionally, two national organizations—the National Network in Solidarity with Migrant Workers (SMJ) and the Zentōitsu Labor Union (ZWU)—established themselves in the early 1990s as network organizations to fight for migrant-labor rights and policy change. While their efforts have garnered international attention, the industrial trainee system remains intact and Japan's borders remain closed to unskilled immigration. Likewise, although the Ministry of Justice announced that it would adopt a more "humanitarian" approach to visa overstayers, special permission to stay in Japan has been granted only on a case-by-case basis (*Japan Times*, October 27, 2009; SOPEMI 2009). Since 2009, even foreign workers with the most privileged "long-term resident" status, the *Nikkei* immigrants from Brazil and Peru, have been paid to "go home."[8]

Why has pro-immigrant advocacy in Japan failed to generate structural reforms regarding migrant-labor rights? Two key features of Korea's migrant rights movement are missing in Japan: (1) mass mobilization and (2) a key ally who played a pivotal role in previous rights movements. Immigrant incorporation in Japan has occurred largely at the local level, with decentralized, grassroots organizations taking the lead. Apichai Shipper (2008: 11–12) uses the term, "associative activism," to describe pro-immigrant advocacy in Japan, which is typically characterized by local attempts to solve specific problems that lead to partnerships involving like-minded activists, NGOs, and local government officials, but that eventually dissolve after the problems are resolved.

Local governments and civil society actors in Japan have applied innovative strategies to solve immediate problems for foreign residents in their local communities and give voice to foreign residents' interests and concerns. Nevertheless, many recurring issues—such as housing discrimination, workplace abuse, and police harassment—are difficult to resolve without national legislation, highlighting the limits of locally based immigrant incorporation programs. While local state and nonstate actors can build a "multicultural coexistence" community that gives voice and agency to foreign residents, they often lack the capacity and authority to respond effectively. Short-lived pro-immigrant advocacy, furthermore, has not generated sufficient momentum for sustained pressure and, ultimately, structural reforms of immigration policies.

In Japan's recent past, however, mass mobilization by foreign residents resulted in significant structural reforms of policies regarding *foreign residents*, most notably the repeal of the fingerprinting requirement. What is missing in the current struggle for migrant workers' rights is therefore not so much the *tradition* of immigrant mass mobilization but rather the leadership of a key ally: the community of multigenerational Korean residents (hereafter zainichi Koreans). Rather than push for immigration reform, zainichi Korean activists have absorbed recent immigrants into programs and movements that reflect more the interests of their multigenerational community and less those of recent immigrants.

By the time that Japan encountered its most recent wave of immigration starting in the late 1980s, zainichi Korean activists and their supporters had reached the final stages of what I call a "noncitizen civil rights movement" (Chung 2010a). Beginning with the landmark Hitachi employment discrimination trial of the early 1970s, in which a Korean plaintiff successfully sued the Hitachi company for employment discrimination, Korean residents have made dramatic gains in claims to citizenship rights and access to the labor market through lawsuits and local campaigns. By 1980, foreign residents were eligible for social welfare benefits and public-sector jobs in cities such as Nagoya, Osaka, Kawasaki, Kobe, and Tokyo. Some of these rights were subsequently centralized following Japan's ratification of the International Covenants on Economic, Social, and Cultural Rights and on Civil and Political Rights in 1979 and the Geneva Convention Relating to the Status of Refugees in 1982. Even without national-level reforms, zainichi Koreans and their advocates succeeded in removing the nationality requirement for employment in public secondary schools, public universities, and semipublic companies, such as the Nippon Telegraph and Telephone Public Corporation (NTT), as well as entry into the Legal Training and Research Institute, which provides mandatory training for those who have passed the bar examination. These series of lawsuits and local campaigns culminated in the largest mass mobilization of Korean residents and their supporters in post-war Japan—the decade-long anti-fingerprinting movement in the 1980s that succeeded in abolishing the fingerprinting requirement for special permanent residents in 1993 and for all foreign residents in 1999 (see Strausz 2006).[9]

Having gained a secure legal status, social welfare benefits, access to public-sector employment, and, in some localities, ethnic or "multicultural" education in public school curricula, as well as the repeal of the fingerprinting requirement, zainichi Koreans and their advocates concentrated on securing local voting rights as growing numbers of new immigrants began to settle in communities throughout Japan. The timing of new immigration in relation to developments in the foreign-resident community already settled in Japan defined the path to political empowerment. On the one hand, immigrants with a secure legal status benefited from earlier movements of zainichi Koreans that made foreign residents eligible for a range of social welfare benefits and legal protections against employment discrimination; these were out of their reach until the late 1970s and early 1980s. Rather than an insular society unprepared for immigration, numerous civil society organizations and local governments had already been engaged in initiatives that directly addressed foreign residents' rights and duties in Japan well before the new immigrants arrived. Although some communities had to create incorporation programs from scratch, local governments with relatively large foreign populations, such as those of Osaka, Kanagawa, and Hyōgo, absorbed new immigrants into a range of existing programs; likewise, networks of grassroots organizations that had provided services and advocacy to zainichi Korean residents expanded the scope of their activities to address the needs of the new immigrant flows.

On the other hand, because existing foreign-resident services and programs were created for permanently settled, highly assimilated, and, in many cases, native-born non-national residents, most local communities were ill-equipped to address some of the specific needs of migrant workers. Although civil society organizations stepped in to advocate for immigrant populations whose needs were overlooked by existing local programs, the residence-based incorporation approach—in contrast to the rights-based approach in Korea—widened the gap between legally registered long-term foreign residents and undocumented workers. Because the zainichi Korean movement from the 1960s made claims to citizenship rights on the basis of their permanent settlement as tax-paying, *law-abiding* residents, temporary and, especially, undocumented, immigrants have no voice in their movement.

DIVERGENCE FROM THE 2000S: THE EMERGENCE OF TWO FRAMEWORKS FOR INCORPORATING IMMIGRANTS

By the mid-2000s, Korean and Japanese government officials could no longer turn a blind eye to the swelling ranks of immigrants within their borders, and so they announced comprehensive proposals for immigrant incorporation: the Basic Act on the Treatment of

Foreigners in Korea (Chaehan oegugin ch'ŏu kibonpŏp; hereafter "Basic Act") and the MIC plan for "Multicultural Coexistence Promotion in Local Communities" (Tabunka kyōsei suisin puroguramu; hereafter "MIC Plan") in Japan. Unlike previous legislation that focused on immigration and border control, these plans not only acknowledged the need to manage foreigners settled within each country's borders but also represented the first attempts by each country to establish an overarching framework for their incorporation. At the same time, they diverge dramatically in their degree of centralization, the scope of their reforms, and their target populations.

Korea's Basic Act

Korea's National Assembly passed the 2007 Basic Act after years of debate, research, and negotiations between policymakers and civil society organizations. Following a 2006 meeting of representatives from the major government ministries, migrant advocacy organizations, and the scholarly community, the government announced plans to enact the Basic Act with the stated purpose of promoting immigrant social integration and mutual respect between foreigners and Korean nationals. The act calls for the implementation of a Basic Plan for Immigration Policy every five years that entails the cooperation of national, municipal, and local governments and the designation of a Foreigner Policy Committee to coordinate all policies regarding foreign residents. The First Basic Plan for Immigration Policy (2008–2012; hereafter "First Basic Plan"), which included a total budget of 612.7 billion Korean won, set the basis for designing and funding programs and assigning to specific ministries tasks related to the following four goals: "1) enhancing national competitiveness with a proactive openness policy; 2) pursuing quality social integration; 3) enforcing immigration laws; and 4) protecting human rights of foreigners" (KIS 2009a).

Although the Basic Act is meant to serve as a general guide for drafting the five-year Basic Plan for Immigration Policy, it is notable for its explicit provision to safeguard the human rights of foreign residents in Korea (Article 10). As mentioned, this provision was adopted as one of the four stated goals of the First Basic Plan with the explanation that, as minorities in Korean society who are vulnerable to "human rights abuse," foreigners require "national-level protection against discrimination" (p. 13). In addition to outlining broad plans for reviewing and reforming discriminatory practices and institutions, the First Basic Plan offers specific provisions for protecting migrant women, foreigners in detention facilities, and refugees.

Migrant women, especially marriage migrants, are also central to the First Basic Plan's second goal of "pursuing quality social integration." Among the four major tasks assigned to it are two that are devoted solely to marriage migrants and their children: "helping immigrants through marriage get settled" and "creating a sound environment for multicultural children." In a similar vein, the last task concerns the social integration of co-ethnic immigrants, or the "Korean diaspora." The first task on immigration reforms makes clear that co-ethnics have priority over other foreign nationals in entry and employment rights. This task additionally includes a framework for equalizing working conditions for foreign and Korean workers as well as reducing industrial accidents and protecting foreign workers from workplace abuse. Accordingly, the Basic Act and the First Basic Plan set distinct guidelines for incorporating specific immigrant populations: social integration for marriage migrants, preferential entry and employment rights for co-ethnic immigrants, and human rights protection for migrant workers.

Japan's MIC Plan

Although the Immigration Bureau within the Ministry of Justice is responsible for immigration policies, there is no single agency in Japan that manages *immigrant* policies akin to the KIS. Instead, immigrant integration programs and services in Japan were, until recently, spearheaded by civil society organizations and local governments. In 2001, a network of twenty-one cities and one town established the Convention for Cities and Towns with Concentrations of Foreign Residents (*gaikokujin shuju toshi kaigi*). Local government officials within this network declared that they had exhausted their resources in attempts to incorporate foreign residents in their communities, and called for national legislation to coordinate local immigrant incorporation programs and services. In 2005, the MIC established a Committee for the Promotion of Multicultural Community Building, which conducted a nationwide survey of local governmental programs and policies and, in 2006, announced an unprecedented proposal that called for all of Japan's prefectures and major cities to devise plans for "multicultural community building" (Yamawaki 2008).

Similar to Korea's Basic Act, Japan's MIC plan provides general guidelines for implementing policies and programs; however, whereas Korea's Basic Act assigns policy and program design, implementation, and assessment to the central ministries, the MIC plan is explicitly designed for adoption by local governments with the stipulation that authorities should make adjustments according to local needs and characteristics. The guidelines for implementing the MIC Plan are broadly divided into four tasks: (1) intercultural communication support; (2) assistance in everyday life; (3) development of a "multicultural coexistence" (*tabunka kyōsei*) community; and (4) development of a system to promote multicultural coexistence policies. While the focus on social integration of and coexistence with foreigners is largely similar to the goals of Korea's Basic Act, the methods for achieving these goals vary considerably. Korea's First Basic Plan concentrates on providing *support* and *protection* for foreigners through centralized, top-down policies and programs; the MIC Plan rests on the pillars of *support* and foreign resident *participation* in the local community through decentralized coordination between local governments, civil society organizations, and foreign residents themselves. Unlike Korea's Basic Plan, the MIC neither targets specific groups of foreigners nor offers any specific guidelines for protecting foreign residents' "human rights."

What is striking about the MIC Plan is the inclusion of foreign residents not only as the beneficiaries of incorporation policies and programs but also as active participants of "multicultural coexistence" community building. An entire section is devoted to encouraging participation of foreign-residents through support of their leaders, advisory bodies, participation in local civic associations, and public acknowledgement of their contributions to their local communities. This framework contrasts strikingly with the comparatively thin proposals for "encouraging foreigners' participation in local communities" found in Korea's First Basic Plan. Aside from a brief reference to future research on the living conditions of foreigners in Korea, the only proposals outlined in this section of the Basic Plan refer to "multicultural festivals," cultural events, and the establishment of a "Together Day" and a "Together Week" every May, according to Article 19 of the Basic Act.

CONTROLLING DIVERSITY: PROSPECTS FOR IMMIGRATION PERMANENT SETTLEMENT

The Limits of Blood-Based National Membership

While Japanese and Korean officials routinely link their country's immigration and citizenship policies to claims of ethnic and cultural homogeneity, the inconsistencies in their policies suggest that such claims are highly contingent and flexible. Despite the presence of permanently settled and, in many cases, native-born foreign-resident populations, neither Japan nor Korea revised their nationality laws to introduce elements of *jus soli*, resulting in multiple generations of foreign residents. Also, although both countries have revised their nationality laws, these revisions were not aimed at facilitating the incorporation of each country's largest groups of co-ethnic immigrants: *Nikkei* Brazilians and Peruvians in Japan and ethnic Korean immigrants from China in South Korea.

Japan's revisions to the Nationality Law aimed to resolve the legal status of bicultural children in Japan. The 1985 revision, which followed ratification of the Convention on the Elimination of All Forms of Discrimination against Women, made children of international marriages eligible for Japanese nationality through either their father's or their mother's nationality. In 2008, the Supreme Court ruled that children born out of wedlock to a Japanese father and a foreign mother are to be granted Japanese nationality. Both cases highlighted the need to adjust the laws for those with "mixed" blood, specifically those without Japanese fathers in the first instance and those born out of wedlock in the second.

Korea took a more radical step in 2010, when the National Assembly passed a bill to allow dual nationality, which went into effect in 2011. However, the bill applies only to three categories of foreign nationals: (1) "exceptionally talented foreign nationals in science, economics, culture and sports"; (2) overseas Koreans over the age of 65, ethnic Koreans who lost their Korean nationality as minors, and ethnic Koreans who lost their Korean nationality through marriage; and (3) foreign spouses of Korean nationals. It notably excludes three categories of foreign nationals: (1) so-called "anchor babies" who were born in a country with birthright citizenship and returned to Korea shortly thereafter; (2) divorced foreign nationals previously married to Korean nationals; and (3) native-born generations of *hwagyo* residents (*Korea Times*, April 21, 2010, and May 3, 2010). Although the bill targets "high-quality" overseas Koreans, primarily from the United States and Japan, it does not "welcome home" ethnic Korean immigrants. On the contrary, as the KIS director, Seok Dong-hyeon, proposed, "It [naturalization] should be rectified to help increase the population of Korea" ("Immigration Office to Polish Image of Korea," *Korea Times*, September 13, 2009).

Targeted Incorporation in Korea and Disaggregated Citizenship in Japan

Naturalization and permanent residency rates in Korea and Japan most visibly reflect the countries' divergent approaches to immigrant incorporation. Naturalization rates in Japan

TABLE 13.3
Annual naturalizations in Korea and Japan

	KOREA			JAPAN		
Year	Total[a]	Simplified naturalization (marriage)	Percentage of foreign population[b]	Total	All foreign nationals	Percentage of foreign population
2001	1,680	—	0.8	15,291	10,295	0.9
2002	3,883	—	1.7	14,339	9,188	0.8
2003	7,734	—	2.8	17,633	11,778	1.0
2004	9,262	—	2.0	16,336	11,031	0.9
2005	16,974	7,075	3.5	15,251	9,689	0.8
2006	8,125	3,344	1.6	14,108	8,531	0.7
2007	10,319	4,190	1.6	14,680	8,546	0.7
2008	15,258	7,916	1.9	13,218	7,412	0.6
2009	26,756	17,141	3.0	14,785	7,637	0.7
2010	17,323	10,271	1.9	13,072	6,668	0.6
2011	18,355	10,733	1.9	10,359	5,656	0.5

SOURCE: KIS (2011); Ministry of Justice, Japan (2012); and SOPEMI (2012).
[a]Naturalization figures for Korea include "Reinstatement of Nationality."
[b]Percentage of total registered foreign residents.

remain among the lowest of all industrial democracies and have continually fallen behind those of Korea since 2002 (see Table 13.3). Although zainichi Korean residents are naturalizing at higher rates than ever before—at an annual average rate of about 10,000 since 1995—overall, naturalization rates in Japan remain at less than 1 percent of the total foreign population annually. In contrast, the number of naturalization applications in Korea went up by more than 18 times in less than a decade, from 1,268 in 2000 to 23,846 in 2009 (KIS 2009b). In 2009, 26,756 individuals, or 3 percent of the total foreign resident population, naturalized in Korea, compared to 14,785, or 0.7 percent, in Japan (KIS 2009b; Ministry of Justice, Japan, 2010; SOPEMI 2010).

The informal practices associated with naturalization in Japan have posed considerable hurdles to naturalization. Until 1985, local officials typically required naturalization applicants to adopt a Japanese name (family name and surname) and conducted painstaking evaluations of applicants' cultural assimilation to determine eligibility for the "good behavior and conduct" requirement. While naturalization applicants are no longer required to adopt a Japanese name, the pressure to do so remains, especially for applicants with Chinese-character surnames that are not listed in the official *Jōyōkanji* ("Characters in Common Use") or *Jinmeiyō kanji* ("Name Characters") lists, such as the common Korean surnames "Choi," "Kang," and "Yoon." In some cases, local officials may offer unsolicited advice about the convenience of having a Japanese name over a "foreign" name or the benefits of adopting a Japanese name for the sake of the applicant's children (Okamoto 1994). A third-generation zainichi Korean man married to a Japanese national recalls that the official dealing with his naturalization application suggested that a name change would be good for his marriage: "He said that we would be much happier if we both had the same Japanese family names. If I kept my Korean name, he said my wife might resent me and our children would suffer" (personal interview, December 11, 2009, Tokyo, Japan). With a few exceptions, pro-immigrant groups in Japan rarely encourage foreign residents to naturalize as a means of political empowerment.

Unlike Japan, the Korean government actively encourages specific categories of foreigners—particularly marriage migrants—to naturalize through government-run support centers, the KIS "e-government for Foreigners" website, and simplified naturalization procedures.[10] Although the naturalization process in Korea is not easy, pro-immigrant organizations in Korea, such as the Ansan Migrant Center, routinely help foreign residents with their naturalization applications, and government-sponsored "Multicultural Family Centers" provide preparatory citizenship exam courses and "Korea Immigration and Integration Programs" that eligible applicants can take in lieu of the written exam (personal interviews with Ryu, Sung-hwan of the Ansan Migrant Center, May 25, 2010, Ansan, Korea and Shin, Sang-rok of P'och'ŏn Multicultural Family Support Center, May 24, 2010, P'och'ŏn, Korea).

At the same time, incorporation policies and programs that target marriage migrants and co-ethnic immigrants conspicuously exclude the largest category of foreign nationals in Korea from permanent settlement: migrant workers. Marriage migrants, or spouses of Korean nationals (including those with F-2 resident visas), accompanying spouses (F-3 visa), and co-ethnic immigrants with Overseas Korean (F-4) visas—which allow multiple renewals and confer many of the same rights granted to Korean nationals—made up only 21 percent of the total foreign population in Korea in 2011 (KIS 2011). Permanent foreign residents (with F-5 visas), moreover, make up less than 5 percent of foreign residents. Consequently, immigrants with temporary visas that permit only a single two-year renewal make up the largest category of foreign residents in Korea by far.[11] Thus, Korea appears to be heading toward a type of bifurcated immigrant incorporation pattern that embraces some immigrants as potential citizens and excludes others from permanent settlement.

In Japan's case, low naturalization rates contrast strikingly with the rapid growth of permanent residents among registered foreign residents, from approximately 63,500 in 1995 to more than 943,000 in 2009 (Ministry of Justice, Japan, 1999, 2010). In 2011, permanent residents—including both "general permanent residents"(*ippan eijūsha*, 28.8 percent) and "special permanent residents" (*tokubetsu eijūsha*, 18.7 percent)[12]—accounted for over 47 percent of Japan's total foreign resident population (see Figure 13.1). Among the remaining categories of registered foreign residents are some whose visas allow for unrestricted employment and multiple visa renewals, making them de facto permanent residents.[13] When combined, permanent residents and "quasi-permanent residents" made up over 65 percent of registered foreign residents in 2011.

Rates of naturalization and permanent residency registrations in Korea and Japan highlight divergent patterns of immigrant incorporation as well as potential problems. Korea's policies are rapidly coming to resemble those of traditional countries of immigration, where naturalization is seen as the final step in political incorporation. But because only a small, targeted group of immigrants qualify for naturalization, there are still wide gaps between marriage migrants who are expected to assimilate culturally and politically, Overseas Kore-

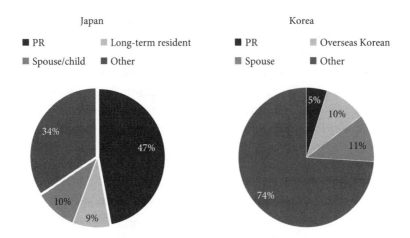

Figure 13.1 Registered foreign residents in Japan and Korea, 2011. *Source:* Korea Immigration Service (2011) and Japanese Ministry of Justice (2012).

ans who already hold quasi–dual citizenship rights, and migrant workers who are expected to leave the country after their temporary contracts expire. When foreign residents no longer fit into their designated categories—because of divorce, injury, or visa expiration—they are likely to be excluded from targeted services as well as denied their group-specific rights. A Catholic priest and long-time activist put it bluntly: "To the government, they [female marriage migrants] are simply baby-makers. When they can't fulfill their obligations or flee from their husbands, they become disposable, just like migrant workers" (personal interview, May 26, 2010, Seoul, Korea). Integration thus becomes a matter not of choice or of will but of survival. A 75-year-old ethnic Korean immigrant from China describes her decision to apply for Korean nationality accordingly: "I was getting too old to work but I couldn't stay in Korea if I didn't have a work permit. If I didn't acquire Korean nationality, then I would have become illegal" (focus group interview, May 29, 2010, Ansan, Korea).

In contrast, foreign permanent residency has become the norm in Japan, despite closed-door immigration policies. Among a wide spectrum of immigrants and local officials alike, permanent residency is treated as the final step in immigrant settlement. A Chinese national who lived in Japan for eleven years recalls that when his permanent residency application was finally accepted, the presiding official remarked, "You're free now. You can do whatever you want" (focus group interview, April 10, 2010, Tokyo, Japan). While this trend may signal the enlargement of foreign-resident rights, it has also contributed to the growth of permanently settled foreign residents who remain indefinitely "migrants-turned-immigrants in an intermediate status," to use Rogers Brubaker's (1989) words, or "denizens," according to Tomas Hammar (1990). Low rates of naturalization combined with high rates of permanent residency among both prewar and postwar immigrants indicate that, regardless of closed-door immigration policies, the *foreign* population in Japan will continue to grow and the problem of political incorporation will multiply, rather than decrease, with successive immigrant generations.

CONCLUSION

Overall, immigration politics in Korea and Japan reflect the interaction between new immigration and existing institutions that have shaped relationships between dominant and minority communities and between state and nonstate actors. In the absence of national incorporation programs and policies for new immigrants, institutions that previously worked to incorporate traditionally disadvantaged groups in each society became central to incorporating new immigrants. Because there was no directive from the national government, local communities and civil society actors used existing tools to confront the challenges faced by both new immigrants and the communities in which they lived. In Japan's case, immigrant incorporation patterns began *prior* to the most recent wave of immigration that started in the late 1980s. Alien rights, labor market access for foreign residents, multicultural programs, and networks of pro-immigrant activists that came out of earlier movements founded by multigenerational Korean residents established pathways for the incorporation of later immigrant flows. In Korea's case, human rights activists, labor unions, and citizen groups that had played central roles in earlier democratization movements applied tools for incorporating labor, women, and the poor within Korean society to make claims for migrant workers' rights. In both cases, existing institutions and strategies provided immigrants with far more political capital than they would have had otherwise, given their recent arrival and relatively small numbers.

Intranational gaps between exclusionary policies and inclusionary outcomes as well as cross-national variations between two seemingly similar systems, in turn, reflect the divergent ways that civil society actors use the tools of democratic institutions and principles to demand democratic accountability. While Japan's policies and programs are more informal and decentralized than those of Korea's, they treat all legal foreign residents essentially as members of their local communities with accordant rights and responsibilities. Permanent foreign residents, moreover, have rights and recognition almost on par with those of Japanese nationals. Korea's policies and programs, in contrast, target specific populations based on visa status, which themselves correspond to occupational, gendered, and ethnic categories. In this way, specific rights are accorded to specific visa holders: local voting rights for permanent residents (F-5 visa holders), dual citizenship rights and social welfare benefits for Overseas Korean (F-4) and Spouse of Korean national (F-3) visa holders, property rights for Overseas Korean (F-4) visa holders, and so forth. In sum, Japan maintains closed borders for unskilled immigration but has one of the most generous systems for granting institutionalized rights to legal foreigners already residing in the country. Since the institutionalization of the EPS in 2004, Korea has had partially open borders, including a guest worker program, with a corporatist model that incorporates specific categories of desirable, long-term immigrants but prohibits the permanent settlement of unskilled foreign labor. Although both countries use ethnic preferences in their immigration policies, not all co-ethnic immigrants are necessarily privileged over other immigrants in the areas of naturalization, citizenship acquisition, and citizenship rights.

In sum, the divergent ways that Japan and Korea have attempted to incorporate different immigrant groups into their societies reflect each country's attempt to absorb greater social diversity while maintaining social stability *and* democratic accountability. Although both have applied the language of "multiculturalism" in their frameworks for incorporating immigrants, neither has embraced cultural pluralism. On the contrary, Korea's "targeted incorporation" and Japan's "disaggregated citizenship" frameworks demonstrate the tensions between each society's acknowledgment of the swelling ranks of immigrants within their borders and their uneasiness with their permanent settlement. Similar to other countries that have experienced large-scale immigration, the combination of immigration and citizenship policies based on monocultural assumptions has forced Korea and Japan to redefine the meaning, terms, and rights of political and social membership.

NOTES

This chapter is a revised, expanded, and updated version of Chung (2010b).

1. The *CIA World Factbook* calculates the net migration rate based on the difference between the number of persons entering and leaving a country during the year per 1,000 persons (based on mid-year population). See https://www.cia.gov/library/publications/the-world-factbook/fields/2112.html.

2. In 1988, the Ministry of Justice revised the application procedures for "entertainer" visas to prevent the entry of those whose actual work was in the *mizu shōbai* and sex industries (see Komai 1995: 74–75).

3. The revision, modeled after US immigration laws, subjected employers hiring undocumented workers, and brokers facilitating their employment, to up to three years of imprisonment and fines up to ¥2 million (Komai 2001: 5–6).

4. Only four other visa categories permit unrestricted economic activities: special permanent resident, permanent resident, spouse or child of a Japanese national, and spouse or child of a permanent resident. Although Japan's borders officially remain closed to unskilled labor, the revision further allows precollege and college students as well as "trainees" to work for a limited amount of time.

5. Since the 2003 amendment, ethnic Koreans from China and the former Soviet Union must formally apply for a change of status to that of Overseas Korean to be eligible for the aforementioned benefits. However, the thousands of co-ethnic immigrants from China with undocumented status are not eligible.

6. With the institutionalization of dual nationality in Korea in 2010, however, all Overseas Koreans over the age of 65 are eligible for dual nationality in Korea, as are ethnic Koreans who lost their Korean nationality as minors or through marriage.

7. The provision for renewal was inserted a few years after policymakers ratified the initial EPS proposal partially in response to heavy pressure from migrant worker organizations.

8. Under the so-called repatriation plan announced in April 2009, the Japanese government provides a lump sum of 300,000 yen for airfare, with an additional 200,000 yen for each dependent, with the stipulation that the recipients cannot reapply for a "long-term resident" visa until the economy recovers (see Tabuchi 2009).

9. The fingerprinting requirement for foreign residents was reinstated in 2007 for all but special permanent residents.

10. Foreign spouses of Korean nationals are eligible to apply for naturalization after two years of residency in Korea (while married) or, for those who have been married for longer than three years, one year of residency (www.hikorea.go.kr).

11. Overseas Koreans with Work-Visit (H-2) visas, who made up approximately 22 percent of all foreign residents in 2011, are given preferences in employment and entry under the EPS but cannot reside continuously in Korea for more than four years and ten months.

12. Only former colonial subjects and their descendants are eligible for the status of "special permanent resident," the vast majority of whom are South Korean and *Chōsen* (de facto North Korean) nationals. Chinese nationals made up the largest group among "general permanent residents" in 2011.

13. The three visa categories that allow for unrestricted employment are (1) spouse or child of a permanent resident, (2) spouse or child of a Japanese national, and (3) long-term resident. In 2011, Brazilians made up the largest group among the last two categories, while Chinese nationals made up the largest group among the first (Ministry of Justice, Japan, 2012).

REFERENCES

Brubaker, Rogers. 1989. "Citizenship and Naturalization: Policies and Politics." In *Immigration and the Politics of Citizenship in Europe and North America*, edited by Rogers Brubaker, 99–127. Lanham, MD: University Press of America.

Caprio, Mark. 2009. *Japanese Assimilation Policies in Colonial Korea, 1910–1945*. Seattle: University of Washington Press.

Chen, Edward I-te. 1984. "The Attempt to Integrate the Empire: Legal Perspectives." In *The Japanese Colonial Empire, 1895–1945*, edited by Ramon H. Myers and Mark R. Peattie, 240–74. Princeton, NJ: Princeton University Press.

Chung, Erin Aeran. 2010a. *Immigration and Citizenship in Japan*. New York: Cambridge University Press.

———. 2010b. "Workers or Residents? Diverging Patterns of Immigrant Incorporation in Korea and Japan." *Pacific Affairs* 83 (4): 675–96.

Chung, Erin Aeran, and Daisy Kim. 2012. "Citizenship and Marriage in a Globalizing World: Multicultural Families and Monocultural Nationality Laws in Korea and Japan." *Indiana Journal of Global Legal Studies* 19 (1): 195–219.

Flowers, Petrice R. 2008. "Failure to Protect Refugees? Domestic Institutions, International Organizations, and Civil Society in Japan." *Journal of Japanese Studies* 34 (2): 333–61.

Hammar, Tomas. 1990. *Democracy and the Nation State: Aliens, Denizens, and Citizens in a World of International Migration*. Brookfield, VT: Gower.

Kim, Joon. 2003. "Insurgency and Advocacy: Unauthorized Foreign Workers and Civil Society in South Korea." *Asian and Pacific Migration Journal* 12 (3): 237–69.

Komai, Hiroshi. 1995. *Migrant Workers in Japan*. London: Kegan Paul International.

———. 2001. *Foreign Migrants in Contemporary Japan*. Melbourne: Trans Pacific Press.

Korea Immigration Service (KIS). 2009a. "First Basic Plan for Immigration Policy, 2008–2012."

———. 2009b. "Korea Immigration Service (KIS) Statistics 2009."

———. 2010. "Korea Immigration Service (KIS) Statistics 2010."

———. 2011. "Korea Immigration Service (KIS) Statistics 2011."

Lee, Chulwoo. 2002. "'Us' and 'Them' in Korean Law: The Creation, Accommodation, and Exclusion of Outsiders in Korean Law." In *East Asian Law: Universal Norms and Local Cultures*, edited by Arthur Rosett, Lucie Cheng, and Margaret Woo, 105–34. London: RoutledgeCurzon.

Lee, Hye-Kyung. 2008. "International Marriage and the State in South Korea: Focusing on Governmental Policy." *Citizenship Studies* 12 (1): 107–23.

Lee, Yong Wook, and Hyemee Park. 2005. "The Politics of Foreign Labor Policy in Korea and Japan." *Journal of Contemporary Asia* 35 (2): 143–65.

Lie, John. 2001. *Multiethnic Japan*. Cambridge, MA: Harvard University Press.

Lim, Timothy C. 2003. "Racing from the Bottom in South Korea? The Nexus between Civil Society and Transnational Migrants." *Asian Survey* 43 (3): 423–42.

———. 2006. "NGOs, Transnational Migrants, and the Promotion of Rights in South Korea." In *Local Citizenship in Recent Countries of Immigration: Japan in Comparative Perspective*, edited by Takeyuki Tsuda, 235–69. Lanham, MD: Lexington Books.

———. 2010. "Rethinking Belongingness in Korea: Transnational Migration, 'Migrant Marriages' and the Politics of Multiculturalism." *Pacific Affairs* 83 (1): 22.

Messina, Anthony M. 2007. *The Logics and Politics of Post-WWII Migration to Western Europe*. New York: Cambridge University Press.

Ministry of Justice, Japan. 1989. "Statistics for Foreign Residents in Japan" [Zairyu Gaikokujin Tokei].

———. 2010. "Heisei 21-Nenmatsu Genzaini Okeru Gaikokujin Tōrokusha Tōkeini Tsuite" [Report on Current Foreign Resident Statistics at the End of 2009].

———. 2011. "Heisei 22-Nenmatsu Genzaini Okeru Gaikokujin Tōrokusha Tōkeini Tsuite" [Report on Current Foreign Resident Statistics at the End of 2010].

———. 2012. "Heisei 23-Nenmatsu Genzaini Okeru Gaikokujin Tōrokusha T ōkeini Tsuite" [Report on Current Foreign Resident Statistics at the End of 2011].

Moon, Katharine. 2000. "Strangers in the Midst of Globalization: Migrant Workers and Korean Nationalism." In *Korea's Globalization*, edited by Samuel S. Kim, 147–69. New York: Cambridge University Press.

Mori, Hiromi. 1997. *Immigration Policy and Foreign Workers in Japan*. New York: St. Martin's Press.

Morris-Suzuki, Tessa. 2010. *Borderline Japan: Frontier Controls, Foreigners and the Nation in the Postwar Era*. New York: Cambridge University Press.

Okamoto, Makiko. 1994. "Shokuminchi jidaini okeru zainichi chōsenjinno senkyo undō: 1930 nendai gohan made" [The Electoral Movement of Korean Residents in Japan during the Colonial Period: Until the Latter Half of the 1930s]. *Zainichi chōsenjinshi kenkyū* [Historical Research on Korean Residents in Japan] 24: 1–36.

Park, Jung-Sun, and Paul Y. Chang. 2005. "Contention in the Construction of a Global Korean Community: The Case of the Overseas Korean Act." *Journal of Korean Studies* 10: 1–27.

Sellek, Yoko. 2001. *Migrant Labour in Japan*. New York: Palgrave.

Seol, Dong-Hoon. 2000. "Past and Present of Foreign Workers in Korea 1987–2000." *Asia Solidarity Quarterly* 2: 1–17.

Seol, Dong-Hoon, and John D. Skrentny. 2009. "Why Is There So Little Migrant Settlement in East Asia?" *International Migration Review* 43 (3): 578–620.

Shipper, Apichai W. 2008. *Fighting for Foreigners: Immigration and Its Impact on Japanese Democracy.* Ithaca, NY: Cornell University Press.

Skrentny, John D., Stephanie Chan, Jon Fox, and Denis Kim. 2007. "Defining Nations in Asia and Europe: A Comparative Analysis of Ethnic Return Migration Policy." *International Migration Review* 41 (4): 793–825.

SOPEMI. 2007. *International Migration Outlook: Annual Report.* Paris: Organisation for Economic Co-operation and Development.

———. 2008. *International Migration Outlook: Annual Report.* Paris: Organisation for Economic Co-operation and Development.

———. 2009. *Trends in International Migration: Continuous Reporting System on Migration.* Paris: Organisation for Economic Co-operation and Development.

———. 2010. *Trends in International Migration: Continuous Reporting System on Migration.* Paris: Organisation for Economic Co-operation and Development.

———. 2012. *Trends in International Migration: Continuous Reporting System on Migration.* Paris: Organisation for Economic Co-operation and Development.

Strausz, Michael. 2006. "Minorities and Protest in Japan: The Politics of the Fingerprinting Refusal Movement." *Pacific Affairs* 79 (4): 641–56.

Tabuchi, Hiroko. 2009. "Japan Pays Foreign Workers to Go Home." *New York Times,* April 22.

Tsuda, Takeyuki. 2003. *Strangers in the Ethnic Homeland: Japanese Brazilian Return Migration in Transnational Perspective.* New York: Columbia University Press.

Yamawaki, Keizo. 2008. "The Challenges for Japanese Immigrant Integration Policy." *Around the Globe* 4 (2): 42–44.

COMMENTARY

Dietrich Thränhardt

Comparing Japan and Korea is enlightening because we can identify an East Asian pattern of reluctant opening on the one hand and register the differences between the political systems of Japan and South Korea on the other. Both countries are characterized as zero net immigration, meaning that immigration does not surpass emigration. That is important to keep in mind before we go into detail about the dilemmas that immigration poses for these two rich countries. Japan and even more so Korea have some of the lowest fertility rates in the world and the fastest-aging populations. Both governments were able to implement strict immigration controls and to lower the numbers of illegal immigrants, in spite of intensifying tourism and trade connections worldwide and the relaxing of visa requirements for tourists from mainland China, with its 1.3 billion inhabitants and 200 million internal migrant workers. Other parallels are the general de-skilling of migrant labor and the deferential acceptance of ethnic immigrants, which allows them to work but does not grant them full rights. These striking parallels can be explained by the close but not easy connections between both countries and their common history, even if Korea has tried to liberate itself from the past colonial domination. Thus we find an East Asian pattern of immigration (or nonimmigration) policy, different from those of North America and Europe.

The differences between Japan and Korea go to the heart of their political systems: after decades of dictatorship, Korea now has a two-party system with alternative political outlooks and styles. This translates into government policies, including immigration, integration, and particularly human rights. In Japan, on the other hand, despite long and complex debates between ministries, pressure groups, and specialists (of which we have detailed knowledge thanks to Chiavacci's profound study; see Chiavacci 2011a, 2011b), the Justice Ministry and its bureaucrats maintain their hold on policy decisions. This is visible even in the OECD's SOPEMI committee, in which Japan is the only member with two representatives: one from the Labor Ministry to provide the information and the other from the Justice Ministry to control the policy (SOPEMI 2010: 355). This situation has not changed since 1991, when I had a chance to interview both labor and justice officials (Thränhardt 1999). Not even three changes in governing party or coalition had any effect on policies. Nor did the lively public discussion, with dozens of plans, concepts, newspaper articles, and television programs, influence government decisions. The Japanese situation can be summarized with the headline: "A nonimmigration country discusses migration" (Kibe and Thränhardt 2010). There were two waves of discussion: one focusing on guest worker schemes in the boom years around 1990, the second focusing on demography, human trafficking, sexual exploitation, and immigrant crime around 2000, a period of rising unemployment.

In the absence of national integration policies, local government and civil society become more important, and many studies about Japanese immigration concentrate on their activities. This parallels the situation in Southern European countries like Italy and Greece, where the state does not provide care and governance with respect to immigrants. In countries with more organized immigration policies, civil society and local government can concentrate on additional integration programs—for example, cultural, civic, and leisure activities—and integrate immigrants into social and political structures. In the end, that brought immigrants to important positions such as leadership of the Belgian Socialist Party or the mayoralty of Rotterdam. In Japan, this happened only in some special business sectors and in popular culture but not in politics or in the core business realm.

On the other hand, local special interest was important for shaping the side-door policies that brought immigrants into Japan, with trainee schemes deliberately constructed to use their labor but denying them status security and not paying them full wages. Over the years, these schemes were modified, to keep trainees at work longer, to push them to small and medium-size firms, and to keep them dependent (Chiavacci 2011a). Criticism from concerned lawyers, activists, and humanitarian organizations did not help. The umbrella organization administering the program is a place for ex-bureaucrats to land profitable jobs after retirement (*amakudari*). Language students and ethnic Japanese from Latin America (*Nikkeijin*) are also in an exposed position. They cannot naturalize easily yet successive generations stay in Japan (Green 2011).

Korea not only gave more rights to foreign workers but also expanded the definition of Korean co-ethnics. Whereas Germany eliminated any special immigration status for ethnic Germans abroad between 1990 and 2005, Korea granted special immigration status for Koreans in China and North Korea and opportunities for these groups were opened up step by step (Brubaker and Kim 2011; Weiner 1989). This reflects the state of external relations. In contrast to Europe, Korea still exists in a Cold War environment. Like West Germany between 1951 and 1989, it can use its position as a rich, developed, and free country to attract people of Korean extraction from the North, from China, and later, possibly, from Kazakhstan and Russia. Moreover, this strengthens the country's self-esteem and internal coherence. In the years before Korea's economic take-off and democratization, such a policy was not possible and the South Korean authoritarian regime feared ideological diversion from the Communist North.

We should do some justice to the Japanese bureaucrats who have been criticized so much in migration literature. They achieved something that many Western governments and much of public opinion would have wanted to have: keeping out unqualified labor; controlling and even reducing the number of informal migrants through strict controls at the borders and in the country; and, in a limited number of cases, regularizing immigrants

(Kondo 2006: 219). Only under US pressure, did Japan accept a limited number of Vietnamese boat people and successfully integrate them (Kosaka-Isleif 1991). At the same time, Japan opened itself for tourists. Chinese and Korean tourist groups can now enter the country without visas, and 7,000 former students were granted permission to work in Japan (SOPEMI 2010: 216)—even though language students are another side-door immigrant group. More and more Chinese specialists work in China-related posts in Japanese companies (Liu-Farrer 2011). At the same time, the strict controls did not prevent strong and explicit negative public opinion of the newcomers (Herbert 1993), who recently replaced Koreans as outsiders in the media.

Finally, it is important to put these rich countries into an East Asian context. Mainland China now hosts 4 million foreign workers—two times the official number of foreigners in Japan—indicating that the borders of this totalitarian country seem to be more porous than those of Japan. There are about 200 million internal migrant workers in China, and China's population grew by 74 million in 2011, a rate much slower than that of India or Vietnam.

REFERENCES

Brubaker, Rogers, and Jaeeun Kim. 2011. "Transborder Membership Politics in Germany and Korea." *Archives Européennes de Sociologie* 52: 21–75.

Chiavacci, David. 2011a. *Japans neue Immigrationspolitik: Ostasiatisches Umfeld, ideelle Diversität und institutionelle Fragmentierung*. Wiesbaden: VS Verlag für Sozialwissenschaften.

———. 2011b. "Vom Training für Ausländer zum Technischen Praktikumsprogramm—Geschichte, Struktur und Debatte des japanischen 'Gastarbeiterprogramms.'" *Japan-Jahrbuch 2011*. Zurich: Vereinigung für Sozialwissenschaftliche Japanforschung.

Green, Paul. 2011. "The Enemy Within? Explorations of Personhood, Friendship and Difference amongst Brazilian Nationals in Japan." *Journal of Ethnic and Migration Studies* 37: 373–88.

Herbert, Wolfgang. 1993. *Die asiatische Gefahr: Ausländerkriminalität in Japan als Argument in der Diskussion um ausländische "illegal" ArbeitsmigratInnen*. Vienna: Institut für Japanologie.

Kibe, Takashi, and Dietrich Thränhardt. 2010. "Japan: A Non-Immigration Country Discusses Migration." In *National Paradigms of Migration Research*, edited by Dietrich Thränhardt and Michael Bommes, 233–57. Osnabrück: V&R Unipress.

Kondo, Atsushi. 2006. "Summary of the Legal Position of Migrants in Japan." law.meijo-u.ac.jp/association/contents/57-3/570306_kondo.pdf.

Kosaka-Isleif, Fumiko. 1991. *Integration südostasiatischer Flüchtlinge in der Bundesrepublik Deutschland und in Japan*. Saarbrücken: Breitenbach.

Liu-Farrer, Gracia. 2011. "Making Careers in the Occupational Niche: Chinese Students in Corporate Japan's Transnational Business." *Journal of Ethnic and Migration Studies* 37: 785–803.

SOPEMI. 2010. *International Migration Outlook*. Paris: Organisation for Economic Co-operation and Development.

Thränhardt, Dietrich. 1999. "Closed Doors, Back Doors, Side Doors: Japan's Nonimmigration Policy in Comparative Perspective." *Journal of Comparative Policy Analysis: Research and Practice* 1: 203–33.

Weiner, Michael. 1989. *The Origins of the Korean Community in Japan, 1910–1923.* Manchester: Manchester University Press.

COMMENTARY

Midori Okabe

The purpose of this commentary is to review Erin Aeran Chung's analysis in light of three points brought up by James Hollifield as the original idea behind *Controlling Immigration*: the relevance of the "gap hypothesis," the meaning of (immigration) control, and the definition of "dilemma" as it applies to immigration control. Before making my remarks, I would like to reconsider in what way these three points can be used as an effective theoretical framework for explaining and understanding Chung's study.

The "gap hypothesis" refers to the "gap between the goals of national immigration policy (laws, regulations, executive actions, etc.) and the actual results of policies in this area (policy outcomes)" (Cornelius, Martin, and Hollifield 1994: 3). This analytical hypothesis continues to be highly valid even now as an effective tool of observation of policymaking, implementation, and results, often recognized as changes in sociopolitical relations within a state. The target of observation need not be limited to immigration policy but can be extended to almost every policy area: foreign affairs, taxation, economic stimulus, social security, and the like. However, in immigration policy in particular, it is extremely difficult to achieve the shared understanding necessary for setting policy goals, both among policymakers and where consensus among political actors and the public is to be achieved. For the time being, in many receiving counties of immigration (including all that are covered in this volume), policy failure is increasingly evident in the sense that government officials find it less easy to "effectively regulate immigration flows and employment of unauthorized foreign workers" (Cornelius, Martin, and Hollifield 1994: 4) than they used to. Whether or not this "failure" is for the same reasons, however, is not certain. There are several factors to explain this.

THE TIME LAG FACTOR

The time lag factor is closely related to the "convergence hypothesis" (Cornelius, Martin, and Hollifield 1994: 3–5). Differences are found by chronological observation of several cases of political activities in states that have a comparatively long history of receiving immigrants (both authorized and unauthorized) and those that do not. These differences need to be observed not only to determine whether a state's immigration policy per se is in development but also to determine whether or not (or how far) the liberal ideology of a state is projected into immigration policymaking. Not all states that have a restrictive immigration policy are illiberal. Just as many advanced countries of immigration (the United States, Australia, Canada, and many European countries) are confronted with the agonizing dilemma of immigration, so too are "latecomers" at least when we focus on the situation in which the political intention of opening doors to foreigners is often spinning out, distorted, and even hampered by the decision-making process.

The development of immigration policies in various states in simple chronological order needs to be questioned here because it cannot be known if policy failure could have been avoided until a certain policy is fully "mature" (in any light). Moreover, studies on advanced receiving states have shown that the liberal principle does not necessarily and sufficiently improve policy in the sense that it ensures successful immigration control and the integration of immigrants.

CHANGES IN WHAT CONSTITUTES PUSH AND PULL FACTORS

As is aptly described in this volume, immigration policy (especially regarding acceptance) is more and more affected by supply factors generated in potential migrant-sending countries and by the international environment that facilitates the rise in international migration. Although it appears that immigration policy is defined by the receiving states—they have the ability to determine *who* may enter, thus influencing (would-be) immigrants' decisions on *which* states they will enter and *how*—it also has an impact on the acceptance decision indirectly but with increasing significance. This insight permits an explanation of why many states encounter "unwanted" immigration.

It is important to examine intermediate factors here, not only as the object of government regulation and punishment but also as the means by which the course of migration policy might be altered. Migration patterns and the nexus between the origin and the destination of migration have changed over the last decades, and intermediate factors have played a significant role in this regard: they denounce not only, but notably, human trafficking but also the labor demands of enterprises that are often either unseen or not under control by the government. Whether or not the state is "attractive" in the eyes of potential immigrants—if you can make a fortune there, if you can run a business (even an underground one!) freely, or if you can live safely—these are also important considerations. They are not to be seen just as the "environment" but also as explanatory variables for contemporary migration, especially for governments receiving unwanted immigrants against their will.

THE RELATIVIZATION OF IMMIGRATION POLICY ANALYSIS

Third and most important, a clear and shared understanding is needed of the lack of consensus on what is "successful" immigration policy and on ways of measuring success. On what grounds is an open immigration policy (if any) regarded as *good*? For whom and for what purpose are foreign labor recruitment and social integration of immigrants? What precise conditions does a country have to meet in order to clean up its restrictive image? Do the citizens of the receiving country make the judgment or do immigrants? How are the UN and third-country actors involved?

Quite often, an evaluation of immigration policy is made in accordance with such universal norms as human dignity and fundamental rights, but in the political real world, it is made in a more *relativized* manner: policy is constructed out of numerous political activities within the state and even within the environment where international relations matter. In particular, bilateral relations between immigrant-sending and immigrant-receiving states, together with a state's position internationally, heavily depend on immigration policymaking as well as policy interpretation, and it often leads to the outcome being seen as a failure or a success. This point relates to the meaning of immigration control.

What is immigration control? Who does it and for purpose? On what legitimate grounds do policymakers set its purpose? Can we say that the success of immigration control is determined by whether a policy has accomplished its goal? On the contrary, I find immigration control to entail a rather ontological meaning because it is always accompanied by questions of inclusion and exclusion and often a longer-term perspective. In other words, in contemporary political discourse, immigration control can be judged as effective (or as ineffective) when its outcome is expected to lead to social stability (or not).

In such discourse, control can be a balancing act between nationals and non-nationals, involving not just the policy design itself but also the possible adjustment of the policymaking process, and at an even earlier stage of mass mobilization (which Chung accurately describes in her chapter) so as to move the immigration issue higher up on the political agenda. From this viewpoint, it can be seen that further study of discontent in the existing domestic political system is needed. Again, we need to be careful, especially in any comparative study that attempts to account for discontent. We need to avoid defining it in such a way as to explain which country's immigration policy is "in progress" and which is not. Rather, independent variables are to be set free from such normative criteria.

This approach of disaggregation, especially from a moral standard, might enable empirical research on varied cases where the state encounters the "liberal dilemma." As Hollifield describes it, the liberal dilemma derives from the concept of (human) rights (Cornelius, Martin, and Hollifield 1994: 9–11; Brettell and Hollifield 2008: 196–98) and the different ways in which individual states institutionalize it, including their commitment to it across place and time. Because this means that what constitutes the liberal dilemma may be different in each stage of immigration politics development as well as in each country, there is still room for study from this perspective.

Based on these premises, Dr. Chung successfully argues that it is not entirely correct (or relevant) to say that East Asian countries (including Korea and Japan) follow the exclusionary model of immigrant integration. As she aptly points out, this restrictive image often fails to take into account legislation and activities that are in fact intended to integrate foreign residents. Her observation is precise, as can be seen in her concluding remarks: "Immigration politics in Korea and Japan reflect not new countries of immigration but, rather, the interaction between new immigration and existing institutions." Also, her insights on mass mobilization in both Korea and Japan show us how immigrant rights are guaranteed to a great extent by the support of native labor associations and by minorities in the form of women's groups and those who are in a socially lower class.

Dr. Chung closely analyzes the peculiar similarity between the two countries in their comparatively "restrictive" official stance on immigrant inclusion, which strangely but somehow tactfully coincides with proactive efforts toward integration made by intermediate actors—that is, local governments and grassroots organizations. Her observations and arguments prove that the scientific analysis on which she bases them is free from value judgments.

Meanwhile, her explanation of the mechanisms by which immigrants are incorporated into the two host societies (these mechanisms may be diverse but they do exist) is not entirely convincing. Of note is her implication that the attainment of policy goals equals full integration of immigrants and, furthermore, that the success of integration equals naturalization. In this Dr. Chung fails to examine the advantages of naturalization both to the host society and to the individual immigrant. This is a criticism that can be leveled at many studies (especially sociological ones): they regard various kinds of entitlement proffered to foreign residents as dynamic and evolving, leading inevitably to naturalization as the ultimate goal of social integration. What she claims as "targeted incorporation (Korea)" and "disaggregated citizenship (Japan)" can only be explained either in terms of political inaction or in terms of reluctance to support the (often discriminated against) minority.

Japan provides both quasi-naturalization (to "permanent residents") and regular naturalization (nominally to any foreign nationalities as long as they meet stated conditions). Is this necessarily to be deemed a lack of policy consistency? In this regard, although Dr. Chung correctly points out that "low rates of naturalization combined with high rates of permanent residency . . . indicate that . . . the *foreign* population in Japan will continue to grow and the problem of political incorporation will multiply, rather than decrease, with successive immigrant generations," she does not explore what kind of (multiplying) problems could emerge and under what circumstances. What is significantly missing in her chapter is any discussion of the relevance of international relations between the receiving country (in this case Korea and Japan) and the (potential) sending country.

Take Japan as an example, where certain aspects of official immigration policy provide evidence that low rates of naturalization are better explained in terms of international relations than in terms of domestic politics, given the fact that it is significantly less difficult to become naturalized than it used to be. Bilateral agreements (including extradition treaties) as well as diplomatic relations may play an important role. The degree of confidence building between Japan and a sending country may have an effect on changes in the number of those who are naturalized as opposed to the number of those who adhere to their "permanent resident" status. The unsettled security problems ranging from postwar reparation to territorial disputes might hamper the attempts of some permanent residents of Korean and Chinese descent to become Japanese citizens.

When issues such as these are elaborated, it becomes clear that an analysis is needed that examines the status quo in light of Pareto efficiency, where not only domestic associations but the state itself is an actor in immigration policymaking.

REFERENCES

Brettell, Caroline, and James F. Hollifield, eds. 2008. *Migration Theory: Talking across Disciplines*. New York: Routledge.

Cornelius, Wayne A., Philip L. Martin, and James F. Hollifield, eds. 1994. *Controlling Immigration: A Global Perspective*. Stanford, CA: Stanford University Press.

V | THE EUROPEAN UNION AND GLOBAL MIGRATION
GOVERNANCE

14 THE EUROPEAN UNION

Supranational Governance and the Remaking of European Migration Policy and Politics

Andrew Geddes

INTRODUCTION

European immigration politics and policy cannot be understood without accounting for the role now played by the European Union (EU). This chapter shows how the EU as a form of regionalized supranational governance changes the dynamics of migration politics and policymaking for twenty-eight European countries. It also explains why, where, and with what effects European integration drives Europe-wide policy convergence. European integration categorically does not mean that national politics and member states are somehow written out of the analytical equation, but it does mean that we have to rethink their place and role and, by doing so, also rethink some key issues that underpin the study of international migration, at least in the European context. The chapter shows: (1) that there is a common EU migration and asylum policy that is particularly but not exclusively focused on asylum and unauthorized immigration; (2) that policy effects are particularly but not only evident in newer immigration countries and newer member states; (3) that, while there is evidence of convergence, this does not conform with "fortress Europe" accounts that posit a race to the bottom in the form of lowest-common-denominator, restrictive policies; and (4) that the shift to EU action can highlight in new ways the observed gap between policy goals and policy outcomes and contribute to populist and extremist mobilizations by political parties that target both immigration and European integration.

The EU framework has developed quite rapidly since the late 1990s, but remains partial and has highly differential effects. Thus, it is necessary to ground discussion in a broader perspective on the EU as a political system (Hix 2005). The EU is neither an international regime nor a federation, but an evolving system of multilevel governance with common institutions within which powers are defined by treaty and with significant variation across policy areas (Bache and Flinders 2004; Bache 2008). Responsibilities in a wide range of policy areas are now distributed and shared across subnational, national, and supranational levels of governance. Intra-EU free movement by nationals of member states (since 1993, EU citizens) has been central to the European project (Maas 2005). Policy relating to non-EU migrants, or third-country nationals (TCNs), is a newcomer. To cut through some of the complexities of EU action, this analysis distinguishes between policies designed to restrict immigration (primarily asylum and unauthorized immigration), those that relate to admissions policy, and those aimed at extending rights to non-EU migrants (Geddes 2008).

These points are developed through close assessment of the development of EU action in the areas of free movement, immigration, and asylum. Table 14.1 provides a chronological overview of key immigration and asylum-related measures. This analysis is particularly focused on the period since 1989, when the end of the Cold War changed the scope and reach of European integration and brought immigration and asylum firmly onto the EU agenda. Since 1989, there has been a geopolitical widening of immigration in Europe with the result that all EU member states are sending, destination, and transit countries, and usually a combination of all three (Geddes 2005a).

TABLE 14.1
Evolution of EU free movement, immigration, and asylum policy

Year	Measure	Key features
1957	Treaty of Rome	Benelux countries, France, Germany, and Italy found the EC with economic and political objectives, including creation of a "common market" to reduce trade barriers and promote free movement of goods, services, capital, and people
1973	First enlargement	Denmark, Ireland, and UK join EC (membership now 9 countries)
1975	Trevi group founded	Informal cooperation, outside the treaty framework, on internal security issues
1981	Second enlargement	Greece joins EC (membership now 10 countries)
1985	Schengen Agreement	Benelux countries, France, and Germany resolve to move more quickly toward free movement goal with compensating internal security measures outside main treaty framework
1986	Single European Act	Defines Europe as an area without internal frontiers in which free movement of people, services, goods, and capital should be assured
1986	Third enlargement	Portugal and Spain join EC (membership now 12 countries)
1990	Schengen Implementing Convention	Outlines specific measures needed to attain free movement and internal security objectives
1990	Dublin Convention	Lays down "one-stop" principles informing European asylum system
1992	Maastricht Treaty	Creates intergovernmental pillar dealing with justice and home affairs (JHA), including immigration and asylum
1995	Fourth enlargement	Austria, Finland, and Sweden join EU (membership now 15 countries)
1999	Amsterdam Treaty	Defines EU as "Area of Freedom, Security and Justice"; moves immigration and asylum into a chapter of main treaty and links them to free movement; brings Schengen framework into main treaty
1999	Tampere conclusions	Heads of government agreement on a 5-year plan to develop the Amsterdam Treaty provisions on immigration and asylum
2001	Nice Treaty	Reforms decision making, including extended role for qualified majority voting (QMV) in Council of Ministers on immigration and asylum issues
2004	Hague programme	Second 5-year plan on internal security, including immigration and asylum
2004	Fifth enlargement	Cyprus, Czech Republic, Estonia, Hungary, Latvia, Lithuania, Malta, Poland, Slovakia, and Slovenia join EU (membership now 25 countries)
2008	Sixth enlargement	Bulgaria and Romania join EU (membership now 27 countries)
2009	Lisbon Treaty	Brings immigration and asylum fully within the EU's common institutional structure and ordinary legislative procedures
2010	Stockholm programme	5-year plan until 2014 for internal security, including immigration and asylum
2013	Seventh enlargement	Croatia joins EU (membership now 28 countries)

CONVERGENT MIGRATION POLICIES?

Discussion of EU migration and asylum policy requires two components. The first centers on interstate negotiation and effects on decision making. In a classic statement of the neorealist position, Hoffmann (1966) argued that European states would be prepared to play Russian roulette with state sovereignty only so long as the gun was filled with blanks. This view has found echoes in other work on multilateral cooperation that is skeptical about potential development in immigration and asylum policy (Meyers 2002; Keohane, Macedo, and Moravcsik 2009). The EU has, however, developed a constitutionalized free movement framework that applies to twenty-eight countries stretching from Finland to Malta and from France to Bulgaria (Guild 1998). There has also been agreement, as we will see, on aspects of immigration and asylum policy that are primarily focused on restriction, but also cover migrants' rights, social integration, and admissions. There is not necessarily a normative component to this policy convergence. Both progressive and repressive measures represent a shift in the locus of action as marked by a strong EU role that must necessarily change dynamics between EU states and thus the meaning and practice of sovereignty in the EU system (Clark 1999). It can be more helpful to think in terms of "sovereignty bargains" where participation in EU integration increases the likelihood of attaining domestic objectives. This idea is further developed by the consideration of associated "capacity bargains" later in this chapter.

The second component focuses on what happens next or on the effects of "Europeanization" on domestic structures (and on nonmember states, too). This analysis shows differential effects, with some EU states more exposed to convergence pressures than others. These pressures have consequences for domestic governance structures and capacity within the EU states, a matter that is discussed more fully later.

Both the shift to Europe, as a result of interstate negotiation, and the impacts of such decisions on domestic politics in member states can be seen as indicators of convergence. European integration also interacts with other convergence-inducing factors, such as mobilizations on immigration issues and the role of courts (Hollifield 1992; Freeman 2006).

There is growing attention in the public policy literature on convergence linked to factors such as globalization and Europeanization (Bennett 1991; Drezner 2001; Busch and Jorgens 2005; Heichel, Pape, and Sommerer 2005; Holzinger and Knill 2005; Starke, Obinger, and Castles 2008). Convergence has been defined as:

> Any increase in the similarity between one or more characteristics of a certain policy (e.g.,
> policy objectives, policy instruments, policy settings) across a given set of political jurisdic-
> tions (supranational institutions, states, regions, local authorities) over a given period of time.
> Policy convergence thus describes the end result of a process of policy change over time to-
> wards some common point, regardless of the causal processes. (Holzinger and Knill 2005: 5)

If the EU were to induce change leading to convergence, then there are different kinds of similarity. Barro and Sala-i-Martin (1992) distinguish between α convergence, which is a decrease in variation, and β convergence, which denotes "an inverse relationship between the initial value of a particular policy indicator and its subsequent growth rate or change"

(Starke, Obinger, and Castles 2008: 980). This can be when laggards catch up with leaders, such as "new" immigration countries in Central, Eastern, and Southern Europe catching up with "older" immigration countries, which has been seen as a core EU dynamic (Cornelius 1994). Then there is δ change, which can be in relation to an exemplary model, such as the EU *acquis* or a specific "twinning" exercise linking a new member or accession state with a longer-standing member state. Finally, γ convergence can result from changes in country rankings as a result of benchmarking exercises, which have become an increasingly popular "soft" governance tool.

Cornelius (1994, 2004) identifies the scope for convergence in immigration policy and politics along four dimensions: growing similarity in policy instruments (especially for un-authorized immigration and refugee flows); the results or efficacy of policy; social integra-tion policies; and public reactions to immigration flows and policy. While not explicitly on convergence, accounts of EU immigration and asylum have often focused on the "Fortress Europe" trope—that is, that European integration leads to lowest-common-denominator, restriction-oriented policies. The analysis in this chapter departs from accounts of Europe as a "fortress." There are restrictive aspects to EU immigration and asylum policies, but European integration is not a simple, deterministic process with a single predicted location for convergence. For example, there are measures that can be seen as rights-enhancing for TCNs, such as the directive on the rights of long-term residents that grants legally resident TCNs rights equivalent to those of EU citizens following five years of legal residence. This suggests that it is the "ability of states to co-operate and their ability to agree on norms of governance [that] determines the extent of policy convergence" (Drezner 2001: 78).

There is not a single governance norm. A security-driven impetus competes with other policy drivers, such as the legal and political dynamics arising from the original core, eco-nomic purposes, as well as rights-based and anti-discrimination logics that have acquired some purchase at the national and international levels and may well be reinforced as a result of the growing role of the EU's court, the European Court of Justice (ECJ). No single predicted outcome of convergence also points to the necessity of overcoming what Walker (2004) refers to as an unhelpful polarization in EU analysis between "structural fatalists," who are pessimis-tic about the possibility of real progress, and "naïve separatists," who have unrealistic expecta-tions about integration divorced from any real understanding of political context.

To assess potential effects, it is possible to distinguish five variables. The first is time and timing. The "timescape" is an integral component of Freeman's (1995) analysis of con-vergence. The key point about newer EU immigration countries in Central, Eastern, and Southern Europe is that the onset of immigration is closely associated with the obligations of EU membership.

The second variable is the proximity of the migration policy type to the EU's legal and political framework. The core economic rationale has provided a powerful momentum for creation of an intra-EU mobility framework. "Flexibility" within the treaty structure can also facilitate convergence, taking the form of opt-outs from a treaty and derogations entered by member states into the texts of legislation. Flexibility is "a political rather than a legal concept" (Papagianni 2001: 127) and a potentially least-worst solution to the prac-tical problems of cooperation and integration in contentious areas. It is consistent with established norms and practices, not a deviation from them. Those member states that are "out" can use negotiations and derogations to define their position in relation to agreed measures. Opt-outs may also disguise the extent of engagement. The United Kingdom has a reputation as a reluctant state, but it is extensively engaged with EU policies on unauthorized migration and asylum, which means that in these areas "the UK does not act like an opt-out" (Adler-Nissen 2009: 69; see also Geddes 2005b).

The third variable, the experience of similar problem pressures such as demographic change, skills shortages, or high levels of irregular immigration, can induce convergence. These pressures play out unevenly with differences in population profile, labor market characteristics, and exposure to irregular flows.

The fourth variable, locational factors, are likely to be important, but again with variation in their effects. The central issue here is, of course, the scale, extent, and location of Europe's borders. Table 14.2 shows the EU's "green" land borders in Central and Southeastern Europe. Table 14.3 shows its southern maritime "blue" borders. These borders have a particular resonance in the context of the EU's "fight against illegal immigration."

The fifth factor, again with variable resonance, is scope for imitation and policy learning. This is most obvious in the form of accession criteria for new member states as they face a steep learning curve and a requirement to adapt as a condition of membership (Lavenex 1999; Grabbe 2000; Schimmelfennig and Sedelmeier 2004). Transnational communication can facilitate lesson drawing and the diffusion of policy ideas and practices. The European Commission can play a key role in this, as can other international migration organizations with a project delivery focus, such as the United Nations High Commissioner for Refugees (UNHCR), the International Organization for Migration (IOM), and the International Centre for Migration Policy Development (ICMPD).

TABLE 14.2
EU external "green" land borders, 2008

Border between		Length (km)
Finland	Russia	1,340
Estonia	Russia	455
Latvia	Russia	276
Lithuania	Belarus	651
Lithuania	Russia (Kaliningrad)	272
Poland	Russia (Kaliningrad)	232
Poland	Belarus	418
Poland	Ukraine	535
Slovakia	Ukraine	98
Hungary	Ukraine	136
Romania	Ukraine (east/west of Moldova)	649
Romania	Moldova	681
Bulgaria	Turkey	259
Greece	Turkey	215
Greece	Albania	282
Greece	Macedonia	246
Bulgaria	Macedonia	165
Bulgaria	Serbia	341
Romania	Serbia	546
Total		7,958

SOURCE: House of Lords (2008: 16).

TABLE 14.3
EU southern "blue" maritime borders

Country	Length (km)
Portugal (including Azores and Madeira)	2,555
Spain (including Canaries)	4,964
France	4,720
Slovenia	48
Italy	7,600
Greece (including over 3,000 islands)	13,676
Malta (including Gozo)	253
Cyprus	293
Total	34,109

SOURCE: House of Lords (2008: 17).

THE DEVELOPMENT OF THE EU MIGRATION FRAMEWORK

Before moving on to explore forms of convergence and the impact of its variables, it is important to establish the context of EU action. This section briefly surveys the relative role of intra- and extra-EU migration and identifies how a notion of "virtuous" (albeit relatively small-scale) mobility for nationals of member states who, since the Maastricht Treaty of 1993, are also EU citizens contrasts with the more negative connotations associated with non-EU migration by TCNs. The intention is to sketch key features of the EU framework and identify themes to which the analysis will return as it develops.

Mobility rights were central to the emergence of the EU during the 1950s. Initially, these were provided for nationals of the six founder member states to move within what was known as the Common Market. Such provisions were central to the EU's founding treaty signed in Rome in March 1957. The foundations of the Common Market and the removal of impediments to free movement were largely in place in the national legal frameworks of the six founder member states by 1968. The key point here is that mobility for EU citizens is a central, defining feature that is closely linked to the union's core economic purposes. There has also been over time a progressive extension of the categories of people entitled to move freely, with the result that free movement has become a generalized right with only limited and highly circumscribed exceptions. While there may be high-flown rhetoric about the political dimension of European integration, it is the pursuit of economic objectives that has been and continues to be fundamental to the shape and form taken by European integration. This economic rationale became clearer when free movement rights were extended by the aspiration to create a single European market contained within the Single European Act (1986) that defined the EU as "an area without internal frontiers" within which free movement of people, services, goods, and capital would be assured.

There were no provisions for movement by non-EU nationals in the founding treaties. Not until the Maastricht Treaty came into effect in 1993 was there even weak informal cooperation outside of the formal treaty structure on Justice and Home Affairs (JHA, including immigration and asylum). There were, however, highly significant developments outside the main treaty in the form of the Schengen Agreement (named after the eponymous town in Luxembourg), signed in June 1985 by Belgium, France, Germany, Luxembourg, and the

Netherlands. This agreement sought to achieve the removal of frontier controls between these five very pro-integration-minded states that were keen to move more quickly toward ambitious objectives. Flexibility circumvented the likely opposition of more reluctant states, such as the United Kingdom. The Schengen states agreed to work outside of the formal treaty framework in pursuit of integrative objectives. Schengen has been characterized as a laboratory (Monar 2001) within which the "compensating" internal security implications of free movement were developed. Equally important, Schengen institutionalized cooperation between ministers and officials from interior ministries and security agencies in the twenty-five participating states (all EU members except the United Kingdom and Ireland, with Bulgaria, Croatia, and Romania currently adapting to the requirements of membership, and Iceland, Norway, and Switzerland having observer status). Wallace (2005) refers to the development of networks of transgovernmental action, which presents a useful and powerful way of understanding patterns of cooperation that have been institutionalized for relatively long periods of time and that have a strong sectoral focus.

Schengen provides a powerful link to EU action on migration and asylum. In fact, fourteen years after it was signed, the Schengen Agreement, as it developed in the intervening years, was incorporated into the EU by the Amsterdam Treaty (1999). Prior to Amsterdam, developments had been slower and constrained by the preferences of the more reluctant member states, such as the United Kingdom and Denmark. As will be discussed below, the Maastricht Treaty created informal structures of intergovernmental cooperation on Justice and Home Affairs. The Amsterdam Treaty then brought together free movement, migration, and asylum within one chapter of the treaty and within the framework of the EU's common institutional structure, to which we now briefly turn.

A key distinguishing feature of the EU as an international organization is that it has the power to turn treaties in public international law, agreed to by participating states, into laws that bind these states (Sandholtz and Stone Sweet 1997). It does so through a set of common institutions located primarily in Brussels that are separate but not detached from member states and that are central to the remaking of migration policy and politics in Europe. There are four main institutions at the EU level. The European Commission (hereafter "the Commission") performs executive roles through its responsibility for policy management and implementation. It also has a more "political" component, as it makes policy proposals and thus can seek to shape European integration. Indeed, the title "Commission" is slightly misleading because there is a high level of internal differentiation between policy fields. A Directorate General (DG)—the basic organizational unit within the Commission—was created only to deal with migration and asylum issues in 1999, but it grew rapidly in size. In 2010, the JHA DG was split into two news DGs: one dealing with home affairs (within which immigration and asylum reside) and one dealing with justice. It is important to see the Commission and its units as actors in the integration process and not as some kind of apolitical bureaucracy (Boswell and Geddes 2010).

The Council (of Ministers; hereafter "the Council") is composed of ministers from member-state governments at one time performed the legislative role, but this role is now increasingly shared with the European Parliament. While there is technically "a" Council, there are actually a series of configurations depending on the issue being discussed. This means that there is a JHA Council meeting and a network of groups and committees comprising the national and EU-level officials that support it. At a senior official level is the Committee of Permanent Representatives (COREPER) comprising senior Brussels-based national officials. Of central importance in the area of migration and asylum are the various working groups that inform the Council's work. The Strategic Committee on Immigration, Frontiers and Asylum (SCIFA) was established in 1999 to bring together national officials from interior ministries and internal security agencies. SCIFA itself breaks down into a series of working groups dealing with, for example, migration and expulsion.

While cooperation remained intergovernmental during the 1990s, the Council was the dominant actor, with all decisions made on the basis of unanimity. The Commission did make efforts to secure a seat at the table during the 1980s and 1990s, but within the informal setting had significant constraints on its role and, in the case of Schengen, was formally excluded until Schengen was brought into the treaty structure in 1999. Supranational institutions were largely excluded. These dynamics changed quite rapidly during the 1990s, with growing roles for the European Parliament (EP) and the European Court of Justice (ECJ). There is now a provision for co-decision between the EP and the Council. The first issue decided using this procedure was the return directive of 2008, more on which below.

The Lisbon Treaty (2009) created an enhanced role for the ECJ in national legal systems in the areas of migration and asylum. It did so by allowing the ECJ to consider the scope for annulment of legislation and to rule on any failure to act or to fulfill obligations. The ECJ was also given the power to issue "preliminary rulings" regarding migration and asylum. A key aspect of the EU legal framework has been its provision for lower member state tribunals to clarify questions of EU laws for interpretation in national legal systems. Until the Lisbon Treaty came into force in 2009, the ECJ could only issue such rulings following a reference from the highest court in a member-state system. This provision has now been changed so that preliminary rulings can also be sought by lower tribunals, which creates the possibility of a more active role for the ECJ in the politics of migration and asylum and the further opening of "social and political spaces" for migrants at the EU level (Acosta and Geddes 2013).

To summarize, free movement rights have been central both to the economic logic underpinning European integration and to the governance system that has developed since the late 1950s. Extra-EU migration by TCNs has been on the agenda only as subject to common institutional rules and procedures since 1999, but there has been rapid policy and institutional development since that time. It is also important to factor into the analysis the development of the Schengen area outside of the formal treaty framework until its inclusion in 1999, and the associated importance of transgovernmental action that has changed the strategic content of decision making on migration and asylum in Europe.

EU ACTION ON IMMIGRATION AND ASYLUM

This section explores the development of EU action on immigration and asylum and contextualizes the subsequent section, which explores specific EU measures under the broad headings of restriction, rights, and admissions. Rather than take a chronological approach and survey the development of various measures and instruments since the 1980s, this section instead asks, "How did we get here?" This is a question that helps to avoid the potential problem of a lengthy description of the various stages in the development of EU action over more than twenty years, and it facilitates efforts to delineate the key components of cooperation and integration. Indeed, this distinction between cooperation and integration is important. Before 1999, EU action on immigration was by intergovernmental cooperation between member states acting on the basis of unanimity. Since 1999, there has been a move toward integration in the EU's common institutional structures and processes—that is, the governance system referred to at the start of this chapter. Immigration and asylum policy cannot be neatly characterized as "intergovernmental" or "supranational." Wallace (2005) has shown that cooperation on immigration and asylum can best be understood as "intensive transgovernmentalism," with patterns of intense collaboration between ministers, officials, and other actors, such as the Commission and members of the European Parliament (MEPs), with a sectoral focus that cannot be captured by a supranational versus intergovernmental dichotomy.

To refer back to this section's first paragraph, the "here" to which the question refers is a common EU migration and asylum policy governed by the framework created by the Lisbon Treaty and with a plan of action through 2014 specified in the "Stockholm programme" of 2010.

The Lisbon Treaty marked the full incorporation of migration and asylum within the treaty framework. In terms of institutional competence, this means qualified majority voting (a weighted voting system) in the Council and co-decision between the Council and EP and ECJ jurisdictions. Articles 77–80 set out the main provisions on migration and asylum.

Article 77 provides for the absence of internal border controls between member states, checks at external borders, and integrated border management. In effect, this means scope for common policy covering visas, short-term residence permits, checks of those crossing external borders, conditions under which TCNs are free to travel within the EU, the gradual establishment of an integrated management system for external borders, and the absence of controls on those crossing internal borders. Where necessary, the Council can also adopt measures on passports, identity cards, residence permits, and other such documents, but it must act on the basis of unanimity and only has to "consult" the European Parliament (i.e., these measures are not covered by co-decision).

Article 78 deals with a common policy on asylum, subsidiary protection, and temporary protection. It provides for a uniform status of asylum valid throughout the EU, a uniform status of subsidiary protection for TCNs, a common system of temporary protection for displaced persons in the event of a massive inflow, common procedures for granting and withdrawing uniform asylum or subsidiary protection status, criteria and mechanisms for allocating responsibility for asylum claims, standards for receipt of applications for asylum or subsidiary protection, and partnership and cooperation with third countries to manage inflows of persons applying for asylum or for subsidiary or temporary protection.

Article 79 sets out the basis for a common immigration policy comprising conditions for entry and residence and standards governing long-term visas and residence permits; definition of the rights of TCNs legally residing in a member state, including free movement and residence in other member states; illegal immigration and unauthorized residence; and combating people trafficking. Article 79(3) allows the conclusion of readmission agreements between the EU and third countries, and Article 79(4) provides for the possibility of incentive measures to promote integration of legally resident TCNs. Importantly, Article 79(5) states that immigration measures "do not affect the right of member states to determine volumes of admission of TCNs coming from third countries." This is a very important provision that maintains the national prerogative to determine the basis for decisions about non-EU migration, although jurisdiction with regard to EU citizens has, of course, been ceded.

Finally, Article 80 provides for "solidarity and fair sharing of responsibility in the areas of migration and asylum." This has been tested in the wake of uprisings in the Middle East and North Africa. Italy, for example, found that its claims for EU solidarity in the face of migration from Libya to the island of Lampedusa to the south of Sicily did not resonate with other governments. This suggests that distributive norms that have informed EU cohesion policy are not similarly powerful in migration and asylum policy (Thielemann 2004).

While the Lisbon Treaty specified competence, it was also necessary to set a policy agenda and establish priorities for action. The EU thus produced in 2009 the Stockholm programme, which is the third in a series of five-year plans (the other two being the Tampere agreement covering 1999–2004 and the Hague programme covering 2005–2009), designed to provide road maps for policymakers. In the same way that Lisbon built on previous treaties, Stockholm built on the Tampere and Hague programmes. It identifies a number of priority areas:

- Integrated management of external borders, including further development of the role of the EU agency created to promote operational cooperation on border security and controls, FRONTEX, and further developments of both the European Surveillance System (Eurosur), on the borders of the Union's eastern and southern member states, and the Schengen Information System (SIS, evolving into SIS II), as well as a Visa Information System (VIS).

- "Responsibility, solidarity and partnership in migration and asylum matters," ensure that the Union affirms its commitment to what is known as the Global Approach to Migration and Mobility (CEC 2011). This emphasizes cooperation with countries of origin and transit and thus raises the importance of the "external" dimension of EU action on migration and asylum and on the foreign policy dimension of EU migration policy (Lavenex and Kunz 2008). The "Global Approach" is broad ranging and touches on migration and development, integration, unauthorized immigration, and unaccompanied minors.

- The aim in asylum policy is to create "a common area of protection and solidarity" with a common asylum procedure and a uniform status for those granted international protection. The Dublin system is the cornerstone of the Common European Asylum System (CEAS), building on Article 78 of the Lisbon Treaty.

The treaty framework, with its most recent iteration in Lisbon, provides the legal basis for action, but "five-year plans" (Stockholm being the latest), the common institutional framework, and the ordinary legislative procedure determine the ways in which treaties agreed between states in public international law are turned into legal outputs that bind participating states. The key legal outputs are regulations and directives. Both are binding and have a direct effect, which means that they must be implemented. Both regulations and directives specify the objective to be achieved, but directives allow more scope for variation in implementation so long as the objective is secured. There is, for example, Regulation (EC) No 539/2001, which specifies the member states whose nationals can enter the EU without a visa, while Directive 2003/9/EC specifies minimum standards for the reception of asylum seekers.

We now move on to assess EU action under three headings: restriction, rights, and admission.

Restriction

Cornelius (1994, 2004) argues that convergence is most evident in policy instruments related to unauthorized immigration and asylum. This section assesses EU action on asylum and unauthorized immigration and describes the development of an EU asylum system that emphasizes minimum standards and efforts to increase border control capacity in the face of unauthorized flows into member states seen as most exposed to migration flows. There is evidence of adaptation to an EU template as newer immigration countries and accession states "catch up" either voluntarily or through compulsion. This arises, in particular, from the timing of immigration, exposure to similar problem pressures, and proximity to sending states and regions. There has also been scope for international policy learning for newer immigration countries and newer member states (categories that often coincide), either from member states in the form of twinning exercises or from international organizations.

The EU has developed a particular focus on external frontier control and, in particular, the development of enforcement and response capacity in newer immigration countries and newer member states in Central, Eastern, and Southern Europe. EU action in these areas has been relatively long standing. Concern about "unwanted" flows drove early-stage cooperation within the informal structures created by the Maastricht Treaty, and it was central to the venue-shopping argument developed by Guiraudon (2001).

EU action on asylum provides insight both into the scope and content of EU action and the institutional dynamics of multilevel migration politics. The basic principle informing policy development is the "Dublin" system, first agreed in 1990 and since reinforced by regulations of 2003 and 2014 (Noll 2000). Dublin provides for a system of mutual recognition or a "one-stop" asylum procedure whereby claims must be made by an applicant in the first state entered, and a decision in that state is valid for all other member states. The Amsterdam Treaty specified competence in relation to criteria for determining which state is responsible for processing an asylum application and "minimum standards" for reception conditions, qualification of TCNs as refugees, the granting or withdrawing of refugee status, and temporary protection. The second phase of the development of the Common European Asylum System was implemented in 2014 and 2015.

The focus on minimum standards has been criticized. Indeed, a 2011 European Court of Human Rights judgment argued that the Dublin system was flawed because asylum seekers being returned to Greece under its "one-stop" provision were not even granted minimal protections. This can be construed as an indictment of the EU system, but it is more likely to lead to efforts to increase capacity in Greece and to further develop the EU system. This leads to another point: common asylum standards, even though initially set at a low level, have actually led to some upward pressure in terms of standards of provision in some member states that had previously been set, particularly in newer immigration countries and accession states (Kaunert and Leonard 2012). Finally, the institutional configuration and dynamics around asylum have changed. One manifestation of this is the increased role for the Commission, which has been the source of more progressive policy proposals in the area of asylum that have then been watered down by member states during negotiation in the Council. Another important change post-Lisbon is that asylum issues now fall within the domain of the ECJ. Given the track record of courts at national levels, it is not unreasonable to suppose that asylum is likely to be a growth area in ECJ jurisprudence.

An issue of central importance in restriction policy is the link between asylum and irregular migration, or what the EU calls its "fight against illegal immigration." Here too we see the EU framework acting as a powerful driver of convergence. Of central importance is the Schengen framework, which was brought into the EU's legal and institutional procedures by the Amsterdam Treaty. The Schengen Convention came into effect with nine participating states in 1995; it abolished checks at internal borders and created a single external border where entry checks for access to the Schengen area would be carried out. These checks are based on a common set of rules, such as a common visa policy, police and judicial cooperation, and a Schengen Information System (SIS) to pool and share data. Adaptation to the Schengen framework was a central component of the 2004 and 2007 enlargements. In 2006, the Commission identified its policy priorities in the fight against illegal immigration (CEC 2006). These priorities had a strong "external focus" and thus distracted attention from the fact that most migrants who become irregular actually enter legally and then overstay. Such a focus on external frontiers can perpetuate a "myth of invasion" (de Haas 2007). The priorities identified were cooperation with non-EU states, particularly in Sub-Saharan Africa and the Mediterranean; Integrated Border Management (IBM); the fight against human trafficking; combating illegal employment; return policy and the return directive; improving information exchange; and carriers' liability.

The return directive is particularly significant for a number of reasons, not least that it was the first measure to be agreed using co-decision involving both the EP and the Council. It emerged after three years of negotiations based on the original Commission proposals. Finally adopted by the European Parliament on June 18, 2008, it aims to standardize the procedures regulating the expulsion of irregular migrants. EU member states cannot adopt harsher rules than the ones laid out in the directive, but they can retain more liberal rules or adopt new more permissive ones.

The return directive stipulates that, once a decision is taken to deport an individual who cannot claim asylum or refugee status, there will be a voluntary departure period (seven to thirty days). If the deportee does not leave, a removal order can be issued, which can include an entry ban lasting up to five years. Article 15 of the directive sets a maximum period of custody at six months, with a possible twelve-month extension (for a total of eighteen months). Families and children can be held in custody only as a last resort and for up to six months. Unaccompanied minors will be repatriated only if they can be returned to their families or to "adequate reception facilities." Legal aid is provided to immigrants without resources and a €676 million return fund, set up by the Commission for the period 2008–2013, can be used to cover its cost. Member states are forbidden to return people to unsafe countries, and procedural safeguards for asylum seekers are left unaffected.

There is evidence of convergence on restriction. This is marked by adaptation to fairly specific and prescriptive EU requirements in the EU *acquis* that leads to a strong focus on border controls and efforts to create a common approach to asylum. The factors driving convergence are timing of immigration, exposure to similar problem pressures, and proximity to migrant-sending states or regions. The focus has been on legislative adaptation and on "hard" governance, although, as discussed below, this does not mean that formal compliance equates with on-the-ground implementation.

Rights

We now explore EU action that extends rights to migrants, which presents a challenge to accounts of multilateral cooperation that are skeptical of the scope for member states to reach agreement on issues that relate so closely to sovereignty and are prone to provoke controversy in domestic politics (Keohane, Macedo, and Moravcsik 2009). Four measures enter into consideration: the two anti-discrimination directives of June and November 2000, the family reunion directive of 2003, and the 2003 directive on the rights of long-term residents. These directives are interesting because they demonstrate the links between national and EU politics. They exist because of national-level concern over the social integration of migrants that manifested itself in EU negotiation and led to the insertion of integration provisions in both the family reunion and long-term residents directives. In this area, we see that proximity to the EU *acquis* made a difference in the scope and pace of development, particularly regarding the legitimation of EU action to expand migrants' rights on the basis of the market-making rationale informing economic integration. Specific legal resources developed to support free movement within the market—the prohibition in the Treaty of Rome against discrimination on the grounds of nationality and the Equal Treatment directive of 1976, among others—provided legal and discursive resources for campaign groups. This has led to both harder and softer governance mechanisms, including not only the legal resources provided by the directives but also recourse to measures such as benchmarking exercises, with the Commission keen to co-opt scientific expertise in support of its arguments for an enhanced EU role in this area. (CEC 2004, 2005a, 2005b).

The anti-discrimination directives drew directly from UK and Dutch national legal provisions in that they sought to tackle both direct and indirect discrimination on the grounds of race and ethnic origin (Tyson 2001). This has led to adaptation pressure in newer immigration countries and newer member states, as well as pressure on "older" immigration countries such as France that did not share the British and Dutch approach—indeed, they had a positive aversion to it. French objections were accommodated in a derogation that allowed for attainment of the directive's objectives without having to collect data on ethnic origin (Geddes and Guiraudon 2004). Here too it is evident that "flexibility" facilitated the attainment of broader objectives.

The family reunion and long-term residents directives were both agreed in 2003 and are interesting for a number of reasons, the first of which has already been alluded to: the inclusion of integration provisions (Groenendijk 2004; Groenendijk et al. 2007). The family reunion directive emerged following a three-year negotiation process during which there was movement away from the Commission's more liberal proposals to a stronger emphasis on integration of migrants and their families. The Commission's original proposals conceptualized "integration" as the promotion of social stability through, for example, training and education for family members. In negotiations, the Austrian and German governments sought inclusion of integration provisions in accordance with their national laws.

The family reunion directive provides for the right to family reunification of TCNs who reside lawfully in a member state, and specifies conditions under which family members can enter and reside in a member state. It also lists the rights of family members once the application for family reunification has been accepted regarding, for example, education and training. The directive gives member states the right to impose conditions on family migration and gives them a margin in which to do so in relation to factors such as definition of the family, waiting periods, and integration measures. There was dispute between the Council, the Commission and EP over the directive's content. The EP sought its annulment and argued that certain articles were not in line with fundamental rights, such as those specified by the European Convention on Human Rights (ECHR) (specifically Article 8, on the right to family life, and Article 14, on nondiscrimination on grounds of age) and a number of other international agreements. The ECJ rejected EP calls for annulment, arguing that, while member states must have regard for a child's interests, the EU's framework of fundamental rights does not create an individual right for family members to enter the territory of a member state, because member states have a "certain margin of appreciation" when examining applications for family reunification. The ECJ also ruled that integration was a legitimate factor to be taken into account, but not as the basis for a quota system or a three-year waiting period imposed without regard to the circumstances of specific cases.

The long-term residents directive defined a new EU status, "long-term resident," for all TCNs who had been living in a member state for five years or more, giving them a legal status comparable to that of citizens of that state. Long-term residents can reside in a second member state for *more than* three months for the purpose of economic activity, as either employed or self-employed, to pursue studies or vocational training, or for other purposes. During negotiations, the Austrian, Dutch, and German delegations insisted on the inclusion of integration provisions.

There has been convergence linked to European integration in rights-related areas. There are, of course, constraints, and these can be linked to the dynamics of multilevel politics, as made evident, for example, in interstate and interinstitutional negotiations. Care was taken to ensure EU standards would be consistent with national frameworks and national political sensitivities, but EU-level legal and political resources now exist that change the dynamics of law and policy in three key areas and raise the prospect of future developments following the extension of the ordinary legislative procedure to immigration and asylum, which means that all of these areas are now justiciable at the EU level (Acosta and Geddes 2013).

Admissions

There is considerable skepticism in the international relations (IR) literature about the scope for states to agree on admissions policy given its close link to national sovereignty, and the fact that an excess supply of migrant workers in the international system means that states are able to meet their labor market needs without recourse to agreements that may constrain them in times of economic downturn (Meyers 2002). However, there has been some movement on admissions policy—or, more particularly, on the approximation of measures concerning admissions—which means that even in this area we see some evidence of convergence, albeit nascent and weak. That said, we should not neglect the fact that a free movement area incorporating twenty-eight member states does have major effects on admissions policies and perhaps knock-on effects on TCN admissions because of the potential for labor market gaps to be filled by citizens of other member states.

In this area, we see "softer" governance mechanisms that do not impinge on the ability of member states to determine the numbers of migrants to be admitted—in fact, Article 79(5) of the Lisbon Treaty specifically precludes this kind of involvement. A Commission "Green Paper" of January 2005, on an "EU Approach to Managing Economic Migration" set out ideas for a common admission procedure for economic migrants and linked these to an economic, market-making frame. Such measures, it was claimed would help "meet the needs of the EU labor market and ensure Europe's prosperity" (CEC 2005b). Actual legislative achievements were far less grand. A Council directive of December 2004 dealt with the "conditions of admission of third-country nationals for the purposes of studies, pupil exchange, unremunerated training or voluntary service," while an October 2005 directive covered "a specific procedure for admitting TCNs for the purposes of scientific research."

The "Blue Card" directive, agreed on in May 2009, covers conditions for entry and residence of TCNs for the purpose of high-skilled employment. "Blue Card" holders are granted permits of between one to four years, under which they and their family members benefit from a range of rights, including equal working conditions, access to education and training, recognition of qualifications, and various national provisions on social security and pensions. After a stay of eighteen months in one EU country, and under certain conditions, a Blue Card holder may travel to another country to seek employment without going through the usual national procedures for admission. The caveats are important: the card only covers those with relevant skills and experience and who have a job offer. Member states retain the right to determine the number of migrants entering under such a scheme, and they can declare themselves, or certain regions or sectors, exempt from Blue Card provisions. Using these flexibility provisions, the United Kingdom, Ireland, and Denmark have all opted-out. The Commission has since sought to further develop its role with proposals currently in negotiation on intracorporate transferees and seasonal workers (the latter agreed to in January 2014).

In admission policy, there is also evidence of some convergence, although with an emphasis on softer governance mechanisms. Majone (1992) refers to processes of "softening up" whereby the Commission devotes itself to the technical aspects of its proposals and to gathering relevant information by, for example, commissioning scientific research. Such processes are important at the EU level and need to be seen as a part of the convergence process that cannot be captured by a focus on interstate and interinstitutional negotiation alone.

EUROPEANIZATION AND THE "GAP"

The preceding analysis of policy convergence identified a partial policy framework with differential effects on member states and a variety of harder and softer governance mechanisms that change the dynamics of migration policy and politics. This section extends the analysis by exploring the effects of European integration on domestic governance structures, which raises the question of implementation and the observed gap between policy goals and policy outcomes. The EU does not itself seek to regulate migration flows because it does not possess the resources. Rather, it seeks to build and develop member-state capacity.

Capacity, a key focus of this section, is linked to an EU system within which there is "policy without politics" (Schmidt 2006). While it can be argued that the EU may facilitate domestic change, it is also the case that European integration may increase the perception of a lack of control held by electorates over key issues and a shift to distant EU institutions and collective decision-making processes (Mair 2007). For example, in Italy economic and monetary union in the 1990s was represented as a *vincolo esterno* (external constraint) that added credibility to domestic adjustment. In migration and asylum, the EU has been more of a *capro espiatorio* (scapegoat). The gap between objectives and outcomes can be filled not just by anti-immigration mobilizations but also by mobilizations that target the EU. There has been a marked upturn in the electoral fortunes of anti-immigration, Euroskeptic political parties across the EU, including in traditional pro-integration states such as the Netherlands.

The capacity bargain builds on the idea of sovereignty bargains referred to earlier, to which there are three dimensions. First, a functional element compensates to some extent for the weakness of the "input" side of integration and EU rule making by balancing increased policy effectiveness against the perceived democratic deficit (Scharpf 1997). Adjustment to EU policies can then be justified by the prospect of "better" policy, or at least a policy that conforms to EU practices. The second element is political and refers to potential benefits that arise from closing the gap between (sovereign) national capabilities and the commitments a state is required to undertake as a part of the EU. This can reduce adaptation costs, but, as in the case of Italy, the EU can be targeted as a reason for failure to achieve domestic policy objectives. The third element is administrative and refers to the ways in which unrepresented or poorly represented interests can secure access to the policymaking process, or—far more likely in the case of immigration and asylum—how domestic actors can be incorporated into "transgovernmental networks" (Menon and Weatherill 2006: 408).

The capacity bargain aims to make states more able to assume the responsibilities of membership. In the case of immigration and asylum this has meant adapting to the Schengen *acquis*. However, the "gap" becomes wider and potentially even more politically significant as responsibility for immigration and asylum shifts to the EU level. Political parties that seek to exploit anti-immigration sentiment tend to do so on nationalist or populist terms that also make it easier to combine hostility to immigration with skepticism about the EU. This is becoming a potent combination in contemporary EU politics, and it is one that is not easy for the EU to resolve because its measures tend to focus on the regulatory aspects of external-border frontier control and the "fight against illegal immigration" projected outward to source countries. This leads to a particular kind of capacity bargain with an external focus. Such a bargain is not well placed to resolve the more complex mix of regulatory and distributive issues once migrants are "in," and is one in which the EU has only limited capacity to intervene. Rather, it leads to an increased exposure to blame.

REFERENCES

Acosta, D., and A. Geddes. 2013. "The Development, Application and Implications of an EU Rule of Law in the Area of Migration Policy." *Journal of Common Market Studies* 51 (2): 179–93.

Adler-Nissen, R. 2009. "Behind the Scenes of Differentiated Integration: Circumventing National Opt-Outs in Justice and Home Affairs." *Journal of European Public Policy* 16 (1): 62–80.

Bache, I. 2008. *Europeanization and Multi-Level Governance.* Lanham, MD: Rowman & Littlefield.

Bache, I., and M. Flinders. 2004. *Multi-Level Governance.* Oxford: Oxford University Press.

Barro, R., and X. Sala-i-Martin. 1992. "Convergence." *Journal of Political Economy* 100: 223–51.

Bennett, C. 1991. "Review Article: What Is Policy Convergence and What Causes It?" *British Journal of Political Science* 21 (1): 215–33.

Boswell, C., and A. Geddes. 2010. *Migration and Mobility in the European Union.* London: Palgrave Macmillan.

Busch, P., and H. Jorgens. 2005. "The International Sources of Policy Convergence: Explaining the Spread of Environmental Policy Innovations." *Journal of European Public Policy* 12 (5): 841–59.

CEC (Commission of the European Communities). 2004. *Handbook on Integration for Policy Makers and Practitioners.* Brussels: Directorate General for Justice, Freedom and Security.

———. 2005a. *A Common Agenda for Integration: Framework for the Integration of Third Country Nationals in the EU.* Brussels: CEC.

———. 2005b. *Policy Plan on Legal Migration.* Brussels: CEC.

———. 2006. *Policy Priorities in the Fight against Illegal Immigration.* Brussels: CEC.

———. 2011. *The Global Approach to Migration and Mobility.* Brussels: CEC.

Clark, I. 1999. *Globalization and International Relations Theory.* Oxford: Oxford University Press.

Cornelius, W. 1994. "Spain: The Uneasy Transition from Labor Exporter to Labor Importer." In *Controlling Immigration: A Global Perspective,* edited by W. Cornelius, P. Martin, and J. Hollifield, 331–70. Stanford, CA: Stanford University Press.

———. 2004. "Spain: The Uneasy Transition from Labor Exporter to Labor Importer." In *Controlling Immigration: A Global Perspective,* edited by W. Cornelius, T. Tsuda, P. Martin, and J. Hollifield, 387–429. 2nd ed. Stanford, CA: Stanford University Press.

de Haas, H. 2007. *The Myth of Invasion: Irregular Migration from West Africa to the Maghreb and the European Union.* Oxford: International Migration Institute.

Drezner, D. 2001. "Globalization and Policy Convergence." *International Studies Review* 3 (1): 53–78.

Freeman, G. 1995. "Modes of Immigration Politics in Liberal Democratic States." *International Migration Review* 29 (4): 881–902.

———. 2006. "National Models, Policy Types and the Politics of Immigration in Liberal Democracies." *West European Politics* 29 (2): 227–47.

Geddes, A. 2005a. "Europe's Border Relationships and International Migration Relations." *Journal of Common Market Studies* 43 (4): 787–806.

———. 2005b. "Getting the Best of Both Worlds: Britain, the EU and Migration Policy." *International Affairs* 81 (4): 723–40.

———. 2008. *Immigration and European Integration: Beyond Fortress Europe?* 2nd ed. Manchester: Manchester University Press.

Geddes, A., and V. Guiraudon. 2004. "Britain and France and EU Anti-Discrimination Policy: The Emergence of an EU Policy Paradigm." *West European Politics* 27 (2): 334–53.

Grabbe, H. 2000. "The Sharp Edges of Europe: Extending Schengen Eastwards." *International Affairs* 76 (3): 519–36.

Groenendijk, K. 2004. "Legal Concepts of Integration in EU Migration Law." *European Journal of Migration and Law* 6 (2): 111–26.

Groenendijk, K., R. Fernhout, D. van Dam, R. van Oers, and T. Strik. 2007. *The Family Reunification Directive in EU Member States: The First Year of Implementation.* Nijmegen: Wolf Legal Publishers.

Guild, E., ed. 1998. *The Legal Framework and Social Consequences of Free Movement of Persons in the European Union.* The Hague: Kluwer Law International.

Guiraudon, V. 2001. "European Integration and Migration Policy: Vertical Policy-Making as Venue Shopping." *Journal of Common Market Studies* 27 (2): 334–53.

Heichel, S., J. Pape, and T. Sommerer. 2005. "Is There Convergence in Convergence Research? An Overview of Empirical Studies on Policy Convergence." *Journal of European Public Policy* 12 (5): 817–40.

Hix, S. 2005. *The Political System of the European Union.* London: Palgrave Macmillan.

Hoffmann, S. 1966. "Obstinate or Obsolete? The Fate of the Nation State and the Case of Western Europe." *Daedalus* 95 (3): 862–915.

Hollifield, J. 1992. *Immigrants, States and Markets: The Political Economy of Migration in Europe.* Cambridge, MA: Harvard University Press.

Holzinger, K., and C. Knill. 2005. "Causes and Conditions of Cross-National Policy Convergence." *Journal of European Public Policy* 12 (5): 775–96.

Kaunert, C., and S. Leonard. 2012. "The Development of EU Asylum Policy: Venue Shopping in Perspective." *Journal of European Public Policy* 19 (9): 1396–1413.

Keohane, R., S. Macedo, and A. Moravcsik. 2009. "Democracy Enhancing Multilateralism." *International Organization* 63 (1): 1–31.

Lavenex, S. 1999. *Safe Third Countries: Extending the EU Asylum and Immigration Policies to Central and Eastern Europe.* Budapest: Central European University Press.

Lavenex, S., and R. Kunz. 2008. "The Migration-Development Nexus in EU External Relations." *Journal of European Integration* 30 (3): 439–57.

Maas, W. 2005. "The Genesis of European Rights." *Journal of Common Market Studies* 43 (5): 1009–25.

Mair, P. 2007. "Political Opposition and the European Union." *Government and Opposition* 42 (1): 1–17.

Majone, G. 1992. "Regulatory Federalism in the European Community." *Government and Policy* 10: 299–316.

Menon, A., and S. Weatherill. 2006. "Transnational Legitimacy in a Globalising World: How the European Union Rescues Its States." *West European Politics* 31 (3): 397–416.

Meyers, E. 2002. "Multilateral Co-Operation in International Labor Migration." Working Paper wrkg61, Center for Comparative Immigration Studies, San Diego.

Monar, J. 2001. "The Dynamics of Justice and Home Affairs: Laboratories, Driving Factors and Costs." *Journal of Common Market Studies* 39 (4): 747–64.

Noll, G. 2000. *Negotiating Asylum: The EU Acquis, Extra-Territorial Protection and the Common Market of Deflection.* Leiden: Martinus Nijhoff.

Papagianni, G. 2001. "Flexibility in Justice and Home Affairs: An Old Phenomenon Taking New Forms." In *The Many Faces of Differentiation in EU Law*, edited by B. de Witte, D. Hanf, and E. Vos, 101–28. New York: Intersentia.

Sandholtz, W., and A. Stone Sweet, eds. 1997. *European Integration and Supranational Governance.* Oxford: Oxford University Press.

Scharpf, F. 1997. "Economic Integration, Democracy and the Welfare State." *Journal of European Public Policy* 4 (1): 219–42.

Schimmelfennig, F., and U. Sedelmeier. 2004. "Governance by Conditionality: EU Rule Transfer to the Candidate Countries of Central and Eastern Europe." *Journal of European Public Policy* 11 (4): 661–79.

Schmidt, V. 2006. *Democracy in Europe: The EU and National Polities.* Oxford: Oxford University Press.

Starke, P., H. Obinger, and F. G. Castles. 2008. "Convergence towards Where: In What Ways, If Any, Are Welfare States Becoming More Similar?" *Journal of European Public Policy* 15 (7): 975–1000.

Thielemann, E. 2004. "Why European Policy Harmonization Undermines Refugee Burden-Sharing." *European Journal of Migration and Law* 6 (1): 43–61.

Tyson, A. 2001. "The Negotiation of the European Community Directive on Anti-Discrimination." *European Journal of Migration and Law* 3 (2): 199–229.

Walker, N. 2004. *Europe's Area of Freedom, Security and Justice.* Oxford: Oxford University Press.

Wallace, H. 2005. "An Institutional Anatomy and Five Policy Models." In *Policy-Making in the EU*, edited by H. Wallace, W. Wallace, and M. Pollack, 49–50. 5th ed. Oxford: Oxford University Press.

COMMENTARY

Alexander Betts

Within political science, there is a division between comparative politics, which tends to explain states' behavior by looking inside the state, and international relations, which tend to explain that behavior by looking outside the state. One approach is incomplete without the other, and an account of the politics of immigration control needs to combine both.

Most of the previous chapters take a comparative approach. They start within the state, taking immigration states one at a time and assuming that the variables that explain (1) preferences and (2) the ability to "control" are largely endogenous to that state. Andrew Geddes's chapter is an exception to this approach and is unique in this volume. It highlights how an intergovernmental institutional structure leads to policy convergences across states. Geddes not only documents what the institutions are and where they have come from; he also touches on the question of how they lead to variation in policy change within particular states. In other words, international institutions shape domestic immigration control policies.

I want to build on that observation to make a simple argument, one that I believe is missing from this volume but is crucial in explaining immigration control policies. The argument is that *interstate politics (as opposed to simply domestic politics) shapes a state's ability to control immigration*. Individual state preferences and capabilities in immigration control cannot be adequately explained by looking at individual states in isolation.

What other states do (collectively and individually) shapes what you can do as a state. Crudely illustrated, a migrant can only be in one country at a time; if you admit a particular migrant, he cannot be on another state's territory, or if you refuse to admit a particular migrant, he has to be on another state's territory. By definition, one state's migration policies impose positive and negative externalities on other states. This recognition of strategic interaction in the politics of migration has given rise to emerging patterns of conflict and cooperation in migration which define the boundaries of the possible for immigration states.

One aspect of this is the emergence of what I call global migration governance (Betts 2011a, 2011b). Global governance can be defined in either procedural or substantive terms. On a procedural level, it can be understood as the process by which states engage in collective action to address common problems in a particular issue area. This process takes place through agenda setting, negotiation, monitoring, implementation, and enforcement. On a substantive level, global governance is identifiable by the norms, rules, principles, and decision making procedures that regulate the behavior of states (and other transnational actors) in a particular issue area.

In recent years, a more focused debate has emerged on the global governance of migration. It has begun to reflect on the forms of international cooperation that can best meet states' migration interests. At the policy level, publications such as the Doyle Report (2002) and the Global Commission on International Migration (2003–2005) outlined gaps in the institutional architecture governing migration. The Global Forum on Migration and Development (GFMD) has emerged as a site for multilateral dialogue on migration, and the UN High Level Dialogue on Migration and Development (UNHLD) in 2013 focused in particular on discussions of the multilateral institutional architecture regulating migration. Meanwhile, in academia a number of publications have started to address issues of global migration governance, exploring what it is and how we can base claims for what "better" migration governance might look like (Betts 2011a; Hansen, Koehler, and Money 2011; Koser 2010; Koslowski 2011; Kunz, Lavenex, and Panizzon 2011; Newland 2010).

In most policy fields that involve transboundary movements across borders, such as climate change, international trade, finance, and communicable disease, states have developed institutionalized cooperation, primarily through the United Nations system. However, despite the inherently transboundary nature of international migration and the interdependence of states' migration policies, there is no formal or coherent multilateral institutional framework regulating states' responses to international migration. There is no UN migration organization and no international migration regime; thus, sovereign states retain a significant degree of autonomy in determining their migration policies.

It has become increasingly common to argue that there is limited global migration governance or none at all. While it may be true that such governance within a formal multilateral and UN context remains limited, and that progress in the UN "migration and development" debate has been limited, this is not a basis on which to claim that no global migration governance exists. It is simply of a different and—arguably—more complex type than many of the issue areas in which more neatly compartmentalized regimes emerged after the Second World War. Indeed, it is possible to conceive of global migration governance as existing at five broad levels: multilateralism, embedded governance, regionalism, bilateralism, and unilateralism with extraterritorial scope.

At the first level, there is a thin layer of multilateralism with origins in the interwar years. As Koslowski (2011) indicates, if one divides the global governance of migration into three broad "global mobility regimes"—refugee, international travel, and labor—each one of these can be identified as having its origins in the interwar years. The global refugee regime, based on the 1951 Convention Relating to the Status of Refugees and the role of UNHCR, is the migration regime with formalized UN-based multilateralism (Loescher 2001; Loescher, Betts, and Milner 2008). The international travel regime, insofar as it is a regime, has built on the passport regime. Over time, cooperation on technical standards for travel document security has become ever more complex, with The International Civil Aviation

Organization (ICAO) playing an increasingly important role in standards setting (Koslowski 2011; Salter 2009). Finally, the labor migration regime, although extremely limited, is nevertheless underpinned by a range of labor standards developed through International Labour Organization (ILO) treaties (Kuptsch and Martin 2011). Along with these more formal areas, the GFMD now provides informal "facilitative" multilateral governance through which states share knowledge practices in ways that contribute to the development of formal bilateral agreements.

In addition, a significant amount of multilateral migration governance might be referred to as *embedded governance*. The concept of "embeddedness" is widely used in anthropology to refer to a situation where an area of social life does not exist as a recognized and compartmentalized area but is an integrated part of the larger social system. Much of global migration governance is not explicitly labeled as such, but it nevertheless regulates how states can and do behave regarding migration. At the level of norms, states' responses to migration are regulated by their obligations in a host of other areas. Many areas of public international law shape the boundaries of acceptable state behavior in migration. For example, international human rights law, international humanitarian law, World Trade Organization (WTO) law, maritime law, and labor law all represent important elements of global migration governance. It is as a result of these embedded institutions that some international lawyers have argued for conceiving of the existence of International Migration Law (IML) based on these pre-existing bodies of law (Cholewinski, MacDonald, and Perruchoud 2007). Similarly, at the level of international organizations, the mandates of a host of pre-existing UN and non-UN agencies may not explicitly mention migration but indirectly touch on it.

At a third level, there is a growing amount of *regional governance*, including inter- and transregional governance mechanisms. Formal regional economic communities (RECs) such as the EU and NAFTA have increasingly developed mechanisms for greater internal mobility alongside stronger border control. Meanwhile, a range of informal networks called regional consultative processes (RCPs) have emerged, almost with universal coverage. Examples of RCPs include the Intergovernmental Consultations on Asylum, Refugees and Migration (IGC), the Regional Consultative Mechanism (RCM), the Bali Process, and the Southern African Dialogue on International Migration (MIDSA). Many RCPs may be understood as transregional insofar as their funding, training, and knowledge often come from outside of the regions involved.

At a fourth level is a complex array of *bilateral agreements* between states, spanning visas, readmission, circular migration, knowledge sharing, border management, and rescue at sea. It is these bilateral agreements that make up the most substantive component of global migration governance—many are cross-regional, along north–south lines, or between neighboring states. For example, the EU has consciously sought to develop partnership agreements with third countries as part of its migration management. Its "Global Approach," beginning with pilot partnerships with Moldova and Cape Verde, has encompassed partnerships on circular and irregular migration as well as migration and development.

In addition, one may conceive of some aspects of *unilateralism* as comprising global migration governance—insofar as these aspects have extraterritorial scope. Emigration states such as the Philippines, India, and Mexico, in their attempts to engage their diasporas may be thought of as performing global governance. When northern states engage in asylum and immigration management through unilateral policies that exert external control over other states and their populations, they may also be thought of as performing global governance.

Beyond describing this array of international institutions, the challenge is to examine their causal effects on states' immigration control. How do particular institutions constrain or constitute states? In other words, how do they change the incentives for states or the dominant ideas and common standards that states apply to immigration control? Do they have differential effects across states? To understand this, can the same "convergence literature" examined by Geddes be drawn on?

In conclusion, in order to explain state behavior in relation to immigration, states cannot simply be looked at individually. In an era of globalization, external factors, including interstate interaction and the resulting institutional structures have a significant influence on state immigration control. Interstate politics—both in terms of competition and cooperation—shapes the boundaries of the possible for all states in immigration control.

REFERENCES

Betts, A., ed. 2011a. *Global Migration Governance*. Oxford: Oxford University Press.

———. 2011b. "The Global Governance of Migration and the Role of Trans-Regionalism." In *Multi-Layered Migration Governance*, edited by R. Kunz, S. Lavenex, and M. Panizzon. London: Routledge.

Cholewinski, R., E. MacDonald, and R. Perruchoud, ed. 2007. *International Migration Law: Developing Paradigms and Key Challenges*. Cambridge: Cambridge University Press.

Hansen, R., J. Koehler, and J. Money, eds. 2011. *Migration, the Nation-State and International Cooperation*. London: Routledge.

Koser, K. 2010. "International Migration and Global Governance." *Global Governance* 16 (3): 301–16.

Koslowski, R., ed. 2011. *Global Mobility Regimes*. London: Palgrave Macmillan.

Kunz, R., S. Lavenex, and M. Panizzon, eds. 2011. *Multi-Layered Migration Governance*. London: Routledge.

Kuptsch, C., and P. Martin. 2011. "Low-Skilled Labor Migration." In *Global Migration Governance*, edited by A. Betts, 34–59. Oxford: Oxford University Press.

Loescher, G. 2001. "The UNHCR and World Politics: State Interests versus Institutional Autonomy." *International Migration Review* 35 (1): 33–56.

Loescher, G., A. Betts, and J. Milner. 2008. *The United Nations High Commissioner for Refugees (UNHCR): The Politics and Practice of Refugee Protection into the Twenty-First Century*. London: Routledge.

Newland, K. 2010. "The Governance of International Migration: Mechanisms, Processes and Institutions." *Global Governance* 16 (3): 331–44.

Salter, M. 2009. "The North Atlantic Field of Aviation Security." Working paper.

COMMENTARY

Gallya Lahav

The editors of this volume should be lauded for welcoming, at long last, Geddes's important contribution of the EU to the immigration control story. Indeed, this chapter's premise derives from what is by now a near truism. That is, no analysis of European immigration politics today can be devoid of the dynamics of EU politics. This commonly held assumption derives from international relations (IR) theories of globalization and interdependence and, in many ways is supported by the efforts herein to explain national "loss of control."

The changes wrought by "globalization" not only justify the revised title of this third edition of *Controlling Immigration*, but may also lend credence to the editors' overarching hypotheses on "convergence" and "gap." In this line of argument, globalization and regional integration can be understood as exogenous factors related to the international system that have generated national convergence and have furthered the gap between liberal international and market norms and protectionist national and political pressures.

Immigration policymaking in Europe is influenced by regional integration in two broad ways: institutionally and normatively. Institution building and consolidation in the EU present all sorts of struggles—between national and supranational forces, between political parties, and between national actors (e.g., justice, labor, security). These struggles affect not only how Europe is organized but also the kinds of immigration outcomes that are considered optimal.

The second component of European integration that shapes migration thinking is related to the psychological processes and norms that buttress the emergent community: the identification of "in groups" and "out groups." The conflict of whether to identify with one's nation or with Europe as a whole is indeed real and it impacts the politics of inclusion and exclusion. "Europeanness," the identification with a larger community, as I have elsewhere described, may be seen as a mobilizing force of inclusiveness that inherently excludes foreigners or outsiders. This attitudinal component of European integration is particularly sensitive to questions of national identity and citizenship, and it may account for what Geddes aptly refers to as the differential effects of cooperation pressures.

Despite the robust weight of cross-national evidence to support the convergence thesis, the penultimate test of "control" in a changing global context is whether international or, in this case, EU norms are commensurate with national interests. Is the capacity of states to implement rational and self-serving immigration and immigrant policies constrained or enhanced in an environment of increasing international interdependence and globalization? To a large degree, the answers to these questions may be measured by migration developments on the EU front.

Given national pressures to "control immigration" (a theme well covered in the two previous editions of this volume), the detailed longitudinal evidence of cooperation offered by Geddes regarding the free movement of persons (both EU and non-EU), and their rights, is compelling. Since the Treaty of Rome gave birth to the European *Economic* Community in 1957, the EU has steadily transformed itself from an economic actor into a significant political player. Though initially driven by economic motives (i.e., the movement of workers, labor), the EU's incursion into other policy areas is momentous. Over time, rights to free movement of "people" (as well as the definition and scope of who those "people" are) have been expanded through the Single European Act (SEA) and the Maastricht, Amsterdam, and Lisbon treaties. The plethora of common rules and practices on migration and asylum established by treaties, conventions, and summits, especially since the 1990s, which Geddes carefully outlines, underscores the remarkable transformation of a "peoples' Europe" into a full-fledged political community.

The interesting question is no longer about the existence of cooperation on immigration and asylum policies but about why it has occurred the way it did. More important, what happened to national interests? Notwithstanding this foregone conclusion, considerable debate remains regarding the independent variables used to explain both convergence and cooperation. These questions have preoccupied European immigration scholars since the 1990s (Geddes 2000; Lahav 2004), when national policy trends began to increasingly converge.

To be sure, the interactive effects of regional integration and migration issues suggest that cooperation is predicated on some convergent national interests. Whether they have resulted from what Geddes refers to as "timescape," or from proximity, experience, location, policy learning, or a combination of all of these factors, incentives for cooperation are intricately bound to some level of convergent interests. Given that the lines between traditional immigration countries and traditional emigration countries have all but disappeared, as Geddes importantly notes, heightened sensitivities to immigration even in less experienced countries is ubiquitous. Convergence may be an outcome of international learning (Weil and Crowley 1994), a reluctant recognition of policy limitations at the national level (Butt Philip 1994), a narrowing of the range of treatment of populations (Heisler 1992), or the threat of European integration to the nation-state.

Cooperation may reflect domestic societal pressures (i.e., immigration flows, party and electoral politics, public opinion, economic constraints, extreme-right politics). Alternatively, exogenous variables related to European integration may be more relevant in explaining it. Global structural changes may mobilize some consensus in immigration thinking, and it may serve either to justify unpopular yet necessary politics (i.e., "blame avoidance" or the "Europe to the rescue" syndrome" (Weaver 1986; Messina and Thouez 2002), or serve as a correlate to spillover effects. For example, the "externalities" of EU migration policies mean that they are increasingly interdependent with other policy domains (from foreign affairs to welfare), and thus their effect on migration flows may be mediated by developments elsewhere (Lavenex and Ucarer 2002; Geddes 2000). Especially in an institutionally "thick" environment, well captured by Geddes's multigovernance reference, it is plausible that international institutions and transnational actors have been able to diffuse shared understandings about the treatment of foreigners so as to change and shape the views of domestic state and societal actors—something that constructivists argue has been the case in other areas (Finnemore 1996; Wapner 1995).

Irrespective of causal mechanisms, the normative implications of EU cooperation on policy outcomes remain questionable. While Geddes offers ample evidence of a common EU migration and asylum policy—particularly but not exclusively focused on illegal immigration—his skepticism regarding "fortress Europe" does not logically follow. Consider that the policies most convivial to the "partial" Europeanization of migration have been on visas, asylum, and illegal migration, where protectionism has been most desirable. These issue areas often involve policing the EU's porous southern and eastern frontiers. The EU has now established a common border patrol (FRONTEX), a common format for visas, a common list of countries whose nationals are granted visa-free entry, and common databases (the Visa Informational System, the Schengen Information System, and the EURODAC for asylum seekers) containing biometric data on foreign entrants. Thus, by pooling resources and joining efforts, national politicians can appear "tough" even as they give up control over these issues (e.g., visas and border guards)—that in some ways defines the nation-state's sovereignty.

Furthermore, despite that and because European integration may increase the perception of a lack electoral control, it may offer national policymakers more capacity to maneuver competing interests (Lahav and Guiraudon 2000). More important, it allows national actors to circumvent the most liberal constitutional and political constraints at home. In short, Europeanization of migration, ironically, has most advanced in migration policy areas that satisfy the desire of national politicians to keep foreigners out.

To a large degree, then, Geddes's normative conclusions about restrictive convergence are debatable, even more so because of his own persuasive thesis about policy convergence among newer immigration countries/ member states. The enthusiasm of such new states for jumping on the bandwagon of this lowest-common-denominator equation compels us to question the metric employed to evaluate the scale. Insofar as convergence is based on compatible interests to secure effective state control over migration, cooperation may bolster—not compromise—state sovereignty and sanction more restrictive immigration and asylum policies. In this scenario, the causal direction of the so-called gap between policy goals and outcomes may be reversed. The populist and extremist mobilizations against both immigration and European integration that Geddes describes may in fact be less a consequence or reaction to the gap and more a driver of a gap that exists between the vociferous voices of European elites managing the issue at the "top" and national politicians trying to implement it at the "bottom."

To a large degree, evidence of convergence coincides with more restrictive policies of a "fortress Europe" mentality. Cooperation may reinforce national interests and open up new channels and opportunities for control. A longitudinal analysis of immigration cooperation in the EU suggests that, at least in nationally sensitive areas such as immigration, cooperation may be marked by more protectionist impulses. Because the regional integration project has evidently assumed new sectors beyond the economy, the incorporation of migration issues now coincides with political and security concerns. These concerns were institutionalized in the comprehensive mission of the newly formed AFSJ in 1999, which succeeded in conflating the different and often competing arms of "freedom, security, and justice.[1] With justice and freedoms being subsumed by security, the program for a common immigration policy has assumed a restrictionist character.

This has also been the trajectory of refugee matters, which have been shown to be less about establishing a common European asylum system and more about reducing migration pressures and compensating for the perceived losses of internal security as a result of a frontier-free Europe (Lavenex 2001: 869). Similarly, the Dublin Convention—an instrument of humanitarian policy that was supposedly based on the Geneva Convention, its more internationally revered prototype—represented an effort to deter asylum shopping as well as establish accelerated procedures and safe-third-country principles more than it did an initiative to facilitate refuge. As its name implies—Convention Determining the State Responsible for Examining Applications for Asylum Lodged in One Member State of the EC—Dublin aimed to establish the principle that only one EU state should be responsible for determining the validity of an asylum claim. Indeed, with specific exceptions (e.g., highly skilled labor, the Reception Conditions Directive [RCD]), cooperation on migration has predominantly existed in the form of prevention or exclusion.

The mounting development of a European common response to immigration and asylum seekers is of considerable political significance because it places under a common EU treaty issues long entrenched in national political and judicial systems. However, the blurring of internal and external lines of security, the joint management of external borders, the increasing coordination of national police forces in the fight against crime, the harmonization of national criminal and civil law, the creation of specialized EU bodies such as Europol, Eurojust, and FRONTEX—all have followed a protectionist security logic. They imply that, in more classic terms, a "frontier-free" Europe can simultaneously rather than alternatively *be* a "fortress Europe."

Given that cooperation *and* protectionism operate at both levels of Tomas Hammar's (1985) traditionally distinct policy areas (immigration/admissions and immigrant/rights), it behooves us to consider the value of characterizing either level by a simple dichotomy of liberal versus restrictive norms. To definitively identify policy sets according to such norms is to deny that impulses to restrictionism run through the veins of both policy areas. Though such EU directives on students and researchers (which do not so galvanize public alarm) have generated some expansiveness, for the most part steps toward harmonized standards have continued to be met with criticism by NGOs, the EP, and the ECHR for human rights violations (Lahav and Luedtke 2013). With some exceptions (e.g., the ERF), asylum measures have also allowed member states to lower their refugee protection standards (van der Klaauw 2004).

To be fair to Geddes's insightful analysis, it is important to keep in mind that any deterministic account of restrictive norms belies the fact that, when it comes to immigration regulation, the EU is far less a regime than a multigovernance entity. Such a nuanced perspective of the piecemeal nature of EU migration regulation compels us to evaluate the "gap" thesis by locating the predominant input and actors driving policy outcomes. Regulating migration in the contemporary global world involves not only reconciling national interests but also balancing an immigration equilibrium composed of distinct parts. In the classical Eastonian systems framework, it requires us to reconsider the new "black box" and the environment within which it operates.

NOTES

1. According to the Amsterdam Treaty (1999), the mission of the Area of Freedom, Security and Justice (AFSJ) was "to provide citizens with a high level of safety within an area of freedom, security, and justice by developing common action among the member states in police, judicial cooperation, and criminal matters and by preventing and combating racism and xenophobia."

REFERENCES

Butt Philip, A. 1994. "European Union Immigration Policy: Phantom, Fantasy or Fact?" *West European Politics* 17 (2): 169–91.

Finnemore, M. 1996. "Norms, Culture and World Politics: Insights from Sociology's Institutionalism." *International Organization* 50 (Spring): 325–48.

Geddes, A. 2000. *Immigration and European Integration: Towards Fortress Europe?* Manchester: Manchester University Press.

Guiraudon, V., and G. Lahav. 2000. "A Reappraisal of the State Sovereignty Debate: The Case of Migration Control." *Comparative Political Studies* 33 (2): 163–95.

Hammar, T. ed. 1985. *European Immigration Policy: A Comparative Study*. Cambridge: Cambridge University Press.

Heisler, M. 1992. "Migration, International Relations and the New Europe: Theoretical Perspectives from Institutional Political Sociology." *International Migration Review* 26 (Summer): 596–622.

Lahav, G. 2004. *Immigration and Politics in the New Europe: Reinventing Borders*. Cambridge: Cambridge University Press.

Lahav, G., and A. Luedtke. 2013. "The Europeanization of Immigration Policy." In *Contemporary European Politics: Transition and Europeanization*, edited by M. Mannin and C. Bretherton, 109–22. London: Palgrave.

Lavenex, S. 2001. "The Europeanization of Refugee Policies: Normative Challenges and Institutional Legacies." *Journal of Common Market Studies* 39 (5): 851–74.

Lavenex, S., and E. Ucarer. 2002. *Migration and the Externalities of European Integrations*. Lanham, MD: Rowman & Littlefield.

Messina, A. M., and C. V. Thouez. 2002. "The Logics and Politics of a European Immigration Regime." In *West European Immigration and Immigrant Policy in the New Century: A Continuing Quandary for States and Societies*, edited by A. M. Messina, 97–120. New York: Praeger.

van der Klaauw, J. 2004. "The Future Common Asylum System: Between a Closed-Circuit and an Open-Ended Scheme?" In *Justice and Home Affairs in the EU: Liberty and Security Issues after Enlargement*, edited by J. Apap, 235–58. Northampton, UK: Edward Elgar.

Wapner, P. 1995. "Politics beyond the State: Environmental Activism and World Civic Politics." *World Politics* 47: 311–40.

Weaver, K. 1986. "The Politics of Blame Avoidance." *Journal of Public Policy* 6 (4): 371–98.

Weil, P., and J. Crowley. 1994. "Integration in Theory and Practice: A Comparison of France and Britain." *West European Politics* 17 (2): 110–26.

INDEX

INDEX

Italic page numbers indicate material in figures and tables.